NCERT EXEMPLAR

Problems - Solutions

Chemistry 12th

BEST Solution Guaranteed •••

NCERT EXEMPLAR

Problems – Solutions

Chemistry 12th

Author
Pankaj Mittal

ARIHANT PRAKASHAN (Series), MEERUT

卐 Administrative & Production Offices

Regd. Office

'Ramchhaya' 4577/15, Agarwal Road, Darya Ganj, New Delhi -110002
Tele: 011- 47630600, 43518550

卐 Head Office

Kalindi, TP Nagar, Meerut (UP) - 250002
Tel: 0121-7156203, 7156204

卐 Sales & Support Offices

Agra, Ahmedabad, Bengaluru, Bareilly, Chennai, Delhi, Guwahati, Hyderabad, Jaipur, Jhansi, Kolkata, Lucknow, Nagpur & Pune.

卐 **PRICE** ₹385.00

卐 **PO No.** : TXT-59-T071602-6-26

Published by Arihant Publications (India) Ltd.

For further information about the books published by Arihant, log on to www.arihantbooks.com or e-mail at info@arihantbooks.com

Follow us on   

PREFACE

NCERT Exemplar Problems, published by the NCERT, are designed to provide students with a diverse range of quality questions in formats such as Multiple Choice Questions, Multiple Choice Questions (More Than One Options), Short Answer Type Questions, Matching The Coloumns, Assertion and Reason and Long Answer Type Questions, catering to varying levels of difficulty.

These problems are essential for success in school and board exams, as well as competitive exams like engineering and medical entrances. Regular practice with these problems prepares students to tackle challenging questions effectively.

This book, **NCERT Exemplar Problems-Solutions Chemistry 12th**, offers precise and detailed solutions to all the questions in the NCERT Exemplar Chemistry textbook. Each solution is complemented by explanatory notes and authentic explanations, enabling students to deepen their conceptual understanding and enhance their analytical skills.

Key features

- **Thinking Process** Provides simple steps to approach and solve the question, clearing up any confusion.
- **Concept Insight** Explains the main ideas and concepts needed to answer the questions correctly.
- **Mistake Alert!** Points out common mistakes students might make and helps them avoid these errors.
- **Notes** Highlights important points and useful tips to make learning easier.

I hope this book proves to be a valuable resource, aiding students in their academic journey and leading them to great success.

Author

CONTENTS

***Note(*)** These Chapters have been deleted from latest NCERT.*

Chapter 01

Solid State*

Multiple Choice Questions (MCQs)

Q.1 Which of the following conditions favours the existence of a substance in the solid state?

(a) High temperature
(b) Low temperature
(c) High thermal energy
(d) Weak cohesive forces

Ans. ***(b)*** At low temperature, existence of a substance in solid state is due to

(a) slow molecular motion and

(b) strong cohesive forces

These two forces hold the constituent particles together thus, causes existence of substance in solid state.

Q.2 Which of the following is **not** a characteristic of a crystalline solid?

(a) Definite and characteristic heat of fusion

(b) Isotropic nature

(c) A regular periodically repeated pattern of arrangement of constituent particles in the entire crystal

(d) A true solid

Thinking Process This problem is based on the concept of crystalline solid and its characteristics. A crystalline solid usually consists of a large number of small crystals, having definite characteristic geometrical shape. The arrangement of these particles in a crystal is ordered and repetitive in three-dimensions.

Ans. ***(b)*** Crystalline solid is anisotropic in nature as this solid shows different physical properties such as electrical resistance, refractive index in different directions.

Note Isotropic and anisotropic properties are related to amorphous solid and crystalline solid which can be clearly understood as

Property	Types of solid	Physical properties
Isotropy	Amorphous solid	Same value
Anisotropy	Crystalline solid	Different values

Q.3 Which of the following is an amorphous solid?

(a) Graphite (C)
(b) Quartz glass (SiO_2)
(c) Chrome alum
(d) Silicon carbide (SiC)

Ans. ***(b)*** Quartz glass (SiO_2) is an amorphous solid due to its short range order of constituent particles.

Note Quartz is a crystalline solid while quartz glass is an amorphous solid.

Note (*) This chapter has been deleted from latest NCERT.

Q.4 Which of the following arrangements shows schematic alignment of magnetic moments of antiferromagnetic substances?

(a) ↑ ↑ ↑ ↑ ↑ ↑

(b) ↓ ↓ ↓ ↓ ↓ ↓

(c) ↑ ↑ ↓ ↑ ↑ ↓

(d) ↑ ↓ ↑ ↓ ↑ ↓

Ans. ***(d)*** The substances which have domain structure, which are oppositely oriented and cancel each other's magnetic field are known as antiferromagnetic substances.

↑ ↓ ↑ ↓ ↑ ↓

Schematic arrangement of antiferromagnetic substance

Q.5 Which of the following is true about the value of refractive index of quartz glass?

(a) Same in all directions
(b) Different in different directions
(c) Cannot be measured
(d) Always zero

Ans. ***(a)*** Since, quartz glass is an amorphous solid having short range order of constituents. Hence, value of refractive index is same in all directions, can be measured and not be equal to zero always.

Q.6 Which of the following statement is **not** true about amorphous solids?

(a) On heating they may become crystalline at certain temperature.
(b) They may become crystalline on keeping for long time.
(c) Amorphous solids can be moulded by heating.
(d) They are anisotropic in nature.

● **Concept Insight** This solution includes the concept of amorphous solid and its properties.

Ans. ***(d)*** Amorphous solids are isotropic in nature because it has no long range order and any physical property will be same in all directions. On the other hand, anisotropic nature is a characteristic feature of crystalline solid.

Q.7 The sharp melting point of crystalline solids is due to ....

(a) a regular arrangement of constituent particles observed over a short distance in the crystal lattice
(b) a regular arrangement of constituent particles observed over a long distance in the crystal lattice
(c) same arrangement of constituent particles in different directions
(d) different arrangement of constituent particles in different directions

Ans. ***(b)*** Crystalline solid has regular arrangement of constituent particles observed over a long distance in the crystal lattice. Due to this regular arrangement, crystalline solid have sharp melting point.

Q.8 Iodine molecules are held in the crystal lattice by ....

(a) London forces
(b) dipole-dipole interactions
(c) covalent bonds
(d) coulombic forces

- **Concept Insight** This solution includes the concept of non-polar molecular solids, where molecules like iodine are held together by weak dipersion forces or London forces making them soft, non-conductive and having low melting and boiling points.

Ans. ***(a)*** Iodine molecules are a class of non-polar molecular solid in which constituents molecules are held together by weak London or dispersion forces. These solids are soft and non-conductors of electricity.

Q.9 Which of the following is a network solid?

(a) SO_2 (solid)
(b) I_2
(c) Diamond
(d) H_2O (ice)

Ans. ***(c)*** Diamond is a giant molecule in which constituent atoms are held together by covalent bond. Hence, this is a network solid.

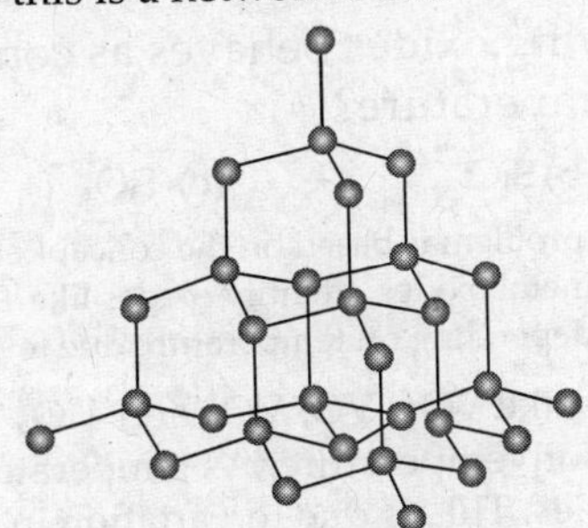

Network structure of atoms

Q.10 Which of the following solids is **not** an electrical conductor?

1. Mg(s)
2. TiO (s)
3. I_2 (s)
4. H_2O (s)

(a) Only 1
(b) Only 2
(c) 3 and 4
(d) 2, 3 and 4

Ans. ***(c)*** Iodine is a non-polar molecular solid in which iodine molecules are held together by London forces or dispersion forces. This is soft and non-conductor of electricity.

Water is a hydrogen bonded molecular solid in which H and O are held together by polar covalent bond and each water molecule is held together by hydrogen bonding. Due to non-ionic nature, they are not electrical conductor.

Q.11 Which of the following is **not** the characteristic of ionic solids?

(a) Very low value of electrical conductivity in the molten state.
(b) Brittle nature.
(c) Very strong forces of interactions.
(d) Anisotropic nature.

Ans. ***(a)*** Ionic solids easily dissociated into its ions in molten state and show high electrical conductivity. So, statement (a) is incorrect. Ionic solids are anisotropic and brittle. They are linked with very strong forces of interactions.

Q.12 Graphite is a good conductor of electricity due to the presence of ....

(a) lone pair of electrons
(b) free valence electrons
(c) cations
(d) anions

Ans. ***(b)*** Graphite is a good conductor of electricity due to presence of free valence electrons. In graphite, each carbon is sp^2 hybridised having one free electron which makes graphite a good conductor of electricity.

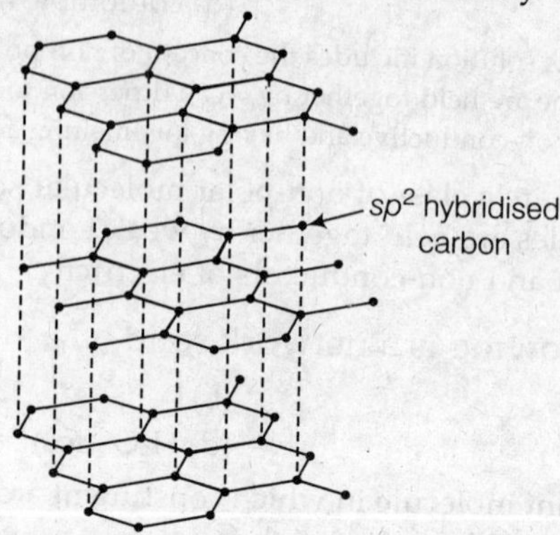

Q.13 Which of the following oxides behaves as conductor or insulator depending upon temperature?

(a) TiO (b) SiO_2 (c) TiO_3 (d) MgO

Thinking Process This problem is based on the concept of temperature dependent electrical properties of metal oxides. Identify oxides like TiO_3, which can act as a conductor or insulator depending on temperature due to change in their band structure.

Ans. ***(c)*** Certain metal oxides like VO_2, VO, VO_3 and TiO_3 show metallic or insulating property depending upon temperature. As temperature varies, metallic or insulating property varies. This is due to variation in energy gap between conduction band and valence band.

Q.14 Which of the following oxides shows electrical properties like metals?

(a) SiO_2 (b) MgO (c) $SO_2(s)$ (d) CrO_2

Ans. ***(d)*** CrO_2, TiO and ReO_3 are some typical metal oxides which show electrical conductivity similar to metals. While SiO_2, MgO and SO_2 are oxides of metal, semimetal and non-metal which do not show electrical properties.

Q.15 The lattice site in a pure crystal **cannot** be occupied by ....

(a) molecule (b) ion (c) electron (d) atom

Ans. ***(c)*** Each point in a lattice is known as lattice point which are occupied by either atom or molecule or ion which are joined together by a straight line to bring out geometry of lattice in pure crystal. Constituents in pure crystal are arranged in fixed stoichiometric ratio.

Hence, existence of free electrons are not possible.

Q.16 Graphite **cannot** be classified as ....

(a) conducting solid (b) network solid
(c) covalent solid (d) ionic solid

Ans. ***(d)*** Graphite cannot be classified as ionic solid as graphite is not made up of ions. It is made up of carbon atoms covalently bonded to three carbon atoms so, it is a covalent solid.

Since, the formation of covalent bond occurs throughout the crystal, therefore it is a type of network solid. Due to presence of free electron, graphite is also classified as conductor solid.

Q.17 Cations are present in the interstitial sites in ....

(a) Frenkel defect
(b) Schottky defect
(c) Vacancy defect
(d) Metal deficiency defect

Thinking Process This solution includes the concept of frenkel defect, a type of defect in crystals where a smaller ion, typically a cation, moves from its regular lattice site to an interstitial position, causing a vacancy.

Ans. ***(a)*** When smaller ion (usually cation) is dislocated from its normal site in crystal and move to an interstitial site, then it is known as Frenkel defect which can be shown below as :

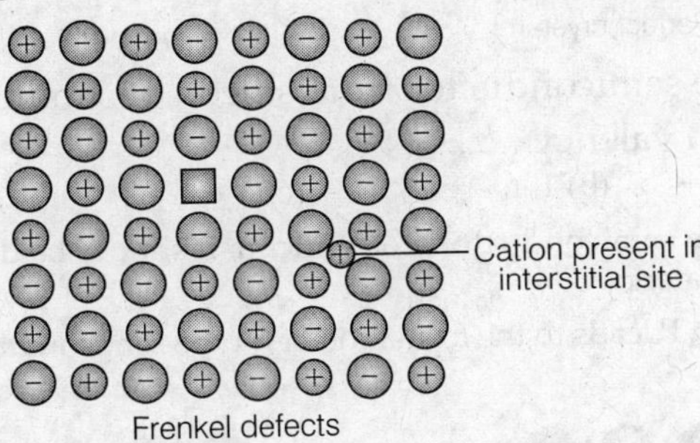

Frenkel defects

Q.18 Schottky defect is observed in crystals when ....

(a) some cations move from their lattice site to interstitial sites
(b) equal number of cations and anions are missing from the lattice
(c) some lattice sites are occupied by electrons
(d) some impurity is present in the lattice

Ans. ***(b)*** Schottky defect is observed in crystals when equal number of cations and anions are missing from the lattice. Thus, density of solid decreases.

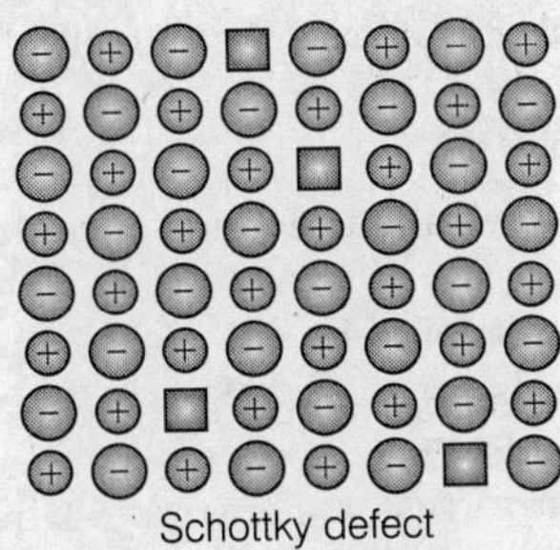
Schottky defect

When some cations move from their lattice site to interstitial site, then it is known as Frenkel defect. When some impurity is present on crystal it is known as impurity defect.

When lattice site is occupied by electron, this type of defect is known as metal excess defect. Hence, except (b) all statements are incorrect regarding Schottky defect.

Q.19 Which of the following is true about the charge acquired by p - type semiconductors?

(a) Positive
(b) Neutral
(c) Negative
(d) Depends on concentration of p impurity

Ans. ***(b)*** When group 13 elements are doped in group 14 element, it creates a hole in a molecule but the molecule as a whole remains neutral. Thus, p-type semiconductor is neutral in nature.

Positive hole (no electron)

B

Perfect crystal

p-type

Q.20 To get a n-type semiconductor from silicon, it should be doped with a substance with valency ....

(a) 2 (b) 1 (c) 3 (d) 5

Ans. ***(d)*** To get a n-type semiconductor from silicon, it should be doped with a substance with valency 5.

e.g., Si doped with P leads to the formation of n-type semiconductor as shown below

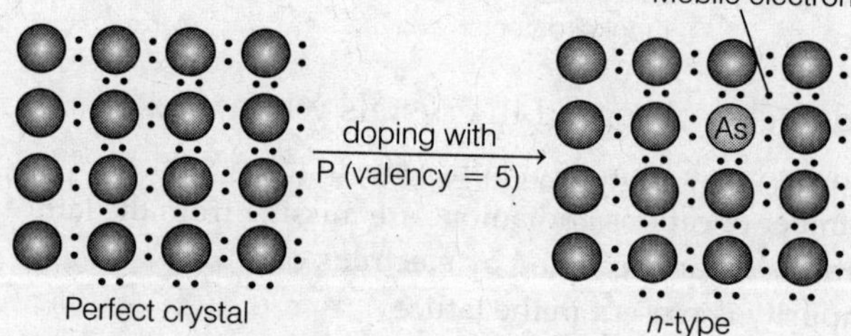

Perfect crystal

n-type

Q.21 The total number of tetrahedral voids in the face centred unit cell is... .

(a) 6 (b) 8 (c) 10 (d) 12

Thinking Process If number of atoms in fcc unit cell = N

Number of tetrahedral voids = 2 N

Number of octahedral voids = N

Ans. ***(b)*** Fcc unit cell contains 8 tetrahedral voids at centre of each 8 smaller cube of an unit cell as shown below

Number of atoms in fcc unit cell = 4

Number of octahedral voids = 4

Number of tetrahedral voids = 8

Eight tetrahedral voids per fcc unit cell

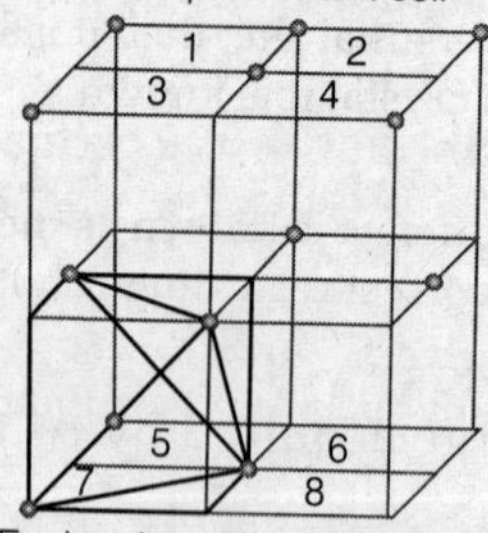

Each cube represented by numeric 1, 2, 3, 4, 5, 6, 7, 8 contain one tetrahedral voids.

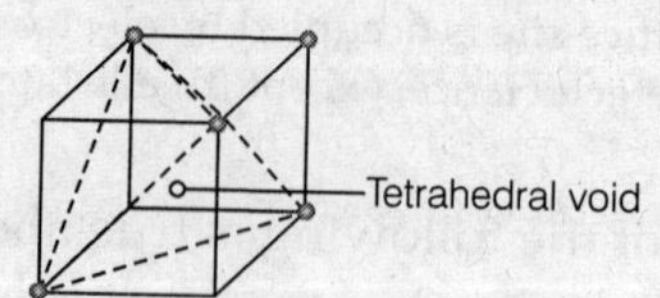

Each cube contain one tetrahedral void at its body centre as shown above

Q.22 Which of the following point defects are shown by AgBr(*s*) crystals?

1. Schottky defect
2. Frenkel defect
3. Metal excess defect
4. Metal deficiency defect

(a) 1 and 2 (b) 3 and 4 (c) 1 and 3 (d) 2 and 4

Thinking Process This problem involves identifying point defects in ionic crystals. Analyse the structure and properties of AgBr to determine defects.

Frenkel defect arises due to the displacement of smaller Ag^+ ions to interstitial sites.

Schottky defect occurs because both Ag^+ and Br^- ions leave the lattice, creating vacancies.

Ans. ***(a)*** AgBr shows both Schottky as well as Frenkel defect. In AgBr, both Ag^+ and Br^- ions are absent from the lattice causing Schottky defect. However, Ag^+ ions are mobile so they have a tendency to move aside the lattice and get trapped in interstitial site hence, cause Frenkel defect.

Q.23 In which pair most efficient packing is present?

(a) hcp and bcc
(b) hcp and ccp
(c) bcc and ccp
(d) bcc and simple cubic cell

Ans. ***(b)*** Packing efficiency is the percentage of total filled space by particles and it can be calculated as packing efficiency

$$= \frac{\text{Volume occupied by four spheres in the unit cell}}{\text{Total volume of unit cell}} \times 100$$

Packing efficiency for hcp or ccp is calculated to be 74%, which is maximum among all type of crystals.

Q.24 The percentage of empty space in a body centred cubic arrangement is ....

(a) 74 (b) 68 (c) 32 (d) 26

Ans. ***(c)*** Packing efficiency for bcc arrangement is 68%, which represents total filled space in the unit cell. Hence, empty space in a body centred arrangement is $100 - 68 = 32\,\%$.

Mistake Alert! *One can make a mistake of confusing the packing efficiency percentage with percentage of empty space. Here, empty space in bcc arrangement is asked, therefore empty space in any crystal packing can be calculated as, empty space in unit cell = 100 − packing efficiency.*

Q.25 Which of the following statement is **not** true about the hexagonal close packing?

(a) The coordination number is 12
(b) It has 74% packing efficiency
(c) Tetrahedral voids of the second layer are covered by the spheres of the third layer
(d) In this arrangement spheres of the fourth layer are exactly aligned with those of the first layer

Ans. *(d)* Hexagonal close packing can be done by arranging two layers *A* and *B* one over another which can be diagramatically represented as :

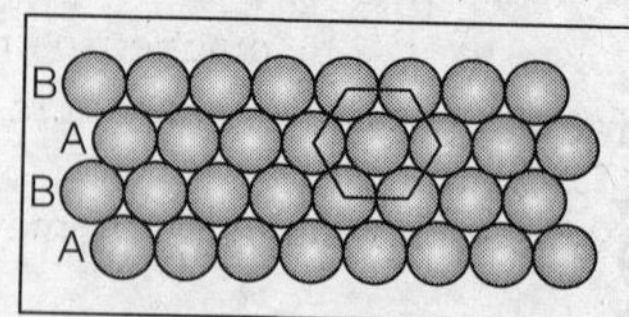

Here, we can see easily that 1st layer and 4th layer are not exactly aligned. Thus, statement (d) is not correct while other statements (a), (b) and (c) are true.

Q.26 In which of the following structures coordination number for cations and anions in the packed structure will be same?

(a) Cl^- ions form fcc lattice and Na^+ ions occupy all octahedral voids of the unit cell.

(b) Ca^{2+} ions form fcc lattice and F^- ions occupy all the eight tetrahedral voids of the unit cell.

(c) O^{2-} ions form fcc lattice and Na^+ ions occupy all the eight tetrahedral voids of the unit cell.

(d) S^{2-} ions form fcc lattice and Zn^{2+} ions go into alternate tetrahedral voids of the unit cell.

Ans. *(a)* NaCl crystal have rock salt structure having fcc lattice in which Cl^- ions are present at fcc lattice points and face centre and Na^+ occupies all the octahedral void of given unit cell.

Here, coordination number of $Na^+ = 6$

coordination number of $Cl^- = 6$

Q.27 What is the coordination number in a square close packed structure in two dimensions?

(a) 2 (b) 3 (c) 4 (d) 6

Ans. *(c)* Coordination number in a square closed packed structure in two dimensions is equal to 4 as shown below

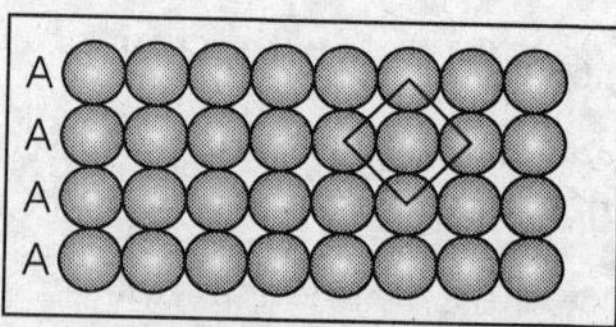

Cubic closed structure

Q.28 Which kind of defects are introduced by doping?

(a) Dislocation defect (b) Schottky defect

(c) Frenkel defect (d) Electronic defect

Ans. *(d)* When electron rich or electron deficient impurity is added to a perfect crystal it introduces electronic defect in them.

Q.29 Silicon doped with electron rich impurity forms ....

(a) *p*-type semiconductor (b) *n*-type semiconductor

(c) intrinsic semiconductor (d) insulator

Ans. *(b)* Silicon doped with electron rich impurity such as phosphorus forms a *n*-type semiconductor. This is due to presence of mobile electron.

Q.30 Which of the following statements is **not** true?

(a) Paramagnetic substances are weakly attracted by magnetic field.

(b) Ferromagnetic substances cannot be magnetised permanently.

(c) The domains in antiferromagnetic substances are oppositely oriented with respect to each other.

(d) Pairing of electrons cancels their magnetic moment in the diamagnetic substances.

Thinking Process This problem is based on the magnetic properties of materials. Analyse the given statements, using the definitions of paramagnetic, ferromagnetic, antiferromagnetic and diamagnetic substances.

Ans. *(b)* Ferromagnetic substances can be magnetised by applying magnetic field to it and magnetic property persist within it even after removal of magnetic field.

Hence, statement (b) is incorrect, answer while other three statements are correct.

Q.31 Which of the following is **not** true about the ionic solids?

(a) Bigger ions form the close packed structure.

(b) Smaller ions occupy either the tetrahedral or the octahedral voids depending upon their size.

(c) Occupation of all the voids is not necessary.

(d) The fraction of octahedral or tetrahedral voids occupied depends upon the radii of the ions occupying the voids.

Ans. *(d)* The fraction of octahedral or tetrahedral voids occupied depends upon the radii of the ions present at the lattice points. As we know the radii of octahedral or tetrahedral void, is related to radii of atoms (r) as

$$\text{Radius of octahedral void } (R_0) = 0.414\, r$$

$$\text{Radius of tetrahedral void } (R_t) = 0.225\, r$$

where, r = radius of bigger atom involved.

Q.32 A ferromagnetic substance becomes a permanent magnet when it is placed in a magnetic field because ....

(a) all the domains get oriented in the direction of magnetic field

(b) all the domains get oriented in the direction opposite to the direction of magnetic field

(c) domains get oriented randomly

(d) domains are not affected by magnetic field

Thinking Process This problem is based on the alignment of magnetic domains in ferromagnetic substances under an external magnetic field, leading to permanent magnetisation.

Ans. *(a)* When a ferromagnetic substance is placed in a magnetic field it becomes a permanent magnet because all the domains get oriented in the direction of magnetic field even after removal of applied magnetic field.

Q.33 The correct order of the packing efficiency in different types of unit cells is ....

(a) fcc < bcc < simple cubic

(b) fcc > bcc > simple cubic

(c) fcc < bcc > simple cubic

(d) bcc < fcc > simple cubic

Ans. *(b)* Packing efficiency in different types of unit cells can be tabulated as

Unit cell	Packing efficiency
fcc	74%
bcc	68%
Simple cubic	52%

Hence, correct order is fcc (74%) > bcc (68%) > simple cubic (52%).

Q.34 Which of the following defects is also known as dislocation defect?

(a) Frenkel defect
(b) Schottky defect
(c) Non-stoichiometric defect
(d) Simple interstitial defect

Ans. *(a)* Frenkel defect is also known as dislocation defect because in Frenkel defect atoms present in crystal lattice is dislocated to interstitial site.

Q.35 In the cubic close packing, the unit cell has ....

(a) 4 tetrahedral voids each of which is shared by four adjacent unit cells
(b) 4 tetrahedral voids within the unit cell
(c) 8 tetrahedral voids each of which is shared by four adjacent unit cells
(d) 8 tetrahedral voids within the unit cells

Ans. *(d)* In the cubic close packing, the unit cell has 8 tetrahedral voids within it and they are located at each eight smaller cube of a unit cell.

Q.36 The edge lengths of the unit cells in terms of the radius of spheres constituting fcc, bcc and simple cubic unit cells are respectively ....

(a) $2\sqrt{2}r, \frac{4r}{\sqrt{3}}, 2r$
(b) $\frac{4r}{\sqrt{3}}, 2\sqrt{2}r, 2r$
(c) $2r, 2\sqrt{2}r, \frac{4r}{\sqrt{3}}$
(d) $2r, \frac{4r}{\sqrt{3}}, 2\sqrt{2}r$

Ans. *(a)* Edge length for different types of unit cells can be tabulated as

Types of unit cell	Edge length
fcc	$2\sqrt{2}r$
bcc	$\frac{4}{\sqrt{3}}r$
scc	2r

Q.37 Which of the following represents correct order of conductivity in solids?

(a) $\kappa_{metals} >> \kappa_{insulators} < \kappa_{semiconductors}$
(b) $\kappa_{metals} << \kappa_{insulators} < \kappa_{semiconductors}$
(c) $\kappa_{metals} \simeq > \kappa_{semiconductors} > \kappa_{insulators} = \text{zero}$
(d) $\kappa_{metals} < \kappa_{semiconductors} > \kappa_{insulators} \neq \text{zero}$

Thinking Process Look at the options and choose the correct answer by using the concept that metals have maximum value of κ and insulators have minimum value.

Ans. *(a)* Conductivity of metal, insulator and semiconductors can be represented in the term of κ (Kappa), which depends upon energy gap between valence band and conduction band.

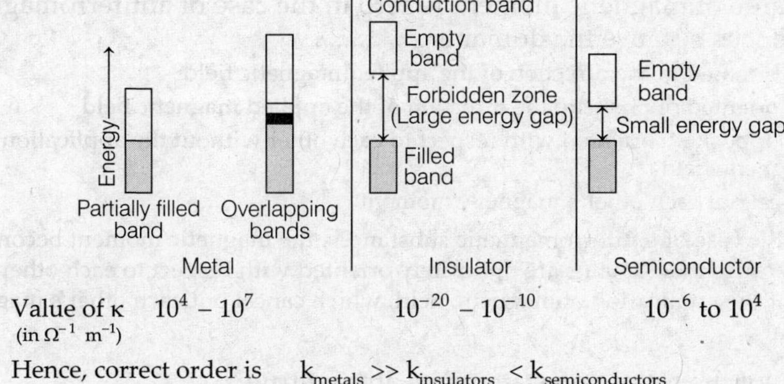

Value of κ (in Ω^{-1} m^{-1})	$10^4 - 10^7$	$10^{-20} - 10^{-10}$	10^{-6} to 10^4

Hence, correct order is $k_{metals} >> k_{insulators} < k_{semiconductors}$

Multiple Choice Questions (More Than One Options)

Q.38 Which of the following is **not** true about the voids formed in 3 dimensional hexagonal close packed structure?

(a) A tetrahedral void is formed when a sphere of the second layer is present above triangular void in the first layer.

(b) All the triangular voids are not covered by the spheres of the second layer.

(c) Tetrahedral voids are formed when the triangular voids in the second layer lie above the triangular voids in the first layer and the triangular shapes of these voids do not overlap.

(d) Octahedral voids are formed when the triangular voids in the second layer exactly overlap with similar voids in the first layer.

Ans. ***(c, d)*** Tetrahedral voids are formed when the triangular void in the second layer lie exactly above the triangular voids in the first layer and the triangular shape of these voids oppositely overlap.

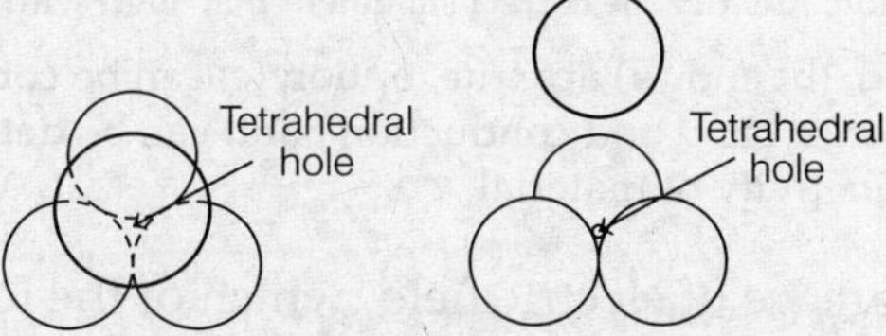

Octahedral voids are formed when triangular void of second layer does not exactly overlap with similar void in first layer.

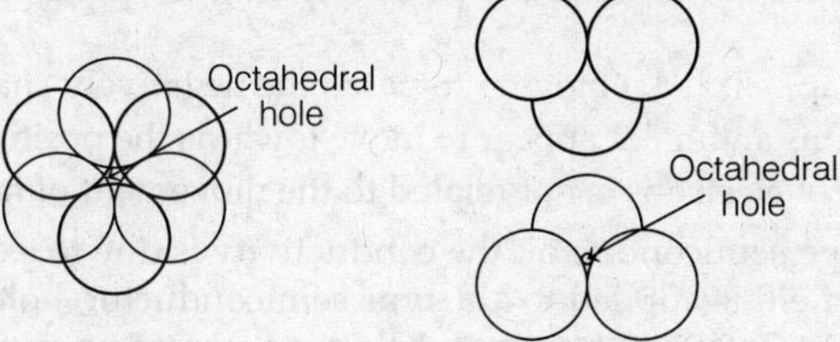

Q.39 The value of magnetic moment is zero in the case of antiferromagnetic substances because the domains ....

(a) get oriented in the direction of the applied magnetic field

(b) get oriented opposite to the direction of the applied magnetic field

(c) are oppositely oriented with respect to each other without the application of magnetic field

(d) cancel out each other's magnetic moment

Ans. *(c, d)* In the case of antiferromagnetic substances, the magnetic moment becomes zero because the domains are oppositely oriented with respect to each other without the application of magnetic field, which cancel out each other's magnetic moment.

Q.40 Which of the following statements are **not** true?

(a) Vacancy defect results in a decrease in the density of the substance.

(b) Interstitial defects results in an increase in the density of the substance.

(c) Impurity defect has no effect on the density of the substance.

(d) Frenkel defect results in an increase in the density of the substance.

Ans. *(c, d)* Statements (c) and (d) can be correctly written as

(c) Impurity defect changes the density of substance as impurity has different density than the ions present on perfect crystal, e.g. When $SrCl_2$ is added to the NaCl crystal it causes impurity defect.

(d) Frenkel defect results in neither decrease nor increase in density of the substance.

Q.41 Which of the following statements are true about metals?

(a) Valence band overlaps with conduction band.

(b) The gap between valence band and conduction band is negligible.

(c) The gap between valence band and conduction band cannot be determined.

(d) Valence band may remain partially filled.

Thinking Process This problem is based on the electronic bond structure of solids. To solve this question, identify the correct statement that align with the metallic behavior.

Ans. *(a, b, d)* Option (a), (b) and (d) are true, option (c) can be correctly stated as the gap between valence band and conduction band can be determined and it decides the conductivity of material.

Q.42 Under the influence of electric field, which of the following statement is true about the movement of electrons and holes in a *p*-type semiconductor?

(a) Electron will move towards the positively charged plate through electron holes.

(b) Holes will appear to be moving towards the negatively charged plate.

(c) Both electrons and holes appear to move towards the positively charged plate.

(d) Movement of electrons is not related to the movement of holes.

Ans. *(a, b)* In a *p*-type semiconductor, the conductivity is due to existence of hole. When electric field is applied to a *p*-type semiconductor, hole starts moving towards negatively charged plate and electron towards positively charged plate.

Q.43 Which of the following statements are true about semiconductors?

(a) Silicon doped with electron rich impurity is a p-type semiconductor.

(b) Silicon doped with an electron rich impurity is an n-type semiconductor.

(c) Delocalised electrons increase the conductivity of doped silicon.

(d) An electron vacancy increases the conductivity of n-type semiconductor.

Ans. *(b, c)* Silicon doped with an electron rich impurity is a n-type semiconductor. Conductivity of n-type semiconductor is due to presence of free electron. Delocalisation of electrons increases the conductivity of doped silicon due to increase in mobility of electrons.

Q. 44 An excess of potassium ions makes KCl crystals appear violet or lilac in colour since ....

(a) some of the anionic sites are occupied by an unpaired electron

(b) some of the anionic sites are occupied by a pair of electrons

(c) there are vacancies at some anionic sites

(d) F-centres are created which impart colour to the crystals

Ans. *(a, d)* When KCl crystals are heated, it leads to the deposition of potassium ion on surface of KCl. The Cl^- ions diffuse to the surface of crystal and potassium atom loses electron to form K^+ ion. The released electron occupies anionic site which is known as F-centre and impart colour to the crystal.

Q.45 The number of tetrahedral voids per unit cell in NaCl crystal is ....

(a) 4

(b) 8

(c) twice the number of octahedral voids

(d) four times the number of octahedral voids

Ans. *(b, c)* NaCl has a rock salt type structure having fcc arrangement.
Total number of atoms per unit cell = 4

$\therefore$ Number of tetrahedral voids = $2 \times 4 = 8$

Number of octahedral voids = 4

Hence, (b) and (c) are correct choices.

Q.46 Amorphous solids can also be called ....

(a) pseudo solids
(b) true solids
(c) super cooled liquids
(d) super cooled solids

- **Concept Insight** This solution includes the concept of amorphous solids and their properties. such as short-range order, slow flow behaviour and their classification as pseudo solids or super cooled liquids.

Ans. *(a, c)* Amorphous solid has a short range order which has a tendency to flow very slowly. Hence, it is also known as pseudo solids or super cooled liquids. Glass panes fixed to windows or doors of old buildings are invariably observed to be thicker at bottom than at the top. These are examples of amorphous solids.

Q.47 A perfect crystal of silicon (fig.) is doped with some elements as given in the options. Which of these options shows n-type semiconductors?

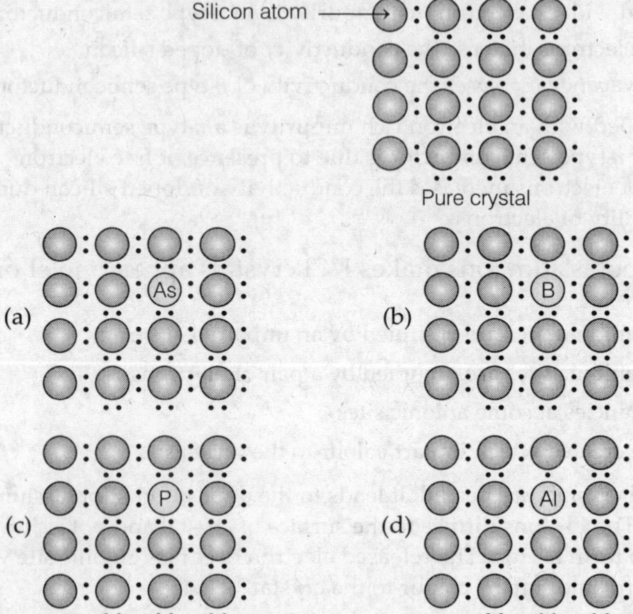

Ans. ***(a, c)*** **n-type semiconductor** When group 15 elements are doped into a perfect crystal it leads to the formation of n-type semiconductor.

Here, in (a) As (group 15, period 3) is doped to perfect Si-crystal and in (c) P (group 15, period 2) is doped to perfect Si-crystal.

Q.48 Which of the following statements are correct?

(a) Ferrimagnetic substances lose ferrimagnetism on heating and become paramagnetic.
(b) Ferrimagnetic substances do not lose ferrimagnetism on heating and remain ferrimagnetic.
(c) Antiferromagnetic substances have domain structures similar to ferromagnetic substances and their magnetic moments are not cancelled by each other.
(d) In ferromagnetic substances, all the domains get oriented in the direction of magnetic field and remain as such even after removing magnetic field.

Ans. ***(a, d)*** Ferrimagnetic substances lose ferrimagnetism on heating and become paramagnetic. In ferrimagnetic substance domains are alligned in parallel and antiparallel direction in unequal numbers.

In ferromagnetic substances, all the domains get oriented in the direction of magnetic field and remain as such even after removing magnetic field.
Hence, (a) and (d) are correct choices.

Q.49 Which of the following features are **not** shown by quartz glass?

(a) This is a crystalline solid.
(b) Refractive index is same in all the directions.
(c) This has definite heat of fusion.
(d) This is also called super cooled liquid.

Thinking Process This problem is based on the properties of quartz glass, which is an amorphous solid.

Ans. ***(a, c)*** Quartz glass is an amorphous solid so it does not have definite heat of fusion. This is due to short range order of molecules while, quartz glass is also known as super cooled liquid and it is isotropic in nature.

Q.50 Which of the following **cannot** be regarded as molecular solid?

(a) SiC (silicon carbide) (b) AlN

(c) Diamond (d) I_2

Ans. ***(a, b, c)*** SiC, AlN and diamond are examples of network solid as they have three dimensional structure. I_2 is a molecular solid because in I_2, solid particles are held together by dipole-dipole interactions.

Q.51 In which of the following arrangements octahedral voids are formed?

(a) hcp (b) bcc (c) simple cubic (d) fcc

Ans. ***(a, d)*** In hcp and fcc arrangement, octahedral voids are formed. In fcc the octahedral voids are observed at edge and centre of cube, while in bcc and simple cubic, no any octahedral voids are observed.

Q.52 Frenkel defect is also known as ....

(a) stoichiometric defect (b) dislocation defect

(c) impurity defect (d) non-stoichiometric defect

Ans. ***(a, b)*** Frenkel defect arises when the smaller ion (usually cation) is dislocated from its original site to interstitial site, this is also known as dislocation defect. Since, stoichiometry of substance persist so, it is categorised as stoichiometric defect.

Mistake Alert! *Students may confuse Frenkel defect with other defects, thinking it alters stoichiometry like schottky defect. They might also overlook that Frenkel defect is both a stoichiometric and a dislocation defect.*

Q.53 Which of the following defects decrease the density?

(a) Interstitial defect (b) Vacancy defect

(c) Frenkel defect (d) Schottky defect

Ans. ***(b, d)*** Vacancy and Schottky defects lead to decrease in the density and both are the types of a stoichiometric defect. In case of Frenkel defect and interstitial defect, there is no change in density of substance.

Short Answer Type Questions

Q.54 Why are liquids and gases categorised as fluids?

Ans. Liquids and gases have the tendency to flow, *i.e.*, their molecules can move freely from one place to another. Therefore, they are known as fluids.

Q.55 Why are solids incompressible?

Ans. The distance between the constituent particles is very less in solids. On bringing them closer repulsion will start between electron clouds of these particles. Hence, they cannot be brought further close together and are incompressible.

Q.56 Inspite of long range order in the arrangement of particles why are the crystals usually not perfect?

Ans. Crystals have long range repeated pattern of arrangement of constituent particles, but in the process of crystallisation some deviations from the ideal arrangement (i.e. defects) may be introduced, therefore, crystals are usually not perfect.

Q.57 Why does table salt, NaCl sometimes appear yellow in colour?

Ans. Yellow colour in NaCl is because of to metal excess defect, due to which unpaired electrons occupy anionic sites, known as F-centres. These electrons absorb energy from the visible region for the excitation, which makes crystal appear yellow.

Q.58 Why is FeO(s) not formed in stoichiometric composition?

Ans. In the crystals of FeO, some of the Fe^{2+} cations are replaced by Fe^{3+} ions. Three Fe^{2+} ions are replaced by two Fe^{3+} ions to make up the loss of positive charge. Eventually, there would be less amount of metal as compared to stoichiometric composition.

Q.59 Why does white ZnO (*s*) becomes yellow upon heating?

Ans. On heating, ZnO loses oxygen as follows

$$ZnO \xrightarrow{\text{Heat}} Zn^{2+} + \frac{1}{2}O_2 + 2e^-$$

Zn^{2+} ions and electrons move to interstitial sites and F-centres are formed which impart yellow colour to ZnO(*s*).

Q.60 Why does the electrical conductivity of semiconductors increase with rise in temperature?

Ans. The gap between conduction band and valence band is small in semiconductors. Therefore, electrons from the valence band can jump to the conduction band on increasing temperature. Thus, they become more conducting as the temperature increases.

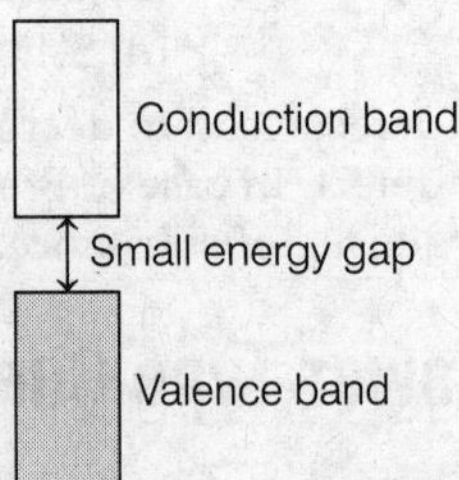

Q.61 Explain why does conductivity of germanium crystals increase on doping with galium?

Ans. On doping germanium with galium, some of the positions of lattice of germanium are occupied be galium. Galium atom has only three valence electrons. Therefore, fourth valency of nearby germanium atom is not satisfied and the place remains vacant.

This place is deficient of electrons and is therefore called electron hole or electron vacancy. Electron from neighbouring atom comes and fills the hole, thereby creating a hole in its original position.

Under the influence of electric field, electrons move towards positively charged plates through these and conduct electricity. The holes appear to move towards negatively charged plates.

Q.62 In a compound, nitrogen atoms (N) make cubic close packed lattic and metal atoms (*M*) occupy one-third of the tetrahedral voids present. Determine the formula of the compound formed by *M* and N?

Ans. Let the number of N atoms in ccp is x

$$\therefore \quad \text{Number of tetrahedral voids} = 2x$$

$$\therefore \quad \text{Number of } M \text{ atoms} = \frac{1}{3} \times 2x$$

$$\frac{\text{Number of } N \text{ atoms}}{\text{Number of } M \text{ atoms}} = \frac{3x}{2x} = \frac{3}{2}$$

So, the formula of the compound is M_2N_3.

Q.63 Under which situations can an amorphous substance change to crystalline form?

Ans. On heating, amorphous substances change to crystalline form at some temperature. Some objects from ancient civilisation are found to be milky in appearancem due to crystallisation.

Matching The Columns

Q.64 Match the defects given in Column I with the statements in given Column II.

	Column I		Column II
A.	Simple vacancy defect	1.	Shown by non-ionic solids and increases density of the solid.
B.	Simple interstitial defect	2.	Shown by ionic solids and decreases density of the solid.
C.	Frenkel defect	3.	Shown by non-ionic solids and density of the solid decreases.
D.	Schottky defect	4.	Shown by ionic solids and density of the solid remains the same.

Ans. A. → (3) B. → (1) C. → (4) D. → (2)

A. When some of lattice sites are vacant in any non-ionic solid, the crystal is said to have vacancy defect and due to decrease in number of particles present in crystal lattice the density of crystal decreases.

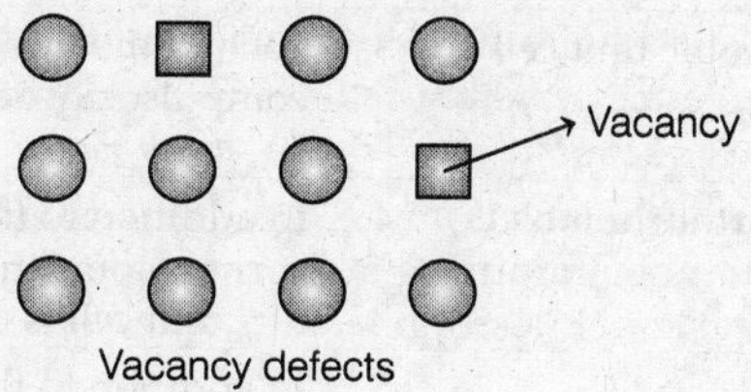

Vacancy defects

B. Simple interstitial defect are shown by non-ionic solids in which constituent particles is displaced from its normal site to an interstitial site. Hence, density of solid increases.

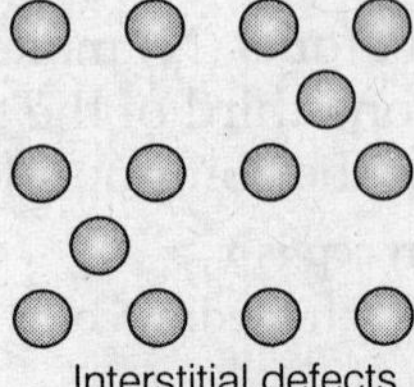

Interstitial defects

C. Frenkel defect is shown by ionic solids in which smaller ions get dislocated from its normal site to its interstitial site which lead to no change its density.

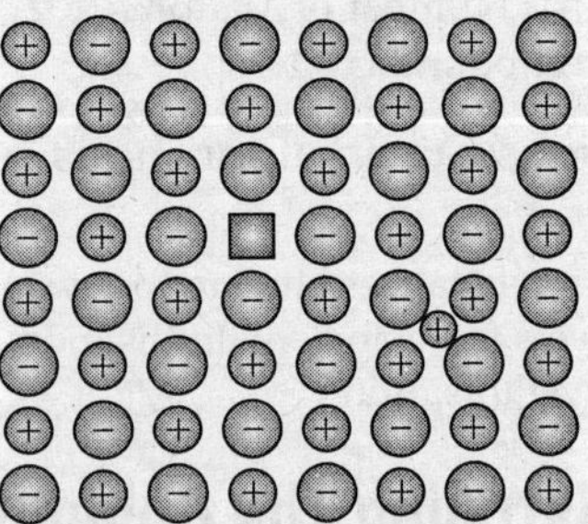

Frenkel defects

D. Schottky defect is shown by ionic solids in which equal number of cations and anions get missed from ionic solids and thus, density of solid decreases.

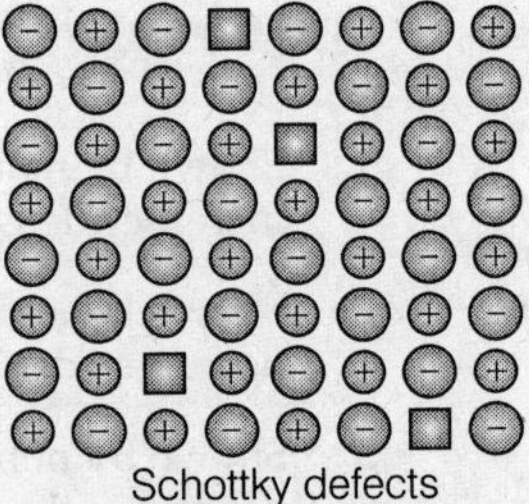

Schottky defects

Q.65 Match the type of unit cell given in Column I with the features given in Column II.

	Column I		Column II
A.	Primitive cubic unit cell	1.	Each of the three perpendicular edges compulsorily have the different edge length *i.e.*, $a \neq b \neq c$
B.	Body centred cubic unit cell	2.	Number of atoms per unit cell is one
C.	Face centred cubic unit cell	3.	Each of the three perpendicular edges compulsorily have the same edge length *i.e.*, $a = b = c$
D.	End centred orthorhombic unit cell	4.	In addition to the contribution from the corner atoms the number of atoms present in a unit cell is one
		5.	In addition to the contribution from the corner atoms the number of atoms present in a unit cell is three

Ans. **A.** → (2, 3) **B.** → (3, 4) **C.** → (3, 5) **D.** → (1, 4)

A. For primitive unit cell, $a = b = c$
Total number of atoms per unit cell $= 1/8 \times 8 = 1$
Here, 1/8 is due to contribution of each atom present at corner.

B. For body centred cubic unit cell, $a = b = c$
This lattice contain atoms at corner as well as body centre. Contribution due to atoms at corner $= 1/8 \times 8 = 1$ and contribution due to atoms at body centre = 8

C. For face centred unit cell, $a = b = c$
Total constituent ions per unit cell present at corners $= \frac{1}{8} \times 8 = 1$

Total constituent ions per unit cell present at face centre $= \frac{1}{2} \times 6 = 3$

D. For end centered orthorhombic unit cell, $a \neq b \neq c$
Total contribution of atoms present at corner $= \frac{1}{8} \times 8 = 1$

Total contribution of atoms present at end centre $= \frac{1}{2} \times 2 = 1$

Hence, other than corner, it contain total one atom per unit cell.

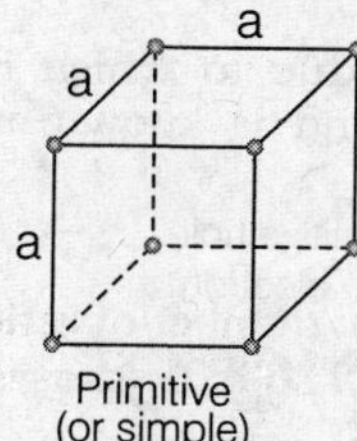

Primitive (or simple)

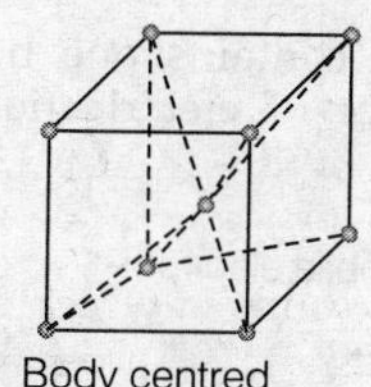
Body centred

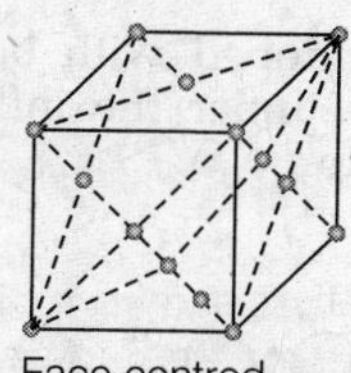
Face centred

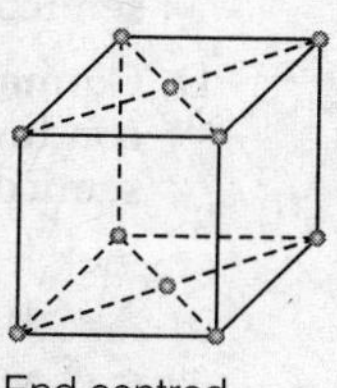
End centred

Q.66 Match the types of defect given in Column I with the statement given in Column II.

	Column I		Column II
A.	Impurity defect	1.	NaCl with anionic sites called F-centres
B.	Metal excess defect	2.	FeO with Fe^{3+}
C.	Metal deficiency defect	3.	NaCl with Sr^{2+} and some cationic sites vacant

Ans. **A.** → (3) **B.** → (1) **C.** → (2)

A. Impurity defect arises due to replacement of one common ion present in any crystal by another uncommon ion.

B. Metal excess defect is due to missing of cation from an ideal ionic solid which leads to creation of a F-centre generally occupied by unpaired electrons. *e.g.*, NaCl with anionic site.

C. In FeO, Fe^{3+} exists along with Fe^{2+} which leads to decrease in metal ion(s), so this is a type of metal deficiency defect.

Q.67 Match the items given in Column I with the items given in Column II.

	Column I		Column II
A.	Mg in solid state	1.	*p*-type semiconductor
B.	$MgCl_2$ in molten state	2.	*n*-type semiconductor
C.	Silicon with phosphorus	3.	Electrolytic conductors
D.	Germanium with boron	4.	Electronic conductors

Ans. A. → (4) **B.** → (3) **C.** → (2) **D.** → (1)

A. Mg in solid state shows electronic conductivity due to presence of free electrons. Hence, they are known as electronic conductors.

B. $MgCl_2$ in molten state show electrolytic conductivity due to presence of electrolytes in molten state.

C. Silicon doped with phosphorus contains one extra electron due to which it shows conductivity under the influence of electric field and is known as *n-type* semiconductor.

D. Germanium doped with boron contains one hole due to which it shows conductivity under the influence of electric field and is known as *p*-type semiconductor.

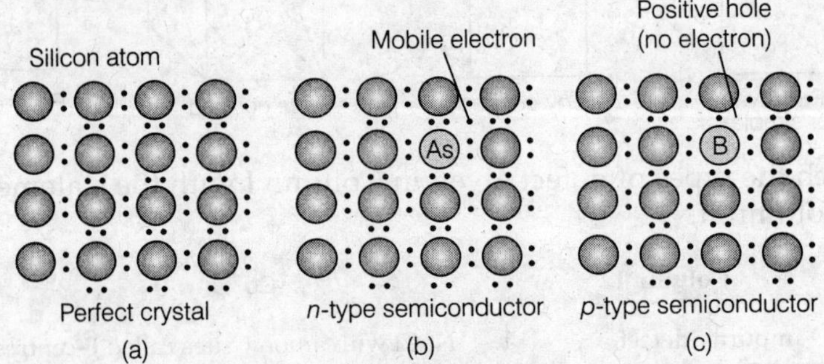

Perfect crystal (a) *n*-type semiconductor (b) *p*-type semiconductor (c)

Q.68 Match the type of packing given in Column I with the items given in Column II.

	Column I		Column II
A.	Square close packing in two dimensions	1.	Triangular voids
B.	Hexagonal close packing in two dimensions	2.	Pattern of spheres is repeated in every fourth layer
C.	Hexagonal close packing in three dimensions	3.	Coordination number = 4
D.	Cubic close packing in three dimensions	4.	Pattern of sphere is repeated in alternate layers

Ans. **A.** → (3) **B.** → (1) **C.** → (4) **D.** → (2)

A. In square close packing in two dimensions, each sphere have coordination number 4, as shown below

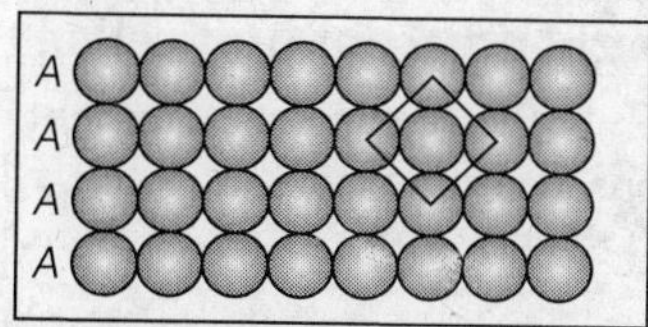

B. In hexagonal close packing in two dimensions, each sphere have coordination number 6 as shown below and creates a triangular void.

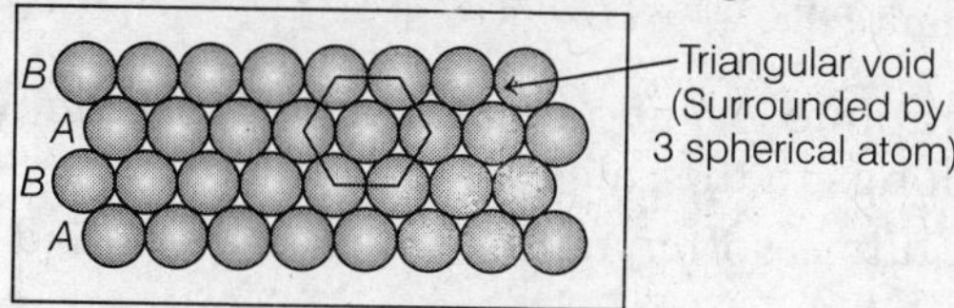

C. In hexagonal close packing in 3 dimensions, there is a repeated pattern of sphere in alternate layers, also known as *ABAB* pattern.

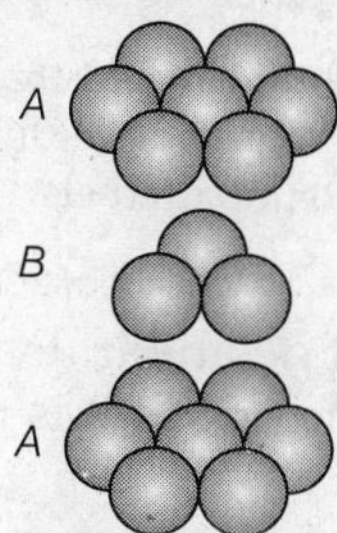

D. In cubic close packing in a 3 dimensions, there is a repeating pattern of sphere in every fourth layer also known as *ABCABC* pattern.

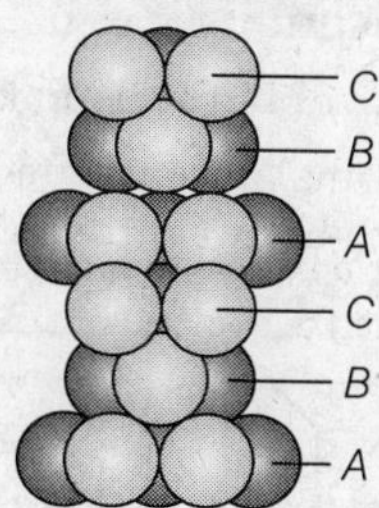

Assertion and Reason

In the following questions a statement of Assertion followed by a statement of Reason is given. Choose the correct answer out of the following choices.

(a) Assertion and Reason both are correct statements and Reason is correct explanation for Assertion.

(b) Assertion and Reason both are correct statements but Reason is not correct explanation for Assertion.

(c) Assertion is correct statement but Reason is wrong statement.

(d) Assertion is wrong statement but Reason is correct statement.

Q.69 **Assertion** The total number of atoms present in a simple cubic unit cell is one.

Reason Simple cubic unit cell has atoms at its corners, each of which is shared between eight adjacent unit cells.

Ans. *(a)* Assertion and reason both are correct statements and reason is correct explanation for assertion. In simple cubic unit cell, each atom is present at corners having contribution 1/8. Hence, total number of atoms present per unit cell in scc is $\frac{1}{8} \times 8 = 1$.

Simple cubic unit cell has atoms at its corners, each of which is shared between eight adjacent unit cells.

Q.70 **Assertion** Graphite is a good conductor of electricity however diamond belongs to the category of insulators.

Reason Graphite is soft in nature on the other hand diamond is very hard and brittle.

Ans. *(b)* Assertion and Reason both are correct, but Reason is not correct explanation of Assertion.

Correct explanation is that graphite have layered structure with free electrons due to which it is a good conductor of electricity. On the other hand, diamond have tetrahedral arrangement with no unpaired electron. Therefore, diamond is hard, brittle and insulator.

Q.71 **Assertion** Total number of octahedral voids present in unit cell of cubic close packing including the one that is present at the body centre, is four.

Reason Besides the body centre there is one octahedral void present at the centre of each of the six faces of the unit cell and each of which is shared between two adjacent unit cells.

Ans. *(c)* Assertion is correct statement but Reason is incorrect statement.

Assertion is true as in ccp, atoms present at face centre and corner of each unit cell creates octahedral void at each body centre and all twelve edges of a unit cell as shown below

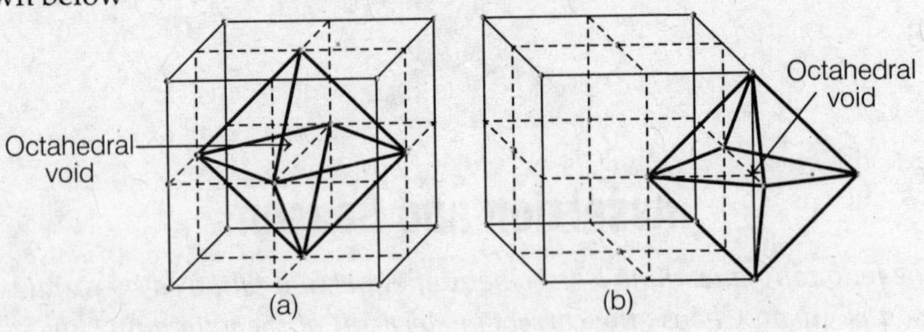

Correct reason is that beside the body centre there is one octahedral void at centre of each of 12 edges which is surrounded by six atoms.

Out of six atoms four belongs to same unit cell (2 at corner and 2 at face centre) and 2 atoms belong to adjacent unit cell.

Q.72 **Assertion** The packing efficiency is maximum for the fcc structure.
Reason The coordination number is 12 in fcc structures.

Ans. *(b)* Assertion and Reason both are correct statements, but reason is not the correct explanation of Assertion.

Correct reason is that, packing efficiency is maximum for fcc structure because it consists of total four atoms per unit cell.

Packing efficiency is maximum in fcc structure which is equal to 74%.

Q.73 **Assertion** Semiconductors are solids with conductivities in the intermediate range from $10^{-6} - 10^{4}$ ohm^{-1}m^{-1}.
Reason Intermediate conductivity in semiconductor is due to partially filled valence band.

Ans. *(c)* Assertion is correct statement, but reason is incorrect statement.

Semiconductors are solids with conductivities in the intermediate range varying from $10^{-6} - 10^{4}\ \Omega^{-1}\ m^{-1}$. Intermediate conductivity is due to small energy gap between valence band and conduction band.

(Also, refer to Q. 60)

Long Answer Type Questions

Q.74 With the help of a labelled diagram show that there are four octahedral voids per unit cell in a cubic close packed structure.

Ans. Cubic close packed structure contains one atom at each of eight corners of a unit cell and one atom at each of six faces which can be represented below.

As we know that any atom surrounded by six atoms (hard sphere) creates an octahedral void. In case of fcc, body centre is surrounded by six identical atoms present at face centre. Hence, there is a octahedral void at body centre of each unit cell.

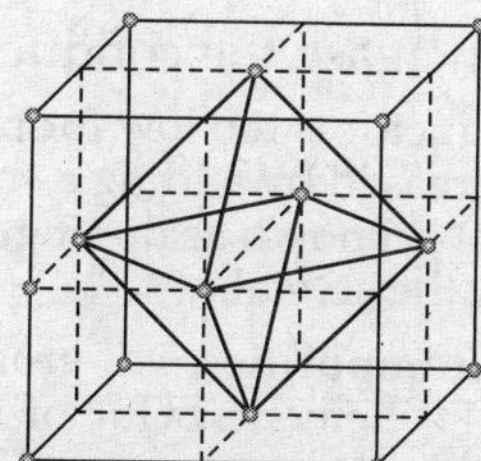

Location of octahedral voids per unit cell of ccp or fcc lattice at the body centre of the cube

Beside the body centre there is one octahedral void at centre of each of 12 edge as shown below

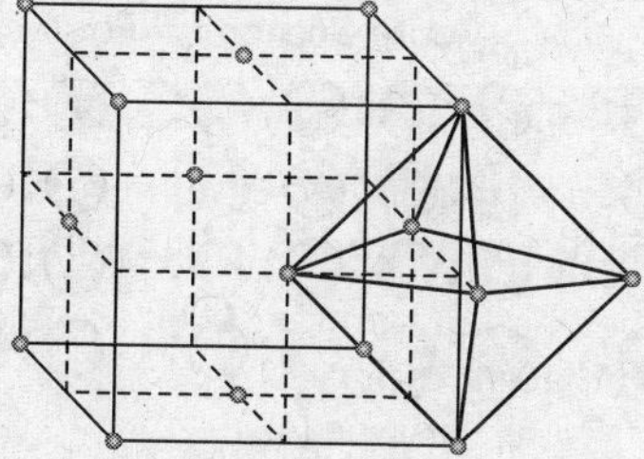

Octahedral void at centre of each edge

Since, each void is shared by 4 unit cell. Therefore, contribution of octahedral void to each edge of a unit cell is $\frac{1}{4}$.

Number of octahedral void at centre of 12 edges $= \frac{1}{4} \times 12 = 3$

Number of octahedral void at body centre = 1

Therefore, total number of octahedral void at each ccp lattice = 3 + 1 = 4

Q.75 Show that in a cubic close packed structure, eight tetrahedral voids are present per unit cell.

Ans. Cubic close packed structure contains one atom at each corner of an unit cell and at face centre of each unit cell. Each unit cell consists of 8 small cubes.

Each small cube contains 4 atoms at its alternate corner, when these atoms are joined to each other, it leads to creation of a tetrahedral void as shown below.

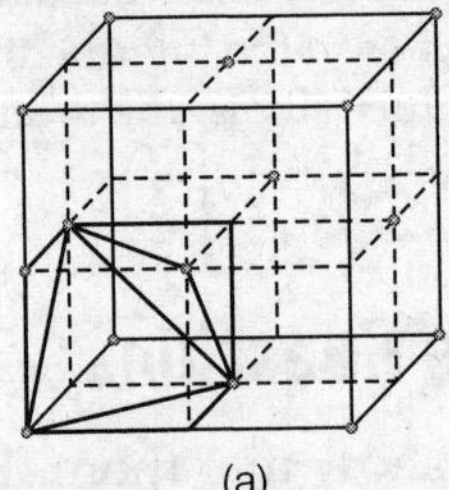

(a)

Eight tetrahedral voids per unit cell of ccp structure

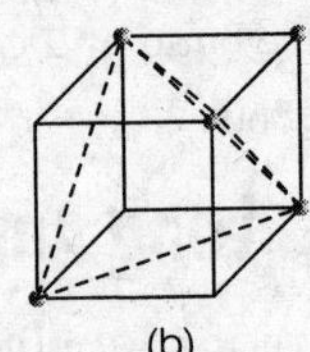

(b)

One tetrahedral void showing the geometry

Since, there are total 8 smaller cubes present at one unit cell and each smaller cube has one tetrahedral void hence, total number of tetrahedral void present in each unit cell is equal to eight.

As we know ccp structure has 4 atoms per unit cell. Thus, total number of tetrahedral void in one ccp unit cell is equal to 8.

Q.76 How does the doping increase the conductivity of semiconductors?

Ans. Conductivity of a semiconductor is too low for practical use. The conductivity of a semiconductor can be increased by adding a suitable amount of impurity to perfect crystal. This process is known as doping. It can be done by adding either of two types of impurity to the crystal.

(A) By adding **electron rich impurities,** *i.e.,* group 15 elements to the silicon and germanium of group 14 elements. Out of 4 valence electrons of group 14 elements and 5 valence electrons of group 15 elements, four electrons of each element led to formation of four covalent bonds while the one extra electron of group 15 elements become delocalised.

Thus, this increases conductivity of semiconductor. This type of semiconductor is known as *n*-type semiconductor.

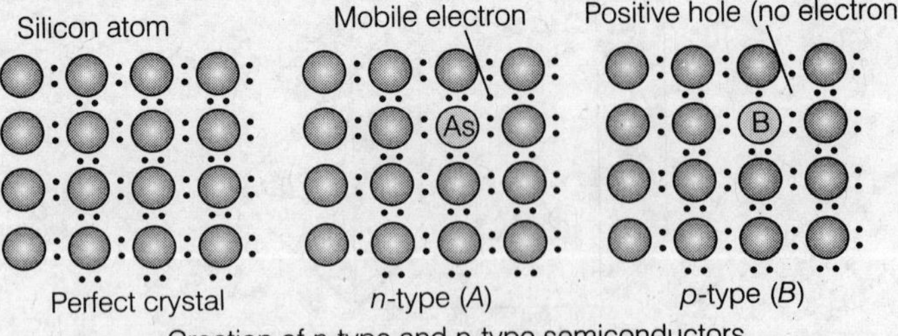

Creation of *n*-type and *p*-type semiconductors by doping groups 15 and 13 elements

(B) By adding **electron deficient impurity,** *i.e.,* when group 13 element is doped to group 14 element, it leads to creation of a hole in the ideal crystal which is known as electron hole or electron vacancy.

An electron from the neighbouring atom comes and fill the electron hole, in doing so an electron from the neighbour leaves an electron hole in its original position. Thus, it increases the conductivity of semiconductor. This type of semiconductor is known as *p*-type semiconductor.

Q.77 A sample of ferrous oxide has actual formula $Fe_{0.93}O_{1.00}$. In this sample, what fraction of metal ions are Fe^{2+} ions? What type of non-stoichiometric defect is present in this sample?

Thinking Process Consider the number of Fe^{2+} and Fe^{3+} ions as x and y, then write their sum equal to 0.93. Write another equation in terms of x and y by taking the sum of their total charge equal to 2 [charge on oxygen]. Now using the substitution method. Calculate the value of x and y, then calculate fraction of Fe^{2+} ion present in this sample.

Ans. Let the formula of the sample be $(Fe^{2+})_x\ (Fe^{3+})_y\ O$

On looking at the given formula of the compound

$$x + y = 0.93 \quad \text{...(i)}$$

Total positive charge on ferrous and ferric ions should balance the two units of negative charge on oxygen

Therefore,

$$2x + 3y = 2 \quad \text{...(ii)}$$

$$\Rightarrow \quad x + \frac{3}{2}y = 1 \quad \text{...(iii)}$$

On subtracting equation (i) from equation (iii) we have,

$$\frac{3}{2}y - y = 1 - 0.93$$

$$\Rightarrow \quad \frac{1}{2}y = 0.07$$

$$\Rightarrow \quad y = 0.14$$

On putting the value of y in equation (i), we get

$$x + 0.14 = 0.93$$

$$\Rightarrow \quad x = 0.93 - 0.14$$

$$\Rightarrow \quad x = 0.79$$

Fraction of Fe^{2+} ions present in the sample $= \frac{0.79}{0.93} = 0.849$

Metal deficiency defect is present in the sample because iron is less in amount than that required for stoichiometric composition.

Chapter

02 Solutions

Multiple Choice Questions (MCQs)

Q.1 Which of the following unit is useful in relating concentration of solution with its vapour pressure?

(a) Mole fraction (b) Parts per million

(c) Mass percentage (d) Molality

Ans. *(a)* According to Henry's law, partial pressure of gas in the solution is proportional to the mole fraction of gas in the solution.

$$p = K_H x$$

where, K_H = Henry's constant

Hence, (a) mole fraction is the correct choice.

Q.2 On dissolving sugar in water at room temperature solution feels cool to touch. Under which of the following cases dissolution of sugar will be most rapid?

(a) Sugar crystals in cold water.

(b) Sugar crystals in hot water.

(c) Powdered sugar in cold water.

(d) Powdered sugar in hot water.

Thinking Process Use the concept of solubility and effect of temperature on solubility to answer this question.

Ans. *(d)* Dissolution of sugar in water will be most rapid when powdered sugar is dissolved in hot water because powdered sugar has large surface area and thus, dissolves faster in hot water. As dissolution of sugar in water is an endothermic process. Hence, high temperature will favour the rapid dissolution of sugar in water.

Q.3 At equilibrium the rate of dissolution of a solid solute in a volatile liquid solvent is ....

(a) less than the rate of crystallisation

(b) greater than the rate of crystallisation

(c) equal to the rate of crystallisation

(d) zero

Ans. *(c)* At equilibrium the rate of dissolution of solid in a volatile liquid solvent is equal to the rate of crystallisation.

Q.4 A beaker contains a solution of substance 'A'. Precipitation of substance 'A' takes place when small amount of 'A' is added to the solution. The solution is ....

(a) saturated (b) supersaturated (c) unsaturated (d) concentrated

Thinking Process Use the concept of saturated, unsaturated, supersaturated and concentrated solution.

Ans. ***(b)*** When solute is added to the solution, three cases may arise

(i) If it dissolves into solution then solution is unsaturated.

(ii) If it does not dissolve in the solution then solution is known as saturated.

(iii) When solute gets precipitated, solution is known as supersaturated solution.

Q.5 Maximum amount of a solid solute that can be dissolved in a specified amount of a given liquid solvent does not depend upon ....

(a) temperature (b) nature of solute
(c) pressure (d) nature of solvent

Ans. ***(c)*** Solubility of a solid in liquid solvent does not depend upon pressure because solid and liquid are highly incompressible and practically remain unaffected by change in pressure.

Q.6 Low concentration of oxygen in the blood and tissues of people living at high altitude is due to ....

(a) low temperature
(b) low atmospheric pressure
(c) high atmospheric pressure
(d) Both low temperature and high atmospheric pressure

Ans. ***(b)*** At high altitudes, the partial pressure of oxygen is less than at the ground level and atmospheric pressure decreases which leads to low concentrations of oxygen in the blood and tissues of people living at high altitudes.

Q.7 Considering the formation, breaking and strength of hydrogen bond, predict which of the following mixtures will show a positive deviation from Raoult's law?

(a) Methanol and acetone (b) Chloroform and acetone
(c) Nitric acid and water (d) Phenol and aniline

Ans. ***(a)*** In pure methanol, molecules are hydrogen bonded. On adding acetone, its molecules get in between the host molecules and break some of the hydrogen bonds between them.

Therefore, the intermolecular attractive forces between the solute-solvent molecules are weaker than those between the solute-solute and solvent-solvent molecules.

On the other hand, other three remaining options will show negative deviation from Raoult's law, where the intermolecular attractive forces between the solute-solvent molecules are stronger than those between the solute-solute and solvent-solvent molecules.

Q.8 Colligative properties depend on ....

(a) the nature of the solute particles dissolved in solution.
(b) the number of solute particles in solution.
(c) the physical properties of the solute particles dissolved in solution.
(d) the nature of solvent particles.

- **Concept Insight** This solution includes the concept of colligative properties and their applications.

Ans. ***(b)*** Colligative properties depend upon the number of the solute particles in solution irrespective of their nature. Colligative property is used to determine the molecular mass of a particle.

Q.9 Which of the following aqueous solutions should have the highest boiling point?

(a) 1.0 M NaOH (b) 1.0 M Na_2SO_4
(c) 1.0 M NH_4NO_3 (d) 1.0 M KNO_3

Thinking Process This problem includes concept of van't Hoff factor and boiling point. Calculate van't Hoff factor then correlate it with boiling point of the solution.

Ans. ***(b)*** As we know greater the value of van't Hoff factor, higher will be the elevation in boiling point and hence higher will be the boiling point of solution.

Solution	van't Hoff factor (i)
1.0 M NaOH	2
1.0 M Na_2SO_4	3
1.0 M NH_4NO_3	2
1.0 M KNO_3	2

Hence, 1.0 M Na_2SO_4 has highest value of boiling point.

Q.10 The unit of ebullioscopic constant is

(a) K kg mol^{-1} or K $(molality)^{-1}$ (b) mol kg K^{-1} or K^{-1} (molality)
(c) kg mol^{-1} K^{-1} or K^{-1} $(molality)^{-1}$ (d) K mol kg^{-1} or K (molality)

Thinking Process Write the formula of ebullioscopic constant then put the values of their units to calculate unit of ebullioscopic constant.

Ans. ***(a)*** As we know from elevation in boiling point that

$$\Delta T_b = K_b m$$

$$K_b = \frac{\Delta T_b}{m}$$

$$\text{Unit of } K_b = \frac{\text{unit of } \Delta T_b}{\text{unit of } m} = \frac{\text{K}}{\text{mol kg}^{-1}} = \text{kg K mol}^{-1} \text{ or K (molality)}^{-1}$$

Q.11 In comparison to a 0.01 M solution of glucose, the depression in freezing point of a 0.01 M $MgCl_2$ solution is ....

(a) the same (b) about twice
(c) about three times (d) about six times

Thinking Process Calculate the value of van't Hoff factor then correlate it with colligative property of given solution.

Ans. *(c)* As we know depression in freezing point is directly related to van't Hoff factor (i), according to which greater the value of i greater will be the depression in freezing point.

Solution	i
0.01 M glucose	1
0.01 M $MgCl_2$	3

Hence, depression in freezing point of 0.01 M $MgCl_2$ is about 3 times of 0.01M glucose.

Q. 12 An unripe mango placed in a concentrated salt solution to prepare pickle shrivels because ....

(a) it gains water due to osmosis

(b) it loses water due to reverse osmosis

(c) it gains water due to reverse osmosis

(d) it loses water due to osmosis

Thinking Process Use the concept of osmosis and its effect to solve this question.

Ans. *(d)* When an unripe mango is placed in a concentrated salt solution to prepare pickle then mango loose water due to osmosis and get shrivel.

Q.13 At a given temperature, osmotic pressure of a concentrated solution of a substance ....

(a) is higher than that of a dilute solution

(b) is lower than that of a dilute solution

(c) is same as that of a dilute solution

(d) cannot be compared with osmotic pressure of dilute solution

Ans. *(a)* According to definition of osmotic pressure we know that $\pi = CRT$. For concentrated solution C has higher value than dilute solution.

Hence, as concentration of solution increases, osmotic pressure will also increase.

Q.14 Which of the following statements is false?

(a) Two different solutions of sucrose of same molality prepared in different solvents will have the same depression in freezing point.

(b) The osmotic pressure of a solution is given by the equation $\pi = CRT$ (where, C is the molarity of the solution).

(c) Decreasing order of osmotic pressure for 0.01 M aqueous solutions of barium chloride, potassium chloride, acetic acid and sucrose is

$$BaCl_2 > KCl > CH_3COOH > \text{sucrose}.$$

(d) According to Raoult's law, the vapour pressure exerted by a volatile component of a solution is directly proportional to its mole fraction in the solution.

Ans. *(a)* According to definition of depression in freezing point

$$\Delta T_f = K_f m$$

where, K_f = freezing point depression constant, value of K_f depends upon nature of solvent. Thus, two different solutions of sucrose of same molality prepared in different solvents will have the different depression in freezing point.

Q.15 The values of van't Hoff factors for KCl, NaCl and K_2SO_4 respectively are ....

(a) 2, 2 and 2
(b) 2, 2 and 3
(c) 1, 1 and 2
(d) 1, 1 and 1

Ans. ***(b)*** Number of total ions present in the solution is known as van't Hoff factors (*i*).

Substances	van't Hoff factor (*i*)
For KCl ($K^+ + Cl^-$)	2
For NaCl ($Na^+ + Cl^-$)	2
For K_2SO_4 ($2K^+ + SO_4^{2-}$)	3

Hence, correct choice is (b).

Q.16 Which of the following statements is false?

(a) Units of atmospheric pressure and osmotic pressure are the same.
(b) In reverse osmosis, solvent molecules move through a semipermeable membrane from a region of lower concentration of solute to a region of higher concentration.
(c) The value of molal depression constant depends on nature of solvent.
(d) Relative lowering of vapour pressure, is a dimensionless quantity.

Ans. ***(b)*** In reverse osmosis, solvent molecules move through a semipermeable membrane from a region of higher concentration of solute to lower concentration.

Mistake Alert! *One can make a mistake of confusing osmosis with reverse osmosis.*

Q.17 Value of Henry's constant K_H ....

(a) increases with increase in temperature
(b) decreases with increase in temperature
(c) remains constant
(d) first increases then decreases

Ans. ***(a)*** Value of Henry's constant (K_H) increases with increase in temperature representing the decrease in solubility.

Q.18 The value of Henry's constant, K_H is ....

(a) greater for gases with higher solubility
(b) greater for gases with lower solubility
(c) constant for all gases
(d) not related to the solubility of gases

Ans. ***(b)*** According to Henry's law,

$$p \propto x$$

$$\Rightarrow \quad p = K_H x$$

At a given pressure when value of K_H increases, the solubility of gas in liquid decreases.

Q.19 Consider the figure and mark the correct option.

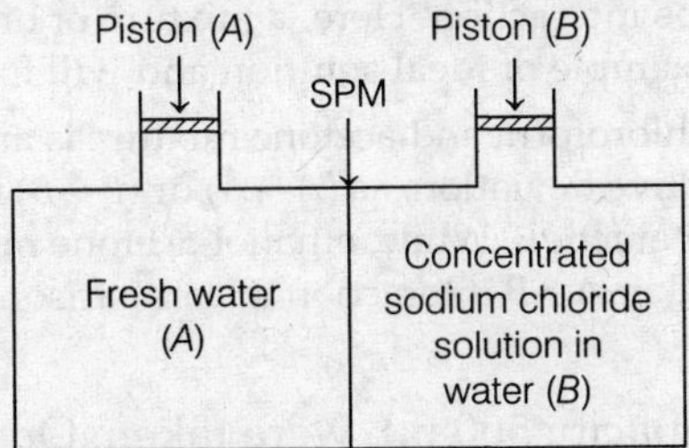

(a) Water will move from side (A) to side (B) if a pressure lower then osmotic pressure is applied on piston (B).

(b) Water will move from side (B) to side (A) if a pressure greater than osmotic pressure is applied on piston (B).

(c) Water will move from side (B) to side (A) if a pressure equal to osmotic pressure is applied on piston (B).

(d) Water will move from side (A) to side (B) if pressure equal to osmotic pressure is applied on piston (A).

Ans. ***(b)*** We know that, if a pressure higher than the osmotic pressure is applied on the solution, the solvent will flow from the solution into the pure solvent through semi-permeable membrane. This process is called reverse osmosis.

Thus, in this case, water will move from side (B) to side (A) if a pressure greater than osmotic pressure is applied on piston (B).

Q.20 We have three aqueous solutions of NaCl labelled as 'A', 'B' and 'C' with concentrations 0.1 M, 0.01 M and 0.001 M, respectively. The value of van't Hoff factor for these solutions will be in the order ....

(a) $i_A < i_B < i_C$ (b) $i_A > i_B > i_C$ (c) $i_A = i_B = i_C$ (d) $i_A < i_B > i_C$

Ans. ***(c)*** As NaCl is a strong electrolyte, it undergoes dissociation completely. Thus, the value of van't Hoff factor will be $i_A = i_B = i_C$. It means the value of i is same for all three solutions.

Q.21 On the basis of information given below mark the correct option.

Information

(i) In bromoethane and chloroethane mixture intermolecular interactions of A—A and B—B type are nearly same as A—B type interactions.

(ii) In ethanol and acetone mixture A—A or B—B type intermolecular interactions are stronger than A—B type interactions.

(iii) In chloroform and acetone mixture A—A or B—B type intermolecular interactions are weaker than A—B type interactions.

(a) Solution (ii) and (iii) will follow Raoult's law.

(b) Solution (i) will follow Raoult's law.

(c) Solution (ii) will show negative deviation from Raoult's law.

(d) Solution (iii) will show positive deviation from Raoult's law.

Ans. *(b)* For an ideal solution, the $A-A$ or $B-B$ type intermolecular interaction is near by equal to $A-B$ type interaction. Here, a mixture of bromoethane and chloroethane is an example of ideal solution and will follow Raoult's law.

On the other hand, chloroform and acetone mixture is an example of non-ideal solution having negative deviation, as $(A-A)$ or $(B-B)$ interaction must be weaker than $A-B$ interaction. While, ethanol-acetone mixture shows positive deviation due to weaker $A-B$ interaction in comparison to $A-A$ or $A-B$ interaction.

Q.22 Two beakers of capacity 500 mL were taken. One of these beakers, labelled as "A", was filled with 400 mL water whereas the beaker labelled "B' was filled with 400 mL of 2M solution of NaCl. At the same temperature both the beakers were placed in closed containers of same material and same capacity as shown in figure.

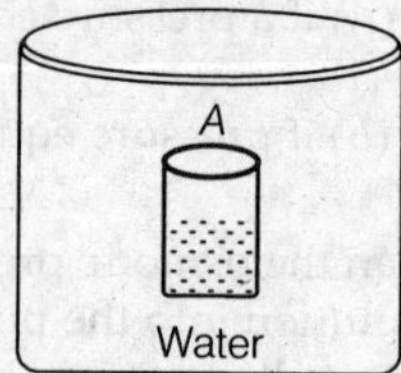

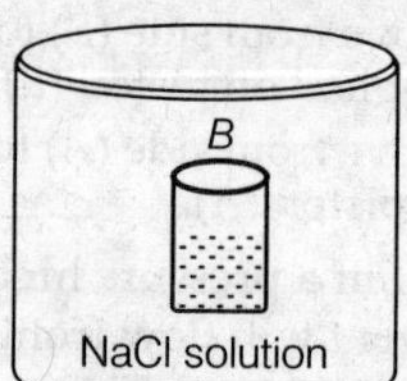

At a given temperature, which of the following statement is correct about the vapour pressure of pure water and that of NaCl solution?

(a) Vapour pressure in container (A) is more than that in container (B).
(b) Vapour pressure in container (A) is less than that in container (B).
(c) Vapour pressure is equal in both the containers.
(d) Vapour pressure in container (B) is twice the vapour pressure in container (A).

Ans. *(a)* NaCl is a non-volatile solute. When it is added to water to make the NaCl solution, the vapour pressure of the solution decreases due to the fact that the solute particles occupy the surface area of the solvent. This leads to decrease in the number of solvent molecule, escaping from the surface corresponding to pure solvent.

Hence, vapour pressure in container (A) is more than container (B).

Q.23 If two liquids A and B form minimum boiling azeotrope at some specific composition then.

(a) A—B interactions are stronger than those between A—A or B—B.
(b) vapour pressure of solution increases because more number of molecules of liquids A and B can escape from the solution.
(c) vapour pressure of solution decreases because less number of molecules of only one of the liquids escape from the solution.
(d) A—B interactions are weaker than those between A—A or B—B.

Ans. *(d)* If two liquids A and B form minimum boiling azeotrope at some specific composition then $A-B$ interactions are weaker than those of A—A and B—B. Due to positive deviation of solution from Rault's law, we get minimum boiling azeotropes, while in case of negative deviation, we get maximum boiling azeotropes.

Q.24 4 L of 0.02 M aqueous solution of NaCl was diluted by adding 1 L of water. The molality of the resultant solution is ....

(a) 0.004 (b) 0.008 (c) 0.012 (d) 0.016

Thinking Process To calculate the strength of solution when it is diluted by adding solvent. Write all the given values M_1, V_1, M_2 and V_2. Then calculate required parameter using formula,

$$M_1V_1 = M_2V_2$$

where, V_1 = volume of solution before dilution
V_2 = volume of solution after dilution
M_1 = strength of solution before dilution
M_2 = strength of solution after dilution

Ans. *(d)* Given, $M_1 = 0.02\text{M},\ V_1 = 4\text{L},\ M_2 = ?,\ V_2 = 4\text{L} + 1\text{L} = 5\text{L}$

As we know,

$$M_1V_1 = M_2V_2$$
$$0.02 \times 4\text{L} = M_2 \times 5\text{L}$$
$$M_2 = \frac{0.08}{5} = 0.016\text{ M}$$

Q.25 On the basis of information given below mark the correct option.

Information On adding acetone to methanol some of the hydrogen bonds between methanol molecules break.

(a) At specific composition methanol-acetone mixture will form minimum boiling azeotrope and will show positive deviation from Raoult's law.
(b) At specific composition methanol-acetone mixture will form maximum boiling azeotrope and will show positive deviation from Raoult's law.
(c) At specific composition methanol-acetone mixture will form minimum boiling azeotrope and will show negative deviation from Raoult's law.
(d) At specific composition methanol-acetone mixture will form maximum boiling azeotrope and will show negative deviation from Raoult's law.

Ans. *(a)* At specific composition methanol-acetone mixture will form minimum boiling azeotrope and will show positive deviation. This is due to weaker $A—B$ interaction than $A—A$ or $B—B$ interaction. *i.e.*, $A—B < A—A$ and $B—B$

Q.26 K_H value for Ar(*g*), CO_2 (*g*), HCHO (*g*) and CH_4(*g*) are 40.39, 1.67, 1.83×10^{-5} and 0.413 respectively.

Arrange these gases in the order of their increasing solubility.

(a) $HCHO < CH_4 < CO_2 < Ar$ (b) $HCHO < CO_2 < CH_4 < Ar$
(c) $Ar < CO_2 < CH_4 < HCHO$ (d) $Ar < CH_4 < CO_2 < HCHO$

Thinking Process Higher the value of K_H at a given pressure, the lower is the solubility of the gas in the liquid.

Ans. *(c)* Value of K_H depends upon nature of gases dissolved in water.

Gas	Temperature (K)	K_H/k bar
Ar	298 K	40.39
CO_2	298 K	1.67
CH_4	298 K	0.413
HCHO	298 K	1.83×10^{-5}

Hence, correct order of increasing solubility is $Ar < CO_2 < CH_4 < HCHO$ and correct choice is (c).

Multiple Choice Questions (More Than One Options)

Q.27 Which of the following factor(s) affect the solubility of a gaseous solute in the fixed volume of liquid solvent?

(i) Nature of solute (ii) Temperature

(iii) Pressure

(a) (i) and (iii) at constant T (b) (i) and (ii) at constant p

(c) (ii) and (iii) (d) Only (iii)

Ans. ***(a, b)*** Solubility of gaseous solute in the fixed volume of liquid solvent always depends upon nature of solute but it also depends upon pressure at constant temperature and depends upon temperature at constant pressure.

Hence, (a) and (b) both are correct.

Q.28 Intermolecular forces between two benzene molecules are nearly of same strength as those between two toluene molecules. For a mixture of benzene and toluene, which of the following are not true?

(a) $\Delta_{mix} H$ = zero

(b) $\Delta_{mix} V$ = zero

(c) These will form minimum boiling azeotrope.

(d) These will not form ideal solution.

Ans. ***(c, d)*** The solution which follows Raoult's law is known as an ideal solution. For an ideal solution intermolecular forces between two benzene molecules are nearly of same strength as those between two toluene molecules. For an ideal solution.

$$\Delta V_{mix}\ H = 0 \text{ and } \Delta H_{mix} V = 0$$

Thus, the mixture of benzene and toluene is an example of an ideal solution. Hence, option (c) is incorrect as minimum boiling azeotropes are formed by non-ideal solution.

Q.29 Relative lowering of vapour pressure is a colligative property because ....

(a) it depends on the concentration of a non-electrolyte solute in solution and does not depend on the nature of the solute molecules.

(b) it depends on number of particles of electrolyte solute in solution and does not depend on the nature of the solute particles.

(c) it depends on the concentration of a non-electrolyte solute in solution as well as on the nature of the solute molecules.

(d) it depends on the concentration of an electrolyte or non-electrolyte solute in solution as well as on the nature of solute molecules.

Ans. ***(a, b)*** Relative lowering of vapour pressure is a colligative property because

(i) It does not depend upon nature of solute.

(ii) It depends upon number of solute particles.

(iii) It depends upon concentration of non-electrolyte solute in solution.

Hence, options (a) and (b) are correct.

Q.30 van't Hoff factor (i) is given by the expression ....

(a) $i = \dfrac{\text{normal molar mass}}{\text{abnormal molar mass}}$ (b) $i = \dfrac{\text{abnormal molar mass}}{\text{normal molar mass}}$

(c) $i = \dfrac{\text{observed colligative property}}{\text{calculated colligative property}}$ (d) $i = \dfrac{\text{calculated colligative property}}{\text{observed colligative property}}$

Ans. ***(a, c)*** van't Hoff factor (i) is a measure of extent of association or dissociation of solute particles which can be calculated as

$$i = \frac{\text{normal molar mass}}{\text{abnormal molar mass}}$$

or,

$$= \frac{\text{observed colligative property}}{\text{calculated colligative property}}$$

Q.31 Isotonic solutions must have the same ....

(a) solute (b) density

(c) elevation in boiling point (d) depression in freezing point

Ans. ***(c, d)*** Isotonic solutions have same osmotic pressure and same concentration. Elevation in boiling point and depression in freezing point are the colligative properties, which depend upon concentration.

As the molar concentration is same for isotonic solutions, so elevation in boiling point and depression in freezing point of isotonic solutions must be same.

Q.32 Which of the following binary mixtures will have same composition in liquid and vapour phase?

(a) Benzene-Toluene (b) Water-Nitric acid

(c) Water-Ethanol (d) *n*-hexane- *n*-Heptane

Thinking Process Identify if the mixture forms an azeotrope or follows Raoult's law ideally. Azeotropes have the same composition in both liquid and vapour phases.

Ans. ***(b, c)*** Mixtures having same composition in liquid and vapour phase are known as azeotropes. Azeotropes boil at a constant temperature.

Here, water-nitric acid and water-ethanol mixtures are non-ideal solutions. Hence, water-nitric acid and water-ethanol are examples of azeotropes.

While benzene-toluene and *n*-hexane-*n*-heptane are examples of ideal solution.

Mistake Alert ! *Students may confuse that ideal mixtures like benzene-toluene or n-hexane - n -heptane will always have the same composition in both liquid and vapour phases.*

Q.33 In isotonic solutions ....

(a) solute and solvent both are same.

(b) osmotic pressure is same.

(c) solute and solvent may or may not be same.

(d) solute is always same, solvent may be different.

Ans. ***(b, c)*** The two solutions having same osmotic pressure are known as isotonic solutions. For isotonic solutions, the solute and solvent particles may or may not be same but osmotic pressure must be same.

Q.34 For a binary ideal liquid solution, the variation in total vapour pressure *versus* composition of solution is given by which of the curves?

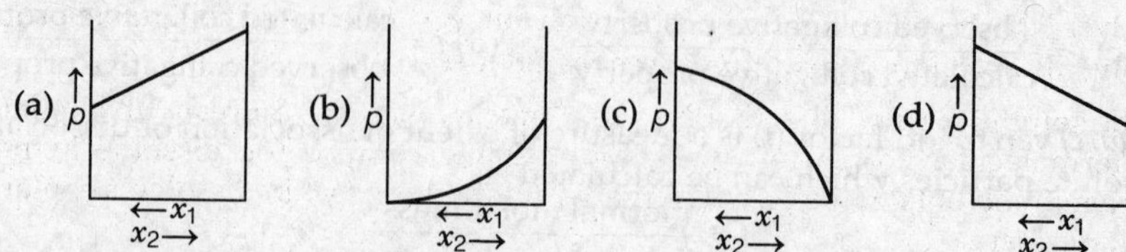

- **Concept Insight** This solution is based on the concept of Raoult's law, which states that in an ideal solution, the total vapour pressure is a linear function of the mole fraction.

Ans. ***(a,d)*** Depending on the vapour pressures of the pure components 1 and 2, total vapour pressure over the solution increases as the more fraction of more volatile components increases. Therefore, the graph of total vapour pressure versus composition will be a straight line.

Q.35 Colligative properties are observed when ....

(a) a non-volatile solid is dissolved in a volatile liquid
(b) a non-volatile liquid is dissolved in another volatile liquid
(c) a gas is dissolved in non-volatile liquid
(d) a volatile liquid is dissolved in another volatile liquid

Ans. ***(a, b)*** As the colligative properties depend only upon the number of solute particles, so if any one of the component of binary mixture either solute or solvent is volatile, the value of colligative properties deviates.
Hence, options (a) and (b) are correct.

Short Answer Type Questions

Q.36 Components of a binary mixture of two liquids *A* and *B* were being separated by distillation. After some time separation of components stopped and composition of vapour phase became same as that of liquid phase. Both the components started coming in the distillate. Explain why this happened?

Ans. Both components appear in both the liquid and vapour phases, indicating an azeotropic mixture. This means the mixture boils at a constant temperature and cannot be seperated by distillation or fractional distillation. Azeotropic solutions show significant positive or negative deviations from Raoult's law, depending on the intermolecular interactions.

Q.37 Explain why on addition of 1 mole of NaCl to 1 L of water, the boiling point of water increases, while addition of 1 mole of methyl alcohol to 1 L of water decreases its boiling point.

Ans. NaCl is a non-volatile solute. So, its addition to water lowers the vapour pressure of the water. Hence, boiling point of water (solution) increases. Whereas methyl alcohol is more volatile than water. So, its addition to water increases the total vapour pressure over the solution. It results in the decreas in of boiling point of water.

Q.38 Explain the solubility rule "like dissolves like" in terms of intermolecular forces that exist in solutions.

Ans. If the intermolecular interactions are similar in both constituents, *i.e.*, solute and solvent, then solute dissolves in the solvent. *e.g.*, polar solutes dissolve in polar solvents and non-polar solutes in non-polar solvents.

The solubility rule "like dissolves like" means that substances with similar type of intermolecular forces mix well. *e.g.*, organic compounds dissolve in non-polar organic solvents while polar inorganic compounds (salts) dissolve in polar solvent (like water).

Q.39 Concentration terms such as mass percentage, ppm, mole fraction and molality are independent of temperature, however molarity is a function of temperature. Explain.

Thinking Process To solve this problem notice the role of temperature in component of concentration term such as volume, mass, number of moles, etc.

Ans. Concentration terms like mass percentage, PPM, mole fraction and molality are unaffected by temperature because they depend on mass, which does not change with temperature. However, molarity depends on the volume of the solution, which changes with change in temperature.

Since molarity is defined as moles of solute per litre of solution, any temperature change affecting the solution's volume will also affect its molarity.

Q.40 What is the significance of Henry's law constant K_H?

Ans. According to Henry's law, $p \propto x \Rightarrow p = K_H x$

Higher the value of Henry's law constant K_H, the lower is the solubility of the gas in a liquid. Thus, the solubility of a gas in the given liquid can be increased by increasing pressure.

Q.41 Why are aquatic species more comfortable in cold water in comparision to warm water?

Ans. Aquatic species are more comfortable in cold water due to the presence of more oxygen. Solubility of oxygen in water increases with decrease in temperature as the solubility of a gas in a given liquid decreases with increase in temperature.

Q.42 (a) Explain the following phenomena with the help of Henry's law.

(i) Painful condition known as bends.

(ii) Feeling of weakness and discomfort in breathing at high altitude.

(b) Why soda water bottle kept at room temperature fizzes on opening?

Ans. (a) (i) Henry's law represents a relation between solubility of gases in liquid and pressure. Scuba divers have high concentrations of dissolved gases in blood due to high pressure underwater. When the divers come towards surface, the pressure gradually decreases. This reduces pressure releases the dissolves gases present in blood and leads to formation of bubbles of nitrogen in the blood.

This creates a painful and dangerous condition by blocking capillaries known as bends.

(ii) At high altitudes, atmospheric pressure is low as compared to surface. This leads to low concentrations of oxygen in the blood and tissues of climbers or people living at high altitude. Low blood onygen causes difficulty in breathing and climbers feel weakness and discomfort.

(b) Soda water bottle kept at room temperature fizzes on opening due to different pressure inside and outside the bottle. Inside the sealed bottle, the partial pressure of CO_2 is high,increasing the solubility of CO_2 in the liquid but when the bottle is opened, the pressure decreases, reducing the solubility of CO_2, causing it to escape as bubbles.

Q.43 Why is the vapour pressure of an aqueous solution of glucose lower than that of water?

Ans. In pure liquid, the entire surface of liquid is occupied by the molecules of water. When a non-volatile solute, *e.g.*, glucose is dissolved in water, the fraction of surface covered by the solvent molecules gets reduced because some positions are occupied by glucose molecules.

So, number of solvent molecules escaping from the surface is reduced. That is why vapour pressure of aqueous solution of glucose is reduced.

Q.44 How does sprinkling of salt help in clearing the snow covered roads in hilly areas? Explain the phenomenon involved in the process.

Ans. When salt is spread over snow covered roads, snow starts melting from the surface because depression in freezing point of water takes place due to addition of salt as the addition of salt to snow introduces colligative properties. It helps in clearing of snow covered roads in hilly areas.

Q.45 What is "semipermeable membrane"?

Ans. Continuous sheets or films (natural or synthetic) which contain a network of submicroscopic holes or pores through which only small solvent molecules (water etc.) can pass, but solute molecules of bigger size cannot pass are called semipermeable membrane. *e.g.*, cellophane membrane.

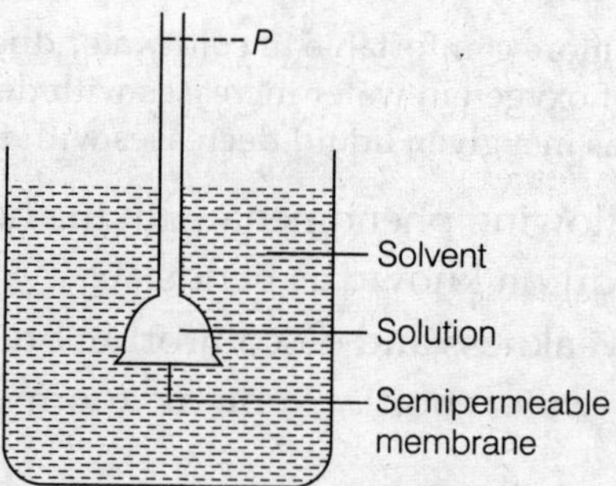

Q.46 Give an example of a material used for making semipermeable membrane for carrying out reverse osmosis.

Ans. Since pressure required for the reverse osmosis is very high, cellulose acetate placed over a suitable support is used for making semipermeable membrane. Cellulose acetate is permeable to water but impermeable to impurities and ions present in sea water.

Matching The Columns

Q.47 Match the items given in Column I and Column II.

Column I	Column II
A. Saturated solution	1. Solution having same osmotic pressure at a given temperature as that of given solution.
B. Binary solution	2. A solution whose osmotic pressure is less than that of another.
C. Isotonic solution	3. Solution with two components.
D. Hypotonic solution	4. A solution which contains maximum amount of solute that can be dissolved in a given amount of solvent at a given temperature.
E. Solid solution	5. A solution whose osmotic pressure is more than that of another.
F. Hypertonic solution	6. A solution in solid phase.

Ans. **A.** → (4) **B.** → (3) **C.** → (1) **D.** → (2) **E.** → (6) **F.** → (5)

A. **Saturated solution** A solution which contains maximum amount of solute that can be dissolved in a given amount of solvent at a given temperature.

B. **Binary solution** A solution with two components is known as a binary solution.

C. **Isotonic solution** A solution having same osmotic pressure at a given temperature as that of given solution is known as isotonic solution.

D. **Hypotonic solution** A solution whose osmotic pressure is less than another is known as hypotonic solution.

E. **Solid solution** A solution in solid phase is known as solid solution.

F. **Hypertonic solution** A solution whose osmotic pressure is greater than that of another is known as hypertonic solution.

Q.48 Match the items given in Column I with the type of solutions given in Column II.

Column I	Column II
A. Soda water	1. A solution of gas in solid
B. Sugar solution	2. A solution of gas in gas
C. German silver	3. A solution of solid in liquid
D. Air	4. A solution of solid in solid
E. Hydrogen gas in palladium	5. A solution of gas in liquid
	6. A solution of liquid in solid

Ans. **A.** → (5) **B.** → (3) **C.** → (4) **D.** → (2) **E.** → (1)

A. **Soda water** A solution of gas in liquid. *e.g.*, CO_2 in soft drinks.

B. **Sugar solution** A solution of solid in liquid in which sugar particles (soild) are dissolved in water (liquid).

C. **German silver** German silver is an alloy which is a solid solution of solid in solid. It is an alloy of Cu, Zn and Ni.

D. **Air** A solution of gas in gas. Air is a mixture of various gases.

E. **Hydrogen gas in palladium** is an example of solution of gas in solid. This is used as a reducing agent.

Q.49 Match the laws given in Column I with expressions given in Column II.

Column I	Column II
A. Raoult's law	1. $\Delta T_f = K_f m$
B. Henry's law	2. $\pi = CRT$
C. Elevation of boiling point	3. $p = x_1 p_1^\circ + x_2 p_2^\circ$
D. Depression in freezing point	4. $\Delta T_b = K_b m$
E. Osmotic pressure	5. $p = K_H \cdot x$

Ans. **A.** → (3) **B.** → (5) **C.** → (4) **D.** → (1) **E.** → (2)

A. **Raoult's law** Mathematical representation of Raoult's law

$$p = x_1 p_1^\circ + x_2 p_2^\circ$$

B. **Henry's law** $p = K_H \cdot x$

C. **Elevation of boiling point** Mathematical representation, $\Delta T_b = K_b \cdot m$

D. **Depression in freezing point** Mathematical representation, $\Delta T_f = K_f \cdot m$

E. **Osmotic pressure** Mathematical representation, $\pi = CRT$

Q.50 Match the terms given in Column I with expressions given in Column II.

Column I	Column II
A. Mass percentage	1. $\frac{\text{Number of moles of the solute component}}{\text{Volume of solution in litres}}$
B. Volume percentage	2. $\frac{\text{Number of moles of a component}}{\text{Total number of moles of all the components}}$
C. Mole fraction	3. $\frac{\text{Volume of the solute component in solution}}{\text{Total volume of solution}} \times 100$
D. Molality	4. $\frac{\text{Mass of the solute component in solution}}{\text{Total mass of the solution}} \times 100$
E. Molarity	5. $\frac{\text{Number of moles of the solute components}}{\text{Mass of solvent in kilograms}}$

Ans. **A.** → (4) **B.** → (3) **C.** → (2) **D.** → (5) **E.** → (1)

Column I (Concentration terms)		Column II (Mathematical formula)
A.	Mass percentage	$\frac{\text{Mass of the solute component in solution}}{\text{Total mass of the solution}} \times 100$
B.	Volume percentage	$\frac{\text{Volume of the solute component in solution}}{\text{Total volume of solution}} \times 100$
C.	Mole fraction	$\frac{\text{Number of moles of a component}}{\text{Total number of moles of all the components}}$
D.	Molality	$\frac{\text{Number of moles of the solute components}}{\text{Mass of solvent in kilograms}}$
E.	Molarity	$\frac{\text{Number of moles of the solute component}}{\text{Volume of solution in litres}}$

Assertion and Reason

In the following questions a statement of assertion (A) *followed by a statement of reason* (R) *is given. Choose the correct answer out of the following choices.*

(a) Assertion and reason both are correct statements and reason is correct explanation for assertion.

(b) Assertion and reason both are correct statements but reason is not correct explanation for assertion.

(c) Assertion is correct statement but reason is wrong statement.

(d) Assertion and reason both are incorrect statements.

(e) Assertion is wrong statement but reason is correct statement.

Q.51 **Assertion** (A) Molarity of a solution in liquid state changes with temperature.

Reason (R) The volume of a solution changes with change in temperature.

Ans. *(a)* Assertion and reason both are correct statements and reason is the correct explanation of assertion.

Volume of solutions is a function of temperature which varies with temperature. Hence, molarity of solution in liquid state changes with temperature.

$$\text{Molarity} = \frac{\text{moles of solute}}{\text{volume of solution in litre}}$$

Q.52 **Assertion** (A) When methyl alcohol is added to water, boiling point of water increases.

Reason (R) When a volatile solute is added to a volatile solvent elevation in boiling point is observed.

Ans. *(d)* Assertion and Reason both are incorrect statements.

When methyl alcohol is added to water, boiling point of water decreases because methyl alcohol is a volatile causes the vapour pressure of the solution to the higher than that for pure water. Hence, the solution boils at a lower temperature. When a non-volatile solute is added to a volatile solvent, elevation in boiling point is observed.

Q.53 **Assertion** (A) When NaCl is added to water a depression in freezing point is observed.

Reason (R) The lowering of vapour pressure of a solution causes depression in the freezing point.

Ans. ***(a)*** Assertion and reason both are correct and reason is correct explanation of assertion. When NaCl (non-volatile solute) is added to water a depression in freezing point is observed. This is due to lowering of vapour pressure of a solution. Lowering of vapour pressure is observed due to intermolecular interaction of solvent-solute particles.

Q.54 **Assertion** (A) When a solution is separated from the pure solvent by a semipermeable membrane, the solvent molecules pass through it from pure solvent side to the solution side.

Reason (R) Diffusion of solvent occurs from a region of high concentration solution to a region of low concentration solution.

Ans. ***(c)*** Assertion is correct statement but reason is wrong statement.
When a solution is separated from the pure solvent by a semipermeable membrane, the solvent molecules pass through it from pure solvent side to the solution side. Solvent molecules always flow from lower concentration to higher concentration solution.

Long Answer Type Questions

Q.55 Define the following modes of expressing the concentration of a solution? Which of these modes are independent of temperature and why?

(a) *w/w* (mass percentage) (b) *V/V* (volume percentage)
(c) *w/V* (mass by volume percentage) (d) ppm (parts per million)
(e) χ (mole fraction) (f) *M* (molarity)
(g) *m* (molality)

Ans. (a) *w/w* (mass percentage) Mass percentage of a component of a solution can be expressed as

$$\text{Mass \% of component} = \frac{\text{mass of component in the solution}}{\text{total mass of solution}} \times 100$$

Thus, the percentage by mass means the mass of the solute in grams present in 100g of the solution.

(b) *V/V* (volume percentage) is defined as

$$\text{Volume percentage} = \frac{\text{volume of the component}}{\text{total volume of solution}} \times 100$$

Thus, volume percentage means the volume of the liquid solute in cm^3 present in 100 cm^3 of the solution.

(c) *w/V* (mass by volume percentage) = mass of solute dissolved in 100 mL of solution.

(d) **ppm** (parts per million) This parameter is used to express the concentration of very dilute solution.

$$\text{ppm} = \frac{\text{number of parts of component}}{\text{total number of parts of all components of solution}} \times 10^6$$

(e) χ (mole fraction) Mole fraction is an unitless quantity used to determine extent of any particular component present in total solution.

$$\chi = \frac{\text{number of moles of the component}}{\text{total number of moles of all components}}$$

(f) *M* (molarity) Number of moles of solute dissolved in per litre of solution is known as molarity.

$$M = \frac{\text{number of moles of solute}}{\text{volume of solution in litre}}$$

(g) *m* (Molality) Molality of any solution can be defined as number of moles of solute dissolved in per kg of solvent.

$$m = \frac{\text{number of moles of solute}}{\text{mass of solvent in kg}}$$

Concentration terms like mass percentage, ppm, mole fraction and molality are independent of temperature because they are based on mass, which remains constant with change in temperature.

Q.56 Using Raoult's law explain how the total vapour pressure over the solution is related to mole fraction of components in the following solutions.

(a) $CHCl_3$ (*l*) and CH_2Cl_2 (*l*) (b) NaCl (*s*) and H_2O (*l*)

Ans. According to Raoult's law, for any solution the partial vapour pressure of each volatile component in the solution is directly proportional to its mole fraction.

$$p_1 = p_1^\circ x_1$$

(a) $CHCl_3$ (*l*) and CH_2Cl_2 (*l*) both are volatile components.

Hence, for a binary solution in which both components are volatile liquids, the total pressure will be $p = p_1 + p_2 = x_1 p_1^\circ + x_2 p_2^\circ$

$$= x_1 p_1^\circ + (1 - x_1)\, p_2^\circ = (p_1^\circ - p_2^\circ)\, x_1 + p_2^\circ$$

where, p = total vapour pressure

p_1 = partial vapour pressure of component 1

p_2 = partial vapour pressure of component 2

(b) NaCl (*s*) and H_2O (*l*) contains non-volatile solute.

Hence, for a solution containing non-volatile solute, the Raoult's law is applicable only to vaporisable component and total vapour pressure can be written as

$$p = p_1 = x_1 p_1^\circ$$

Q.57 Explain the terms ideal and non-ideal solutions in the light of forces of interactions operating between molecules in liquid solutions.

Ans. **Ideal Solution** The solutions which obey Raoult's law over the entire range of concentration are known as ideal solutions. For an ideal solution $\Delta H_{mix} = 0$ and $\Delta V_{mix} = 0$. The ideal behaviour of the solutions can be explained by considering two components *A* and *B*.

In pure components, the intermolecular attractive interactions will be of $A-A$ type and $B-B$ type, whereas in the binary solutions in addition to these two, $A-B$ type of interaction will also be present. If $A-A$ and $B-B$ intermolecular forces are nearly equal to those between $A-B$, this leads to the formation of ideal solution *e.g.*, solution of *n*-hexane and *n*-heptane.

Non-Ideal Solution When a solution does not obey-Raoult's law over the entire range of concentration, then it is called a non-ideal solution. The vapour pressure of such a solution is either higher or lower than that predicted by Raoult's law.

If vapour pressure is higher, the solution exhibits positive deviation and if it is lower it exhibits negative deviation from Raoult's law. In case of positive deviation, $A-B$ interactions are weaker than those between $A-A$ or $B-B$. *i.e.*, the attractive forces between solute-solvent molecules are weaker than those between solute-solute and solvent-solvent molecules *e.g.*, mixture of ethanol and acetone.

For such solutions $\Delta H_{\text{mixing}} = +\text{ ve}$ and $\Delta V_{\text{mixing}} = +\text{ ve}$

On the other hand, in case of negative deviation the intermolecular attractive forces between $A-A$ and $B-B$ are weaker than those between $A-B$ molecules. Thus, the escaping tendency of A and B types of molecules from the solution becomes less than from the pure liquids *i.e.*, mixture of chloroform and acetone.

For such solutions $\Delta H_{\text{mix}} < 0$, $\Delta V_{\text{mix}} < 0$

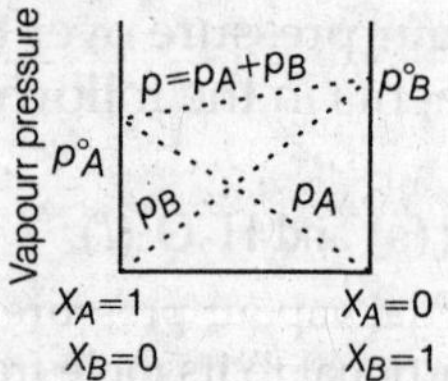

Graph for ideal solution

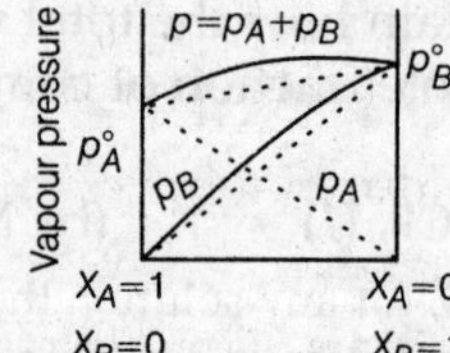

Graph showing +ve deviation

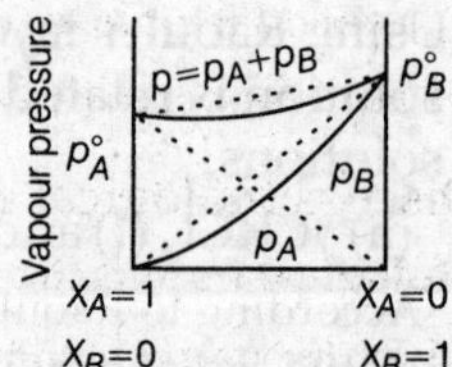

Graph showing –ve deviation

Q.58 Why is it not possible to obtain pure ethanol by fractional distillation? What general name is given to binary mixtures which show deviation from Raoult's law and whose components cannot be separated by fractional distillation. How many types of such mixtures are there?

Ans. The solution or mixture having same composition in liquid as well as in vapour phase and boils at a constant temperature is known as azeotropes. Due to constant composition it cannot be separated by fractional distillation. There are two types of azeotropes

(i) **Minimum boiling azeotropes** Solutions which show large positive deviation from Raoult's law form minimum boiling azeotropes at a specific composition. *e.g.*, ethanol—water mixture

(ii) **Maximum boiling azeotropes** Solutions which show large negative deviation from Raoult's law form maximum boiling azeotropes. *e.g.*, solution having composition 68% HNO_3 and 32% water by mass.

Q.59 When kept in water, raisin swells in size. Name and explain the phenomenon involved with the help of a diagram. Give three applications of the phenomenon.

Ans. This phenomenon is called endo osmosis, *i.e.*, movement of water inside the raisin and shown with the help of diagram as it can be

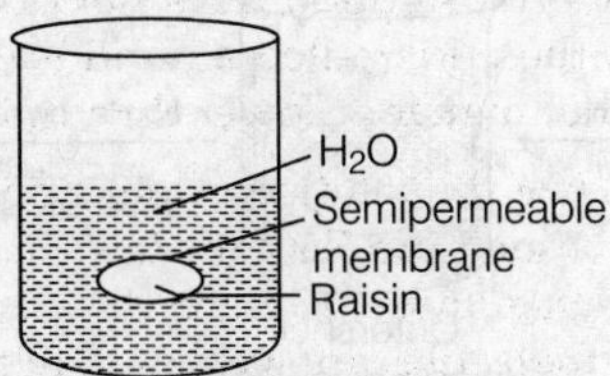

The process of osmosis is of immense biological as well as industrial importance.. It is evident from the following examples.

Application of Osmosis

(i) Movement of water from soil into plant roots and subsequently into upper portion of the plant is partly due to osmosis.

(ii) Preservation of meat against bacterial action by addition of salt.

(iii) Preservation of fruits against bacterial action by adding sugar. Bacterium in canned fruit loses water through the process of osmosis and become inactive.

(iv) Reverse-osmosis is used in desalination of water.

Q.60 Discuss biological and industrial importance of osmosis.

Ans. **Biological importance of osmosis**

(i) **Water movement in animals** Osmosis regulates the movement of water between different parts of the body.

(ii) **Plant growth and germination** Osmosis plays a key role in plant growth and seed germination by facilitating water absorption.

(iii) **Control of plant movements** Processes like the opening and closing of flower and leaves are influenced by osmosis.

Industrial importance of osmosis

(i) **Water purification** Reverse osmosis is widely used for dessalination and purification of water.

(ii) **Food preservation** Osmosis is used in food preservation such as in salting and sugaring, to draw water out of food and prevent spoilage.

(iii) **Medical applications** Osmosis helps in processes like dialysis, where it is used to remove waste from the blood.

Q.61 How can you remove the hard calcium carbonate layer of the egg without damaging its semipermeable membrane? Can this egg be inserted into a bottle with a narrow neck without distorting its shape? Explain the process involved.

Thinking Process The question can be answered using the concept of solubility, osmosis, reverse-osmosis, hypertonic solution and hypotonic solution.

Ans. When egg is placed in mineral acid solution, outershell of egg dissolves.

Egg is now removed and placed in hypertonic solution. Size of egg gets reduced and egg shrivels due to osmosis. Egg is now placed in a bottle with narrow neck. Finally on adding hypotonic solution egg regains its shape due to osmosis. Diagramatically it can be represented as

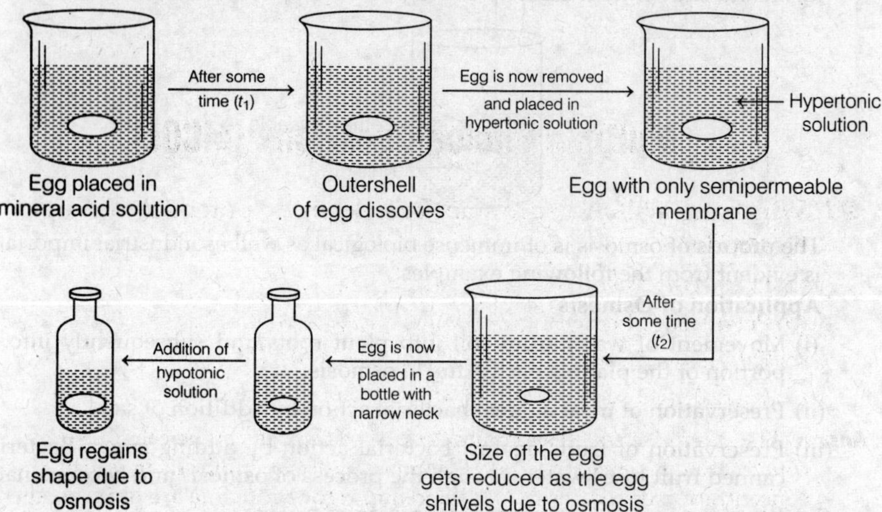

Q.62 **Why is the mass determined by measuring a colligative property in case of some solutes abnormal? Discuss it with the help of van't Hoff factor.**

Ans. Certain compounds when dissolved in suitable solvents either dissociate or associate. *e.g.*, ethanoic acid dimerises in benzene due to H-bonding, while in water, it dissociates and forms ions.

As a result the number of chemical species in solution increases or decreases as compared to the number of chemical species of solute added to form the solution.

Since, the magnitude of colligative property depends on the number of solute particles, it is expected that the molar mass determined on the basis of colligative properties will be either higher or lower than the expected value or the normal value and is called abnormal molar mass.

In order to account for the extent of dissociation or association of molecules in solution, van't Hoff introduced a factor, *i*, known as the van't Hoff factor.

$$i = \frac{\text{expected molar mass}}{\text{abnormal molar mass}} = \frac{\text{observed colligative property}}{\text{calculated colligative property}}$$

$$= \frac{\text{total number of moles of particles after association or dissociation}}{\text{total number of moles of particles before association or dissociation}}$$

Chapter

03

Electrochemistry

Multiple Choice Questions (MCQs)

Q.1 Which cell will measure standard electrode potential of copper electrode?

(a) Pt (s) $|H_2(g, 0.1 \text{ bar})|H^+(aq., 1 \text{ M})||Cu^{2+}(aq., 1 \text{ M})|Cu$

(b) Pt (s) $|H_2(g, 1 \text{ bar})|H^+(aq., 1 \text{ M})||Cu^{2+}(aq., 2 \text{ M})|Cu$

(c) Pt (s) $|H_2(g. 1 \text{ bar})|H^+(aq., 1 \text{ M})||Cu^{2+}(aq., 1 \text{ M})|Cu$

(d) Pt (s) $|H_2(g\ 1 \text{ bar})|H^+(aq., 0.1 \text{ M})||Cu^{2+}(aq., 1 \text{ M})|Cu$

Ans. *(c)* Standard electrode potential of copper electrode can be calculated by constructing a concentration cell composed of two half cells in which concentration of species on left hand and right hand side are unity. In such case cell potential is equal to standard electrode potential.

$$\underbrace{Pt(s)|H_2(g, 1 \text{ bar})||H^+(aq, 1 \text{ M})}_{\text{Oxidation half cell}}||\underbrace{Cu^{2+}(aq, 1 \text{ M})|Cu}_{\text{Reduction half cell}}$$

Q.2 Electrode potential for Mg electrode varies according to the equation

$E_{Mg^{2+}/Mg} = E^{\ominus}_{Mg^{2+}/Mg} - \frac{0.059}{2} \log \frac{1}{[Mg^{2+}]}$. The graph of $E_{Mg^{2+}/Mg}$ vs $\log [Mg^{2+}]$ is

(a) [graph: $E_{Mg^{2+}/Mg}$ vs log[Mg^{2+}]→]

(b) [graph: $E_{Mg^{2+}/Mg}$ vs log[Mg^{2+}]→]

(c) [graph: $E_{Mg^{2+}/Mg}$ vs log[Mg^{2+}]→]

(d) [graph: $E_{Mg^{2+}/Mg}$ vs log[Mg^{2+}]→]

Thinking Process This problem includes concept of Nernst equation and its transformation to equation of straight line.

Ans. *(b)* Electrode potential for Mg electrode varies according to the equation

$$E_{Mg^{2+}/Mg} = E^{\circ}_{Mg^{2+}/Mg} - \frac{0.059}{2} \log \frac{1}{[Mg^{2+}]}$$

$$E_{Mg^{2+}/Mg} = E^{\circ}_{Mg^{2+}/Mg} + \frac{0.059}{2} \log [Mg^{2+}]$$

$$E_{Mg^{2+}/Mg} = \frac{0.059}{2} \log [Mg^{2+}] + E^{\circ}_{Mg^{2+}/Mg}$$

This equation represents equation of straight line. It can be correlated with the equation of straight line ($y = mx + c$) as

$$\underset{Y}{\underset{\uparrow}{E_{Mg^{2+}/Mg}}} = \underset{M}{\underset{\uparrow}{\left(\frac{0.059}{2}\right)}} \underset{X}{\underset{\uparrow}{\log [Mg^{2+}]}} + \underset{C}{\underset{\uparrow}{E^{\circ}_{Mg^{2+}/Mg}}}$$

So, intercept (C) = $E^{\circ}_{Mg^{2+}/Mg}$

Thus, equation can be diagramatically represented as

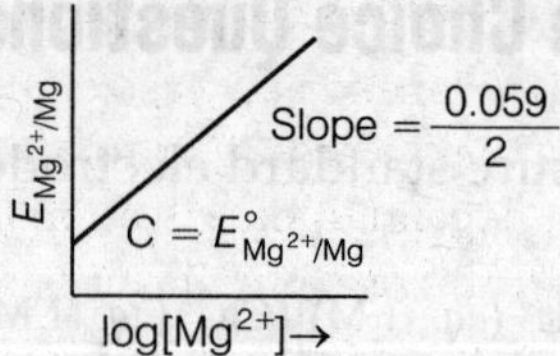

Q.3 Which of the following statement is correct?

(a) E_{cell} and $\Delta_r G$ of cell reaction both are extensive properties.
(b) E_{cell} and $\Delta_r G$ of cell reaction both are intensive properties.
(c) E_{cell} is an intensive property while $\Delta_r G$ of cell reaction is an extensive property.
(d) E_{cell} is an extensive property while $\Delta_r G$ of cell reaction is an intensive property.

Thinking Process This problem is based on thermodynamical concept of intensive and extensive property. Intensive property is independent of the quantity or size of matter present in the system and extensive property is dependent on both quantity and size of the matter.

Ans. ***(c)*** E_{cell} is an intensive property as it does not depend upon mass of species (number of particles) but $\Delta_r G$ of the cell reaction is an extensive property because this depends upon mass of species (number of particles).

Q.4 The difference between the electrode potentials of two electrodes when no current is drawn through the cell is called.........

(a) cell potential
(b) cell emf
(c) potential difference
(d) cell voltage

Ans. ***(b)*** The difference between the electrode potential of two electrodes when no current is drawn through the cell is called cell emf.

Q.5 Which of the following statement is not correct about an inert electrode in a cell?

(a) It does not participate in the cell reaction.
(b) It provides surface either for oxidation or for reduction reaction.
(c) It provides surface for conduction of electrons.
(d) It provides surface for redox reaction.

Ans. ***(d)*** An inert electrode in a cell does not take part in a chemical reaction. It provides surface either for oxidation or reduction reactions and for the conduction of electrons. It does not provide surface for redox reaction.

Q.6 An electrochemical cell can behave like an electrolytic cell when ....

(a) $E_{cell} = 0$ (b) $E_{cell} > E_{ext}$ (c) $E_{ext} > E_{cell}$ (d) $E_{cell} = E_{ext}$

Ans. *(c)* An electrochemical cell behaves like an electrolytic cell when the external potential applied to it is greater than its own cell potential.

When an external potential greater than the cell's emf is applied in the opposite direction, it forces the reaction to reverse, causing the cell to behave like an electrolytic cell, where a non-spontaneous reaction is driven by the external voltage.

Q.7 Which of the statements about solutions of electrolytes is **not** correct?

(a) Conductivity of solution depends upon size of ions.
(b) Conductivity depends upon viscosity of solution.
(c) Conductivity does not depend upon solvation of ions present in solution.
(d) Conductivity of solution increases with temperature.

Ans. *(c)* Solution consisting of electrolytes is known as electrolytic solution and conductivity of electrolytic solution depends upon the following factors.

(i) **Size of ions** As ion size increases, ion mobility decreases and conductivity decreases.
(ii) **Viscosity of solution** Greater the viscosity of the solvent, lesser will be the conductivity of the solution.
(iii) **Solvation of ions** Greater the solvation of ions of an electrolyte, lesser will be the electrical conductivity of the solution.
(iv) **Temperature of medium** Conductivity of solution increases with increase in temperature.

Q.8 Using the data given below find out the strongest reducing agent.

$$E^\ominus_{Cr_2O_7^{2-}/Cr^{3+}} = 1.33\text{ V};\quad E^\ominus_{Cl_2/Cl^-} = 1.36\text{ V}$$
$$E^\ominus_{MnO_4^-/Mn^{2+}} = 1.51\text{ V};\quad E^\ominus_{Cr^{3+}/Cr} = -0.74\text{ V}$$

(a) Cl^- (b) Cr (c) Cr^{3+} (d) Mn^{2+}

Thinking Process This problem includes concept of electrochemical series and standard reduction potential of the metal.

Higher the negative value of standard reduction potential, strongest will be the reducing agent. As value of standard reduction potential increases from negative to positive value, nature of species changes from reducing to oxidising nature.

Ans. *(b)* Here out of given four options, standard reduction potential of chromium has highest negative value. Hence, most powerful reducing agent is chromium.

$$Cr \longrightarrow Cr^{3+} + 3e^- \text{ (oxidation)}$$

Q.9 Use the data given in Q. 8 and find out which of the following is the strongest oxidising agent?

(a) Cl^- (b) Mn^{2+} (c) MnO_4^- (d) Cr^{3+}

Ans. *(c)* Higher the positive value of standard reduction potential of metal ion higher will be its oxidising capacity.

Since, $E^\circ_{MnO_4^-/Mn^{2+}}$ has value equal to 1.51 V. Hence, it is the strongest oxidising agent.

Mistake Alert! *Students may make a mistake in considering that a higher standard reduction potential indicates stronger reducing capacity instead of greater oxidising capacity.*

Q.10 Using the data given in Q.8 find out in which option the order of reducing power is correct.

(a) $Cr^{3+} < Cl^- < Mn^{2+} < Cr$ (b) $Mn^{2+} < Cl^- < Cr^{3+} < Cr$

(c) $Cr^{3+} < Cl^- < Cr_2O_7^{2-} < MnO_4^-$ (d) $Mn^{2+} < Cr^{3+} < Cl^- < Cr$

Ans. *(b)*

Species (ions)	SRP values
Mn^{2+}	1.51 V
Cl^-	1.36 V
Cr^{3+}	1.33 V
Cr	– 0.74 V

On moving from top to bottom Standard Reduction Potential value decreases from positive to negative value which will increase the reducing capacity. So, the correct option is (b).

Q.11 Use the data given in Q. 8 and find out the most stable ion in its reduced form.

(a) Cl^- (b) Cr^{3+} (c) Cr (d) Mn^{2+}

Ans. *(d)* $E^\circ_{MnO_4^-/Mn^{2+}}$ has +ve SRP value equal to 1.51 V which is highest among given four choices. So, Mn^{2+} is most stable ion in its reduced form.

Q.12 Use the data of Q. 8 and find out the most stable oxidised species.

(a) Cr^{3+} (b) MnO_4^- (c) $Cr_2O_7^{2-}$ (d) Mn^{2+}

Ans. *(a)* $E^\circ_{Cr^{3+}/Cr}$ has most –ve SRP value equal to – 0.74 among given four choices. So, Cr^{3+} is the most stable oxidised species.

Q.13 The quantity of charge required to obtain one mole of aluminium from Al_2O_3 is equal to the number of electrons required to convert Al_2O_3 to Al is ....

(a) 1F (b) 6F (c) 3F (d) 2F

Ans. *(c)* The quantity of charge required to obtain one mole of Aluminum from Al_2O_3.

$$Al_2O_3 \longrightarrow 2Al^{3+} + 3O^{2-}$$

$$2Al^{3+} + 6e^- \longrightarrow 2Al$$

$$\therefore \quad Al^{3+} + 3e^- \longrightarrow Al$$

Hence, 3F charge is required to obtain one mole of Al from Al_2O_3.

Q.14 The cell constant of a conductivity cell ....

(a) changes with change of electrolyte

(b) changes with change of concentration of electrolyte

(c) changes with temperature of electrolyte

(d) remains constant for a cell

Ans. *(d)* Cell constant is defined as the ratio of length of an object and area of cross section.

$$G^* = \frac{l}{A}$$

Since, l and A remain constant for any particular object hence value of cell constant always remains constant.

Q.15 While charging the lead storage battery ....

(a) $PbSO_4$ anode is reduced to Pb (b) $PbSO_4$ cathode is reduced to Pb
(c) $PbSO_4$ cathode is oxidised to Pb (d) $PbSO_4$ anode is oxidised to PbO_2

Ans. ***(a)*** While charging the lead storage battery the reaction occurring in the cell is reversed and $PbSO_4(s)$ on anode and cathode is converted into Pb and PbO_2 respectively.

Hence, option (a) is the correct choice.

The electrode reactions are as follows

At anode $PbSO_4(s)+2e^- \rightarrow Pb(s)+SO_4^{2-}(aq)$ (Reduction)

At cathode $PbSO_4(s)+2H_2O \rightarrow PbO_2(s)+SO_4^{2-}+4H^+ + 2e^-$ (Oxidation)

Overall reaction $2PbSO_4(s)+2H_2O \rightarrow Pb(s)+PbO_2(s)+4H^+(aq.)+2SO_4^{2-}(aq.)$

Q.16 $\overset{\circ}{\Lambda}_{m\,(NH_4OH)}$ is equal to ....

(a) $\overset{\circ}{\Lambda}_{m\,(NH_4OH)} + \overset{\circ}{\Lambda}_{m\,(NH_4Cl)} - \overset{\circ}{\Lambda}_{(HCl)}$ (b) $\overset{\circ}{\Lambda}_{m\,(NH_4Cl)} + \overset{\circ}{\Lambda}_{m\,(NaOH)} - \overset{\circ}{\Lambda}_{(NaCl)}$
(c) $\overset{\circ}{\Lambda}_{m\,(NH_4Cl)} + \overset{\circ}{\Lambda}_{m\,(NaCl)} - \overset{\circ}{\Lambda}_{(NaOH)}$ (d) $\overset{\circ}{\Lambda}_{m\,(NaOH)} + \overset{\circ}{\Lambda}_{m\,(NaCl)} - \overset{\circ}{\Lambda}_{(NH_4Cl)}$

Thinking Process This question is based on the concept of Kohlrausch law and can be solved by using the concept involved in calculation of limiting molar conductivity of any salt. According to Kohlrausch law, limiting molar conductivity of any salt is equal to sum of limiting molar conductivity of individual cations and anions of electrolyte *i.e.*, $\overset{\circ}{\Lambda}_m = v_+ \overset{\circ}{\lambda}_+ \; v_- \overset{\circ}{\lambda}_-$

Ans. ***(b)***

$$\overset{\circ}{\Lambda}_{m\,(NH_4Cl)} = \overset{\circ}{\Lambda}_{m\,(NH_4^+)} + \overset{\circ}{\Lambda}_{m\,(Cl^-)}$$
$$\overset{\circ}{\Lambda}_{m\,(NaOH)} = \overset{\circ}{\Lambda}_{m\,(Na^+)} + \overset{\circ}{\Lambda}_{m\,(OH^-)}$$
$$\overset{\circ}{\Lambda}_{m\,(NaCl)} = \overset{\circ}{\Lambda}_{m\,(Na^+)} + \overset{\circ}{\Lambda}_{m\,(Cl^-)}$$
$$-\qquad -\qquad -$$
$$\overset{\circ}{\Lambda}_{m\,(NH_4Cl)} + \overset{\circ}{\Lambda}_{m\,(NaOH)} - \overset{\circ}{\Lambda}_{m\,(NaCl)} = \overset{\circ}{\Lambda}_{m\,(NH_4OH)}$$

Hence, option (b) is correct option.

Q.17 In the electrolysis of aqueous sodium chloride solution which of the half cell reaction will occur at anode?

(a) $Na^+(aq)+e^- \longrightarrow Na\,(s);\; E^\ominus_{cell} = -2.71\text{ V}$
(b) $2H_2O\,(l) \longrightarrow O_2\,(g) + 4H^+\,(aq) + 4e^-;\; E^\ominus_{cell} = 1.23\text{ V}$
(c) $H^+\,(aq) + e^- \longrightarrow \frac{1}{2}H_2\,(g);\; E^\ominus_{cell} = 0.00\text{ V}$
(d) $Cl^-\,(aq) \longrightarrow \frac{1}{2}Cl_2\,(g) + e^-;\; E^\ominus_{cell} = 1.36\text{ V}$

Ans. ***(d)*** In case of electrolysis of aqueous NaCl, oxidation reaction occurs at anode which is as follows

$$Cl^-\,(aq) \longrightarrow \frac{1}{2}Cl_2(g)+e^- \qquad \overset{\circ}{E}_{cell} = 1.36\text{ V}$$
$$2H_2O\,(l) \longrightarrow O_2(g)+4H^+(aq.)+4e^-. \qquad \overset{\circ}{E}_{cell} = 1.23\text{ V}$$

The reaction with lower E°_{cell} value should occur at anode, *i.e.*, water should get oxidised in preference to $Cl^-(aq)$. However, this does not take place and Cl^- is oxidised to $Cl_2(g)$ at anode.

This unexpected result is explained on the basis of the concept of 'overpotential', *i.e.*, water needs greater voltage for oxidation to O_2 (as it is kinetically slow process) than that needed for oxidation of Cl^- ions to Cl_2. Thus, the correct option is (d).

Multiple Choice Questions (More Than One Options)

Q.18 The positive value of the standard electrode potential of Cu^{2+}/Cu indicates that..........

(a) this redox couple is a stronger reducing agent than the H^+/H_2 couple
(b) this redox couple is a stronger oxidising agent than H^+/H_2
(c) Cu can displace H_2 from acid
(d) Cu cannot displace H_2 from acid

Ans. ***(b, d)*** 'Lesser the E° value of redox couple higher the reducing power''

$$Cu^{2+} + 2e^- \longrightarrow Cu \qquad E^\circ = 0.34\text{ V}$$
$$2H^+ + 2e^- \longrightarrow H_2 \qquad E^\circ = 0.00\text{ V}$$

Since, $2H^+/H_2$ has lesser standard reduction potential than Cu^{2+}/Cu redox couple. Therefore,

(i) Cu^{2+}/Cu redox couple is a stronger oxidising agent than H^+/H_2.

(ii) Cu can't displace H_2 from acid.

Hence, (b) and (d) are correct options.

Q.19 $E^\ominus_{cell}$ for some half cell reactions are given below. On the basis of these mark the correct answer.

(a) $H^+(aq) + e^- \longrightarrow \frac{1}{2}H_2(g);\ E^\ominus_{cell} = 0.00V$

(b) $2H_2O(l) \longrightarrow O_2(g) + 4H^+(aq) + 4e^-;\ E^\ominus_{cell} = 1.23V$

(c) $2SO_4^{2-}(aq) \longrightarrow S_2O_8^{2-}(aq) + 2e^-;\quad E^\ominus_{cell} = 1.96V$

(a) In dilute sulphuric acid solution, hydrogen will be reduced at cathode.
(b) In concentrated sulphuric acid solution, water will be oxidised at anode.
(c) In dilute sulphuric acid solution, water will be oxidised at anode.
(d) In dilute sulphuric acid solution, SO_4^{2-} ion will be oxidised to tetrathionate ion at anode.

Ans. ***(a, c)*** During the electrolysis of dilute sulphuric acid, hydrogen will be reduced at cathode and H_2O will be oxidised at anode.

Oxidation half cell reactions possible at anode are as follows

$$2SO_4^{2-}(aq) \longrightarrow S_2O_8{}^{2-}(aq) + 2e^- \qquad E^\circ_{cell} = 1.96V$$
$$2H_2O(l) \longrightarrow O_2(g) + 4H^+(aq) + 4e^-; \qquad E^\circ_{cell} = 1.23V$$

Reaction having lower value of E°_{cell} will undergo faster oxidation. So, reaction of oxidation of $H_2O(l)$ to $O_2(g)$ is preferred at anode.

The reaction occurs at cathode is

$$H^+(aq) + e^- \longrightarrow \frac{1}{2}H_2(g)$$

Hence, options (a) and (c) are correct.

Q.20 $E^\circ_{cell} = 1.1$ V or Daniel cell. Which of the following expressions are correct description of state of equilibrium in this cell?

(a) $1.1 = K_C$ (b) $\frac{2.303\,RT}{2F}\log K_C = 1.1$

(c) $\log K_C = \frac{2.2}{0.059}$ (d) $\log K_C = 1.1$

Ans. ***(b, c)*** At state of equilibrium

$$\Delta G = -RT \ln K_C$$

$$-nFE^\circ = -RT\,2.303 \log K_C$$

$$E^\circ = \frac{RT\,2.303\ \log K_C}{2F} \qquad (n = 2 \text{ for Daniel cell})$$

$\because$ At equilibrium $E^\circ = 1.1$

$$\therefore \quad \frac{2.303\,RT}{2\,F} \log K_C = 1.1$$

$$\log K_C = \frac{2.2}{0.059} \qquad \text{[on solving]}$$

Hence, options (b) and (c) are the correct choices.

Q.21 Conductivity of an electrolytic solution depends on ....

(a) nature of electrolyte
(b) concentration of electrolyte
(c) power of AC source
(d) distance between the electrodes

● **Concept insight** This solution includes the concept of conductivity of an electrolytic solution and how it depends on different factors.

Ans. ***(a, b)*** Conductivity of an electrolytic solution is due to the presence of mobile ions in the solution. This type of conductance is known as ionic conductance.
Conductivity of these type of solutions depend upon

(i) the nature of electrolyte added.
(ii) size of the ion produced and their solvatian.
(iii) concentration of electrolyte.
(iv) nature of solvent and its viscosity.
(v) temperature.

While power of AC source and distance between electrodes have no effect on conductivity of electrolytic solution.
Hence, options (a) and (b) are the correct choices.

Q.22 $\Lambda^\circ_m H_2O$ is equal to.......

(a) $\Lambda^\circ_{m\,(HCl)} + \Lambda^\circ_{m\,(NaOH)} - \Lambda^\circ_{m\,(NaCl)}$
(b) $\Lambda^\circ_{m\,(HNO_3)} + \Lambda^\circ_{m\,(NaNO_3)} - \Lambda^\circ_{m\,(NaOH)}$
(c) $\Lambda^\circ_{m\,(HNO_3)} + \Lambda^\circ_{m\,(NaOH)} - \Lambda^\circ_{m\,(NaNO_3)}$
(d) $\Lambda^\circ_{m\,(NH_4OH)} + \Lambda^\circ_{m\,(HCl)} - \Lambda^\circ_{m\,(NH_4Cl)}$

Thinking Process This problem includes concept of Kohlrausch law and its application in determination of molar conductivity of species. This problem can be solved by following three steps.

(i) Write the molar conductance of each species in terms of sum of their constituent ions.
(ii) Now operate the equation of each option given above by using information provided in the question.
(iii) At last if the sum of molar conductivity remaining constituent ions is equal to the molar conductivity of species asked (here $\Lambda^\circ_{m(H_2O)}$) then that will be the correct choice.

Ans. (a, c)

(a)

$$\overset{\circ}{\Lambda}_{m\,(HCl)} = \overset{\circ}{\Lambda}_{m\,(H^+)} + \overset{\circ}{\Lambda}_{m\,(Cl^-)}$$
$$\overset{\circ}{\Lambda}_{m\,(NaOH)} = \overset{\circ}{\Lambda}_{m\,(Na^+)} + \overset{\circ}{\Lambda}_{m\,(OH^-)}$$
$$\underline{\overset{\circ}{\Lambda}_{m\,(NaCl)} = \overset{\circ}{\Lambda}_{m\,(Na^+)} + \overset{\circ}{\Lambda}_{m\,(Cl^-)}}$$
$$\overset{\circ}{\Lambda}_{m\,(HCl)} + \overset{\circ}{\Lambda}_{m\,(NaOH)} - \overset{\circ}{\Lambda}_{m\,(NaCl)} = \overset{\circ}{\Lambda}_{m(H^+)} + \overset{\circ}{\Lambda}_{m\,(HO^-)} = \overset{\circ}{\Lambda}_{m\,(H_2O)}$$

(b)

$$\overset{\circ}{\Lambda}_{m\,(HNO_3)} = \overset{\circ}{\Lambda}_{m\,(H^+)} + \overset{\circ}{\Lambda}_{m\,(NO_3^-)}$$
$$\overset{\circ}{\Lambda}_{m\,(NaNO_3)} = \overset{\circ}{\Lambda}_{m\,(Na^+)} + \overset{\circ}{\Lambda}_{m\,(NO_3^-)}$$
$$\underline{\overset{\circ}{\Lambda}_{m\,(NaOH)} = \overset{\circ}{\Lambda}_{m\,(Na^+)} + \overset{\circ}{\Lambda}_{m\,(OH^-)}}$$
$$\overset{\circ}{\Lambda}_{m\,(HNO_3)} + \overset{\circ}{\Lambda}_{m\,(NaNO_3)} - \overset{\circ}{\Lambda}_{m\,(NaOH)} = \overset{\circ}{\Lambda}_{m\,(H^+)} + 2\overset{\circ}{\Lambda}_{m\,(NO_3^-)} - \overset{\circ}{\Lambda}_{m\,(OH^-)}$$

Option (b) is incorrect.

(c)

$$\overset{\circ}{\Lambda}_{m\,(HNO_3)} = \overset{\circ}{\Lambda}_{m\,(H^+)} + \overset{\circ}{\Lambda}_{m\,(NO_3^-)}$$
$$\overset{\circ}{\Lambda}_{m\,(NaOH)} = \overset{\circ}{\Lambda}_{m\,(Na^+)} + \overset{\circ}{\Lambda}_{m\,(OH^-)}$$
$$\underline{\overset{\circ}{\Lambda}_{m\,(NaNO_3)} = \overset{\circ}{\Lambda}_{m\,(Na^+)} + \overset{\circ}{\Lambda}_{m\,(NO_3^-)}}$$
$$\overset{\circ}{\Lambda}_{m\,(HNO_3)} + \overset{\circ}{\Lambda}_{m\,(NaOH)} - \overset{\circ}{\Lambda}_{m\,(NaNO_3)} = \overset{\circ}{\Lambda}_{m\,(H^+)} + \overset{\circ}{\Lambda}_{m\,(OH^-)} = \overset{\circ}{\Lambda}_{m\,(H_2O)}$$

(d)

$$\overset{\circ}{\Lambda}_{m\,(NH_4OH)} = \overset{\circ}{\Lambda}_{m\,(NH_4^+)} + \overset{\circ}{\Lambda}_{m\,(OH^-)}$$
$$\overset{\circ}{\Lambda}_{m\,(HCl)} = \overset{\circ}{\Lambda}_{m\,(H^+)} + \overset{\circ}{\Lambda}_{m\,(Cl^-)}$$
$$\underline{\overset{\circ}{\Lambda}_{m\,(NH_4Cl)} = \overset{\circ}{\Lambda}_{m\,(NH_4^+)} + \overset{\circ}{\Lambda}_{m\,(Cl^-)}}$$
$$\overset{\circ}{\Lambda}_{m\,(NH_4OH)} + \overset{\circ}{\Lambda}_{m\,(HCl)} - \overset{\circ}{\Lambda}_{m\,(NH_4Cl)} = \overset{\circ}{\Lambda}_{m\,(H^+)} + \overset{\circ}{\Lambda}_{m\,(OH^-)} = \overset{\circ}{\Lambda}_{m\,(H_2O)}$$

Decomposition of NH_4OH is not possible due to its weak basic strength. Hence, options (a) and (c) are the correct choices.

Q.23 What will happen during the electrolysis of aqueous solution of $CuSO_4$ by using platinum electrodes?

(a) Copper will deposit at cathode.
(b) Copper will deposit at anode.
(c) Oxygen will be released at anode.
(d) Copper will dissolve at anode.

Thinking Process This problem is based on electrolysis of electrolytes.

Ans. (a, c) For electrolysis of aqueous solution of $CuSO_4$.

$$CuSO_4\,(aq) \longrightarrow Cu^{2+} + SO_4^{2-}$$
$$H_2O \longrightarrow 2H^+ + O^{2-}$$

At cathode,
$$Cu^{2+} + 2e^- \longrightarrow Cu; \quad E^\circ_{cell} = 0.34\text{ V}$$
$$H^+ + e^- \longrightarrow \frac{1}{2}H_2; \quad E^\circ_{cell} = 0.00\text{ V}$$

Reaction with higher value of E° will take place at cathode. Hence, Cu will deposit at cathode.

At anode,
$$2SO_4^{2-} \longrightarrow S_2O_8^{2-} + 2e^-; \quad E^\circ_{cell} = 1.96\text{ V}$$
$$2H_2O \longrightarrow O_2 + 4H^+ + 4e^-; \quad E^\circ_{cell} = 1.23\text{ V}$$

Reaction with lower value of $E°$ will be prefered at anode. Hence, **oxygen will be** released at anode.

Hence, options (a) and (c) are the correct choices.

Q.24 What will happen during the electrolysis of aqueous solution of $CuSO_4$ in the presence of Cu electrodes?

(a) Copper will deposit at cathode (b) Copper will dissolve at anode

(c) Oxygen will be released at anode (d) Copper will deposit at anode

Ans. ***(a, b)*** Electrolysis of $CuSO_4$ can be represented by two half cell reactions occurring at cathode and anode respectively as

At cathode $Cu^{2+} + 2e^- \longrightarrow Cu(s)$

At anode $Cu(s) \longrightarrow Cu^{2+} + 2e^-$

Here, Cu will deposit at cathode while copper will dissolve at anode.

Hence, options (a) and (b) are the correct choices.

Q.25 Conductivity κ, is equal to.........

(a) $\frac{1}{R}\frac{l}{A}$ (b) $\frac{G^*}{R}$ (c) Λ_m (d) $\frac{l}{A}$

Ans. ***(a, b)*** As we know that, conductance is reciprocal of resistance and conductivity is the conductance of $1\,cm^3$ of substance. Also,conductivity is reciprocal of resistivity.

$$\kappa = \frac{1}{\rho}$$

$$\because \quad R = \rho\frac{l}{A}$$

$$\rho = \frac{R \cdot A}{l} \Rightarrow \kappa = \frac{1}{\left(\frac{R \cdot A}{l}\right)}$$

$$\kappa = \frac{1}{R} \cdot \frac{l}{A} = \frac{1}{R} \times G^* = \frac{G^*}{R}$$

Hence, options (a) and (b) are the correct choices.

Q.26 Molar conductivity of ionic solution depends on ....

(a) temperature

(b) distance between electrodes

(c) concentration of electrolytes in solution

(d) surface area of electrodes

Ans. ***(a, c)*** Molar conductivity is the conductivity due to ions furnished by one mole of electrolyte in solution. Molar conductivity of ionic solution depends on

(a) **Temperature** Molar conductivity of an electrolyte solution increases with increase in temperature.

(c) **Concentration of electrolytes in solution** As concentration of electrolyte increases, molar conductivity decreases.

$$\therefore \quad \lambda_m = \frac{\kappa}{c}$$

Hence, options (a) and (c) are the correct choices.

Q.27 For the given cell, $Mg \mid Mg^{2+} \parallel Cu^{2+} \mid Cu$

(a) Mg is cathode
(b) Cu is cathode
(c) The cell reaction is $Mg + Cu^{2+} \longrightarrow Mg^{2+} + Cu$
(d) Cu is the oxidising agent

Ans. ***(b, c)*** Left side of cell reaction represents oxidation half cell *i.e.*, oxidation of Mg and right side of cell represents reduction half cell reactions, *i.e.*, reduction of copper.

(i) Cu is reduced and reduction occurs at cathode.

(ii) Mg is oxidised and oxidation occurs at anode.

(iii) Whole cell reaction can be written as

Oxidation

$$Mg + Cu^{2+} \rightarrow Mg^{2+} + Cu$$

Reduction

Hence, options (b) and (c) are correct choices.

Short Answer Type Questions

Q.28 Can absolute electrode potential of an electrode be measured ?

Ans. No, only the difference in potential between two electrodes can be measured. This is due to the reason that oxidation or reduction cannot occur alone. So, when we measure electrode potential of any electrode we have to take a reference electrode.

Q.29 Can E°_{cell} or $\Delta_r G^{\circ}$ for cell reaction ever be equal to zero ?

Ans. No, otherwise the reaction become non-feasible.
The reaction is feasible only at E°_{cell} = positive or $\Delta_r G^{\circ}$ = negative .
when $E^{\circ} = \Delta_r G^{\circ} = 0$ the reaction reaches at equilibrium.

Q.30 Under what condition is $E_{cell} = 0$ or $\Delta_r G = 0$?

Ans. At the stage of chemical equilibrium in the cell,

$$E_{cell} = 0$$
$$\Delta_r G - nF\, E_{cell}$$
$$= - n \times F \times 0 = 0$$

Q.31 What does the negative sign in the expression $E^{\ominus}_{Zn^{2+}/Zn} = -0.76$ V mean?

Ans. Greater the negative value of standard reduction potential of metal, greater is its reactivity. It means that Zn is more reactive than hydrogen. When zinc electrode will be connected to standard hydrogen electrode, Zn will get oxidised and H^+ will get reduced.

Thus, zinc electrode will be the anode of the cell and hydrogen electrode will be the cathode of the cell.

Q.32 Aqueous copper sulphate solution and aqueous silver nitrate solution are electrolysed by 1 ampere current for 10 minutes in separate electrolytic cells. Will the mass of copper and silver deposited on the cathode be same or different? Explain your answer.

Ans. Different masses of Cu and Ag will be deposited at cathode. According to Faraday's second law of electrolysis amount of different substances liberated by keeping the same quantity of electricity passing through electrolyte solution, is directly proportional to their chemical equivalent weight.

$$\frac{W_1}{W_2} = \frac{E_1}{E_2}$$

where, E_1 and E_2 have different values depending upon number of electrons required to reduce the metal ion. Thus, masses of Cu and Ag deposited will be different.

Q.33 Depict the galvanic cell in which the cell reaction is

$$Cu + 2Ag^+ \longrightarrow 2Ag + Cu^{2+}$$

Ans. In a galvanic cell, oxidation half reaction is written on left hand side and reduction half reaction is on right hand side. Salt bridge is represented by parallel lines. $Cu \mid Cu^{2+} \parallel Ag^+ \mid Ag$.

Q 34 Value of standard electrode potential for the oxidation of Cl^- ions is more positive than that of water, even then in the electrolysis of aqueous sodium chloride, why is Cl^- oxidised at anode instead of water?

Ans. Under the condition of electrolysis of aqueous sodium chloride, oxidation of water at anode requires over potential. So, Cl^- is oxidised at anode instead of water.

Possible oxidation half cell reactions occurring at anode are

$$Cl^-(aq) \longrightarrow \frac{1}{2}Cl_2(g) + e^-; \qquad E^{\ominus}_{cell} = 1.36\text{ V}$$

$$2H_2O(l) \longrightarrow O_2(g) + 4H^+(aq) + 4e^-; \qquad E^{\circ}_{cell} = 1.23\text{ V}$$

Species having lower E°_{Cell} undergo oxidation first than the higher value but oxidation of H_2O to O_2 is kinetically so slow, that it needs some over voltage.

Mistake Alert! *One can make a mistake of not considering the factor of overpotential while finding out the product of electrolysis of* NaCl*(aq) solution at anode.*

Q.35 What is electrode potential?

Ans. The potential difference between the electrode and the electrolyte in an electrochemical cell is called electrode potential.

Q.36 Consider the following diagram in which an electrochemical cell is coupled to an electrolytic cell. What will be the polarity of electrodes '*A*' and '*B*' in the electrolytic cell?

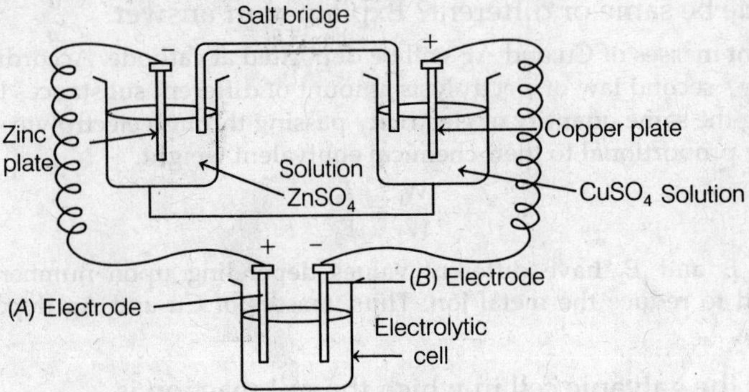

Ans. The cell drawn above represents electrochemical cell in which two different electrodes are fitted in their respective electrolytic solutions and the cell drawn at bottom represents electrolytic cell.

Cell representation can be represented as $Zn \mid Zn^{2+} \parallel Cu^{2+} \mid Cu$.

Zn is loosing electrons which are going towards electrode (*A*) and copper is accepting electron from electrode *B*.Hence,

Charge on electrode *A* = +

Charge on electrode *B* = –

Q.37 Why is alternating current used for measuring resistance of an electrolytic solution?

Ans. Alternating current is used in electrolysis so that concentration of ions in the solution remains constant and exact value of resistance can be measured.

Q.38 A galvanic cell has electrical potential of 1.1V. If an opposing potential of 1.1V is applied to this cell, what will happen to the cell reaction and current flowing through the cell ?

Ans. When an opposing potential of 1.1V is applied to a galvanic cell having electrical potential of 1.1V, then cell reaction stops completely and no current will flow through the cell.

Q.39 How will the pH of brine (*aq*. NaCl solution) be affected when it is electrolysed?

Ans. The pH of the solution will rise as NaOH (strong base) is formed in the electrolytic cell.

Chemical reactions occurring at cell when aqueous brine solution is electrolysed are as follows

$$NaCl\,(aq) \xrightarrow{H_2O} Na^+(aq) + Cl^-(aq)$$

Cathode $$H_2O(l) + e^- \longrightarrow \frac{1}{2}H_2(g) + OH^-(aq)$$

Anode $$Cl^-(aq) \longrightarrow \frac{1}{2}Cl_2(g) + e^-$$

Net reaction, $$NaCl\,(aq) + H_2O\,(l) \longrightarrow Na^+(aq) + OH^-(aq) + \frac{1}{2}H_2(g) + \frac{1}{2}Cl_2(g)$$

Q.40 Unlike dry cell, the mercury cell has a constant cell potential throughout its useful life. Why ?

Ans. Life time of any cell depends upon ions present in the cell. Ions are not involved in the overall cell reaction of mercury cell. Hence, mercury cell has a constant cell potential throughout its useful life.

Q.41 Solutions of two electrolytes *A* and *B* are diluted. The Λ_m of '*B*' increases 1.5 times while that of *A* increases 25 times. Which of the two is a strong electrolyte? Justify your answer.

Ans. Strong electrolytes dissociate almost completely even on high concentration. Therefore, concentration of such solutions remain almost same on dilution. Electrolyte '*B*' is stronger than '*A*' because in '*B*' the number of ions remains the same on dilution, but only interionic attraction decreases.
Therefore, Λ_m increases only by 1.5 times. While in case of weak electrolyte on dilution, number of constituent ions increases.

Q.42 When acidulated water (dil. H_2SO_4 solution) is electrolysed, will the pH of the solution be affected? Justify your answer.

Ans. Since pH of the solution depends upon concentration of H^+ present in solutions. pH of the solution will not be affected as $[H^+]$ remains constant.

At anode $2H_2O \longrightarrow O_2 + 4H^+ + 4e^-$

At cathode $4H^+ + 4e^- \longrightarrow 2H_2 \uparrow$

Q.43 In an aqueous solution how does specific conductivity of electrolytes change with addition of water?

Ans. Conductivity of solution due to total ions present in per unit volume of solution is known as specific conductivity. Specific conductivity decreases due to decrease in the number of ions per unit volume. When water is added to an aqueous solution.

Q.44 Which reference electrode is used to measure the electrode potential of other electrodes?

Ans. Standard hydrogen electrode (SHE) is the reference electrode whose electrode potential is taken to be zero. The electrode potential of other electrodes are measured with respect to it.

Q.45 Consider a cell given below

$$Cu \mid Cu^{2+} \parallel Cl^- \mid Cl_2, Pt$$

Write the reactions that occur at anode and cathode.

Ans. Cell reaction represented in the question is composed of two half cell reactions. These reactions are as follows

At anode $Cu \longrightarrow Cu^{2+} + 2e^-$

At cathode $Cl_2 + 2e^- \longrightarrow 2Cl^-$

overall reaction, $Cu + Cl_2 \longrightarrow Cu^{2+} + 2Cl^-$

Copper is getting oxidised at anode. Cl_2 is getting reduced at cathode.

Q.46 Write the Nernst equation for the cell reaction in the Daniel cell. How will the E_{cell} be affected when concentration of Zn^{2+} ions is increased?

Ans. $Zn + Cu^{2+} \longrightarrow Zn^{2+} + Cu$

$$E_{cell} = E^{\circ}_{cell} - \frac{0.0591}{2} \log \left[\frac{Zn^{2+}}{Cu^{2+}}\right]$$

$$E_{cell} = E^{\circ}_{cell} + \frac{0.0591}{2} \log \left[\frac{Cu^{2+}}{Zn^{2+}}\right]$$

According to this equation,

E°_{cell} is directly dependent on concentration of Cu^{2+} and inversely dependent upon concentration of Zn^{2+} ions.

E_{cell} decreases when concentration of Zn^{2+} ions is increased.

Q.47 What advantage do the fuel cells have over primary and secondary batteries ?

Ans. Primary batteries contain a limited amount of reactants and are discharged when the reactants have been consumed. Secondary batteries can be recharged but it takes a long time. Fuel cell run continuously as long as the reactants are supplied to it and products are removed continuously.

Q.48 Write the cell reaction of a lead storage battery when it is discharged. How does the density of the electrolyte change when the battery is discharged?

Ans. When a lead storage battery is discharged then the following cell reaction takes place

$$Pb + PbO_2 + 2H_2SO_4 \longrightarrow 2PbSO_4 + 2H_2O$$

Density of electrolyte depends upon number.of constituent ions present in per unit volume of electrolyte solution. In this case, density of electrolyte decreases as water is formed and sulphuric acid is consumed as the product during discharge of the battery.

Q.49 Why on dilution the Λ_m of CH_3COOH increases drastically, while that of CH_3COONa increases gradually?

Ans. In the case of CH_3COOH, which is a weak electrolyte, the number of ions increases on dilution due to an increase in degree of dissociation. Thus, Λ_m of CH_3COOH increases drastically.

$$CH_3COOH + H_2O \rightleftharpoons CH_3COO^- + H_3O^+$$

In case of strong electrolyte CH_3COONa the number of ions remains the same but the interionic attraction decreases. Thus, Λ_m of CH_3COONa increases gradually.

Matching The Columns

Q.50 Match the terms given in Column I with the units given in Column II.

Column I		Column II	
A.	$\wedge_m$	1.	$S\,cm^{-1}$
B.	E_{cell}	2.	m^{-1}
C.	κ	3.	$S\,cm^2\,mol^{-1}$
D.	G^*	4.	V

Ans. A. → (3) B. → (4) C. → (1) D. → (2)

	Column I	Column II (Unit of parameter)
A.	$\wedge_m$	$S\,cm^2\,mol^{-1}$
B.	E_{cell}	V
C.	κ (conductivity)	$S\,cm^{-1}$
D.	$G^* = \frac{l}{a}$	m^{-1}

Q.51 Match the terms given in Column I with the items given in Column II.

Column I		Column II	
A.	$\wedge_m$	1.	Intensive property
B.	$E^{\ominus}_{cell}$	2.	Depends on number of ions/volume
C.	κ	3.	Extensive property
D.	$\Delta_r G_{cell}$	4.	Increases with dilution

Ans. A. → (4) B. → (1) C. → (2) D. → (3)

A. $\wedge_m$ (molar conductivity) is the conductivity due to number of ions furnished by one mole of electrolyte. As dilution increases, number of ions present in the solution increases, hence molar conductivity increases.

B. E°_{cell} of any atom/ion does not depend upon number of atom/ion, hence E°_{cell} of any atom/ion is an intensive properties.

C. κ represents specific conductivity which depends upon number of ions present in the solution in per unit volume.

D. $\Delta_r G_{cell}$ is an extensive property as it depends upon number of particles(species).

Q.52 Match the items of Column I and Column II.

Column I		Column II	
A.	Lead storage battery	1.	Maximum efficiency
B.	Mercury cell	2.	Prevented by galvanisation
C.	Fuel cell	3.	Gives steady potential
D.	Rusting	4.	Pb is anode, PbO_2 is cathode

Ans. **A.** → (4) **B.** → (3) **C.** → (1) **D.** → (2)

A. Chemical reaction occurring on lead storage battery can be represented as

At anode $Pb(s) + SO_4^{2-}(aq) \longrightarrow PbSO_4(s) + 2e^-$

At cathode $PbO_2\ (s) + SO_4^{2-}(aq) + 4H^+(aq) \xrightarrow{+2e^-} 2PbSO_4(s) + 2H_2O(l)$

Thus, Pb is anode and PbO_2 is cathode.

B. Mercury cell does not include ions during their function, hence it produces steady current.

C. Fuel cell has maximum efficiency as it produces energy due to combustion reaction of fuel.

D. Rusting is prevented by galvanisation.

Q.53 Match the items of Column I and Column II.

Column I		Column II	
A.	κ	1.	$I \times t$
B.	$\wedge_m$	2.	$\wedge_m / \overset{\circ}{\wedge}_m$
C.	α	3.	$\dfrac{\kappa}{C}$
D.	Q	4.	$\dfrac{G^*}{R}$

Ans. **A.** → (4) **B.** → (3) **C.** → (2) **D.** → (1)

A. Conductivity $(\kappa) = \dfrac{G^*}{R}$

B. Molar conductivity $(\wedge_m) = \dfrac{\kappa}{C}$

C. Degree of dissociation $(\alpha) = \dfrac{\wedge_m}{\overset{\circ}{\wedge}_m}$

D. Charge $Q = I \times t$

where, Q is the quantity of charge in coulomb when I ampere of current is passed through an electrolyte for t second.

Q.54 Match the items of Column I and Column II.

	Column I		Column II
A.	Lechlanche cell	1.	Cell reaction $2H_2 + O_2 \longrightarrow 2H_2O$
B.	Ni-Cd cell	2.	Does not involve any ion in solution and is used in hearing aids.
C.	Fuel cell	3.	Rechargeable
D.	Mercury cell	4.	Reaction at anode, $Zn \longrightarrow Zn^{2+} + 2e^-$
		5.	Converts energy of combustion into electrical energy

Ans. **A.** → (4) **B.** → (3) **C.** → (1, 5) **D.** → (2)

A. The electrode reactions occuring in Lechlanche cell are

At anode $Zn\,(s) \longrightarrow Zn^2 + 2e^-$

At cathode $MnO_2 + NH_4^+ + e^- \longrightarrow MnO(OH) + NH_3$

B. Ni-Cd cell is rechargeable. So, it has more life time.

C. Fuel cell produces energy due to combustion. So, fuel cell converts energy of combustion into electrical energy *e.g.*, $2H_2 + O_2 \longrightarrow 2H_2O$

D. Mercury cell does not involve any ion in solution and is used in hearing aids.

Q.55 Match the items of Column I and Column II on the basis of data given below

$$E^\ominus_{F_2/F^-} = 2.87\,V,\ E^\ominus_{Li^+/Li} = -3.5\,V,$$
$$E^\ominus_{Au^{3+}/Au} = 1.4\,V,\ E^\ominus_{Br_2/Br^-} = 1.09\,V$$

	Column I		Column II
A.	F_2	1.	Metal is the strongest reducing agent
B.	Li	2.	Metal ion which is the weakest oxidising agent
C.	Au^{3+}	3.	Non-metal which is the best oxidising agent
D.	Br^-	4.	Unreactive metal
E.	Au	5.	Anion that can be oxidised by Au^{3+}
F.	Li^+	6.	Anion which is the weakest reducing agent
G.	F^-	7.	Metal ion which is an oxidising agent

Ans. **A.** → (3) **B.** → (1) **C.** → (7) **D.** → (5) **E.** → (4) **F.** → (2) **G.** → (6)

A. F_2 is a non-metal and best oxidising agent because SRP of F_2 is + 2.87 V.

B. Li is a metal and strongest reducing agent because SRP of Li is – 3.05 V.

C. Au^{3+} is a metal ion which is an oxidising agent as SRP of Au^{3+} is +1.40 V.

D. Br^- is an anion that can be oxidised by Au^{3+} as $E°$values of Au^{3+} ($E° = 1.40$) is greater than Br^-($E° = 1.09$ V).

E. Au is an unreactive metal.

F. Li^+ is a metal ion having least value of SRP (– 3.05 V), hence it is the weakest oxidising agent.

G. F^- is an anion which is the weakest reducing agent as F^- / F_2 has low oxidation potential (–2.87 V).

Assertion and Reason

In the following questions a statement of assertion followed by a statement of reason is given. Choose the correct answer out of the following choices.

(a) Both assertion and reason are true and the reason is the correct explanation of assertion.

(b) Both assertion and reason are true and reason is not the correct explanation of assertion.

(c) Assertion is true but the reason is false.

(d) Both assertion and reason are false.

(e) Assertion is false but reason is true.

Q.56 Assertion Cu is less reactive than hydrogen.

Reason $E^\ominus_{Cu^{2+}/Cu}$ is negative.

Ans. *(c)* Assertion is true but the reason is false. Electrode potential of Cu^{2+} / Cu is + 0.34 V and electrode potential of $2H^+ / H_2$ is 0.00 V.

Hence, correct reason is due to positive $E°$ value of Cu^{2+} / Cu, it looses electron to H^+ and get reduce, while H_2 gas evolves out.

Q.57 Assertion E_{cell} should have a positive value for the cell to function.

Reason $E_{cathode} < E_{anode}$

Ans. *(a)* Both assertion and reason are true and the reason is the correct explanation of assertion. Feasibility of chemical reaction depends on Gibbs free energy which is related to E°_{cell} as

$$\Delta G^\circ = - nFE^\circ_{cell}$$

When value of $E^\ominus_{cell}$ is positive then $\Delta G^\ominus$ becomes negative. Hence, reaction becomes feasible.

Since, $E^\circ_{cell} = E^\circ_{cathode} - E^\circ_{anode}$

Then for $E^\circ_{cell} > 0$, $E^\circ_{cathode} - E^\circ_{anode} > 0$

$\Rightarrow$ $E^\circ_{cathode} > E^\circ_{anode}$

Q.58 Assertion Conductivity of all electrolytes decreases on dilution.

Reason On dilution number of ions per unit volume decreases.

Ans. *(a)* Both assertion and reason are correct and reason is the correct explanation of assertion.

Since, conductivity depends upon number of ions per unit volume. Therefore, the conductivity of all electrolytes decreases on dilution due to decrease in number of ions per unit volume.

Q.59 **Assertion** Λ_m for weak electrolytes shows a sharp increase when the electrolytic solution is diluted.

Reason For weak electrolytes degree of dissociation increases with dilution of solution.

Ans. *(a)* Assertion and reason are true and the reason is the correct explanation of the assertion.

Molar conductivity of weak electrolytic solution increases on dilution, because as we add excess water to increase the dilution, degree of dissociation increases which lead to increase in number of ions in the solution. Thus, Λ_m shows a very sharp increase.

Q.60 **Assertion** Mercury cell does not give steady potential.

Reason In the cell reaction, ions are not involved in solution.

Ans. *(e)* Assertion is false but reason is true. Correct assertion is mercury cell gives steady potential.

Reason is correct as ions are not involved in the cell reaction.

Q.61 **Assertion** Electrolysis of NaCl solution gives chlorine at anode instead of O_2.

Reason Formation of oxygen at anode requires over voltage.

Ans. *(a)* Both assertion and reason are correct and reason is the correct explanation of assertion.

Electrolysis of NaCl is represented by following chemical reactions

At cathode $\quad H^+ (aq) + e^- \longrightarrow \frac{1}{2} H_2(g)$

At anode $\quad Cl^-(aq) \longrightarrow \frac{1}{2} Cl_2 + e^-; \ E^\circ_{cell} = 1.36V$

$$2H_2O\,(aq) \longrightarrow O_2(g) + 4H^+\ (aq) + 4e^-;\ E^\circ_{cell} = 1.23\ V$$

E°_{cell} for the second reaction has lower value, but formation of oxygen at anode requires over potential.

Q.62 **Assertion** For measuring resistance of an ionic solution an AC source is used.

Reason Concentration of ionic solution will change if DC source is used.

Ans. *(a)* Both assertion and reason are correct and reason is the correct explanation of assertion.

Concentration of ionic solution changes on using DC current as a source of energy, whereas, while on passing AC current, concentration of ionic solution does not change. Hence, AC source is used for measuring resistance.

Q.63 **Assertion** Current stops flowing when $E_{cell} = 0$.

Reason Equilibrium of the cell reaction is attained.

Ans. *(a)* Both assertion and reason are correct and reason is the correct explanation of assertion.

Current stop flowing when $E_{cell} = 0$. As at $E_{cell} = 0$ reaction reaches the equilibrium.

Q.64 **Assertion** $E_{Ag^+/Ag}$ increase with increase in concentration of Ag^+ ions.

Reason(R) $E_{Ag^+/Ag}$ has a positive value.

Ans. ***(b)*** Both assertion and reason are correct but reason is not the correct explanation of assertion.

$$Ag^+ + e^- \longrightarrow Ag$$

$$E = E° \frac{0.0591}{1} \log \frac{1}{[Ag^+]}$$

$$E = E° + 0.059 \log [Ag^+]$$

Thus, $E_{Ag^+/Ag}$ increases with increase in concentration of Ag^+. Also, it has a positive value.

Q.65 **Assertion** Copper sulphate can be stored in zinc vessel.

Reason Zinc is less reactive than copper.

Ans. ***(d)*** Both assertion and reason are false.

Copper sulphate cannot be stored in zinc vessel as zinc is more reactive than copper due to negative value of standard reduction potential of Zn.

Long Answer Type Questions

Q.66 Consider the figure and answer the following questions.

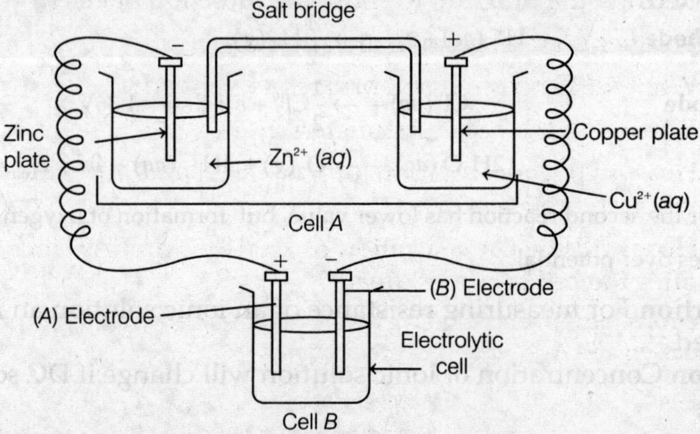

(i) Cell 'A' has $E_{cell} = 2V$ and Cell 'B' has $E_{cell} = 1.1$ V. Which of the two cells 'A' or 'B' will act as an electrolytic cell. Which electrode reactions will occur in this cell?

(ii) If cell 'A' has $E_{cell} = 0.5V$ and cell 'B' has $E_{cell} = 1.1$ V then what will be the reactions at anode and cathode?

Thinking Process This problem includes concept of electrochemical cell, electrolytic cell and charge on electrode. To solve this problem identify the charge on each electrode first.

Ans. (i) Cell '*B*' will act as electrolytic cell due to its lesser value of emf.

The electrode reactions will be

At cathode $Zn^{2+} + 2e^- \longrightarrow Zn$

At anode $Cu \longrightarrow Cu^{2+} + 2e^-$

(ii) If cell '*B*' has higher emf, it acts as galvanic cell. Now it will push electrons into cell '*A*'

In this case, the reactions will be

$$Zn \longrightarrow Zn^{2+} + 2e^- \text{ (At anode)}$$

$$Cu^{2+} + 2e^- \longrightarrow Cu \text{ (At cathode)}$$

Q.67 Consider figure from the above question and answer the questions (i) to (vi) given below.

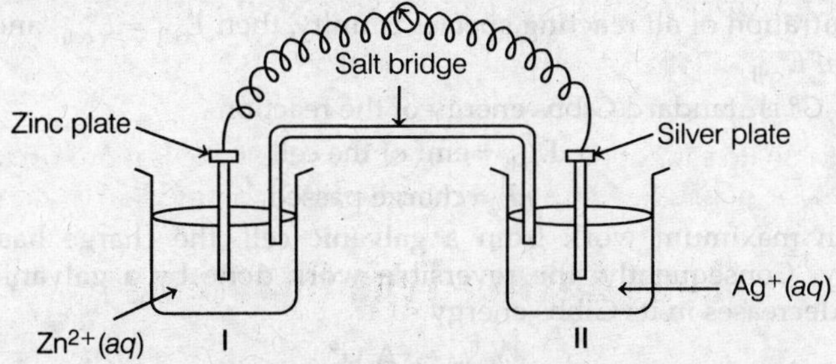

(i) Redraw the diagram to show the direction of electron flow.

(ii) Is silver plate the anode or cathode?

(iii) What will happen if salt bridge is removed?

(iv) When will the cell stop functioning?

(v) How will concentration of Zn^{2+} ions and Ag^+ ions be affected when the cell functions?

(vi) How will the concentration of Zn^{2+} ions and Ag^+ ions be affected after the cell becomes 'dead'?

Ans. (i) Electrons move from Zn to Ag as E° is more negative for Zn, so Zn undergoes oxidation and Ag^+ undergoes reduction.

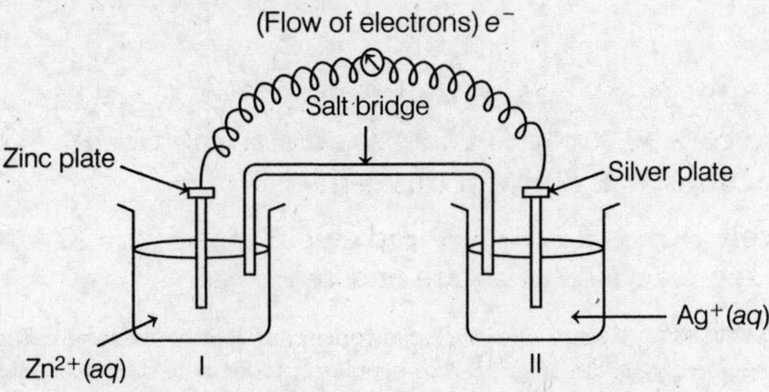

(ii) Ag is the cathode as it is the site of reduction where Ag^+ takes electrons from medium and deposit at cathode.

(iii) When salt bridge is removed, cell stops functioning because cell potential drops to zero. At $E = 0$ reaction reaches equilibrium.

(iv) When $E_{cell} = 0$, cell stops functioning because at this condition reaction reaches to equilibrium.

(v) Concentration of Zn^{2+} ions will increase and concentration of Ag^{+} ions will decrease because during redox reaction, Zn is converted into Zn^{2+} and Ag^{+} is converted into Ag.

(vi) When $E_{cell} = 0$, equilibrium is reached and concentration of Zn^{2+} ions and Ag^{+} will not change.

Q.68 What is the relationship between Gibbs free energy of the cell reaction in a galvanic cell and the emf of the cell? When will the maximum work be obtained from a galvanic cell?

Ans. If concentration of all reacting species is unity, then $E_{cell} = E^{\circ}_{cell}$ and $\Delta G^{\circ} = -nFE^{\circ}_{cell}$

where, $\Delta_r G^{\circ}$ is standard Gibbs energy of the reaction

E°_{cell} = emf of the cell

nF = charge passed

To obtain maximum work from a galvanic cell, the charge has to be passed reversibly. Consequently, the reversible work done by a galvanic cell becomes equal to decreases in its Gibbs energy.

i.e., $$W_{max} = -\Delta_r G^{\circ}$$

Chapter

04 Chemical Kinetics

Multiple Choice Questions (MCQs)

Q.1 The role of a catalyst is to change ....

(a) Gibbs energy of reaction
(b) enthalpy of reaction
(c) activation energy of reaction
(d) equilibrium constant

Ans. *(c)* The role of a catalyst is to change the activation energy of reaction. This is done by either increasing or decreasing activation energy of molecule. A catalyst does not change Gibbs energy (ΔG) of a reaction and equilibrium constant.

Note Catalyst are of two types one is positive catalyst which increases rate of reaction by decreasing activation energy and another is negative catalyst which decreases rate of reaction by increasing energy of activation.

Q.2 In the presence of a catalyst, the heat evolved or absorbed during the reaction ....

(a) increases
(b) decreases
(c) remains unchanged
(d) may increase or decrease

Ans. *(c)* In the presence of catalyst, the heat absorbed, or evolved during the reaction remains unchanged as it does not participate in the reaction.

Mistake Alert! *Enthalpy change of a reaction remains constant even if a catalyst is added in the reaction.*

Q.3 Activation energy of a chemical reaction can be determined by ....

(a) determining the rate constant at standard temperature
(b) determining the rate constant at two temperatures
(c) determining probability of collision
(d) using catalyst

Ans. *(b)* Activation energy of a chemical reaction is related to rate constant of a reaction at two different temperatures *i.e.,* k_1 and k_2 respectively

$$\ln\left(\frac{k_2}{k_1}\right) = -\frac{E_a}{R}\left[\frac{1}{T_1} - \frac{1}{T_2}\right]$$

where,
E_a = activation energy
T_2 = higher temperature
T_1 = lower temperature
k_1 = rate constant at temperature T_1
k_2 = rate constant at temperature T_2

This equation is known as Arrhenius equation.

Q.4 Consider figure and mark the correct option.

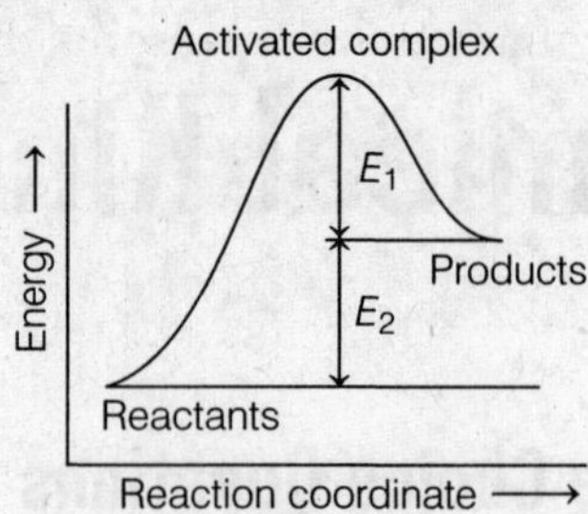

(a) Activation energy of forward reaction is $E_1 + E_2$ and product is less stable than reactant.

(b) Activation energy of forward reaction is $E_1 + E_2$ and product is more stable than reactant.

(c) Activation energy of both forward and backward reaction is $E_1 + E_2$ and reactant is more stable than product.

(d) Activation energy of backward reaction is E_1 and product is more stable than reactant.

Ans. ***(a)*** Activation energy is the minimum energy required to convert reactant molecules to product molecules. Here, the energy gap between reactants and activated complex is sum of E_1 and E_2.

$\therefore$ Activation energy $= E_1 + E_2$

Also, product is less stable than reactant as energy of product is greater than the reactant.

Q.5 Consider a first order gas phase decomposition reaction given below

$$A(g) \longrightarrow B(g) + C(g)$$

The initial pressure of the system before decomposition of A was p_i. After lapse of time 't', total pressure of the system increased by x units and became 'p_t'. The rate constant k for the reaction is given as ....

(a) $k = \frac{2.303}{t} \log \frac{p_i}{p_i - x}$

(b) $k = \frac{2.303}{t} \log \frac{p_i}{2p_i - p_t}$

(c) $k = \frac{2.303}{t} \log \frac{p_i}{2p_i + p_t}$

(d) $k = \frac{2.303}{t} \log \frac{p_i}{p_i + x}$

Thinking Process This problem is based on first order rate of reaction. To solve this question determine the value of total pressure then calculate value of x followed by rate constant.

where, $x =$ pressure of gas transform to product

Ans. ***(b)***

	$A(g) \rightarrow$	$B(g) +$	$C(g)$
Initially	p_i	0	0
At time t	$p_i - x$	x	x

$$p_t = p_i - x + x + x = p_i + x$$

For first order reaction

$$x = p_t - p_i$$

$$k = \frac{2.303}{t} \log \frac{p_i}{p_i - x}$$

$$= \frac{2.303}{t} \log \frac{p_i}{p_i - (p_t - p_i)} = \frac{2.303}{t} \log \frac{p_i}{2p_i - p_t}$$

Q.6 According to Arrhenius equation rate constant k is equal to $A\,e^{-E_a/RT}$. Which of the following options represents the graph of $\ln k$ vs $\frac{1}{T}$?

(a) 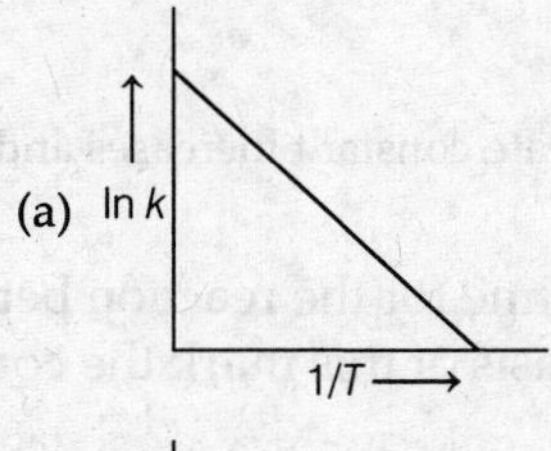

(b) 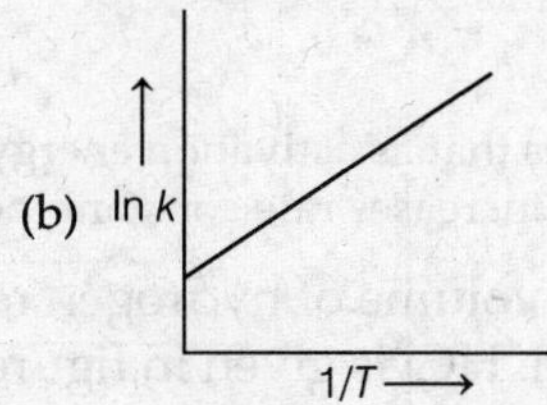

(c) 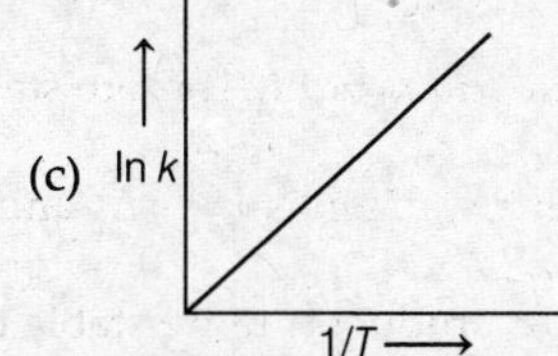

(d) 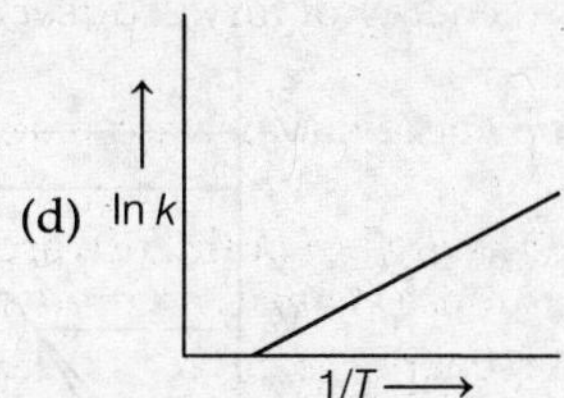

Thinking Process This problem includes graphical representation of Arrhenius equation. To solve this problem transform the Arrhenius equation into equation of straight line taking ln k on x–axis and $\frac{1}{T}$ *on y -axis*

Ans. ***(a)*** According to Arrhenius equation, $k = A\,e^{-E_a/RT}$

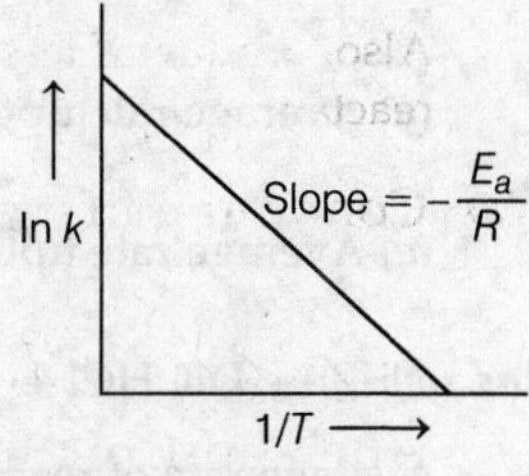

Taking log on both side $\ln k = \ln(A.e^{-\frac{E_a}{RT}})$

$$\ln k = \ln A - \frac{E_a}{RT}$$

$$\ln k = \frac{-E_a}{R} \times \frac{1}{T} + \ln A$$

$$y = m\,x + c$$

This equation can be related to equation of straight line as shown above.

From the graph, it is very clear that slope of the plot $= \frac{-E_a}{R}$ and intercept = ln A.

Q.7 Consider the Arrhenius equation given below and mark the correct option.

$$k = A\,e^{-\frac{E_a}{RT}}$$

(a) Rate constant increases exponentially with increasing activation energy and decreasing temperature.

(b) Rate constant decreases exponentially with increasing activation energy and decreasing temperature.

(c) Rate constant increases exponentially with decreasing activation energy and decreasing temperature.

(d) Rate constant increases exponentially with decreasing activation energy and increasing temperature.

Ans. ***(d)*** According to Arrhenius equation $k = A\,e^{-E_a/RT}$

Here,
$$k \propto e^{-E_a}$$
$$k \propto e^{\frac{-1}{T}}$$
$$k \propto e^{T}$$

This indicates that as activation energy decreases rate constant increases and as temperature increases rate constant increases.

Q.8 A graph of volume of hydrogen released *vs* time for the reaction between zinc and dil. HCl is given in figure. On the basis of this mark the correct option.

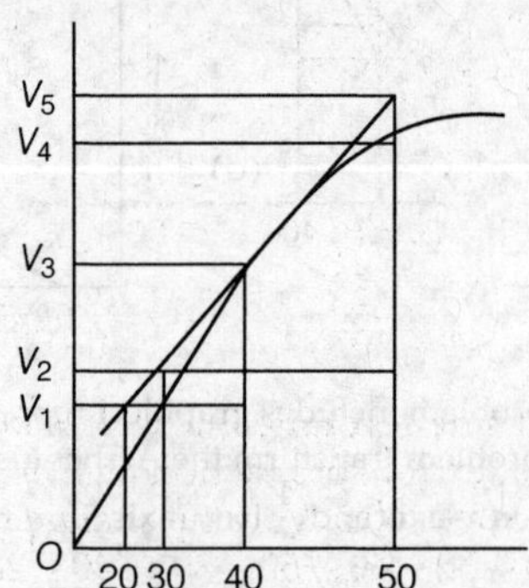

(a) Average rate upto 40 s is $\dfrac{V_3 - V_2}{40}$

(b) Average rate upto 40 s is $\dfrac{V_3 - V_2}{40 - 30}$

(c) Average rate upto 40 s is $\dfrac{V_3}{40}$

(d) Average rate upto 40 s is $\dfrac{V_3 - V_1}{40 - 20}$

Ans. ***(c)*** $Zn + \text{Dil. } HCl \longrightarrow ZnCl_2 + H_2 \uparrow$

$$\text{Average rate of reaction} = \frac{\text{Change in concentration of } H_2}{\text{Change in time}} = \frac{V_3 - 0}{40 - 0} = \frac{V_3}{40}$$

Q.9 Which of the following statements is **not** correct about order of a reaction?

(a) The order of a reaction can be a fractional number.

(b) Order of a reaction is experimentally determined quantity.

(c) The order of a reaction is always equal to the sum of the stoichiometric coefficients of reactants in the balanced chemical equation for a reaction .

(d) The order of a reaction is the sum of the powers of molar concentration of the reactants in the rate law expression .

Ans. ***(c)*** Out of the given four statements, statement (c) is not correct.

Order of Reaction

Order of reaction is equal to the sum of powers of concentration of the reactants in rate law expression.

For any chemical reaction

$$xA + yB \longrightarrow \text{Product}$$
$$\text{Rate} = k\,[A]^x[B]^y$$
$$\text{Order} = x + y$$

Order of a reaction can be a fraction also. It is not always equal to the sum of the stoichiometric coefficients of reactants in the balanced chemical equation. It is an experimentally determined quantity.

Q.10 Consider the graph given in figure. Which of the following options does **not** show instantaneous rate of reaction at 40th second?

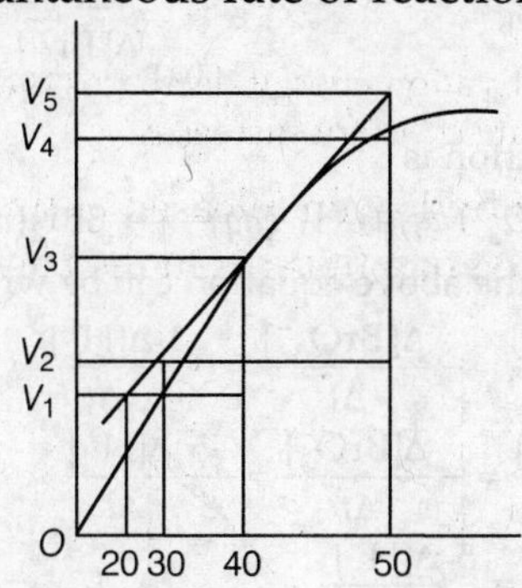

(a) $\frac{V_5 - V_2}{50 - 30}$ (b) $\frac{V_4 - V_2}{50 - 30}$ (c) $\frac{V_3 - V_2}{40 - 30}$ (d) $\frac{V_3 - V_1}{40 - 20}$

Ans. ***(b)*** Reaction occurring at smallest time interval is known as instantaneous rate of reaction *e.g.,* instantaneous rate of reaction at 40 s is rate of reaction during a small interval of time close to 40 s. Volume change during a small time interval close to 40 s *i.e.,* 40 – 30 s, 50 – 40 s, 50 – 30 s, 40 – 20 s.

$$\text{Instantaneous rate of reaction} = \frac{\text{Change in volume}}{\text{Time interval close to 40 s}}$$

(a) r_{inst} (20 s) $= \frac{V_5 - V_2}{50 - 30}$ correct

(b) r_{inst} (20 s) $= \frac{V_4 - V_3}{50 - 30}$ is incorrect,as V_4 does not link to any other line corresponding to time in the graph.

(c) r_{inst} (10 s) $= \frac{V_3 - V_2}{40 - 30}$ correct

(d) r_{inst} (20 s) $= \frac{V_3 - V_1}{40 - 20}$ correct

Q.11 Which of the following statements is correct?

(a) The rate of a reaction decreases with passage of time as the concentration of reactants decreases.

(b) The rate of a reaction is same at any time during the reaction.

(c) The rate of a reaction is independent of temperature change.

(d) The rate of a reaction decreases with increase in concentration of reactant(s).

Ans. ***(a)*** According to rate law expression, Rate $\propto [R]$

$$\text{Rate of reaction} = \frac{\text{Rate of disappearance of reactant}}{\text{Time taken}}$$

$$r = \frac{-dx}{dt}$$

Thus, as the concentration of reactant decreases with passage of time, rate of reaction decreases.

Q.12 Which of the following expressions is correct for the rate of reaction given below?

$$5\,Br^-(aq) + BrO_3^-(aq) + 6\,H^+(aq) \rightarrow 3\,Br_2(aq) + 3\,H_2O(l)$$

(a) $\frac{\Delta[Br^-]}{\Delta t} = 5\frac{\Delta[H^+]}{\Delta t}$ (b) $\frac{\Delta[Br^-]}{\Delta t} = \frac{6}{5}\frac{\Delta[H^+]}{\Delta t}$

(c) $\frac{\Delta[Br^-]}{\Delta t} = \frac{5}{6}\frac{\Delta[H^+]}{\Delta t}$ (d) $\frac{\Delta[Br^-]}{\Delta t} = 6\frac{\Delta[H^+]}{\Delta t}$

Ans. *(c)* Given, chemical reaction is

$$5\,Br^-(aq) + BrO_3^-(aq) + 6H^+(aq) \longrightarrow 3Br_2(aq) + 3H_2O(l)$$

Rate law expression for the above equation can be written as

$$-\frac{1}{5}\frac{\Delta[Br^-]}{\Delta t} = -\frac{\Delta[BrO_3^-]}{\Delta t} = \frac{-1}{6}\frac{\Delta[H^+]}{\Delta t} = \frac{+1}{3}\frac{\Delta[Br_2]}{\Delta t}$$

$$\Rightarrow \quad -\frac{\Delta[Br^-]}{\Delta t} = -\frac{\Delta[BrO_3^-]}{\Delta t} = \frac{-5}{6}\frac{\Delta[H^+]}{\Delta t}$$

$$\Rightarrow \quad \frac{\Delta[Br^-]}{\Delta t} = \frac{5}{6}\frac{\Delta[H^+]}{\Delta t}$$

Q.13 Which of the following graphs represents exothermic reaction?

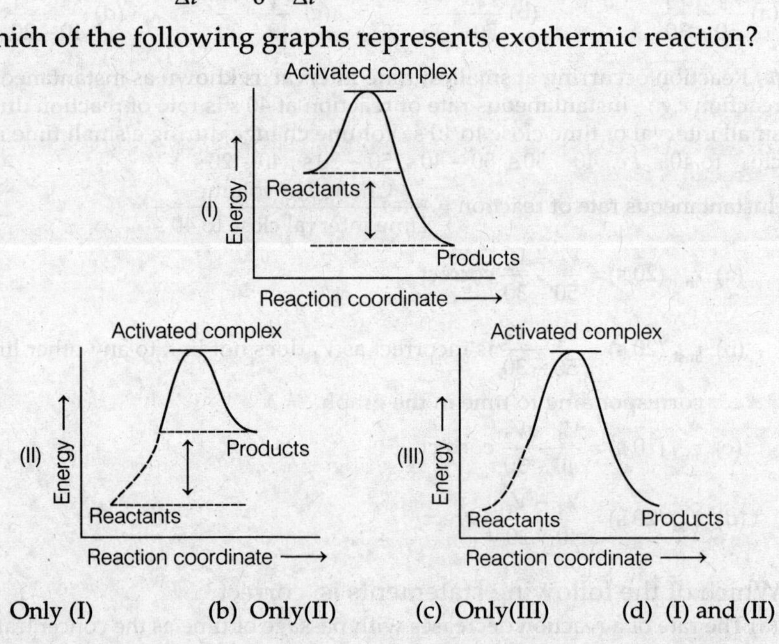

(a) Only (I) (b) Only(II) (c) Only(III) (d) (I) and (II)

Ans. *(a)* The chemical reaction in which energy is evolved during the reaction is known as exothermic reaction, *i.e.*, activation energy of product is greater than activation energy of reactants.

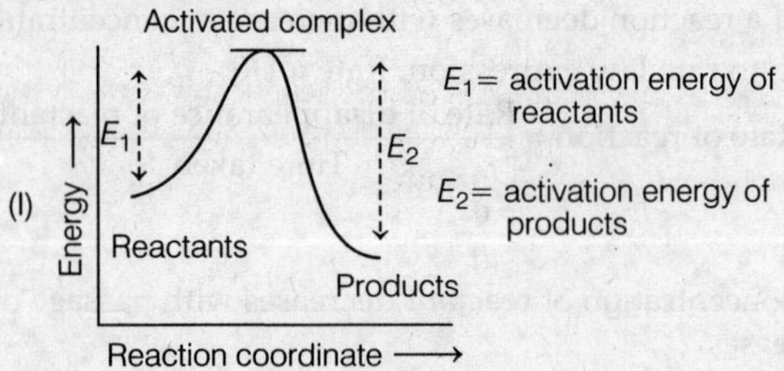

For exothermic reaction,

$$\Delta H = -ve$$

$$\Delta H = E_a(\text{Forward reaction}) - E_a(\text{backward reaction})$$

for ΔH to be negative, $E_{a,b} > E_{a,f}$.

Here, only (I) denotes correct picture of exothermic reaction.

Q.14 Rate law for the reaction $A + 2B \longrightarrow C$ is found to be

$$\text{Rate} = k[A][B]$$

Concentration of reactant 'B' is doubled, keeping the concentration of 'A' constant, the value of rate constant will be.......... .

(a) the same
(b) doubled
(c) quadrupled
(d) halved

Ans. ***(a)*** Rate constant (k) is independent of the concentration of the reactant and thus it will remains same.

Doubling the concentration of reactent 'B' on keeping the concentration of 'A' constant will only double the rate of the reaction.

Hence, (a) is the correct choice.

Q.15 Which of the following statements is **incorrect** about the collision theory of chemical reaction?

(a) It considers reacting molecules or atoms to be hard spheres and ignores their structural features.
(b) Number of effective collisions determines the rate of reaction.
(c) Collision of atoms or molecules possessing sufficient threshold energy results into the product formation.
(d) Molecules should collide with sufficient threshold energy and proper orientation for the collision to be effective.

- **Concept Insight** This solution includes the concept of collision theory.

Ans. ***(c)*** According the postulates of collision theory there are following necessary conditions for any reaction to occur.

(i) Molecule should collide with sufficient threshold energy.
(ii) Their orientation must be proper.
(iii) The collision must be effective.

Q.16 A first order reaction is 50% completed in 1.26×10^{14} s. How much time would it take for 100% completion?

(a) 1.26×10^{15} s
(b) 2.52×10^{14} s
(c) 2.52×10^{28} s
(d) Infinite

Ans. ***(d)*** The time taken for half the reaction to complete, *i.e.*, the time in which the concentration of a reactant is reduced to half of its original value is called half-life period of the reaction.

But it is impossible to perform 100% of the reaction. Whole of the substance never reacts because in every half-life , 50% of the substance reacts. Hence, time taken for 100% completion of a reaction is infinite.

But it is impossible to perform 100% of the reaction. Whole of the substance never reacts because in every half-life , 50% of the substance reacts. Hence, time taken for 100% completion of a reaction is infinite.

Q.17 Compounds '*A*' and '*B*' react according to the following chemical equation.

$$A(g) + 2B(g) \longrightarrow 2C(g)$$

Concentration of either '*A*' or '*B*' were changed keeping the concentrations of one of the reactants constant and rates were measured as a function of initial concentration. Following results were obtained. Choose the correct option for the rate equations for this reaction.

Experiment	Initial concentration of $[A]/\text{mol L}^{-1}$	Initial concentration of $[B]/\text{mol L}^{-1}$	Initial rate of formation of $[C]/\text{mol L}^{-1}\text{s}^{-1}$
1.	0.30	0.30	0.10
2.	0.30	0.60	0.40
3.	0.60	0.30	0.20

(a) Rate $= k[A]^2[B]$ (b) Rate $= k[A][B]^2$
(c) Rate $= k[A][B]$ (d) Rate $= k[A]^2[B]^0$

Ans. ***(b)*** Rate of reaction is change in concentration of reactant with respect to time.

$$r = k[A]^x[B]^y$$

$$0.1 = k(0.3)^x(0.3)^y \quad ...(i)$$

$$0.4 = k(0.3)^x(0.6)^y \quad ...(ii)$$

$$0.2 = k(0.6)^x(0.3)^y \quad ...(iii)$$

Dividing (ii) by (i) we get,

$$\frac{0.4}{0.1} = \frac{(0.6)^y}{(0.3)^y} \Rightarrow 4 = (2)^y$$

$$\Rightarrow \quad (2)^2 = (2)^y$$

$$\Rightarrow \quad y = 2$$

Dividing (iii) by (i) we get

$$\frac{0.2}{0.1} = \frac{(0.6)^x}{(0.3)^x}$$

$$\Rightarrow \quad (2)^1 = (2)^x$$

$$\therefore \quad x = 1$$

$$\therefore \quad \text{Rate} = k[A]^x[B]^y$$

$$\text{Rate} = k[A]^1[B]^2$$

Q.18 Which of the following statement is **not** correct for the catalyst?

(a) It catalyses the forward and backward reactions to the same extent.

(b) It alters ΔG of the reaction.

(c) It is a substance that does not change the equilibrium constant of a reaction.

(d) It provides an alternate mechanism by reducing activation energy between reactants and products.

Ans. ***(b)*** Characteristics of catalyst

(a) It catalyses the forward and backward reaction to the same extent as it decreases energy of activation hence, increases the rate of both the reactions.

(b) Since, reaction quotient is the relation between concentration of reactants and products. Hence, catalyst does not alter Gibbs free energy as it is related to reaction quotient. Thus, Gibbs free energy does not change during the reaction when catalyst is added to it.

$$\Delta G = \Delta G^\circ + RT \ln Q$$

where, Q = reaction quotient , ΔG° = standard state free energy

(c) It does not alter equilibrium constant of reaction as equilibrium constant is also concentration dependent term.

(d) It provides an alternate mechanism by reducing activation energy between reactants and products.

Q.19 The value of rate constant of a pseudo first order reaction ....

(a) depends on the concentration of reactants present in small amount
(b) depends on the concentration of reactants present in excess
(c) is independent of the concentration of reactants
(d) depends only on temperature

Ans. ***(b)*** The value of rate constant of a pseudo first order reaction depends on concentration of reactant present in excess amount. Pseudo first order reaction behaves as first order reaction under certain conditions, although they are higher order reactions.

Hence, option (b) is correct.

Q.20 Consider the reaction $A \longrightarrow B$. The concentration of both the reactants and the products varies exponentially with time. Which of the following figures correctly describes the change in concentration of reactants and products with time?

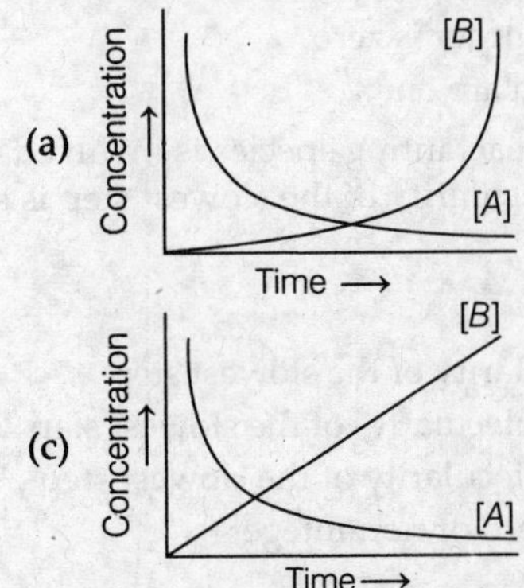

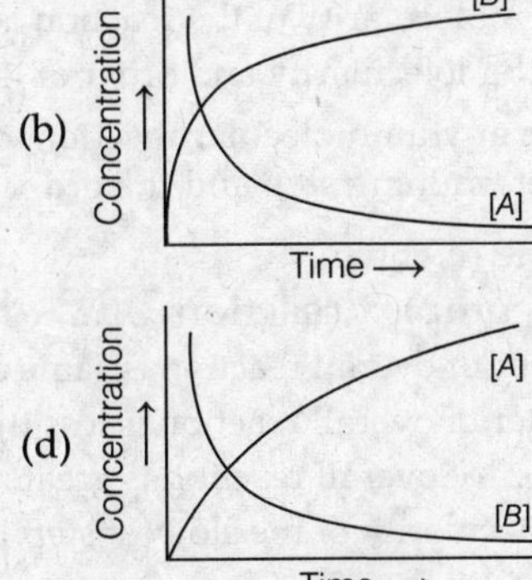

Ans. ***(b)*** In a reaction, $A \longrightarrow B$

Concentration of reactants and products varies exponentially *w.r.t* time.

(i) Concentration of reactant (here, A) decreases exponentially *w.r.t* time.

(ii) Concentration of product (here, B) increases exponentially *w.r.t* time. Hence, the correct graphical representation is (b).

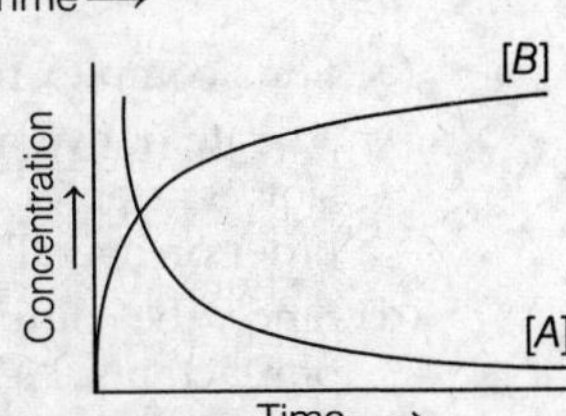

Multiple Choice Questions (More Than One Options)

Q.21 Rate law cannot be determined from balanced chemical equation if ....

(a) reverse reaction is involved
(b) it is an elementary reaction
(c) it is a sequence of elementary reactions
(d) any of the reactants is in excess

Ans. *(a, c, d)* Rate law can be determined from balanced chemical equation if it is an elementary reaction.

Q.22 Which of the following statements are applicable to a balanced chemical equation of an elementary reaction?

(a) Order is same as molecularity.
(b) Order is less than the molecularity.
(c) Order is greater than the molecularity.
(d) Molecularity can never be zero.

Ans. *(a, d)* For a balanced chemical equation of an elementary reactions order is same as molecularity and molecularity can never be zero. If molecularity of a reaction is considered to be zero it means that no reactant is going to transform into product. Consider a chemical reaction.

$$2NO(g) + O_2(g) \longrightarrow 2NO_2(g)$$

Differential rate law expression can be written as

$$\frac{dR}{dt} = k[NO]^2\ [O_2]$$

Here, molecularity = 3, order = 3

Q.23 In any unimolecular reaction ....

(a) only one reacting species is involved in the rate determining step
(b) the order and the molecularity of slowest step are equal to one
(c) the molecularity of the reaction is one and order is zero
(d) both molecularity and order of the reaction are one

Ans. *(a, b)* In any unimolecular reaction, only one reactanting species is involved in the rate determining step and the order and molecularity of the slowest step is equal to one.

Q.24 For a complex reaction ....

(a) order of overall reaction is same as molecularity of the slowest step
(b) order of overall reaction is less than the molecularity of the slowest step
(c) order of overall reaction is greater than molecularity of the slowest step
(d) molecularity of the slowest step is never zero or non-integer

Ans. *(a, d)*

(a) For a complex reaction, order of overall reaction = molecularity of slowest step
As rate of overall reaction depends upon total number of molecules involved in slowest step of the reaction. Hence, molecularity of the slowest step is equal to order of overall reaction.

(d) Since, the completion of any chemical reaction is not possible in the absence of reactants. Hence, slowest step of any chemical reaction must contain at least one reactant. Thus, molecularity of the slowest step is never zero or non-integer.

Q.25 At high pressure the following reaction is zero order.

$$2NH_3(g) \xrightarrow[\text{Platinum catalyst}]{1130\,K} N_2(g) + 3H_2(g)$$

Which of the following options are correct for this reaction?

(a) Rate of reaction = Rate constant.

(b) Rate of the reaction depends on concentration of ammonia.

(c) Rate of decomposition of ammonia will remain constant until ammonia disappears completely.

(d) Further increase in pressure will change the rate of reaction.

Ans. ***(a, c, d)*** Given, chemical reaction is

$$2NH_3(g) \xrightarrow[\text{Platinum catalyst}]{1130\,K} N_2(g) + 3H_2(g)$$

At very high pressure rate of reaction becomes independent of concentration of ammonia *i.e.*, zero order reaction.

Hence, $\text{Rate} = k[p_{NH_3}]^0$

$\text{Rate} = k$

(a) Rate of reaction = Rate constant

(b) Rate of decomposition of ammonia will remain constant until ammonia disappears completely.

(c) Since, formation of ammonia is a reversible process further increase in pressure will change the rate of reaction. According to Le-Chatelier principle, increase in pressure will favour backward reaction.

Q.26 During decomposition of an activated complex

(a) energy is always released

(b) energy is always absorbed

(c) energy does not change

(d) reactants may be formed

Ans. ***(a, d)*** When the reactant molecules collide with each other they lead to formation of an activated complex. It has the highest energy among reactants, products and activated complex. When it decomposes to give product, energy is released and stability of product increases.

Since, the entire concentration of activated complex do not convert into products hence, some activated complex may give reactants also.

Q.27 According to Maxwell, Boltzmann distribution of energy,......... .

(a) the fraction of molecules with most probable kinetic energy decreases at higher temperatures

(b) the fraction of molecules with most probable kinetic energy increases at higher temperatures

(c) most probable kinetic energy increases at higher temperatures

(d) most probable kinetic energy decreases at higher temperatures

Ans. ***(a, c)*** Distribution of kinetic energy may be described by plotting a graph of fraction of molecules *versus* kinetic energy.

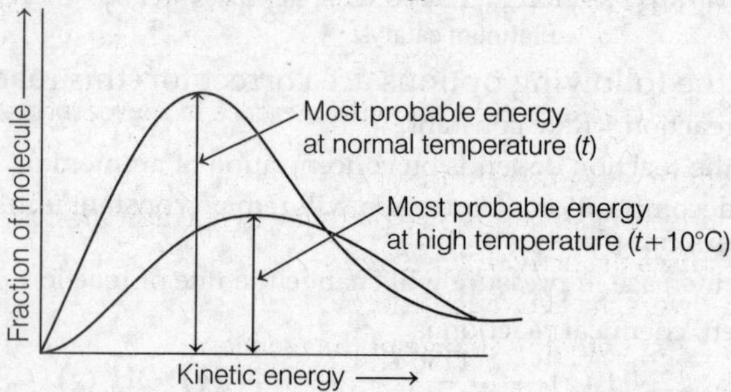

Kinetic energy of maximum fraction of molecule is known as most probable kinetic energy. It is important to note that with increase in temperature, peak shifts forward but downward. This means that with increase in temperature,

(i) most probable kinetic energy increases at higher temperature.

(ii) the fractions of molecules possessing most probable kinetic energy decreases.

Q.28 In the graph showing Maxwell, Boltzmann distribution of energy ....

(a) area under the curve must not change with increase in temperature

(b) area under the curve increases with increase in temperature

(c) area under the curve decreases with increase in temperature

(d) with increase in temperature curve broadens and shifts to the right hand side

Ans. ***(a, d)*** According to Maxwell Boltzmann distribution curve, area under the curve remains same with increase in temperature.

But with increase in temperature curve broadens and shift towards right hand side due to decrease in fraction of molecules having most probable kinetic energy.

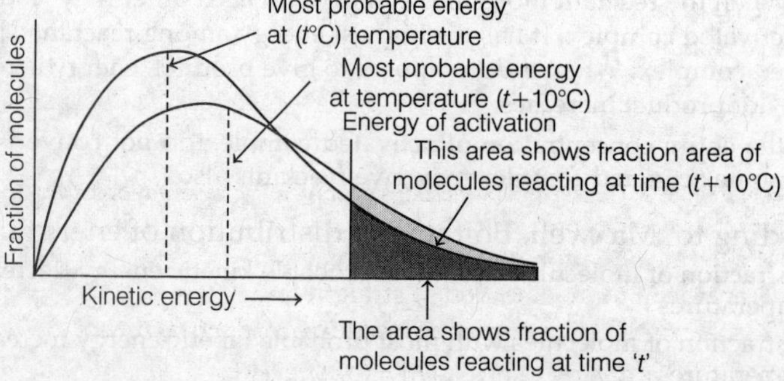

Q.29 Which of the following statements are in accordance with the Arrhenius equation?

(a) Rate of a reaction increases with increase in temperature.

(b) Rate of a reaction increases with decrease in activation energy.

(c) Rate constant decreases exponentially with increase in temperature.

(d) Rate of reaction decreases with decrease in activation energy.

Ans. ***(a, b)*** Arrhenius equation can be written as $k = A.e^{\frac{-E_a}{RT}}$

$k \propto e^{-E_a}$ *i.e.*, rate of reaction increases with decrease in activation energy.

$$k \propto e^{\frac{-1}{T}}$$

$k \propto e^{T}$, *i.e.*, rate of reaction increases with increase in temperature.

Q.30 Mark the **incorrect** statements.

(a) Catalyst provides an alternative pathway to reaction mechanism.
(b) Catalyst raises the activation energy.
(c) Catalyst lowers the activation energy.
(d) Catalyst alters enthalpy change of the reaction.

Thinking Process The problem includes the effects of the catalyst on the rate of reaction.

Ans. ***(b, d)*** **Function of Catalyst** As the catalyst is added to the reaction medium rate of reaction increases by decreasing the activation energy of molecule. Hence, it follows an alternative pathway.

Catalyst does not change the enthalpy change of the reaction. Energy of reactant and product remain same in both catalysed and uncatalysed reaction.

Hence, (b) and (d) are incorrect statements.

Q.31 Which of the following graphs is correct for a zero order reaction?

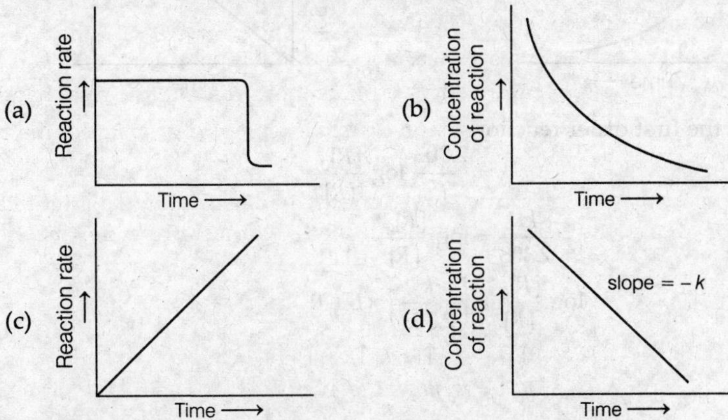

Thinking Process This problem includes graphical representation of zero order reaction. To solve this problem.

(i) Write rate equation of zero order reaction.
(ii) Transform it into equation of straight line.
(iii) Transform it into a curve representing rate *versus* time.

Ans. ***(a, d)*** For a zero order reaction $[R] = (-k)\,t + [R]_0$ ...(i)

$$\begin{matrix} [R] = & (-k) & t & + [R]_0 \\ \uparrow & \uparrow & \uparrow & \uparrow \\ y = & m \times & x & + c \end{matrix}$$

On comparing with Eq. of straight line

$y = [R]$ (concentration)

$x = t$ (time)

Slope $(m) = -k$ (rate constant)

Intercept $(c) = [R]_0$ (initial concentration)

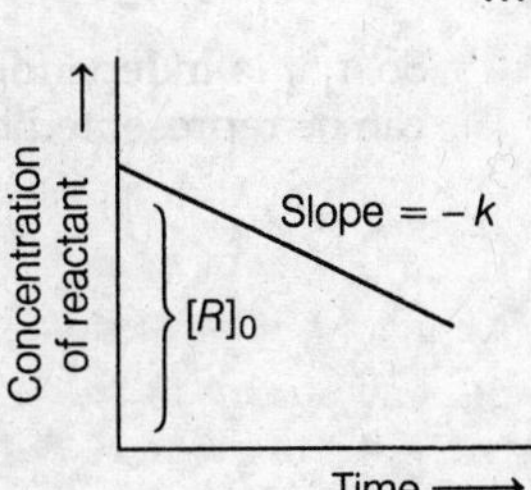

On rearranging Eq. (i)

$$\frac{[R]-[R]_0}{t} = -k$$

$$\frac{[R]-[R]_0}{t} = -kt^0$$

$$\text{Rate} \propto t^0$$

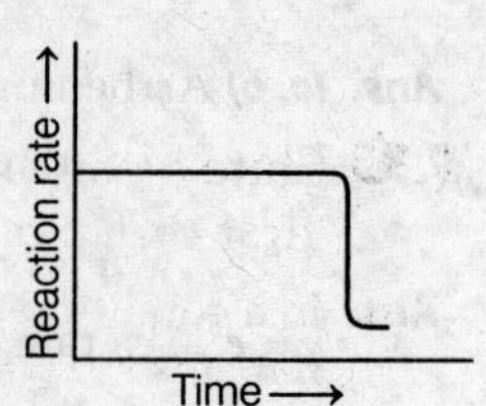

Hence, options (a) and (d) are representing correct graph for zero order reaction.

Q.32 Which of the following graphs is correct for a first order reaction?

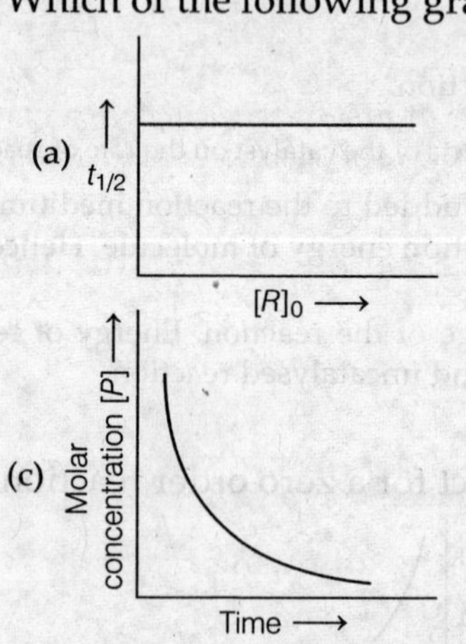

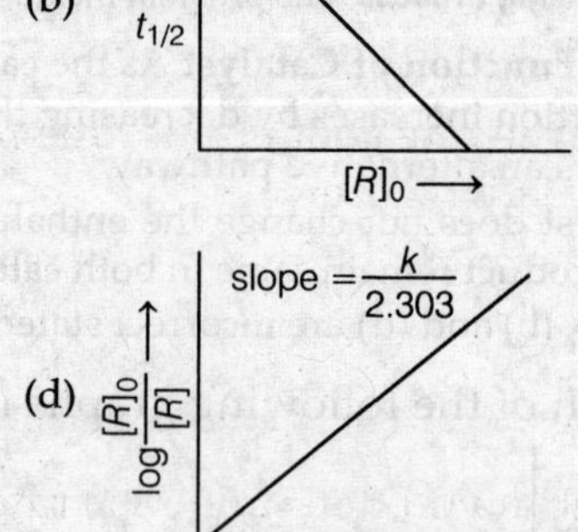

Ans. ***(a, d)*** For the first order reaction

$$k = \frac{2.303}{t}\log\frac{[R]_0}{[R]}$$

$$\frac{kt}{2.303} = \log\frac{[R]_0}{[R]}$$

$$\log\frac{[R]_0}{[R]} = \left(\frac{k}{2.303}\right) \times t + 0$$

$$\uparrow \quad \uparrow \quad \uparrow \quad \uparrow$$

$$y \;=\; m \quad x + c$$

Correct plot of $\log\frac{[R]_0}{[R]}$ v/s time can be represented by (d)

where, $\quad \text{slope} = \frac{k}{2.303}$

For first order reaction, $\quad t_{1/2} = \frac{2.303}{k}\log 2$

$\Rightarrow \quad t_{1/2} = \frac{0.693}{k}$

So, $t_{1/2}$ is independent of initial concentration. Hence, correct plot of $t_{1/2}$ and $[R]_0$ can be represented by (a).

Short Answer Type Questions

Q.33 State a condition under which a bimolecular reaction is kinetically first order reaction.

Ans. In a condition where one of the reactant is in excess, such that its concentration remains constant and rate of this type of reaction depends upon concentration of one reactant only under this condition, a bimolecular reaction behaves like a first order reaction and it is known as pseudo first order reaction *e.g.*, acid catalysed hydrolysis of ethyl acetate.

$$\underset{\text{Ethyl acetate}}{CH_3COOC_2H_5} + H_2O \xrightarrow{H^+} \underset{\text{Acetic acid}}{CH_3COOH} + \underset{\text{Ethyl alcohol}}{C_2H_5OH}$$

This reaction is bimolecular but is found to be of first order as experimentally it is observed that rate of reaction depends upon the concentration of ethyl acetate not on water as it is present in excess.

Q.34 Write the rate equation for the reaction $2A + B \longrightarrow C$ if the order of the reaction is zero.

Ans. For reaction $2A + B \longrightarrow C$ if the rate of reaction is zero then it can be represented as

$$\text{Rate} = k\,[A]^0\,[B]^0 = k$$

i.e., rate of reaction is independent of concentration of *A* and *B*.

Q.35 How can you determine the rate law of the following reaction?

$$2NO(g) + O_2\,(g) \longrightarrow 2NO_2\,(g)$$

Ans. We can determine the rate of this reaction as a function of initial concentrations either by keeping the concentration of one of the reactants constant and changing the concentration of the other reactant or by changing the concentration of both the reactants. *e.g.*, for the given reaction,

(i) Keeping $[O_2]$ constant, if the concentration of NO is doubled, rate is found to become four times. This shows that,

$$\text{Rate} \propto [NO]^2$$

(ii) Keeping [NO] constant, if the concentration of $[O_2]$ is doubled, rate is also found to become double. This shows that,

$$\text{Rate} \propto [O_2]^2$$

Hence, overall rate law will be

$$\text{Rate} = k\,[NO]^2\,[O_2]^2$$

Q.36 For which type of reactions, order and molecularity have the same value?

Ans. If the reaction is elementary reaction then order and molecularity have same value because elementary reaction proceeds in a single step.

Q.37 In a reaction if the concentration of reactant *A* is tripled, the rate of reaction becomes twenty seven times. What is the order of the reaction?

Ans. Rate of any elementary reaction can be represented as

$$r = k[A]^n \qquad \text{...(i)}$$

After changing concentration of *A* to its triple value, $A = 3A$, *r* becomes $27r$

$$27r = k[3A]^n \qquad \text{...(ii)}$$

Divide equaton (i) by (ii)

$$\frac{r}{27r} = \frac{k[A]^n}{k[3A]^n}$$

$$\frac{1}{27} = \left[\frac{1}{3}\right]^n \Rightarrow \left[\frac{1}{3}\right]^3 = \left[\frac{1}{3}\right]^n$$

Hence, $n = 3$

Order of reaction is three.

Q.38 Derive an expression to calculate time required for completion of zero order reaction.

Ans. For zero order reaction $[R] = [R]_0 - kt$

For completion of the reaction $[R] = 0$

$$\therefore \quad t = \frac{[R]_0}{k}$$

Q.39 For a reaction $A + B \longrightarrow$ Products, the rate law is —Rate $= k[A][B]^{3/2}$. Can the reaction be an elementary reaction? Explain.

Ans. During an elementary reaction, the number or atoms or ions colliding to react is referred to as molecularity. For an elementary reaction, the order of reaction and the molecularity should be the same. For this reaction molecularity is 2 and the order with respect to B would have been 1, but in the given rate law it is $\frac{3}{2}$. This indicates that the reaction is not an elementary reaction. Hence, this reaction must be a complex reaction.

Q.40 For a certain reaction large fraction of molecules has energy more than the threshold energy, yet the rate of reaction is very slow. Why?

Ans. According to collision theory apart from the energy considerations, the colliding molecules should also have proper orientation for effective collision.

Since, this condition is not fulfilled in the reaction. So the rate of reaction is very slow.

Q.41 For a zero order reaction will the molecularity be equal to zero? Explain.

Ans. No, the molecularity can never be zero or a fractional number as it shows the number of reactants taking part in a reaction.

Q.42 For a general reaction $A \rightarrow B$, plot of concentration of A *vs* time is given in figure. Answer the following questions on the basis of this graph.

(i) What is the order of the reaction?

(ii) What is the slope of the curve?

(iii) What are the units of rate constant?

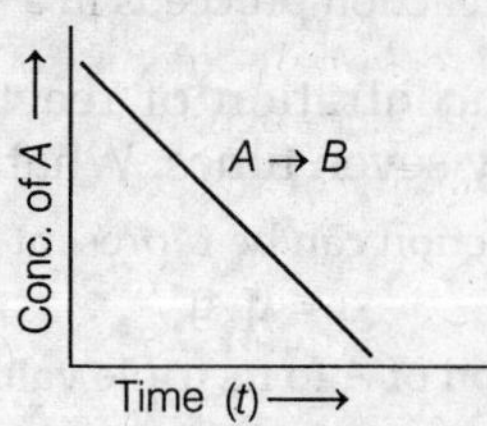

Ans. (i) For $A \longrightarrow B$ the given graph shows a zero order reaction. Mathematically represented as

$$[R] = -kt + [R]_0$$

which is equation of straight line. ($y = mx + c$) Hence, reaction is a zero order.

(ii) Slope = $-k$

(iii) Unit of rate constant for zero order reaction is mole $L^{-1}\ s^{-1}$.

Q.43 The reaction between $H_2(g)$ and $O_2(g)$ is highly feasible yet allowing the gases to stand at room temperature in the same vessel does not lead to the formation of water. Explain.

Ans. The reaction between hydrogen and oxygen ($H_2(g) + O_2(g)$) does not take place at room temperature due to the high activation energy of reaction. At high temperature H—H and O—O bonds break and colliding particles cross the energy barrier.

This is why reaction between $H_2(g)$ and $O_2(g)$ does not lead to formation of water at room temperature while keeping in the same vessel.

Q.44 Why does the rate of a reaction increase with rise in temperature?

Ans. At higher temperatures, larger fraction of colliding particles can cross the energy barrier (*i.e.*, the activation energy) which leads to faster rate of a reaction.

Q.45 Oxygen is available in plenty in air yet fuels do not burn by themselves at room temperature. Explain.

Ans. For combustion reactions, activation energy of fuels is very high at room temperature. So, fuels do not burn by themselves at room temperature.

Q.46 Why is the probability of reaction with molecularity higher than three very rare?

Ans. According to collision theory, we know that to complete any chemical reaction there must be effective collision between reactant particles and they must have minimum sufficient energy. The probability of more than three molecules colliding simultaneously is very small. Hence, possibility of reaction with molecularity more than three is very rare.

Q.47 Why does the rate of any reaction generally decreases during the course of the reaction?

Ans. The rate of a reaction depends on the concentration of the reactants. As the reaction proceeds in forward direction, concentration of reactant decreases and that of products increases. So, the rate of reaction generally decreases during the course of reaction.

Q.48 Thermodynamic feasibility of the reaction alone cannot decide the rate of the reaction. Explain with the help of one example.

Ans. Thermodynamically the conversion of diamond to graphite is highly feasible but this reaction is very slow because its activation energy is high.

Hence, thermodynamic feasibility of the reaction alone cannot decide the rate of reaction.

Q.49 Why in the redox titration of $KMnO_4$ *vs* oxalic acid, we heat oxalic acid solution before starting the titration?

Ans. As we know with increase in temperature, rate of reaction increases. Hence, we heat oxalic acid solution before starting of titration to increase the rate of reaction. Heating solution increases the kinetic energy of the molecules, which makes more reactant particles available for the reaction.

Q.50 Why can't molecularity of any reaction be equal to zero?

Ans. Molecularity of the reaction is the number of molecules taking part in an elementary step. For this we require at least a single molecule leading to the value of minimum molecularity to one. Hence, molecularity of any reaction can never be equal to zero.

Q.51 Why molecularity is applicable only for elementary reactions and order is applicable for elementary as well as complex reactions?

Ans. A complex reaction occurs through a number of steps *i.e.*, elementary reactions. Number of molecules involved in each elementary reaction may be different, *i.e.*, the molecularity of each step may be different. Therefore, it is meaningless to talk of molecularity of the overall complex reaction.

On the other hand, order of complex reaction depends upon the molecularity of the slowest step. Hence, it is not meaningless to talk of the order of a complex reaction.

Q.52 Why can we not determine the order of a reaction by taking into consideration the balanced chemical equation?

Ans. Balanced chemical equation often leads to incorrect order or rate law. *e.g.*, the of following reaction seems to be a tenth order reaction

$$KClO_3 + 6FeSO_4 + 3H_2SO_4 \longrightarrow KCl + 3H_2O + 3Fe_2(SO_4)_3$$

This is actually a second order reaction. The reaction is complex and occurs in several steps. The order of such reaction is determined by the slowest step in the reaction mechanism.

Order is determined experimentally and is confined to the dependence of observed rate of reaction on the concentration of reactants.

Hence, the order of a reaction can not be determined by a balanced chemical equation.

Matching The Columns

Q.53 Match the graph given in Column I with the order of reaction given in Column II. More than one item in Column I may link to the same item of Column II.

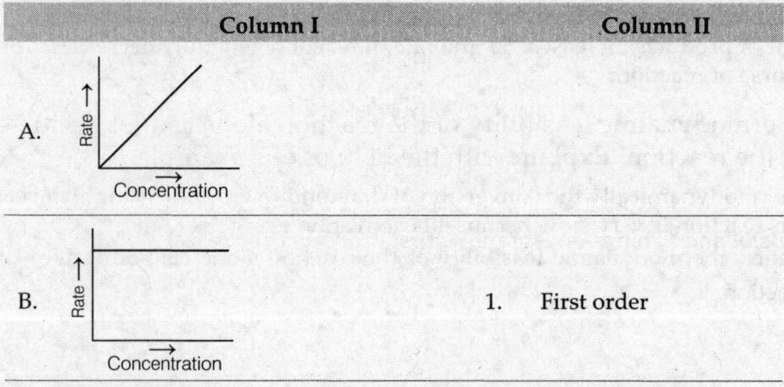

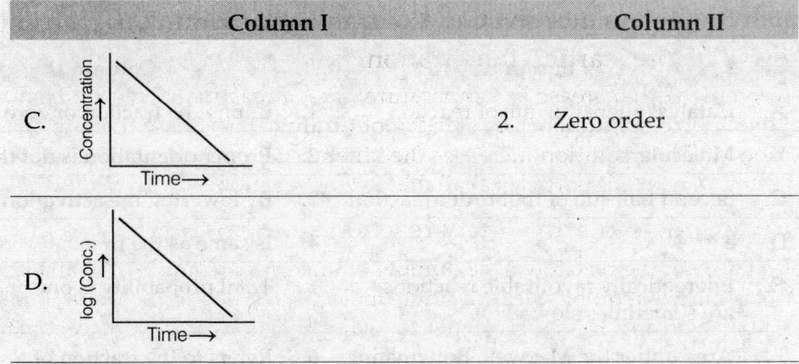

Ans. **A.** → (1) **B.** → (2) **C.** → (2) **D.** → (1)

For zero order reaction, rate equation may be written as

$$[R] = -kt + [R_0] \quad \ldots(i)$$

Which denotes a straight line equation similar to $y = mx + c$

On transforming (i) $\frac{[R]-[R_0]}{t} = -k$

$$k = \frac{[R_0]-[R]}{t}$$

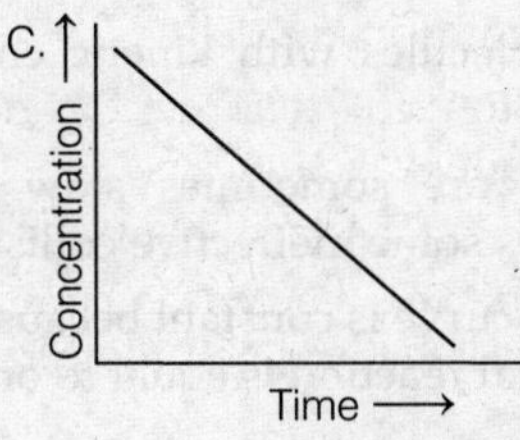

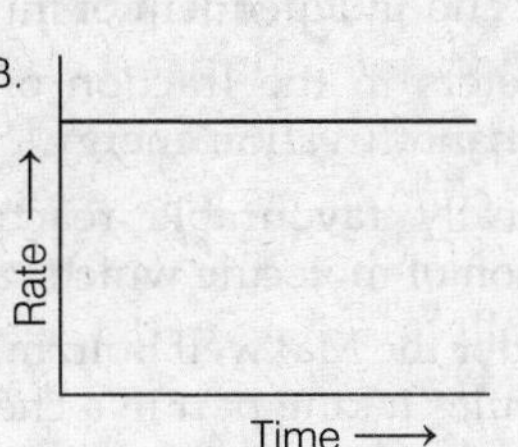

$$k = \text{Rate}$$
$$\text{Rate} = k \cdot [t]^0$$
$$\text{Rate} \propto [t]^0$$

Hence, *B* and *C* represents graph of zero order reaction.

For a first order reaction, $\frac{dx}{dt} \propto [\text{concentration}]^1$

∴ Graph between rate and concentration may be drawn as

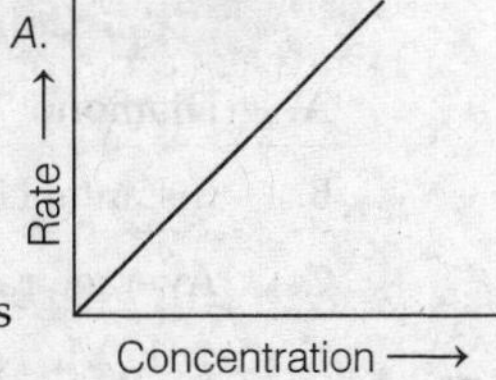

$$k = \frac{2.303}{t} \log \frac{[R]_0}{[R]}$$

$$\frac{kt}{2.303} = \log\left[\frac{R_0}{[R]}\right]$$

$$\frac{kt}{2.303} = \log[R]_0 - \log[R]$$

$$\log[R] = \underbrace{\left(\frac{-k}{2.303}\right)}_{\text{Slope}} t + \underbrace{\log[R]_0}_{\text{Intercept}}$$

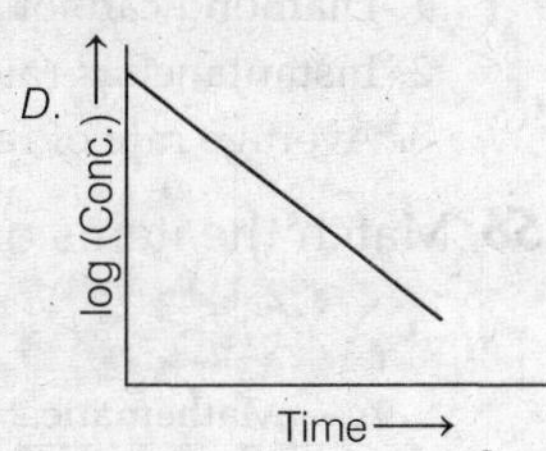

Thus, *A* and *D* represents graph of first order reaction.

Q.54 Match the statements given in Column I and Column II.

	Column I		Column II
A.	Catalyst alters the rate of reaction	1.	Cannot be fraction or zero
B.	Molecularity	2.	Proper orientation is not there
C.	Second half-life of first order reaction	3.	By lowering the activation energy
D.	$e^{-E_a/RT}$	4.	Is same as the first
E.	Energetically favourable reactions are sometimes slow	5.	Total probability is one
F.	Area under the Maxwell, Boltzmann curve is constant	6.	Refers to the fraction of molecules with energy equal to or greater than activation energy

Ans. **A.** → (3) **B.** → (1) **C.** → (4) **D.** → (6) **E.** → (2) **F.** → (5)

1. Catalyst alters the rate of reaction by lowering the activation energy.
2. Molecularity cannot be fraction or zero. If molecularity is zero, then reaction is not possible.
3. Second half-life of first order reaction is same as first because half-life time is constant and independent of initial concentration of the reactant.
4. $e^{-E_a/RT}$ refers to the fraction of molecules with kinetic energy equal to or greater than activation energy.
5. Energetically favourable reactions are sometimes slow due to improper orientation of molecule which causes some ineffective collision of molecules.
6. Area under the Maxwell Boltzmann curve is constant because total probability of molecules taking part in a chemical reaction is equal to one.

Q.55 Match the items of Column I and Column II.

	Column I		Column II
A.	Diamond	1.	Short interval of time
B.	Instantaneous rate	2.	Ordinarily rate of conversion is imperceptible
C.	Average rate	3.	Long duration of time

Ans. A → (2) B → (1) C → (3)

1. Diamond cannot be converted into graphite under ordinary condition.
2. Instantaneous rate of reaction completes at very short span of time.
3. Average rate of reaction to is calculated over a long duration of time.

Q.56 Match the items of Column I and Column II.

	Column I		Column II
A.	Mathematical expression for rate of reaction	1.	Rate constant
B.	Rate of reaction for zero order reaction is equal to	2.	Rate law
C.	Units of rate constant for zero order reaction is same as that of	3.	Order of slowest step
D.	Order of a complex reaction is determined by	4.	Rate of reaction

Ans. A → (2) B → (1) C → (4) D → (3)

1. Mathematical expression for rate of reaction is known as rate law.
2. Rate of reaction for zero order reaction is equal to rate constant

$$r = k[A]^0$$

$$\therefore \quad r = k$$

3. Unit of rate of reaction for zero order reaction is same as that of rate of reaction (*i.e.*, mol L^{-1} S^{-1}).
4. Order of complex reaction is determined by order of the slowest step.

Assertion and Reason

In the following questions a statement of Assertion followed by a statement of Reason is given. Choose the correct answer out of the following choices.

(a) Both assertion and reason are correct and the reason is correct explanation of assertion.
(b) Both assertion and reason are correct, but reason does not explain assertion.
(c) Assertion is correct, but reason is incorrect.
(d) Both assertion and reason are incorrect.
(e) Assertion is incorrect, but reason is correct.

Q.57 Assertion Order of the reaction can be zero or fractional.
Reason We cannot determine order from balanced chemical equation.

Ans. ***(b)*** Both assertion and reason are correct, but the reason is not the correct explanation of assertion.

Order of reaction can be zero or fractional as order of reaction is directly related to sum of power of reactants. Reason is a correct statement but not the correct explanation.

Q.58 Assertion Order and molecularity are same.
Reason Order is determined experimentally and molecularity is the sum of the stoichiometric coefficient of rate determining elementary step.

Ans. ***(e)*** Assertion is incorrect and reason is correct.

Order and molecularity may or may not be the same as order of reaction is sum of power of reactant which can be determined experimentally. But molecularity is sum of stoichiometric coefficient of rate determining elementary step.

Q.59 Assertion The enthalpy of reaction remains constant in the presence of a catalyst.

Reason A catalyst participating in the reaction forms, different activated complex and lowers down the activation energy but the difference in energy of reactant and product remains the same.

Ans. ***(a)*** Assertion and reason both are correct and reason is the correct explanation of assertion.

Enthalpy of reaction, *i.e.*, difference of total enthalpy of reactants and product remains constant in the presence of a catalyst. As a catalyst participating in the reaction forms different activated complex and lowers down the activation energy, but the difference in energy of reactant and product remains same.

Q.60 Assertion All collision of reactant molecules lead to product formation.
Reason Only those collisions in which molecules have correct orientation and sufficient kinetic energy lead to compound formation.

Ans. *(e)* Assertion is incorrect, but reason is correct.

Correct assertion is "only effective collision leads to the formation of product." Reason defines correct meaning of effective collision, and criterion of collision theory for completion of reaction.

Only those collisions in which molecules have correct orientation and sufficient energy can lead to the formation of product.

Q.61 Assertion The Rate constant determined from Arrhenius equation are fairly accurate for simple as well as complex molecules.
Reason Reactant molecules undergo chemical change irrespective of their orientation during collision.

Ans. *(c)* Assertion is correct, but reason is incorrect.

Rate constant determined from Arrhenius equation are fairly accurate for simple and complex molecules because only those molecules which have proper orientation during collision (*i.e.*, effective collision) and sufficient kinetic energy leads to the chemical change.

Long Answer Type Questions

Q.62 All energetically effective collisions do not result in a chemical change. Explain with the help of an example.

Ans. Only effective collisions lead to the formation of products. It means that collisions in which molecules collide with sufficient kinetic energy (called threshold energy = activation energy + energy possessed by reacting species) and proper orientation lead to a chemical change because it facilitates the breaking of bonds between reactant molecules and formation of bonds, in products.

e.g., formation of methanol from bromomethane depends upon the orientation of the reactant molecules.

$$CH_3Br + OH^- \longrightarrow CH_3OH + Br^-$$

$$H_3\overset{+\delta}{C}-\overset{-\delta}{Br} + OH^- \xrightarrow[\text{orientation}]{\text{Improper}} H_3\overset{+\delta}{C}-\overset{-\delta}{Br}\ \ \bar{O}H \longrightarrow \text{No products}$$

$$HO^- + H_3\overset{+\delta}{C}-\overset{-\delta}{Br} \xrightarrow[\text{orientation}]{\text{Proper}} \left[\overset{-\delta}{HO}\text{---}CH_3\text{---}\overset{-\delta}{Br}\right] \longrightarrow HO-CH_3 + Br^-$$

Intermediate

The proper orientation of reactant molecules leads to bond formation whereas improper orientation makes them simply bounce back and no products are formed. To account for effective collisions, another factor P (probability or steric factor) is introduced, Rate $= PZ_{AB}e^{-E_a/RT}$.

Q.63 What happens to most probable kinetic energy and the energy of activation with increase in temperature?

Ans. Kinetic energy is directly proportional to the absolute temperature and the number of molecules possessing higher energies increases with increase in temperature, *i.e.*, most probable kinetic energy increases with increase in temperature.

Energy of activation is related to temperature by the following Arrhenius equation,

$$k = Ae^{-E_a/RT}$$

As temperature increases, activation energy decreases which increases the rate of reaction.

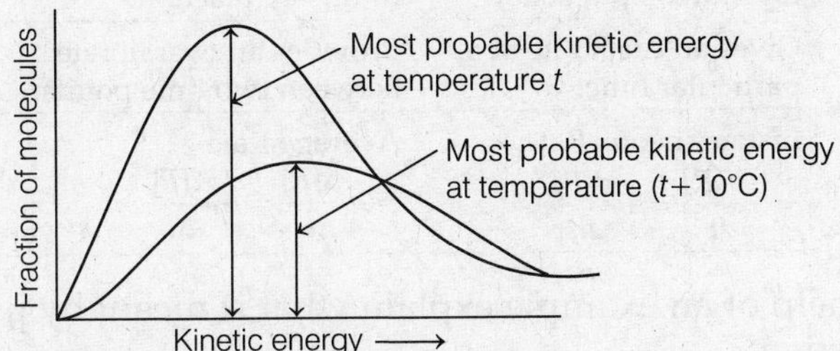

Q.64 Describe how does the enthalpy of reaction remain unchanged when a catalyst is used in the reaction?

Ans. A catalyst is a substance which increases the speed of a reaction without itself undergoing any chemical change.

According to "intermediate complex formation theory" reactants first combine with the catalyst to form an intermediate complex which is short-lived and decomposes to form the products and regenerating the catalyst.

The intermediate formed has much lower potential energy than the intermediate complex formed between the reactants in the absence of the catalyst.

Thus, the presence of catalyst lowers the potential energy barrier and the reaction follows a new alternate pathway which requires less activation energy.

We know that, lower the activation energy, faster is the reaction because more reactant molecules can cross the energy barrier and change into products.

Enthalpy, ΔH is a state function. Enthalpy of reaction, *i.e.*, difference in energy between reactants and products is constant, which is clear from potential energy diagram.

Potential energy diagram of catalysed reaction is given as,

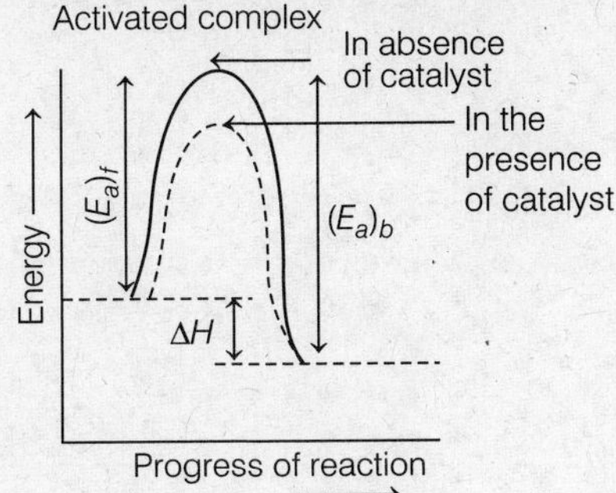

Q.65 Explain the difference between instantaneous rate of a reaction and average rate of a reaction.

Ans. The difference between instantaneous rate of reaction and average rate of a reaction are as below

	Instantaneous rate of reaction	Average rate of reaction
(i)	It occurs within a short span of time.	It occurs during a long interval of time.
(ii)	It cannot be calculated for multistep reaction .	It can be calculated for multistep reaction.
(iii)	Gives an exact rate at a particular time.	Provides an overall rate between two time points.
(iv)	Instantaneous Rate $= \frac{-d[R]}{dt} = +\frac{d[P]}{dt}$.	Average Rate $= \frac{-\Delta[R]}{\Delta t} = +\frac{\Delta[P]}{\Delta t}$

Q.66 With the help of an example explain what is meant by pseudo first order reaction.

Ans. A reaction in which one reactant is present in large amount and its concentration does not get altered during the course of the reaction, behaves as first order reaction. Such reaction is called pseudo first order reaction.

e.g., (i) hydrolysis of ethyl acetate (ester)

$$CH_3COOC_2H_5 + H_2O \xrightarrow{H^+} CH_3COOH + C_2H_5OH$$

	$CH_3COOC_2H_5$	H_2O	CH_3COOH	C_2H_5OH
Conc. $t = 0$	0.01 mol	10 mol	0 mol	0 mol
Conc. at t	0 mol	9.99 mol	0.01 mol	0.01 mol

$$\text{Rate of reaction} = k\,[CH_3COOC_2H_5]$$

where, $k = k'\,[H_2O]$

e.g., (ii) inversion of cane sugar

$$\underset{}{C_{12}H_{22}O_{11}} + H_2O \xrightarrow{H^+} \underset{\text{Glucose}}{C_6H_{12}O_6} + \underset{\text{Fructose}}{C_6H_{12}O_6}$$

Rate of reaction $= k[C_{12}H_{22}O_{11}]$

where, $k = k'[H_2O]$

Chapter

05

Surface Chemistry*

Multiple Choice Questions (MCQs)

Q.1 Which of the following process does **not** occur at the interface of phases?

(a) Crystallisation
(b) Heterogeneous catalysis
(c) Homogeneous catalysis
(d) Corrosion

Ans. *(c)* Homogeneous catalysis does not occur at the interface of phases, as in case of homogeneous catalysis reactant and catalyst have same phase and their distribution is uniform throughout.

Q.2 At the equilibrium position in the process of adsorption ....

(a) $\Delta H > 0$
(b) $\Delta H = T\Delta S$
(c) $\Delta H > T\Delta S$
(d) $\Delta H < T\Delta S$

Ans. *(b)* As we know that, at equilibrium, $\Delta G = 0$

$$\Delta H - T\Delta S = 0$$

$$\Delta H = T\Delta S$$

Hence, at equilibrium enthalpy change is equal to product of temperature and entropy change.

Q.3 Which of the following interface **cannot** be obtained?

(a) Liquid-liquid
(b) Solid-liquid
(c) Liquid-gas
(d) Gas-gas

Thinking Process This problem is based on the concept of interfaces between different states of matter.

Ans. *(d)* Gas-gas interface cannot be obtained as they are completely miscible in nature.

e.g., air is a mixture of various gases such as, O_2, N_2, CO_2, etc.

Q.4 The term 'sorption' stands for ....

(a) absorption
(b) adsorption
(c) Both absorption and adsorption
(d) desorption

Ans. *(c)* Sorption stands for both absorption and adsorption. We can understand this by using following figures.

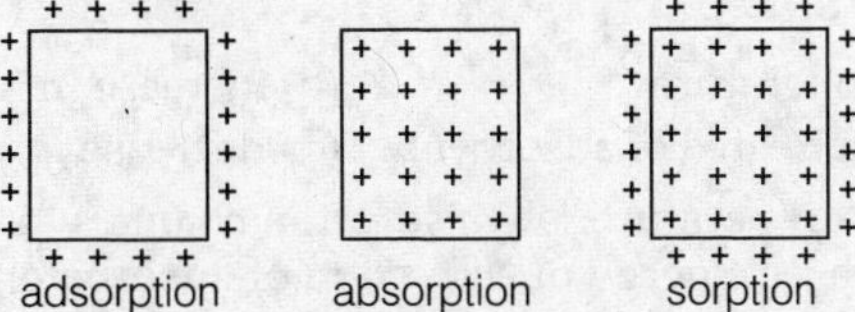

Note (*) This chapter has been deleted from latest NCERT.

Q.5 Extent of physisorption of a gas increases with ....

(a) increase in temperature.
(b) decrease in temperature.
(c) decrease in surface area of adsorbent.
(d) decrease in strength of van der Waals' forces.

Ans. ***(b)*** Extent of physisorption of a gas increases with decrease in temperature. Because in physisorption particles are held to the surface by weak van der Waals force of attraction. Hence on increasing temperature they get desorbed easily.

Q.6 Extent of adsorption of adsorbate from solution phase increases with ....

(a) increase in amount of adsorbate in solution
(b) decrease in surface area of adsorbent
(c) increase in temperature of solution
(d) decrease in amount of adsorbate in solution

Ans. ***(a)*** Extent of adsorption of adsorbate from solution phase increases with increase in amount of adsorbate in solution. As amount of adsorbate in the solution increases, interaction of adsorbate with adsorbent increases which lead to increase in extent of adsorption.

Q.7 Which one of the following is **not** applicable to the phenomenon of adsorption?

(a) $\Delta H > 0$ (b) $\Delta G < 0$ (c) $\Delta S < 0$ (d) $\Delta H < 0$

Ans. ***(a)*** For phenomenon of adsorption $\Delta H < 0$, *i.e.*, enthalpy change during phenomenon of adsorption is negative because during adsorption, there is always a decrease in residual forces of the surface which leads to decrease in surface energy which appears as heat.

So, adsorption is an exothermic process and $\Delta H < 0$.

Q.8 Which of the following is **not** a favourable condition for physical adsorption?

(a) High pressure
(b) Negative ΔH
(c) Higher critical temperature of adsorbate
(d) High temperature

Ans. ***(d)*** Physisorption is a process in which adsorbate gets adsorbed on the adsorbent surface by weak van der Waals force of attraction. On increasing temperature, the interaction between adsorbate and adsorbent becomes weak and adsorbate particles get desorbed.

Hence, physical adsorption is favoured at low temperature.

Q.9 Physical adsorption of a gaseous species may change to chemical adsorption with ....

(a) decrease in temperature (b) increase in temperature
(c) increase in surface area of adsorbent (d) decrease in surface area of adsorbent

Ans. ***(b)*** On increasing temperature, physisorption changes to chemisorption. As temperature increases, energy of activation of adsorbate particles increases, which lead to formation of chemical bond between adsorbate and adsorbent. Hence, physisorption transforms into chemisorption.

Q.10 In physisorption adsorbent does not show specificity for any particular gas because ....

(a) involved van der Waals forces are universal
(b) gases involved behave like ideal gases
(c) enthalpy of adsorption is low
(d) it is a reversible process

Ans. **(a)** In physisorption, adsorbent does not show specificity for any particular gas because involved van der Waals forces are universal. It means extent of van der Waals interaction between adsorbate and adsorbent is constant for all gases.

Q.11 Which of the following is an example of absorption?

(a) Water on silica gel
(b) Water on calcium chloride
(c) Hydrogen on finely divided nickel
(d) Oxygen on metal surface

Ans. **(b)** Absorption means penetration of adsorbate molecules into the bulk of the adsorbent *e.g.*, water on calcium chloride. When water is spread over calcium chloride, water penetrates into bulk of the calcium chloride.

Q.12 On the basis of data given below predict which of the following gases shows least adsorption on a definite amount of charcoal?

Gas	CO_2	SO_2	CH_4	H_2
Critical temp./K	304	630	190	33

(a) CO_2
(b) SO_2
(c) CH_4
(d) H_2

Thinking Process This problem includes the concept of extent of adsorption and critical temperature. Extent of adsorption is directly related to critical temperature of gases.

Ans. **(d)** Lesser the value of critical temperature of gases lesser will be the extent of adsorption. Here, H_2 has lowest value of critical temperature, *i.e.*, 33.
Hence, hydrogen gas shows least adsorption on a definite amount of charcoal.

Q.13 In which of the following reactions heterogeneous catalysis is involved?

(i) $2SO_2(g) + O_2(g) \xrightarrow{NO(g)} 2SO_3(g)$
(ii) $2SO_2(g) \xrightarrow{Pt(s)} 2SO_3(g)$
(iii) $N_2(g) + 3H_2(g) \xrightarrow{Fe(s)} 2NH_3(g)$
(iv) $CH_3COOCH_3(l) + H_2O(l) \xrightarrow{HCl(l)} CH_3COOH(aq) + CH_3OH(aq)$

(a) (ii), (iii)
(b) (ii), (iii) and (iv)
(c) (i), (ii) and (iii)
(d) (iv)

Ans. **(a)** (i) Reaction in which catalyst is in different phase than other reactants and products is known as heterogeneous catalysis.

(ii) $2SO_2(g) \xrightarrow{Pt(s)} 2SO_3(g)$

Here, reactant SO_2 and product SO_3 are in gaseous phase while platinum is in solid phase. So, this reaction represents a heterogeneous catalysis.

(iii) $N_2(g) + 3H_2(g) \xrightarrow{Fe(s)} 2NH_3(g)$

Similarly, here N_2 and H_2 reactants and NH_3 product are in gaseous phase while iron catalyst is in solid phase. So this reaction also represents a heterogeneous catalysis.

Hence, option (a) is the correct choice.

Q.14 At high concentration of soap in water, soap behaves as ....

(a) molecular colloid (b) associated colloid
(c) macromolecular colloid (d) lyophilic colloid

Ans. ***(b)*** **Associated colloid** At high concentration of soap in water, soap particles present in the solution gets associated around and leads to the formation of associated colloid.

Q.15 Which of the following will show Tyndall effect?

(a) Aqueous solution of soap below critical micelle concentration.
(b) Aqueous solution of soap above critical micelle concentration.
(c) Aqueous solution of sodium chloride.
(d) Aqueous solution of sugar.

- **Concept Insight** This solution includes the concept of colloidal solutions and their properties, emphasising on the Tyndall effect, which demonstrates the scattering of light by colloidal particles.

Ans. ***(b)*** Aqueous solution of soap above critical micelle concentration leads to the formation of colloidal solution. Tyndall effect is a characteristic of colloidal solution in which colloidal particles scatter the light when passed through it.

Q. 16 Method by which lyophobic sol can be protected.

(a) By addition of oppositely charged sol.
(b) By addition of an electrolyte.
(c) By addition of lyophilic sol.
(d) By boiling.

Ans. ***(c)*** Lyophobic sol can be protected by addition of lyophilic sol. As lyophobic sols are readily precipitated on addition of small amount of electrolytes or shaking, or heating hence, they are made stable by adding lyophillic sol which stabilises the lyophobic sols.

Q.17 Freshly prepared precipitate sometimes gets converted to colloidal solution by ....

(a) coagulation (b) electrolysis
(c) diffusion (d) peptisation

Ans. ***(d)*** Freshly prepared precipitate sometimes gets converted to colloidal solution by peptisation. Peptisation is a process in which by addition of a suitable peptising agent, precipitate gets converted into colloidal solution.

Q. 18 Which of the following electrolytes will have maximum coagulating value for Ag/Ag^+ sol?

(a) Na_2S (b) Na_3PO_4
(c) Na_2SO_4 (d) NaCl

Thinking Process This problem includes the concept of Hardy-Schulze law. According to which higher charge on oppositely charge ion of electrolyte decides the coagulating power of colloid.

Ans. ***(b)*** According to Hardy-Schulze law, greater the charge on anion greater will be its coagulating power.

Electrolytes	Anionic part	Charge on anion
Na_2S	S^{2-}	2
Na_3PO_4	PO_4^{3-}	3
Na_2SO_4	SO_4^{2-}	2
NaCl	Cl^-	1

Here, PO_4^{3-} have highest charge. Hence, PO_4^{3-} have highest coagulating power.

Q.19 A colloidal system having a solid substance as a dispersed phase and a liquid as a dispersion medium is classified as ....

(a) solid sol (b) gel (c) emulsion (d) sol

Ans. **(d)** Sol is a colloidal system in which solid substance is a dispersed phase and a liquid is a dispersion medium. *e.g.*, paint, cell fluids, etc.

In paints, solid colouring particles are dissolved in liquid dispersion medium.

Q.20 The values of colligative properties of colloidal solution are of small order in comparison to those shown by true solutions of same concentration because of colloidal particles ....

(a) exhibit enormous surface area
(b) remain suspended in the dispersion medium
(c) form lyophilic colloids
(d) are comparatively less in number

Thinking Process This problem is based on the concept of colligative properties and particle concentration.

Ans. **(d)** The value of colligative properties of colloidal solution are of small order in comparison to those of true solution of same concentration because colloidal particles are comparatively less in number.

This is due to slight large size of colloidal particles in comparison to particles present in true solution. Size of colloidal particles is in between 1 nm to 1000 nm.

Q.21 Arrange the following diagrams in correct sequence of steps involved in the mechanism of catalysis, in accordance with modern adsorption theory.

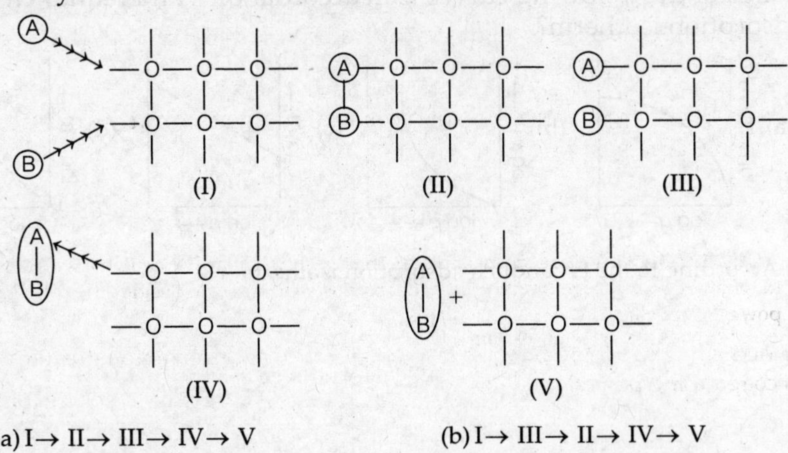

(a) I→ II→ III→ IV→ V (b) I→ III→ II→ IV→ V
(c) I→ III→ II→ V→ IV (d) I→ II→ III→ V→ IV

Ans. ***(b)*** Correct sequence is I→ III → II→ IV→ V

Each transformation denotes a meaningful process as follows :

I : adsorption of *A* and *B* on surface

III → II : interaction between *A* and *B* to form intermediate

II → IV : starting desorption of *A*—*B*

IV → V : complete desorption

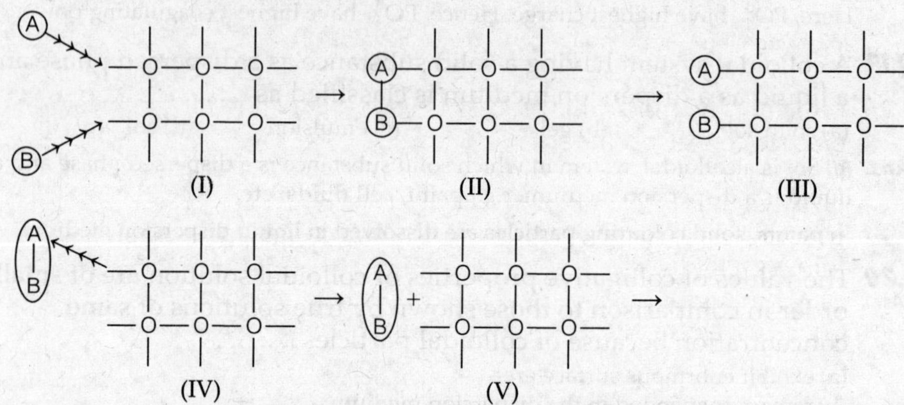

Q.22 Which of the following process is responsible for the formation of delta at a place where rivers meet the sea?

(a) Emulsification (b) Colloid formation

(c) Coagulation (d) Peptisation

● **Concept Insight** This solution includes the concept of coagulation of colloidal particles. The electrolytes in sea water neutralise the charge on colloidal clay particles in river water, leading to their aggregation and setting at the point of contact.

Ans. ***(c)*** River water is a colloidal solution of clay and sea. Water contains various electrolytes. When river water comes in contact with sea water, then the electrolytes present in sea water coagulates the suspended colloidal particles which ultimately settle down at the point of contact.

Q.23 Which of the following curves is in accordance with Freundlich adsorption isotherm?

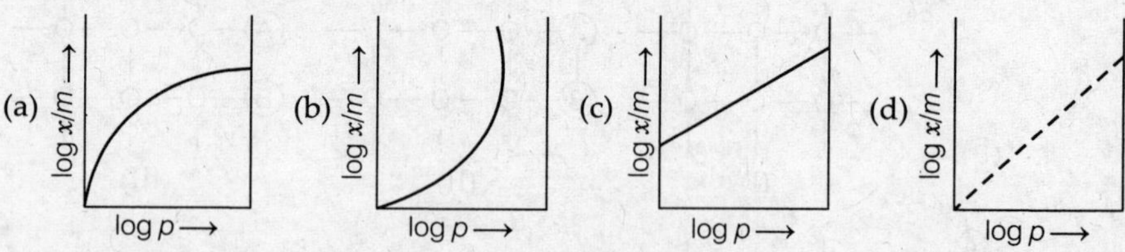

Ans. ***(c)*** According to the Freundlich adsorption isotherm

$$\frac{x}{m} = kp^{\frac{1}{n}}$$

Taking log on both sides, $\log \frac{x}{m} = \left(\frac{1}{n}\right) \log p + \log k$

$$\begin{matrix} \uparrow & & \uparrow & \uparrow & & \uparrow \\ Y & = & m & x & + & C \end{matrix}$$

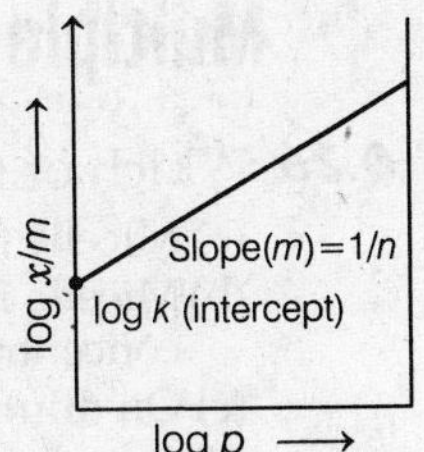

On comparing it with equation of straight line and drawing the graph $\log \frac{x}{m}$ *versus* $\log p$, we get a straight line with intercept $\log k$ and slope of the straight line gives the value of $\frac{1}{n}$.

Q.24 Which of the following process is **not** responsible for the presence of electric charge on the sol particles?

(a) Electron capture by sol particles.
(b) Adsorption of ionic species from solution.
(c) Formation of Helmholtz electrical double layer.
(d) Absorption of ionic species from solution.

Ans. ***(d)*** Absorption of ionic species from solution is not responsible for the presence of electric charge on the sol particles. Charge on the sol particles is due to

(i) electrons capture by sol particles during electro dispersion of metal.
(ii) preferential adsorption of ionic species from solution.
(iii) formation of Helmholtz electrical double layer.

Q.25 Which of the following phenomenon is applicable to the process shown in the figure?

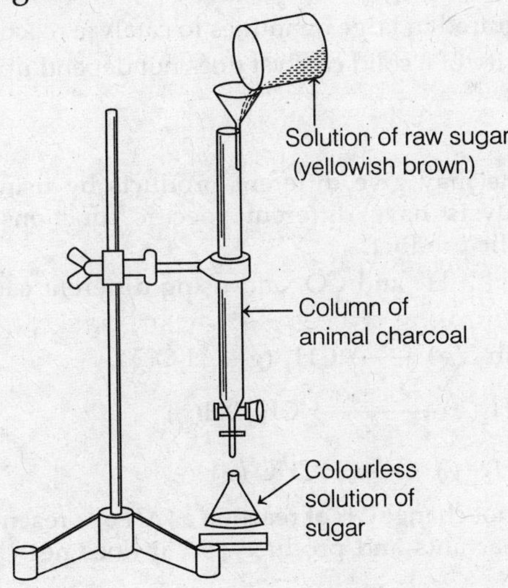

(a) Absorption
(b) Adsorption
(c) Coagulation
(d) Emulsification

Ans. ***(b)*** Above figure represents adsorption of yellowish brown colour of raw sugar by animal charcoal.

Here, aqueous solution of raw sugar is filtered by using animal charcoal. Yellowish brown colour of raw sugar is adsorbed and filterate is colourless which gives white colour on cystallisation. Hence, this phenomenon is adsorption.

Multiple Choice Questions (More Than One Options)

Q.26 Which of the following options are correct?

(a) Micelle formation by soap in aqueous solution is possible at all temperatures.

(b) Micelle formation by soap in aqueous solution occurs above a particular concentration.

(c) On dilution of soap solution micelles may revert to individual ions.

(d) Soap solution behaves as a normal strong electrolyte at all concentrations.

Thinking Process This problem is based on concept of micelle formation and CMC (critical micelle concentration).

Ans. *(b, c)* **Micelle formation** Some substances at low concentration behaves as a normal electrolyte but at higher concentration exhibits colloidal behaviour due to formation of micelles.

CMC (Critical Micelle Concentration) The concentration above which it behaves as a micelle known as critical micelle concentration.

e.g., soap solution in aqueous solution above particular concentration (called CMC $= 10^{-4} - 10^{3}$ mol L^{-1}) forms soap micelles.

On dilution, soap solution behaves as a normal electrolyte and after adding excess of water, intermolecular forces of attraction between the soap particles decreases and soap solution micelles may revert to individual ions.

Q.27 Which of the following statements are correct about solid catalyst?

(a) Same reactants may give different products by using different catalysts.

(b) Catalyst does not change ΔH of reaction.

(c) Catalyst is required in large quantities to catalyse reactions.

(d) Catalytic activity of a solid catalyst does not depend upon the strength of chemisorption.

Ans. *(a, b)*

(a) Same reactants may give different products by using different catalysts as different catalysts have different specific functions to drive the reaction towards specific product.

e.g., starting with H_2 and CO, and using different catalysts, we get different products.

(i) $CO(g) + 3H_2(g) \xrightarrow{Ni} CH_4(g) + H_2O(g)$

(ii) $CO(g) + 2H_2(g) \xrightarrow[Cr_2O_3]{Cu/ZnO} CH_3OH(g)$

(iii) $CO(g) + H_2(g) \xrightarrow{Cu} HCHO(g)$

(b) Catalyst does not change ΔH of reaction as ΔH of a reaction is difference between enthalpy of reactants and products. So, it does not change during catalysed reaction.

Q.28 Freundlich adsorption isotherm is given by the expression $\frac{x}{m} = kp^{\frac{1}{n}}$.

Which of the following conclusions can be drawn from this expression?

(a) When $\frac{1}{n} = 0$, the adsorption is independent of pressure.

(b) When $\frac{1}{n} = 0$, the adsorption is directly proportional to pressure.

(c) When $n = 0$, $\frac{x}{m}$ *vs* p graph is a line parallel to x-axis.

(d) When $n = 0$, plot of $\frac{x}{m}$ *vs* p is a curve.

Thinking Process To solve this problem follow steps given below.
Write Freundlich equation and transform it into different form depending upon the value of n, then choose the correct answer.

Ans. ***(a, c)*** According to Freundlich adsorption isotherm,

$$\frac{x}{m} \propto p^{\frac{1}{n}} \Rightarrow \frac{x}{m} = kp^{\frac{1}{n}}$$

(a) At $\frac{1}{n} = 0$ this equation becomes $\frac{x}{m} = kp^0 = k$

Extent of adsorption is independent of pressure.

(c) At $x = 0$, $\frac{x}{m} = kp^{\frac{1}{0}} = kp^{\infty}$

Hence, $\frac{x}{m}$ *vs* p graph is a line parallel to x-axis.

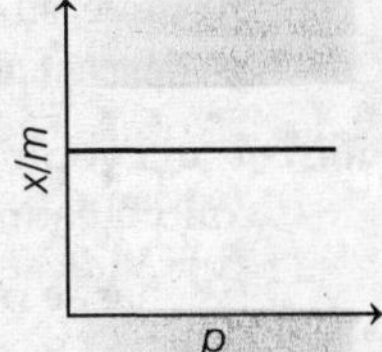

Q.29 H_2 gas is adsorbed on activated charcoal to a very little extent in comparison to easily liquefiable gases due to ....

(a) very strong van der Waals interaction.
(b) very weak van der Waals' forces.
(c) very low critical temperature.
(d) very high critical temperature.

Ans. ***(b, c)*** H_2 gas is adsorbed on activated charcoal to a very little extent in comparison to easily liquefiable gases due to

(i) very low van der Waals forces and
(ii) very low critical temperature

Q.30 Which of the following statements are correct?

(a) Mixing two oppositely charged sols neutralises their charges and stabilises the colloid.

(b) Presence of equal and similar charges on colloidal particles provides stability to the colloids.

(c) Any amount of dispersed liquid can be added to emulsion without destabilising it.

(d) Brownian movement stabilises sols.

Ans. ***(b, d)*** Presence of equal and similar charges on colloidal particles provides stability to colloids as repulsive forces between charge particles having same charge prevents them from colliding when they come closer to each other.

Q.31 An emulsion cannot be broken by .... and ....

(a) heating
(b) adding more amount of dispersion medium
(c) freezing
(d) adding emulsifying agent

Ans. ***(b, d)*** Emulsions are liquid-liquid colloidal system. They cannot be broken by adding more amount of dispersion medium and by adding emulsifying agent as on adding more amount of dispersion medium, they become dilute and on adding emulsifying agent they get stabilised.

Q.32 Which of the following substances will precipitate the negatively charged emulsions?

(a) KCl (b) Glucose (c) Urea (d) NaCl

Ans. ***(a, d)*** The droplets present in emulsion has negative charge. It can be precipitated by adding electrolyte such as KCl, NaCl etc, Since, glucose and urea do not produce ions on dissolving in water. Hence, they are non-electrolyte and do not precipitate the negatively charged emulsion.

Q.33 Which of the following colloids **cannot** be coagulated easily?

(a) Lyophobic colloids (b) Irreversible colloids
(c) Reversible colloids (d) Lyophilic colloids

● **Concept Insight** This solution includes the concept of protective action of lyophilic sols.

Ans. ***(c, d)*** Lyophilic colloids (liquid loving colloids) which are also known as reversible colloid cannot be coagulated easily. The stability of these colloids are due to

(i) charge on colloidal particles and (ii) solvation of colloidal particles.

Q.34 What happens when a lyophilic sol is added to a lyophobic sol?

(a) Lyophobic sol is protected.
(b) Lyophilic sol is protected.
(c) Film of lyophilic sol is formed over lyophobic sol.
(d) Film of lyophobic sol is formed over lyophilic sol.

Ans. ***(a, c)*** Lyophobic sol is unstable in nature. When lyophilic sol is added to lyophobic sol then lyophobic sol is protected because a film of lyophilic sol is formed over lyophobic sol.

Hence, options (a) and (c) are correct.

Q.35 Which phenomenon occurs when an electric field is applied to a colloidal solution and electrophoresis is prevented?

(a) Reverse osmosis takes place.
(b) Electroosmosis takes place.
(c) Dispersion medium begins to move.
(d) Dispersion medium becomes stationary.

Thinking Process This problem is based on the concept of electroosmosis.

Ans. ***(b, c)*** The movement of colloidal particles under an applied electric potential is called electrophoresis. When this movement of particles is prevented by some suitable means, it is observed that the dispersion medium begins to move in an electric field. This phenomenon is termed as electroosmosis.

Q.36 In a reaction, catalyst changes ....
(a) physically (b) qualitatively (c) chemically (d) quantitatively

Ans. *(a, b)* In a reaction, catalyst changes physically and qualitatively as it is unaltered during the reaction. It remains quantitatively intact after completion of reaction and it does not change chemically.

Q.37 Which of the following phenomenon occurs when a chalk stick is dipped in ink?
(a) Adsorption of coloured substance.
(b) Adsorption of solvent.
(c) Absorption and adsorption both of solvent.
(d) Absorption of solvent.

Ans. *(a, d)* When a chalk stick is dipped in ink adsorption as well as absorption both occurs. Adsorption of coloured substance and absorption of solvent takes place.

Short Answer Type Questions

Q.38 Why is it important to have clean surface in surface studies?

Ans. Clean surface in surface studies facilitate the adsorption of desired species. If surface is covered by the gases of air then it will not be available for adsorption of desired gases. So, it is very important to have a clean surface in surface studies, *i.e.*, study of surface chemistry.

Q.39 Why is chemisorption referred to as activated adsorption?

Ans. Chemisorption is referred to as activated adsorption as it involves chemical bond formation between reactant and adsorbent molecules. Formation of chemical bond requires high activation energy. So, it is activated on increasing temperature.

Q.40 What type of solutions are formed on dissolving different concentrations of soap in water?

Ans. At lower concentration, soap behaves as a normal solution of electrolyte in water. However, after a certain concentration, called critical micelle concentration, colloidal solution is formed due to aggregation of colloidal particles.
CMC for soap solution is 10^{-4} to 10^{-3} mol L^{-1}.

Q.41 What happens when gelatin is mixed with gold sol?

Ans. Gold sol is a solvent repelling sol, *i.e.*, a lyophobic sol and is unstable in nature. Addition of gelatin stabilises the gold sol because gelatin forms lyophilic sol and act as a protective colloid.

Q.42 How does it become possible to cause artificial rain by spraying silver iodide on the clouds?

Ans. As we know artificial rainfall occurs when oppositely charged clouds meet. Since, clouds are colloidal in nature and carry charge. Spray of silver iodide, an electrolyte from aeroplane results in coagulation of colloidal water particles leading to rain. Sometimes electrified sand is also used for this purpose.

Q.43 Gelatin which is a peptide is added in ice-creams. What can be its role?

Ans. Emulsifying agent is added to an emulsion to stabilise it. Emulsifying agent forms a layer between the suspended particles and the medium and hence stabilises the emulsion. Ice cream (emulsion) is stabilised by emulsifying agent like gelatin.

Q.44 What is collodion?

Ans. 4% solution of nitrocellulose in a mixture of alcohol and ether is called collodion.

Q. 45 Why do we add alum to purify water?

Ans. We add alum to purify water as alum coagulates the colloidal impurities present in water, so that these impurities get settles down and can be removed by decantation or filtration. Thus, water gets purified by adding alum to water.

Q.46 What happens when electric field is applied to colloidal solution?

Ans. When electric potential is applied to colloidal solution, the colloidal particles move towards one or other electrode. Positively charged particles move towards the cathode, while negatively charged particles move towards the anode.

Q.47 What causes Brownian motion in colloidal dispersion?

Ans. Brownian movement may be defined as continuous *zig-zag* movement of colloidal particles in a colloidal sol. A state of continuous *zig-zag* motion of colloidal particles appears to be in view due to unbalanced bombardment of the particles of dispersed phase by molecules of dispersion medium. This Brownian movement stabilises the sol.

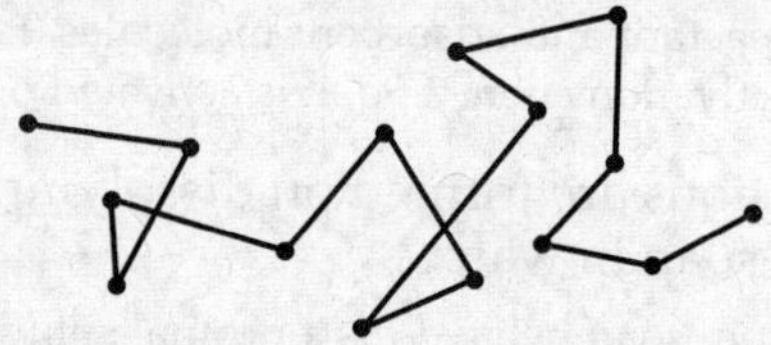

Q 48 A colloid is formed by adding $FeCl_3$ in excess of hot water. What will happen if excess sodium chloride is added to this colloid?

Ans. Positively charged ions coagulate the negatively charged sol and negatively charged ions coagulate the positively charged sol. Positively charged sol of hydrated ferric oxide is formed when $FeCl_3$ is added in excess of hot water. On adding excess of NaCl to this sol, negatively charged Cl^- ions coagulate the positively charged sol of hydrated ferric oxide.

Q.49 How do emulsifying agents stabilise the emulsion?

Ans. Emulsifying agents stabilise the emulsion by forming an interfacial layer between suspended particles and the dispersion medium. *e.g.*, gelatin is added to ice cream to stabilise it.

Q.50 Why are some medicines more effective in the colloidal form?

Ans. Some medicines are more effective in colloidal form because they have large surface area so they are easily assimilated in the body.

Q.51 Why does leather get hardened after tanning?

Ans. Animal hide is colloidal in nature and has positively charged particles. When it is soaked in tanin a negatively charged colloid, it results in mutual coagulation and gets hardened. Thus, leather gets hardened after tanning.

Q.52 How does the precipitation of colloidal smoke take place in Cottrell precipitator?

Ans. In Cottrell precipitator, smoke particles (charged) are passed through a chamber containing plates with charge opposite to the smoke particles thus, smoke particles lose their charge on the plates and gets precipitated.

Q.53 How will you distinguish between dispersed phase and dispersion medium in an emulsion?

Ans. To distinguish between dispersed phase and dispersion medium, we increase the concentration of any one dispersion medium or dispersed phase and then notice the change.

When dispersion medium is added to an emulsion, it gets diluted to any extent. But on adding dispersed phase, it forms a separate layer, if added in excess.

Q.54 On the basis of Hardy-Schulze rule explain why the coagulating power of phosphate is higher than chloride?

Ans. Minimum quantity of an electrolyte required to cause precipitation of a sol is called its coagulating value. Greater the charge on flocculating ion and smaller is the amount of electrolyte required for precipitation, higher is the coagulating power of coagulating ion (Hardy-Schulze Law).

Phosphate ion carries – 3 charge while chloride ion carries only –1 charge and due to high charge phosphate ion has high coagulating power than that of chloride ion.

Q.55 Why does bleeding stop by rubbing moist alum?

Ans. Blood is a colloidal sol. When we rub the injured part with moist alum then coagulation of blood takes place. Hence, main reason is coagulation, which stops the bleeding.

Q.56 Why is $Fe(OH)_3$ colloid positively charged, when prepared by adding $FeCl_3$ to hot water?

Ans. Charge on sol is decided by adsorption of ions present in medium. Adsorption of positively charged Fe^{3+} ions takes place by the sol of hydrated ferric oxide. Thus, $Fe(OH)_3$ colloid has positive charge when prepared by adding $Fe(OH)_3$ to hot water.

Q.57 Why do physisorption and chemisorption behave differently with rise in temperature?

Ans. Behaviour of physisorption and chemisorption on increase in temperature can be explained on the basis of nature of forces present to bind their particles.

Physisorption involves weak van der Waals forces which weakens with increase in temperature.

Chemisorption involves formation of chemical bond which requires activation energy, hence, it is favoured by rise in temperature.

Q.58 What happens when dialysis is prolonged?

Ans. Traces of electrolyte which stabilises the colloids is removed completely, making the colloid unstable. So, coagulation occurs on prolonged dialysis.

Q.59 Why does the white precipitate of silver halide become coloured in the presence of dye eosin?

Ans. White coloured precipitate of silver halide becomes coloured in the presence of dye eosin because dye eosin (coloured) gets adsorbed on the surface of silver halide precipitate.

Q.60 What is the role of activated charcoal in gas mask used in coal mines?

Ans. Role of activated charcoal in gas mask can be explained on the basis of adsorption. Activated charcoal adsorbs various poisonous gases on its surface present in coal mines.

Q.61 How does a delta form at the meeting place of sea and river water?

Ans. Formation of delta at the meeting place of sea and river water is due to coagulation. River water (colloid of sea water + clay) has many dissolved electrolytes. The place where river meets sea is the site for coagulation. Deposition of coagulated clay results in delta formation.

Q.62 Give an example where physisorption changes to chemisorption with rise in temperature. Explain the reason for change.

Ans. Adsorption of H_2 on finely divided nickel (physisorption) involves weak van der Waals forces. When temperature is increased, hydrogen molecules dissociate into hydrogen atoms, form chemical bonds with the metal atoms at the surface (chemisorption).

Q.63 Why is desorption important for a substance to act as good catalyst?

Ans. Desorption is important for a substance to act as a good catalyst so that after the reaction, the products formed on the surface separate out (desorbed) to create free surface again for other reactant molecules to approach the surface and react.

Q.64 What is the role of diffusion in heterogeneous catalyst?

Ans. Diffusion of gas molecules occurs at the surface of catalyst (solid) followed by adsorption. In the same way, the product formed diffuse from the surface of the catalyst leaving the surface free for more reactant molecules to get adsorbed and undergo in a reaction.

Q.65 How does a solid catalyst enhance the rate of combination of gaseous molecules?

Ans. When gaseous molecules come in contact with the surface of a solid catalyst, a weak chemical bond is formed between the surface (catalyst) molecules and reactant (gas) molecules. Thus, concentration of reactant molecules increases at the surface.

The rate of reaction increases by adsorption of different molecules side by side facilitating the chemical reaction. Adsorption, being exothermic also help in increasing the rate of reaction (chemisorption increases with rise in temperature).

Q.66 Do the vital functions of the body such as digestion get affected during fever? Explain your answer.

Ans. The optimum temperature range for enzymatic activity is 298-310 K, *i.e.*, enzymes are inactive beyond this temperature range (high or low).

Normal human body temperature being 310 K, is suitable for enzyme-catalysed reactions. If a person is suffering from fever (temperature >310 K), the activity of enzymes may be affected.

Matching The Columns

Q.67 Method of formation of solution is given in Column I. Match it with the type of solution given in Column II.

	Column I		Column II
A.	Sulphur vapours passed through cold water.	1.	Normal electrolyte solution
B.	Soap mixed with water above critical micelle concentration.	2.	Molecular colloids
C.	White of egg whipped with water.	3.	Associated colloid
D.	Soap mixed with water below critical micelle concentration.	4.	Macromolecular colloids

Ans. A. → (2) B. → (3) C. → (4) D. → (1)

A. When sulphur vapours passed through cold water it leads to formation of molecular colloids.

B. When soap is mixed with water above critical micelle concentration it lead to formation of associated colloids.

C. White of egg whipped with water is an example of macromolecular colloids in which high molecular mass proteneous molecule acts as a colloidal particle.

D. Soap mixed with water below critical micelle concentration is known as normal electrolyte solution.

Q.68 Match the statement given in Column I with the phenomenon given in Column II.

	Column I		Column II
A.	Dispersion medium moves in an electric field.	1.	Osmosis
B.	Solvent molecules pass through semipermeable membrane towards solvent side.	2.	Electrophoresis
C.	Movement of charged colloidal particles under the influence of applied electric potential towards oppositely charged electrodes.	3.	Electroosmosis
D.	Solvent molecules pass through semipermeable membranes towards solution side.	4.	Reverse-osmosis

Ans. A. → (3) B. → (4) C. → (2) D. → (1)

A. Dispersion medium moves in an electric field is known as electroosmosis.

B. Solvent molecules pass through semipermeable membrane towards solvent side is known as reverse-osmosis.

C. Movement of charged colloidal particles under the influence of applied electric potential towards oppositely charge electrodes is known as electrophoresis.

D. Solvent molecules pass through semipermeable membranes towards solution side is known as osmosis.

Q.69 Match the items given in Column I and Column II.

	Column I		Column II
A.	Protective colloid	1.	$FeCl_3$ + NaOH
B.	Liquid-liquid colloid	2.	Lyophilic colloids
C.	Positively charged colloid	3.	Emulsion
D.	Negatively charged colloid	4.	$FeCl_3$ + hot water

Ans. A. → (2) B. → (3) C. → (4) D. → (1)

A. Lyophobic colloids (solvent hating colloid) are readily protected by small amount of electrolyte. These colloids are also stabilised by addition of lyophilic colloids which makes a protective layer around lyophobic sol. Hence, lyophilic sol are known as protective colloid.

B. Liquid-liquid colloid is also known as emulsion if they are partially miscible or immiscible liquids.

C. When $FeCl_3$ is added to hot water it leads to the formation of positively charged colloid.

D. When NaOH is added to $FeCl_3$, it leads to the formation of negatively charged colloid.

Q.70 Match the types of colloidal systems given in Column I with the name given in Column II.

	Column I		Column II
A.	Solid in liquid	1.	Foam
B.	Liquid in solid	2.	Sol
C.	Liquid in liquid	3.	Gel
D.	Gas in liquid	4.	Emulsion

Ans. A. → (2) B. → (3) C. → (4) D. → (1)

Colloids are classified on the basis of types of dispersed phase and dispersion medium.

	Dispersed phase	Dispersion medium	Name
A.	Solid in	Liquid	Sol
B.	Liquid in	Solid	Gel
C.	Liquid in	Liquid	Emulsion
D.	Gas in	Liquid	Foam

Q.71 Match the items of Column I and Column II.

Column I	Column II
A. Dialysis	1. Cleansing action of soap
B. Peptisation	2. Coagulation
C. Emulsification	3. Colloidal sol formation
D. Electrophoresis	4. Purification

Ans. **A.** → (4) **B.** → (3) **C.** → (1) **D.** → (2)

A. Purification of colloid can be done by dialysis in which ions/particles are removed from solution through semipermeable membrane.

B. Peptisation is a process in which when small quantity of electrolyte (peptising agent) is added to precipitate. It leads to formation of colloidal solution.

Sol
Water
SPM
Dialysis

C. The process of removing of oily or greasy dirt from the cloth is done by emulsification.

D. Process of settling of colloidal particle is called coagulation. Electrophoresis is a process in which on applying electric potential to the electrodes dipped in sol, the oppositely charged particles of colloidal solution move towards oppositely charged electrodes, get discharged and precipitated.

Q.72 Match the items of Column I and Column II.

Column I	Column II
A. Butter	1. Dispersion of liquid in liquid
B. Pumice stone	2. Dispersion of solid in liquid
C. Milk	3. Dispersion of gas in solid
D. Paints	4. Dispersion of liquid in solid

Ans. **A.** → (4) **B.** → (3) **C.** → (1) **D.** → (2)

A. Butter is an example of dispersion of liquid in solid.

B. Pumice stone is an example of dispersion of gas in solid in which gas bubbles are pearced within solid particles.

C. Milk is a dispersion of liquid in liquid in which fats and protein are dissolved in milk.

D. Paint is an example of solid in liquid.

Assertion and Reason

In the following questions a statement of assertion followed by a statement of reason is given. Choose the correct answer out of the following choices.

(a) Assertion and reason both are correct and the reason is correct explanation of assertion.

(b) Assertion and reason both are correct but reason does not explain assertion.

(c) Assertion is correct, but reason is incorrect.

(d) Both assertion and reason are incorrect.

(e) Assertion is incorrect, but reason is correct.

Q.73 **Assertion** An ordinary filter paper impregnated with collodion solution stops the flow of colloidal particles.

Reason Pore size of the filter paper becomes more than the size of colloidal particle.

Ans. *(c)* Assertion is correct, but reason is incorrect.

An ordinary filter paper impregnated with collodion solution stops the flow of colloidal particles because pore size of the filter paper becomes smaller than the size of colloidal particles.

Q. 74 **Assertion** Colloidal solution show colligative properties.

Reason Colloidal particles are large in size.

Ans. *(b)* Assertion and reason both are correct, but reason does not explain assertion.

Colloidal solutions show colligative properties as colloidal particles have large size. Also, colloidal particles have small value of colligative properties because number of particles are small in comparison to normal solution.

Q.75 **Assertion** Colloidal solutions do not show Brownian motion.

Reason Brownian motion is responsible for stability of sols.

Ans. *(e)* Assertion is incorrect, but reason is correct.

Colloidal solutions show Brownian motion and this Brownian motion is responsible for stability of sols.

Q.76 **Assertion** Coagulation power of Al^{3+} is more than Na^{+}.

Reason Greater the valency of the flocculating ion added, greater is its power to cause precipitation (Hardy–Schulze rule).

Ans. *(a)* Assertion and reason both are correct and reason is correct explanation of assertion.

According to Hardy–Schulze law, greater the charge/valency on flocculating ion added, greater will be its power to cause precipitation.

$$\text{Coagulating power} \propto \text{Valency of flocculating ion}$$

Q.77 **Assertion** Detergents with low CMC are more economical to use.

Reason Cleansing action of detergents involves the formation of micelles. These are formed when the concentration of detergents becomes equal to CMC.

Ans. *(a)* Assertion and reason both are correct and reason is correct explanation of assertion.

Detergents with low CMC are more economical to use as cleansing action of detergents involves the formation of micelles. These are formed when the concentration of detergent becomes equal to CMC. If CMC has lower value then it will form CMC easily and readily.

Long Answer Type Questions

Q.78 What is the role of adsorption in heterogeneous catalysis?

Ans. Heterogeneous catalyst is used to increase rate of reaction in which catalyst is not in phase with reactants and products.

Role of adsorption in heterogeneous catalysis are

(i) Diffusion of reactants to the surface of the catalyst.

(ii) Reactants are adsorbed on the catalyst surface.

(iii) Occurrence of chemical reaction at catalyst surface.

(iv) Desorption of products.

(v) Diffusion of reaction products away from the catalysts surface.

e.g.,

Catalyst surface having free valencies $+ A + B$ (Reacting molecules) $\xrightarrow{\text{Adsorption of reacting molecules}}$ Adsorption of reacting molecules $\downarrow$ Intermediate $\xrightarrow{\text{Desorption of product molecules}}$ Catalyst $+ A + B$ (Product)

Role of adsorption in heterogeneous catalysis

Q.79 What are the applications of adsorption in chemical analysis?

Ans. There are various applications of adsorption in chemical analysis.

Some of which are as follows

(i) **In thin layer chromatography** The lower adsorbing particles comes out readily while other particles, having higher adsorbing tendency come out later. On this basis, compounds are separated or analysed.

(ii) **In adsorption indicators** Surface of certain precipitate has an ability to adsorb some dyes to produce a characteristic colour, *e.g.*, Ag*X* adsorbs eosin dye and thereby produces a characteristic colour at the end point.

(iii) **In qualitative analysis** Specific material has specific adsorption tendency, so particular ion can be identified very easily.

(iv) **In the separation of inert gases** Different inert gases are adsorbed to different extents at different temperatures on coconut charcoal. This forms the basis of their separation from a mixture.

(v) **In froth floatation process** Sulphide ore is concentrated by seperating it from silica and other earthly matter by using pine oil and frothing agent.

Q.80 What is the role of adsorption in froth floatation process used especially for concentration of sulphide ores?

Ans. In froth floatation process sulphide ore is shaken with pine oil and water, the ore particles are adsorbed on froth that floats and the gangue particles settle down in tank.

Role of adsorption in froth floatation can be described as

(i) Adsorption increases the concentration of reactants on the surface of the catalyst.

(ii) Adsorbed molecules get dissociated to make active species like free radicals, which react much faster than molecules.

As sulphide ores are extracted using froth floatation method therefore, only sulphide ore particles will show these type of adsorbing tendency.

Q.81 What do you understand by shape selective catalysis? Why are zeolites good shape selective catalysts?

Ans. The catalytic reaction which depends upon pore structure of catalyst and the size of the reactant and product molecules is known as shape selective catalysts.

Zeolites are good shape selective catalyst because of 'honey comb' like structure.

(i) They are microporous aluminosilicates with Al—O—Si framework and general formula $M_{x/n}\ [(AlO_2)_x(SiO_2)_y].mH_2O$.

(ii) The reactions taking place in zeolites depend upon the size and shape of the reactant and product molecules as well as upon the pores and cavities of the zeolites.

(iii) Zeolites are widely used as catalysts in petrochemical industries for cracking of hydrocarbons and isomerisation. They are also used for removing permanent hardness of water.

(iv) *e.g.*, ZSM-5 is a catalyst used in petroleum industry.

$$\text{Alcohols} \xrightarrow[\text{Dehydration}]{\text{ZSM-5}} \text{Gasoline(petrol)} \quad \text{(A mixture of hydrocarbons)}$$

Chapter

06 General Principle and Processes of Isolation of Elements*

Multiple Choice Questions (MCQs)

Q.1 In the extraction of chlorine by electrolysis of brine ....

(a) oxidation of Cl^- ion to chlorine gas occurs

(b) reduction of Cl^- ion to chlorine gas occurs

(c) for overall reaction $\Delta G^{\ominus}$ has negative value

(d) a displacement reaction takes place

Ans. ***(a)*** Following reaction takes place in the extraction of chlorine by electrolysis.

$$2H_2O(l) + 2Cl^-(aq) \rightarrow H_2(g) + Cl_2(g) + 2OH^-(aq)$$

From the above reaction, it is very clear that the oxidation of Cl^- ion to chlorine gas occurs. Thus, option (a) is the correct answer.

$\Delta^\circ G$ for this reaction is +422kJ. Therefore, thermodynamically reaction is not feasible. We know that,

$$\Delta G^\circ = -nFE^\circ$$

By using this equation value of E° can be calculated. Thus,

$$E^\circ = -\frac{\Delta G^\circ}{nF} = -2.2 \text{ V}$$

Therefore, for the occurrence of this reaction, external potential (emf) greater than 2.2V is required. Due to this fact, (c) is not the correct option.

Mistake Alert ! *Students may make a mistake by choosing reduction instead of oxidation for the formation of chlorine gas. In the electrolysis of brine, oxidation of* Cl^- *ions to chlorine gas occurs at the anode.*

Q.2 When copper ore is mixed with silica, in a reverberatory furnace copper matte is produced. The copper matte contains ....

(a) sulphides of copper (II) and iron (II)

(b) sulphides of copper (II) and iron (III)

(c) sulphides of copper (I) and iron (II)

(d) sulphides of copper (I) and iron (III)

Ans. ***(c)*** When copper ore is mixed with sillica in a reverberatory furnace, copper matte is produced. The copper matte contains sulphide of copper (I) (Cu_2S) and iron (II) (FeS).

Note (*) This chapter has been deleted from latest NCERT.

Q.3 Which of the following reactions is an example of autoreduction?

(a) $Fe_3O_4 + 4CO \longrightarrow 3Fe + 4CO_2$
(b) $Cu_2O + C \longrightarrow 2Cu + CO$
(c) $Cu^{2+}(aq) + Fe(s) \longrightarrow Cu(s) + Fe^{2+}(aq)$
(d) $Cu_2O + \frac{1}{2}Cu_2S \longrightarrow 3Cu + \frac{1}{2}SO_2$

Thinking Process This problem is based on the concept of autoreduction reaction. To solve this question, identify reaction where the same element appears in different oxidation states, allowing it to reduce itself.

Ans. ***(d)*** $Cu_2O + \frac{1}{2}Cu_2S \longrightarrow 3Cu + \frac{1}{2}SO_2$

This reaction includes reduction of copper (I) oxide by copper (I) sulphide. In this process, copper is reduced by itself hence, this process is known as autoreduction. The solidified copper os obtained is known as blister copper.

Q.4 A number of elements are available in earth's crust but most abundant elements are ....

(a) Al and Fe (b) Al and Cu (c) Fe and Cu (d) Cu and Ag

Ans. ***(a)*** Among a number of elements which are available in earth crust, the most abundant elements are aluminium and iron. Aluminium is third most abundant element in earth crust, *i.e.*, 8.3% by weight while iron is present in earth crust with 4.2% by weight. Copper and silver are also found in earth crust but their abundance percentage is low.

Q.5 Zone refining is based on the principle that ....

(a) impurities of low boiling metals can be separated by distillation.
(b) impurities are more soluble in molten metal than in solid metal.
(c) different components of a mixture are differently adsorbed on an adsorbent.
(d) vapours of volatile compound can be decomposed in pure metal.

Concept Insight This solution includes the concept of selective purification through differential solubility of impurities in molten *vs* solid states, as utilised in the zone refining process.

Ans. ***(b)*** Zone refining is based on the principle that the impurities are more soluble in molten state than in solid state of the metal. A circular mobile heater is fixed at one end of an impure metal rod. The molten zone moves along with heater which is moved forward.

As the heater moves forward, the pure metal crystallises out of the melt and the impurities pass on into adjacent molten zone. The process is repeated several times and the heater is moved in the same direction. At one end, impurities get concentrated. This end is cut off. and we get pure metal. *e.g.*, germanium, silicon, gallium, etc., are refined by this method.

Q.6 In the extraction of copper from its sulphide ore, the metal is formed by the reduction of Cu_2O with

(a) FeS (b) CO (c) Cu_2S (d) SO_2

Concept Insight This solution includes the concept of autoreduction reaction in metal extraction, where copper oxide (Cu_2O) is reduced by copper sulphide (Cu_2S) to form metallic copper (blister copper).

Ans. ***(c)*** In the extraction of copper from its sulphide ore, the metal is formed by the reduction of Cu_2O with Cu_2S. This reaction is called as autoreduction.
Chemical reaction occurring in this process is as follows :

$$Cu_2O + \frac{1}{2}Cu_2S \longrightarrow 3Cu + \frac{1}{2}SO_2$$

In this process, copper appears as blister copper.

Q.7 Brine is electrolysed by using inert electrodes. The reaction at anode is ....

(a) $Cl^- (aq.) \rightarrow \frac{1}{2}Cl_2 (g) + e^-$; $E^\circ_{Cell} = 1.36$ V

(b) $2H_2O (l) \rightarrow O_2(g) + 4H^+ + 4e^-$; $E^\circ_{Cell} = 1.23$ V

(c) $Na^+ (aq.) + e^- \rightarrow Na(s)$; $E^\circ_{Cell} = 2.71$ V

(d) $H^+ (aq.) + e^- \rightarrow \frac{1}{2}H_2(g)$; $E^\circ_{Cell} = 0.00$ V

Ans. ***(a)*** Brine is electrolysed by using inert electrodes. The possible reactions occurring at anode are

$$Cl^- (aq) \longrightarrow \frac{1}{2}Cl_2 (g) + e^-; \quad E^\circ_{Cell} = 1.36 \text{ V}$$

$$2H_2O (l) \longrightarrow O_2(g) + 4H^+ + 4e^-; \quad E^\circ_{Cell} = 1.23 \text{ V}$$

The reaction at anode with lower value of E° is preferred and therefore water should get oxidised in preference to $Cl^-(aq.)$. However, Cl_2 is produced instead of O_2. This unexpected result is explained on the basis of the fact that water needs greater voltage for oxidation to O_2 (as it is kinetically slow process) than that needed for oxidation of Cl^- ions to Cl_2.

Q.8 In the metallurgy of aluminium ....

(a) Al^{3+} is oxidised to Al (*s*).

(b) graphite anode is oxidised to carbon monoxide and carbon dioxide.

(c) oxidation state of oxygen changes in the reaction at anode.

(d) oxidation state of oxygen changes in the overall reaction involved in the process.

Ans. ***(b)*** In the metallurgy of aluminium, electrolysis is performed in a steel vessel with lining of carbon which acts as cathode and graphite acts as anode. During this process graphite anode is oxidised to CO and CO_2.
Chemical reaction occurring in this process is as follows

$$2Al_2O_3 + 3C \longrightarrow 4Al + 3CO_2$$

This process is known as Hall-Heroult process. The electrolytic reactions are

At cathode $Al^{3+}(\text{melt}) + 3e^- \longrightarrow Al(l)$

At anode $C(s) + O^{2-}(\text{melt}) \longrightarrow CO(g) + 2e^-$

$$C(s) + 2O^{2-}(\text{melt}) \longrightarrow CO_2 (g) + 4e^-$$

Q.9 Electrolytic refining is used to purify which of the following metals?

(a) Cu and Zn (b) Ge and Si (c) Zr and Ti (d) Zn and Hg

Ans. ***(a)*** Copper and zinc are two metals which are generally purified by using electrolyte refining. In this process, impure metal is used as anode and pure metal is used as a cathode. Impurities from the blister copper or impure zinc deposit as anode mud.

Q.10 Extraction of gold and silver involves leaching the metal with CN^- ion. The metal is recovered by ....

(a) displacement of metal by some other metal from the complex ion.

(b) roasting of metal complex.

(c) calcination followed by roasting.

(d) thermal decomposition of metal complex.

Ans. ***(a)*** Extraction of gold and silver involves leaching the metal with CN^- ion. The metal is recovered by displacement of metal by some other metal from the complex ion.

This is an oxidation reaction.

$$4Au(s) + 8CN^-(aq) + 2H_2O(aq) + O_2(g) \longrightarrow 4[Au(CN)_2]^-(aq) + 4OH^-(aq)$$

$$4[Au(CN)_2](aq) + Zn(s) \longrightarrow 2Au(s) + [Zn(CN)_4]^{2-}(aq)$$

Here, Zn acts as a reducing agent.

Direction (Q. Nos. 11-13) *Answer the questions on the basis of figure.*

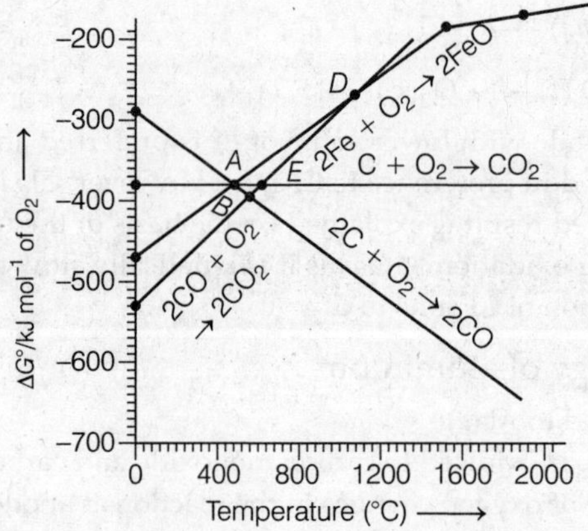

Q.11 Choose the correct option of temperature at which carbon reduces FeO to iron and produces CO.

(a) Below temperature at point *A*.

(b) Approximately at the temperature corresponding to point *A*.

(c) Above temperature at point *A* but below temperature at point *D*.

(d) Above temperature at point *A*.

Thinking Process This problem is based on concept of Ellingham diagram which relates Gibbs free energy of reaction and temperature. The point above which greater the negative value of formation of compound is observed, compound will form at that temperature.

At a particular temperature, compound having higher negative value of Gibbs free energy will be formed first.

Ans. ***(d)*** In the figure shown, above point *A*

$$\Delta_f G^\circ_{(C,CO)} < \Delta_f G^\circ_{(Fe, FeO)}$$

Therefore, above point *A*, *C* reduces FeO to Fe forming carbon monoxide. Hence, reduction of FeO by carbon occurs above point *A* only.

Q.12 Below point 'A' FeO can ....

(a) be reduced by carbon monoxide only.

(b) be reduced by both carbon monoxide and carbon.

(c) be reduced by carbon only.

(d) not be reduced by both carbon and carbon monoxide.

Ans. ***(a)*** Below point A, Gibbs free energy change for the formation of CO_2 from CO ($\Delta G^\circ_{CO,CO_2}$) has lower value (more negative value) than Gibbs free energy change for the formation of FeO ($\Delta G^\circ_{Fe,FeO}$). Hence, FeO will be reduced by CO only below point A.

Q.13 For the reduction of FeO at the temperature corresponding to point D, which of the following statements is correct?

(a) ΔG value for the overall reduction reaction with carbon monoxide is zero.

(b) ΔG value for the overall reduction reaction with a mixture of 1 mol carbon and 1 mol oxygen is positive.

(c) ΔG value for the overall reduction reaction with a mixture of 2 mol carbon and 1 mol oxygen will be positive.

(d) ΔG value for the overall reduction reaction with carbon monoxide is negative.

Ans. ***(a)*** At point D, ΔG curve for formation of CO_2 from CO and FeO from Fe intersect each other. Thus, ΔG° for the reaction $FeO + CO \rightarrow Fe + CO_2$ is zero.

Hence, option (a) is the correct choice.

Multiple Choice Questions (More Than One Options)

Q.14 At the temperature corresponding to which of the points in Fig. FeO will be reduced to Fe by coupling the reaction $2FeO \longrightarrow 2Fe + O_2$ with all of the following reactions?

1. $C + O \longrightarrow CO_2$
2. $2C + O_2 \longrightarrow 2CO$
3. $2CO + O_2 \longrightarrow 2CO_2$

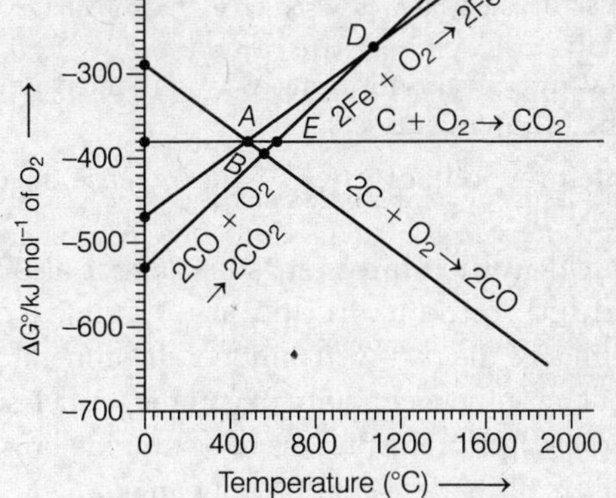

(a) Point A (b) Point B (c) Point D (d) Point E

Ans. ***(b, d)*** Below point B and E, FeO will be reduced to Fe by all the three reactions shown above in the question. $\Delta G^{\circ}_{(C, CO_2)}$, $\Delta G^{\circ}_{(C, CO)}$, $\Delta G^{\circ}_{(C, CO_2)}$ lie below $\Delta_f G^{\circ}_{(Fe, FeO)}$ curve at point B and E. Therefore, FeO will be reduced by all three reactions.

Hence, options (b) and (d) are correct choices.

Q.15 Which of the following options are correct?

(a) Cast iron is obtained by remelting pig iron with scrap iron and coke using hot air blast.

(b) In extraction of silver, silver is extracted as cationic complex.

(c) Nickel is purified by zone refining.

(d) Zr and Ti are purified by van Arkel method.

Thinking Process This question is based on concept of purification techniques and formation of cast iron.

Ans. ***(a, d)*** Correct statements are

(a) Cast iron is obtained by remelting pig iron with scrap iron and coke using hot air blast.

(d) Zr and Ti are purified by van Arkel method as

$$\underset{\text{Impure}}{Zr} + 2I_2 \longrightarrow \underset{\text{Volatile}}{ZrI_4} \xrightarrow{\Delta} \underset{\text{Pure}}{Zr} + 2I_2$$

Statements (b) and (c) can be correctly stated as

(b) In extraction of silver, silver is extracted as anionic complex $[Ag(CN)_2]^-$

(c) Nickel is purified by vapour phase refining method.

$$Ni + 4\,CO \rightarrow Ni(CO)_4 \xrightarrow{450\text{-}470K} Ni + 4CO$$

Q.16 In the extraction of aluminium by Hall-Heroult process, purified Al_2O_3 is mixed with CaF_2 to

(a) lower the melting point of Al_2O_3.

(b) increase the conductivity of molten mixture.

(c) reduce Al^{3+} into Al(*s*).

(d) acts as catalyst.

Thinking Process This problem is based on extraction of aluminium using Hall-Heroult process.

Ans. ***(a, b)*** In the metallurgy of aluminium, Al_2O_3 is mixed with Na_3AlF_6 and CaF_2 which causes the following affects.

(i) Lower the melting point of Al_2O_3 (ii) Increase the conductivity of molten mixture

Q.17 Which of the following statements is correct about the role of substances added in the froth floatation process?

(a) Collectors enhance the non-wettability of the mineral particles.

(b) Collectors enhance the wettability of gangue particles.

(c) By using depressants in the process two sulphide ores can be separated.

(d) Froth stabilisers decrease wettability of gangue.

Thinking Process This problem is based on the method involved in froth floatation process and function of collector and depressants.

Ans. ***(a, c)*** Froth floatation process is used to extract metal from sulphide ore. This method utilises collectors and depressants whose functions are as follows

(a) Collectors enhance the non-wettability of the mineral particles.

(c) By using depressants in the process, two sulphide ores can be separated. *e.g.*, sodium cyanide is used as a depressant to separate lead sulphide ore from zinc sulphide ore.

Q.18 In the froth floatation process, zinc sulphide and lead sulphide can be separated by ....

(a) using collectors
(b) adjusting the proportion of oil to water
(c) using depressant
(d) using froth stabilisers

Ans. ***(b, c)*** Froth floatation method is used to extract metal from sulphide ore. ZnS and PbS can be separated by using depressant and adjusting the proportion of oil to water. Depressant used for this purpose is NaCN. It selectively prevents ZnS from coming to the froth.

Hence, options (b) and (c) are correct choices.

Q.19 Common impurities present in bauxite are ....

(a) CuO (b) ZnO (c) Fe_2O_3 (d) SiO_2

Ans. ***(c, d)*** Bauxite is an ore of aluminium which contains Fe_2O_3 and SiO_2 as common impurities.

Q.20 Which of the following ores are concentrated by froth floatation?

(a) Haematite (b) Galena (c) Copper pyrites (d) Magnetite

Ans. ***(b, c)*** Haematite (Fe_2O_3) and magnetite (Fe_3O_4) are oxide ores while galena (PbS) and copper pyrites ($CuFeS_2$) are sulphide ores. As we know sulphide ores are extracted by using froth floatation method. Hence, (b) and (c) are the correct choices.

Q.21 Which of the following reactions occur during calcination?

(a) $CaCO_3 \longrightarrow CaO + CO_2$
(b) $2FeS_2 + \frac{11}{2}O_2 \longrightarrow Fe_2O_3 + 4SO_2$
(c) $Al_2O_3 \cdot xH_2O \longrightarrow Al_2O_3 + xH_2O$
(d) $ZnS + \frac{3}{2}O_2 \longrightarrow ZnO + SO_2$

Thinking Process This process is based on concept of calcination. Calcination involves heating of the ore below its melting point in the absence of air or in limited supply of air.

Ans. ***(a, c)*** Oxygen containing ores like oxide, hydroxides and carbonates are calcined. Thus, the following reactions occur during calcination.

$$CaCO_3 \xrightarrow{\Delta} CaO + CO_2$$

$$Al_2O_3 \cdot xH_2O \xrightarrow{\Delta} Al_2O_3 + x\,H_2O$$

Q.22 For the metallurgical process of which of the ores calcined ore can be reduced by carbon?

(a) Haematite (b) Calamine (c) Iron pyrites (d) Sphalerite

Ans. ***(a, b)*** In the metallurgical process, the oxide ores are reduced by carbon. Sulphide ore cannot be reduced by carbon. Here, haematite (Fe_2O_3) and calamine (ZnO) are oxide ores of iron and zinc respectively, while iron pyrites (FeS_2) and sphalerite (ZnS) are sulphide ores of iron and zinc respectively.

Therefore, haematite and calamine can be reduced by carbon.

Q.23 The main reactions occurring in blast furnace during extraction of iron from haematite ore ....

(a) $Fe_2O_3 + 3CO \longrightarrow 2Fe + 3CO_2$ (b) $FeO + SiO_2 \longrightarrow FeSiO_3$

(c) $Fe_2O_3 + 3C \longrightarrow 2Fe + 3CO$ (d) $CaO + SiO_2 \longrightarrow CaSiO_3$

Ans. ***(a, d)*** In extraction of iron from haematite ore following reactions take place.

(i) $Fe_2O_3 + 3CO \longrightarrow 2Fe + 3CO_2$

This reaction represents reduction of Fe_2O_3 to Fe.

(ii) Formation of slag $CaO + SiO_2 \longrightarrow \underset{\text{Slag}}{CaSiO_3}$.

Q.24 In which of the following method of purification, metal is converted to its volatile compound which is decomposed to give pure metal?

(a) Heating with stream of carbon monoxide

(b) Heating with iodine

(c) Liquation

(d) Distillation

Thinking Process This problem is based on purification of metal using vapour phase refining method.

Ans. ***(a, b)*** Vapour phase refining method includes

(i) heating of metal with stream of CO

$$Ni + 4CO \rightarrow Ni(CO)_4 \xrightarrow{450-470\text{ K}} Ni + 4CO \text{ (Mond's process)}$$

(ii) heating with iodine

$$Zr + 2I_2 \xrightarrow{870\text{ K}} ZrI_4 \xrightarrow[\text{Tungsten filament}]{2075\text{ K}} Zr + 2I_2 \text{ (van Arkel method)}$$

Q.25 Which of the following statements are correct?

(a) A depressant prevents certain type of particle to come to the froth.

(b) Copper matte contains Cu_2S and ZnS.

(c) The solidified copper obtained from reverberatory furnace has blistered appearance due to evolution of SO_2 during the extraction.

(d) Zinc can be extracted by self-reduction.

Ans. ***(a, c)*** Correct statements are :

(i) A depressant prevents certain type of particle to come to the froth. *e.g.*, NaCN is added as a depressant during separation of PbS and ZnS.

(ii) The solidified copper obtained from reverberatory furnace has blistered appearance due to evolution of SO_2 during the extraction.

(b) and (d) are incorrect statements, and can be correctly stated as :

(iii) Copper matte contains Cu_2S and FeS.

(iv) Zinc can be extracted by reduction of ZnO with carbon.

Mistake Alert! *Students may confuse copper matte composition and self reduction.*

For example, Statment (b) is incorrect because copper matte contains Cu_2S and FeS, not ZnS.

Statement (d) is also incorrect, as zinc cannot be extracted by self-reduction.

Q.26 In the extraction of chlorine from brine ....

(a) $\Delta G°$ for the overall reaction is negative.

(b) $\Delta G°$ for the overall reaction is positive.

(c) $E°$ for the overall reaction has negative value.

(d) $E°$ for the overall reaction has positive value.

Ans. ***(b, c)*** Electrolysis of brine solution is used to extract chlorine. Overall chemical reaction occurring in this process can be shown as S

$$2H_2O(l) + 2Cl^-(aq) \longrightarrow H_2(g) + Cl_2(g) + 2OH^-(aq)$$

For the given reaction, value of $\Delta G°$ is 422 kJ

Using $\Delta G° = -nFE°$, the value of $E° = -2.2V$.

Therefore, $\Delta G°$ for the overall reaction is positive and $E°$ has negative value.

Short Answer Type Questions

Q.27 Why is an external emf of more than 2.2V required for the extraction of Cl_2 from brine?

Ans. $2Cl^-(aq.) + 2H_2O\,(l) \longrightarrow 2\,OH^-(aq.) + H_2(g) + Cl_2(g)$

For the given reaction, value of $\Delta G°$ is + 422 kJ.

Using $\Delta G° = -nFE°$, the value of $E° = -2.2V$.

Therefore, an external emf greater than 2.2V is required for the extraction of Cl_2 from brine.

Q.28 At temperature above 1073 K, coke can be used to reduce FeO to Fe. How can you justify this reduction with Ellingham diagram?

Ans. Using Ellingham diagram, we observe that at temperature greater than 1073 K; $\Delta G_{(C,\,CO)} < \Delta G_{(Fe,\,FeO)}$. We know that according to Ellingham diagram, compound having lower $\Delta_f G°$ undergoes its formation.

$$FeO + C \xrightarrow{>1073} Fe + CO$$

Hence, coke can reduce FeO to Fe.

Q.29 Wrought iron is the purest form of iron. Write a reaction used for the preparation of wrought iron from cast iron. How can the impurities of sulphur, silicon and phosphorus be removed from cast iron?

Ans. (a) $\underset{\text{Haematite lining}}{Fe_2O_3} + \underset{\text{Impurities (present in cast iron)}}{3C} \longrightarrow \underset{\text{Wrought iron}}{2Fe} + 3CO$

This reaction takes place in reverberatory furnace lined with haematite.

(b) The haematite oxidises S to SO_2, Si to SiO_2 and P to P_4O_{10}. Sometimes limestone is added as flux. Impurities of S, Si and P oxidise and pass into slag. The metal is removed and freed from slag by passing through rollers.

Q.30 How is copper extracted from low grade copper ores?

Ans. Copper is extracted from low grade copper ores by using hydrometallurgy method. For this purpose, ore is leached out using bacteria. The solution containing Cu^{2+} is treated with scrap iron and H_2.

$$Cu^{2+}(aq) + H_2(g) \longrightarrow Cu(s) + 2H^+(aq)$$

Q. 31 Write two basic requirements for refining of a metal by Mond process and by van Arkel Method.

Ans. Two basic requirements for refining of a metal by Mond's process and by Van Arkel method are

(i) Metal should form volatile compound with available reagent.

(ii) The volatile compound should be easily decomposable so that it can be recovered easily.

(a) **Mond's process** includes conversion of Ni to $Ni(CO)_4$ and then decomposition of $Ni(CO)_4$ to Ni.

$$Ni + 4CO \longrightarrow Ni(CO)_4$$

$$Ni(CO)_4 \xrightarrow{450-470\text{ K}} Ni + 4CO$$

(b) **Van Arkel method** includes conversion of Zr to volatile ZrI_4 and then decomposition of ZrI_4 to Zr and I_2.

$$Zr + 2I_2 \xrightarrow{870\text{ K}} ZrI_4 \xrightarrow{2075\text{ K}} Zr + 2I_2$$

Q.32 Although carbon and hydrogen are better reducing agents but they are not used to reduce metallic oxides at high temperatures. Why?

Ans. Because at high temperatures, carbon and hydrogen react with metals to form carbides and hydrides respectively. So, carbon and hydrogen are not better reducing agents to reduce metallic oxide.

Q.33 How do we separate two sulphide ores by Froth Floatation Method? Explain with an example.

Ans. Two sulphide ores can be separated by adjusting the proportion of oil and water or by using depressants, *e.g.*, if an ore contains ZnS and PbS both, a depressant NaCN is added during froth floatation. It forms a complex with ZnS and prevents it from coming into froth. PbS comes into the froth and thus gets separated.

Q.34 The purest form of iron is prepared by oxidising impurities from cast iron in a reverberatory furnace. Which iron ore is used to line the furnace? Explain by giving reaction.

Ans. (a) Haematite (Fe_2O_3) ore is used to line the furnace.

(b) $$\underset{\text{Haematite lining}}{Fe_2O_3} + \underset{\substack{\text{Impurities} \\ \text{(present in cast iron)}}}{3C} \longrightarrow \underset{\text{Wrought iron}}{2Fe} + 3CO$$

Q.35 The mixture of compounds *A* and *B* is passed through a column of Al_2O_3 by using alcohol as eluant. Compound *A* is eluted in preference to compound *B*. Which of the compounds *A* or *B*, is more readily adsorbed on the column?

Ans. Compounds which are adsorbed to the more extent comes out later, while the another one which is absorbed to the less extent comes out readily. Since, compound '*A*' comes out before compound '*B*', the compound '*B*' is more readily adsorbed on the column.

Q.36 Why is sulphide ore of copper heated in a furnace after mixing with silica?

Ans. Silica (flux) being an acidic flux removes the impurities of iron oxide, the basic impurity, by reacting with it. Thus, iron silicate (slag) is formed.

$$\underset{\text{Gangue}}{FeO} + \underset{\text{Flux}}{SiO_2} \longrightarrow \underset{\text{Slag}}{FeSiO_3}$$

Q.37 Why are sulphide ores converted to oxide before reduction?

Ans. Because oxides are reduced to metals easily while sulphides are not. So, sulphide ores are converted to oxide before reduction.

Q.38 Which method is used for refining Zr and Ti? Explain with equation.

Ans. Zr and Ti are refined by van Arkel method. It involves 2 steps

(a) **Formation of iodide** *e.g.,* zirconium $Zr + 2I_2 \longrightarrow ZrI_4$

(b) **Decomposition of iodide** $ZrI_4 \xrightarrow{1800\text{ K}} \underset{\text{Pure}}{Zr} + 2I_2$

Q.39 What should be the considerations during the extraction of metals by electrochemical method?

Ans. During extraction of metals by electrochemical method, the following two points must be considered

(i) **Reactivity of metals** If the metals are quite reactive and are expected to react with water then the metals should be extracted by the electrolysis of their purified molten ore rather than their aqueous solution.

(ii) **Suitability of electrodes** The selected electrodes should not react with the product of electrolysis. Also, the electrodes must be made up of a material which is quite cheap since their periodic replacement should not increase the cost of the process.

Q.40 What are the role of flux in metallurgical processes?

Ans. Role of flux in metallurgical process

(i) Flux is used to remove the gangue by combining with it. Thus, slag formation takes place.

(ii) It makes the molten mass more conducting.

Q.41 How are metals used as semiconductors refined? What is the principle of the method used like?

Ans. Metals of high grade like germanium, silicon, etc., used as semiconductors are refined by zone refining method.

Principle This method is based upon the principle that impurities are more soluble in molten state of metal than in solid state.

Q.42 Write down the reactions taking place in blast furnace related to the metallurgy of iron in the temperature range 500-800 K.

Ans. Chemical reactions occurring in blast furnace related to the metallurgy of iron in the temperature range 500-800 K are

(i) $3Fe_2O_3 + CO \longrightarrow 2\,Fe_3O_4 + CO_2$

(ii) $Fe_3O_4 + 4CO \longrightarrow 3Fe + 4CO_2$

(iii) $Fe_2O_3 + CO \longrightarrow 2FeO + CO_2$

Q.43 Give two requirements for vapour phase refining.

Ans. Two requirements for vapour phase refining are

(i) The metal should form a volatile compound with an available reagent.

(ii) The volatile compound should be easily decomposed to give pure metal.

Q.44 Write the chemical reactions involved in the extraction of gold by cyanide process. Also give the role of zinc in the extraction.

Ans. (i) $4Au(s) + 8CN^-(aq) + 2H_2O(aq) + O_2(g) \longrightarrow 4[Au(CN)_2]^-(aq) + 4OH^-(aq)$

(ii) $2[Au(CN)_2]^-(aq) + Zn(s) \longrightarrow [Zn(CN)_4]^{2-}(aq.) + 2Au(s)$

Sodium tetracyano-zincate(II)

Zinc acts as a reducing agent in this reaction.

Matching The Columns

Q.45 Match the items of Column I with items of Column II and assign the correct code.

	Column I		Column II
A.	Pendulum	1.	Chrome steel
B.	Malachite	2.	Nickel steel
C.	Calamine	3.	Na_3AlF_6
D.	Cryolite	4.	$CuCO_3 \cdot Cu(OH)_2$
		5.	$ZnCO_3$

Codes

	A	B	C	D		A	B	C	D
(a)	1	2	3	4	(b)	2	4	5	3
(c)	2	3	4	5	(d)	4	5	3	2

Ans. ***(b)*** **A.** → (2) **B.** → (4) **C.** → (5) **D.** → (3)

A. Pendulum is made up of nickel steel.

B. Molecular formula of malachite is $Cu\,CO_3 \cdot Cu\,(OH)_2$.

C. Molecular formula of calamine is $ZnCO_3$.

D. Molecular formula of cryolite is Na_3AlF_6.

Q.46 Match the items of Column I with the items of Column II and assign the correct code.

	Column I		Column II
A.	Coloured bands	1.	Zone refining
B.	Impure metal to volatile complex	2.	Fractional distillation
C.	Purification of Ge and Si	3.	Mond process
D.	Purification of mercury	4.	Chromatography
		5.	Liquation

Codes

	A	B	C	D		A	B	C	D
(a)	1	2	4	5	(b)	4	3	1	2
(c)	3	4	2	1	(d)	5	4	3	2

Ans. *(b)* **A.** → (4) **B.** → (3) **C.** → (1) **D.** → (2)

A. Coloured bands are observed in chromatography.

B. Impure metal is converted to volatile complex by using Mond process.

C. Ge an Si are purified by zone refining method.

D. Purification of mercury is done by fractional distillation.

Q.47 Match items of Column I with the items of Column II and assign the correct code.

	Column I		Column II
A.	Cyanide process	1.	Ultrapure Ge
B.	Froth floatation process	2.	Dressing of ZnS
C.	Electrolytic reduction	3.	Extraction of Al
D.	Zone refining	4.	Extraction of Au
		5.	Purification of Ni

Codes

	A	B	C	D
(a)	4	2	3	1
(b)	2	3	1	5
(c)	1	2	3	4
(d)	3	4	5	1

Ans. *(a)* **A.** → (4) **B.** → (2) **C.** → (3) **D.** → (1)

A. Cyanide process is used for extraction of Au through formation of anionic complex $[Au\ CN)_2]^-$.

B. Froth floatation process is used for dressing of ZnS.

C. Electrolytic reduction method is used for extraction of aluminium. Graphite electrode is used for this purpose.

D. Zone-refining is used for purification of Ge.

Q.48 Match the items of Column I with the items of Column II and assign the correct code.

	Column I		Column II
A.	Sapphire	1.	Al_2O_3
B.	Sphalerite	2.	NaCN
C.	Depressant	3.	Co
D.	Corundum	4.	ZnS
		5.	Fe_2O_3

Codes

	A	B	C	D
(a)	3	4	2	1
(b)	5	4	3	2
(c)	2	3	4	5
(d)	1	2	3	4

Ans. *(a)* **A.** → (3) **B.** → (4) **C.** → (2) **D.** → (1)

A. Sapphire is a gemstone which contain Co.

B. Molecular formula of sphalerite is ZnS .

C. NaCN is used as a depressant in froth floatation method.

D. Molecular formula of corundum is Al_2O_3.

Q.49 Match the items of Column I with items of Column II and assign the correct code.

	Column I		Column II
A.	Blisterred Cu	1.	Aluminium
B.	Blast furnace	2.	$2Cu_2O + Cu_2S \longrightarrow 6Cu + SO_2$
C.	Reverberatory furnace	3.	Iron
D.	Hall-Heroult process	4.	$FeO + SiO_2 \longrightarrow FeSiO_3$
		5.	$2Cu_2S + 3O_2 \longrightarrow 2Cu_2O + 2SO_2$

Codes

	A	B	C	D		A	B	C	D
(a)	2	3	4	1	(b)	1	2	3	5
(c)	5	4	3	2	(d)	4	5	3	2

Ans. ***(a)*** **A.** → (2) **B.** → (3) **C.** → (4) **D.** → (1)

A. Blisterred Cu can be prepared by means of following chemical reaction

$$2Cu_2O + Cu_2S \longrightarrow 6Cu + SO_2$$

B. Iron is extracted by using blast furnace.

C. In reverberatory furnace formation of slag occurs as

$$FeO + SiO_2 \longrightarrow \underset{\text{Slag}}{FeSiO_3}$$

D. Hall-Heroult process is used for extraction of aluminium.

Assertion and Reason

In the following questions a statement of assertion followed by a statement of reason is given. Choose the correct answer out of the following choices.

(a) Both assertion and reason are true and reason is the correct explanation of assertion.

(b) Both assertion and reason are true but reason is not the correct explanation of assertion.

(c) Assertion is true but reason is false.

(d) Assertion is false but reason is true.

(e) Assertion and reason both are wrong.

Q.50 **Assertion** Nickel can be purified by Mond's process.

Reason $Ni(CO)_4$ is a volatile compound which decomposes at 460 K to give pure Ni.

Ans. ***(a)*** Both assertion and reason are true and reason is the correct explanation of assertion.

Nickel can be purified by Mond's process in which formation of a volatile compound $Ni(CO)_4$ takes place which further decomposes to give pure Ni at 460 K.

Q.51 Assertion Zirconium can be purified by van Arkel method.
Reason ZrI_4 is volatile and decomposes at 1800K.

Ans. *(a)* Both assertion and reason are true and reason is the correct explanation of assertion.

Zirconium can be purified by van Arkel method which includes formation of volatile ZrI_4 which decomposes at 1800 K to give pure Zr.

Q.52 Assertion Sulphide ores are concentrated by Froth Flotation Method.
Reason Cresols stabilise the froth in Froth Floatation Method.

Ans.*(b)* Both assertion and reason are true but reason is not the correct explanation of assertion.

Sulphide ores are concentrated by froth floatation method. Sulphide ore particles are preferentially wetted by oil, become lighter and rise to the surface along with the froth, while gangue particles are preferentially wetted by water, become heavier and thus settle down at the bottom of the tank. Cresols stabilise the froth in Froth Floatation Method.

Formation of froth is main reason for extraction of metal. Metal ore comes out along with froth.

Q.53 Assertion Zone refining method is very useful for producing semiconductors.
Reason Semiconductors are of high purity.

Ans. *(b)* Both assertion and reason are true but reason is not the correct explanation of assertion.

Zone refining method is very useful for producing semiconductors of high purity as in this process pure metal crystallises while impurities pass on into adjacent molten zone when impure metal rod is heated.

Q.54 Assertion Hydrometallurgy involves dissolving the ore in a suitable reagent followed by precipitation by a more electropositive metal.
Reason Copper is extracted by hydrometallurgy.

Ans. *(b)* Assertion and reason both are correct but reason is not the correct explanation of assertion.

Hydrometallurgy involves dissolving the ore in suitable reagent followed by precipitation with the help of more electropositive metal in which pure metal is replaced by more electropositive metal.

Copper is extracted using this method.

Long Answer Type Questions

Q.55 Explain the following.

(a) CO_2 is a better reducing agent below 710 K whereas CO is a better reducing agent above 710 K.

(b) Generally sulphide ores are converted into oxides before reduction.

(c) Silica is added to the sulphide ore of copper in the reverberatory furnace.

(d) Carbon and hydrogen are not used as reducing agents at high temperatures.

(e) Vapour phase refining method is used for the purification of Ti.

Thinking Process This problem is based on the concept of Ellingham diagrams and purification of metal.

Ans. (a) As shown in Ellingham diagram which relates Gibbs free energy and temperature, below 710 K, $\Delta G_{(C,CO_2)} < \Delta G_{(C,CO)}$. So, CO_2 is a better reducing agent than CO, while above 710K, CO becomes a very good reducing agent.

(b) Generally, sulphide ores are converted to oxides before reduction as reduction of oxides can easily be done using C or CO, depending upon metal ore and temperature.

(c) FeO is removed by adding silica flux to the sulphide ore of copper in the reverberatory furnace leading to the formation of slag.

$$\underset{}{FeO}+\underset{\text{Flux}}{SiO_2} \rightarrow \underset{\text{Slag}}{FeSiO_3}$$

(d) Carbon and hydrogen are not used as reducing agents at high temperature. At high temperature, carbon and hydrogen readily form their carbides and hydrides respectively.

(e) Vapour phase refining method is used for the purification of Ti as

$$Ti + 2I_2 \xrightarrow{530\text{ K}} TiI_4 \xrightarrow{1800\text{ K}} Ti + 2I_2$$

Chapter 07

The *p*-block Elements*

Multiple Choice Questions (MCQs)

Q.1 On addition of conc. H_2SO_4 to a chloride salt, colourless fumes are evolved but in case of iodide salt, violet fumes come out. This is because

(a) H_2SO_4 reduces HI to I_2
(b) HI is of violet colour
(c) HI gets oxidised to I_2
(d) HI changes to HIO_3

Ans. *(c)* Hydrogen iodide (HI) is more stronger oxidising agent than H_2SO_4. So, it reduces H_2SO_4 to SO_2 and itself oxidises to I_2. Colour of I_2 is violet.

$$2NaCl + H_2SO_4 \longrightarrow Na_2SO_4 + 2HCl$$

$$2NaI + H_2SO_4 \longrightarrow Na_2SO_4 + 2HI \xrightarrow{H_2SO_4} 2H_2O + SO_2 + I_2$$

Q.2 In qualitative analysis when H_2S is passed through an aqueous solution of salt acidified with dil. HCl, a black precipitate is obtained. On boiling the precipitate with dil. HNO_3, it forms a solution of blue colour. Addition of excess of aqueous solution of ammonia to this solution gives ....

(a) deep blue precipitate of $Cu(OH)_2$
(b) deep blue solution of $[Cu(NH_3)_4]^{2+}$
(c) deep blue solution of $Cu(NO_3)_2$
(d) deep blue solution of $Cu(OH)_2 \cdot Cu(NO_3)_2$

Ans. *(b)* In qualitative analysis, when H_2S is passed through an aqueous solution of salt acidified with dil. HCl, a black ppt. of CuS is obtained.

$$CuSO_4 + H_2S \xrightarrow{\text{dil. HCl}} \underset{\text{black ppt}}{CuS} + H_2SO_4$$

On boiling CuS with dil. HNO_3, it forms a blue coloured solution and the following reactions occur.

$$3CuS + 8HNO_3 \longrightarrow 3Cu(NO_3)_2 + 2NO + 3S + 4H_2O$$

$$S + 2HNO_3 \longrightarrow H_2SO_4 + NO$$

$$2Cu^{2+} + SO_4^{2-} + 2NH_3 + 2H_2O \longrightarrow Cu(OH)_2 \cdot CuSO_4 + 2NH_4OH$$

$$Cu(OH)_2 \cdot CuSO_4 + 8NH_3 \longrightarrow \underset{\substack{\text{Tetraammine copper (II)} \\ \text{(Deep blue solution)}}}{2[Cu(NH_3)_4]SO_4} + 2OH^- + SO_4^{2-}$$

Note (*) This chapter has been deleted from latest NCERT.

Q.3 In a cyclotrimetaphosphoric acid molecule, how many single and double bonds are present?

(a) 3 double bonds; 9 single bonds
(b) 6 double bonds; 6 single bonds
(c) 3 double bonds; 12 single bonds
(d) Zero double bond; 12 single bonds

Ans. ***(c)*** Cyclotrimetaphosphoric acid contains three double bonds and 12 single bonds as shown below.

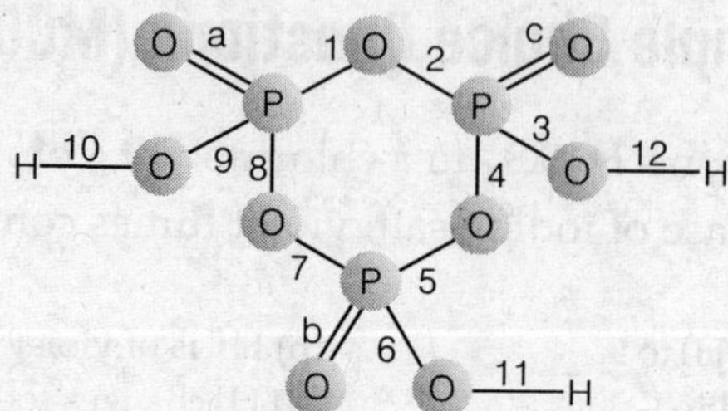

Cyclotrimetaphosphoric acid $(HPO_3)_3$

a, b, c are three π bonds and numerics 1 to 12 are sigma (σ) bonds.

Q.4 Which of the following elements can be involved in $p\pi - d\pi$ bonding?

(a) Carbon
(b) Nitrogen
(c) Phosphorus
(d) Boron

Ans. ***(c)*** Among given four elements, *i.e.*, carbon, nitrogen, phosphorus and boron. Only phosphorus has vacant *d*-orbitals, so only phosphorus has ability to form $p\pi - d\pi$ bonding.

Q.5 Which of the following pairs of ions are isoelectronic and isostructural?

(a) CO_3^{2-}, NO_3^- (b) ClO_3^-, CO_3^{2-} (c) SO_3^{2-}, NO_3^- (d) ClO_3^-, SO_3^{2-}

Ans. ***(a)*** Compounds having same value of total number of electrons are known as isoelectronic.

For CO_3^{2-}

Total number of electrons

$$= 6 + 8 \times 3 + 2$$
$$= 6 + 24 + 2$$
$$= 32$$

For NO_3^-

Total number of electrons

$$= 7 + 8 \times 3 + 1$$
$$= 7 + 25$$
$$= 32$$

Hence, CO_3^{2-} and NO_3^- are isoelectronic. These two ions have similar structure so, they are isostructural.

$$\begin{matrix} {}^{\ominus}O \\ \quad \diagdown \\ \quad\quad C{=}O \\ \quad \diagup \\ {}^{\ominus}O \end{matrix} \qquad \begin{matrix} O \\ \quad \diagdown \\ \quad\quad N{=}O \\ \quad \diagup \\ {}^{\ominus}O \end{matrix}$$

Both have triangular planar structure as in both the species, carbon and nitrogen are sp^2 hybridised. Hence, option (a) is the correct choice.

Q.6 Affinity for hydrogen decreases in the group from fluorine to iodine. Which of the halogen acids should have highest bond dissociation enthalpy?

(a) HF (b) HCl (c) HBr (d) HI

Ans. *(a)* HF | On moving from top to bottom

HCl | • Size of halogen atom increases

HBr | • H–X bond length increases

HI ↓ • Bond dissociation enthalpy decreases

Q.7 Bond dissociation enthalpy of $E—H$ (E= element) bonds is given below. Which of the compounds will act as strongest reducing agent?

Compound	NH_3	PH_3	AsH_3	SbH_3
$\Delta_{diss}(E—H)$ / kJ mol^{-1}	389	322	297	255

(a) NH_3 (b) PH_3 (c) AsH_3 (d) SbH_3

Ans. *(d)* On moving from top to bottom, size of central atom increases. Bond length of X—H bond increases and bond dissociation energy decreases. Hence, reducing nature increases.

NH_3 |

PH_3 | • Bond length increases

AsH_3 | • Bond dissociation energy decreases

SbH_3 ↓ • Reducing character increases

Hence, SbH_3 acts as strongest reducing agent among these.

Q.8 On heating with concentrated NaOH solution in an inert atmosphere of CO_2, white phosphorus gives a gas. Which of the following statement is incorrect about the gas?

(a) It is highly poisonous and has smell like rotten fish.

(b) It's solution in water decomposes in the presence of light.

(c) It is more basic than NH_3.

(d) It is less basic than NH_3.

Ans. *(c)* White phosphorous on reaction with NaOH solution in the presence of inert atmosphere of CO_2, produces phosphine gas which is less basic than NH_3.

$$P_4 + 3NaOH + 3H_2O \longrightarrow \underset{\text{(Phosphine)}}{PH_3} + \underset{\text{(sodium hypophosphite)}}{3NaH_2PO_2}$$

Q.9 Which of the following acids forms three series of salts?

(a) H_3PO_2 (b) H_3BO_3 (c) H_3PO_4 (d) H_3PO_3

● **Concept Insight** This solution includes the concept of stepwise neutralisation of H_3PO_4 and formation of salts corresponding to each ionisation stage.

Ans. *(c)* Structure of H_3PO_4 is

O
||
P
HO / | \ OH
OH

H_3PO_4 has 3 –OH groups, *i.e.*, has three ionisable H-atoms and hence, forms three series of salts. These three possible series of salts for H_3PO_4 are as follows :

$$NaH_2PO_4, Na_2HPO_4 \text{ and } Na_3PO_4$$

Q.10 Strong reducing behaviour of H_3PO_2 is due to

(a) low oxidation state of phosphorus.

(b) presence of two — OH groups and one P — H bond.

(c) presence of one — OH group and two P — H bonds.

(d) high electron gain enthalpy of phosphorus.

Ans. ***(c)*** Strong reducing behaviour of H_3PO_2 is due to presence of two P—H bonds and one P—OH bond.

O

P — H

H OH

Hypophosphorus acid
(Monobasic)

Note The existence of a P—H bond gives phosphorus oxyacids their reducing characteristics.

Q.11 On heating lead nitrate forms oxides of nitrogen and lead. The oxides formed are ....

(a) N_2O, PbO (b) NO_2, PbO (c) NO, PbO (d) NO, PbO_2

Ans. ***(b)*** On heating lead nitrate, it produces brown coloured nitrogen dioxide (NO_2) and lead (II) oxide.

$$2Pb(NO_3)_2 \xrightarrow{\Delta} 4NO_2 + 2PbO + O_2$$

Q.12 Which of the following elements does not show allotropy?

(a) Nitrogen (b) Bismuth (c) Antimony (d) Arsenic

Thinking Process To solve this question, analyse the property of allotropy, which involves the existence of an element in different structural forms.

Ans. ***(a)*** Nitrogen does not show allotropy due to its weak N—N single bond. Therefore, ability of nitrogen to form polymeric structure or more than one structure or form becomes less. Hence, nitrogen does not show allotropy.

Q.13 Maximum covalency of nitrogen is ....

(a) 3 (b) 5 (c) 4 (d) 6

Ans. ***(c)*** Maximum covalency of nitrogen is 4 in which one electron is made available by *s*-orbital and 3 electrons are made available by *p* orbitals. Hence, total four electrons are available for bonding.

Q.14 Which of the following statements is wrong?

(a) Single N—N bond is stronger than the single P—P bond.

(b) PH_3 can act as a ligand in the formation of coordination compound with transition elements.

(c) NO_2 is paramagnetic in nature.

(d) Covalency of nitrogen in N_2O_5 is four.

Ans. ***(a)*** Corrected statement (a) is that single N — N bond is weaker than the single P — P bond. This is why phosphorous show allotropy but nitrogen does not.

Other statements are correct as

(i) PH_3 acts as a ligand in the formation of coordination compound due to presence of lone pair of electrons.

(ii) NO_2 is paramagnetic in nature due to presence of one unpaired electron. Structure of NO_2 is

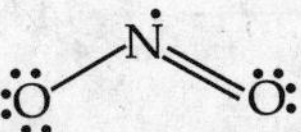

(iii) Covalency of nitrogen in N_2O_5 is 4.

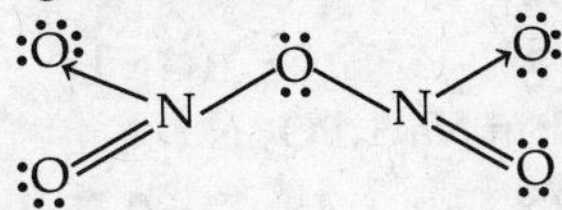

Q.15 A brown ring is formed in the ring test for NO_3^- ion. It is due to the formation of

(a) $[Fe(H_2O)_5(NO)]^{2+}$ (b) $FeSO_4 \cdot NO_2$

(c) $[Fe(H_2O)_4(NO)_2]^{2+}$ (d) $FeSO_4 \cdot HNO_3$

Ans. ***(a)*** When freshly prepared solution of $FeSO_4$ is added in a solution containing NO_3^- ion, it leads to formation of a brown coloured complex. This is known as brown ring test of nitrate.

$$NO_3^- + 3Fe^{2+} + 4H^+ \longrightarrow NO + 3Fe^{3+} + 2H_2O$$

$$[Fe(H_2O)_6]^{2+} + NO \longrightarrow \underset{\text{Brown ring}}{[Fe(H_2O)_5(NO)]^{2+}} + H_2O$$

Q.16 Elements of group- 15 form compounds in +5 oxidation state. However, bismuth forms only one well characterised compound in +5 oxidation state. The compound is

(a) Bi_2O_5 (b) BiF_5 (c) $BiCl_5$ (d) Bi_2S_5

Ans. ***(b)*** Stability of + 5 oxidation state decreases from top to bottom and + 3 oxidation state increases from top to bottom due to inert pair effect. Meanwhile, compound having + 5 oxidation state of Bi is BiF_5. It is due to smaller size and high electronegativity of fluorine.

Q.17 On heating ammonium dichromate and barium azide separately we get

(a) N_2 in both cases.

(b) N_2 with ammonium dichromate and NO with barium azide.

(c) N_2O with ammonium dichromate and N_2 with barium azide.

(d) N_2O with ammonium dichromate and NO_2 with barium azide.

Ans. ***(a)*** On heating ammonium dichromate and barium azide, it produces N_2 gas separately.

$$(NH_4)_2Cr_2O_7 \xrightarrow{\Delta} N_2 + 4H_2O + Cr_2O_3$$

$$Ba(N_3)_2 \longrightarrow Ba + 3N_2$$

Mistake Alert! *Students may make a mistake in writing the incorrect products of thermal decomposition due to the involvement of multiple nitrogen-containing compounds. They might incorrectly assume ammonium dichromate or barium azide products to be* N_2O, NO_2 *or NO.*

Q.18 In the preparation of HNO_3, we get NO gas by catalytic oxidation of ammonia. The moles of NO produced by the oxidation of two moles of NH_3 will be ....

(a) 2 (b) 3 (c) 4 (d) 6

Ans. *(a)* Two moles of NH_3 will produce 2 moles of NO on catalytic oxidation of ammonia in preparation of nitric acid.

$$4NH_3 + 5O_2 \xrightarrow[\text{Pt/ Rh gauge catalyst}]{\Delta} 4\,NO\,(g) + 6H_2O\,(l)$$

Q.19 The oxidation state of central atom in the anion of compound NaH_2PO_2 will be ....

(a) + 3 (b) + 5 (c) + 1 (d) − 3

Ans. *(c)* Let oxidation state of P in NaH_2PO_2 is x.

$$1 + 2 \times 1 + x + 2 \times -2 = 0$$
$$1 + 2 + x - 4 = 0$$
$$x - 1 = 0$$
$$x = +1$$

Q.20 Which of the following is not tetrahedral in shape?

(a) NH_4^+ (b) $SiCl_4$ (c) SF_4 (d) SO_4^{2-}

Ans. *(c)* SF_4 has sea-saw shape as shown below.

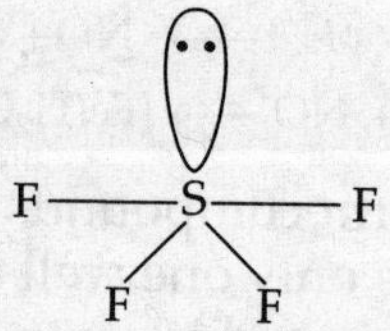

F—S—F (with lone pair on S; two F below)

It has trigonal bipyramidal geometry having sp^3d hybridisation.

Q.21 Which of the following are peroxoacids of sulphur?

(a) H_2SO_5 and $H_2S_2O_8$ (b) H_2SO_5 and $H_2S_2O_7$
(c) $H_2S_2O_7$ and $H_2S_2O_8$ (d) $H_2S_2O_6$ and $H_2S_2O_7$

Ans. *(a)* Peroxoacids of sulphur must contain one —O—O— bond as shown below.

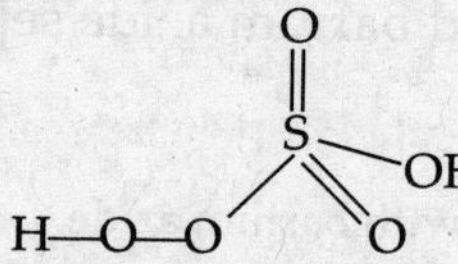

H_2SO_5 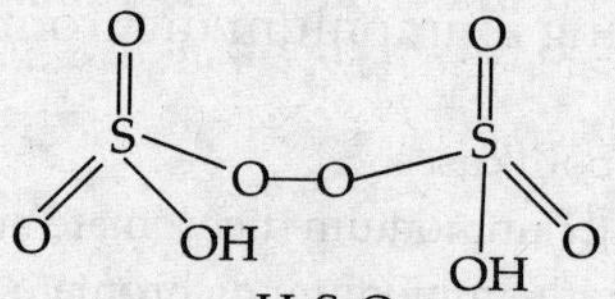 $\qquad$ $H_2S_2O_8$

Q.22 Hot conc. H_2SO_4 acts as moderately strong oxidising agent. It oxidises both metals and non-metals. Which of the following element is oxidised by conc. H_2SO_4 into two gaseous products?

(a) Cu (b) S (c) C (d) Zn

Ans. *(c)* H_2SO_4 is a moderately strong oxidising agent which oxidises both metals and non-metals as shown below.

$$Cu + 2H_2SO_4\,(conc.) \longrightarrow CuSO_4 + SO_2 + 2H_2O$$
$$S + 2H_2SO_4\,(conc.) \longrightarrow 3SO_2 + 2H_2O$$

While carbon on oxidation with H_2SO_4 produces two types of oxides CO_2 and SO_2.

$$C + 2H_2SO_4\,(\text{conc.}) \longrightarrow CO_2 + 2SO_2 + 2H_2O$$

Q.23 A black compound of manganese reacts with a halogen acid to give greenish yellow gas. When excess of this gas reacts with NH_3 an unstable trihalide is formed. In this process the oxidation state of nitrogen changes from ....

(a) – 3 to + 3
(b) – 3 to 0
(c) – 3 to + 5
(d) 0 to – 3

Ans. ***(a)*** Black coloured compound MnO_2 reacts with HCl to produce greenish yellow coloured gas of Cl_2

$$\underset{\text{(Black)}}{MnO_2} + 4HCl \longrightarrow MnCl_2 + 2H_2O + \underset{\text{(greenish yellow gas)}}{Cl_2}$$

Cl_2 on further treatment with NH_3 produces NCl_3.

$$\overset{-3}{N}H_3 + 3Cl_2 \longrightarrow \overset{+3}{N}Cl_3 + 3HCl$$

NH_3 (– 3) changes to NCl_3 (+3) in the above reaction. Hence, option (a) is the correct choice.

Q.24 In the preparation of compounds of Xe, Bartlett had taken $O_2^+PtF_6^-$ as a base compound. This is because

(a) both O_2 and Xe have same size.
(b) both O_2 and Xe have same electron gain enthalpy.
(c) both O_2 and Xe have almost same ionisation enthalpy.
(d) both Xe and O_2 are gases.

Ans. ***(c)*** Bertlett had taken $O_2^+PtF_6^-$ as a base compound because O_2 and Xe both have almost same ionisation enthalpy. The ionisation enthalpies of noble gases are the highest in their respective periods due to their stable electronic configurations.

Q.25 In solid state PCl_5 is a ....

(a) covalent solid
(b) octahedral structure
(c) ionic solid with $[PCl_6]^+$ octahedral and $[PCl_4]^-$ tetrahedral
(d) ionic solid with $[PCl_4]^+$ tetrahedral and $[PCl_6]^-$ octahedral

Ans. ***(d)*** In solid state PCl_5 exists as an ionic solid with $[PCl_4]^+$ tetrahedral and $[PCl_6]^-$ octahedral.

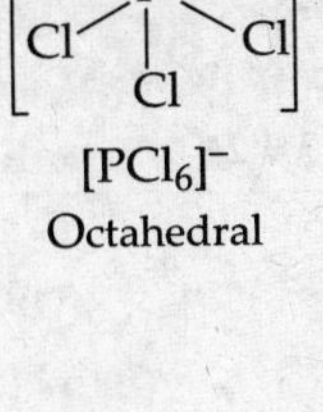

$[PCl_6]^-$
Octahedral

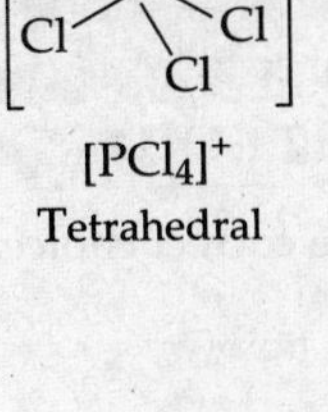

$[PCl_4]^+$
Tetrahedral

Q.26 Reduction potentials of some ions are given below. Arrange them in decreasing order of oxidising power.

Ion	ClO_4^-	IO_4^-	BrO_4^-
Reduction potential $E°/V$	$E° = 1.19$ V	$E^{\ominus} = 1.65$ V	$E^{\ominus} = 1.74$ V

(a) $ClO_4^- > IO_4^- > BrO_4^-$
(b) $IO_4^- > BrO_4^- > ClO_4^-$
(c) $BrO_4^- > IO_4^- > ClO_4^-$
(d) $BrO_4^- > ClO_4^- > IO_4^-$

Thinking Process This problem is based on concept of standard reduction potential of species and oxidising property.

Ans. ***(c)*** Greater the SRP value of species higher will be its oxidising power.

Species	$E°_{cell}$	
ClO_4^-	1.19V	▪ SRP of species increases.
IO_4^-	1.65V	▪ Oxidising power increase.
BrO_4^-	1.74V	↓

Here, SRP = standard reduction potential.

Hence, the decreasing order of oxidising powder is $BrO_4^- > IO_4^- > ClO_4^-$

Q.27 Which of the following is isoelectronic pair?

(a) ICl_2, ClO_2
(b) BrO_2^-, BrF_2^+
(c) ClO_2, BrF
(d) CN^-, O_3

Ans. ***(b)*** Isoelectronic pair have the same number of electrons.

	BrO_2^-	BrF_2^+
Total number of electrons	$= 35 + 2 \times 8 + 1$ $= 52$	$= 35 + 9 \times 2 - 1$ $= 52$

While in another cases this value is not equal.

ICl_2	ClO_2
$53 + 2 \times 17 = 87$	$17 + 16 = 33$

ClO_2	BrF
$17 + 16 = 33$	$35 + 9 = 44$

CN^-	O_3
$6 + 7 + 1 = 14$	$8 \times 3 = 24$

Hence, only (b) is the correct choice.

Multiple Choice Questions (More Than One Options)

Q.28 If chlorine gas is passed through hot NaOH solution, two changes are observed in the oxidation number of chlorine during the reaction. These are .... and ....

(a) 0 to +5 (b) 0 to +3 (c) 0 to −1 (d) 0 to +1

Ans. ***(a, c)*** When chlorine gas is passed through hot NaOH solution, it produces NaCl and $NaClO_3$.

$$6NaOH + 3\overset{0}{Cl_2} \longrightarrow 5Na\overset{-1}{Cl} + NaCl\overset{+5}{O_3} + 3H_2O$$

Oxidation state varies from 0 to − 1 and 0 to + 5.

Q.29 Which of the following options are **not** in accordance with the property mentioned against them?

(a) $F_2 > Cl_2 > Br_2 > I_2$ Oxidising power

(b) $MI > MBr > MCl > MF$ Ionic character of metal halide

(c) $F_2 > Cl_2 > Br_2 > I_2$ Bond dissociation enthalpy

(d) $HI < HBr < HCl < HF$ Hydrogen-halogen bond strength

Ans. ***(b, c)*** As ability to gain electron increases, oxidising property increases. Here, F is the most electronegative element having highest value of SRP hence, it has highest oxidising power. So correct order of oxidising power is $F_2 > Cl_2 > Br_2 > I_2$.

Order of ionic character of metal halides,

$$MI < MBr < MCl < MF$$

As electronegativity difference between metal and halogen increases ionic character increases.

$F_2 > Cl_2 > Br_2 > I_2$ is incorrect order of bond dissociation energy. Correct order is $Cl_2 > Br_2 > F_2 > I_2$ due to electronic repulsion among lone pairs in F_2 molecule.

Q.30 Which of the following is correct for P_4 molecule of white phosphorus?

(a) It has 6 lone pairs of electrons.

(b) It has six P — P single bonds.

(c) It has three P — P single bonds.

(d) It has four lone pairs of electrons.

Ans. ***(b, d)*** Structure of P_4 molecule can be represented as.

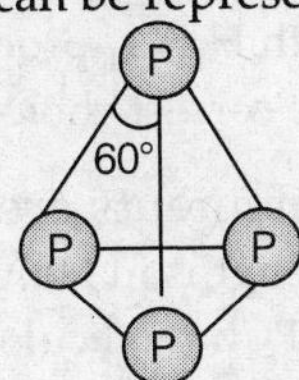

It has total four lone pairs of electrons situated at each P-atom.

It has six P—P single bond.

Q.31 Which of the following statements are correct?

(a) Among halogens, radius ratio between iodine and fluorine is maximum.

(b) Leaving F — F bond, all halogens have weaker $X - X$ bond than $X - X'$ bond in interhalogens.

(c) Among interhalogen compounds maximum number of atoms are present in iodine fluoride.

(d) Interhalogen compounds are more reactive than halogen compounds.

Ans. *(a, c, d)*

(a) Among halogens, radius ratio between iodine and fluorine is maximum because iodine has maximum radius and fluorine has minimum radius.

(b) It can be correctly stated as in general interhalogen compounds are more reactive than halogens. This is because $X - X'$ bond in interhalogen is weaker than $X - X$ bond in halogens except F—F bond.

(c) Among interhalogen compounds maximum number of atoms are present in iodine fluoride because radius ratio of iodine and fluorine has maximum value.

(d) Interhalogen compounds are more reactive than halogen compounds due to weaker $X - X'$ bond as compared to $X - X$ of halogen compounds.

Q.32 Which of the following statements are correct for SO_2 gas?

(a) It acts as bleaching agent in moist conditions.

(b) Its molecule has linear geometry.

(c) Its dilute solution is used as disinfectant.

(d) It can be prepared by the reaction of dilute H_2SO_4 with metal sulphide.

Ans. *(a, c)*

(a) In moist condition SO_2 gas acts as a bleaching agent.

e.g., it converts Fe (III) to Fe (II) ion and decolourises acidified $KMnO_4$ (VII).

$$2Fe^{3+} + SO_2 + 2H_2O \longrightarrow 2Fe^{2+} + SO_4^{2-} + 4H^+$$

(b) is incorrect as SO_2 has bent structure.

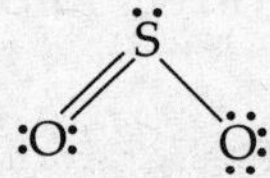

(c) Its dilute solution is used as a disinfectant.

(d) It can be prepared by the reaction of O_2 with sulphide ore,

$$4\,FeS_2 + 11O_2 \longrightarrow 2Fe_2O_3 + 8SO_2$$

While metal on treatment with H_2SO_4 produces H_2S.

Hence, options (a) and (c) are correct choices.

Q.33 Which of the following statements are correct?

(a) All the three N — O bond lengths in HNO_3 are equal.

(b) All P — Cl bond lengths in PCl_5 molecule in gaseous state are equal.

(c) P_4 molecule in white phosphorus have angular strain therefore white phosphorus is very reactive.

(d) PCl_5 is ionic in solid state in which cation is tetrahedral and anion is octahedral.

Ans. ***(c, d)***

(a) All the three N—O bond lengths in HNO_3 are not equal.

(b) All P—Cl bond lengths in PCl_5 molecule in gaseous state are not equal. Axial bond is longer than equatorial bond.

(c) P_4 molecule in white phosphorous have angular strain therefore white phosphorous is very reactive.

(d) PCl_5 is ionic in solid state in which cation is tetrahedral and anion is octahedral.

Cation – $[PCl_4]^+$
Anion – $[PCl_6]^-$

Q.34 Which of the following orders are correct as per the properties mentioned against each?

(a) $As_2O_3 < SiO_2 < P_2O_3 < SO_2$	Acid strength.
(b) $AsH_3 < PH_3 < NH_3$	Enthalpy of vapourisation.
(c) $S < O < Cl < F$	More negative electron gain enthalpy.
(d) $H_2O > H_2S > H_2Se > H_2Te$	Thermal stability.

Ans. ***(a, d)***

(a) $\xrightarrow[\text{acidic strength increases}]{As_2O_3 < SiO_2 < P_2O_3 < SO_2}$

(b) Correct order is $\xleftarrow[\text{enthalpy of vaporisation}]{AsH_3 > PH_3 > NH_3}$

(c) $S < O < F < Cl$ More negative electron gain enthalpy.

(d) $H_2O > H_2S > H_2Se > H_2Te$ Thermal stability decreases on moving from top to bottom due to increase in its bond length.

Q.35 Which of the following statements are correct?

(a) S—S bond is present in $H_2S_2O_6$.

(b) In peroxosulphuric acid (H_2SO_5) sulphur is in +6 oxidation state.

(c) Iron powder along with Al_2O_3 and K_2O is used as a catalyst in the preparation of NH_3 by Haber's process.

(d) Change in enthalpy is positive for the preparation of SO_3 by catalytic oxidation of SO_2.

Ans. ***(a, b)*** (a) Structure of $H_2S_2O_6$ is as shown below.

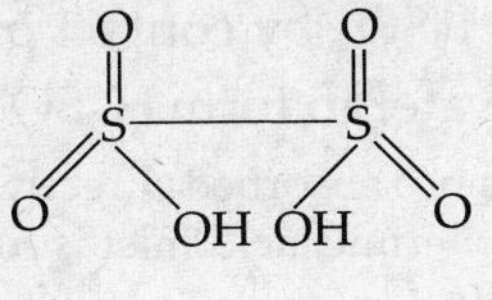

O O
S—S
O OH OH O

It contains one S—S bond.

(b) In peroxosulphuric acid (H_2SO_5) sulphur is in + 6 oxidation state.

Structure of H_2SO_5 is

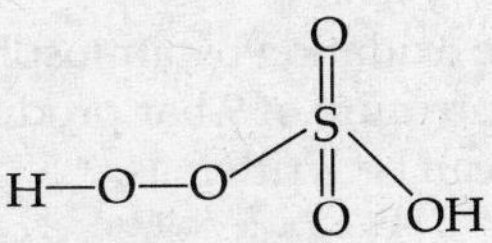

O
H—O—O—S—OH
O

In H_2SO_5, there is a peroxo-linkage.

(c) During preparation of ammonia, iron oxide with small amount of K_2O and Al_2O_3 is used as a catalyst to increase the rate of attainment of equilibrium.

(d) Change in enthalpy is negative for preparation of SO_3 by catalytic oxidation of SO_2.

Q.36 In which of the following reactions conc. H_2SO_4 is used as an oxidising reagent?

(a) $CaF_2 + H_2SO_4 \longrightarrow CaSO_4 + 2HF$

(b) $2HI + H_2SO_4 \longrightarrow I_2 + SO_2 + 2H_2O$

(c) $Cu + 2H_2SO_4 \longrightarrow CuSO_4 + SO_2 + 2H_2O$

(d) $NaCl + H_2SO_4 \longrightarrow NaHSO_4 + HCl$

Ans. *(b, c)* In the above given four reactions, (b) and (c) represent oxidising behaviour of H_2SO_4. As we know that oxidising agent reduces itself as oxidation state of central atom decreases.

Here, $$2\overset{-1}{HI} + H_2\overset{+6}{S}O_4 \longrightarrow \overset{0}{I_2} + \overset{+4}{S}O_2 + 2H_2O$$

$$\overset{0}{Cu} + 2H_2\overset{+6}{S}O_4 \longrightarrow \overset{+2}{Cu}SO_4 + \overset{+4}{S}O_2 + 2H_2O$$

Q.37 Which of the following statements are true?

(a) Only type of interactions between particles of noble gases are due to weak dispersion forces.

(b) Ionisation enthalpy of molecular oxygen is very close to that of xenon.

(c) Hydrolysis of XeF_6 is a redox reaction.

(d) Xenon fluorides are not reactive.

Ans. *(a, b)*

(a) Only one type of interactions between particles of noble gases are due to weak dispersion forces.

(b) Ionisation enthalpy of molecular oxygen is very close to that of xenon. This is the reason for the formation of xenon oxides.

(c) Hydrolysis of XeF_6 $(\overset{+6}{Xe}\overset{-1}{F_6} + 3\overset{+1}{H_2}\overset{-2}{O} \longrightarrow \overset{+6}{Xe}\overset{-2}{O_3} + 3\overset{+1}{H}\overset{-1}{F})$ is not a redox reaction.

(d) Xenon fluorides are highly reactive and they undergo hydrolysis readily even by traces of water.

Short Answer Type Questions

Q.38 In the preparation of H_2SO_4 by contact process, why is SO_3 not absorbed directly in water to form H_2SO_4?

Ans. In Contact process, SO_3 is not absorbed directly in water to from H_2SO_4 because the reaction is highly exothermic, acid mist is formed. Hence, the reaction becomes difficult to handle.

Q.39 Write a balanced chemical equation for the reaction showing catalytic oxidation of NH_3 by atmospheric oxygen.

Ans. Ammonia (NH_3) on catalytic oxidation by atmospheric oxygen in presence of Rh/Pt gauge at 500K under pressure of 9 bar produces nitrous oxide.
Balanced chemical reaction can be written as.

$$4NH_3 + \underset{\text{From air}}{5O_2} \xrightarrow[\text{500 K; 9 bar}]{\text{Pt/Rh gauge catalyst}} 4NO + 6H_2O$$

Q.40 Write the structure of pyrophosphoric acid.

Ans. Molecular formula of pyrophosphoric acid is $H_4P_2O_7$ and its structure is as follows.

Pyrophosphoric acid ($H_4P_2O_7$)

Q.41 PH_3 forms bubbles when passed slowly in water but NH_3 dissolves. Explain why?

Ans. Dissolution of NH_3 and PH_3 in water can be explained on the basis of H-bonding. NH_3 forms H-bond with water, so it is soluble but PH_3 does not form H-bond with water so it remains as gas and forms bubble in water.

Q.42 In PCl_5, phosphorus is in sp^3d hybridised state but all its five bonds are not equivalent. Justify your answer with reason.

Ans. PCl_5 has trigonal bipyramidal geometry, in which two Cl atoms occupy axial position while three occupy equatorial positions. All five P—Cl bonds are not identical. There are two types of bond lengths (i) Axial bond lengths (ii) Equatorial bond lengths

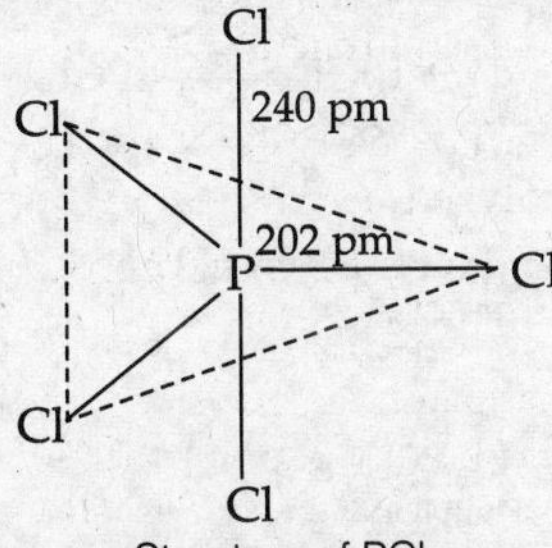

Structure of PCl_5

Thus, difference in bond length is due to fact that axial bond pairs suffer more repulsion as compared to equatorial bond pairs.

Q.43 Why is nitric oxide paramagnetic in gaseous state but the solid obtained on cooling it is diamagnetic?

Ans. In gaseous state, NO_2 exists as a monomer which has one unpaired electron but in solid state, it dimerises to N_2O_4, so no unpaired electron left. Therefore, NO_2 is paramagnetic in gaseous state but diamagnetic in solid state.

Gaseous state (Monomer) → Solid state (Dimer)

Q.44 Give one reason to explain why ClF_3 exists but FCl_3 does not exist?

Ans. Existence of ClF_3 and FCl_3 can be explained on the basis of size of central atom. Because fluorine is more electronegative as compared to chlorine and has smaller size, thus, one large Cl atom can accomodate three smaller F atoms but reverse is not true.

Q.45 Out of H_2O and H_2S, which one has higher bond angle and why?

Ans. Bond angle of H_2O (H—O—H = 104.5°) is larger than that of H_2S (H—S—H = 92°) because oxygen is more electronegative than sulphur therefore, bond pair electron of O—H bond will be closer to oxygen and there will be more bond pair—bond pair repulsion between bond pairs of two O—H bonds.

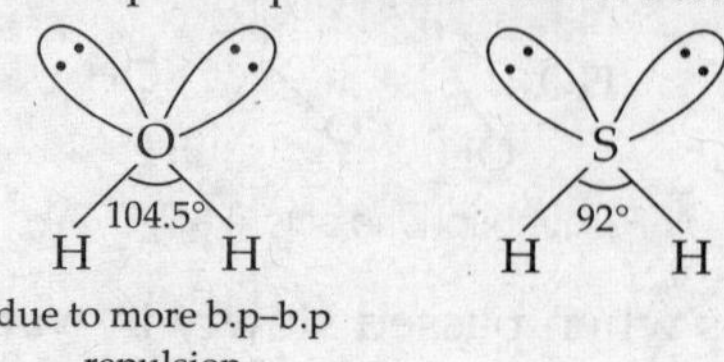

due to more b.p–b.p repulsion

Q.46 SF_6 is known but SCl_6 is not. Why?

Ans. Fluorine atom is smaller in size so, six F^- ions can surround a sulphur atom. The case is not so with chlorine atom due to its large size. So, SF_6 is known but SCl_6 is not known due to interionic repulsion between larger Cl^- ions.

Q.47 On reaction with Cl_2, phosphorus forms two types of halides '*A*' and '*B*'. Halide '*A*' is yellowish-white powder but halide '*B*' is colourless oily liquid. Identify *A* and *B* and write the formulae of their hydrolysis products.

Ans. Phosphorus on reaction with Cl_2 forms two types of halides *A* and *B*. '*A*' is PCl_5 and '*B*' is PCl_3.

$$P_4 + 10Cl_2 \longrightarrow 4PCl_5$$
$$P_4 + 6Cl_2 \longrightarrow 4PCl_3$$

When '*A*' and '*B*' are hydrolysed

(a) $\underset{\substack{[A]\\\text{Phosphorus}\\\text{pentachloride}}}{PCl_5} + 4H_2O \longrightarrow \underset{\substack{\text{Phosphoric}\\\text{acid}}}{H_3PO_4} + 5HCl$

(b) $\underset{\substack{[B]\\\text{Phosphorus}\\\text{trichloride}}}{PCl_3} + 3H_2O \longrightarrow \underset{\substack{\text{Phosphorus}\\\text{acid}}}{H_3PO_3} + 3HCl$

Q.48 In the ring test of NO_3^- ion, Fe^{2+} ion reduces nitrate ion to nitric oxide, which combines with Fe^{2+} (*aq*) ion to form brown complex. Write the reactions involved in the formation of brown ring.

Ans. $NO_3^- + 3Fe^{2+} + 4H^+ \longrightarrow NO + 3Fe^{3+} + 2H_2O$

$[Fe(H_2O)_6]^{2+} + NO \longrightarrow \underset{\text{Brown ring}}{[Fe(H_2O)_5NO]^{2+}} + H_2O$

This test is known as brown ring test of nitrates generally used to identify the presence of nitrate ion in given solution.

Q.49 Explain why the stability of oxoacids of chlorine increases in the order given below.

$$HClO < HClO_2 < HClO_3 < HClO_4$$

Ans. Oxygen is more electronegative than chlorine, therefore dispersal of negative charge present on chlorine increases from ClO^- to ClO_4^- ion because number of oxygen atoms attached to chlorine is increasing.Therefore, stability of ions will increase in the order given below.

$$ClO^- < ClO_2^- < ClO_3^- < ClO_4^-$$

Due to increase in stability of conjugate base, acidic strength of corresponding acid increases in the same order.

$$HClO < HClO_2 < HClO_3 < HClO_4$$

Q.50 Explain why ozone is thermodynamically less stable than oxygen?

Ans. Ozone is thermodynamically less stable than oxygen because its decomposition into oxygen results in the liberation of heat (ΔH is negative) and an increase in entropy (ΔS is positive). These two effects reinforce each other, resulting in large negative Gibbs energy change (ΔG) for its conversion into oxygen.

Q.51 P_4O_6 reacts with water according to equation $P_4O_6 + 6H_2O \longrightarrow 4H_3PO_3$. Calculate the volume of 0.1 M NaOH solution required to neutralise the acid formed by dissolving 1.1 g of P_4O_6 in H_2O.

● **Concept Insight** This problem includes conceptual mixing of chemical properties of oxides of phosphorus, mole concept and stoichiometry.

Ans. $P_4O_6 + 6H_2O \longrightarrow 4H_3PO_3$ ...(i)

Neutralisation $H_3PO_3 + 2NaOH \longrightarrow Na_2HPO_3 + 2H_2O] \times 4$ ...(ii)

Adding Eqs. (i) and (ii)

$$\underset{1\text{mol}}{P_4O_6} + \underset{8\text{ mol}}{8NaOH} \longrightarrow 4Na_2HPO_3 + 2H_2O \quad ...(iii)$$

Number of moles of P_4O_6, $n = \frac{m}{M} = \frac{1.1}{220} = \frac{1}{200}$ mol

(Molar mass of $P_4O_6 = (4 \times 31) + (6 \times 16) = 220$)

$\because$ Product formed by 1 mole of P_4O_6 is neutralised by 8 moles NaOH.

$\therefore$ Product formed by $\frac{1}{200}$ moles of P_4O_6 will be neutralised by NaOH

$$= 8 \times \frac{1}{200} = \frac{8}{200} \text{ mole NaOH.}$$

Given, Molarity of NaOH = 0.1 M = 0.1 mol/L

$$\text{Molarity} = \frac{\text{Number of moles}}{\text{Volume in litres}}$$

$$\text{Volume} = \frac{\text{Number of moles}}{\text{Molarity}} = \frac{8}{200} \times \frac{1}{0.1} = 0.4 \text{ L or } 400 \text{ mL}$$

$\therefore$ 400 mL NaOH is required.

Q.52 White phosphorus reacts with chlorine and the product hydrolyses in the presence of water. Calculate the mass of HCl obtained by the hydrolysis of the product formed by the reaction of 62 g of white phosphorus with chlorine in the presence of water.

Thinking Process This problem is based on the concept of chemical reaction of phosphorus and stoichiometry. Write balanced chemical reaction and then calculate the amount of HCl produced.

Ans. Equations for the reactions

$$P_4 + 6Cl_2 \longrightarrow 4PCl_3$$

$$PCl_3 + 3H_2O \longrightarrow H_3PO_3 + 3HCl] \times 4 \text{ (}PCl_3\text{ is hydrolysed)}$$

$$\underset{\substack{1\text{ mol}\\31 \times 4 = 124\text{ g}}}{P_4} + 6Cl_2 + 12H_2O \longrightarrow 4H_3PO_3 + \underset{\substack{12\text{ mol}\\12 \times 36.5 = 438.0\text{ g}}}{12HCl}$$

$\because$ 124 g of white phosphorus produces HCl = 438 g

$\therefore$ 62 g of white phosphorus will produces HCl $= \frac{438}{124} \times 62 = 219.0$ g HCl

Q.53 Name three oxoacids of nitrogen. Write the disproportionation reaction of that oxoacid of nitrogen in which nitrogen is in + 3 oxidation state.

Ans. Three oxoacids of nitrogen having oxidation state + 3 are

(a) HNO_2, nitrous acid

(b) HNO_3, nitric acid

(c) Hyponitrous acid, $H_2N_2O_2$

In HNO_2, N is in + 3 oxidation state and its disproportionation reaction is :

$$3HNO_2 \xrightarrow{\text{Disproportionation}} HNO_3 + H_2O + 2NO$$

Q.54 Nitric acid forms an oxide of nitrogen on reaction with P_4O_{10}. Write the reaction involved. Also write the resonating structures of the oxide of nitrogen formed.

Ans. P_4O_{10} on reaction with HNO_3 forms HPO_3 and N_2O_5.

$$4HNO_3 + P_4O_{10} \longrightarrow 4HPO_3 + 2N_2O_5$$

Resonating structures of N_2O_5 are

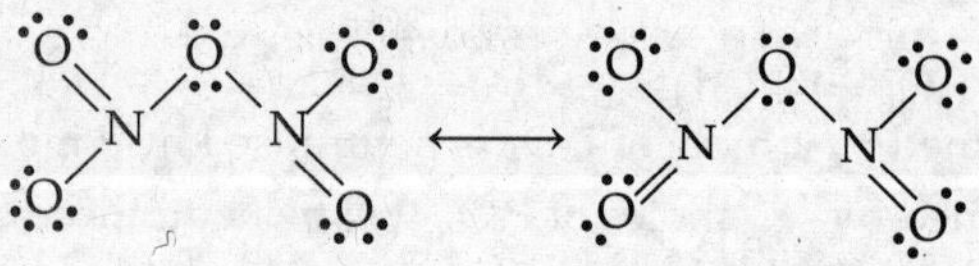

Q.55 Phosphorus has three allotropic forms—(i) white phosphorus (ii) red phosphorus and (iii) black phosphorus. Write the difference between white, red and black phosphorus on the basis of their structure and reactivity.

Ans. Phosphorus has three allotropic forms

	White phosphorus	Red phosphorus	Black phosphorus
1.	It is less stable form of P	More stable than white P.	It is most stable form of P
2.	It is highly reactive.	Less reactive than white P.	It is least reactive.
3.	It has regular tetrahedron structure.	It has polymeric structure.	It has a layered structure.

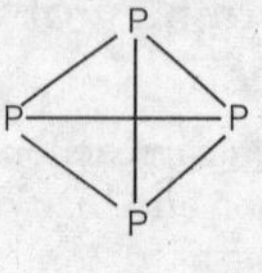

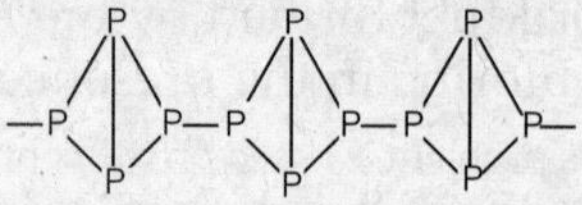

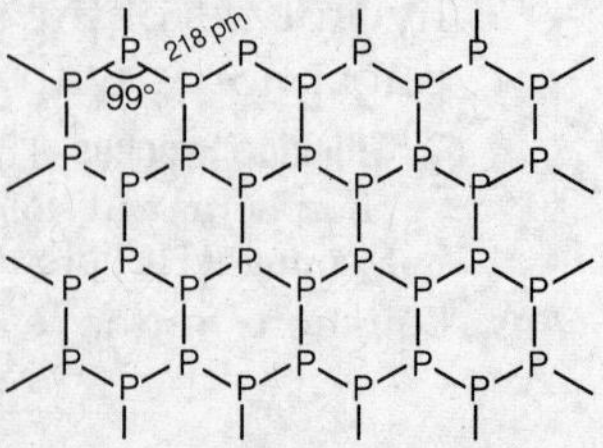

Q.56 Give an example to show the effect of concentration of nitric acid on the formation of oxidation product.

Ans. Effect of concentration of nitric acid on the formation of oxidation product can be understood by its reaction with copper. Dilute and concentrated nitric acid give different oxidation products on reaction with copper metal.

$$3Cu + 8HNO_3(Dil.) \longrightarrow 3Cu(NO_3)_2 + 2NO + 4H_2O$$
$$Cu + 4HNO_3(Conc.) \longrightarrow Cu(NO_3)_2 + 2NO_2 + 2H_2O$$

Q.57 PCl_5 reacts with finely divided silver on heating and a white silver salt is obtained, which dissolves on adding excess aqueous NH_3 solution. Write the reactions involved to explain what happens.

Ans. PCl_5 on reaction with finely divided silver produced silver halide.

$$PCl_5 + 2Ag \longrightarrow 2AgCl + PCl_3$$

AgCl on further reaction with aqueous ammonia solution produces a soluble complex of $[Ag(NH_3)_2]^+Cl^-$

$$AgCl + 2NH_3(aq) \longrightarrow \underset{\text{Soluble complex}}{[Ag(NH_3)_2]^+Cl^-}$$

Q.58 Phosphorus forms a number of oxoacids. Out of these oxoacids, phosphinic acid has strong reducing property. Write its structure and also write a reaction showing its reducing behaviour.

Ans. Among various forms of oxoacids, phosphinic acid (H_3PO_2) has stronger reducing property.

```
      O
      ‖
      P
   H ⁄ ⁄ \ OH
     H
```

Structure of phosphinic acid

Reaction showing reducing behaviour of phosphinic acid is as follows.

$$4AgNO_3 + 2H_2O + H_3PO_2 \longrightarrow 4Ag\downarrow + 4HNO_3 + H_3PO_4$$

Matching The Columns

Q.59 Match the compounds given in Column I with the hybridisation and shape given in Column II and mark the correct option.

Column I	Column II
A. XeF_6	1. sp^3d^3-distorted octahedral
B. XeO_3	2. sp^3d^2-square planar
C. $XeOF_4$	3. sp^3-pyramidal
D. XeF_4	4. sp^3d^2-square pyramidal

Codes

	A	B	C	D		A	B	C	D
(a)	1	3	4	2	(b)	1	2	4	3
(c)	4	3	1	2	(d)	4	1	2	3

Ans. (a) **A.** → (1) **B.** → (3) **C.** → (4) **D.** → (2)

S. No.	Compound	Hybridisation
A.	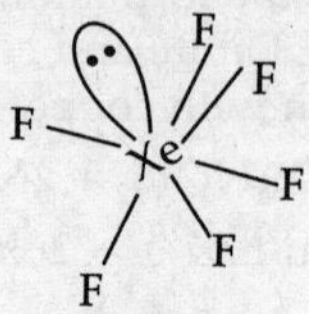 XeF_6	sp^3d^3-distorted octahedral
B.	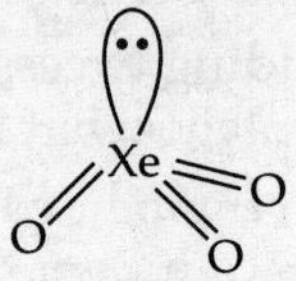 XeO_3	sp^3-pyramidal
C.	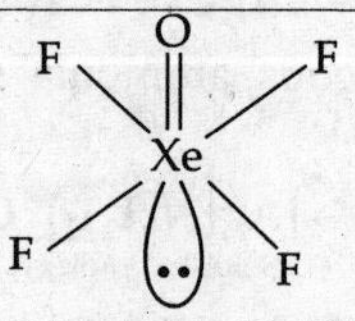 $XeOF_4$	sp^3d^2-square pyramidal
D.	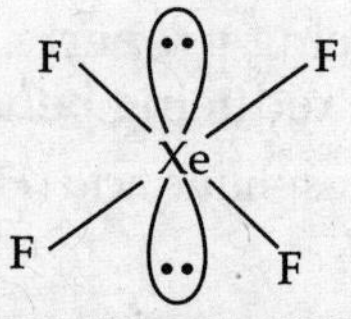 XeF_4	sp^3d^2-square planar

Q.60 Match the formulas of oxides given in Column I with the type of oxide given in Column II and mark the correct option.

Column I		Column II	
A.	Pb_3O_4	1.	Neutral oxide
B.	N_2O	2.	Acidic oxide
C.	Mn_2O_7	3.	Basic oxide
D.	Bi_2O_3	4.	Mixed oxide

Codes

	A	B	C	D
(a)	1	2	3	4
(b)	4	1	2	3
(c)	3	2	4	1
(d)	4	3	1	2

Ans. (b) **A.** → (4) **B.** → (1) **C.** → (2) **D.** → (3)

	Formulas of the compound	Type of oxide
A.	Pb_3O_4 $(PbO \cdot Pb_2O_3)$	Mixed oxide
B.	N_2O	Neutral oxide
C.	Mn_2O_7	Acidic oxide
D.	Bi_2O_3	Basic oxide

Note Mn_2O_7 on dissolution in water produces acidic solution.
Bi_2O_3 on dissolution in water produces basic solution.

Q.61 Match the items of Columns I with column II and mark the correct option.

Column I		Column II	
A.	H_2SO_4	1.	Highest electron gain enthalpy
B.	CCl_3NO_2	2.	Chalcogen
C.	Cl_2	3.	Tear gas
D.	Sulphur	4.	Storage batteries

Codes

	A	B	C	D		A	B	C	D
(a)	4	3	1	2	(b)	3	4	1	2
(c)	4	1	2	3	(d)	2	1	3	4

Ans. ***(a)*** **A.** → (4) **B.** → (3) **C.** → (1) **D.** → (2)

A. H_2SO_4 is used in storage batteries.

B. CCl_3NO_2 is known as tear gas.

C. Cl_2 has highest electron gain enthalpy.

D. Sulphur is a member of chalcogen, *i.e.*, ore producing elements.

Q.62 Match the species given in Column I with the shape given in Column II and mark the correct option.

Column I		Column II	
A.	SF_4	1.	Tetrahedral
B.	BrF_3	2.	Pyramidal
C.	BrO_3^-	3.	See-saw shaped
D.	NH_4^+	4.	Bent T-shaped

Codes

	A	B	C	D		A	B	C	D
(a)	3	2	1	4	(b)	3	4	2	1
(c)	1	2	3	4	(d)	1	4	3	2

Ans. ***(b)*** **A.** → (3) **B.** → (4) **C.** → (2) **D.** → (1)

	Species	Shape	Structure
A.	SF_4	See-saw shaped	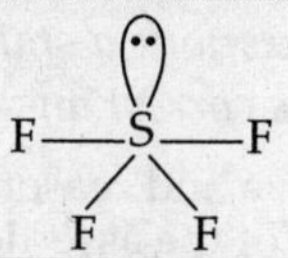 F—S—F, F, F (with lone pair on S)
B.	BrF_3	Bent T-shaped	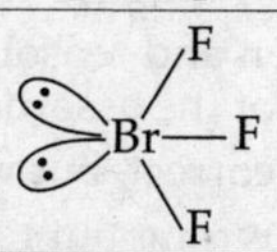 Br—F, F, F (with two lone pairs on Br)
C.	BrO_3	Pyramidal	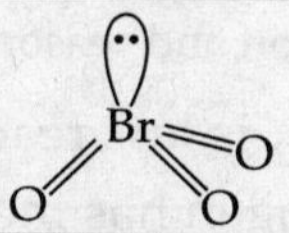 Br=O, O, O (with lone pair on Br)
D.	NH_4^+	Tetrahedral	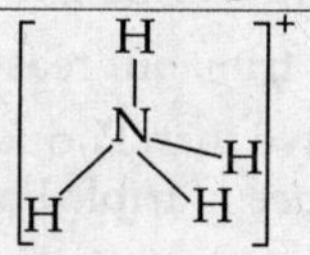 $[NH_4]^+$: N bonded to H, H, H, H

Q.63 Match the items of Columns I with Column II and mark the correct option.

	Column I		Column II
A.	Its partial hydrolysis does not change oxidation state of central atom.	1.	He
B.	It is used in modern diving apparatus.	2.	XeF_6
C.	It is used to provide inert atmosphere for filling electrical bulbs.	3.	XeF_4
D.	Its central atom is in sp^3d^2 hybridisation.	4.	Ar

Codes

	A	B	C	D		A	B	C	D
(a)	1	4	2	3	(b)	1	2	3	4
(c)	2	1	4	3	(d)	1	3	2	4

Ans. ***(c)*** **A.** → (2) **B.** → (1) **C.** → (4) **D.** → (3)

(A) Partial hydrolysis of XeF_6 does not change oxidation state of central atom.

$$\overset{+6}{Xe}F_6 + 2H_2O \longrightarrow \overset{+6}{Xe}O_3 + 6HF$$

(B) He is used in modern diving apparatus.

(C) Ar is used to provide inert atmosphere for filling electrical bulbs.

(D) Central atom (Xe) of XeF_4 is in sp^3d^2 hybridisation.

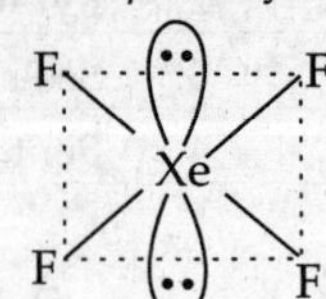

Square planar geometry

Assertion and Reason

In the following questions a statement of Assertion followed by a statement of Reason is given. Choose the correct answer out of the following choices.

(a) Both assertion and reason are correct statements, and reason is the correct explanation of the assertion.

(b) Both assertion and reason are correct statements, and reason is not the correct explanation of the assertion.

(c) Assertion is correct, but reason is wrong statement.

(d) Assertion is wrong but reason is correct statement.

(e) Both assertion and reason are wrong statements.

Q.64 **Assertion** N_2 is less reactive than P_4.

Reason Nitrogen has more electron gain enthalpy than phosphorus.

Ans. ***(c)*** Assertion is true, but reason is false.

N_2 is less reactive than P_4 due to its high value of bond dissociation energy which is due to presence of triple bond between two N-atoms of N_2 molecule.

Q.65 Assertion HNO_3 makes iron passive.

Reason HNO_3 forms a protective layer of ferric nitrate on the surface of iron.

Ans. *(c)* Assertion is true, but reason is false.
HNO_3 makes iron passive due to formation of passive form of oxide on the surface. Hence, Fe does not dissolve in conc. HNO_3 solution.

Q.66 Assertion HI cannot be prepared by the reaction of KI with concentrated H_2SO_4.

Reason HI has lowest H—X bond strength among halogen acids.

Ans. *(b)* Both assertion and reason are correct statements, but reason is not the correct explanation of the assertion.

HI cannot be prepared by the reaction of KI with concentrated H_2SO_4 because HI is converted into I_2 on reaction with H_2SO_4.

HI has the lowest H–*X* bond strength among halogen acids because of the largest size of iodine among the halogens.

Q.67 Assertion Both rhombic and monoclinic sulphur exist as S_8 but oxygen exists as O_2.

Reason Oxygen forms $p\pi$ - $p\pi$ multiple bond due to small size and small bond length but $p\pi$ - $p\pi$ bonding is not possible in sulphur.

Ans. *(a)* Both assertion and reason are correct statements, and reason is the correct explanation of the assertion.

Both rhombic and monoclinic sulphur exist as S_8 but oxygen exists as O_2, because oxygen forms $p\pi$ - $p\pi$ multiple bond due to its small size and small bond length. But $p\pi$ -$p\pi$ bonding is not possible in sulphur due to its bigger size as compared to oxygen.

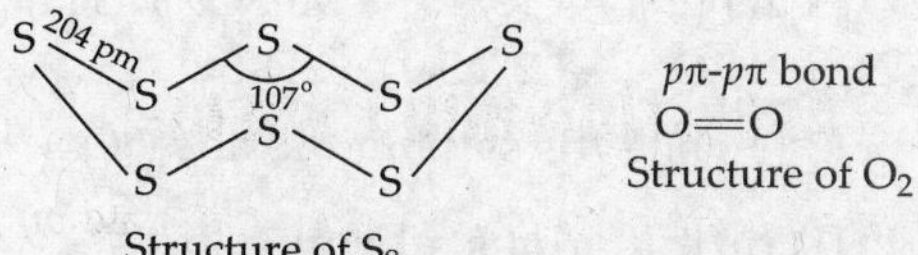

Structure of S_8

Structure of O_2

Q.68 Assertion NaCl reacts with concentrated H_2SO_4 to give colourless fumes with pungent smell. But on adding MnO_2 the fumes become greenish yellow.

Reason MnO_2 oxidises HCl to chlorine gas which is greenish yellow.

Ans. *(a)* Both assertion and reason are correct statements, and reason is the correct explanation of the assertion.

NaCl reacts with concentrated H_2SO_4 to give colourless fumes with pungent smell. Pungent smell is due to formation of HCl.

$$NaCl + H_2SO_4 \longrightarrow Na_2SO_4 + 2HCl$$

But on adding MnO_2 the fumes become greenish yellow due to formation of chlorine gas.

$$MnO_2 + 2H_2SO_4 + 2NaCl \longrightarrow MnSO_4 + Na_2SO_4 + Cl_2 + 2H_2O$$

Q.69 **Assertion** SF_6 cannot be hydrolysed but SF_4 can be.

Reason Six F-atoms in SF_6 prevent the attack of H_2O on sulphur atom of SF_6.

Ans. *(a)* Assertion and reason both are true and reason is the correct explanation of assertion.

SF_4 can be hydrolysed but SF_6 cannot because six F-atoms in SF_6 prevent the attack of H_2O on sulphur atoms of SF_6.

Long Answer Type Questions

Q.70 An amorphous solid "A" burns in air to form a gas "B" which turns lime water milky. The gas is also produced as a by-product during roasting of sulphide ore. This gas decolourises acidified aqueous $KMnO_4$ solution and reduces Fe^{3+} to Fe^{2+}. Identify the solid "A" and the gas "B" and write the reactions involved.

Thinking Process This problem is based on concept of properties of sulphur and its oxide.

Ans. $\underset{\text{(Amorphous solid)}}{A} \xrightarrow{\text{Burn in air}} \underset{\text{(gas)}}{B}$ Since, the by-product of roasting of sulphide ore is SO_2, so

$'A' = S_8$; $'B' = SO_2$

Reactions

(i) $S_8 + 8O_2 \longrightarrow \underset{(B)}{8SO_2}$

(ii) $2ZnS + 3O_2 \longrightarrow 2ZnO + \underset{(B)}{2SO_2}$

(iii) $2KMnO_4 + 5SO_2 + 2H_2O \longrightarrow K_2SO_4 + MnSO_4 + 2H_2SO_4$

(iv) $Fe_2(SO_4)_3 + SO_2 + 2H_2O \longrightarrow 2FeSO_4 + 2H_2SO_4$

Hence, *A* is sulphur (S_8) while *B* is sulphur dioxide (SO_2).

Q.71 On heating lead (II) nitrate gives a brown gas "*A*". The gas "*A*" on cooling changes to colourless solid "*B*". Solid "*B*" on heating with NO changes to a blue solid '*C*'. Identify '*A*', '*B*' and '*C*' and also write reactions involved and draw the structures of '*B*' and '*C*'.

Thinking Process This problem is based on the preparation and properties of NO_2.

Ans. $Pb(NO_3)_2$ on heating produces a brown coloured gas which may be NO_2. On cooling NO_2 changes to N_2O_4 and on heating N_2O_4 with NO, it changes to N_2O_3.

$$2Pb(NO_3)_2 \xrightarrow{\text{Heat}} 2PbO + \underset{(A)}{4NO_2} + O_2$$

$$2NO_2 \xrightarrow{\text{cooling}} \underset{(B)}{N_2O_4}$$

$$2NO + \underset{(B)}{N_2O_4} \xrightarrow{\text{Heating}} \underset{\substack{\text{(Blue Solid)} \\ (C)}}{2N_2O_3}$$

Structures

(i) N_2O_4

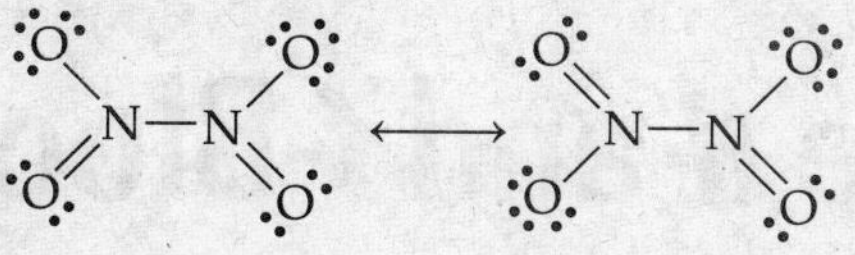

(ii) N_2O_3

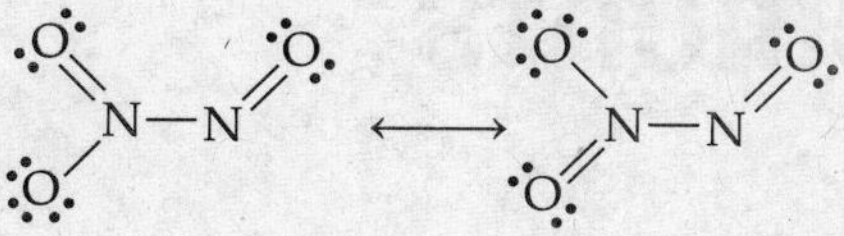

Q.72 On heating compound gives a gas (*B*) which is a constituent of air. This gas when treated with 3 moles of hydrogen (H_2) in the presence of a catalyst gives another gas (*C*) which is basic in nature. Gas *C* on further oxidation in moist condition gives a compound (*D*) which is a part of acid rain. Identify compounds to (*D*) and also give necessary equations of all the steps involved.

Ans. The main constituents of air are nitrogen (78%) and oxygen (21%). Only N_2 reacts with three moles of H_2 in the presence of a catalyst to give NH_3 (ammonia) which is a gas having basic nature. On oxidation, NH_3 gives NO_2 which is a part of acid rain. So, the compounds *A* to *D* are

$$A = NH_4NO_2;\ B = N_2;\ C = NH_3;\ D = HNO_3$$

Reactions involved can be given as

(i) $\underset{(A)}{NH_4NO_2} \xrightarrow{\Delta} \underset{(B)}{N_2} + 2H_2O$

(ii) $\underset{(B)}{N_2} + 3H_2 \underset{\text{Catalyst}}{\rightleftharpoons} \underset{(C)}{2NH_3}$

(iii) $4NH_3 + 5O_2 \xrightarrow{\text{Oxidation}} 4NO + 6H_2O$

(iv) $2NO + O_2 \longrightarrow 2NO_2$

(v) $3NO_2 + H_2O \longrightarrow \underset{(D)}{2HNO_3} + NO$

Chapter 08

The *d* and *f*-Block Elements

Multiple Choice Questions (MCQs)

Q.1 Electronic configuration of a transition element X in +3 oxidation state is $[Ar]3d^5$. What is its atomic number?

(a) 25 (b) 26 (c) 27 (d) 24

Ans. ***(b)*** Electronic configuration of X^{3+} is $[Ar]3d^5$

It represents the total number of $e^{\ominus}$ and oxidation state.

Therefore, atomic number of X = 18 + 5 + 3 = 26

Hence, option (b) is correct.

Q.2 The electronic configuration of Cu(II) is $3d^9$ whereas that of Cu (I) is $3d^{10}$. Which of the following is correct?

(a) Cu(II) is more stable

(b) Cu(II) is less stable

(c) Cu(I) and Cu(II) are equally stable

(d) Stability of Cu(I) and Cu(II) depends on nature of copper salts

Ans. ***(a)*** Cu (II) is more stable than Cu (I) despite Cu(I) having a more stable $3d^{10}$ configuration, while Cu (II) has $3d^9$ configuration. The greater effective nuclear charge in Cu(II) makes it more stable as it holds 17 electrons compared to 18 in Cu(I).

Q.3 Metallic radii of some transition elements are given below. Which of these elements will have highest density?

Element	Fe	Co	Ni	Cu
Metallic radii/pm	126	125	125	128

(a) Fe (b) Ni (c) Co (d) Cu

Thinking Process This problem is based on the concept of decreasing metallic radius and increasing atomic mass across a period, leading to higher density for elements like Cu.

Ans. ***(d)*** On moving from left to right along a period, metallic radius decreases while atomic mass increases. Decrease in metallic radius coupled with increase in atomic mass results in increase in density of metal. (Density is mass by volume (r^3)).

Hence, among the given four choices, Cu belongs to right side of Periodic Table in transition metal, and it has highest density (89 g/cm^3).

Q.4 Generally, transition elements form coloured salts due to the presence of unpaired electrons. Which of the following compounds will be coloured in solid state?

(a) Ag_2SO_4 (b) CuF_2 (c) ZnF_2 (d) Cu_2Cl_2

- **Concept Insight** This solution includes the concept of electron pairing in transition metal compounds.

Ans. ***(b)*** CuF_2 is colored in the solid state due to the unpaired electron in Cu^{2+}, which undergoes electronic transition by absorbing light energy.

Q.5 On addition of small amount of $KMnO_4$ to concentrated H_2SO_4, a green oily compound is obtained which is highly explosive in nature. Identify the compound from the following.

(a) Mn_2O_7 (b) MnO_2
(c) $MnSO_4$ (d) Mn_2O_3

Ans. ***(a)*** On addition of $KMnO_4$ to concentrated H_2SO_4, a green oily compound Mn_2O_7 is obtained, which is highly explosive in nature.

$$2KMnO_4 + 2H_2SO_4(\text{Conc.}) \longrightarrow Mn_2O_7 + 2KHSO_4 + H_2O$$

Q.6 The magnetic nature of elements depends on the presence of unpaired electrons. Identify the configuration of transition element, which shows highest magnetic moment.

(a) $3d^7$ (b) $3d^5$ (c) $3d^8$ (d) $3d^2$

Thinking Process This problem is based on the calculation of magnetic moment can be done as Magnetic moment $(\mu) = \sqrt{n(n+2)}$ BM.

Ans. ***(b)*** Greater the number of unpaired electron, higher will be its value of magnetic moment.

Since, $3d^5$ has 5 unpaired electrons, hence, it has highest magnetic moment.

$$\mu = \sqrt{5(5+2)}$$
$$= \sqrt{35} = 5.95 \text{ BM}$$

Q.7 Which of the following oxidation state is common for all lanthanoids?

(a) +2 (b) +3 (c) +4 (d) +5

Ans. ***(b)*** Lanthanoids generally show +3 oxidation state, but some can also exhibit +2 or +4 states. These occur when element attains a stable f^0, f^7, f^{14} configuration.

Q.8 Which of the following reactions are disproportionation reactions?

(i) $Cu^+ \longrightarrow Cu^{2+} + Cu$

(ii) $3MnO_4^{2-} + 4H^+ \longrightarrow 2MnO_4^- + MnO_2 + 2H_2O$

(iii) $2KMnO_4 \longrightarrow K_2MnO_4 + MnO_2 + O_2$

(iv) $2MnO_4^- + 3Mn^{2+} + 2H_2O \longrightarrow 5MnO_2 + 4H^+$

(a) (i), (ii) (b) (i), (ii) and (iii)
(c) (ii), (iii) and (iv) (d) (i) and (iv)

Ans. ***(a)*** The reaction in which oxidation as well as reduction, occur upon same atom simultaneously is known as disproportionation reaction.

e.g.,

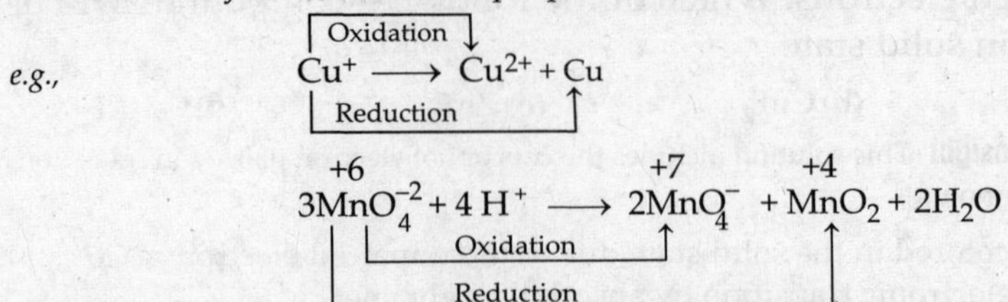

Q.9 When $KMnO_4$ solution is added to oxalic acid solution, the decolourisation is slow in the beginning but becomes instantaneous after some time because

(a) CO_2 is formed as the product.
(b) reaction is exothermic.
(c) MnO_4^- catalyses the reaction.
(d) Mn^{2+} acts as autocatalyst.

Ans. ***(d)*** When $KMnO_4$ solution is added to oxalic acid solution, the decolourisation is slow in the beginning but becomes instantaneous after some time because Mn^{2+} acts as autocatalyst.

Reduction half $\quad MnO_4^- + 8H^+ + 5e^- \longrightarrow Mn^{2+} + 4H_2O] \times 2$

Oxidation half $\quad C_2O_4^{2-} \longrightarrow 2CO_2 + 2e^-] \times 5$

Overall equation

$$2MnO_4^- + 16H^+ + 5C_2O_4^{2-} \longrightarrow 2Mn^{2+} + 10CO_2 + 8H_2O$$

Q.10 There are 14 elements in actinoid series. Which of the following elements does not belong to this series?

(a) U (b) Np (c) Tm (d) Fm

Ans. ***(c)*** Tm ($Z = 69$) does not belong to actinoid series. The actinoid series includes elements with atomic numbers 90 to 103. Thulium (Tm) has atomic number 69 and it belongs to lanthanoid series (4*f* series).

Q.11 $KMnO_4$ acts as an oxidising agent in acidic medium. The number of moles of $KMnO_4$ that will be needed to react with one mole of sulphide ions in acidic solution is

(a) $\frac{2}{5}$ (b) $\frac{3}{5}$

(c) $\frac{4}{5}$ (d) $\frac{1}{5}$

Ans. ***(a)*** The reaction of $KMnO_4$ in which it acts as an oxidising agent in acidic medium is

$$2KMnO_4 + 3H_2SO_4 \longrightarrow K_2SO_4 + 2MnSO_4 + 3H_2O + 5[O]$$
$$H_2S + [O] \longrightarrow H_2O + S] \times 5$$
$$\overline{2KMnO_4 + 3H_2SO_4 + 5H_2S \longrightarrow K_2SO_4 + 2MnSO_4 + 8H_2O + 5S}$$

5 moles of S^{2-} ions react with 2 moles of $KMnO_4$. So, 1 mole of S^{2-} ion will react with $\frac{2}{5}$ moles of $KMnO_4$.

Q.12 Which of the following is amphoteric oxide?

$$Mn_2O_7, CrO_3, Cr_2O_3, CrO, V_2O_5, V_2O_4$$

(a) V_2O_5, Cr_2O_3 (b) Mn_2O_7, CrO_3
(c) CrO, V_2O_5 (d) V_2O_5, V_2O_4

Thinking Process This problem is based on the concept of amphoteric oxides. It can be solved by recognising that V_2O_5 and Cr_2O_3 react with both acids and bases.

Ans. ***(a)*** V_2O_5 and Cr_2O_3 are amphoteric oxides because they both react with alkalies as well as acids.

Q.13 Gadolinium belongs to 4*f* series. Its atomic number is 64. Which of the following is the correct electronic configuration of gadolinium?

(a) $[Xe]\,4f^7 5d^1 6s^2$ (b) $[Xe]\,4f^6 5d^2 6s^2$
(c) $[Xe]\,4f^8 6d^2$ (d) $[Xe]\,4f^9 5s^1$

Ans. ***(a)*** Gadolinium belongs to 4*f* series and has atomic number 64. The correct electronic configuration of gadolinium is

$$_{64}Gd = _{54}[Xe]\,4f^7 5d^1 6s^2$$

It has extra stability due to half-filled 4*f* subshell.

Q.14 Interstitial compounds are formed when small atoms are trapped inside the crystal lattice of metals. Which of the following is not the characteristic property of interstitial compounds?

(a) They have high melting points in comparison to pure metals.
(b) They are very hard.
(c) They retain metallic conductivity.
(d) The are chemically very reactive.

Ans. ***(d)*** Interstitial compounds are formed when small atoms are trapped inside the crystal lattice of metals. Some of their important characteristics are as follows :

(i) They are very hard and rigid.
(ii) They have high melting point which are higher than those of the pure metals.
(iii) They show conductivity like that of the pure metal.
(iv) They acquire chemical inertness.

Q.15 The magnetic moment is associated with its spin angular momentum and orbital angular momentum. Spin only magnetic moment value of Cr^{3+} ion is

(a) 2.87 B.M. (b) 3.87 B.M. (c) 3.47 B.M. (d) 3.57 B.M.

Ans. ***(b)*** The magnetic moment is associated with its spin angular momentum and orbital angular momentum.

Electronic configuration of Cr^{3+} ion is $3d^3$

Hence, its spin only magnetic moment $(\mu) = \sqrt{n(n+2)}$ B.M.

$$= \sqrt{3(3+2)} = \sqrt{15}$$

$$= 3.87 \text{ B.M.}$$

Q.16 $KMnO_4$ acts as an oxidising agent in alkaline medium. When alkaline $KMnO_4$ is treated with KI, iodide ion is oxidised to ....

(a) I_2 (b) IO^- (c) IO_3^- (d) IO_4^-

Ans. *(c)* $KMnO_4$ acts as an oxidising agent in alkaline medium. When alkaline $KMnO_4$ is treated with KI, iodide ion is oxidised to IO_3^-.

Reaction $2KMnO_4 + H_2O + KI \longrightarrow 2MnO_4 + 2KOH + KIO_3$

or, $I^- + 6OH^- \longrightarrow IO_3^- + 3H_2O + 6e^-$

Mistake Alert ! *Students may make a mistake in considering that iodide (I^-) are oxidised to iodine (I_2) or iodate (IO_4^-) instead of the iodate (IO_3^-) in alkaline medium.*

Q.17 Which of the following statements is **not** correct?

(a) Copper liberates hydrogen from acids.

(b) In its higher oxidation states, manganese forms stable compounds with oxygen and fluorine.

(c) Mn^{3+} and Co^{3+} are oxidising agents in aqueous solution.

(d) Ti^{2+} and Cr^{2+} are reducing agents in aqueous solution.

Thinking Process Cu is less reactive than hydrogen in the electrochemical series, so it cannot displace hydrogen gas from acids.

Ans. *(a)* Copper lies below hydrogen in the electrochemical series and hence does not liberate H_2 from acids. Therefore, statement (a) is not correct.

Other three statements (b, c, d) are correct.

Q.18 When acidified $K_2Cr_2O_7$ solution is added to Sn^{2+} salts then Sn^{2+} changes to

(a) Sn (b) Sn^{3+} (c) Sn^{4+} (d) Sn^+

Ans. *(c)* When acidified $K_2Cr_2O_7$ solution is added to Sn^{2+} salts then Sn^{2+} changes to Sn^{4+}. (by oxidation) and Cr in $K_2Cr_2O_7$ is reduced to Cr^{3+}.

The reaction is given below,

$$\overset{+6}{Cr_2}O_7^{2-} + 14H^+ + 3Sn^{2+} \longrightarrow 2Cr^{3+} 3Sn^{4+} + 7H_2O$$

Oxidation

Reduction

Q.19 Highest oxidation state of manganese in fluoride is +4 (MnF_4) but highest oxidation state in oxides is +7 (Mn_2O_7) because

(a) fluorine is more electronegative than oxygen

(b) fluorine does not possess *d* orbitals

(c) fluorine stabilises lower oxidation state

(d) in covalent compounds, fluorine can form single bond only while oxygen forms double bond

Ans. *(d)* In covalent compound, manganese has a highest oxidation state of +4 in fluorides (MnF_4) and +7 in oxides (Mn_2O_7). This is because fluorine forms single bonds, while oxygen can form double bonds, allowing for higher oxidation states in oxides.

Q.20 Although zirconium belongs to 4*d* transition series and Hafniun to 5*d* transition series even then they show similar physical and chemical properties because ....

(a) both belong to *d*-block

(b) both have same number of electrons

(c) both have similar atomic radius

(d) both belong to the same group of the Periodic Table

Ans. ***(c)*** Due to lanthanoid contraction, Zr and Hf possess nearly same atomic and ionic radii, *i.e.*, Zr = 160 pm and Hf = 159 pm, Zr^{4+} = 79 pm and Hf^{4+} = 78 pm. Therefore, these two elements show similar physical and chemical properties.

Q.21 Why is HCl not used to make the medium acidic in oxidation reactions of $KMnO_4$ in acidic medium?

(a) Both HCl and $KMnO_4$ act as oxidising agents.

(b) $KMnO_4$ oxidises HCl into Cl_2 which is also an oxidising agent.

(c) $KMnO_4$ is a weaker oxidising agent than HCl.

(d) $KMnO_4$ acts as a reducing agent in the presence of HCl.

Thinking Process This problem is based on the concept of redox reactions, illustrating how HCl can interfere by producing Cl_2, which competes as an oxidising agent with $KMnO_4$.

Ans. ***(b)*** HCl is not used to acidify $KMnO_4$oxidation reactions because the oxygen produced can partially oxidize HCl to Cl_2, which then acts as an oxidising agent interfering with the reaction.

Multiple Choice Questions (More Than One Options)

Q.22 Generally transition elements and their salts are coloured due to the presence of unpaired electrons in metal ions. Which of the following compounds are coloured?

(a) $KMnO_4$ (b) $Ce(SO_4)_2$ (c) $TiCl_4$ (d) Cu_2Cl_2

Ans. ***(a, b)*** $KMnO_4$ is coloured due to charge transfer rather than unpaired electron. Similarly, in $Ce(SO_4)_2$, cerium has +4 oxidation state with $4f^{\circ}$ configuration and is colored yellow for the same reason.

Q.23 Transition elements show magnetic moment due to spin and orbital motion of electrons. Which of the following metallic ions have almost same spin only magnetic moment?

(a) Co^{2+} (b) Cr^{2+} (c) Mn^{2+} (d) Cr^{3+}

Ans. ***(a, d)*** Electronic configuration of Co^{2+} = [Ar] $3d^7$; Number of unpaired electrons = 3
Electronic configuration of Cr^{2+} = [Ar] $3d^4$; Number of unpaired electrons = 4
Electronic configuration of Mn^{2+} = [Ar] $3d^5$; Number of unpaired electrons = 5
Electronic configuration of Cr^{3+} = [Ar] $3d^3$; Number of unpaired electrons = 3
Hence, it is clearly seen that both Co^{2+} and Cr^{3+} have same number of unpaired electrons, *i.e.*, 3 thus, will have same magnetic moment (as $\mu = \sqrt{n(n+2)}$)

Q.24 In the form of dichromate, Cr(VI) is a strong oxidising agent in acidic medium but Mo(VI) in MoO_3 and W(VI) in WO_3 are not because ....

(a) Cr (VI) is more stable than Mo(VI) and W(VI).

(b) Mo (VI) and W (VI) are more stable than Cr(VI).

(c) Higher oxidation states of heavier members of group-6 of transition series are more stable.

(d) Lower oxidation states of heavier members of group-6 of transition series are more stable.

- **Concept Insight** This solution includes the concept of oxidation state stability in *d*-block elements, where havier elements like Mo and W,. Stabilise higher oxidation states better than Cr, affecting their oxidising abilities.

Ans. ***(b, c)*** In *d*-block elements, for heavier elements, the higher oxidation states are more stable. Hence, Mo(VI) and W(VI) are more stable than Cr(VI). Thats why, Cr(VI) in the form of dichromate is a stronger oxidising agent in acidic medium whereas MoO_3 and WO_3 are not.

Mistake Alert! *An element less stable in a higher oxidation state tends to be a stronger oxidising agent as it has a higher tendency to accept electrons and get reduced.*

Q.25 Which of the following actinoids show oxidation states upto +7?

(a) Am
(b) Pu
(c) U
(d) Np

Ans. ***(b, d)*** The oxidation states of the following actinoids are :

(a) Americium (Z = 95); Electronic configuration = $[Rn]5f^7 6d^0 7s^2$
Oxidation states shown by Am = + 3, + 4, + 5, + 6.

(b) Plutonium (Z = 94); Electronic configuration = $[Rn]\ 5f^6 6d^0 7s^2$
Oxidation states shown by Pu = + 3, + 4, + 5, + 6, + 7.

(c) Uranium (Z = 92); Electronic configuration = $[Rn]\ 5f^3 6d^1 7s^2$
Oxidation states shown by U = + 3, + 4, + 5, + 6.

(d) Neptunium (Z = 93); Electronic configuration = $[Rn]\ 5f^4 6d^1 7s^2$
Oxidation states shown by Np = + 3, + 4, + 5, + 6, + 7.

Thus, among the given, Pu and Np show oxidation states upto +7.

Q.26 General electronic configuration of actinoids is $(n-2)f^{1-14}(n-1)d^{0-2}\ ns^2$. Which of the following actinoids have one electron in 6*d* orbital?

(a) U (Atomic number. 92)
(b) Np (Atomic number. 93)
(c) Pu (Atomic number. 94)
(d) Am (Atomic number. 95)

Ans. ***(a, b)*** General electronic configuration of actinoids is $(n-1)f^{1-14}(n-1)d^{0-2}ns^2$. U and Np each have one electron in 6*d* orbital. (*Also, refer to Q.* 25)

Q.27 Which of the following lanthanoids show +2 oxidation state besides the characteristic oxidation state +3 of lanthanoids?

(a) Ce
(b) Eu
(c) Yb
(d) Ho

Ans. ***(b, c)***

(a) Cerium (Z = 58) ⇒ Electronic configuration = $[Xe]4f^1 5d^1 6s^2$
Oxidation state of Ce = +3, +4

(b) Europium (Z = 63) ⇒ Electronic configuration = $[Xe]4f^7 5d^0 6s^2$
Oxidation state of Eu = +2, +3

(c) Ytterbium (Z = 70) ⇒ Electronic configuration = $[Xe]\ 4f^{14} 5d^0 6s^2$
Oxidation state of Yb = +2, +3

(d) Holmium (Z = 67) ⇒ Electronic configuration = $[Xe]\ 4f^{11} 5d^0 6s^2$
Oxidation state of Ho = +3

Q.28 Which of the following ions show higher spin only magnetic moment value?

(a) Ti^{3+} (b) Mn^{2+} (c) Fe^{2+} (d) Co^{3+}

Ans. ***(b, c)*** As,

$$Ti^{3+} = [Ar]\,3d^1$$
$$Mn^{2+} = [Ar]\,3d^5, (t_{2g}^3 e_g^2)$$
$$Fe^{2+} = [Ar]\,3d^6, (t_{2g}^4 e_{2g}^2)$$
$$Co^{3+} = [Ar]\,3d^6, (t_{2g}^6 e_g^0)$$

Crystal field splitting energy (CFSE) is high in Co^{3+}, thus electrons pair up in t_{2g}. Hence, only Fe^{2+} and Mn^{2+} show higher spin magnetic moment value.

Q.29 Transition elements form binary compounds with halogens. Which of the following elements will form MF_3 type compounds?

(a) Cr (b) Co (c) Cu (d) Ni

Ans. ***(a, b)*** Transition elements such as Cr and Co form binary compounds with halogens, *i.e.*, CrF_3 and CoF_3 whereas Cu and Ni do not form CuF_3 and NiF_3.

Q.30 Which of the following will **not** act as oxidising agents?

(a) CrO_3 (b) MoO_3 (c) WO_3 (d) CrO_4^{2-}

Ans. ***(b, c)*** A species can act as oxidising agent only when metal is present in high oxidation state and its lower oxidation state shows stability. As higher oxidation states of W and Mo are more stable, therefore they will not act as oxidising agents.

Q.31 Although +3 is the characteristic oxidation state for lanthanoids but cerium also shows +4 oxidation state because ....

(a) it has variable ionisation enthalpy

(b) it has a tendency to attain noble gas configuration

(c) it has a tendency to attain f^0 configuration

(d) it resembles Pb^{4+}

Ans. ***(b, c)*** Electronic configuration of $_{58}Ce = [Xe]\,4f^1 5d^1 6s^2$.

Therefore, electronic configuration of $Ce^{4+} = {}_{54}[Xe]\;4f^0$.

Thus, it has a tendency to attain noble gas configuration and attain f^0 configuration.

Short Answer Type Questions

Q.32 Why does copper not replace hydrogen from acids?

Ans. Copper does not replace hydrogen from acids because Cu has positive $E°$ value, *i.e.*, it is less reactive than hydrogen which has electrode potential 0.00V.

Q.33 Why $E°$ values for Mn, Ni and Zn are more negative than expected?

Ans. Negative values of Mn^{2+} and Zn^{2+} are related to stabilities of half-filled and completely filled configurations respectively. But for Ni^{2+}, $E°$ value is related to the highest negative enthalpy of hydration.

Hence, $E°$ values for Mn, Ni and Zn are more negative than expected.

Q.34 Why first ionisation enthalpy of Cr is lower than that of Zn?

Ans. Ionisation enthalpy of Cr is less than that of Zn. Cr has electronic configuration of $[Ar]3d^5 4s^1$ whereas zinc has electronic configuration of $[Ar]\ 3d^{10} 4s^2$. When Cr loses its first electron, it will lose it from the 4s orbital, leaving behind a stable half-filled *d*-orbital ($3d^5$). Zn loses its first electron from fully filled 4*s*-orbital, which requires more energy.

Q.35 Transition elements show high melting points. Why?

Thinking Process This problem is based on the concept of metallic bonding, where both $(n-1)d$ and ns electrons in transition elements contribute to strong interatomic bonds, resulting in high melting points

Ans. Transition elements show high melting point, due to involvement of greater number of electrons in the interatomic bonding from $(n-1)$ *d*-orbitals in addition to *ns* electrons in forming metallic bond. Thus, large number of electrons participate in formation of large number of metallic bonds.

Q.36 When Cu^{2+} ion is treated with KI, a white precipitate is formed. Explain the reaction with the help of chemical equation.

Ans. When Cu^{2+} ion is treated with KI, it produces Cu_2I_2 as white precipitate in the final product.

$$2Cu^{2+} + 4I^- \longrightarrow \underset{\text{(White ppt.)}}{Cu_2I_2} + I_2$$

(In this reaction, CuI_2 is formed which being unstable, dissociates into Cu_2I_2 and I_2).

Q.37 Out of Cu_2Cl_2 and $CuCl_2$, which is more stable and why?

Ans. Among Cu_2Cl_2 and $CuCl_2$, $CuCl_2$ is more stable. Stability of complex can be explained on the basis of stability of oxidation state of copper. $Cu^{2+}(aq)$ is more stable than $Cu^+(aq)$ because its hydration energy (ΔH_{hyd}) is much more negative which more than compensates for the energy needed for the second ionisation of Cu.

Q.38 When a brown compound of manganese (*A*) is treated with HCl it gives a gas (*B*). The gas taken in excess, reacts with NH_3 to give an explosive compound (*C*). Identify compounds *A*, *B* and *C*.

Thinking Process This problem is based on the properties of MnO_2 and preparation of NCl_3.

Ans. MnO_2 is the brown compound of Mn which reacts with HCl to give Cl_2 gas. This gas forms an explosive compound NCl_3 when treated with NH_3. Thus, $A = MnO_2$; $B = Cl_2$; $C = NCl_3$ and reactions are as follows.

(i) $\underset{[A]}{MnO_2} + 4HCl \longrightarrow MnCl_2 + \underset{[B]}{Cl_2} + 2H_2O$

(ii) $NH_3 + \underset{\text{(Excess)}}{3Cl_2} \longrightarrow \underset{[C]}{NCl_3} + 3HCl$

Q.39 Although fluorine is more electronegative than oxygen, but the ability of oxygen to stabilise higher oxidation states exceeds that of fluorine. Why?

Concept Insight This solution includes the concept of bonding capabilities of elements.

Ans. Oxygen can form multiple bonds with metals, while fluorine cannot form multiple bond with metals. Hence, oxygen has more ability to stabilize higher oxidation state rather than fluorine.

Q.40 Although Cr^{3+} and Co^{2+} ions have same number of unpaired electrons but the magnetic moment of Cr^{3+} is 3.87 B.M. and that of Co^{2+} is 4.87 B.M. Why?

Ans. Magnetic moment of any metal ion can be decided on the basis of spin as well as orbital contribution of electron. Due to symmetrical electronic configuration, there is no orbital contribution in Cr^{3+} ion. However, appreciable orbital contribution takes place in Co^{2+} ion and hence it has a larger magnetic moment value than Cr^{3+}.

Q.41 Ionisation enthalpies of Ce, Pr and Nd are higher than Th, Pa and U. Why?

Ans. Ce, Pr and Nd are lanthanoids and have incomplete $4f$ shell while Th, Pa and U are actinoids and have $5f$ shell incompletely filled.

In the beginning, when $5f$-orbitals begin to be occupied, they will penetrate less into the inner core of electrons. The $5f$-electrons will be more effectively shielded from the nuclear charge than $4f$ electrons of the corresponding lanthanoids.

Therefore, outer electrons are less firmly held and they are available for bonding in the actinoids.

Hence, Th, Pa and U have lower ionisation enthalpies.

Q.42 Although Zr belongs to $4d$ and Hf belongs to $5d$ transition series but it is quite difficult to separate them, Why?

- **Concept Insight** This solution includes the concept of lanthanoid contraction.

Ans. Separation of Zr and Hf are quite difficult because of lanthanoid contraction. Due to lanthanoid contraction, they have almost same size (Zr = 160 pm and Hf = 159 pm) and thus, similar chemical properties. That is why it is very difficult to separate them by chemical methods.

Q 43 Although +3 oxidation states is the characteristic oxidation state of lanthanoids but cerium shows +4 oxidation state also. Why?

Ans. It is due to the fact that after losing one more electron Ce acquires stable $4f^0$ electronic configuration. So, Ce shows +4 oxidation state also alongwith +3 oxidation state.

Q 44 Explain why does colour of $KMnO_4$ disappear when oxalic acid is added to its solution in acidic medium?

Ans. When oxalic acid is added to acidic solution of $KMnO_4$, its colour disappear due to reduction of MnO_4^- ion to Mn^{2+}. Chemical reaction occurring during this neutralisation reaction is as follows

$$5C_2O_4^{2-} + \underset{\text{(Coloured)}}{2MnO_4^-} + 16H^+ \longrightarrow \underset{\text{(Colourless)}}{2Mn^{2+}} + 8H_2O + 10CO_2$$

Q.45 When orange solution containing $Cr_2O_7^{2-}$ ion is treated with an alkali, a yellow solution is formed and when H^+ ions are added to yellow solution, an orange solution is obtained. Explain why does this happen?

Ans. When orange solution containing $Cr_2O_7^{2-}$ ion is treated with an alkali, a yellow solution of CrO_4^{2-} is obtained.

When H^+ ions are added to yellow solution, an orange solution is obtained due to interconversion of CrO_4^{2-} to $Cr_2O_7^{2-}$.

$$Cr_2O_7^{2-} + 2OH^- \longrightarrow 2CrO_4^{2-} + H_2O$$

$$2CrO_4^{2-} + 4H^+ \longrightarrow Cr_2O_7^{2-} + H_2O$$

Q.46 **A solution of $KMnO_4$ on reduction yields either a colourless solution or a brown precipitate or a green solution depending on pH of the solution. What different stages of the reduction do these represent and how are they carried out?**

Ans. Oxidising behaviour of $KMnO_4$ depends on pH of the solution.

In acidic medium (pH < 7)

$$MnO_4^- + 8H^+ + 5e^- \longrightarrow \underset{\text{Colourless}}{Mn^{2+}} + 4H_2O$$

In alkaline medium (pH > 7)

$$MnO_4^- + e^- \longrightarrow \underset{\text{(Green)}}{MnO_4^{2-}}$$

In neutral medium (pH = 7)

$$MnO_4^- + 2H_2O + 3e^- \longrightarrow \underset{\text{(Brown ppt)}}{MnO_2} + 4OH^-$$

Q.47 **The second and third rows of transition elements resemble each other much more than they resemble the first row. Explain, why?**

Thinking Process Due to poor shileding of $4f$ orbital electrons, effective nuclear charge increases and there is a decrease in the size of the third row transition elements. This contraction in size is called Lanthanoid contraction.

Ans. Due to lanthanoid contraction, the atomic radii of the second and third row transition elements is almost same. So, they resemble each other much more as compared to first row elements and show similar character.

Q.48 **$E^\ominus$ of Cu is +0.34V while that of Zn is –0.76 V. Explain.**

Ans. $E^\ominus$ value of Cu is positive because of the fact that sum of sublimation enthalpy and ionisation enthalpy to convert Cu(*s*) to Cu^{2+} (*aq*) is so high that it is not compensated by its hydration enthalpy. E° value for Zn is negative because of the fact that after removal of electrons from 4s orbital, stable $3d^{10}$ configuration is obtained.

Q.49 **The halides of transition elements become more covalent with increasing oxidation state of the metal. Why?**

Thinking Process This problem is based on concept of Fajan's rule and its application.

Ans. As the oxidation state increases, size of the ion of transition element decreases. As per Fajan's rule, as the size of metal ion decreases, covalent character of the bond formed increases.

Therefore, the halide of transition elements become more covalent with increasing oxidation state of the metal.

Q.50 **While filling up of electrons in the atomic orbitals, the 4s orbital is filled before the 3*d* orbital but reverse happens during the ionisation of the atom. Explain why?**

Ans. During filling up of electrons ($n + l$) rule is followed. Here 4*s* has lower energy than 3*d* orbital so, it is filled before 3*d*-orbital. After the orbitals are filled, 4s goes beyond 3*d*, *i.e.*, 4*s* goes farther from nucleus than 3*d*. So, electron from 4*s* is removed earlier than from 3*d*.

Q.51 Reactivity of transition elements decreases almost regularly from Sc to Cu. Explain.

Ans. Reactivity of transition elements depends mostly upon their ionisation enthalpies. As we move from left to right in the periodic table (Sc to Cu), ionisation enthalpies increases almost regularly.

Hence, their reactivity decreases almost regularly from Sc to Cu.

Matching The Columns

Q.52 Match the catalysts given in Column I with the processes given in Column II.

	Column I (Catalyst)		Column II (Process)
A.	Ni in the presence of hydrogen	1.	Ziegler-Natta catalyst
B.	Cu_2Cl_2	2.	Contact process
C.	V_2O_5	3.	Vegetable oil to ghee
D.	Finely divided iron	4.	Sandmeyer reaction
E.	$TiCl_4 + Al(CH_3)_3$	5.	Haber's process
		6.	Decomposition of $KClO_3$

Ans. A. → (3) B. → (4) C. → (2) D. → (5) E. → (1)

Catalyst	Process
A. Ni in the presence of hydrogen	3. Vegetable oil to ghee
B. Cu_2Cl_2	4. Sandmeyer reaction
C. V_2O_5	2. Contact process $SO_2 \xrightarrow{V_2O_5} SO_3$
D. Finely divided iron	5. Haber's process $N_2 + 3H_2 \xrightarrow{Fe} 2NH_3$
E. $TiCl_4 + Al(CH_3)_3$	1. Ziegler-Natta catalyst

Q.53 Match the compounds/elements given in Column I with uses given in Column II.

	Column I (Compound/element)		Column II (Use)
A.	Lanthanoid oxide	1.	Production of iron alloy
B.	Lanthanoid	2.	Television screen
C.	Misch metall	3.	Petroleum cracking
D.	Magnesium based alloy is constituent of	4.	Lanthanoid metal + iron
E.	Mixed oxides of lanthanoids are employed	5.	Bullets
		6.	X-ray screen

Ans. A. → (2) B. → (1) C. → (4) D. → (5) E. → (3)

	Compound /Element	Use
A.	Lanthanoid oxide	2. Television screen
B.	Lanthanoid	1. Production of iron alloy
C.	Misch metall	4. Lanthanoid metal + iron
D.	Magnesium based alloy is constitute of	5. Bullets
E	Mixed oxides of lanthanoids are employed	3. Petroleum cracking

Q.54 Match the properties given in Column I with the metals given in Column II.

	Column I (Property)		Column II (Metal)
A.	An element which can show +8 oxidation state	1.	Mn
B.	3*d* block element that can show upto +7 oxidation state	2.	Cr
C.	3*d* block element with highest melting point	3.	Os
		4.	Fe

Ans. A. → (3) B. → (1) C. → (2)

A. Osmium is an element which can show +8 oxidation state.

B. 3*d* block element that can show upto +7 oxidation state is manganese.

C. 3*d* block element with highest melting point is chromium.

Q.55 Match the statements given in Column I with the oxidation states given in Column II.

	Column I		Column II
A.	Oxidation state of Mn in MnO_2 is	1.	+ 2
B.	Most stable oxidation state of Mn is	2.	+ 3
C.	Most stable oxidation state of Mn in oxides is	3.	+ 4
D.	Characteristic oxidation state of lanthanoids is	4.	+ 5
		5.	+ 7

Ans. **A.** → (3) **B.** → (1) **C.** → (5) **D.** → (2)

A. Oxidation state of Mn in MnO_2 is + 4.

B. Most stable oxidation state of Mn is + 2.

C. Most stable oxidation state of Mn in oxides is + 7.

D. Characteristic oxidation state of lanthanoids is + 3.

Q.56 Match the solutions given in Column I and the colours given in Column II.

	Column I (Aqueous solution of salt)		Column II (Colour)
A.	$FeSO_4 \cdot 7H_2O$	1.	Green
B.	$NiCl_2 \cdot 4H_2O$	2.	Light pink
C.	$MnCl_2 \cdot 4H_2O$	3.	Blue
D.	$CoCl_2 \cdot 6H_2O$	4.	Pale green
E.	Cu_2Cl_2	5.	Pink
		6.	Colourless

Ans. **A.** → (4) **B.** → (1) **C.** → (2) **D.** → (5) **E.** → (6)

	Aqueous solution of salt	Colour
A.	$FeSO_4 \cdot 7H_2O$	4. Pale green
B.	$NiCl_2 \cdot 4H_2O$	1. Green
C.	$MnCl_2 \cdot 4H_2O$	2. Light pink
D.	$CoCl_2 \cdot 6H_2O$	5. Pink
E.	Cu_2Cl_2	6. Colourless

Q.57 Match the property given in Column I with the element given in Column II.

	Column I (Property)		Column II (Element)
A.	Lanthanoid which shows +4 oxidation state	1.	Pm
B.	Lanthanoid which can show +2 oxidation state	2.	Ce
C.	Radioactive lanthanoid	3.	Lu
D.	Lanthanoid which has $4f^7$ electronic configuration in +3 oxidation state	4.	Eu
E.	Lanthanoid which has $4f^{14}$ electronic configuration in +3 oxidation state	5.	Gd
		6.	Dy

Ans. **A.** → (2) **B.** → (4) **C.** → (1) **D.** → (5) **E.** → (3)

A. Lanthanoid which shows +4 oxidation state is cerium.

$_{58}Ce = [Xe]4f^1 5d^1 6s^2$; Oxidation state = + 3, + 4

B. Lanthanoid which can show +2 oxidation state is europium.

$_{63}Eu = [Xe]4f^7 5d^0 6s^2$; Oxidation state = + 2, + 3

C. Radioactive lanthanoid is promethium. It is the only synthetic (man-made) radioactive lanthanoid.

D. Lanthnoid which has $4f^7$ electronic configuration in +3 oxidation state is gadolinium.

$_{64}Gd = [Xe]4f^7 5d^1 6s^2$; Oxidation state = +3

E. Lanthanoid which has $4f^{14}$ electronic configuration in +3 oxidation state is lutetium.

$_{71}Lu = [Xe]4f^{14} 5d^1 6s^2$; Oxidation state = +3

Q.58 Match the properties given in Column I with the metals given in Column II.

	Column I (Property)		Column II (Metal)
A.	Element with highest second ionisation enthalpy	1.	Co
B.	Element with highest third ionisation enthalpy	2.	Cr
C.	M in $M(CO)_6$ is	3.	Cu
D.	Element with highest heat of atomisation	4.	Zn
		5.	Ni

Ans. **A.** → (3) **B.** → (4) **C.** → (2) **D.** → (1)

A. $Cu^+ = 3d^{10}$ is very stable configuration due to fully-filled orbitals. Hence, removal of second electron requires very high energy.

B. $Zn^{2+} = 3d^{10}$ is very stable configuration due to completely filled *d*-orbital. Hence, removal of third electron requires very high energy.

C. Metal carbonyl with formula $M(CO)_6$ is $Cr(CO)_6$.

D. Nickel (Ni) is the element with highest heat of atomisation.

Assertion and Reason

In the following questions a statement of assertion followed by a statement of reason is given. Choose the correct answer out of the following choices.

(a) Both assertion and reason are true, and reason is the correct explanation of the assertion.

(b) Both assertion and reason are true but reason is not the correct explanation of assertion.

(c) Assertion is not true but reason is true.

(d) Both assertion and reason are false.

Q.59 Assertion Cu^{2+} iodide is not known.
Reason Cu^{2+} oxidises I^- to iodine.

Ans. *(a)* Assertion and reason both are correct and reason is the correct explanation of assertion.

Copper (II) iodide (CuI_2) is not known because Cu^{2+} oxidises I^- to iodine.

Q.60 Assertion Separation of Zr and Hf is difficult.
Reason Because Zr and Hf lie in the same group of the periodic table.

Ans. *(b)* Assertion and reason are true but reason is not correct explanation of assertion.

Separation of Zr and Hf is difficult, not because they are in the same group of periodic table, but due to the lanthanoid contraction, which makes their atomic radii almost identical and they show similar physical and chemical properties.

Q.61 Assertion Actinoids form relatively less stable complexes as compared to lanthanoids.
Reason Actinoids can utilise their $5f$ orbitals alongwith $6d$ orbitals in bonding but lanthanoids do not use their $4f$ orbital for bonding.

Ans. *(c)* Assertion is not true but reason is true.

Actinoids form relatively more stable complexes as compared to lanthanoids because actinoids can utilise their $5f$ orbitals along with $6d$ orbitals in bonding but lanthanoids do not use their $4f$ orbitals for bonding.

Q.62 Assertion Cu cannot liberate hydrogen from acids.
Reason Because it has positive electrode potential.

Ans. *(a)* Assertion and reason both are correct and reason is correct explanation of assertion.

Cu cannot liberate hydrogen from acids because it has positive electrode potential. Metals having negative value of electrode potential liberate H_2 gas from acids..

Q.63 Assertion The highest oxidation state of osmium is +8 .
Reason Osmium is a $5d$-block element.

Ans. *(b)* Assertion and reason both are correct but reason is not the correct explanation of assertion.

The highest oxidation state of osmium is +8 due to its ability to expand their octet by using its all of the 8 electrons (2 from $6s$ and 6 from $5d$).

Long Answer Type Questions

Q.64 Identify A to E and also explain the reaction involved.

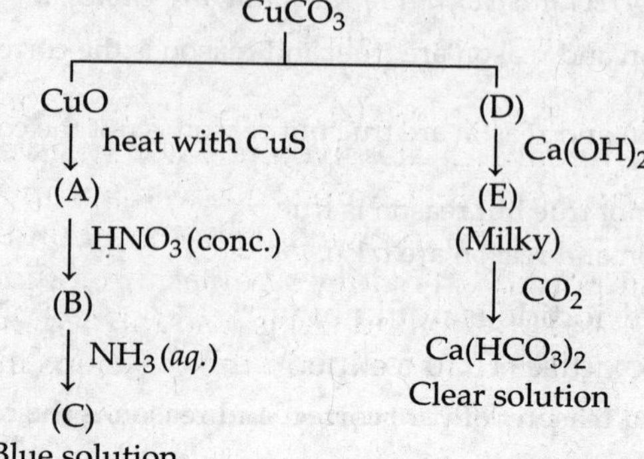

Ans. The substances from A to E are

$$A = Cu;\ B = Cu(NO_3)_2;\ C = [Cu(NH_3)_4]^{2+};\ D = CO_2;\ E = CaCO_3$$

Reactions

(i) $CuCO_3 \xrightarrow{\Delta} CuO + \underset{[D]}{CO_2}] \times 2$

(ii) $2CuO + CuS \longrightarrow \underset{[A]}{3Cu} + SO_2$

(iii) $\underset{[A]}{Cu} + 4HNO_3(\text{conc.}) \longrightarrow \underset{[B]}{Cu(NO_3)_2} + 2NO_2 + 2H_2O$

(iv) $\underset{[B]}{Cu^{2+}} + 4NH_3 \longrightarrow \underset{\substack{[C] \\ \text{(Blue solution)}}}{[Cu(NH_3)_4]}$

(v) $Ca(OH)_2 + \underset{[D]}{CO_2} \longrightarrow \underset{\substack{[E] \\ \text{(Milky)}}}{CaCO_3} + H_2O$

(vi) $\underset{[E]}{CaCO_3} + H_2O + CO_2 \longrightarrow \underset{\text{(Clear solution)}}{Ca(HCO_3)_2}$

Q.65 When a chromite ore (A) is fused with sodium carbonate in free excess of air and the product is dissolved in water, a yellow solution of compound (B) is obtained. After treatment of this yellow solution with sulphuric acid, compound (C) can be crystallised from the solution. When compound (C) is treated with KCl, orange crystals of compound (D) crystallise out. Identify A to D and also explain the reactions.

Thinking Process This problem is based on the preparation method of potassium dichromate from chromite ore.

Ans. $K_2Cr_2O_7$ is an orange compound. It is formed when $Na_2Cr_2O_7$ reacts with KCl. In acidic medium, yellow coloured CrO_4^{2-} (chromate ion) changes into dichromate. The given process is the preparation method of potassium dichromate from chromite ore.

$$A = FeCr_2O_4;\ B = Na_2CrO_4;\ C = Na_2Cr_2O_7;\ D = K_2Cr_2O_7.$$

(i) $\underset{[A]}{4FeCr_2O_4} + 8Na_2CO_3 + 7O_2 \longrightarrow \underset{[B]}{8Na_2CrO_4} + 2Fe_2O_3 + 8CO_2$

(ii) $2Na_2CrO_4 + 2H^+ \longrightarrow \underset{[C]}{Na_2Cr_2O_7} + 2Na^+ + H_2O$

(iii) $\underset{[C]}{Na_2Cr_2O_7} + 2KCl \longrightarrow \underset{[D]}{K_2Cr_2O_7} + 2NaCl$

Q.66 When an oxide of manganese (*A*) is fused with KOH in the presence of an oxidising agent and dissolved in water, it gives a dark green solution of compound (*B*). Compound (*B*) disproportionates in neutral or acidic solution to give purple compound (*C*). An alkaline solution of compound (*C*) oxidises potassium iodide solution to a compound (*D*) and compound (*A*) is also formed. Identify compounds *A* to *D* and also explain the reactions involved.

Thinking Process This problem is based on the concept of preparation and properties of potassium permanganate.

Ans. It is the method of preparation of potassium permanganate (purple).

Thus, $(A) = MnO_2$ $(B) = K_2MnO_4$

$(C) = KMnO_4$ $(D) = KIO_3$

$$\underset{[A]}{2MnO_2} + 4KOH + O_2 \longrightarrow \underset{[B]}{2K_2MnO_4} + 2H_2O$$

$$3MnO_4^{2-} + 4H^+ \longrightarrow \underset{[C]}{2MnO_4^-} + MnO_2 + 2H_2O$$

$$\underset{[C]}{2MnO_4^-} 2MnO_4^- + H_2O + KI \longrightarrow \underset{[A]}{2MnO_2} + 2OH^- + \underset{[D]}{KIO_3}$$

Q.67 On the basis of lanthanoid contraction, explain the following:

(i) Nature of bonding in La_2O_3 and Lu_2O_3.
(ii) Trends in the stability of oxo salts of lanthanoids from La to Lu.
(iii) Stability of the complexes of lanthanoids.
(iv) Radii of 4*d* and 5*d* block elements.
(v) Trends in acidic character of lanthanoid oxides.

Ans. (i) As the size decreases, covalent character increases. Therefore, La_2O_3 is more ionic and Lu_2O_3 is more covalent (as size decreases from La to Cu).

(ii) As the size decreases from La to Lu, stability of oxo salts also decreases.

(iii) Stability of complexes increases as the size of lanthanoids decreases.

(iv) Radii of 4*d* and 5*d*-block elements will be almost same.

(v) Acidic character of oxides increases from La to Lu.

Q.68 (a) Answer the following questions

(i) Which element of the first transition series has highest second ionisation enthalpy?

(ii) Which element of the first transition series has highest third ionisation enthalpy?

(iii) Which element of the first transition series has lowest enthalpy of atomisation?

(b) Identify the metal and justify your answer.

(i) Carbonyl $M(CO)_5$ (ii) MO_3F

Ans. (a) (i) Cu has highest second ionisation energy because the electronic configuration of Cu is $3d^{10}4s^1$. So, second electron needs to be removed from completely filled *d*-orbital which is very difficult.

(ii) Zinc has highest third ionisation energy because the electronic configuration of Zn = $3d^{10}4s^2$ and $Zn^{2+} = 3d^{10}$, which is fully filled and hence is very stable. Removal of third electron requires very high energy.

(iii) Zinc has lowest enthalpy of atomisation because it has completely filled 3*d* subshell and no unpaired electron is available for metallic bonding.

(b) (i) Carbonyl $M(CO)_5$ is $Fe(CO)_5$

According to EAN rule, the effective number of a metal in a metal carbonyl is equal to the atomic number of nearest inert gas. EAN is calculated as :

$$\text{EAN} = \text{number of electrons in metal} + 2 \times (CO)$$
$$= \text{atomic number of nearest inert gas}$$

In $M(CO)_5 = x + 2 \times (5) = 36$ (Kr is the nearest inert gas)

$$x = 26 \text{ (atomic number of metal)}$$

So, the metal is Fe(iron).

(ii) MO_3F is MnO_3F.

In MO_3F,

Let us assume that oxidation state of M is x

$$x + 3 \times (-2) + (-1) = 0$$

or, $x = +7$, *i.e.*, M is in +7 oxidation state which can only be shown by Mn metal. Hence, the given compound is MnO_3F.

Q.69 Mention the type of compounds formed when small atoms like H, C and N get trapped inside the crystal lattice of transition metals. Also give physical and chemical characteristics of these compounds.

Ans. When small atoms like H, C and N get trapped inside the crystal lattice of transition metals.Such compounds are called interstitial compounds *e.g.*, Tic, Mn_4N, Fe_3H, etc.

Their characteristic properties are

(i) They have melting points, higher than those of pure metals.
(ii) They are very hard.
(iii) They retain metallic conductivity.
(iv) They are chemically inert.

Q.70 (a) Transition metals can act as catalysts because these can change their oxidation state. How does Fe(III) catalyse the reaction between iodide and persulphate ions?

(b) Mention any three processes where transition metals act as catalysts.

Ans. (a) Reaction between iodide and persulphate ions is

$$2I^- + S_2O_8^{2-} \xrightarrow{Fe(III)} I_2 + 2SO_4^{2-}$$

Role of Fe(III) ions $2Fe^{3+} + 2I^- \longrightarrow 2Fe^{2+} + I_2$

$$2Fe^{2+} + S_2O_8^{2-} \longrightarrow 2Fe^{3+} + 2SO_4^{2-}$$

(b) (i) Vanadium (V) oxide is used in Contact process for oxidation of SO_2 to SO_3.

(ii) Finely divided iron in Haber's process is used in conversion of N_2 and H_2 to NH_3.

(iii) MnO_2 is used in the preparation of oxygen from $KClO_3$.

Q.71 A violet compound of manganese (*A*) decomposes on heating to liberate oxygen and compounds (*B*) and (*C*) of manganese are formed. Compound (*C*) reacts with KOH in the presence of potassium nitrate to give compound (*B*). On heating compound (*C*) with conc. H_2SO_4 and NaCl, chlorine gas is liberated and a compound (D) of manganese along with other products is formed. Identify compounds *A* to *D* and also explain the reactions involved.

Thinking Process This problem is based on preparation and properties of $KMnO_4$, K_2MnO_4 and MnO_2.

Ans. Compound (C) is manganese oxide (MnO_2), it produces Cl_2 gas when treated with conc. H_2SO_4 and NaCl · MnO_2 is also formed along with MnO_4^{2-}, when $KMnO_4$ (violet) is heated.

Thus, $(A) = KMnO_4$ $(B) = K_2MnO_4$

$(C) = MnO_2$ $(D) = MnCl_2$

$$\underset{[A]}{KMnO_4} \xrightarrow{\Delta} \underset{[B]}{K_2MnO_4} + \underset{[C]}{MnO_2} + O_2$$

$$\underset{[C]}{2MnO_2} + 4KOH + O_2 \longrightarrow \underset{[B]}{2K_2MnO_4} + 2H_2O$$

$$\underset{[C]}{MnO_2} + 4NaCl + 4H_2SO_4 \longrightarrow \underset{[D]}{MnCl_2} + 4NaHSO_4 + 2H_2O + Cl_2$$

Chapter 09

Coordination Compounds

Multiple Choice Questions (MCQs)

Q.1 Which of the following complexes formed by Cu^{2+} ions is most stable?

(a) $Cu^{2+} + 4NH_3 \longrightarrow [Cu(NH_3)_4]^{2+}$, $\log K = 11.6$
(b) $Cu^{2+} + 4CN^- \longrightarrow [Cu(CN)_4]^{2-}$, $\log K = 27.3$
(c) $Cu^{2+} + 2en \longrightarrow [Cu(en)_2]^{2+}$, $\log K = 15.4$
(d) $Cu^{2+} + 4H_2O \longrightarrow [Cu(H_2O)_4]^{2+}$, $\log K = 8.9$

- **Concept Insight** This solution includes the concept of equilibrium constant (K) and its relationship with the stability of complex compounds.

Ans. ***(b)*** Greater the value of log *K*, greater will be stability of complex compound formed.

For reaction,

$$Cu^{2+} + 4CN^- \longrightarrow [Cu(CN)_4]^{2-}$$

$$K = \frac{[(Cu(CN)_4)^{2-}]}{[Cu^{2+}][CN^-]^4} \text{ and } \log K = 27.3$$

For this reaction, log *K* has highest value among the given four reactions. Hence, *K* will also be higher among these four, *i.e.*, stability of the complexes will be highest among these four complexes.

Q.2 The colour of the coordination compounds depends on the crystal field splitting. What will be the correct order of absorption of wavelength of light in the visible region, for the complexes, $[Co(NH_3)_6]^{3+}$, $[Co(CN)_6]^{3-}$, $[Co(H_2O)_6]^{3+}$

(a) $[Co(CN)_6]^{3-} > [Co(NH_3)_6]^{3+} > [Co(H_2O)_6]^{3+}$
(b) $[Co(NH_3)_6]^{3+} > [Co(H_2O)_6]^{3+} > [Co(CN)_6]^{3-}$
(c) $[Co(H_2O)_6]^{3+} > [Co(NH_3)_6]^{3+} > [Co(CN)_6]^{3-}$
(d) $[Co(CN)_6]^{3-} > [Co(NH_3)_6]^{3+} > [Co(H_2O)_6]^{3+}$

Thinking Process This problem is based on the concept of crystal field splitting and colour of coordination compounds. Follow the steps to answer this question

(i) Arrange the given complexes in increasing order of their crystal field splitting energy.
(ii) Now arrange them in decreasing order of the wavelength of light.
(iii) As energy and wavelength are related as $\Delta E = h\nu = \frac{hc}{\lambda}$

Ans. ***(c)*** As we know that, strong field ligand split the five degenerate energy levels with more energy separation than weak field ligand, *i.e.*, as strength of ligand increases crystal field splitting energy increases.

Hence, $$\Delta E = \frac{hc}{\lambda}$$

$\Rightarrow$ $$\Delta E \propto \frac{1}{\lambda} \Rightarrow \lambda \propto \frac{1}{\Delta E}$$

As energy separation increases, the wavelength decreases.

Thus, the correct order of absorption of wavelength of light in visible region is

$$[Co(H_2O)_6]^{3+} > [Co(NH_3)_6]^{3+} > [Co(CN)_6]^{3-}$$

Here, as strength of ligand increases, ΔE increases, CFSE increases and λ absorbed decreases.

Hence, correct choice is option (c).

Mistake Alert! *Energy is inversely proportional to the wavelength.* $E = \frac{hc}{\lambda}$

Q.3 When 0.1 mol $CoCl_3(NH_3)_5$ is treated with excess of $AgNO_3$, 0.2 mol of AgCl are obtained. The conductivity of solution will correspond to

(a) 1 : 3 electrolyte (b) 1 : 2 electrolyte
(c) 1 : 1 electrolyte (d) 3 : 1 electrolyte

Ans. ***(b)*** One mole of $AgNO_3$ precipitates one mole of chloride ion. In the above reaction, when 0.1 mole $CoCl_3(NH_3)_5$ is treated with excess of $AgNO_3$, 0.2 mole of AgCl are obtained thus, there must be two free chloride ions in the solution of electrolyte.

So, molecular formula of complex will be $[Co(NH_3)_5Cl]\,Cl_2$ and electrolytic solution must contain $[Co(NH_3)_5Cl]^{2+}$ and two Cl^- as constituent ions. Thus, it is 1 : 2 electrolyte.

$$[Co(NH_3)_5Cl]Cl_2 \longrightarrow [Co(NH_3)_5Cl]^{2+}(aq) + 2Cl^-(aq)$$

Hence, option (b) is correct.

Mistake Alert! *Only* Cl^- *present as primary valency is ionisable and gives white precipitate with* $AgNO_3$ *solution.*

Q.4 When 1 mole of $CrCl_3 \cdot 6H_2O$ is treated with excess of $AgNO_3$, 3 moles of AgCl are obtained. The formula of the complex is :

(a) $[CrCl_3(H_2O)_3] \cdot 3H_2O$ (b) $[CrCl_2(H_2O)_4]Cl \cdot 2H_2O$
(c) $[CrCl(H_2O)_5]Cl_2 \cdot H_2O$ (d) $[Cr(H_2O)_6]Cl_3$

Ans. ***(d)*** 1 mole of $AgNO_3$ precipitates one free chloride ion (Cl^-).

Here, 3 moles of AgCl are precipitated by excess of $AgNO_3$. Hence, there must be three free Cl^- ions.

So, the formula of the complex can be $[Cr(H_2O)_6]Cl_3$ and correct choice is (d).

Q.5 The correct IUPAC name of $[Pt(NH_3)_2Cl_2]$ is

(a) Diamminedichloridoplatinum (II) (b) Diamminedichloridoplatinum (IV)
(c) Diamminedichloridoplatinum (0) (d) Dichloridodiammineplatinum (IV)

Thinking Process This problem is based on IUPAC nomenclature of coordination : compound. IUPAC nomenclature of any coordination compound can be done as follows

(i) Positively charged ions are named first.

(ii) Negatively charged ions are named in alphabetical order of ligands including their numbers followed by metal ending with –ium and oxidation state in the bracket.

Ans. ***(a)*** The complex compound is $[Pt(NH_3)_2Cl_2]$.
Hence, correct IUPAC name of $[Pt(NH_3)_2Cl_2]$ is
Diammine dichloridoplatinum (II)
So, (a) option is correct.

Q.6 The stabilisation of coordination compounds due to chelation is called the chelate effect. Which of the following is the most stable complex species?

(a) $[Fe(CO)_5]$ (b) $[Fe(CN)_6]^{3-}$ (c) $[Fe(C_2O_4)_3]^{3-}$ (d) $[Fe(H_2O)_6]^{3+}$

Ans. ***(c)*** Chelation (formation of cycle by linkage between metal ion and ligand) stabilises the coordination compound. The ligand which chelates the metal ion is known as chelating ligand.

Here, only $[Fe(C_2O_4)_3]^{3-}$ is a coordination compound which contains oxalate ion as a chelating ligand. Hence, it stabilises coordination compound by chelating Fe^{3+} ion.

Q.7 Indicate the complex ion which shows geometrical isomerism.

(a) $[Cr(H_2O)_4Cl_2]^+$ (b) $[Pt(NH_3)_3Cl]$ (c) $[Co(NH_3)_6]^{3+}$ (d) $[Co(CN)_5(NC)]^{3-}$

Thinking Process This problem includes concept of isomerism in coordination compound. Complex of MA_4B_2 type show geometrical isomerism.

Ans. ***(a)*** $[Cr(H_2O)_4Cl_2]^+$ shows geometrical isomerism because it is a MA_4B_2 type coordination compound which contains two set of equivalent ligands, four H_2O and 2 Cl.

Hence, the possible geometrical isomers are

Cl; H_2O, H_2O; Cr; H_2O, H_2O; Cl — and — Cl; H_2O, Cl; Cr; H_2O, H_2O; H_2O

trans-isomer *cis*-isomer

Hence, correct choice is option (a).

Q.8 The CFSE for octahedral $[CoCl_6]^{4-}$ is 18,000 cm^{-1}. The CFSE for tetrahedral $[CoCl_4]^{2-}$ will be

(a) 18,000 cm^{-1} (b) 16,000 cm^{-1} (c) 8,000 cm^{-1} (d) 20,000 cm^{-1}

Ans. ***(c)*** CFSE for octahedral and tetrahedral complexes are closely related to each other by formula $\Delta_t = \frac{4}{9}\Delta_0$.

where, Δ_0 = CFSE for octahedral complex, Δ_t = CFSE for tetrahedral complex

According to question, $\Delta_0 = 18,000\ cm^{-1}$

$$\therefore \quad \Delta_t = \frac{4}{9}\Delta_0 = \frac{4}{9} \times 18,000\ cm^{-1}$$

$$= 4 \times 2,000\ cm^{-1} = 8,000\ cm^{-1}$$

Q.9 Due to the presence of ambidentate ligands coordination compounds show isomerism. Palladium complexes of the type $[Pd(C_6H_5)_2(SCN)_2]$ and $[Pd(C_6H_5)_2(NCS)_2]$ are

(a) linkage isomers (b) coordination isomers
(c) ionisation isomers (d) geometrical isomers

Ans. *(a)* The ligand(s) which have two different bonding sites are known as ambidentate ligands *e.g.*, NCS, NO_2, etc.

Here, NCS has two binding sites, at N and S.

Hence, NCS (thiocyanate) can bind to the metal ion in two ways

$$M \leftarrow \text{NCS or } M \leftarrow \text{SNC}$$

Thus, coordination compounds containing NCS as a ligand can show linkage isomerism *i.e.*, $[Pd(C_6H_5)_2(SCN)_2]$ and $[Pd(C_6H_5)_2(NCS)_2]$ are linkage isomers.

Hence, correct choice is option (a).

Q.10 The compounds $[Co(SO_4)(NH_3)_5]Br$ and $[Co(SO_4)(NH_3)_5]Cl$ represent

(a) linkage isomerism (b) ionisation isomerism

(c) coordination isomerism (d) no isomerism

Ans. *(d)* Compounds having same molecular formula but different structural formula are known as isomers. $[Co(SO_4)(NH_3)_5]Br$ and $[Co(SO_4)(NH_3)_5]Cl$ do not have same molecular formula. Hence, they are not isomers.

Q.11 A chelating agent has two or more than two donor atoms to bind to a single metal ion. Which of the following is **not** a chelating agent?

(a) Thiosulphato (b) Oxalato

(c) Glycinato (d) Ethane-1, 2-diamine

Ans. *(a)* A chelating ligand has two or more binding donor atoms to a single metal ion

e.g.,

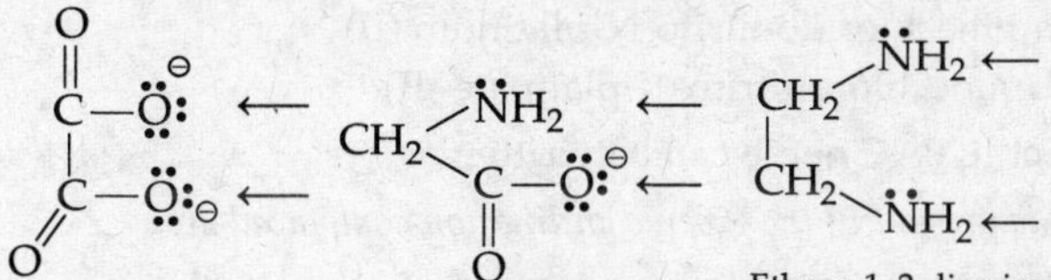

Oxalato Glycinato Ethane-1, 2-diamine

Here (←) denotes binding site.

Thiosulphato ($S_2O_3^{2-}$) is not a chelating ligand because geometrically it is not favourable for $S_2O_3^{2-}$ to chelate a metal ion.

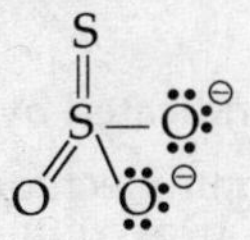

Mistake Alert! *Students may mistakenly think thiosulphate is a chelating agent due to its two atoms, but it typically binds through only one atom. True chelating agents, like oxalato, glycinato and ethane -1, 2-diamine, binds through two donor atoms to form a ring with the metal ion.*

Q.12 Which of the following species is **not** expected to be a ligand?

(a) NO (b) NH_4^+

(c) $NH_2CH_2CH_2NH_2$ (d) CO

Ans. *(b)* Ligand must donate a pair of electron or loosely held electron pair to metal and form a *M*—*L* bond.

e.g., $\ddot{N}= O, \ddot{N}H_2CH_2CH_2\ddot{N}H_2, :CO,$

Among the given options, $\overset{+}{N}H_4$ does not have any pair of electron. Hence $\overset{+}{N}H_4$ is not a ligand.

Q.13 What kind of isomerism exists between $[Cr(H_2O)_6]Cl_3$ (violet) and $[Cr(H_2O)_5Cl]Cl_2 \cdot H_2O$ (greyish-green)?

(a) Linkage isomerism
(b) Solvate isomerism
(c) Ionisation isomerism
(d) Coordination isomerism

Thinking Process This problem is based on the concept of isomerism in coordination compounds. To identify the correct isomerism, examine the formulas :

$[Cr(H_2O)_6] Cl_3$and $[Cr(H_2O)_5Cl]Cl_2 \cdot H_2O$

These compounds differ in the placement of water molecules inside and outside the coordination sphere, indicating solvate isomerism.

Ans. *(b)* Coordination compounds $[Cr(H_2O)_6]Cl_3$ and $[Cr(H_2O)_5Cl]H_2O \cdot Cl_2$ are solvate isomers, because water is exchanged by chloride ion. This is why both of them show different colour on exposure to sunlight.

Q.14 IUPAC name of $[Pt(NH_3)_2Cl(NO_2)]$ is

(a) Platinum diaminechloronitrite
(b) Chloronitrito-N-ammineplatinum (II)
(c) Diamminechloridonitrito-N-platinum (II)
(d) Diamminechloronitrito-N-platinate (II)

Ans. *(c)* Correct IUPAC name can be written as

The ligands present in the given coordination compound are

(i) (NH_3) represented as amine

(ii) Cl^- represented as chlorido

(iii) NO_2^- represented as nitrito-N

According to IUPAC rule, ligands are named in an alphabetical order before central atom. Prefex di-will be used to indicate the number of NH_3 ligands present.

Oxidation state of metal is indicated by Roman numeral in parenthesis.

So, IUPAC name will be diamminechloridonitrito-N-platinum (II)

Multiple Choice Questions (More Than One Options)

Q.15 Atomic number of Mn, Fe and Co are 25, 26 and 27 respectively. Which of the following inner orbital octahedral complex ions are diamagnetic?

(a) $[Co(NH_3)_6]^{3+}$
(b) $[Mn(CN)_6]^{3-}$
(c) $[Fe(CN)_6]^{4-}$
(d) $[Fe(CN)_6]^{3-}$

Thinking Process This problem is based on magnetic property of coordination compound. Coordination compounds containing at least one unpaired electron(s) are paramagnetic and coordination compounds containing all paired electrons are diamagnetic in nature.

Ans. *(a, c)* Molecular orbital electronic configuration of Co^{3+} in $[Co(NH_3)_6]^{3+}$ is

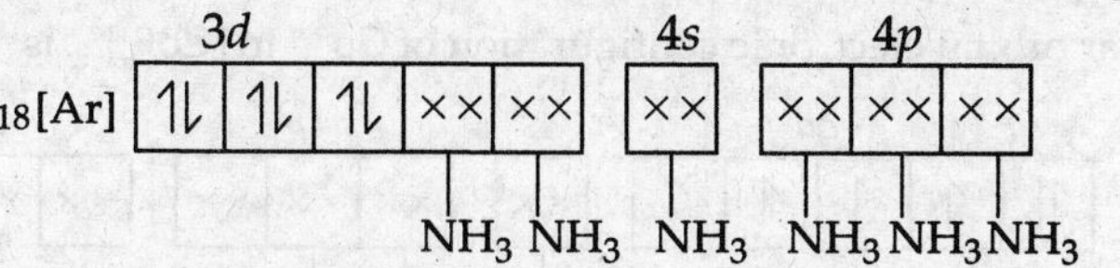

Number of unpaired electron = 0

Magnetic property = Diamagnetic

Molecular orbital electronic configuration of Mn^{3+} in $[Mn(CN)_6]^{3-}$

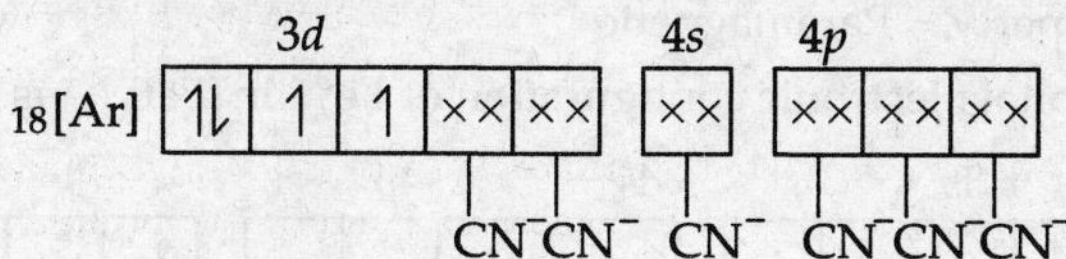

Number of unpaired electrons = 2

Magnetic property = Paramagnetic

Molecular orbital electronic configuration of Fe^{2+} in $[Fe(CN)_6]^{4-}$ is

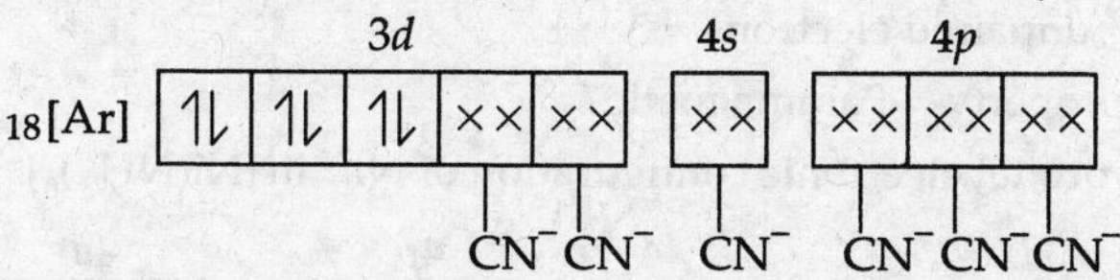

Number of unpaired electron = 0

Magnetic property = Diamagnetic

Molecular orbital electronic configuration of Fe^{3+} in $[Fe(CN)_6]^{3-}$

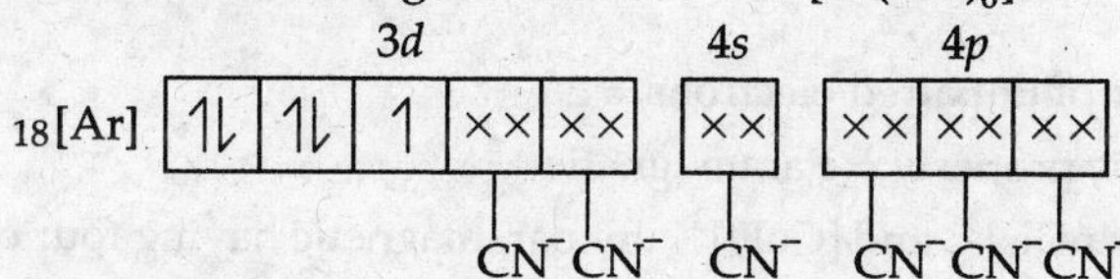

Number of unpaired electron = 1

Magnetic property = Paramagnetic

Thus, $[Co(NH_3)_6]^{3+}$ and $[Fe(CN)_6]^{4-}$ are diamagnetic.

Hence, correct choices are options (a) and (c).

Q.16 Atomic number of Mn, Fe, Co and Ni are 25, 26, 27 and 28 respectively. Which of the following outer orbital octahedral complexes have same number of unpaired electrons?

(a) $[MnCl_6]^{3-}$ (b) $[FeF_6]^{3-}$

(c) $[CoF_6]^{3-}$ (d) $[Ni(NH_3)_6]^{2+}$

Ans. *(a, c)*

Molecular orbital electronic configuration of Mn^{3+} in $[MnCl_6]^{3-}$ is

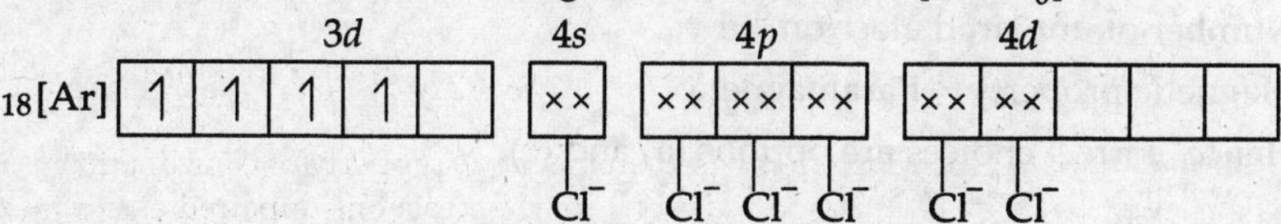

Number of unpaired electrons = 4

Magnetic property = Paramagnetic

Molecular orbital electronic configuration of Co^{3+} in $[CoF_6]^{3-}$ is

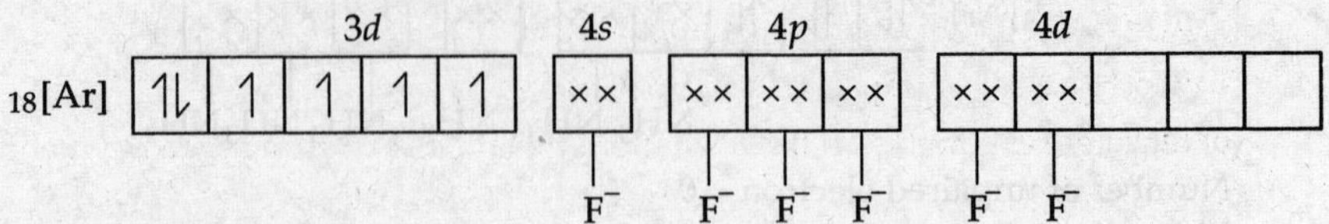

Number of unpaired electrons = 4

Magnetic property = Paramagnetic

Molecular orbital electronic configuration of Fe^{3+} in $[FeF_6]^{3-}$ is

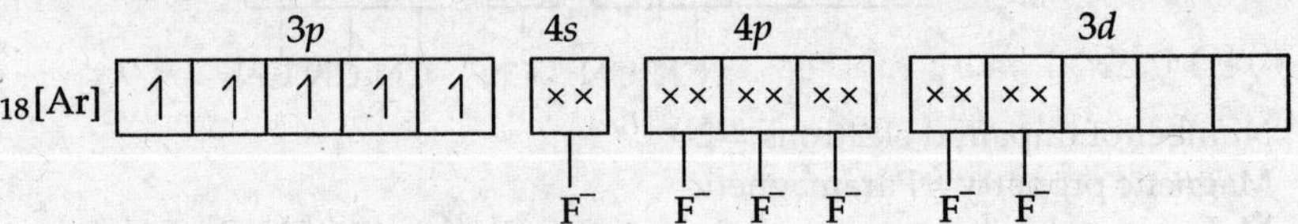

Number of unpaired electrons = 5

Magnetic property = Paramagnetic

Molecular orbital electronic configuration of Ni^{2+} in $[Ni(NH_3)_6]^{2+}$ is

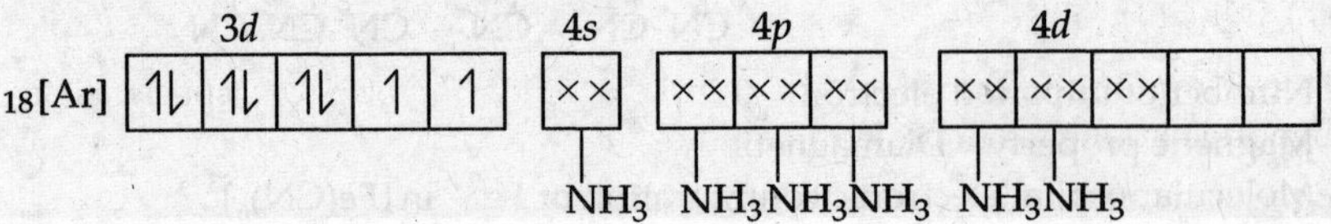

Number of unpaired electrons = 2

Magnetic property = Paramagnetic

Thus, $[MnCl_6]^{3-}$ and $[CoF_6]^{3-}$ are paramagnetic having four electrons each.

Hence, correct choices are options (a) and (c).

Q.17 Which of the following options are correct for $[Fe(CN)_6]^{3-}$ complex?

(a) d^2sp^3 hybridisation (b) sp^3d^2 hybridisation

(c) Paramagnetic (d) Diamagnetic

Ans. *(a, c)* According to VBT, the molecular orbital electronic configuration of Fe^{3+} in $[Fe(CN)_6]^{3-}$ is

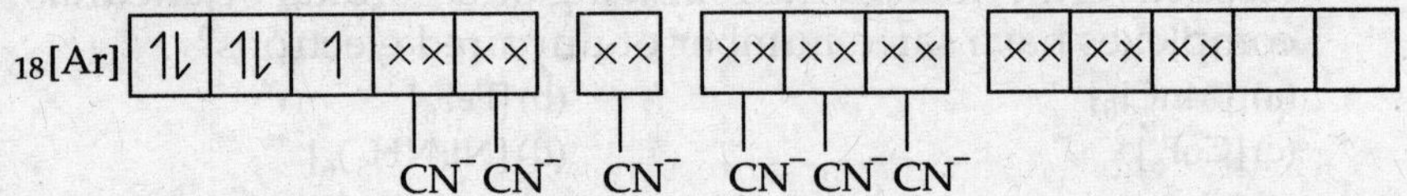

Hybridisation = d^2sp^3

Number of unpaired electron = 1

Magnetic property = Paramagnetic

Hence, correct choices are options (a) and (c).

Q.18 An aqueous pink solution of cobalt(II) chloride changes to deep blue on addition of excess of HCl. This is because ....

(a) $[Co(H_2O)_6]^{2+}$ is transformed into $[CoCl_6]^{4-}$

(b) $[Co(H_2O)_6]^{2+}$ is transformed into $[CoCl_4]^{2-}$

(c) tetrahedral complexes have smaller crystal field splitting than octahedral complexes

(d) tetrahedral complexes have larger crystal field splitting than octahedral complex

Ans. *(b, c)* Aqueous pink solution of cobalt (II) chloride is due to electronic transition of electron from t_{2g} to e_g energy level of $[Co(H_2O)_6]^{2+}$ complex. When excess of HCl is added to this solution,

(i) $[Co(H_2O)_6]^{2+}$ is transformed into $[CoCl_4]^{2-}$.

(ii) Tetrahedral complexes have smaller crystal field splitting than octahedral complexes because $\Delta_t = \frac{4}{9}\Delta_0$

Hence, options (b) and (c) are correct choices.

Q. 19 Which of the following complexes are homoleptic?

(a) $[Co(NH_3)_6]^{3+}$
(b) $[Co(NH_3)_4Cl_2]^+$
(c) $[Ni(CN)_4]^{2-}$
(d) $[Ni(NH_3)_4Cl_2]$

Ans. *(a, c)* **Homoleptic complex** The complex containing only one species or group as ligand is known as homoleptic ligand.

e.g., $[Co(NH_3)_6]^{3+}$, $[Ni(CN)_4]^{2-}$

Here, $[Co(NH_3)_6]^{3+}$ contains only NH_3 as a ligand and $[Ni(CN)_4]^{2-}$ contains CN^- as a ligand. While other two complexes, $[Co(NH_3)_4Cl_2]^+$ and $[Ni(NH_3)_4Cl_2]$ contain NH_3 and Cl as ligands.

Hence, options (a) and (c) are correct choices.

Q.20 Which of the following complexes are heteroleptic?

(a) $[Cr(NH_3)_6]^{3+}$
(b) $[Fe(NH_3)_4Cl_2]^+$
(c) $[Mn(CN)_6)]^{4-}$
(d) $[Co(NH_3)_4Cl_2]$

Ans. *(b, d)* **Heteroleptic complexes** Coordination complexes which contain more than one type of ligands are known as heteroleptic complexes.

e.g., $[Fe(NH_3)_4Cl_2]^+$ contains NH_3 and Cl^- as ligands and is a heteroleptic complex. Similarly, $[Co(NH_3)_4Cl_2]$ contains NH_3 and Cl^- as ligands is also a heteroleptic complex.

Hence, options (b) and (d) are correct choices.

Q.21 Identify the optically active compounds from the following

(a) $[Co(en)_3]^{3+}$

(b) *trans* $-[Co(en)_2Cl_2]^+$

(c) *cis* $-[Co(en)_2Cl_2]^+$

(d) $[Cr(NH_3)_5Cl]$

Ans. (a, c) $[Co(en)_3]^{3+}$ and *cis* $-[Co(en)_2Cl_2]^+$ are optically active compounds because their mirror images are non-superimposable isomer.

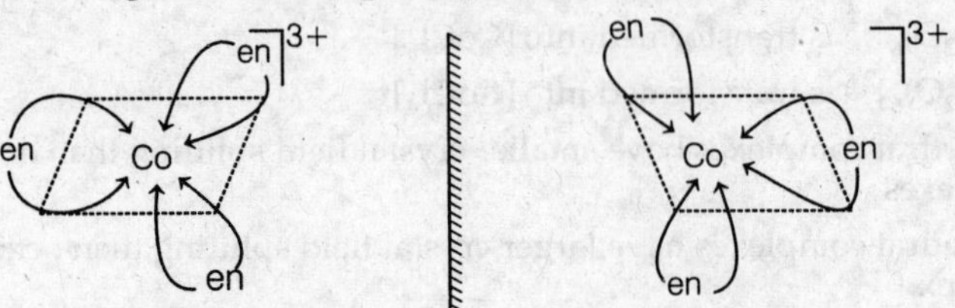

Non-superimposable isomers of $[Co(en)_3]^{3+}$

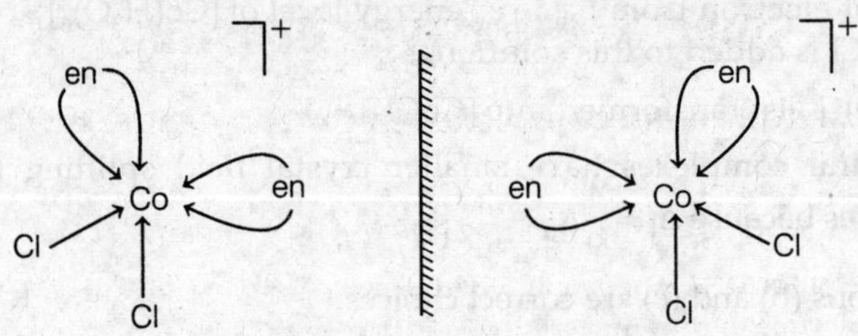

Non-superimposable isomers of $[Co(en)_2Cl_2]^+$

Hence, options (a) and (c) are correct choices.

Q.22 Identify the correct statements for the behaviour of ethane-1, 2-diamine as a ligand.

(a) It is a neutral ligand. (b) It is a didentate ligand.
(c) It is a chelating ligand. (d) It is a unidentate ligand.

Ans. (a, b, c) Molecular formula of ethane-1, 2-diamine is

$$\begin{array}{l} CH_2-\ddot{N}H_2 \\ | \\ CH_2-\ddot{N}H_2 \end{array}$$

(a) Ethane-1, 2-diamine is a neutral ligand due to absence of any charge.

(b) It is a didentate ligand due to presence of two donor sites, one at each nitrogen atom of amino group.

(c) It is a chelating ligand due to its ability to chelate with the metal.

Hence, options (a), (b) and (c) are correct choices.

Q.23 Which of the following complexes show linkage isomerism?

(a) $[Co(NH_3)_5(NO_2)]^{2+}$ (b) $[Co(H_2O)_5CO]^{3+}$
(c) $[Cr(NH_3)_5SCN]^{2+}$ (d) $[Fe(en)_2Cl_2]^+$

Ans. (a, c) Coordination compounds containing a ligand with more than one non-equivalent binding position (known as ambidentate ligand) show linkage isomerism.

e.g., $[Co(NH_3)_5(NO_2)]^+$ contains NO_2 ligand, which have two donor sites N and O that can be shown by arrow (→) as

$$\rightarrow N\begin{matrix} \nearrow O \\ \searrow O \\ \uparrow \end{matrix}$$

$[Cr(NH_3)_5SCN]^{2+}$ contains SCN ligand, which have two different donor sites S and N that can be shown by arrow (→) as

$$\rightarrow S-C\equiv N\leftarrow$$

Hence, $[Co(NH_3)_5(NO_2)]^{2+}$ and $[Cr(NH_3)_5SCN]^{2+}$ show linkage isomerism. While $[Co(H_2O)_5CO]^{3+}$ and $[Fe(en)_2Cl_2]^+$ have no ambidentate ligand. So, these two will not show linkage isomerism.

Hence, options (a) and (c) are correct choices.

Short Answer Type Questions

Q.24 Arrange the following complexes in the increasing order of conductivity of their solution

$[Co(NH_3)_3Cl_3]$, $[Co(NH_3)_4Cl_2]Cl$, $[Co(NH_3)_6]Cl_3$, $[Cr(NH_3)_5Cl]Cl_2$

Thinking Process This problem is based on the concept of conductivity of coordination compound. Greater the number of ions in the solution, greater is the conductivity of coordination compound.

Ans. Ions or molecules present outside the coordination sphere are ionisable. A complex which gives more ions on dissolution, is more conducting.

$$\underset{(1\ \text{ion})}{[Co(NH_3)_3Cl_3]} < \underset{(2\ \text{ions})}{[Co(NH_3)_4Cl_2]Cl} < \underset{(3\ \text{ions})}{[Cr(NH_3)_5Cl]Cl_2} < \underset{(4\ \text{ions})}{[Co(NH_3)_6]Cl_3}$$

Here, number of ions increases and conductivity increases.

Q.25 A coordination compound $CrCl_3 \cdot 4H_2O$ precipitates silver chloride when treated with silver nitrate. The molar conductance of its solution corresponds to a total of two ions. Write structural formula of the compound and name it.

Ans. Formation of white precipitate with $AgNO_3$ shows that atleast one Cl^- ion is present outside the coordination sphere. Moreover only two ions are obtained in solution, so only one Cl^- is present outside the sphere.

Thus, the formula of the complex is $[Co(H_2O)_4Cl_2]Cl$ and its IUPAC name is Tetraaquadichloridocobalt (III) chloride.

Q.26 A complex of the type $[M(AA)_2X_2]^{n+}$ is known to be optically active. What does this indicate about the structure of the complex? Give one example of such complex.

Ans. An optically active complex of the type $[M(AA)_2X_2]^{n+}$ indicates *cis*-octahedral structure, *e.g.*, *cis*-$[Pt(en)_2Cl_2]^{2+}$ or *cis*-$[Cr(en)_2Cl_2]^+$ because its mirror image isomers are non-superimposable.

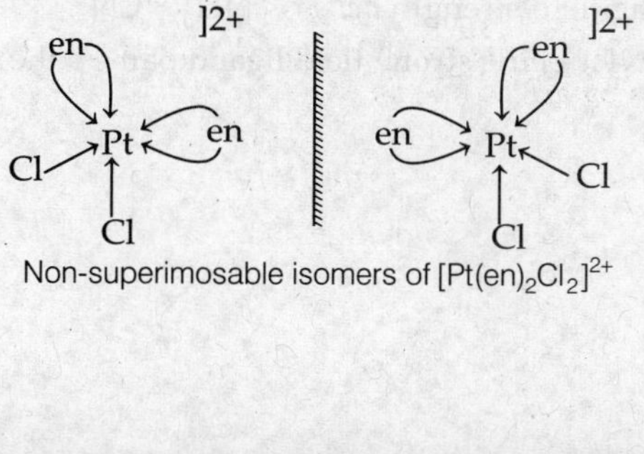

Non-superimosable isomers of $[Pt(en)_2Cl_2]^{2+}$

Q.27 Magnetic moment of $[MnCl_4]^{2-}$ is 5.92 BM. Explain giving reason.

Ans. The magnetic moment 5.92 BM shows that there are five unpaired electrons present in the *d*-orbitals of Mn^{2+} ion. As a result, the hybridisation involved is sp^3 rather than dsp^2. Thus, tetrahedral structure of $[MnCl_4]^{2-}$ complex will show 5.92 BM magnetic moment value.

Q.28 On the basis of crystal field theory explain why Co(III) forms paramagnetic octahedral complex with weak field ligands whereas it forms diamagnetic octahedral complex with strong field ligands.

Ans. With weak field ligands; $\Delta_o < P$, (pairing energy) so, the electronic configuration of Co (III) will be $t_{2g}^4 e_g^2$ *i.e.,* it has 4 unpaired electrons and is paramagnetic.

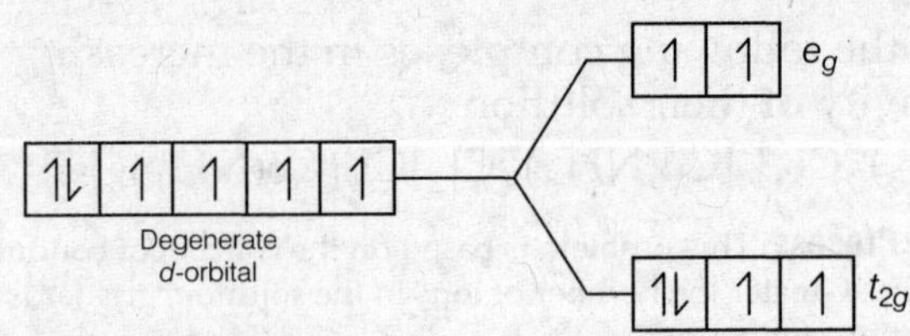

With strong field ligands, $\Delta_o > P$ (pairing energy), so pairing occurs thus, the electronic configuration will be $t_{2g}^6 e_g^0$. It has no unpaired electrons and is diamagnetic.

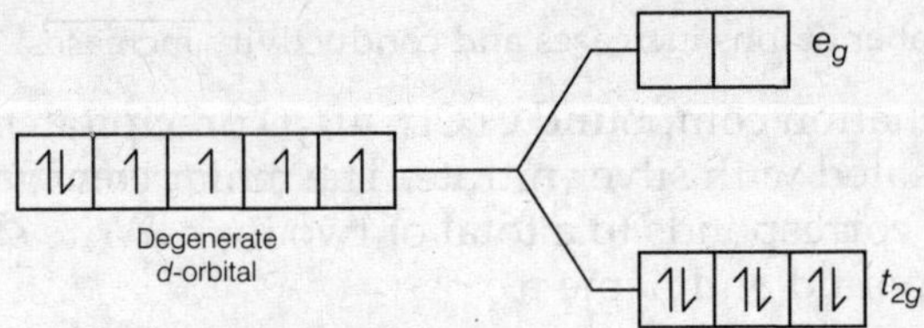

Q.29 Why are low spin tetrahedral complexes not formed?

Ans. In a tetrahedral complex, the *d*-orbital splitting is small as compared to octahedral complex. For same metal and same ligand, $\Delta_t = \frac{4}{9}\Delta_0$.

The crystal field stabilisation energy is lower than pairing energy. As a result, low spin configurations are rarely observed in tetrahedral complexes.

Q.30 Give the electronic configuration of the following complexes on the basis of crystal field splitting theory. $[CoF_6]^{3-}$, $[Fe(CN)_6]^{4-}$ and $[Cu(NH_3)_6]^{2+}$.

Ans. According to spectrochemical series, ligands can be arranged in a series in the order of increasing field strength *i.e.,* $F^- < NH_3 < CN^-$.

Hence, CN^- and NH_3 being strong field ligand pair up the t_{2g} electrons before filling e_g set.

$[CoF_6]^{3-}; Co^{3+} = (3d^6)\, t_{2g}^4 e_g^2$

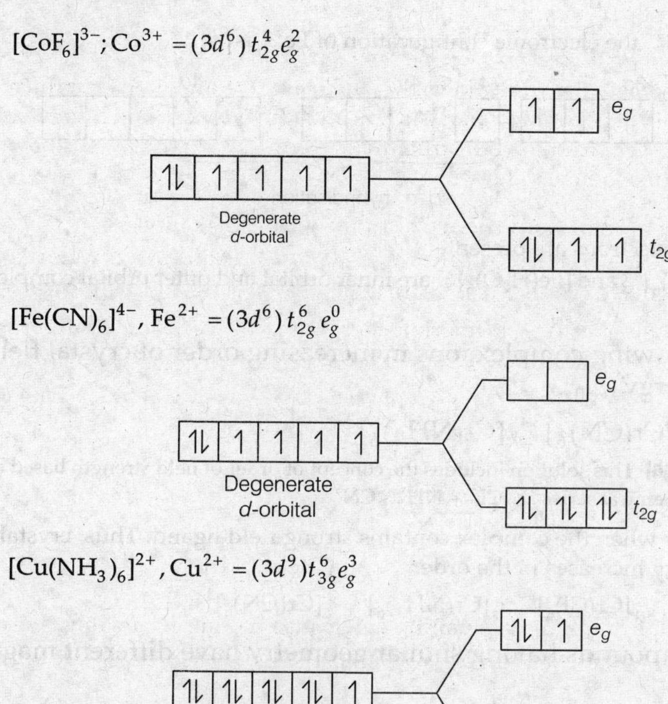

$[Fe(CN)_6]^{4-}, Fe^{2+} = (3d^6)\, t_{2g}^6\, e_g^0$

$[Cu(NH_3)_6]^{2+}, Cu^{2+} = (3d^9) t_{3g}^6 e_g^3$

Q.31 Explain why $[Fe(H_2O)_6]^{3+}$ has magnetic moment value of 5.92 BM whereas $[Fe(CN)_6]^{3-}$ has a value of only 1.74 BM?

Ans. As we know, $\mu_m = \sqrt{n(n+2)}$ BM

where, μ_m = magnetic moment

n = number of unpaired electrons

If $\mu_m = 1.74$ *i.e.,* $n = 1$

and $\mu_m = 5.92$ *i.e.,* $n = 5$

$[Fe(CN)_6]^{3-}$ involves d^2sp^3 hybridisation with one unpaired electron (as shown by its magnetic moment 1.74 BM) and $[Fe(H_2O)_6]^{3+}$ of involves sp^3d^2 hybridisation with five unpaired electrons (because magnetic moment equal to 5.92 BM).

For $[Fe(CN)_6]^{3-}$ the electronic configuration of Fe^{3+} is

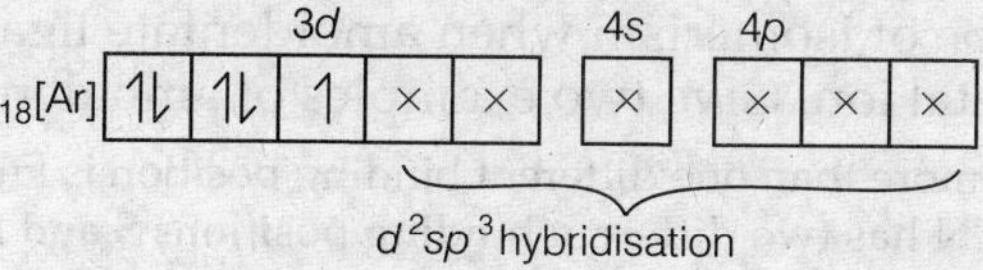

One unpaired electron is present.

For [Fe $(H_2O)_6]^{3+}$ the electronic configuration of Fe^{3+} is

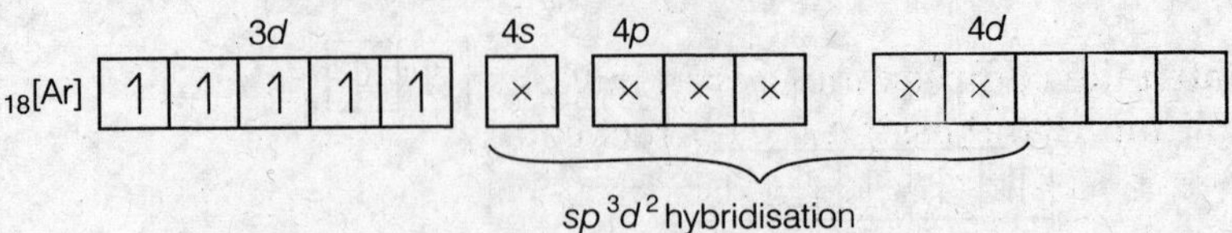

Five unpaired electrons are present.
Hence, $[Fe(CN)_6]^{3-}$ and $[Fe(H_2O)_6]^{3+}$ are inner orbital and outer orbital complexes respectively.

Q.32 Arrange following complex ions in increasing order of crystal field splitting energy (Δ_0).

$[Cr(Cl)_6]^{3-}$, $[Cr(CN)_6]^{3-}$, $[Cr(NH_3)_6]^{3+}$.

- **Concept Insight** This solution includes the concept of order of field strength based on the spectrochemical series *i.e.*, $Cl^- < NH_3 < CN^-$.

Ans. CFSE is higher when the complex contains strong field ligand. Thus, crystal field splitting energy increases in the order

$$[Cr(Cl)_6]^{3-} < [Cr(NH_3)_6]^{3+} < [Cr(CN)_6]^{3-}.$$

Q.33 Why do compounds having similar geometry have different magnetic moment?

Ans. It is due to the presence of weak and strong field ligands in complexes. If CFSE is high, the complex will show low value of magnetic moment and *vice-versa, e.g.*, $[CoF_6]^{3-}$ and $[Co(NH_3)_6]^{3+}$, the former is paramagnetic, and the latter is diamagnetic because F^- is a weak field ligand and NH_3 is a strong field ligand while both have similar octahedral geometry.

$[CoF_6]^{3-}$ (Co with six F) and $[Co(NH_3)_6]^{3+}$ (Co with six NH_3)

Q.34 $CuSO_4 \cdot 5H_2O$ is blue in colour while $CuSO_4$ is colourless. Why?

Ans. In $CuSO_4 \cdot 5H_2O$, water acts as ligand and causes crystal field splitting. Hence, *d-d* transition is possible, thus $CuSO_4 \cdot 5H_2O$ is coloured. In the anhydrous $CuSO_4$ due to the absence of water (ligand), crystal field splitting is not possible and hence, it is colourless.

Q.35 Name the type of isomerism when ambidentate ligands are attached to central metal ion. Give two examples of ambidentate ligands.

Ans. Ligand having more than one different binding position is known as ambidentate ligand. *e.g.*, SCN has two different binding positions S and N. Coordination compound containing ambidentate ligands is considered to show linkage isomerism due to presence of two different binding positions.

e.g., (i) $[Co(NH_3)_5SCN]^{3+}$ and (ii) $[Fe(NH_3)_5(NO_2)]^{3+}$

Matching The Columns

Q.36 Match the complex ions given in Column I with the colours given in Column II and assign the correct code.

Column I (Complex ion)	Column II (Colour)
A. $[Co(NH_3)_6]^{3+}$	1. Violet
B. $[Ti(H_2O)_6]^{3+}$	2. Green
C. $[Ni(H_2O)_6]^{2+}$	3. Pale blue
D. $[Ni(H_2O)_4(en)]^{2+}(aq)$	4. Yellowish orange
	5. Blue

Codes

	A	B	C	D		A	B	C	D
(a)	1	2	4	5	(b)	4	3	2	1
(c)	3	2	4	1	(d)	4	1	2	3

Ans. ***(b)*** A. → (4) **B.** → (3) **C.** → (2) **D.** → (1)

Colour of coordination compound is closely related to CFSE of coordination compound. Depending upon the CFSE of given coordination compounds, correct matching will be as follows

Column I (Complex ion)	Column II (Colour)
A. $[Co(NH_3)_6]^{3+}$	4. Yellowish orange
B. $[Ti(H_2O)_6]^{3+}$	3. Pale blue
C. $[Ni(H_2O)_6]^{2+}$	2. Green
D. $[Ni(H_2O)_4(en)]^{2+}$ (aq)	1. Violet

Hence, correct choice is option (b).

Q.37 Match the coordination compounds given in Column I with the central metal atoms given in Column II and assign the correct code.

Column I (Coordination compound)	Column II (Central metal atom)
A. Chlorophyll	1. Rhodium
B. Blood pigment	2. Cobalt
C. Wilkinson catalyst	3. Calcium
D. Vitamin B_{12}	4. Iron
	5. Magnesium

Codes

	A	B	C	D		A	B	C	D
(a)	5	4	1	2	(b)	3	4	5	1
(c)	4	3	2	1	(d)	3	4	1	2

Ans. *(a)* A. → (5) B. → (4) C. → (1) D. → (2)

Central metal ions present on coordination compounds determine the properties of coordination compound and their biological role.

	Column I (Coordination compound)		Column II (Central metal atom)
A.	Chlorophyll	5.	Magnesium
B.	Blood pigment	4.	Iron
C.	Wilkinson catalyst	1.	Rhodium
D.	Vitamin-B_{12}	2.	Cobalt

Hence, correct choice is (a).

Q.38 Match the complex ions given in Column I with the hybridisation and number of unpaired electrons given in Column II and assign the correct code

	Column I (Complex ion)		Column II (Hybridisation, number of unpaired electrons)
A.	$[Cr(H_2O)_6]^{3+}$	1.	dsp^2, 1
B.	$[Co(CN)_4]^{2-}$	2.	sp^3d^2, 5
C.	$[Ni(NH_3)_6]^{2+}$	3.	d^2sp^3, 3
D.	$[MnF_6]^{4-}$	4.	sp^3, 4
		5.	sp^3d^2, 2

Codes

	A	B	C	D		A	B	C	D
(a)	3	1	5	2	(b)	4	3	2	1
(c)	3	2	4	1	(d)	4	5	2	3

Ans. *(a)* A. → (3) B. → (1) C. → (5) D. → (2)

Formation of inner orbital complex and outer orbital complex determine hybridisation of molecule which *inturn* depend upon field strength of ligand and number of vacant *d* orbitals.

(i) Strong field ligand forms inner orbital complex with hybridisation d^2sp^3.

(ii) Weak field ligand forms outer orbital complex with hybridisation sp^3d^2.

According to VBT, hybridisation and number of unpaired electrons of coordination compounds can be calculated as

A. $[Cr(H_2O)_6]^{3+}$

Molecular orbital electronic configuration of Cr^{3+} in $[Cr(H_2O)_6]^{3+}$ is

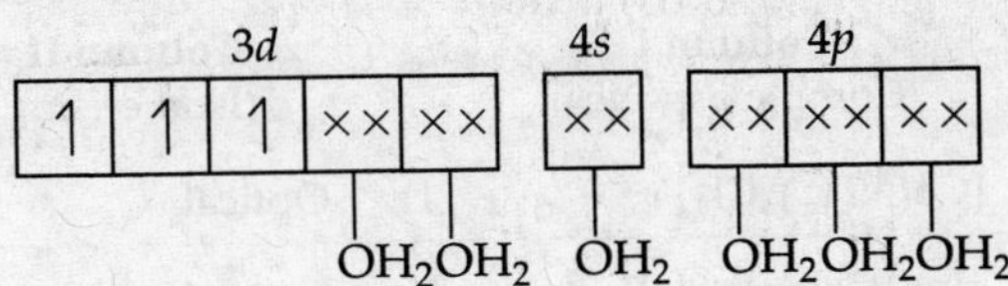

Hybridisation = d^2sp^3

n (number of unpaired electrons) = 3

B. $[Co(CN)_4]^{2-}$

Molecular orbital electronic configuration of Co^{2+} in $[Co(CN)_4]^{2-}$ is

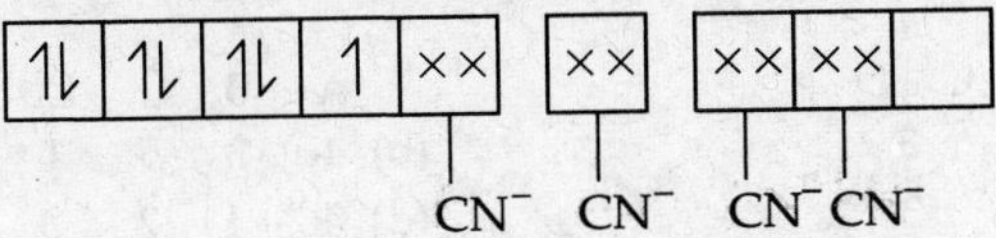

Hybridisation = dsp^2

$n = 1$

C. $[Ni(NH_3)_6]^{2+}$

Molecular orbital electronic configuration of Ni^{2+} in $[Ni(NH_3)_6]^{2+}$ is

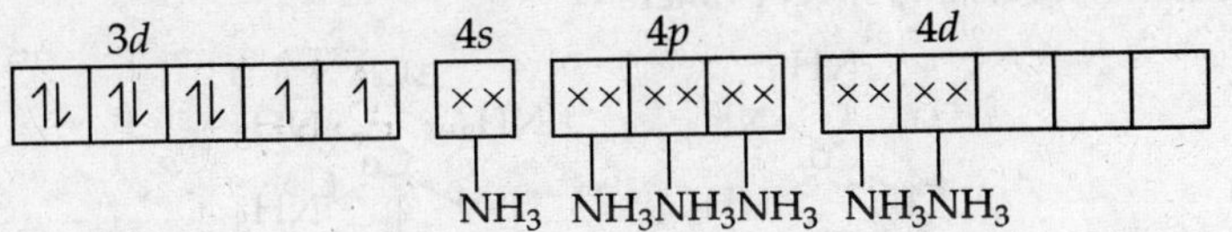

Hybridisation = sp^3d^2

$n = 2$

D. $[MnF_6]^{4-}$

Molecular orbital electronic configuration of Mn^{2+} in $[MnF_6]^{4-}$ is

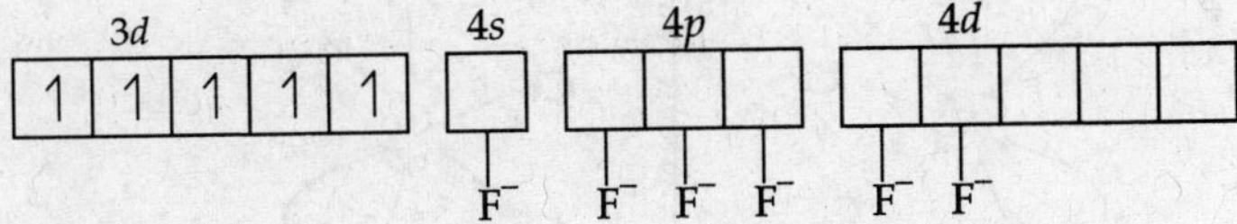

Hybridisation = sp^3d^2

$n = 5$

Hence, correct choice can be represented by (a).

Q.39 Match the complex species given in Column I with the possible isomerism given in Column II and assign the correct code.

Column I (Complex species)	Column II (Isomerism)
A. $[Co(NH_3)_4Cl_2]^+$	1. Optical
B. *cis* – $[Co(en)_2Cl_2]^+$	2. Ionisation
C. $[Co(NH_3)_5(NO_2)]Cl_2$	3. Coordination
D. $[Co(NH_3)_6][Cr(CN)_6]$	4. Geometrical
	5. Linkage

Codes

	A	B	C	D		A	B	C	D
(a)	1	2	4	3	(b)	4	3	5	1
(c)	4	1	5	3	(d)	4	1	2	3

Ans. *(c)* **A.** → (4) **B.** → (1) **C.** → (5) **D.** → (3)

Isomerism in coordination compound is decided by type of ligands and geometry of coordination and arrangement of ligands.

A. $[Co(NH_3)_4Cl_2]^+$ shows geometrical isomerism due to presence of two types of ligand whose $[Co(NH_3)_4Cl_2]^+$ arrangement around central metal ion leads to formation of *cis* and *trans*-isomers.

cis-isomer *trans*-isomer

B. *cis* – $[Co(en)_2Cl_2]^+$ shows optical isomer due to its non-superimposable mirror image relationship.

C. $[Co(NH_3)_5(NO_2)]Cl_2$ shows linkage isomerism due to the presence of ambidentate ligand NO_2 inside the ionisation sphere.

D. $[Co(NH_3)_6][Cr(CN)_6]$ shows coordination isomer due to interchanging of ligand in between two metal ions from one coordination sphere to another coordination sphere.

Hence, correct choice is option (c).

Q.40 Match the compounds given in Column I with the oxidation state of cobalt present in it (given in column II) and assign the correct code.

Column I (Compound)		Column II (Oxidation state of Co)	
A.	$[Co(NCS)(NH_3)_5](SO_3)$	1.	+4
B.	$[Co(NH_3)_4Cl_2]SO_4$	2.	0
C.	$Na_4[Co(S_2O_3)_3]$	3.	+1
D.	$[Co_2(CO)_8]$	4.	+2
		5.	+3

Code

	A	B	C	D		A	B	C	D
(a)	1	2	4	5	(b)	4	3	2	1
(c)	5	1	4	2	(d)	4	1	2	3

Ans. *(c)* **A.** → (5) **B.** → (1) **C.** → (4) **D.** → (2)

Oxidation state of CMI (central metal ion) can be calculated by considering the oxidation state of whole molecule as equal to charge present on coordination sphere.

A. $[Co(NCS)(NH_3)_5]SO_3$.

Let oxidation state of Co is x.

$$x - 1 + 5 \times 0 = +2$$

$$x = +2 + 1 = +3$$

B. $[Co(NH_3)_4Cl_2]SO_4$

Let oxidation state of Co = x

$$\Rightarrow \quad x + 4 \times 0 + 2 \times (-1) = +2$$

$$\Rightarrow \quad x - 2 = +2$$

$$x = 4$$

C. $Na_4[Co(S_2O_3)_3]$

Let oxidation state of Co = x

$$x + 3 \times (-2) = -4$$

$$x - 6 = -4$$

$$x = -4 + 6 = +2$$

D. $[Co(CO)_8]$

Let oxidation state of Co = x

$$x - 8 \times 0 = 0$$

$$x = 0$$

Hence, correct choice is option (c).

Assertion and Reason

In the following questions a statement of assertion followed by a statement of reason is given. Choose the correct answer out of the following choices.

(a) Assertion and reason both are true, reason is correct explanation of assertion.

(b) Assertion and reason both are true but reason is not the correct explanation of assertion.

(c) Assertion is true, reason is false.

(d) Assertion is false, reason is true.

Q.41 **Assertion** Toxic metal ions are removed by the chelating ligands.
Reason Chelate complexes tend to be more stable.

Ans. ***(a)*** Assertion and reason both are correct and reason is the correct explanation of assertion.

Toxic metal ions are removed by chelating ligands. When a solution of chelating ligand is added to solution containing toxic metals, ligands chelates the metal ions by formation of stable complex.

Q.42 **Assertion** $[Cr(H_2O)_6]Cl_2$ and $[Fe(H_2O)_6]Cl_2$ are reducing in nature.
Reason Unpaired electrons are present in their *d*-orbitals.

Ans. ***(b)*** Assertion and reason both are true but reason is not correct explanation of assertion.

$[Cr(H_2O)_6]Cl_2$ and $[Fe(H_2O)_6]Cl_2$ are reducing in nature due to formation of more stable complex ion after gaining of electron.

Q.43 **Assertion** Linkage isomerism arises in coordination compounds containing ambidentate ligand.
Reason Ambidentate ligand has two different donor atoms.

Ans. ***(a)*** Assertion and reason both are correct and reason is correct explanation of assertion. Linkage isomerism arises in coordination compounds containing ambidentate ligands because ambidentate ligand has two different donor atoms. *e.g.*, SCN, NO_2 etc.

Q.44 **Assertion** Complexes of MX_6 and MX_5L type (X and L are unidentate) do not show geometrical isomerism.
Reason Geometrical isomerism is not shown by complexes of coordination number 6.

Ans. ***(b)*** Assertion and reason both are correct and reason is not correct explanation of assertion.

Complexes of MX_6 and MX_5 L type (X and L are unidentate) do not show geometrical isomerism due to presence of plane of symmetry and necessary condition for showing geometrical isomerism is that complex must be of MA_4B_2 type or $[M(AB)_2X_2]$ type

L
X X
M
X X
X Plane of symmetry

Q.45 Assertion $[Fe(CN)_6]^{3-}$ ion shows magnetic moment corresponding to two unpaired electrons.
Reason Because it has d^2sp^3 type hybridisation.

Ans. ***(d)*** Assertion is false but reason is true.

According to VBT, Molecular orbital electronic configuration of Fe^{3+} in $[Fe(CN)_6]^{3-}$ is

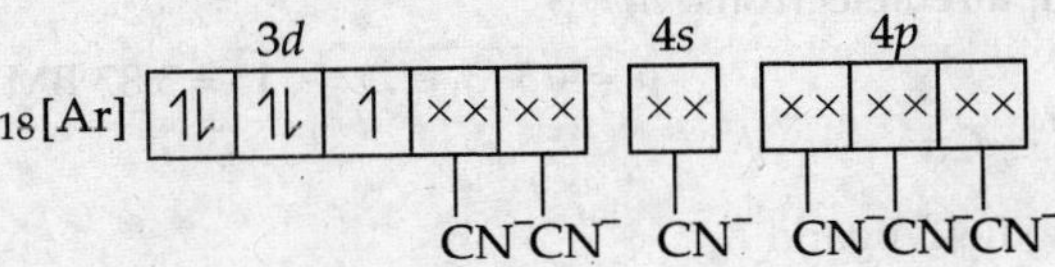

Hybridisation = d^2sp^3

$n = 1$

Hence, correct assertion is : $[Fe(CN)_6]^{3-}$ ion shows magnetic moment corresponding to one unpaired electron.

i.e., $\mu = \sqrt{n(n+2)} = \sqrt{1(1+2)} = \sqrt{3} = 1.73\,\text{BM}$

Long Answer Type Questions

Q.46 Using crystal field theory, draw energy level diagram, write electronic configuration of the central metal atom/ion and determine the magnetic moment value in the following

(a) $[CoF_6]^{3-}$, $[Co(H_2O)_6]^{2+}$, $[Co(CN)_6]^{3-}$

(b) FeF_6^{3-}, $[Fe(H_2O)_6]^{2+}$, $[Fe(CN)_6]^{4-}$

Thinking Process This problem includes concepts mixing of crystal field theory and magnetic moment (μ) determination.

$\mu = \sqrt{n(n+2)}$ BM where, n = number of unpaired electrons

Ans. ***(a)*** $[CoF_6]^{3-}$.

F^- is a weak field ligand.

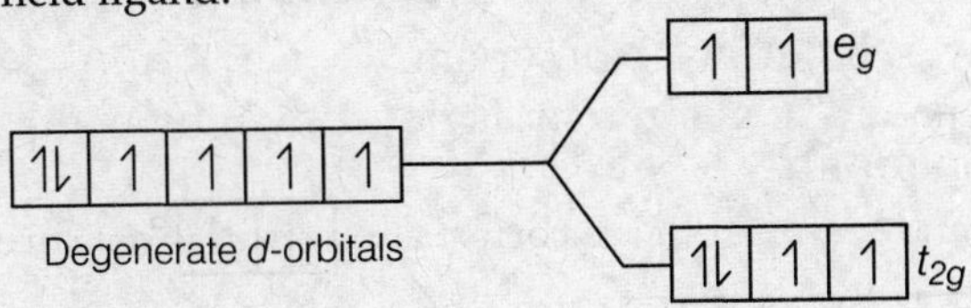

Configuration of $Co^{3+} = 3d^6$ (or $t_{2g}^4\, e_g^2$)

Number of unpaired electrons (n) = 4

Magnetic moment (μ) = $\sqrt{n(n+2)} = \sqrt{4(4+2)} = \sqrt{24} = 4.9\,\text{BM}$

$[Co(H_2O)_6]^{2+}$,

H_2O is a weak field ligand.

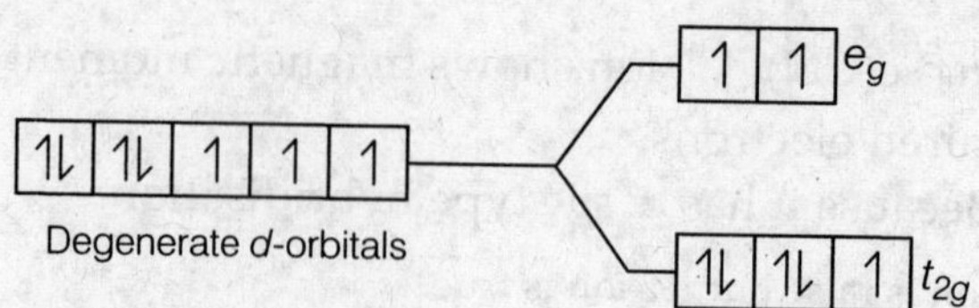

Configuration of $Co^{2+} = 3d^7 (\text{or } t_{2g}^5 e_g^2)$
Number of unpaired electrons (n) = 3

$$\mu = \sqrt{3(3+2)} = \sqrt{15} = 3.87 \text{ BM}$$

$[Co(CN)_6]^{3-}$ *i.e.*, Co^{3+}

∵ CN is strong field ligand.

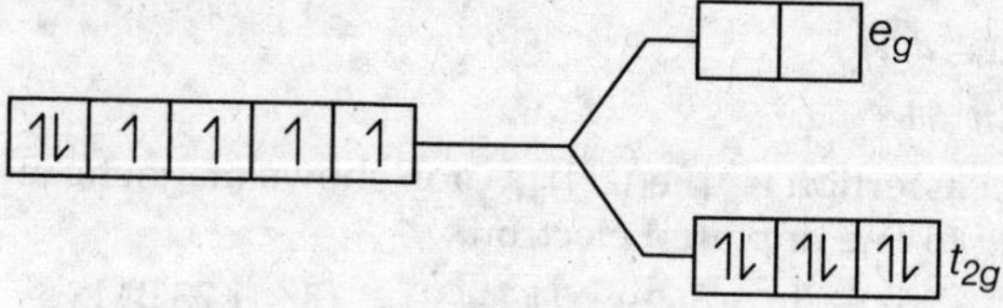

$$Co^{3+} = 3d^6 (\text{or } t_{2g}^6 e_g^0)$$

There is no unpaired electron, so it is diamagnetic.

$$\mu = 0$$

(b) $[FeF_6]^{3-}$,

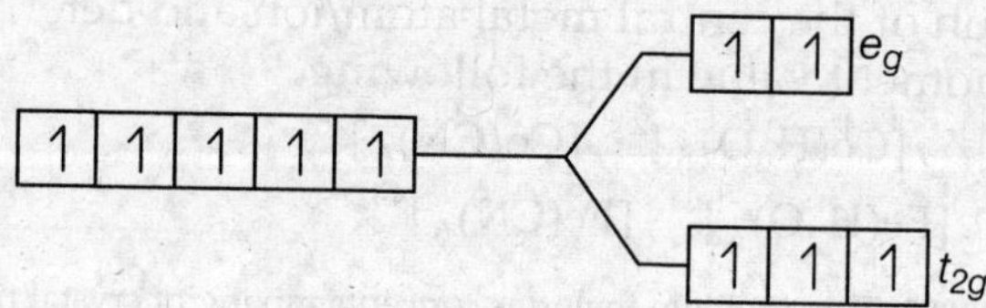

$$Fe^{3+} = d^5 \ (\text{or } t_{2g}^3 e_g^2)$$

Number of unpaired electrons, $n = 5$

$$\mu = \sqrt{5(5+2)}$$
$$= \sqrt{35} = 5.92 \text{ BM}$$

$[Fe(H_2O)_6]^{2+}$

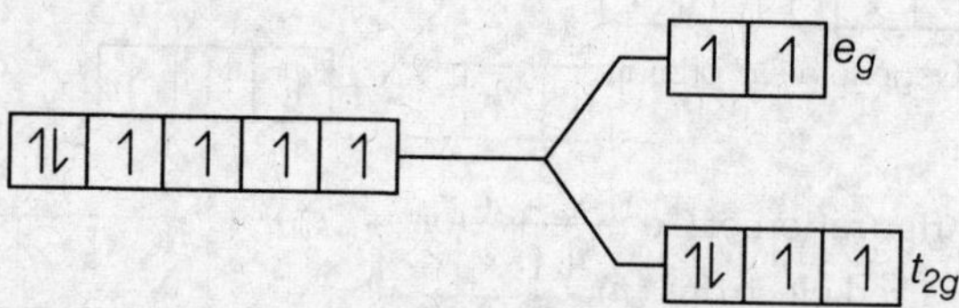

$$Fe^{2+} = 3d^6 \ (\text{or } t_{2g}^4 e_g^2)$$

Number of unpaired electrons, $n = 4$

$$\mu = \sqrt{4(4+2)}$$
$$= \sqrt{24} = 4.98 \text{ BM}$$

$[Fe(CN)_6]^{4-}$

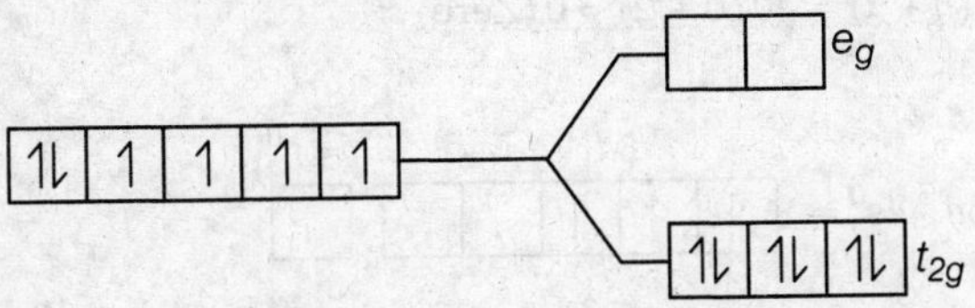

Since, CN^- is a strong field ligand, all the electrons get paired.

$$Fe^{2+} = 3d^6 \text{ (or } t_{2g}^6 e_g^0)$$

Because there is no unpaired electron, so it is diamagnetic in nature.

Q.47 Using valence bond theory, explain the following in relation to the complexes given below

$$[Mn(CN)_6]^{3-}, [Co(NH_3)_6]^{3+}, [Cr(H_2O)_6]^{3+}, [FeCl_6]^{4-}$$

(a) Type of hybridisation
(b) Inner or outer orbital complex
(c) Magnetic behaviour
(d) Spin only magnetic moment value

Ans. (I) $[Mn(CN)_6]^{3-}$

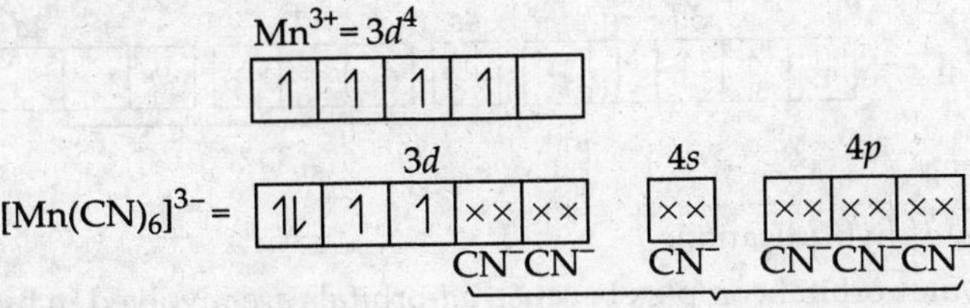

(i) d^2sp^3 hybridisation.
(ii) Inner orbital complex because $(n-1)$ d-orbitals are used.
(iii) Paramagnetic, as two unpaired electrons are present.
(iv) Spin only magnetic moment $(\mu) = \sqrt{2(2+2)} = \sqrt{8} = 2.82$ BM

(II) $[Co(NH_3)_6]^{3+}$

$Co^{3+} = 3d^6\ 4s^0$

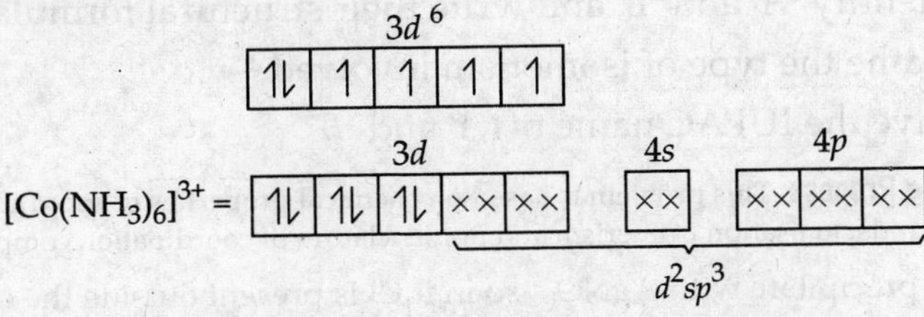

(NH_3 being strong field ligand, pairs up the unpaired $3d$ electrons.)
(i) d^2sp^3 hybridisation
(ii) Inner orbital complex because of the involvement of $(n-1)$ d-orbital in bonding.

(iii) Diamagnetic, as no unpaired electron is present.

(iv) $\mu = \sqrt{n(n+2)} = \sqrt{0(0+2)} = 0$ (Zero)

(III) $[Cr(H_2O)_6]^{3+}$

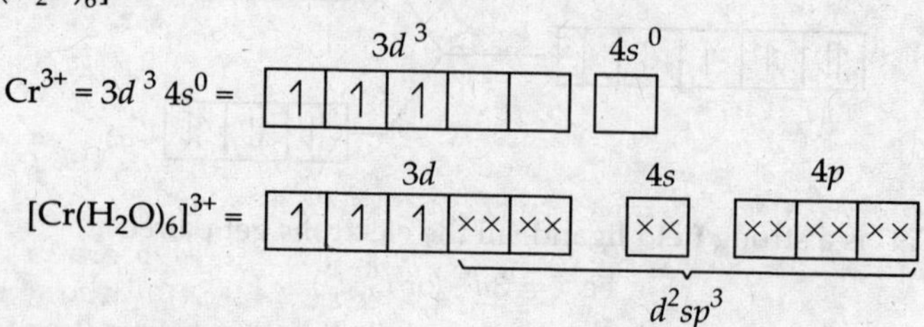

(i) d^2sp^3 hybridisation.

(ii) Inner orbital complex (as $(n-1)$ d-orbital takes part).

(iii) Paramagnetic (as three unpaired electrons are present.)

(iv) $\mu = \sqrt{n(n+2)} = \sqrt{3(3+2)} = \sqrt{15} = 3.87$ BM

(IV) $[FeCl_6]^{4-}$

$Fe^{2+} = 3d^6$

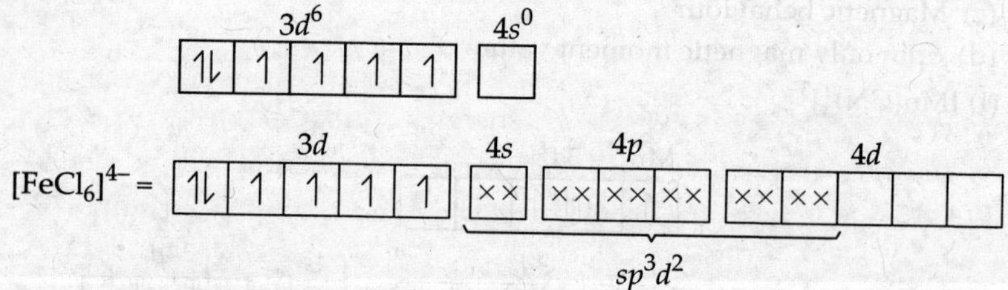

(i) sp^3d^2 hybridisation.

(ii) Outer orbital complex because nd-orbitals are involved in hybridisation.

(iii) Paramagnetic (because of the presence of four unpaired electrons).

(iv) $\mu = \sqrt{n(n+2)} = \sqrt{4(4+2)} = \sqrt{24} = 4.9$ BM

Q.48 $CoSO_4Cl \cdot 5NH_3$ exists in two isomeric forms 'A' and 'B'. Isomer 'A' reacts with $AgNO_3$ to give white precipitate, but does not react with $BaCl_2$. Isomer 'B' gives white precipitate with $BaCl_2$ but does not react with $AgNO_3$. Answer the following questions.

(a) Identify 'A' and 'B' and write their structural formulae.

(b) Name the type of isomerism involved.

(c) Give the IUPAC name of 'A' and 'B'.

Thinking Process This problem is based on chemical properties of coordination compounds, ionisation isomerism and nomenclature of coordination compounds.

Ans. 'A' gives precipitate with $AgNO_3$, so in it Cl is present outside the coordination sphere.

'B' gives precipitate with $BaCl_2$, so in it SO_4^{2-} is present outside the coordination sphere.

(a) So, A - $[Co(NH_3)_5SO_4]$ Cl

B-$[Co(NH_3)_5Cl]$ SO_4

(b) Ionisation isomerism (as give different ions when subjected to ionisation.)

(c) [A], Pentaamminesulphatocobalt (III) chloride.

[B], Pentaamminechloridocobalt (III) sulphate.

Q.49 What is the relationship between observed colour of the complex and the wavelength of light absorbed by the complex?

Ans. When white light falls on the complex, some part of it is absorbed. Higher the crystal field splitting energy, lower will be the wavelength absorbed by the complex. The observed colour of complex is the complementary colour generated from the wavelength of light absorbed by the complex.

e.g., if green light is absorbed, the complex appears red.

Q.50 Why are different colours observed in octahedral and tetrahedral complexes for the same metal and same ligands?

Ans. Extent of splitting of *d*-orbitals is different in octahedral and tetrahedral field. CFSE in octahedral and tetrahederal field are closely related as.

$$\Delta_t = \left(\frac{4}{9}\right)\Delta_o$$

where, Δ_t = crystal field splitting energy in tetrahedral field

Δ_0 = crystal field splitting energy in octahedral field

Wavelength of light and CFSE are related to each other by formula,

$$\Delta_0 = E = \frac{hc}{\lambda}$$

$$E \propto \frac{1}{\lambda}$$

Octahedral complexes generally show larger CFSE than tetrahedral complexes, so they absorb light at shorter wavelength and consequently give rise to complexes of different colour for the same metal and ligands (these complexes have different geometry *i.e.*, tetrahedral or octahedral and on the basis of this the wavelength of light absorbed and the complementary colour given out by the complex is decided).

Chapter

10

Haloalkanes and Haloarenes

Multiple Choice Questions (MCQs)

Q.1 The order of reactivity of following alcohols with halogen acids is ....

(A) $CH_3CH_2—CH_2—OH$

(B) $CH_3CH_2—\underset{\displaystyle CH_3}{\underset{|}{CH}}—OH$

(C) $CH_3CH_2—\underset{\displaystyle CH_3}{\underset{|}{\overset{\displaystyle CH_3}{\overset{|}{C}}}}—OH$

(a) (A) > (B) > (C)
(b) (C) > (B) > (A)
(c) (B) > (A) > (C)
(d) (A) > (C) > (B)

Ans. ***(b)*** Tertiary alcohols react more readily with halogen acids than secondary and primary alcohols due to carbocation stability in the S_N1 mechanism.

Here, (C) is a tertiary alcohol, (B) is secondary alcohol and (A) is primary alcohol, making the reactivity order (C) > (B) > (A)

Hence, the correct option is (b).

Note Higher the stability of intermediate, higher will be the reactivity of compound and higher will be the yield of the desired product.

Q.2 Which of the following alcohols will yield the corresponding alkyl chloride on reaction with concentrated HCl at room temperature?

(a) $CH_3CH_2— CH_2— OH$

(b) $CH_3CH_2—\underset{\displaystyle CH_3}{\underset{|}{CH}}— OH$

(c) $CH_3CH_2 —\underset{\displaystyle CH_3}{\underset{|}{CH}}— CH_2OH$

(d) $CH_3CH_2 —\underset{\displaystyle CH_3}{\underset{|}{\overset{\displaystyle CH_3}{\overset{|}{C}}}}— OH$

Thinking Process To solve this problem, keep in mind that tertiary alcohol being most reactive, reacts at room temperature.

Ans. ***(d)*** When alcohols are treated with conc., HCl at room temperature then alkyl chloride is formed. This reaction follows S_N1 mechanism. S_N1 mechanism completes in two steps. In first step, a carbocation is formed and this carbocation is attacked by a nucleophile in second step.

The attack of nucleophile to the carbocation is possible only if the carbocation is stable. Compound present in option (d) will give a tertiary carbocation in step I. Tertiary carbocation is most stable so it is further attacked by Cl^- nucleophile as follows

***Step* I** $CH_3-CH_2-C(CH_3)_2-OH \longrightarrow CH_3-CH_2-\overset{\oplus}{C}(CH_3)_2 + \bar{O}H$

***Step* II** $CH_3-CH_2-\overset{\oplus}{C}(CH_3)_2 + Cl^- \longrightarrow H_3C-CH_2-C(CH_3)_2-Cl$

Q.3 Identify the compound Y in the following reaction.

$$C_6H_5NH_2 \xrightarrow[273\text{-}278\ K]{NaNO_2+HCl} C_6H_5N_2^+Cl^- \xrightarrow{Cu_2Cl_2} Y + N_2$$

(a) chlorobenzene (b) benzene (c) 1,3-dichlorobenzene (d) 1,4-dichlorobenzene

Ans. ***(a)*** When a primary aromatic amine is dissolved or suspended in cold aqueous mineral acid and treated with sodium nitrite, a diazonium salt is formed. When this freshly prepared diazonium salt is mixed with cuprous chloride, then diazonium group is replaced by —Cl.

Chlorobenzene is formed which is y in this reaction.

$$C_6H_5NH_2 \xrightarrow[273\text{-}278\ K]{NaNO_2+HCl} C_6H_5N_2^+Cl^- \xrightarrow{Cu_2Cl_2} \underset{(y)}{C_6H_5Cl} + N_2$$

Hence, option (a) is correct.

Q.4 Toluene reacts with a halogen in the presence of iron (III) chloride giving *ortho* and *para* halo compounds. The reaction is

(a) electrophilic elimination reaction

(b) electrophilic substitution reaction

(c) free radical addition reaction

(d) nucleophilic substitution reaction

Ans. ***(b)*** Toluene reacts with a halogen in the presence of iron (III) chloride giving *ortho* and *para* halo compounds. The reaction is electrophilic substitution reaction.

It has the following mechanism

$$Cl-Cl \xrightarrow{FeCl_3} FeCl_4^- + Cl^+$$

$$C_6H_5CH_3 + Cl^+ \longrightarrow \text{(arenium ion, Cl and H at ortho position)} \text{ or } \text{(arenium ion, Cl and H at para position)}$$

$$\text{(arenium ion)} + [FeCl_4]^- \longrightarrow o\text{-}ClC_6H_4CH_3 + HCl + FeCl_3$$

In this mechanism, electrophile Cl^+ is attacked by electron rich benzene ring and replaces hydrogen. So, the reaction is electrophilic substitution reaction.

Q.5 Which of the following is halogen exchange reaction?

(a) $RX + NaI \rightarrow RI + NaX$

(b) $>C=C< + HX \longrightarrow >C(H)-C(X)<$

(c) $R{-}OH + HX \xrightarrow{ZnCl_2} R{-}X + H_2O$

(d) $C_6H_5CH_3 + X_2 \xrightarrow[\text{dark}]{\text{Fe}} o\text{-}XC_6H_4CH_3 + p\text{-}XC_6H_4CH_3$

Ans. *(a)* Halogen exchange reactions are those reactions in which one halide replaces another. In option (a) halogen $(-X)$ is replaced by iodine. This reaction is named as Finkelstein reaction.

In option (b), there is the addition of hydrogen halide on alkene.

In option (c), halogen replaces alcoholic group.

While in option (d), halogen replaces the hydrogen of benzene ring.

Q.6 Which reagent will you use for the following reaction?

$$CH_3CH_2CH_2CH_3 \longrightarrow CH_3CH_2CH_2CH_2Cl + CH_3CH_2CHClCH_3$$

(a) Cl_2 / UV light

(b) $NaCl + H_2SO_4$

(c) Cl_2 gas in dark

(d) Cl_2 gas in the presence of iron in dark

Ans. *(a)* The given reaction is a substitution reaction. It involves the replacement of 1° and 2° hydrogen of alkanes by chlorine. It occurs in presence of ultraviolet light or at high temperature.

The chlorination does not occur at room temperature in absence of light. In this reaction, light is absorbed by the chlorine molecule and activated chlorine initiates the reaction as follows :

***Step* 1** $$Cl{-}Cl \xrightarrow[\text{light}]{\text{UV}} 2\dot{C}l$$

$$\dot{C}l + CH_3{-}CH_2{-}CH_2{-}CH_3 \longrightarrow CH_3CH_2CH_2{-}\dot{C}H_2 + HCl$$

***Step* 2** $$CH_3{-}CH_2{-}CH_2{-}\dot{C}H_2 + Cl_2 \longrightarrow CH_3{-}CH_2{-}CH_2{-}CH_2Cl + \dot{C}l$$

***Step* 3** $$CH_3{-}CH_2{-}CH_2{-}\dot{C}H_2 + \dot{C}l \longrightarrow CH_3CH_2CH_2CH_2Cl$$

Q.7 Arrange the following compounds in the increasing order of their densities.

(i) benzene (ii) chlorobenzene (iii) 1,3-dichlorobenzene (iv) 1-bromo-3-chlorobenzene

(a) (i) < (ii) < (iii) < (iv) (b) (i) < (iii) < (iv) < (ii)
(c) (iv) < (iii) < (ii) < (i) (d) (ii) < (iv) < (iii) < (i)

- **Concept Insight** This solution is based on the concept that density is influenced by molecular mass. Compound with higher molecular mass generally have greater density.

Ans. *(a)* Density is directly related to molecular mass. Higher the molecular mass, higher will be the density of the compound. Among the four given compounds, the order of molecular mass is :

benzene < chlorobenzene < dichlorobenzene < bromochlorobenzene

Therefore, the increasing order of their densities are same as above.

Hence, option (a) is correct.

Q.8 Arrange the following compounds in increasing order of their boiling points.

(i) $(CH_3)_2CH{-}CH_2Br$ (ii) $CH_3CH_2CH_2CH_2Br$

(iii) $H_3C{-}C(CH_3)(Br){-}CH_3$

(a) (ii) < (i) < (iii) (b) (i) < (ii) < (iii)
(c) (iii) < (i) < (ii) (d) (iii) < (ii) < (i)

Ans. *(c)* Boiling point of a compound depends upon the surface area. Higher the surface area, higher will be the boiling point of a compound. Surface area decreases with increase in branching. If the compound has branching, so its boiling point will be minimum.

Thus, the increasing order of their boiling points is

$H_3C{-}C(CH_3)(Br){-}CH_3$ (Maximum branching; lowest b.p.) < $(H_3C)_2CH{-}CH_2Br$ (Branching) < $CH_3CH_2CH_2CH_2Br$ (Straight chain; higher b.p.)

Hence, option (c) is correct choice.

Q.9 In which of the following molecules carbon atom marked with asterisk (*) is asymmetric?

(i) I–C*(H)(Br)–Cl (ii) I–C*(D)(Br)–Cl (iii) OH–C*(H)(C_2H_5)–CH_3 (iv) H–C*(H)(C_2H_5)–CH_3

(a) (i), (ii), (iii) and (iv)
(b) (i), (ii) and (iii)
(c) (ii), (iii) and (iv)
(d) (i), (iii) and (iv)

Ans. ***(b)*** Asymmetric/chiral carbon atom is that in which all of its four valencies is satisfied with four different groups or atoms. In compound (iv), carbon satisfies two of its valencies with two hydrogen atoms *i.e.*, similar atom. So, it is not an asymmetric carbon atom while rest of the three molecules have asymmetric carbon as each carbon has satisfied all four valencies with four different groups or atoms.

So, the correct option is (b).

Q.10 Which of the following structures is enantiomeric with the molecule (*A*) given below?

H, CH_3, H_5C_2, C, Br

(*A*)

(a) H, C_2H_5, H_3C, C, Br

(b) CH_3, H, Br, C, C_2H_5

(c) H, Br, H_3C, C, C_2H_5

(d) Br, H, H_5C_2, C, CH_3

Ans. ***(a)*** The stereoisomers related to each other as non-superimposable mirror images are called enantiomers. They only differ with respect to the rotation of plane polarised light. If one of the enantiomer is dextro rotatory, the other will be laevo rotatory.

Here, the enantiomer of molecule (*A*) is compound in option (a).

Mirror

H, CH_3, H_5C_2, C, Br | H, C_2H_5, H_3C, C, Br

Q.11 Which of the following is an example of *vic*-dihalide?

(a) Dichloromethane (b) 1, 2-dichloroethane
(c) Ethylidene chloride (d) Allyl chloride

Ans. ***(b)*** *vic*-dihalides are those halides in which two halogen atoms are present on the two adjacent carbon atoms.

The structures of the given compounds are

```
     H                               H   Cl
     |                               |   |
Cl — C — Cl   CH2 — CH2       H — C — C — H    Cl
     |        |     |             |   |        |
     H        Cl    Cl            H   Cl       CH2 — CH = CH2
Dichloromethane  1, 2-Dichloroethane  Ethylidene chloride  Allyl chloride
```

In 1, 2-dichloroethane, the two chlorine atoms are attached to two adjacent carbon atoms.

Hence, option (b) is correct.

Q.12 The position of —Br in the compound in $CH_3CH{=}CHC(Br)(CH_3)_2$ can be classified as ....

(a) allyl (b) aryl (c) vinyl (d) secondary

● **Concept Insight** This solution includes the concept of classification of halides based on the type of carbon atom (sp^2 or sp^3) bonded to the halogen. allyl, aryl, vinyl and secondary alkyl halides are categorised by the bonding structure and hybridisation of the carbon to which halogen is attached.

Ans. ***(a)*** Allyl halides are those compounds in which the halogen atom is bonded to sp^3 hybridised carbon atom next to carbon-carbon double bond.

e.g., $CH_2 = CH — CH_2X$ and $CH_3CH = CHC(Br)(CH_3)_2$.

Aryl halides are the compounds in which the halogen atom is bonded to the sp^2 hybridised carbon atom of an aromatic ring.

e.g.,

X

Vinyl halides are the compounds in which the halogen atom is bonded to the sp^2 hybridised carbon atom of a carbon-carbon double bond.

e.g., $CH_2{=}CH — X$

Secondary alkyl halides are the compounds in which the halogen atom is bonded to the sp^3 hybridised carbon atom which is further bonded to two alkyl groups and one hydrogen atom.

e.g.,

```
    R
    |
R — C — X
    |
    H
```

Q.13 Chlorobenzene is formed by reaction of chlorine with benzene in the presence of $AlCl_3$. Which of the following species attacks the benzene ring in this reaction?

(a) Cl^- (b) Cl^+ (c) $AlCl_3$ (d) $[AlCl_4]^-$

Ans. ***(b)*** In this reaction, $AlCl_3$ is a catalyst which activates the chlorine molecule to show heterolytic cleavage. $AlCl_3$ is electron deficient molecule and forms $AlCl_4^-$ and Cl^+ when reacted with Cl_2. Electron rich benzene ring attacks the Cl^+ electrophile to form chlorobenzene.

$$AlCl_3 + Cl_2 \longrightarrow [AlCl_4]^- + Cl^+$$

$$C_6H_6 + Cl^+ \longrightarrow C_6H_5Cl$$

Chlorobenzene

Q.14 Ethylidene chloride is a/an ....

(a) *vic*-dihalide (b) *gem*-dihalide (c) allylic halide (d) vinylic halide

Ans. ***(b)*** In *vic*-dihalides, halogen atoms are present on the adjacent carbon atoms.

In *gem*-dihalides, halogen atoms are present on the same carbon atom. They are known as alkylidene halides.

In allylic halides, halogen atom is bonded to sp^3 hybridised carbon atom next to carbon-carbon double bond.

In vinylic halides, halogen atom is bonded to sp^2 hybridised carbon atom of a carbon-carbon double bond.

In ethylidene chloride ($H_3C—CHCl_2$) both halogen atoms are present on same carbon atom, so it is a *gem*-dihalide.

Q.15 What is '*A*' in the following reaction?

$$C_6H_5—CH_2—CH=CH_2 + HCl \longrightarrow A$$

(a) o-Chloro substituted $C_6H_4(Cl)—CH_2—CH=CH_2$

(b) $C_6H_5—CH_2—CH_2—CH_2—Cl$

(c) $C_6H_5—CH_2—CH(Cl)—CH_3$

(d) $C_6H_5—CH(Cl)—CH_2—CH_3$

Ans. ***(c)*** In this reaction, addition of HCl takes place on doubly bonded carbons in accordance with Markovnikov's rule *i.e.*, addition of Cl^- will take place on that carbon which has lesser number of hydrogen.

Thus,

$$C_6H_5—CH_2—CH=CH_2 + HCl \longrightarrow C_6H_5—CH_2—CH(Cl)—CH_3$$

Hence, option (c) is correct.

Q.16 A primary alkyl halide would prefer to undergo ....
(a) S_N1 reaction (b) S_N2 reaction (c) α-Elimination (d) Racemisation

Thinking Process This problem is based on the concept of nucleophilic substitution reactions. Primary alkyl halides have less steric hindrance making them more likely to undergo S_N2 reaction rather than S_N1.

Ans. ***(b)*** A primary alkyl halide would prefer to undergo S_N2 reaction.

(a) S_N2 reactions occur only if the intermediate carbocation is stable, *i.e.*, 3° carbocation.

(b) S_N2 reactions occur if there is less steric hinderance on to the α-carbon of alkyl halide. In case of primary alkyl halides, carbocation is highly unstable and steric hinderance is very less. So, primary alkyl halide would prefer to undergo S_N2 reaction.

(c) In α-elimination, proton and the leaving group are present on same atom.

(d) Racemisation is the process of conversion of enantiomer into a racemic mixture.

Q.17 Which of the following alkyl halides will undergo S_N1 reaction most readily?
(a) $(CH_3)_3C—F$ (b) $(CH_3)_3C—Cl$ (c) $(CH_3)_3C—Br$ (d) $(CH_3)_3C—I$

Concept Insight This solution is based on the concept of leaving group ability and bond strength in S_N1 reactions.

Ans. ***(d)*** All the given compounds are tertiary alkyl halides but the bond formed between carbon and iodine (C— I) bond is the weakest bond due to large difference in the size of carbon and iodine. So, $(CH_3)_3C—I$ gives S_N1 reaction most readily. In other words, iodine is a better leaving group.

Q.18 Which is the correct IUPAC name for $CH_3—\underset{\underset{C_2H_5}{|}}{CH}—CH_2—Br$?

(a) 1-Bromo-2-ethylpropane (b) 1-Bromo-2-ethyl-2-methylethane
(c) 1-Bromo-2-methylbutane (d) 2-Methyl-1-bromobutane

Ans. ***(c)*** The correct IUPAC name of the given compound is

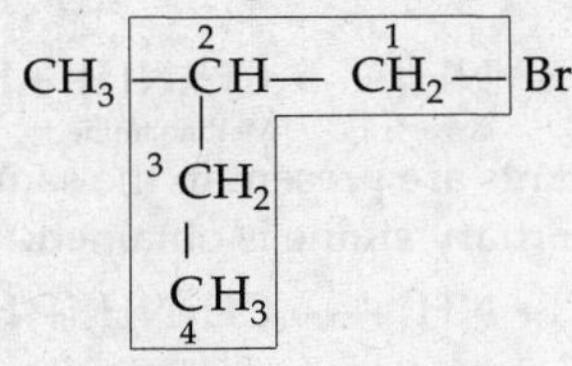

1-Bromo-2-methylbutane

Q.19 What should be the correct IUPAC name for diethylbromomethane?
(a) 1-Bromo-1, 1-diethylmethane (b) 3-Bromopentane
(c) 1-Bromo-1-ethylpropane (d) 1-Bromopentane

Ans. ***(b)*** Structure of the diethylbromomethane is given below :

$$\underset{5}{H_3C}—\underset{4}{H_2C}—\underset{3}{\overset{\overset{Br}{|}}{HC}}—\underset{2}{CH_2}—\underset{1}{CH_3}$$

So, the IUPAC name is 3-bromopentane.

Q.20 The reaction of toluene with chlorine in the presence of iron and in the absence of light yields ....

(a) $C_6H_5CH_2Cl$ (benzyl chloride, ring with CH_2Cl)

(b) ring with CH_3 and ortho Cl

(c) $H_3C-C_6H_4-Cl$

(d) Mixture of (b) and (c)

Ans. ***(d)*** The reaction of toluene with chlorine in the presence of iron and in the absence of light, gives the substitution reaction in the benzene ring. The $—CH_3$ group of toluene is *o* and *p*-directing then product is the mixture of (b) and (c) *i.e.,* *o*-chlorotoluene and *p*-chlorotoluene.

$$\underset{\text{Toluene}}{C_6H_5CH_3} + Cl_2 \xrightarrow[\text{(Dark)}]{\text{Fe}} \underset{o\text{-Chlorotoluene}}{o\text{-}ClC_6H_4CH_3} + \underset{p\text{-Chlorotoluene}}{p\text{-}ClC_6H_4CH_3}$$

Q.21 Chloromethane on treatment with excess of ammonia yields mainly

(a) N, N-Dimethylmethanamine $\left(CH_3—N\begin{matrix}CH_3\\CH_3\end{matrix}\right)$

(b) N-Methylmethanamine ($CH_3—NH—CH_3$)

(c) Methanamine (CH_3NH_2)

(d) Mixture containing all these in equal proportion

Ans. ***(c)*** Chloromethane on treatment with excess of ammonia yields mainly methanamine.

$$CH_3Cl + \underset{\text{Excess}}{NH_3} \longrightarrow \underset{\text{Methanamine}}{CH_3NH_2} + HCl$$

However, if the two reactants are present in the same amount, then the mixture of primary, secondary and tertiary amine is obtained.

$$CH_3Cl + NH_3 \longrightarrow \underset{\text{(Primary amine)}}{CH_3NH_2} + HCl$$

$$CH_3NH_2 + CH_3Cl \longrightarrow \underset{\text{(Secondary amine)}}{(CH_3)_2NH} + HCl$$

$$(CH_3)_2NH + CH_3Cl \longrightarrow \underset{\text{(Tertiary amine)}}{(CH_3)_3N} + HCl$$

$$(CH_3)_3N + CH_3Cl \longrightarrow \underset{\text{(Quarternary ammonium salt)}}{(CH_3)_4\overset{+}{N}\overset{-}{Cl}}$$

Q.22 Molecules whose mirror image is non-superimposable over them are known as chiral. Which of the following molecules is chiral in nature?

(a) 2-Bromobutane (b) 1-Bromobutane

(c) 2-Bromopropane (d) 2-Bromopropan-2-ol

Ans. ***(a)*** Chiral/asymmetric carbon is that carbon in which carbon has formed four bonds with four different groups. The structural formula of the given compounds are

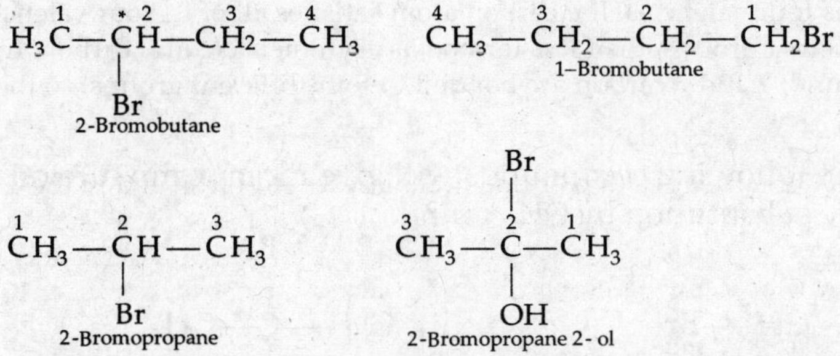

$$\overset{1}{H_3C}-\overset{*\,2}{\underset{\underset{Br}{|}}{CH}}-\overset{3}{CH_2}-\overset{4}{CH_3}$$
2-Bromobutane

$$\overset{4}{CH_3}-\overset{3}{CH_2}-\overset{2}{CH_2}-\overset{1}{CH_2Br}$$
1-Bromobutane

$$\overset{1}{CH_3}-\overset{2}{\underset{\underset{Br}{|}}{CH}}-\overset{3}{CH_3}$$
2-Bromopropane

$$\overset{3}{CH_3}-\underset{\underset{OH}{|}}{\overset{\overset{Br}{|}}{\overset{2}{C}}}-\overset{1}{CH_3}$$
2-Bromopropane 2- ol

With the help of these structural formulae, it is very clear that 2-bromobutane is chiral in nature, in which asterisk marked carbon atom is bonded to four different atoms or groups. Other molecules do not contain four different atoms or groups.

Q.23 Reaction of $C_6H_5CH_2Br$ with aqueous sodium hydroxide follows ....

(a) S_N1 mechanism

(b) S_N2 mechanism

(c) Any of the above two depending upon the temperature of reaction

(d) Saytzeff rule

Ans. ***(a)*** S_N1 mechanism depends upon the stability of carbocation. Higher the stability of carbocation, higher will be the possibility of S_N1 mechanism to take place.

In the given compound, carbocation is $C_6H_5\overset{\oplus}{C}H_2$. This carbocation is stable due to resonance, therefore, it show S_N1 mechanism.

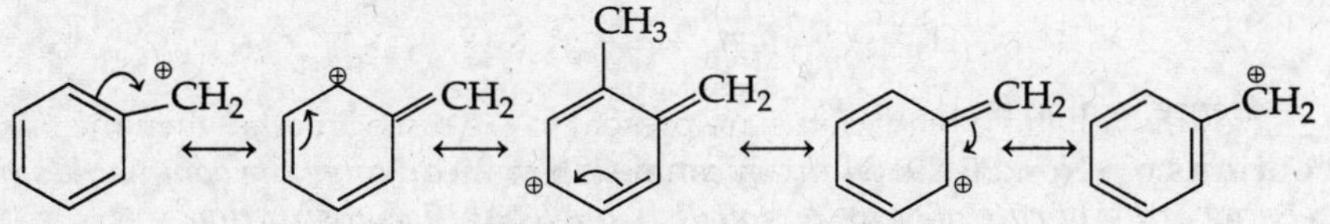

$$C_6H_5\overset{\oplus}{C}H_2 \longleftrightarrow \longleftrightarrow \longleftrightarrow \longleftrightarrow$$

Mistake Alert! *Students may make a mistake about the reaction mechanism, thinking both S_N1 and S_N2 mechanism are possible. However, $C_6H_5CH_2Br$ typically follows S_N1 mechanism with aqueous NaOH because the benzyl carbocation is stabilised by resonance which aids the S_N1 pathway over S_N2.*

Q.24 Which of the carbon atoms present in the molecule given below are asymmetric?

$$HO-\overset{1}{C}(=O)-\overset{2}{C}H(OH)-\overset{3}{C}H(OH)-\overset{4}{C}(=O)-H$$

(a) 1, 2, 3, 4 (b) 2, 3 (c) 1, 4 (d) 1, 2, 3

Ans. ***(b)*** Carbon has four valencies. If a carbon atom satisfies all of its four valencies with four different groups, then it is termed as asymmetric/chiral carbon. In the given compound, 2 and 3 carbon are bonded to four different groups, so these are asymmetric.

Q.25 Which of the following compounds will give racemic mixture on nucleophilic substitution by OH^- ion?

(i) $CH_3-CH(C_2H_5)-Br$ (ii) $CH_3-C(Br)(C_2H_5)-CH_3$

(iii) $CH_3-CH(C_2H_5)-CH_2Br$

(a) (i) (b) (i), (ii) and (iii) (c) (ii) and (iii) (d) (i) and (iii)

Ans. ***(a)*** A mixture containing two enantiomers in equimolar amount have zero optical rotation, as the rotation due to one isomer is cancelled by the rotation due to the other isomer. Such a mixture is known as racemic mixture. All those compounds which follow S_N1 mechanism during nucleophilic substitution reaction form racemic mixture.

Order of reactivity of alkyl halides towards S_N1 reaction is as follows

Tertiary halide > secondary halide > primary halide > CH_3X.

Thus, $CH_3-\overset{*}{C}H(C_2H_5)-Br$ contains a chiral carbon and gives a racemic product.

Hence, option (a) is correct.

Directions (Q. Nos. 26-29) *In the questions 26 to 29 arrange the compounds in increasing order of rate of reaction towards nucleophilic substitution.*

Q.26 (i) chlorobenzene (Cl on benzene ring) (ii) 2-nitrochlorobenzene (Cl, with NO_2 at ortho position) (iii) 3-nitrochlorobenzene (Cl, with NO_2 at meta position)

(a) (i) < (ii) < (iii) (b) (iii) < (ii) < (i)

(c) (i) < (iii) < (ii) (d) (iii) < (i) < (ii)

Thinking Process To solve this question, the point to keep in mind is that the presence of electron withdrawing group at *o* and *p*-position to the halogen atom increases the rate of nucleophilic substitution reaction.

Ans. ***(c)*** Presence of electron withdrawing group $(-NO_2)$ at ortho and para position facilitates nucleophilic substitution. The effect of electron withdrawing group is very less at meta position.

Compound (ii) and (iii) both has one electron withdrawing group but in compound (ii) electron withdrawing $(—NO_2)$ group is present at *ortho* position, so rate of reaction in compound (ii) is more than that of (iii), while (i) has no electron withdrawing group.

Hence, the correct option is (c).

Q.27 (i) 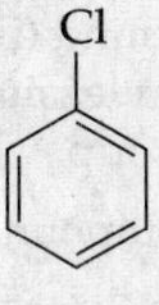 chlorobenzene (ii) 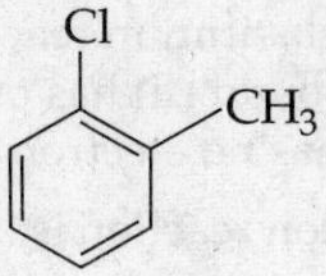 2-methylchlorobenzene (CH_3 ortho to Cl) (iii) 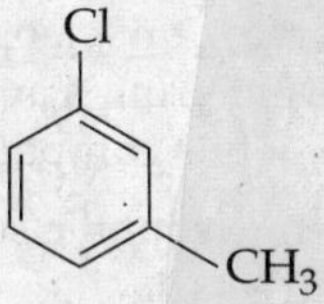 3-methylchlorobenzene (CH_3 meta to Cl)

(a) (i) < (ii) < (iii) (b) (i) < (iii) < (ii)
(c) (iii) < (ii) < (i) (d) (ii) < (iii) < (i)

Ans. ***(d)*** Presence of electron releasing group at *ortho* or *para* position decreases the rate of nucleophilic substitution reaction. In compound (iii), electron releasing group is present at *meta* position *w.r.t.* chlorine, so the impact is less, but in compound (ii) it is present at *ortho* position.

Thus, the rate of reaction towards nucleophilic substitution is least in compound (ii) and highest in compound (i) as there is no electron releasing group present in this compound.

Q.28 (i) 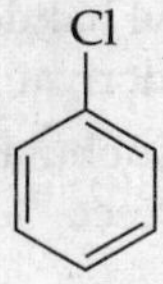 chlorobenzene (ii)  4-nitrochlorobenzene (NO_2 para to Cl) (iii) 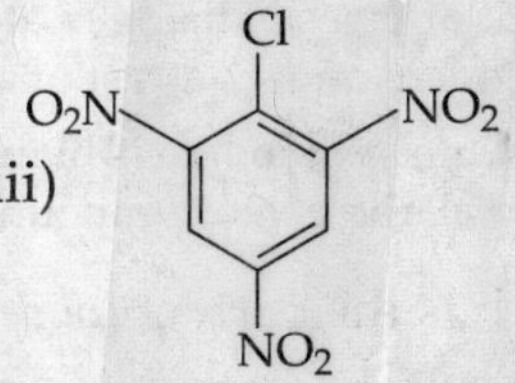 2,4,6-trinitrochlorobenzene (O_2N, NO_2 ortho and NO_2 para to Cl)

(a) (iii) < (ii) < (i) (b) (ii) < (iii) < (i)
(c) (i) < (iii) < (ii) (d) (i) < (ii) < (iii)

Thinking Process For this question, the important point is that electron withdrawing group at ortho and para position decreases the electron density at these positions and increases the rate of reaction. Further, rate of reaction increases with increase in number of electron withdrawing group.

Ans. ***(d)*** Presence of electron withdrawing group at *ortho* and *para* position facilitate the nucleophilic substitution reaction and hence, enhances the rate of reaction.

Compound (iii) has three electron withdrawing groups at *ortho* and *para* positions *w.r.t.* chlorine while compound (ii) has only one electron withdrawing group and there is no electron withdrawing group in compound (i). So, the increasing order of rate of reaction towards nucleophilic substitution is (i) < (ii) < (iii).

Q.29 (i) Chlorobenzene (ii) 4-Chlorotoluene (Cl and CH_3 para) (iii) 2-Chloro-1,5-dimethyl (Cl with CH_3 at ortho and para)

(a) (i) < (ii) < (iii) (b) (ii) < (i) < (iii) (c) (iii) < (ii) < (i) (d) (i) < (iii) < (ii)

Ans. *(c)* Presence of electron releasing group at *otho* and *para* position *w.r.t.* to chlorine decreases the rate of nucleophilic substitution reaction. Compound (iii) has two electron releasing groups and compound (ii) has one electron releasing group *w.r.t.* chlorine, while compound (i) has no electron releasing group.

So, the rate of nucleophilic substitution reaction is highest in compound (i) and order is (iii) < (ii) < (i).

Q.30 Which is the correct increasing order of boiling points of the following compounds?

1-Iodobutane, 1-Bromobutane, 1-Chlorobutane, Butane

(a) Butane < 1-Chlorobutane < 1-Bromobutane < 1-Iodobutane

(b) 1-Iodobutane < 1-Bromobutane < 1-Chlorobutane < Butane

(c) Butane < 1-Iodobutane < 1-Bromobutane < 1-Chlorobutane

(d) Butane < 1-Chlorobutane < 1-Iodobutane < 1-Bromobutane

Ans. *(a)* Higher the surface area, higher will be the intermolecular forces of attraction and thus higher will be the boiling point. Boiling point increases with increase in molecular mass of halogen atom for the similar type of alkyl halides. Butane has no halogen atom and rest of all three compounds are halo derivatives of butane.

Atomic mass of iodine is highest, so the boiling point of 1-iodobutane is maximum among all the given compounds and hence, option (a) is correct.

Q.31 Which is the correct increasing order of boiling points of the following compounds?

1-Bromoethane, 1-Bromopropane, 1-Bromobutane, Bromobenzene

(a) Bromobenzene < 1-Bromobutane < 1-Bromopropane < 1-Bromoethane

(b) Bromobenzene < 1-Bromoethane < 1-Bromopropane < 1-Bromobutane

(c) 1-Bromopropane < 1-Bromobutane < 1-Bromoethane < Bromobenzene

(d) 1-Bromoethane < 1-Bromopropane < 1-Bromobutane < Bromobenzene

Ans. *(d)* Boiling point increases with increase in size of hydrocarbon part for the same haloalkanes. All the given haloalkenes contain same halogen atom *i.e.*, bromine, but the number of carbon atoms in hydrocarbon part of the molecules are increasing from ethane to benzene.

So, the boiling point is minimum for 1-bromoethane and maximum for 1-bromobenzene.

Hence, option (d) is correct.

Multiple Choice Questions (More Than One Options)

Diections *Consider the following reaction and answer the Q. No. 32-34.*

$$\underset{\text{(i)}}{OH^-} + \underset{\text{(ii)}}{H_2C(H)-Cl} \longrightarrow \underset{\text{(iii)}}{\left[HO\cdots \overset{H}{\underset{H\ \ H}{C}} \cdots Cl\right]} \longrightarrow \underset{\text{(iv)}}{HO-CH_3} + \underset{\text{(v)}}{Cl^-}$$

Q.32 Which of the statements are correct about above reaction?

(a) (i) and (v) both are nucleophiles.

(b) In (iii) carbon atom is sp^3 hybridised.

(c) In (iii) carbon atom is sp^2 hybridised.

(d) (i) and (v) both are electrophiles.

Ans. ***(a, c)*** In the above reaction, ^-OH and Cl^- both are electron rich species as they are holding the negative charge. So, they are nucleophiles.

The above reaction show S_N2 mechanism, carbon of alkyl halide is sp^3 hybridised. During this mechanism, the breaking of $C-X$ bond and formation of new bond (C— Nu) occur simultaneously through a transition state in which carbon atom is approximately sp^2 hybridised.

Q.33 Which of the following statements are correct about this reaction?

(a) The given reaction follows S_N2 mechanism.

(b) (ii) and (iv) have opposite configuration.

(c) (ii) and (iv) have same configuration.

(d) The given reaction follows S_N1 mechanism.

Ans. ***(a, b)*** In the given reaction, alkyl halide is primary in nature. Here, a transition state is observed in which one bond is broken and one bond is formed simaltaneously, *i.e.*, in one step. So, it follows S_N2 mechanism.

In this mechanism, nucleophile attacks the carbon at 180° to the leaving group, so the reactant and product have opposite configuration.

Q.34 Which of the following statements are correct about the reaction intermediate?

(a) Intermediate (iii) is unstable because in this carbon is attached to 5 atoms.

(b) Intermediate (iii) is unstable because carbon atom is sp^2 hybridised.

(c) Intermediate (iii) is stable because carbon atom is sp^2 hybridised.

(d) Intermediate (iii) is less stable than the reactant (ii).

Ans. ***(a, d)*** For the given reaction, intermediate (iii) represents transition state, and it is highly unstable. In this transition state, carbon atom is sp^2 hybridised and is partially bonded to two nucleophiles, so it is highly unstable and less stable than the reactant (ii). In reactant (ii), carbon atom is sp^3 hybridised and more stable than intermediate (iii).

Directions *Answer Q. Nos. 35-36 on the basis of the following reactions.*

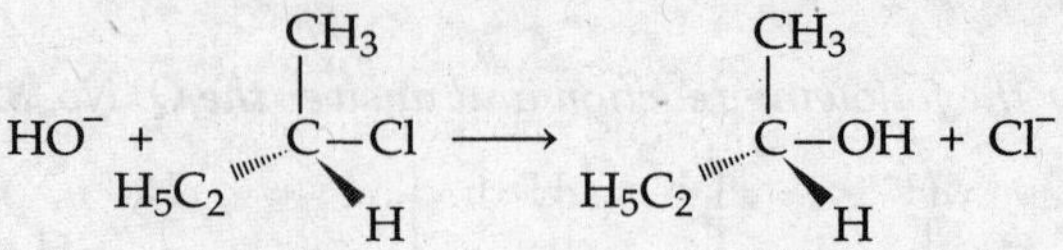

$$HO^- + \underset{(ii)}{H_5C_2\text{—}\overset{CH_3}{\underset{H}{C}}\text{—}Cl} \longrightarrow \underset{(iii)}{H_5C_2\text{—}\overset{CH_3}{\underset{H}{C}}\text{—}OH} + \underset{(iv)}{Cl^-}$$

(i)

Q.35 Which of the following statements are correct about the mechanism of this reaction?

(a) A carbocation will be formed as an intermediate in the reaction.

(b) OH^- will attach the substrate (ii) from one side and Cl^- will leave it simultaneously from other side.

(c) An unstable intermediate will be formed in which OH^- and Cl^- will be attached by weak bonds.

(d) Reaction proceeds through S_N1 mechanism.

Ans. ***(a, d)*** The reactant involved in above reaction is secondary alkyl halide. This 2° alkyl halide contain bulky group, thats why it follow S_N1 mechanism instead of S_N2 mechanism. In S_N1 mechanism, a stable carbocation will be formed as an intermediate. It is further attacked by HO^- nucleophile.

Q.36 Which of the following statements are correct about the kinetics of this reaction?

(a) The rate of reaction depends on the concentration of only (ii).

(b) The rate of reaction depends on concentration of both (i) and (ii).

(c) Molecularity of reaction is one.

(d) Molecularity of reaction is two.

Ans. ***(a, c)*** The above reaction follows S_N1 mechanism. In S_N1 mechanism formation of carbocation is a slow step. So, the rate of reaction depends upon the concentration of (ii). Since, the rate of reaction depends upon the concentration of only (ii) therefore, molecularity of reaction is one.

Q.37 Haloalkanes contain halogen atom(s) attached to the sp^3 hybridised carbon atom of an alkyl group. Identify haloalkane from the following compounds.

(a) 2-Bromopentane

(b) Vinyl chloride (chloroethene)

(c) 2-Chloroacetophenone

(d) Trichloromethane

Ans. ***(a, d)*** In the structure of 2-bromopentane $\left(CH_3\text{—}\underset{Br}{\underset{|}{C}H}\text{—}CH_2\text{—}CH_2\text{—}CH_3\right)$ and trichloromethane $\left(Cl\text{—}\overset{Cl}{\overset{|}{\underset{Cl}{\underset{|}{C}}}}\text{—}H\right)$, halogen atoms are attached to the sp^3 hybridised carbon atom of an alkyl group.

Q.38 Ethylene chloride and ethylidene chloride are isomers. Identify the correct statements.

(a) Both the compounds form same product on treatment with alcoholic KOH.
(b) Both the compounds form same product on treatment with aq. NaOH.
(c) Both the compounds form same product on reduction.
(d) Both the compounds are optically active.

Ans. *(a, c)*

(a) Ethylene chloride and ethylidene chloride on treatment with alc. KOH shows elimination reaction and forms ethyne as the product.

$$\underset{\text{Ethylene chloride}}{Cl-CH_2-CH_2-Cl} \xrightarrow[\text{KOH (excess)}]{\text{Alc.}} \underset{\text{Ethyne}}{CH\equiv CH}$$

$$\underset{\text{Ethylidene chloride}}{CH_3-CHCl_2} \xrightarrow[\text{(excess)}]{\text{Alc. KOH}} CH\equiv CH$$

(b) Both these compounds form different products on treatment with *aq*. NaOH.

$$Cl-CH_2-CH_2Cl \xrightarrow[\text{NaOH}]{Aq.} \underset{\text{Ethylene glycol}}{HO-CH_2-CH_2-OH}$$

$$CH_3-CHCl_2 \xrightarrow[\text{NaOH}]{Aq.} CH_3-CH(OH)_2 \xrightarrow[-H_2O]{} \underset{\text{Ethanal}}{CH_3CHO}$$

(c) Both these compounds form same products on reduction.

$$Cl-CH_2-CH_2-Cl \xrightarrow{\text{Reduction}} \underset{\text{Ethane}}{H_3C-CH_3} + 2HCl$$

$$CH_3-CHCl_2 \xrightarrow{\text{Reduction}} \underset{\text{Ethane}}{H_3C-CH_3} + 2HCl$$

(d) Both these compounds are optically inactive.

Q.39 Which of the following compounds are *gem*-dihalides?

(a) Ethylidene chloride
(b) Ethylene dichloride
(c) Methylene chloride
(d) Benzyl chloride

Ans. *(a, c)* *gem*-dihalides are those dihalides in which two halogen atoms are bonded to the same carbon atom.

The structures of the given compounds are

(a) $\underset{\text{Ethylidene chloride}}{Cl_2-CH-CH_3}$ (b) $\underset{\text{Ethylene dichloride}}{Cl-H_2C-CH_2-Cl}$

(c) $\underset{\text{Methylene chloride}}{CH_2Cl_2}$ (d) $C_6H_5CH_2Cl$ (benzene ring bearing CH_2Cl)

Benzyl chloride

So, in options (a) and (c), two halogen atoms are present on the same carbon atom and they are termed as *gem*-dihalides.

Q.40 Which of the following are secondary bromides?

(a) $(CH_3)_2CHBr$
(b) $(CH_3)_3CCH_2Br$
(c) $CH_3CH(Br)CH_2CH_3$
(d) $(CH_3)_2CBrCH_2CH_3$

Ans.* *(a, c) (a) $H_3C—CH—Br$ with CH_3 on the CH carbon; (c) $H_3C — CH — CH_2 — CH_3$ with Br on the CH carbon

Secondary bromides are those compounds in which α-carbon (*i.e.,* carbon bonded to bromine) is further bonded to two alkyl groups.

In compounds (a) and (c), α-carbon is bonded to two alkyl groups, thats why they are called secondary bromide.

Q.41 Which of the following compounds can be classified as aryl halides?

(a) p-$ClC_6H_4CH_2CH(CH_3)_2$ (b) p-$CH_3CHCl(C_6H_4)CH_2CH_3$
(c) o-$BrH_2C—C_6H_4CH(CH_3)CH_2CH_3$ (d) $C_6H_5—Cl$

Thinking Process Aryl halides represent these compounds in which the halogen atom is bonded to the sp^2 hybridised carbon atom of an aromatic ring.

Ans.* *(a, d) The structure is of the given compounds are :

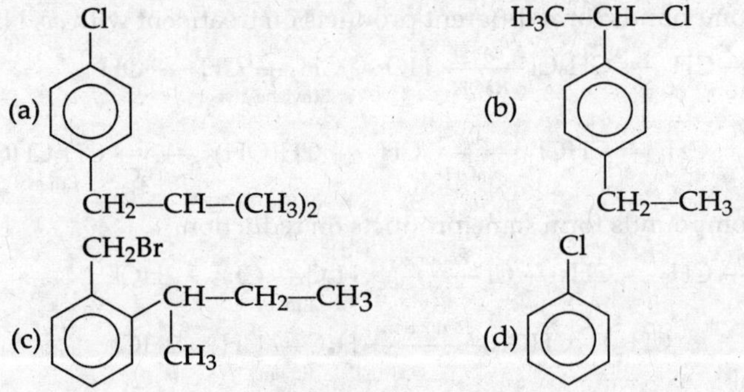

(a) Benzene ring with Cl at the top and $CH_2—CH—(CH_3)_2$ at the bottom

(b) Benzene ring with $H_3C—CH—Cl$ at the top and $CH_2—CH_3$ at the bottom

(c) Benzene ring with CH_2Br and, at the adjacent position, $CH—CH_2—CH_3$ with CH_3 on the CH carbon

(d) Benzene ring with Cl

So, from the above structures it is very clear that in compound (a) and compound (d), halogen atom is directly bonded to aromatic ring, therefore these compounds are classfied as aryl halides.

Q.42 Alkyl halides are prepared from alcohols by treating with

(a) $HCl + ZnCl_2$ (b) Red P + Br_2 (c) H_2SO_4 + KI (d) All of these

Ans.* *(a, b)

(a) Alcohol when treated with $HCl + ZnCl_2$, gives alkyl halide as product.

$$ROH + HCl \xrightarrow{ZnCl_2} \underset{\text{(Alkyl halide)}}{RCl} + H_2O$$

(b) Alcohol when treated with red P and X_2, gives alkyl halide as product.

$$R—OH \xrightarrow{\text{Red P}/Br_2} \underset{\text{(Alkyl halide)}}{R—X}$$

(c) Alcohols when treated with H_2SO_4 and KI, H_2SO_4 oxidises KI to I_2 and does not produce HI. Therefore, alkyl iodide does not form if the alcohols are treated with H_2SO_4 + KI.

Q.43 Alkyl fluorides are synthesised by alkyl chloride/bromide in presence of .... or ....

(a) CaF_2 (b) CoF_2
(c) Hg_2F_2 (d) NaF

Ans. ***(b, c)*** Alkyl fluorides are synthesised by alkyl chloride/bromide in presence of CoF_2 or Hg_2F_2. Only transition metal fluorides react with alkyl chloride/bromide to form alkyl fluorides. Alkali metal fluoride such as NaF and alkaline earth metal fluoride such as CaF_2 do not react to form fluorides.

Note The reaction is termed as Swarts reaction in which alkyl fluorides are synthesised by heating an alkyl chloride/bromide in the presence of AgF, Hg_2F_2, CoF_2.

Short Answer Type Questions

Q.44 Aryl chlorides and bromides can be easily prepared by electrophilic substitution of arenes with chlorine and bromine respectively in the presence of Lewis acid catalysts. But why does preparation of aryl iodides requires presence of an oxidising agent?

Ans. Iodination reactions are reversible in nature.

$$C_6H_6 + I_2 \rightleftharpoons C_6H_5I + HI$$

In this above reaction, hydrogen iodide is formed apart from the required product. It has to be removed from the reaction mixture in order to prevent the backward reaction.

To carry out the reaction in the forward direction, HI formed during the reaction is removed by oxidation by using an oxidising agent. Such as HIO_3 or HNO_3. The reaction is as follow

$$5HI + HIO_3 \longrightarrow 3I_2 + 3H_2O;$$
$$2HI + 2HNO_3 \longrightarrow I_2 + 2NO_2 + 2H_2O$$

By using a suitable oxidising agent HI is oxidised to give I_2.

Q.45 Out of *o*- and *p*-dibromobenzene which one has higher melting point and why?

Ans. *p*-Dibromobenzene has higher melting point than its *o*-isomer due to symmetry. Due to symmetry, *p*- isomer fits in the crystal lattice better than the *o*-isomer.

Hence, *p*-dibromobenzene has higher melting point.

Q.46 Which of the compounds will react faster in S_N1 reaction with the ^-OH ion?

$$CH_3—CH_2—Cl \text{ or } C_6H_5—CH_2—Cl$$

Ans. S_N1 mechanism depends upon the stability of carbocation that is formed as an intermediate in the mechanism.

$C_6H_5— CH_2 — Cl$ will form $C_6H_5\overset{+}{C}H_2$ carbocation as an intermediate.

This carbocation is resonance stabilised and will react faster in S_N1 reaction.

$\overset{+}{C}H_2$ ⟷ CH_2 ⟷ CH_2 ⟷ CH_2 ⟷ $\overset{+}{C}H_2$

While carbocation formed in CH_3CH_2Cl is $CH_3\overset{+}{C}H_2$. This carbocation is highly unstable and not give S_N1 reaction with ^-OH ion.

Q.47 Why iodoform has appreciable antiseptic property?

Ans. Iodoform liberats I_2 when it comes in contact with skin. Antiseptic property of iodine is due to the liberation of I_2 and not because of iodoform itself.

$$\underset{\text{Iodoform}}{CHI_3} \xrightarrow[\text{skin}]{\text{Contact with}} \underset{\text{Iodine}}{I_2} \text{ (responsible for antiseptic property)}$$

Q.48 Haloarenes are less reactive than haloalkanes and haloalkenes. Explain.

Ans. Due to resonance, C— X bond in haloarenes and haloalkenes have some double bond character. This partial double bond character of C — X bond, strengthens the bond. So, haloarenes and haloalkenes are less reactive than haloalkanes. The resonating structure of the haloarenes and haloalkenes are

$$\overset{\ominus}{C}H_2—CH{=}\overset{\oplus}{Cl}: \quad \longleftrightarrow$$

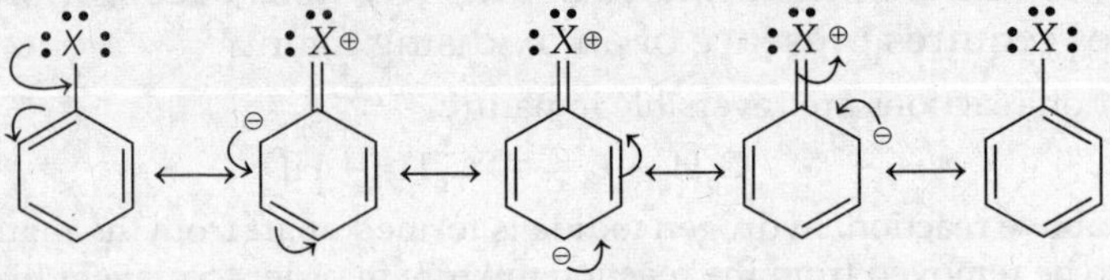

$$CH_2{=}CH—\ddot{X}: \longleftrightarrow \overset{\ominus}{C}H_2—CH{=}\overset{\oplus}{Cl}:$$

Now, more the number of resonating structures higher will be the stability of the compound and lesser will be the reactivity. In haloarenes, more resonating structures are observed than the haloalkenes. So, haloarenes are less reactive than haloalkanes. In haloalkanes, this C— X bond is purely single bond.

Q.49 Discuss the role of Lewis acids in the preparation of aryl bromides and chlorides in the dark.

Ans. Lewis acids are electron deficient species. They are responsible for inducing heterolytic fission in halogen molecule.

Role of Lewis acid is to produce an electrophile. The eletrophile produced will attack on electron rich benzene ring to produce aryl bromides and chlorides.

$$AlCl_3 + Cl_2 \longrightarrow [AlCl_4]^- + Cl^+$$
$$AlBr_3 + Br_2 \longrightarrow [AlBr_4]^- + Br^+$$

This electrophile will further attack on benzene.

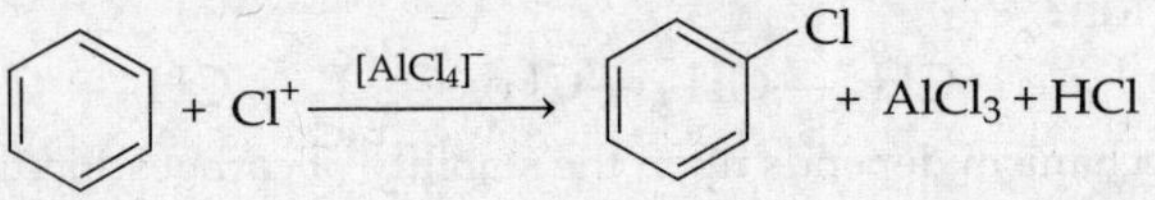

$$C_6H_6 + Cl^+ \xrightarrow{[AlCl_4]^-} C_6H_5Cl + AlCl_3 + HCl$$

Q.50 Which of the following compounds (i) and (ii) will not react with a mixture of NaBr and H_2SO_4. Explain why?

(i) $CH_3CH_2CH_2OH$ (ii) C_6H_5OH

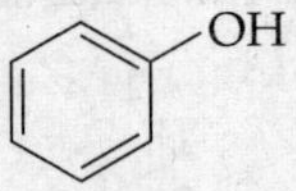

Ans. Partial double bond character of a bond increases the strength of the bond and hence, decreases the stability. Phenol will not react with a mixture of NaBr and H_2SO_4 because it is resonance stabilised. Due to resonance, partial double bond character arises in C— O bond of phenol and it becomes more stable than alcohol ($CH_3CH_2CH_2OH$).

Reaction $2NaBr + 3H_2SO_4 \longrightarrow 2NaHSO_4 + SO_2 + Br_2 + 2H_2O$

$$\text{Phenol} \xrightarrow{Br_2/H_2O} \text{2,4,6-Tribromophenol}$$

$$CH_3CH_2CH_2OH \xrightarrow{Br_2} \text{No reaction}$$

As C — O bond is more stable in phenol (OH on benzene ring) because of resonance.

Q.51 Which of the products will be major product in the reaction given below? Explain.

$$CH_3CH{=}CH_2 + HI \longrightarrow \underset{(A)}{CH_3CH_2CH_2I} + \underset{(B)}{CH_3CHICH_3}$$

Thinking Process The reaction is based on the Markovnikov's rule. Markovnikov's rule states that the negative part of adding molecule get attached that carbon atom of double bond which carries lesser number of hydrogen atom.

Ans. CH_3CHICH_3 is the major product of the reaction. The mechanism of the reaction is as follows $HI \rightleftharpoons H^+ + I^-$

$$CH_3 - CH = CH_2 \xrightarrow{H^{\oplus}} \underset{\substack{(2° \text{ carbocation}) \\ (\text{more stable})}}{CH_3 - \overset{+}{C}H - CH_3} + \underset{\substack{(1° \text{ carbocation}) \\ (\text{less stable})}}{CH_3 - CH_2 - \overset{+}{C}H_2}$$

$$CH_3 - \overset{+}{C}H - CH_3 \xrightarrow{I^-} CH_3 - \underset{\substack{| \\ I}}{CH} - CH_3$$

According to Markovnikov's rule, H atom is added to the C atom with higher number of hydrogen atoms.

Q.52 Why is the solubility of haloalkanes in water very low?

Ans. Haloalkanes are slightly soluble in water. For the solubility to haloalkane in water, energy is required to overcome the attractions between its own molecules and to break the bonds between water molecules.

Since, less energy is released when new attractions are set up between the haloalkanes and the water molecules as these are not as strong as the original hydrogen bonds in water. Therefore, haloalkanes are slightly soluble in water.

Q.53 Draw other resonance structures related to the following structure and find out whether the functional group present in the molecule is *ortho, para* directing or *meta* directing.

Ans. Resonance in halobenzene

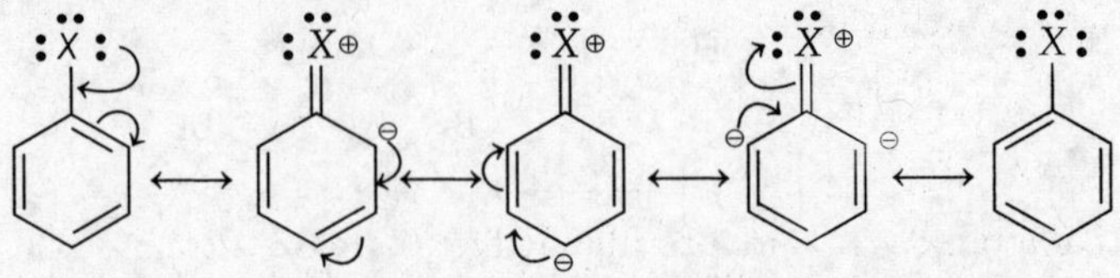

From the above resonating structures it is very clear that electron density is rich at *ortho* and *para* position. Therefore, it is *ortho* and *para* directing and not *meta* directing.

Q.54 Classify the following compounds as primary, secondary and tertiary halides.

(a) 1-Bromobut-2-ene (b) 4-Bromopent-2-ene

(c) 2-Bromo-2-methylpropane

Ans. The structural formulae of the given compounds are :

(a) $H_3C—H_2C = HC—H_2C—Br$
1-Bromobut-2-ene
(Primary halide)

(b) $CH_3—CH(Br)—CH = CH—CH_3$
4-Bromopent-2-ene
(Secondary halide)

(c) $H_3C—C(CH_3)(Br)—CH_3$
2-Bromo-2-methylpropane
(Tertiary halide)

In compound (i), carbon atom to which halogen is bonded is further bonded to two hydrogens and one carbon of hydrocarbon chain. So, it is a primary halide.
In compound (ii), α-carbon is bonded with one hydrogen and two carbons of two hydrocarbons chain. So, it is a secondary halide.
In compound (iii), α-carbon is bonded to three alkyl group, so it is tertiary halide.

Q.55 Compound '*A*' with molecular formula C_4H_9Br is treated with aq. KOH solution. The rate of this reaction depends upon the concentration of the compound '*A*' only. When another optically active isomer '*B*' of this compound was treated with aq. KOH solution, the rate of reaction was found to be dependent on concentration of compound and KOH both.

(i) Write down the structural formula of both compounds '*A*' and '*B*'.

(ii) Out of these two compounds, which one will be converted to the product with inverted configuration.

Ans. (i) As the rate of reaction depends upon the concentration of compound '*A*' (C_4H_9Br) only therefore, the reaction is proceeded by S_N1 mechanism and the given compound will a be tertiary alkyl halide *i.e.*, 2-bromo-2-methylpropane and the structure is as follows

$$H_3C—C(CH_3)_2—Br$$

(*A*)

Optically active isomer of (*A*) is 2-bromobutane (*B*) and its structural formula is

$$CH_3—CH_2—\overset{*}{C}HCH_3 \text{ (with Br on the starred carbon)}$$

(*B*)

(ii) As compound (*B*) is optically active therefore, compound (*B*) must be 2-bromobutane. Since, the rate of reaction of compound (*B*) depends both upon the concentration of compound (*B*) and KOH, hence, the reaction follow S_N2 mechanism. In S_N2 reaction, nucleophile attack from the back side, therefore, the product of hydrolysis will have opposite configuration.

$$(CH_2CH_3)(H)(CH_3)C—Br \longrightarrow HO\cdots C(CH_2CH_3)(H)(CH_3)\cdots Br \longrightarrow (CH_2CH_3)(HO)(H)C—CH_3$$

Q.56 **Write the structures and names of the compounds formed when compound '*A*' with molecular formula C_7H_8 is treated with Cl_2 in the presence of $FeCl_3$.**

Ans. When compound '*A*' with molecular formula, C_7H_8 is treated with Cl_2 in the presence of $FeCl_3$ *o*-chlorotoluene or *p*-chlorotoluene will be formed. The compound *A* with molecular formula C_7H_8 is toluene.

$$\underset{\text{Toluene (M.F } C_7H_8)}{C_6H_5CH_3} \xrightarrow{Cl_2/FeCl_3} \underset{o\text{-chlorotoluene (minor)}}{o\text{-}ClC_6H_4CH_3} + \underset{p\text{-chlorotoluene (major)}}{p\text{-}ClC_6H_4CH_3}$$

Mechanism $Cl—Cl + FeCl_3 \rightarrow [FeCl_4]^- + Cl^+$

$$C_6H_5CH_3 + Cl^+ \longrightarrow [\text{arenium ion with H and Cl, }+] \xrightarrow{[FeCl_4]^-} o\text{-}ClC_6H_4CH_3 + HCl + FeCl_3$$

Q.57 **Identify the products *A* and *B* formed in the following reaction :**

$$CH_3—CH_2—CH{=}CH—CH_3 + HCl \longrightarrow A + B$$

Ans. In the given reaction, addition occur and the following two products (A and B) are possible

$$H_3C—CH_2—CH{=}CH—CH_3 + HCl \longrightarrow \underset{\text{(2-Chloropentane) }(B)}{CH_3—CH_2—CH_2—\underset{Cl}{\underset{|}{C}H}—CH_3}$$

$$+ \underset{\text{(3-Chloropentane) }(A)}{CH_3—CH_2—\underset{Cl}{\underset{|}{C}H}—CH_2—CH_3}$$

The carbocation formed from compound (*A*) is slightly less stable than carbocation leading to the formation of compound (*B*), therefore the amount of 2-chloropentane (*B*) will be slightly more than that of 3- chloropentane (*A*).

Q.58 Which of the following compounds will have the highest melting point and why?

(I) 1,4-dimethyl-2,3-dichlorobenzene; (II) 1,4-dimethyl-2,5-dichlorobenzene; (III) 1,4-dimethyl-2,6-dichlorobenzene

Ans. In compound (II), both the CH_3 groups and Cl atoms at *para*-position to each other. Therefore, compound (II) is more symmetrical and it fits in the crystal lattice better than the other two isomers and hence it has the highest melting point than the others.

Q.59 Write down the structure and IUPAC name for *neo*-pentylbromide.

Ans. The structure of *neo*-pentylbromide is

$$H_3C-C(CH_3)_2-CH_2Br$$

IUPAC name ⇒ 1-Bromo-2,2-dimethylpropane

Common name ⇒ *neo*-pentylbromide

Q.60 A hydrocarbon of molecular mass 72 g mol^{-1} gives a single monochloro derivative and two dichloro derivatives on photo chlorination. Give the structure of the hydrocarbon.

Ans. Since, the molar mass of hydrocarbon is 72 g mol^{-1} thats why the hydrocarbon is C_5H_{12}, *i.e.*, pentane.

On photo chlorination, it gives monochloro derivatives so, all the hydrogen atoms must be equivalent and the structure of the compound will be,

$$\underset{\text{2, 2-Dimethylpropane}}{H_3C-C(CH_3)_2-CH_3} \xrightarrow[hv]{Cl_2} \underset{\text{1-Chloro-2, 2-dimethylpropane (Monochloro derivative)}}{H_3C-C(CH_3)_2-CH_2Cl}$$

$$\underset{\text{2, 2-Dimethylpropane}}{H_3C-C(CH_3)_2-CH_3} \xrightarrow[hv]{Cl_2} \underset{\text{1, 1-Dichloro-2, 2-dimethylpropane (Dichloro derivative)}}{H_3C-C(CH_3)_2-CHCl_2} \text{ or } \underset{\text{1, 3-Dichloro-2, 2-dimethylpropane (Dichloro derivative)}}{Cl-H_2C-C(CH_3)_2-CH_2Cl}$$

Q.61 Name of the alkene which will yield 1-chloro-1-methylcyclohexane by its reaction with HCl. Write the reactions involved.

Ans. Two alkenes are possible,

Methylene cyclohexane $\xrightarrow{HCl}$ 1-Chloro-1-methyl cyclohexane or, 1-Chloro-1-methyl cyclohexane $\xrightarrow{HCl}$ 1-Chloro-1-methyl cyclohexane

Addition takes place in accordance with Markovnikov's rule *i.e.*, negative part of the adding molecule will get attached to that carbon which has lesser number of hydrogen atom.

Q.62 Which of the following haloalkanes reacts with aqueous KOH most easily? Explain giving reason.

(i) 1-Bromobutane (ii) 2-Bromobutane
(iii) 2-Bromo-2-methylpropane (iv) 2-Chlorobutane

Ans. 2-bromo-2-methylpropane (iii), is a tertiary alkyl halide and it will form a stable carbocation on ionisation.

$$(CH_3)_3C{-}Br \xrightarrow[-Br^-]{\text{Ionisation}} (CH_3)_3C^+ \xrightarrow{OH^-} (CH_3)_3C{-}OH$$

2-Bromo-2-methylpropane → 3° carbocation (stable) → 2-Methyl-2-propanal

1-Bromobutane is a primary alkyl halide whereas, 2-bromobutane and 2-Chlorobutane are secondary alkyl halides.

Q.63 Why can aryl halides not be prepared by reaction of phenol with HCl in the presence of $ZnCl_2$?

Ans. Due to resonance in phenol, C— O bond of phenol has some partial double bond character. Partial double bond character strengthens the bond. So, it is difficult to break this C— O bond of phenol while, the C— O bond of alcohol is purely single bond and comparatively weaker bond.

So, alkyl halides can be prepared by the reaction of alcohols with HCl in the presence of $ZnCl_2$ while aryl halides can not be prepared by reaction of phenol with HCl in the presence of $ZnCl_2$.

$$\underset{\text{Phenol}}{C_6H_5OH} \xrightarrow[ZnCl_2]{HCl} \text{NO reaction}$$

$$\underset{\text{Alcohol}}{RCH_2OH} \xrightarrow[ZnCl_2]{HCl} \underset{\text{Alkyl chloride}}{RCH_2Cl} + H_2O$$

Q.64 Which of the following compounds would undergo S_N1 reaction faster and why?

CH_2Cl on cyclohexane ring (*A*) CH_2Cl on benzene ring (*B*)

Ans. Compound (*B*) will give S_N1 reaction faster than compound (*A*) because S_N1 reaction depends upon the stability of carbocation. Benzyl chloride on ionisation gives $C_6H_5\overset{+}{C}H_2$ carbocation which is resonance stabilised while the carbocation obtained from compound (*A*) is not stabilised by resonance.

$$C_6H_5CH_2Cl \xrightarrow{-Cl^-} C_6H_5\overset{+}{C}H_2 \longleftrightarrow \text{(resonance structures)}$$

(resonance stabilised)

$$C_6H_{11}CH_2Cl \xrightarrow{-Cl^-} C_6H_{11}\overset{+}{C}H_2$$

(not stabilised by resonance)

Q.65 Allyl chloride is hydrolysed more readily than *n*-propyl chloride. Why?

Ans. As we know that S_N1 mechanism depends upon the stability of carbocation. Allyl chloride on hydrolysis gives resonance stabilised carbocation while no resonance is observed in the carbocation formed by *n*-propyl chloride.

$$\underset{\text{Allyl chloride}}{CH_2=CH-CH_2Cl} \xrightarrow{-Cl^-} CH_2=CH-\overset{+}{C}H_2 + \overset{-}{Cl}$$

$$CH_2=CH-\overset{+}{C}H_2 \longleftrightarrow \underset{\text{(Resonance stabilised carbocation)}}{\overset{+}{C}H_2-CH=CH_2}$$

$$\underset{n\text{-propyl chloride}}{CH_3-CH_2-CH_2-Cl} \xrightarrow{-Cl^-} \underset{\text{(Not stabilised by resonance)}}{CH_3-CH_2-\overset{+}{C}H_2 + Cl^-}$$

Hence, allyl chloride undergoes hydrolysis much faster than *n*-propyl chloride.

Q.66 Why is it necessary to avoid even traces of moisture during the use of a Grignard reagent?

Ans. Grignard reagents are highly reactive and react with water to give corresponding hydrocarbons.

$$\underset{\text{Grignard reagent}}{RMgX} + H_2O \longrightarrow RH + Mg(OH)X.$$

Q.67 How do polar solvents help in the first step in S_N1 mechanism?

Ans. Polar solvents help in the first step in S_N1 mechanism because leaving group and carbocation both are stabilised by polar solvents. Polarity of a solvent depends upon the value of dielectric constant. Higher the value of dielectric constant, higher will be the polarity of the solvent, faster will be the rate of S_N1 mechanism. These polar solvents can work as a nucleophile and stabilise the carbocation.

Q.68 Write a test to detect the presence of double bond in a molecule.

Ans. Presence of double bond in a molecule is detected by following two methods

(i) **Br_2 in CCl_4 test** When Br_2/CCl_4 is added unsaturated compound then orange colour of bromine disappears and dibromoderivative is formed (colourless).

$$\underset{\text{(Double bond)}}{>C=C<} + \underset{\text{(orange)}}{Br_2} \xrightarrow{CCl_4} \underset{\substack{\text{Dibromo compound}\\\text{(colourless)}}}{-\underset{Br}{\overset{|}{C}}-\underset{Br}{\overset{|}{C}}-}$$

(ii) **Bayer's test** When alkaline solution of $KMnO_4$ is added to the solution of unsaturated compound then its pink colour disappears due to the formation of dihydroxy derivative.

$$\underset{\substack{\text{(Double bond)}\\\text{Pink colour}}}{>C=C<} \xrightarrow[KMnO_4]{\text{Alkaline}} \underset{\text{Colourless}}{>\underset{OH}{C}-\underset{OH}{C}<}$$

Q.69 Diphenyls are potential threat to the environment. How are these produced from aryl halides?

Ans. In environment, diphenyl is formed during the incomplete combustion of mineral oil and coal. It is present in the exhaust gases of vehicles and in exhaust air from residential and industrial heating devices.

Acute exposure to high levels of biphenyl has been observed to cause eye and skin irritation and toxic effects on the liver, kidneys and central/peripheral nervous system. Kidneys of animals are also affected due to the ingestion of biphenyls.

Preparation of diphenyls from aryl halides

$$C_6H_5Cl + 2Na + C_6H_5Cl \xrightarrow{\text{Ether}} C_6H_5-C_6H_5 + 2NaCl$$

Aryl halides when treated with sodium in dry ether give diphenyl. This reaction is named as Fittig reaction.

Q.70 What are the IUPAC names of the insecticide DDT and benzene hexachloride? Why is their use banned in India and other countries?

Ans. The IUPAC name of DDT is 2,2-bis (4-chlorophenyl)-1,1,1-trichloroethane and that of benzene hexachloride is 1,2,3,4,5,6-hexachlorocyclohexane.

They are banned in india because they are non-biodegradable. Instead, they get deposited and stored in fatty tissues. If this ingestion continues at a steady rate, DDT builds up within the animal over time. This will affects the reproductive system of animals.

If animals including humans are exposed to high levels of benzene hexachloride then it may cause acute poisoning. Apart from this, BHC may affect liver functioning in humans.

Q.71 Elimination reactions (especially β – elimination) are as common as the nucleophilic substitution reaction in case of alkyl halides. Specify the reagents used in both cases.

Ans. Elimination reactions are as common as the nucleophilic substitution reaction in case of alkyl halides as two reactions occur simultaneously. Generally, at lower temperature and by using weaker base, nucleophilic substitution reaction occurs, while at higher temperature and by using a stronger base, elimination reactions (especially β – elimination) takes place.

e.g., If ethyl bromide is treated with aq. KOH, at low temperature it gives ethanol while if it is treated with alc. KOH at high temperature then it gives ethene.

$$CH_3CH_2Br \xrightarrow[373K]{Aq.KOH} \underset{Ethanol}{CH_3CH_2OH} \text{ (Nucleophilic substitution reaction)}$$

$$CH_3CH_2Br \xrightarrow[473\text{-}523\,K]{Alc.\ KOH} \underset{Ethene}{CH_2{=}CH_2} \text{ (Elimination reaction)}$$

Q.72 How will you obtain monobromobenzene from aniline?

Ans.

$$\underset{\text{(Aniline, }NH_2\text{)}}{C_6H_5NH_2} + CH_3COCl \xrightarrow{HCl} C_6H_5NHCOCH_3 \xrightarrow{Br_2/FeBr_3} p\text{-}BrC_6H_4NHCOCH_3 + o\text{-}BrC_6H_4NHCOCH_3$$

$$\xrightarrow{HOH} o\text{-}BrC_6H_4NH_2 + p\text{-}BrC_6H_4NH_2$$

Q.73 Aryl halides are extremely less reactive towards nucleophilic substitution. Predict and explain the order of reactivity of the following compounds towards nucleophilic substitution.

(I) 1-Cl-4-NO_2-benzene (Cl, NO_2)

(II) 1-Cl-2,4-diNO_2-benzene (Cl, NO_2, NO_2)

(III) 1-Cl-2,4,6-triNO_2-benzene (Cl, O_2N, NO_2, NO_2)

Ans. Aryl halides are less reactive towards nucleophilic substitution reaction. Presence of electron withdrawing group at *ortho* and *para* position increases the stability of intermediates and hence increases the reactivity of aryl halides towards nucleophilic substitution reaction.

$$\text{p-}O_2N\text{-}C_6H_4\text{-}Cl + \bar{O}H \xrightarrow[\text{Step}]{\text{Slow}} [\text{Cl, OH adduct (Resonance)}] \xrightarrow[\text{Step}]{\text{Fast}} \text{p-}O_2N\text{-}C_6H_4\text{-}OH + Cl^-$$

(Resonance)

Now, more the number of EWG at *ortho* and *para* positions, higher will be the reactivity of aryl halide. Compound (III) has three EWG so, it is most reactive and compound (I) has only one EWG so, it is least reactive.

So, the order of reactivity is (I) < (II) < (III)

Q.74 *tert*-Butylbromide reacts with *aq*. NaOH by S_N1 mechanism while *n*-butylbromide reacts by S_N1 mechanism. Why?

Ans. *tert.* butyl bromide reacts with *aq*. NaOH as follows

$$(CH_3)_3C\text{—}Br \xrightarrow{S_N1} (CH_3)_3C^+ + Br^-$$

tert Butylbromide (3° alkyl halide) → 3° carbocation (more stable)

$$(CH_3)_3C^+ + OH^- \longrightarrow (CH_3)_3C\text{—}OH$$

tert. butyl bromide when treated with aq. NaOH, it forms *tert.*-corbocation which is more stable intermediate. This intermediate is further attacked by ^-OH ion.

As *tert.* carbocation is highly stable so *tert* butylbromide follow S_N1 mechanism.

In case of *n*-butylbromide, primary carbocation is formed which is least stable so, it does not follow S_N1 mechanism. Here, steric hindrance is very less so, it follow S_N2 mechanism. In S_N2 mechanism, ^-OH will attack from backside and a transition state is formed.

The leaving group is then pushed off the eopposite side and the product is formed.

$$CH_3\text{—}CH_2\text{—}CH_2\text{—}CH_2Br \xrightarrow{^-OH} [HO\cdots CH_2(CH_2CH_2CH_3)\cdots Br] \longrightarrow HO\text{—}CH_2\text{—}CH_2\text{—}CH_2\text{—}CH_3 + Br^-$$

n-butyl bromide → transition state → *n*-butyl alcohol

Q.75 Predict the major product formed when HCl is added to isobutylene, Explain the mechanism involved.

Ans. Reaction between the isobutylene added to HCl

$$H_3C-\underset{\underset{CH_3}{|}}{C}=CH_2 + HCl \xrightarrow[\text{rule}]{\text{Markovnikov's}} H_3C-\underset{\underset{CH_3}{|}}{\overset{\overset{Cl}{|}}{C}}-CH_3$$

Isobutylene 2-chloro-2-methylpropane

Electrophilic addition reaction takes place in accordance with Markovnikov's rule.

Mechanism $HCl \longrightarrow H^+ + Cl^-$

$$H_3C-\underset{\underset{CH_3}{|}}{C}=CH_2 + H^+ \longrightarrow CH_3-\underset{\underset{CH_3}{|}}{CH}-\overset{+}{C}H_2 \text{ (1° carbocation) less stable}$$

$$H_3C-\underset{\underset{CH_3}{|}}{C}=CH_2 + H^+ \longrightarrow H_3C-\underset{\underset{CH_3}{|}}{\overset{+}{C}}-CH_3 \text{ (3° carbocation) more stable}$$

We know that 3° carbocation is more stable than 1° carbocation so, in further step, 3° carbocation is further attacked by Cl^- ion.

$$H_3C-\underset{\underset{CH_3}{|}}{\overset{\overset{CH_3}{|}}{C^+}} + Cl^- \longrightarrow H_3C-\underset{\underset{CH_3}{|}}{\overset{\overset{CH_3}{|}}{C}}-Cl$$

2-Chloro-2-methylpropane

Q.76 Discuss the nature of C—*X* bond in the haloarenes.

Ans. In haloarenes, carbon of benzene is bonded to halogen. Electronegativity of halogen is more than that of sp^2 hybridised carbon of benzene ring. So, C— *X* bond is a polar bond. Apart from this, lone pair of electrons of halogen atom are involved in resonance with benzene ring. So, this C— *X* bond has acquired partial bond character.

This C— *X* bond of haloarenes is less polar than C— *X* bond of haloalkanes. This is supported by the fact that dipole moment of chlorobenzene (μ = 1.69 D) is little lower than that of CH_3Cl (μ = 1.83 D)

Q.77 How can you obtain iodoethane from ethanol when no other iodine containing reagent except NaI is available in the laboratory?

Ans. Ethanol is converted to chloroethane and — Cl can be replaced by I.

$$C_2H_5OH + HCl \xrightarrow{ZnCl_2} C_2H_5Cl \xrightarrow{NaI} C_2H_5I$$

Q.78 Cyanide ion acts as an ambident nucleophile. From which end it acts as a stronger nucleophile in aqueous medium? Give reason for your answer.

Ans. Cyanide ion ($:\bar{C} \equiv N$) is an ambident nucleophile because it can react either through carbon or through nitrogen. Since, C—C bond is stronger than C—N bond so, cyanide ion will mainly attack through carbon to form alkyl cyanide

$$\underset{\text{Alkyl halide}}{R—X} + :\bar{C} \equiv N \longrightarrow \underset{\text{Alkyl cyanide}}{R—C \equiv N} + X^-$$

Matching The Columns

Q.79 Match the the compounds given in Column I with the effect given in Column II.

	Column I		Column II
A.	Chloramphenicol	1.	Malaria
B.	Thyroxine	2.	Anaesthetic
C.	Chloroquine	3.	Typhoid fever
D.	Chloroform	4.	Goiter
		5.	Blood substituent

Ans. A. → (3) B. → (4) C. → (1) D. → (2)

A. Chloramphenicol is a broadspectrum antibiotic. It is used in the treatment of typhoid fever.

B. Thyroxine is a hormone secreated by thyroid gland. Execessive secretion of thyroxine in the body is known as hyperthyroidism. Most patient with hyper thyroidism have an enlarged thyroid gland, *i.e.,* goitre.

C. Chloroquine prevents the development of malaria parasite *plasmodium vivax* in the blood.

D. IUPAC name of chloroform is trichloromethane with formula $CHCl_3$. It is a colourless, volatile, sweet-smelling liquid. Its vapours are used to depress the central nervous system and can be used as an anaesthetic.

Q.80 Match the items of Column I and Colum II.

	Column I		Column II
A.	S_N1 reaction	1.	*vic*-dibromides
B.	Chemicals in fire extinguisher	2.	*gem*-dihalides
C.	Bromination of alkenes	3.	Racemisation
D.	Alkylidene halides	4.	Saytzeff rule
E.	Elimination of HX from alkylhalide	5.	Chlorobromocarbons

Ans. A. → (3) B. → (5) C. → (1) D. → (2) E. → (4)

A. A mixture containing two enantiomers in equal proportions will have zero optical rotation, such a mixture is known as racemic mixture. The process of conversion of enantiomer into a racemic mixture is known as racemisation. If an alkyl halide follows S_N1 mechanism then racemisation takes place while if it follows S_N2 mechanism then inversion takes places.

B. Chlorobromocarbons are used in fire extinguishers.

C. In vicinal dihalides, halogen atoms are present on the adjacent carbon atom. Bromination of alkenes will give vicinal dihalides.

D. Alkylidene halides are named as *gem*-dihalides. In *gem*-dihalides halogen atoms are present on same carbon atom.

E. Elimination of HX from alkylhalide follows Saytzeff rule. This rule states that "in dehydrohalogenation reactions, the preferred product is that alkene which has the greater number of alkyl groups attached to the doubly bonded carbon atoms".

Q.81 Match the structures of compounds given in Column I with the classes of compounds given in Column II.

Column I	Column II
A. $CH_3—CH(X)—CH_3$	1. Aryl halide
B. $CH_2=CH—CH_2—X$	2. Alkyl halide
C. C_6H_5X (benzene ring bearing X)	3. Vinyl halide
D. $CH_2=CH—X$	4. Allyl halide

Ans. A. → (2) B. → (4) C. → (1) D. → (3)

A. In alkyl halide, halogen atom is bonded to sp^3 hybridised carbon atom, which may be further bonded to one, two or three alkyl group, *i.e.*, $CH_3—CH(X)—CH_3$

B. Allyl halides are the compounds in which the halogen atom is bonded to sp^3 hybridised carbon atom next to carbon-carbon double bond, *i.e.*, $CH_2—CH—CH_2—X$

C. Aryl halides are the compounds in which the halogen atom is bonded to sp^2 hybridised carbon atom of an aromatic ring, *i.e.*, C_6H_5X

D. Vinyl halides are the compounds in which the halogen atom is bonded to an sp^2 hybridised carbon atom of a carbon-carbon double bond, *i.e.*, $CH_2=CH—X$

Q.82 Match the reactions given in Column I with the types of reactions given in Column II.

Column I	Column II
A. Chlorobenzene $\xrightarrow{Fe/Cl_2}$ 1,2-dichlorobenzene + 1,4-dichlorobenzene	1. Nucleophilic aromatic substitution
B. $CH_3-CH=CH_2 + HBr \longrightarrow CH_3-CH(Br)-CH_3$	2. Electrophilic aromatic substitution
C. $C_6H_5-CH(CH_3)-I \xrightarrow{OH} C_6H_5-CH(CH_3)-OH$	3. Saytzeff elimination
D. 1-Chloro-4-nitrobenzene + NaOH $\longrightarrow$ 4-nitrophenol	4. Electrophilic addition
E. $CH_3CH_2CH(Br)CH_3 \xrightarrow[KOH]{alc.\ KOH} CH_3CH=CH\,CH_3$	5. Nucleophilic substitution (S_N1)

Ans. A. → (2) B. → (4) C. → (5) D. → (1) E. → (3)

A. In this reaction, an electrophile Cl^+ attacks on to the benzene ring and substitution takes place.

B. In this reaction, addition of HBr takes place on to the doubly bonded carbons of propene in accordance with Markovnikov's rule and electrophilic addition takes place.

C. In this reaction, the reactant is secondary halide. Here, halogen atom is substituted by hydroxy ion. As it is secondary halide so it follows S_N1 mechanism.

D. In this reaction, halogen atom is directly bonded to aromatic ring. So, It is nucleophilic aromatic substitution as ^-OH group has substituted halogen of given compound.

E. It is an elimination reaction. It follows Saytzeff elimination rule.

Q.83 Match the structures given in Column I with the names in Column II.

Column I		Column II	
A.	Br	1.	4-Bromopent-2-ene
B.	Br	2.	4-Bromo-3- methylpent-2-ene
C.	Br	3.	1-Bromo-2-methylbut -2-ene
D.	Br	4.	1-Bromo-2-methylpent-2-ene

Ans. A. → (1) B. → (2) C. → (3) D. (4)

A. The IUPAC name of compound (A) is 4-bromopent-2-ene.

B. The IUPAC name of compound (B) is 4-bromo-3-methylpent-2-ene.

C. The IUPAC name of compound (C) is 1-bromo-2- methylbut-2-ene.

D. The IUPAC name of compound (D) is 1-bromo-2-methylpent-2-ene.

Q.84 Match the reactions given in Column I with the names given in Column II.

	Column I		Column II
A.	$-X + RX \xrightarrow{Na} -R$	1.	Fittig reaction
B.	2 (X) $+ 2Na \xrightarrow{Ether} + 2NaX$	2.	Wurtz Fittig reaction
C.	$\overset{+}{N}_2\overset{-}{X} \xrightarrow{Cu_2X_2} X + N_2$	3.	Finkelstein reaction
D.	$C_2H_5Cl + NaI \xrightarrow{\text{Dry acetone}} C_2H_5I + NaCl$	4.	Sandmeyer reaction

Ans. A. → (2) B. → (1) C. → (4) D. → (3)

A. A mixture of an alkyl halide and aryl halide gives an alkylarene when treated with sodium in dry ether and this is called Wurtz-Fittig reaction.

B. Aryl halides give analogous compounds when treated with sodium in dry ether, in which two aryl groups are joined together. It is called Fittig reaction.

C. Diazonium salt when treated with cuprous chloride or cuprous bromide gives chlorobenzene or bromobenzene. The reaction is known as Sandmeyer's reaction.

D. Alkyl iodides are prepared by the reaction of alkyl chlorides with sodium iodide in dry acetone. The reaction is known as Finkelstein reaction.

Assertion and Reason

In the following questions a statement of Assertion followed by a statement of Reason is given. Choose the correct answer out of the following choices.

(a) Assertion and reason both are correct and reason is correct explanation of assertion.

(b) Assertion and reason both are wrong statements.

(c) Assertion is correct but reason is wrong statement.

(d) Assertion is wrong but reason is correct statement.

(e) Assertion and reason both are correct statements but reason is not correct explanation of assertion.

Q.85 Assertion Phosph\orus chlorides (tri and penta) are preferred over thionyl chloride for the preparation of alkyl chlorides from alcohols.

Reason Phosphorus chlorides give pure alkyl halides.

Ans. *(b)* Assertion and reason both are wrong statements.

Correct Assertion Thionyl chloride is preferred over PCl_3 and PCl_5 for the preparation of alkyl chlorides from alcohols.

Correct Reason Thionyl chloride gives pure alkyl halide as other two by products (SO_2 + HCl) are escapable gases.

Q.86 Assertion The boiling points of alkyl halides decrease in the order

$$RI > RBr > RCl > RF$$

Reason The boiling points of alkyl chlorides, bromides and iodides are considerably higher than that of the hydrocarbon of comparable molecular mass.

Ans. *(e)* Assertion and reason both are correct statements but reason is not the correct explanation of assertion. For the same hydrocarbon part, boiling point depends upon the atomic mass of halogen atom. Higher the mass of the halogen atom, higher will be the boiling point. So, we can say that boiling point decreases with decrease in atomic mass of halogen atom.

Q. 87 Assertion KCN reacts with methyl chloride to give methyl isocyanide.

Reason CN^- is an ambident nucleophile.

Ans. *(d)* Assertion is wrong but reason is correct statement.

Correct Assertion KCN reacts with methyl chloride to give the mixture of methyl cyanide and methyl isocyanide in which methyl cyanide predominates because of stable C— C bond in methyl cyanide.

Q.88 Assertion tert-butyl bromide undergoes Wurtz reaction to give 2,2,3,3-tetramethylbutane.

Reason In Wurtz reaction, alkyl halides react with sodium in dry ether to give hydrocarbon containing double the number of carbon atoms present in the halide.

Ans. ***(a)*** Assertion and Reason both are correct and Reason is correct explanation of Assertion. tert-Butyl bromide undergoes Wurtz reaction.

$$CH_3-\underset{CH_3}{\overset{CH_3}{\underset{|}{\overset{|}{C}}}}-Br + 2Na + Br-\underset{CH_3}{\overset{CH_3}{\underset{|}{\overset{|}{C}}}}-CH_3 \xrightarrow[\text{ether}]{\text{Dry}} CH_3-\underset{CH_3}{\overset{CH_3}{\underset{|}{\overset{|}{C}}}}-\underset{CH_3}{\overset{CH_3}{\underset{|}{\overset{|}{C}}}}-CH_3 + 2NaBr$$

2-2-3-3 Tetramethyl-butane

Q.89 **Assertion** Presence of a nitro group at *ortho* or *para* position increases the reactivity of haloarenes towards nucleophilic substitution.

Reason Nitro group, being an electron withdrawing group decreases the electron density over the benzene ring.

Ans. ***(a)*** Assertion and reason both are correct and reason is correct explanation of assertion.

Presence of nitro group at *ortho* or *para* position increases the reactivity of haloarenes towards nucleophilic substitution because — NO_2 group, being an electron withdrawing group decreases the electron density over the benzene ring.

Q.90 **Assertion** In monohaloarenes, further electrophilic substitution occurs at *ortho* and *para* positions.

Reason Halogen atom is a ring deactivator.

Ans. ***(e)*** Assertion and reason both are correct statements but reason is not the correct explanation of assertion.

Correct explanation in monohaloarenes, halogen atom increases the electron density at *ortho* and *para* position. So, further electrophilic substitution occurs at *ortho* and *para* positions.

Q.91 **Assertion** Aryl iodides can be prepared by reaction of arenes with iodine in the presence of an oxidising agent.

Reason Oxidising agent oxidises I_2 into HI.

Ans. ***(c)*** Assertrion is correct but reason is wrong statement.

Correct Reason Oxidising agent oxidises HI into I_2 to prevent the possibility of backward reaction.

$$HI \rightleftharpoons H^+ + I^-$$

The backward reaction will not lead to the formation of aryl iodides.

Q.92 **Assertion** It is difficult to replace chlorine by —OH in chlorobenzene in comparsion to that in chloroethane.

Reason (R) chlorine carbon (C—Cl) bond in chlorobenzene has a partial double bond character due to resonance.

Ans. ***(a)*** **Assertion** and reason both are correct and reason is the correct explanation of assertion. It is difficult to replace chlorine by — OH in chlorobenzene in comparision to that in chloroethane because C— Cl bond in chlorobenzene has a partial bond character due to resonance.

Q.93 Assertion Hydrolysis of (–)-2-bromooctane proceeds with inversion of configuration.
Reason This reaction proceeds through the formation of a carbocation.

Ans. *(c)* Assertion is correct but reason is wrong statement.

Correct Reason This reaction proceeds through S_N2 mechanism, in which ^{-}OH ion attacks at 180° to the halogen atom of 2-bromooctane which leads to the inversion of configuration.

Q.94 Assertion Nitration of chlorobenzene leads to the formation of *m*-nitrochlorobenzene.
Reason —NO_2 group is a *m*-directing group.

Ans. *(d)* Assertion is wrong but reason is correct statement.

Correct Assertion Chlorination of nitrobenzene leads to the formation of *m*-nitrochlorobenzene because —NO_2 group deactivates the ring as it is *meta* directing.

Long Answer Type Questions

Q.95 Some alkyl halides undergo substitution whereas some undergo elimination reaction on treatment with bases. Discuss the structural features of alkyl halides with the help of examples which are responsible for this difference.

Ans. Primary alkyl halides follow S_N2 mechanism in which a nucleophile attacks at 180° to the halogen atom. A transition state is formed in which carbon is bonded to two nucleophiles and finally halogen atom is pushed out. In S_N2 mechanism, substitution of nucleophile takes place as follows

$$H-CH_2-Cl \xrightarrow[\text{(weak base)}]{aq.\ KOH} \left[HO\cdots \underset{H\ \ H}{\overset{H}{C}} \cdots Cl\right] \longrightarrow HO-\underset{H}{\overset{H}{C}}-H + Cl^-$$

Tertiary alkyl halides follow S_N2 mechanism. In this case, *tert* alkyl halides form 3° carbocations. Now, if the reagent used is a weak base then substitution occur while if it is a strong base then instead of substitution, elimination occurs.

$$H_3C-\underset{CH_3}{\overset{CH_3}{C}}-Cl \xrightarrow[\text{KOH (weak base)}]{aq.} H_3C-\overset{CH_3}{\overset{|}{C^{\oplus}}}-CH_3 + Cl^-$$

$$H_3C-\overset{CH_3}{\overset{|}{C^+}}-H_3C + OH^- \longrightarrow H_3C-\underset{CH_3}{\overset{CH_3}{C}}-OH \text{ or } HO-\underset{CH_3}{\overset{CH_3}{C}}-CH_3$$

Here, the reagent used is aq. KOH. It is a weak base so, substitution takes place.

$$H_3C-\underset{CH_3}{\overset{CH_3}{C}}-Cl \xrightarrow[\text{Elimation reaction}]{alc.\ KOH} H_3C-\overset{CH_3}{\overset{|}{C^{\oplus}}}-CH_3 + Cl^-$$

$$\underset{\substack{|\\ CH_3}}{H_3C-\overset{\oplus}{C}-CH_3} \xrightarrow[-H^+]{OH^-} \underset{\text{2-Methylprop-1-ene}}{H_3C-\overset{\overset{CH_3}{|}}{C}=CH_2} + H_2O$$

As alc. KOH is a strong base, so elimination competes over substitution and alkene is formed.

Q.96 Some halogen containing compounds are useful in daily life. Some compounds of this class are responsible for exposure of flora and fauna to more and more of UV light which causes destruction to a great extent. Name the class of these halocompounds. In your opinion, what should be done to minimise harmful effects of these compounds.

Ans. Some halogen containing compounds are useful in daily life are as follows

Dichloromethane It is used as a solvent as a paint remover, as a propellant in aerosols, and as a process solvent in the manufacture of drugs. It is also used as a metal cleaning and finishing solvent.

Trichloromethane It is employed as a solvent for fats, alkaloids, iodine and other substances.

Triodomethane It is used as an antiseptic. Now, it has been replaced by some other compounds because of its objectionable smell.

But some compounds of this class are responsible for exposure of flora and fauna to more and more of UV light which causes destruction to great extent. These are as follows

(i) **Tetrachloromethane** When carbon tetrachloride is released into the air, it rises to the atmosphere and depletes the ozone layer. Depletion of the ozone layer is believed to increase human exposure to UV rays leading to increased skin cancer, eye diseases and disorders, and possible disruption of the immune system. These UV rays cause damage to plants, and reduction of plankton populations in the ocean's photic zone.

(ii) **Freons** Freon (Chlorofluoro carbon compounds of methane and ethane) is likely to remain in the air long enough to reach the upper atomsphere. Here, it provides chlorine atoms which damage the ozone layer. Because of this depletion UV rays enters in our atmosphere and become responsible for damage to great extent.

(iii) $p-p'$-**Dichlorodiphenyl trichloroethane** (DDT)

DDT is not completely biodegradable. Instead, it gets deposited in fatty tissues. If ingestion continues for a long time, DDT builds up within the animal and effect the reproductive system.

To minimise the harmful impacts of these compounds, Multiple halogen groups are present in these compounds, so they are named as polyhalogen compounds. Fluorocarbons and hydrocarbons can be straight used to make refrigerants and air-conditioning equipments. They are stable in the stratosphere and secure for flora and fauna.

Q.97 Why are aryl halides less reactive towards nucleophilic substitution reactions than alkyl halides? How can we enhance the reactivity of aryl halides?

Ans. Aryl halides are less reactive towards nucleophilic substitution reaction due to the following reasons

(i) In haloarenes,the lone pair of electron on halogen are in resonance with benzene ring. So, C— Cl bond acquires partial double bond character which strengthen is C— Cl bond. Therefore, they are less reactive towords nucleophilic substitution reaction.

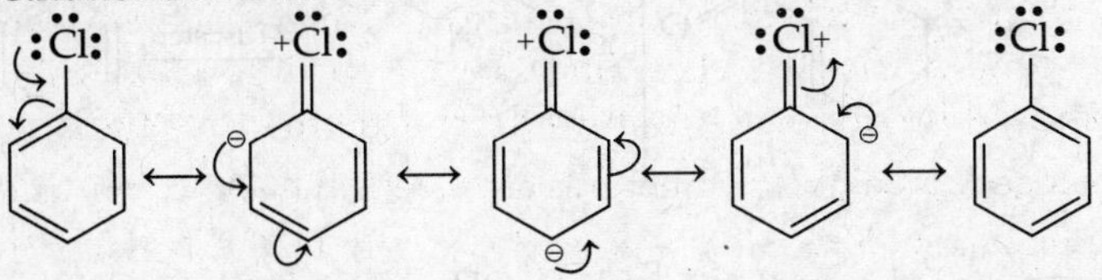

(ii) In haloarenes, the carbon atom attached to halogen is sp^2hybridised. The sp^2 hybridised carbon is more electronegative than sp^3 hybridised carbon. This sp^2-hybridised carbon in haloarenes can hold the electron pair of C—X bond more tightly and make this C— Cl bond shorter than C— Cl bond of haloalkanes.

Since, it is difficult to break a shorter bond than a longer bond, therefore, haloarenes are less reactive than haloalkanes.

In haloarenes, the phenyl cation will not be stabilised by resonance therefore S_N1 mechanism is ruled out.

(iii) Because of the repulsion between the nucleophile and electron rich arenes, aryl halides are less reactive than alkyl halides.

The reactivity of aryl halides can be increased by the presence of an electron withdrawing group (—NO_2) at *ortho* and *para* positions. However, no effect on reactivity of haloarenes is observed by the presence of electron withdrawing group at *meta*-position. Mechanism of the reaction is as depicted with $^-$OH ion.

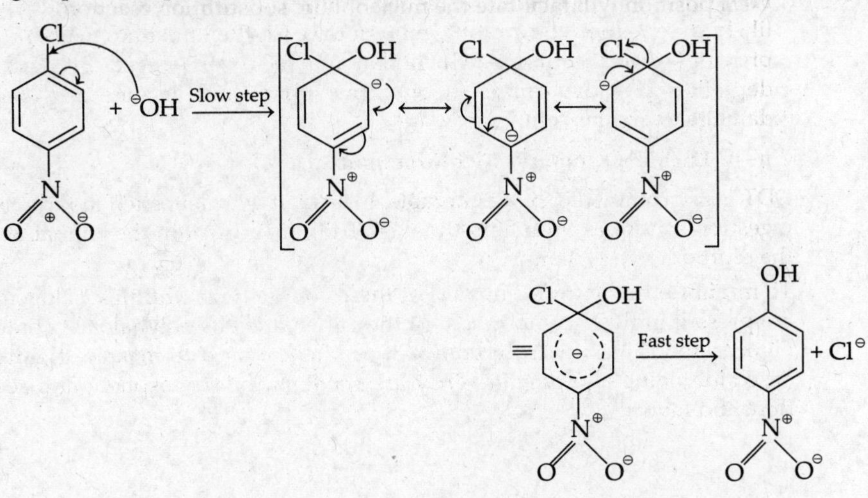

Slow step

Fast step

$+ Cl^{\ominus}$

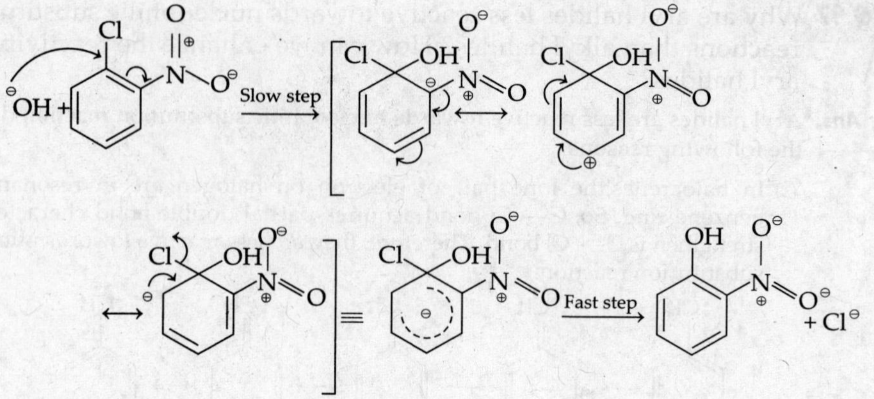

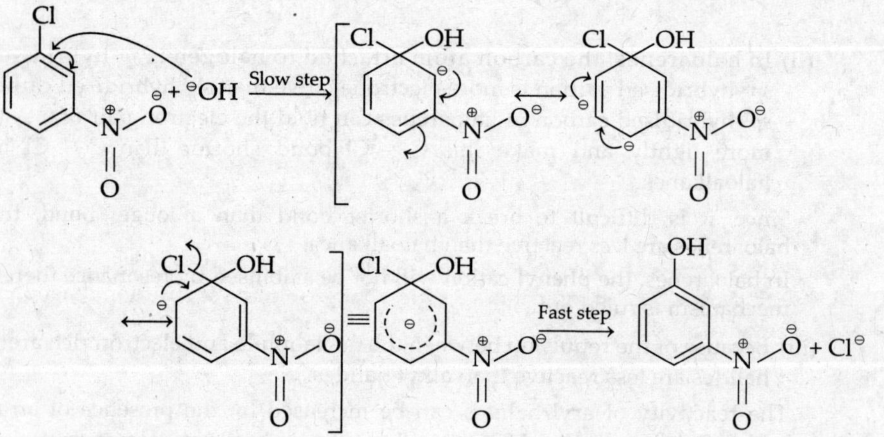

From the above resonance, it is very clear that electron density is rich at *ortho* and *para* positions. So, presence of EWG at *ortho* and *para* postitions and not on *meta* position will facilitate the nucleophilic substitution reaction.

Chapter 11

Alcohols, Phenols and Ethers

Multiple Choice Questions (MCQs)

Q.1 Monochlorination of toluene in sunlight followed by hydrolysis with *aq*. NaOH yields

(a) *o*-cresol (b) *m*-cresol

(c) 2, 4- dihydroxytoluene (d) benzyl alcohol

- **Concept Insight** The solution includes the concept of free radical chlorination (due to sunlight), followed by nucleophilic substitution (SN reaction) to replace the chlorine with a hydroxyl group, converting benzyl chloride to benzyl alcohol.

Ans. ***(d)*** Monochlorination of toluene in sunlight gives benzyl chloride. On hydrolysis with *aq*. NaOH, benzyl chloride shows nucleophilic substitution reaction to give benzyl alcohol.

$$C_6H_5CH_3 \text{ (Toluene)} \xrightarrow[\text{sunlight}]{Cl_2} C_6H_5CH_2Cl \text{ (Benzyl chloride)} \xrightarrow{aq.NaOH} C_6H_5CH_2OH \text{ (Benzyl alcohol)}$$

So, the correct option is (d).

Q.2 How many alcohols with molecular formula $C_4H_{10}O$ are chiral in nature?

(a) 1 (b) 2 (c) 3 (d) 4

Thinking Process It all four groups or atoms attached to the carbon atom are different, such a carbon is called asymmetric carbon or chiral carbon or stereocentre.

Ans. ***(a)*** The three isomers of butanol are possible. Structural formula of these isomers are given below

(i) $CH_3CH_2 — CH_2 — CH_2OH$
Butan–1–ol

No carbon is chiral in this compound as none of the four carbon is bonded to four different substituents.

(ii) $CH_3—CH_2—\overset{*}{C}H—CH_3$ with OH on the starred carbon

Butan-2-ol

In this compound, asterisk marked carbon is chiral carbon as all four substituents attached to it are different.

(iii) $H_3C—C(CH_3)(OH)—CH_3$

2-Methylpropan-2-ol

Here, again carbon is not chiral in nature.

So, only one alcohol is chiral in nature and the correct option is (a).

Q.3 What is the correct order of reactivity of alcohols in the following reaction?

$$R—OH + HCl \xrightarrow{ZnCl_2} R—Cl + H_2O$$

(a) 1° > 2° > 3°
(b) 1° < 2° > 3°
(c) 3° > 2° > 1°
(d) 3° > 1° > 2°

Ans. ***(c)*** The given reaction is nucleophilic substitution reaction in which —OH group is replaced by —Cl. Tertiary alcohols, when react with HCl in presence of $ZnCl_2$, form tertiary carbocation.

This intermediate 3° carbocation is more stable than 2° carbocation as well as 1° carbocation. Higher the stability of intermediate, greater will be the reactivity of reactant molecule.

So, the order of reactivity of alcohols in the given reaction is 3° > 2° > 1° and correct option is (c).

Q.4 CH_3CH_2OH can be converted into CH_3CHO by ....

(a) catalytic hydrogenation
(b) treatment with $LiAlH_4$
(c) treatment with pyridinium chlorochromate
(d) treatment with $KMnO_4$

Ans. ***(c)*** Ethanal (CH_3CHO) is an oxidised product of ethanol. Pyridinium chlorochromate ($C_5H_5\overset{+}{N}HClCr\overset{-}{O}_3$) oxidises primary alcohols to aldehydes. Strong oxidising agents such as $KMnO_4$ are used for getting carboxylic acid from alcohols.

The oxidation process can be stopped at aldehyde stage by using pyridinium chlorochromate $[(C_5H_5NH)^+(CrO_3Cl)^-]$.

Hence, option (c) is correct choice.

$$\underset{\text{Ethanol}}{CH_3CH_2OH} \xrightarrow{PCC} \underset{\text{Ethanal}}{CH_3CHO}$$

Q.5 The process of converting alkyl halides into alcohols involves ....

(a) addition reaction
(b) substitution reaction
(c) dehydrohalogenation reaction
(d) rearrangement reaction

Ans. ***(b)*** The process of converting alkyl halides into alcohols involves a substitution reaction, where halide group is replaced by hydroxyl group (OH^-). Unlike rearrangement reactions, which form structural isomers, substitutions simply replaces the atom or group with another. Therefore, this conversion is an example of nucleophilic substitution.

$$\underset{\text{Alkyl halide}}{R—X} \xrightarrow{OH^-} \underset{\text{Alcohol}}{R—OH}$$

Substitution reaction of alkyl halides

Primary alkyl halides – S_N2

Secondary alkyl halides– S_N1

Tertiary alkyl halides – S_N1

Q.6 Which of the following compounds is aromatic alcohol?

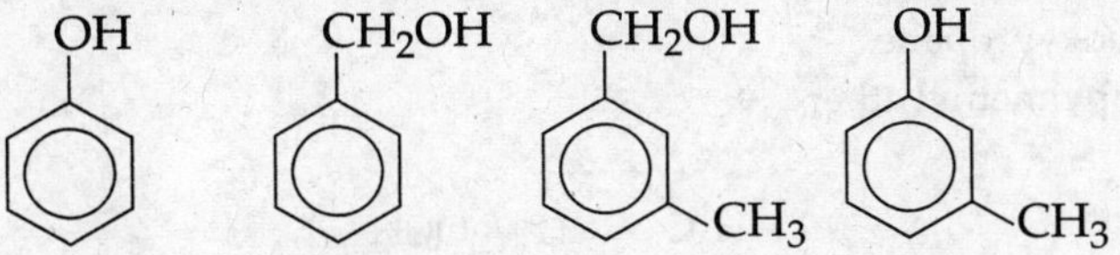

(A) Benzene ring with OH; (B) Benzene ring with CH_2OH; (C) Benzene ring with CH_2OH and CH_3 (meta); (D) Benzene ring with OH and CH_3 (meta)

(a) *A, B, C, D* (b) *A, D* (c) *B, C* (d) *A*

Ans. ***(c)*** Phenol is also known as, 'carbolic acid' and cannot be considered as aromatic alcohol. It is quite separate branch of compound called phenols. So, compound (*A*), *i.e.*, phenol and compound (*D*) *i.e.*, a derivative of phenol cannot be considered as aromatic alcohol.

On the other hand in compounds (*B*) and (*C*), —OH group is bonded to sp^3 hybridised carbon which inturn is bonded to benzene ring. Hence, the correct option is (c).

Q.7 Give IUPAC name of the compound given below.

$$CH_3—\underset{\underset{Cl}{|}}{CH}—CH_2—CH_2—\underset{\underset{OH}{|}}{CH}—CH_3$$

(a) 2-Chloro-5-hydroxyhexane (b) 2-Hydroxy-5-chlorohexane

(c) 5-Chlorohexan-2-ol (d) 2-Chlorohexan-5-ol

Ans. ***(c)***

$$\overset{6}{C}H_3—\underset{\underset{Cl}{|}}{\overset{5}{C}H}—\overset{4}{C}H_2—\overset{3}{C}H_2—\underset{\underset{OH}{|}}{\overset{2}{C}H}—\overset{1}{C}H_3$$

The correct IUPAC name of the compound is 5-chlorohexan-2-ol.

Hence, option (c) is the correct answer.

Q.8 IUPAC name of *m*- cresol is ....

(a) 3-methylphenol (b) 3-chlorophenol

(c) 3-methoxyphenol (d) benzene-1, 3-diol

Ans. ***(a)*** The structure of *m*–cresol is

(benzene ring with CH_3 at position 3 and OH at position 1)

m-cresol

IUPAC name is 3-methylphenol because —OH is the functional group and the (CH_3) methyl is substituent.

Q.9 IUPAC name of the compound $CH_3—\underset{\displaystyle CH_3}{\underset{|}{CH}}—OCH_3$ is ....

(a) 1-methoxy-1-methylethane
(b) 2-methoxy-2-methylethane
(c) 2-methoxypropane
(d) isopropylmethyl ether

Ans. ***(c)***

$$\overset{3}{H_3C}—\overset{2}{\underset{\displaystyle \overset{1}{CH_3}}{\underset{|}{CH}}}—OCH_3$$

IUPAC name of the above compound is 2-methoxypropane and correct option is (c).

Q.10 Which of the following species can act as the strongest base?

(a) $^{\ominus}OH$ (b) $^{\ominus}OR$
(c) $^{\ominus}OC_6H_5$ (d) $\overset{\ominus}{O}$–C_6H_4–NO_2 (*m*-nitrophenoxide)

Thinking Process To compare the species, the point to be noted is that weak acid has strong conjugate base and vice-versa. Write the corresponding acid of the given bases and choose the weakest acid among these.

Ans. ***(b)*** Weakest acid has the strongest conjugate base. ROH is the acid of RO^-

conjugate base, HOH is the acid of ^-OH, C_6H_5OH is the acid of $C_6H_5O^-$ and

HO–C_6H_4–NO_2 (*m*-nitrophenol) is the acid of $\bar{O}$–C_6H_4–NO_2. Among all these acids, ROH is the weakest acid.

Therefore, the strongest base is RO^- and the correct option is (b).

Q.11 Which of the following compounds will react with sodium hydroxide solution in water?

(a) C_6H_5OH (b) $C_6H_5CH_2OH$
(c) $(CH_3)_3COH$ (d) C_2H_5OH

Ans. ***(a)*** Phenol is more acidic than alcohols because it forms a resonance stabilized phenoxide ion after losing a proton. This stability increases its tendency to donate a proton, allowing phenol to dissolve in NaOH, unlike alcohols.

$$C_6H_5OH + NaOH \longrightarrow C_6H_5ONa + H_2O$$

Therefore, option (a) is the correct.

Q.12 Phenol is less acidic than ....

(a) ethanol (b) *o* - nitrophenol
(c) *o* - methylphenol (d) *o* - methoxyphenol

Thinking Process This question is based on the acidic character of phenol. Electron withdrawing group at *o* - and *p*-position *w.r.t.* —OH group of phenol increases the acidic strength.

Ans. ***(b)*** In *o*-nitrophenol, nitro group is present at *ortho* position. Presence of electron withdrawing group at *ortho* position increases the acidic strength. On the other hand, in *o*-methylphenol and in *o*-methoxyphenol, electron releasing group (— CH_3, — OCH_3) are present. Presence of these groups at *ortho* or *para* positions of phenol decreases the acidic strength of phenols. So, phenol is less acidic than *o* - nitrophenol.

Q.13 Which of the following is most acidic?

(a) Benzyl alcohol (b) Cyclohexanol
(c) Phenol (d) *m* - Chlorophenol

Ans. ***(d)*** Alpha carbon of benzyl alcohol and cyclohexanol is sp^3 hybridised while in phenol and m-chlorophenol, it is sp^2 hybridised. In m-chlorophenol electron withdrawing group (—Cl) is present at meta position.

Presence of electron withdrawing group increases the acidic strength. So, *m*-chlorophenol is most acidic among all the given compounds. The correct option is (d).

Mistake Alert ! *Students may confuse the hybridisation of the alpha carbon in phenol and m-chlorophenol, for sp^3 instead of sp^2.*

Q.14 Mark the correct order of decreasing acid strength of the following compounds.

(I) Phenol (C_6H_5OH) (II) *p*-nitrophenol (OH, NO_2 para) (III) *m*-methoxybenzyl alcohol (CH_2OH, OCH_3 meta) (IV) *m*-nitrophenol (OH, NO_2 meta) (V) *p*-methoxyphenol (OH, OCH_3 para)

(a) V > IV > II > I > III (b) II > IV > I > III > V
(c) IV > V > III > II > I (d) V > IV > III > II > I

Ans. ***(b)*** Presence of electron withdrawing group on phenols, increases its acidic strength. So, both compounds, *i.e.*, *p*-nitrophenol (II) and *m*-nitrophenol (IV) are stronger acid than (I). If this — NO_2 group is present at *p*-position, then it exerts both $-I$ and — R effect but if it is present at *meta* position, then it exerts only $-I$ effect. Therefore, *p*-nitrophenol is much stronger acid than *m*-nitrophenol.

On the other hand, presence of electron releasing group on phenol decreases its acidic strength. If — OCH_3 group is present at *meta* position, it will not exert $+R$ effect but exert $-I$ effect.

But, if it is present at *para* position, then it will exert $+R$ effect. Therefore, *m*-methoxy phenol is more acidic than *p*-methoxy phenol.

Hence, the correct option is (b).

Q.15 Mark the correct increasing order of reactivity of the following compounds with HBr/HCl.

CH_2OH (benzene ring) (I) $\quad$ CH_2OH (benzene ring with NO_2 at para) (II) $\quad$ CH_2OH (benzene ring with Cl at para) (III)

(a) I < II < III $\quad$ (b) II < I < III $\quad$ (c) II < III < I $\quad$ (d) III < II < I

Thinking Process This question is based on conceptual mixing of substitution reaction carbocation and reactivity. Nucleophilic substitution reactions depend upon the stability of carbocation. Higher the stability of carbocation (intermediate), higher will be the reactivity of reactant molecule.

Ans. ***(c)*** Reaction of the given compounds with HBr/HCl is a nucleophilic substitution reaction. It follows S_N1 mechanism. S_N1 mechanism depends upon the stability of carbocation. Presence of electron withdrawing group decreases the stability of carbocation. In compound (II) and (III), EWG is present at para position.

Since, — NO_2 group is a stronger EWG than — Cl. So, $NO_2-C_6H_5-\overset{+}{C}H_2$ carbocation will be less stable than $Cl—C_6H_5—\overset{+}{C}H_2$ carbocation.

Thus, the order of stability of carbocation is

$$O_2N-C_6H_4-\overset{+}{C}H_2 < Cl-C_6H_4-\overset{+}{C}H_2 < C_6H_5-\overset{+}{C}H_2$$

Therefore, compound (II) is least reactive and correct option is (c).

Q.16 Arrange the following compounds in increasing order of boiling point.

Propan-1-ol, butan-1-ol, butan-2-ol, pentan-1-ol

(a) Propan-1-ol, butan-2-ol, butan-1-ol, pentan-1-ol

(b) Propan-1-ol, butan-1-ol, butan-2-ol, pentan-1-ol

(c) Pentan-1-ol, butan-2-ol, butan-1-ol, propan-1-ol

(d) Pentan-1-ol, butan-1-ol, butan-2-ol, propan-1-ol

Thinking Process This question is based on the concept of boiling point of the compound. Boiling point increases with increase in the number of carbon atoms and decreases with increase of branching in carbon chain.

Ans. ***(a)*** Boiling point increases with increase in the number of carbon atoms because of increase in molecular mass. So, the boiling point of pentan-1-ol is more than that of all other given compounds. Further, among isomeric alcohols, 1° alcohols have higher boiling points than 2° alcohols because of higher surface area in 1° alcohols. Therefore, boiling point increases in the order.

Propan-1-ol < butan-2-ol < butan-1-ol < pentan-1-ol.

Here, the correct option is (a).

Multiple Choice Questions (More Than One Options)

Q.17 Which of the following are used to convert *R*CHO into *R*CH_2OH?

(a) H_2/Pd
(b) $LiAlH_4$
(c) $NaBH_4$
(d) Reaction with *R*Mg*X* followed by hydrolysis

Ans. ***(a, b, c)*** Conversion of aldehyde into alcohol is a reduction reaction. This reduction can be carried out by adding hydrogen in presence of finely divided metal catalyst such as platinum, palladium or nickel.

$$RCHO \xrightarrow{H_2/Pd} RCH_2OH$$

It can also be prepared by using $NaBH_4$ and $LiAlH_4$ as a reducing agent.

$$RCHO \xrightarrow{NaBH_4} RCH_2OH$$
$$RCHO \xrightarrow{LiAlH_4} RCH_2OH$$

Reaction of *R*Mg*X* with any aldehyde other than methanal gives secondary alcohols not the primary alcohols.

$$RCHO + RMgX \longrightarrow \underset{H}{\overset{R}{>}}C\underset{R}{\overset{OMgX}{<}} \xrightarrow{H_2O} \underset{H}{\overset{R}{>}}C\underset{R}{\overset{OH}{<}}$$

(Where, $R = —C_2H_5, C_3H_7$, etc.)

Q.18 Which of the following reactions will yield phenol?

(a) Chlorobenzene $\xrightarrow[\text{(ii) } H_2O/H^+]{\text{(i) Fusion with NaOH at 300 atm}}$

(b) Aniline (NH_2) $\xrightarrow[\text{(ii) } H_2O \text{ (Warming)}]{\text{(i) } NaNO_2/HCl}$

(c) Benzene $\xrightarrow[\text{(ii) NaOH, (Heating) (iii) } H^+]{\text{(i) Oleum}}$

(d) Chlorobenzene $\xrightarrow[\text{(ii) HCl}]{\text{(i) NaOH (aq.) 298 K/1 atm}}$

Ans. ***(a, b, c)***

(a) $C_6H_5Cl + NaOH \xrightarrow[300 \text{ atm}]{623 \text{ K}} C_6H_5\bar{O}Na^+ \xrightarrow{H_2O/H^+} C_6H_5OH$

(b) Aniline (NH_2) $\xrightarrow[HCl]{NaNO_2}$ Benzenediazonium chloride ($\overset{+}{N_2}Cl^-$) $\xrightarrow[Warming]{H_2O}$ Phenol (OH) $+ N_2 + HCl$

(c) Benzene $\xrightarrow{Oleum}$ Benzenesulphonic acid (SO_3H) $\xrightarrow[H^+]{NaOH}$ Phenol (OH)

Haloarenes are less reactive towards nucleophilic substitution reaction. Therefore, it requires very high temperature and pressure. Chlorobenzene does not undergo hydrolysis on treatment with *aq*. NaOH at 298 K and 1 atm.

Therefore, correct options are (a), (b) and (c).

Q.19 Which of the following reagents can be used to oxidise primary alcohols to aldehydes?

(a) CrO_3 in anhydrous medium (b) $KMnO_4$ in acidic medium
(c) Pyridinium chlorochromate (d) Heat in the presence of Cu at 573K

Ans. ***(a, c, d)*** CrO_3 in anhydrous medium is used to oxidise primary alcohols to aldehydes.

$$RCH_2OH \xrightarrow{CrO_3\ (anhydrous)} RCHO$$

Acidic $KMnO_4$ is a very strong oxidising agent. It oxidises primary alcohols into carboxylic acid.

$$RCH_2OH \xrightarrow{KMnO_4} RCOOH$$

Pyridinium chlorochromate ($C_6H_5\overset{+}{N}HClCrO_3^-$) is a very good reagent for the oxidation of primary alcohols to aldehydes.

$$RCH_2OH \xrightarrow{PCC} RCHO$$

When the vapours of primary alcohols are passed over heated copper at 573 K, dehydrogenation takes place and an aldehyde is formed.

$$RCH_2OH \xrightarrow[573\ K]{Cu} RCHO$$

Q.20 Phenol can be distinguished from ethanol by the reactions with ....

(a) Br_2 /water (b) Na (c) neutral $FeCl_3$ (d) All of these

Ans. ***(a, c)*** Ethanol does not react with Br_2/water while phenol gives 2, 4, 6-tribromophenol as white precipitate.

Phenol (OH) $+ 3Br_2 \longrightarrow$ 2,4,6-tribromophenol (OH; Br, Br, Br)

2, 4, 6-Tribromophenol

Ethanol and phenol both react with sodium, so phenol cannot be distinguished from ethanol by the reaction with sodium.

Ethanol does not give any reaction with neutral $FeCl_3$ solution, while phenol gives purple, blue or red colour when treated with neutral $FeCl_3$.

Therefore, correct options are (a) and (c).

Q.21 Which of the following are benzylic alcohols?

(a) $C_6H_5—CH_2-CH_2OH$ (b) $C_6H_5—CH_2OH$

(c) $C_6H_5—CH(CH_3)—OH$ (d) $C_6H_5—CH_2—CH(CH_3)—OH$

Ans. ***(b, c)*** In benzylic alcohols, the —OH group is attached to a sp^3 hybridised carbon atom next to an aromatic ring. In compound (a) and (d), the – OH group is attached to a sp^3 hybridised carbon atom but this carbon is not attached to the benzene ring.

On the other hand, in compound (a) and (c), the — OH group is attached to a sp^3 hybridised carbon atom next to an aromatic ring.

Short Answer Type Questions

Q.22 What is the structure and IUPAC name of glycerol?

Ans. Glycerol is the trihydric alcohol. Structure of glycerol is

$$HO-\overset{3}{C}H_2-\overset{2}{C}H(OH)-\overset{1}{C}H_2-OH$$

So, IUPAC name is propan- 1, 2, 3-triol.

Q.23 Write the IUPAC name of the following compounds.

(a) $CH_3—CH(CH_3)—CH(OH)—CH(C_2H_5)—CH(OH)—CH_3$

(b) Cyclohexane ring bearing NO_2 and OCH_3 in 1,3-positions

Ans. The correct IUPAC name of the following compounds are given below

(a) $H_3\overset{6}{C}—\overset{5}{C}H(CH_3)—\overset{4}{C}H(OH)—\overset{3}{C}H(C_2H_5)—\overset{2}{C}H(OH)—\overset{1}{C}H_3$

IUPAC name → 3-ethyl-5-methylhexan-2, 4-diol.

(b) Cyclohexane ring: C-3 bears NO_2, C-2, C-1 bears OCH_3

IUPAC name → 1-methoxy-3-nitrocyclohexane.

Q.24 Write the IUPAC name of the compound given below.

$$CH_3—CH_2—\underset{\displaystyle CH_3}{\underset{|}{C}}=\underset{\displaystyle CH_2OH}{\underset{|}{C}}—OH$$

Ans. The IUPAC name of the compound given below is

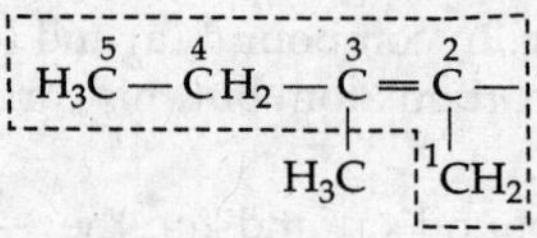

$$\overset{5}{H_3C}—\overset{4}{CH_2}—\underset{\displaystyle H_3C}{\underset{|}{\overset{3}{C}}}=\underset{\displaystyle \overset{1}{CH_2}—OH}{\underset{|}{\overset{2}{C}}}—OH$$

3-Methylpent-2-ene-1, 2-diol.

Q.25 Name the factors responsible for the solubility of alcohols in water.

Ans. Solubility of alcohols in water depends upon the two factors.

(i) **Hydrogen bonding** Higher the extent of hydrogen bonding, higher is the solubility. The hydrogen group of alcohol forms hydrogen bonding. Solubility increases with increase in the number of —OH groups in alcohols of comparable molecular masses.

$$\underset{(I)}{H_3C—CH_2—CH_2—OH} < \underset{(II)}{CH_3—\underset{\displaystyle OH}{\underset{|}{CH}}—CH_2—OH}$$

Compound (II) will form stronger H-bond due to two —OH groups and hence has higher boiling point.

(ii) **Size of alkyl/aryl group** Higher the size of alkyl/aryl group (hydrocarbon part), lower is the extent of hydrogen bonding and lower is the solubility. Hence, the order of boiling point of alcohols as

$$H_3C—CH_2—OH > CH_3CH_2—CH_2OH > CH_3CH_2CH_2—CH_2OH$$

Q.26 What is denatured alcohol?

Ans. Alcohol is widely used in industries as a solvent, so industrial alcohol is made cheaper by mixing it with substances like copper sulphate, pyridine or acetone to make it undrinkable. This process is called denaturation. Denaturated alcohol discourages consumption while keeping costs low for industrial use.

Q.27 Suggest a reagent for the following conversion.

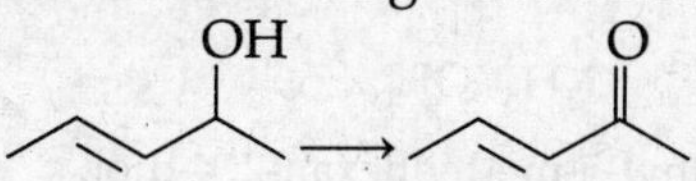

[Skeletal structures: pent-3-en-2-ol (OH) → pent-3-en-2-one (O)]

Ans. The given reactant is $H_3C—CH=CH—\overset{\displaystyle OH}{\overset{|}{CH}}—CH_3$. It is a secondary alcohol. Secondary alcohol ($>$CHOH) gives ketone when oxidises by CrO_3 or pyridinium chlorochromate, without carrying out oxidation at the double bond.

$$H_3C—CH=CH—\overset{\displaystyle OH}{\overset{|}{CH}}—CH_3 \xrightarrow[CrO_3]{PCC/} H_3C—CH=CH—\overset{\displaystyle O}{\overset{||}{C}}—CH_3$$

Q.28 Out of 2-chloroethanol and ethanol which is more acidic and why?

Ans. 2-chloroethanol is more acidic than ethanol. Due to – *I* effect (electron withdrawing group) of the Cl-atom electron density in O—H bond decreases. So, O—H bond of 2-chloroethanol becomes weaker than O—H bond of ethanol. Thus, 2-chloroethanol is more acidic than ethanol.

$$Cl \leftarrow CH_4 \leftarrow CH_2 \leftarrow O \leftarrow CH_3 \leftarrow CH_2 \leftarrow O \leftarrow H$$

(Stronger acid due to – *I* effect of Cl.)

Q.29 Suggest a reagent for conversion of ethanol to ethanal.

Ans. Ethanol can be oxidised into ethanal by using pyridinium chlorochromate. $(C_6H_5\overset{+}{N}HClCrO_3^-)$ in CH_2Cl_2.

$$\underset{\text{Ethanol}}{H_3C—CH_2—OH} \xrightarrow{PCC/CH_2Cl_2} \underset{\text{Ethanal}}{CH_3—CHO.}$$

Q.30 Suggest a reagent for conversion of ethanol to ethanoic acid.

Ans. Ethanol can be converted into ethanoic acid by using acidified $KMnO_4$ or $K_2Cr_2O_7$.

Both $KMnO_4$ and $K_2Cr_2O_7$ are strong oxidising agents.

$$\underset{\text{Ethanol}}{CH_3CH_2OH} \xrightarrow[KMnO_4]{\text{Acidified}} \underset{\text{Ethanoic acid}}{CH_3COOH}$$

Q.31 Out of *o*-nitrophenol and *p*-nitrophenol, which is more volatile? Explain.

Ans. *o*-nitrophenol is more volatile than *p*-nitrophenol due to presence of intramolecular hydrogen bonding. In *para* nitrophenol, intermolecular hydrogen bonding is present. This intermolecular hydrogen bonding causes the association of molecules and is stronger than intramolecular hydrogen bonding.

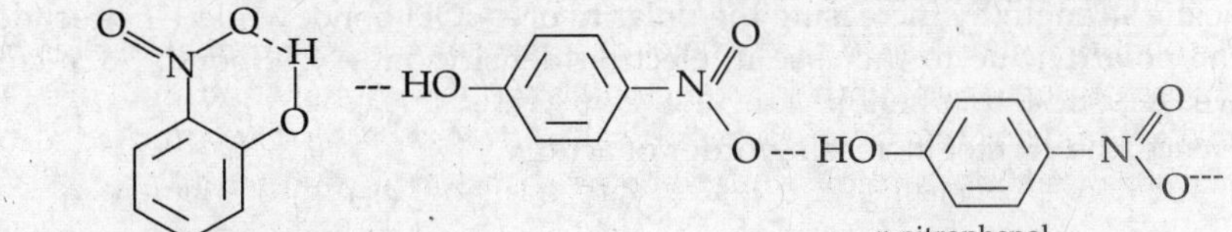

o-nitrophenol
(Intramolecular H-bonding)

p-nitrophenol
(Intermolecular H-bonding)

Q.32 Out of *o*-nitrophenol and *o*-cresol which is more acidic?

Ans. The acidic character of alcohols is due to the polar nature of O—H bond. Higher the polarity of O—H bond, more will be the acidic strength. Due to – *I* and – *R* effect of nitro group, electron density decreases in the O—H bond of *o*-nitrophenol and thus polarity increases.

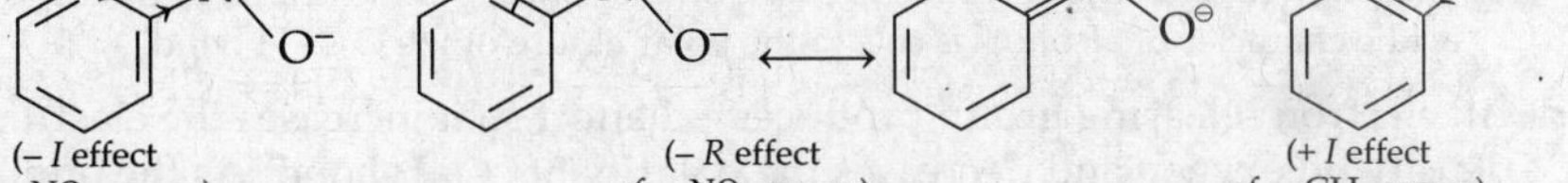

(– *I* effect of —NO_2 group)

(– *R* effect of —NO_2 group)

(+ *I* effect of —CH_3 group)

Whereas due to + *I* effect of — CH_3 group, electron density increases in the O—H bond of *o*-cresol. Thus, O – H bond of *o*-nitrophenol is weaker than O—H bond of *o*-cresol and *o*-nitrophenol is more acidic than *o*-cresol.

Q.33 When phenol is treated with bromine water, white precipitate is obtained. Give the structure and the name of the compound formed.

Ans. When phenol is treated with bromine water, white ppt. of 2, 4, 6 – tribromophenol is obtained.

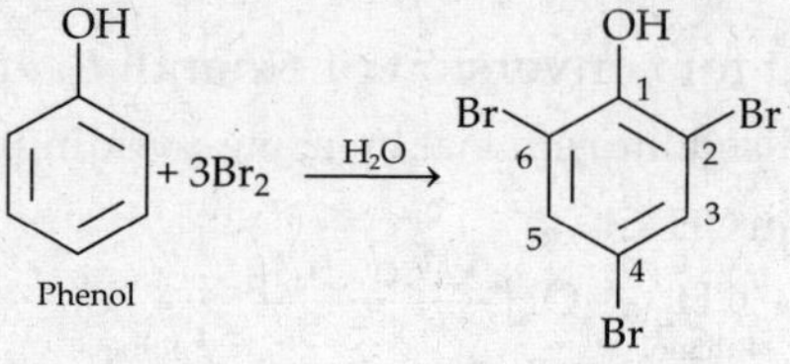

$$\text{Phenol} + 3Br_2 \xrightarrow{H_2O} \text{2,4,6-Tribromophenol}$$

Phenol

2,4,6 –Tribromophenol

Q.34 Arrange the following compounds in increasing order of acidity and give a suitable explanation.

Phenol, *o*-nitrophenol, *o*-cresol

Ans. We know that, nitro group shows – *I* and – *R* effect as follows

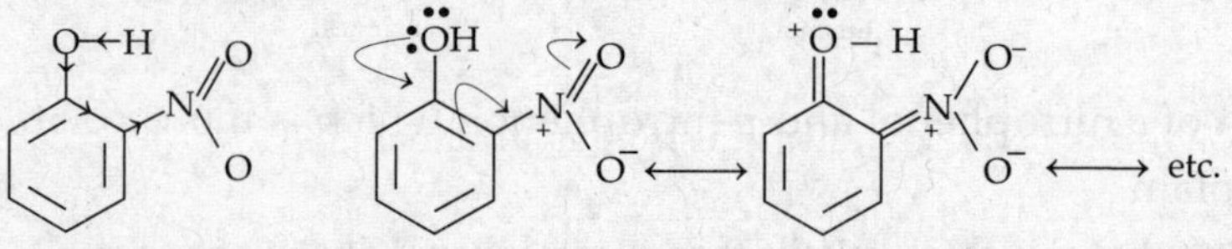

(– *I* effect) (– *R* effect)

Due to this – *I* and – *R* effect of *o*-nitrophenol, it is a stronger acid than phenol. On the other hand, —CH_3 group produces + *I* effect. – *I* and – *R* effect increases the acidic strength by increasing the polarity of — OH bond, while + *I* effect decreases the polarity due to increase in electron density on —OH bond. So, *o*-cresol is a weaker acid than phenol.

Hence, the correct increasing order of acidity.

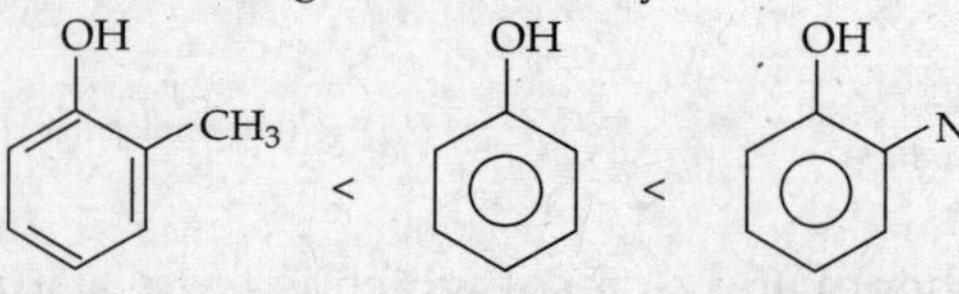

o-cresol < phenol < *o*-nitrophenol

Q. 35 Alcohols react with active metals *e.g.*, Na, K etc., to give corresponding alkoxides. Write down the decreasing order of reactivity of sodium metal towards primary, secondary and tertiary alcohols.

Thinking Process This question is based on the concept of the acidity and reactivity. The acidic character of alcohols is due to the polar nature of the O — H bond.

Ans. An electron releasing group produces + *I* effect so it increases the electron density on oxygen and decreases the polarity of O – H bond. As the number of alkyl group increases from 1° to 3° alcohols, the electron density on the O—H bond increases.

It will finally decrease the polarity and increase the strength of O—H bond in going from 1° to 3° alcohols. Thus, acidic strength decreases in the following order

$$\underset{1^\circ\ \text{alcohol}}{RCH_2OH} > \underset{2^\circ\ \text{alcohol}}{R_2CHOH} > \underset{3^\circ\ \text{alcohol}}{R_3C-OH}$$

As we know that, sodium metal is basic in nature and alcohols are acidic in nature. Thus, reactivity of alcohol with sodium metal decreases with decrease in acidic strength. Therefore, the correct order is 1° > 2° > 3°.

Q.36 What happens when benzene diazonium chloride is heated with water?

Ans. When benzene diazonium chloride is heated with water then phenol is formed.

$$\underset{\text{Benzene diazonium chloride}}{C_6H_5\overset{\oplus}{N_2}\overset{\ominus}{Cl}} \xrightarrow[\text{warm}]{H_2O} \underset{\text{Phenol}}{C_6H_5OH} + N_2 + HCl$$

Q.37 Arrange the following compounds in decreasing order of acidity.

$$H_2O, ROH, HC\equiv CH$$

Ans. A stronger acid displaces a weaker acid from its salt. When *R*ONa is treated with H_2O, it forms *R*OH, so, water is a stronger acid than *R*OH.

$$\underset{\text{Stronger acid}}{HOH} + RONa \longrightarrow NaOH + \underset{\text{Weaker acid}}{ROH}$$

Similarly, when sodium ethynide is treated with water and alcohol, then acetylene is obtained.

$$\underset{\text{Stronger acid}}{HOH} + CH\equiv CNa \longrightarrow \underset{\text{Weak acid}}{HC\equiv CH} + NaOH$$

$$\underset{\text{Stronger acid}}{ROH} + HC\equiv CNa \longrightarrow \underset{\text{Weak acid}}{HC\equiv CH} + RONa$$

Thus, water and alcohol are stronger acid than ethyne and the decreasing order of acidity of given compounds are

$$HOH > ROH > HC\equiv CH$$

Q.38 Name the enzymes and write the reactions involved in the preparation of ethanol from sucrose by fermentation.

Ans. Sucrose is converted to glucose and fructose in the presence of an enzyme, invertase or sucrase. Glucose and fructose undergo fermentation in the presence of another enzyme, zymase. Both these enzymes are present in yeast.

$$\underset{\text{Sucrose}}{C_{12}H_{22}O_{11}} + H_2O \xrightarrow{\text{Invertase/sucrose}} \underset{\text{Glucose}}{C_6H_{12}O_6} + \underset{\text{Fructose}}{C_6H_{12}O_6}$$

$$\underset{\text{Glucose/Fructose}}{C_6H_{12}O_6} \xrightarrow{\text{Zymase}} \underset{\text{Ethanol}}{2CH_3CH_2OH} + 2CO_2$$

Q.39 How can propan-2-one be converted into *tert*-butyl alcohol?

Ans. Propan-2-one is a ketone. Its structural formula is $(H_3C)_2C{=}O$. Ketones when treated with Grignard reagent give tertiary alcohols.

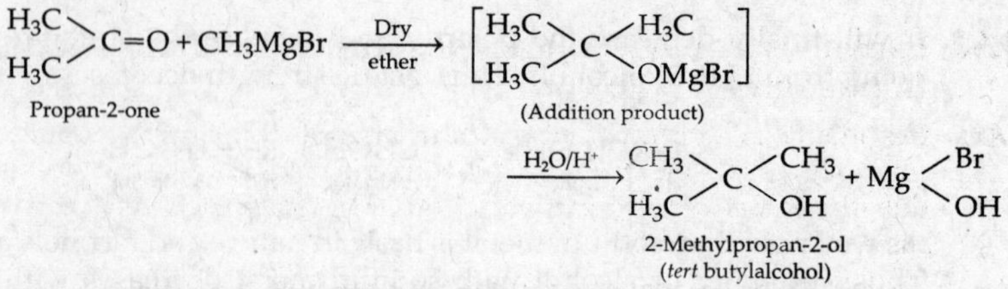

$$\underset{\text{Propan-2-one}}{\begin{matrix} H_3C \\ H_3C \end{matrix}\!\!>C{=}O} + CH_3MgBr \xrightarrow[\text{ether}]{\text{Dry}} \underset{\text{(Addition product)}}{\left[\begin{matrix} H_3C \\ H_3C \end{matrix}\!\!>C<\!\!\begin{matrix} H_3C \\ OMgBr \end{matrix}\right]}$$

$$\xrightarrow{H_2O/H^+} \underset{\substack{\text{2-Methylpropan-2-ol} \\ (\textit{tert}\ \text{butylalcohol})}}{\begin{matrix} CH_3 \\ H_3C \end{matrix}\!\!>C<\!\!\begin{matrix} CH_3 \\ OH \end{matrix}} + Mg<\!\!\begin{matrix} Br \\ OH \end{matrix}$$

Q.40 Write the structures of the isomers of alcohols with molecular formula $C_4H_{10}O$. Which of these exhibits optical activity?

Ans. Some compounds can rotate the plane polarised light, when it is passed through their solution. Such compounds are called optically active compounds. The structures of the isomers of alcohols with molecular formula $C_4H_{10}O$ are as follows.

	Structure	Name
(i)	$CH_3—CH_2—CH_2—CH_2—OH$	Butan-1-ol
(ii)	$CH_3—CH_2—\underset{\large OH}{\underset{\vert}{CH}}—CH_3$	Butan-2-ol
(iii)	$H_3C—\underset{\large CH_3}{\underset{\vert}{CH}}—CH_2OH$	2-Methylpropan-1-ol
(iv)	$H_3C—\overset{\large CH_3}{\overset{\vert}{\underset{\large CH_3}{\underset{\vert}{C}}}}—OH$	2-Methylpropan-2-ol

The asymmetry of the molecule is responsible for the optical activity in a molecule. If all the four substituents attached to the carbon are different then the carbon is called asymmetric or chiral carbon and such a molecule is called asymmetric molecule.

In the above explained structures, it is only butan-2-ol which contains a chiral carbon and hence it is optically active.

Q.41 Explain why is OH group in phenols more strongly held as compared to OH group in alcohols?

Ans. In phenols, the electron pairs on oxygen atom of —OH group are in conjugation (or resonance) with π electrons of the ring and the following resonating structures are possible

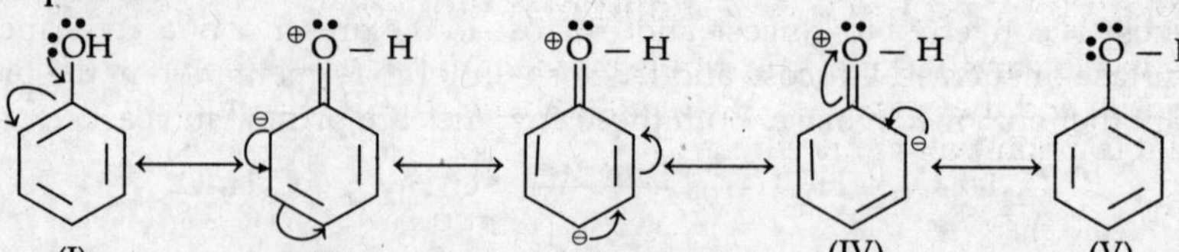

$:\ddot{O}H$ (I) ⟷ $\overset{\oplus}{\ddot{O}}-H$ (II) ⟷ $\overset{\oplus}{\ddot{O}}-H$ (III) ⟷ $\overset{\oplus}{\ddot{O}}-H$ (IV) ⟷ $:\ddot{O}-H$ (V)

Out of these five resonating structures, II, III and IV structures contain a carbon-oxygen double bond character. In other words, carbon-oxygen bond in phenol acquires a partial double bond character due to resonance.

But in alcohols, carbon-oxygen bond in alcohols is purely single bond. Therefore, — OH group in phenols is more strongly held as compared to —OH group in alcohols.

Q.42 Explain why nucleophilic substitution reactions are not very common in phenols?

Ans. Resonance is an important factor in phenols. During resonance — OH group in phenol gives its electrons to the benzene ring. As a result of this, the electron density on benzene ring is very high. This increased electron density on benzene repels nucleophiles.

Therefore, nucleophiles cannot attack the benzene ring and phenols usually do not give nucleophilic substitution reaction.

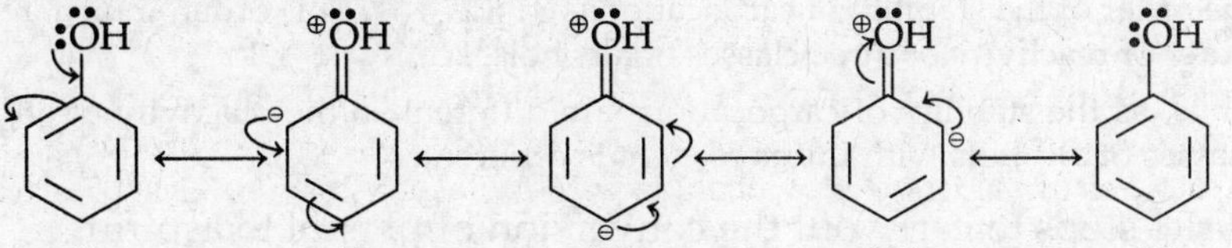

(I) ⟷ (II) ⟷ (III) ⟷ (IV) ⟷ (V)

Resonance in phenols

Q.43 Preparation of alcohols from alkenes involves the electrophilic attack on alkene carbon atom. Explain its mechanism.

Ans. Alcohols can be prepared from alkene by the hydration of alkenes in presence of sulphuric acid.

$$CH_2 = CH_2 + H_2O \xrightarrow{H^+} CH_3CH_2OH$$

This addition reaction takes place in accordance with Markovnikov's rule.

Mechanism The mechanism of the reaction involves the following three steps

Step 1 Protonation of alkene to form carbocation by electrophilic attack of H_3O^+.

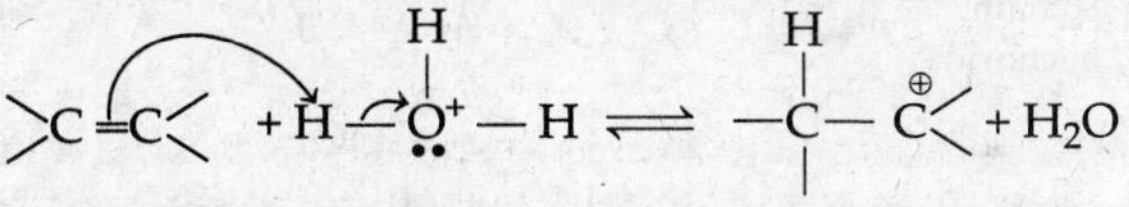

$$>C=C< + H-\ddot{O}^+(H)-H \rightleftharpoons -C(H)-\overset{\oplus}{C}< + H_2O$$

Step 2 Attack of water molecule to the secondary carbocation.

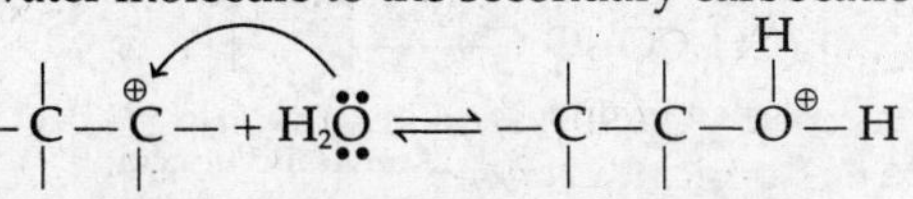

$$-\overset{|}{\underset{|}{C}}-\overset{\oplus}{\underset{|}{C}}- + H_2\ddot{O} \rightleftharpoons -\overset{|}{\underset{|}{C}}-\overset{|}{\underset{|}{C}}-\overset{\oplus}{O}(H)-H$$

Step 3 Loss of the hydrogen from the protonated alcohol.

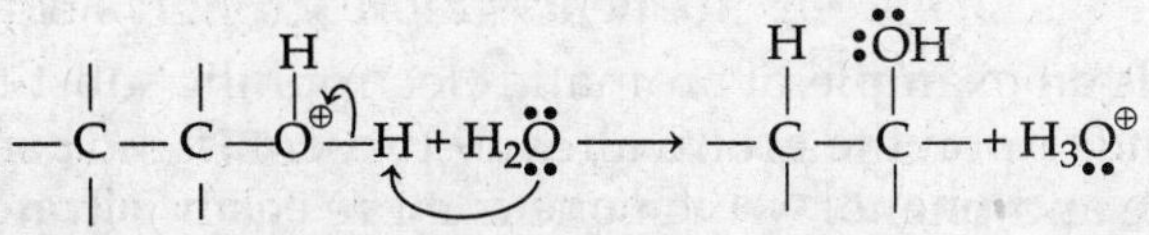

$$-\overset{|}{\underset{|}{C}}-\overset{|}{\underset{|}{C}}-\overset{\oplus}{O}(H)-H + H_2\ddot{O} \longrightarrow -\overset{H}{\underset{|}{C}}-\overset{:\ddot{O}H}{\underset{|}{C}}- + H_3\ddot{O}^{\oplus}$$

Q.44 Explain why is $O=C=O$ non-polar while $R-O-R$ is polar?

Ans. CO_2 is a linear molecule. The dipole moment of two $C=O$ bonds are equal and opposite and they cancel each other, and hence the dipole moment of CO_2 is zero and it is a non-polar molecule.

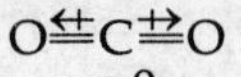

$$O \overset{\leftarrow}{=} C \overset{\rightarrow}{=} O$$
$$\mu = 0$$

While for ethers, two dipoles are pointing in the same direction. These two dipoles do not cancel the effect of each other. Therefore, there is a finite resultant dipole moment and hence $R-O-R$ is a polar molecule.

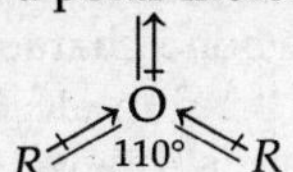

$$R \nearrow O \nwarrow R \quad 110^\circ$$
$$\mu \neq 0$$

Q.45 Why is the reactivity of all the three classes of alcohols with conc. HCl and $ZnCl_2$ (Lucas reagent) different?

Ans. The reaction of alcohols with Lucas reagent (conc. HCl and $ZnCl_2$) follow S_N1 mechanism. S_N1 mechanism depends upon the stability of carbocations (intermediate). More stable the intermediate carbocation, more reactive is the alcohol.

Tertiary carbocations are most stable among the three classes of carbocations and the order of the stability of carbocation is $3° > 2° > 1°$. This order, inturn, reflects the order of reactivity of three classes of alcohols, *i.e.*, $3° > 2° > 1°$.

Thus, as the stability of carbocations are different so the reactivity of all the three classes of alcohols with Lucas reagent is different.

Q.46 Write steps to carry out the conversion of phenol to aspirin.

Ans. Aspirin can be prepared by the reaction of salicylic acid with acetic anhydride. Salicylic acid is prepared by the reaction of phenol with CO_2 and NaOH.

This process is known as Kolbe's reaction. The product salicylic acid is used in the preparation of aspirin. Afterwards, when salicylic acid is treated with acetic anhydride then acetyl group replaces the hydrogen of —OH group, *i.e.*, acetylation occurs at —OH group of salicylic acid. Reaction is as follows

$$\underset{\text{Phenol}}{C_6H_5OH} \xrightarrow[-H_2O]{\text{NaOH}} \underset{\text{Sodium phenoxide}}{C_6H_5ONa} \xrightarrow[\substack{4\text{–}7\text{atm} \\ \text{(Kolbe's reaction)}}]{CO_2/400\text{ K}} \left[C_6H_4(OH)COONa \right] \xrightarrow[-\text{NaCl}]{\text{Dil. HCl}} \underset{\text{Salicylic acid}}{C_6H_4(OH)COOH}$$

$$\underset{\substack{\text{2-Hydroxybenzoic acid} \\ \text{or} \\ \text{Salicylic acid}}}{C_6H_4(OH)COOH} + \underset{\text{Acetic anhydride}}{(CH_3CO)_2O} \xrightarrow{H^+} \underset{\substack{\text{Acetylsalicylic acid} \\ \text{or} \\ \text{2-Acetoxybenzoic acid or aspirin}}}{C_6H_4(OCOCH_3)COOH} + CH_3COOH$$

Q.47 Nitration is an example of aromatic electrophilic substitution and its rate depends upon the group already present in the benzene ring. Out of benzene and phenol, which one is more easily nitrated and why?

Ans. Nitration of benzene and phenol is an electrophilic substitution reaction. During nitration $\overset{+}{N}O_2$ (nitronium ion) is produced as an intermediate as follows

$$HO_3SO—H + H\ddot{O}NO_2 \rightleftharpoons H—\overset{\oplus}{\underset{|}{\overset{H}{O}}}—NO_2 + HSO_4^-$$

$$\underset{\text{(Protonated nitric acid)}}{H—\overset{+}{\underset{\cdot\cdot}{\overset{H}{O}}}—NO_2} \rightleftharpoons \underset{\substack{\text{(Nitronium ion)} \\ \text{(electrophile)}}}{H_2O + \overset{+}{N}O_2}$$

This nitronium ion (electrophile) attacks on benzene or on phenol. Phenol is more easily nitrated than benzene as the presence of —OH group in phenol increases the electron density at *ortho* and *para* positions in benzene ring by + *R* effect.

Phenol has higher electron density than benzene, making it more easily nitrated.

Q.48 In Kolbe's reaction, instead of phenol, phenoxide ion is treated with carbon dioxide. Why?

Ans. In phenoxide ion, the ability to give lone pair of electrons to the benzene ring is more in comparison to phenols. Therefore, the reactivity of phenoxide ion towards electrophilic substitution reaction is more in comparison to phenols.

Thus, phenoxide ion being a stronger nucleophile reacts easily with CO_2 (weak electrophile) than phenols in Kolbe's reaction.

Phenol (OH) $\xrightarrow{NaOH}$ Sodium phenoxide (ONa) $\xrightarrow[\text{(ii) } H^+]{\text{(i) } CO_2}$ 2-Hydroxybenzoic acid (OH, COOH)

(Kolbe's reaciton)

Note Kolbe's process is also known as Kolbe - Schmitt reaction. This reaction is precursor to aspirin formation.

Q.49 Dipole moment of phenol is smaller than that of methanol. Why?

Ans. Dipole moment depends upon the polarity of bonds. Higher the polarity of bonds in molecule, higher will be its dipole moment. In phenol carbon is sp^2 hybridised and due to this reason benzene ring is producing electron withdrawing effect.

On the other hand, carbon of methanol is sp^3 hybridised and produces electron releasing effect (+ *I* effect). Thus, C—O bond in phenol is less polar than C—O bond in methanol and therefore, the dipole moment of phenol is smaller than that of methanol.

Phenol (OH), $\mu = 1.54D$ and CH_3OH, $\mu = 1.71D$

Q.50 Ethers can be prepared by Williamson synthesis in which an alkyl halide is reacted with sodium alkoxide. Di-*tert* -butyl ether can't be prepared by this method. Explain.

Ans. In order to prepare di-*tert*-butyl ether, sodium *tert*-butoxide must be reacted with *tert*-butylbromide. Alkoxides are not only nucleophiles but they are strong base as well. They react with 3° alkyl halides leading to the elimination reaction.

When *tert*-butylbromide reacts with sodium *tert*-butoxide, instead of substitution, elimination takes place. As a result of this elimination reaction, *iso* butylene is formed instead of di-*tert*-butyl ether.

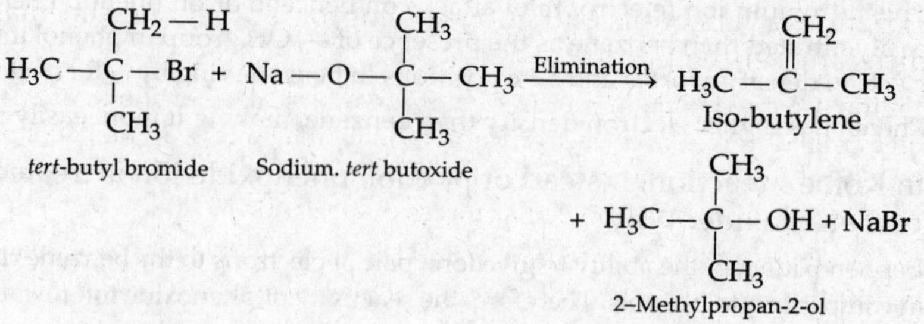

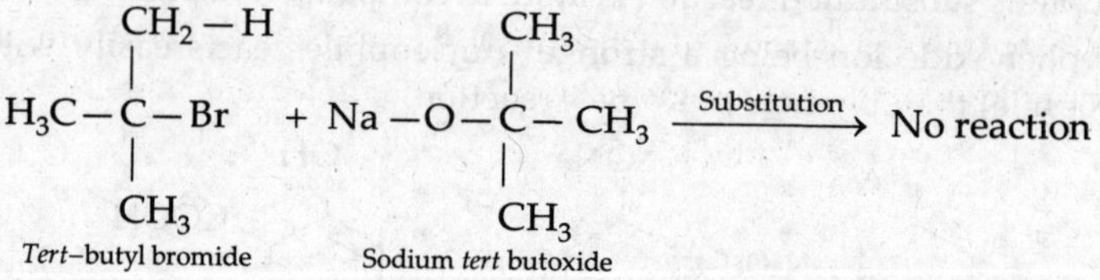

$$\underset{\textit{tert}\text{-butyl bromide}}{H_3C-\overset{CH_2-H}{\underset{CH_3}{C}}-Br} + \underset{\text{Sodium. } \textit{tert} \text{ butoxide}}{Na-O-\overset{CH_3}{\underset{CH_3}{C}}-CH_3} \xrightarrow{\text{Elimination}} \underset{\text{Iso-butylene}}{H_3C-\overset{CH_2}{\overset{\|}{C}}-CH_3}$$

$$+ \underset{\text{2–Methylpropan-2-ol}}{H_3C-\overset{CH_3}{\underset{CH_3}{C}}-OH} + NaBr$$

$$\underset{\textit{Tert}\text{–butyl bromide}}{H_3C-\overset{CH_2-H}{\underset{CH_3}{C}}-Br} + \underset{\text{Sodium } \textit{tert} \text{ butoxide}}{Na-O-\overset{CH_3}{\underset{CH_3}{C}}-CH_3} \xrightarrow{\text{Substitution}} \text{No reaction}$$

Q.51 **Why is the C—O—H bond angle in alcohols slightly less than the tetrahedral angle whereas the C—O—C bond angle in ether is slightly greater?**

Thinking Process To solve this question, it should keep in mind that the order of repulsion between electron pairs is → *lp – lp* > *lp – bp* > *bp – bp*.

Ans. The bond angle in $C-\ddot{\underset{\cdot\cdot}{O}}-H$ in alcohols is slightly less than tetrahedral angle (109°28'). It is due to the repulsion between the unshared electron pairs of oxygen. In alcohols, two lone pair of electrons are present. Therefore, there is comparatively more repulsion and less bond angle.

The C—O—C bond angle in ether is slightly greater than the tetrahedral angle due to the repulsive interaction between the two bulky (– *R*) groups.

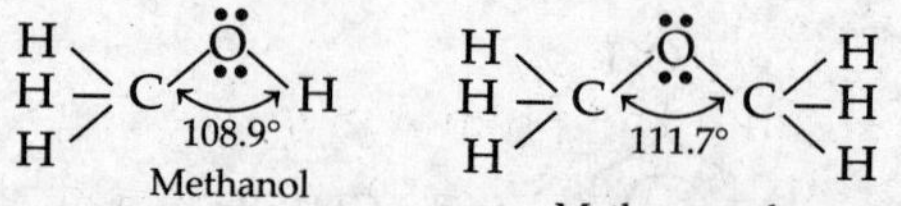

$$\underset{\text{Methanol}}{H_3C-\ddot{O}-H \;(108.9^\circ)} \qquad \underset{\text{Methoxymethane}}{H_3C-\ddot{O}-CH_3 \;(111.7^\circ)}$$

Q.52 **Explain why low molecular mass alcohols are soluble in water?**

Ans. Solubility of alcohols and phenols in water is due to their ability to form hydrogen bonds with water molecule. The hydrocarbon part (*i.e.*, *R* group) tends to prevent the formation of hydrogen bonds.

Alcohols with lower molar mass will have smaller hydrocarbon part and therefore tendency to form hydrogen bonding is more and they are more soluble in water.

$$\underset{\text{(More soluble)}}{CH_3CH_2OH} > \underset{\text{(Less soluble)}}{CH_3CH_2CH_2OH}$$

Q.53 **Explain why *p*-nitrophenol is more acidic than phenol?**

Ans. Nitro group of phenol produces – *I* and – *R* effect. Because of these two effects, $-NO_2$ group is electron withdrawing in nature. So, the electron density in the O—H bond of *p*-nitrophenol decreases relative to the O—H bond of phenol.

The decrease in electron density of the O—H bond of *p*-nitrophenol, causes the polarity of O—H bond to decrease and in turn makes it more acidic than phenol.

Q.54 Explain why alcohols and ethers of comparable molecular mass have different boiling points?

Ans. Boiling point depends upon the strength of intermolecular forces of attraction. Higher these forces of attraction, more will be the boiling point. Alcohols undergo intermolecular hydrogen bonding. So, the molecules of alcohols are held together by strong intermolecular forces of attraction.

But in ethers no hydrogen atom is bonded to oxygen. Therefore, ethers are held together by weak dipole-dipole forces, not by strong hydrogen bond.

Since, lesser amount of energy is required to break weak dipole-dipole forces in ethers than to break strong hydrogen bonds in alcohol. Therefore, alcohols have higher boiling points than ethers of comparable molecular mass.

$$CH_3CH_2-O-H \text{.....} \underset{\displaystyle H}{\underset{|}{O}}-CH_2-CH_3$$

Hydrogen bond in alcohols

Q.55 The carbon-oxygen bond in phenol is slightly stronger than that in methanol. Why ?

Ans. Positive resonance effect is observed in phenols. Due to this + R effect, lone pair of electrons of —OH group are in conjugation with π electrons of the ring and the following resonance hybrid are obtained.

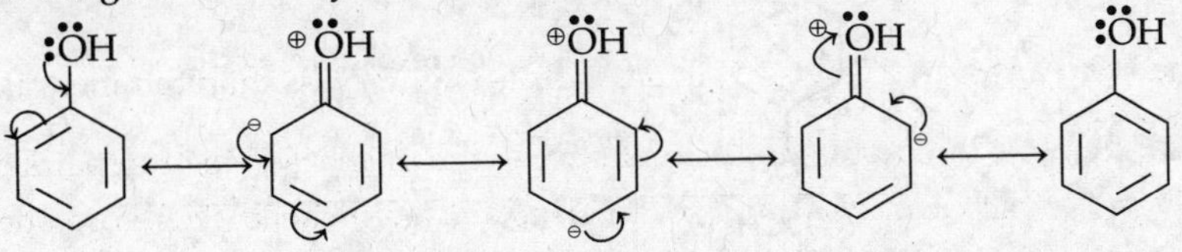

From the above resonating structures, it is very clear that C—O bond of phenol acquires some partial double bond character, while the C—O bond of methanol is purely single bond. Therefore, the carbon-oxygen bond in phenol is slightly stronger than that in methanol.

Q.56 Arrange water, ethanol and phenol in increasing order of acidity and give reason for your answer.

Ans. The phenoxide ion obtained after the removal of a proton is resonance stabilised as follows

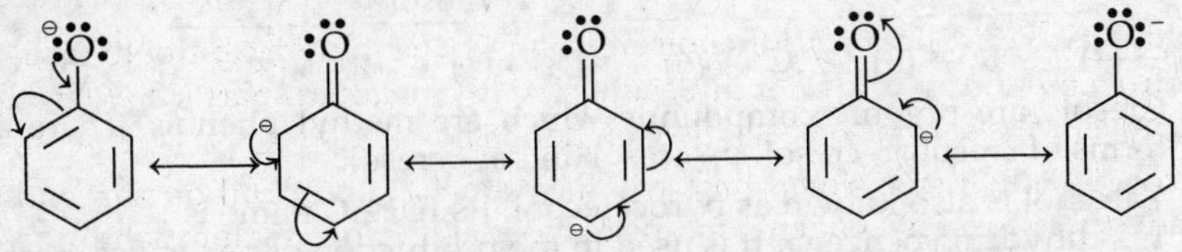

Whereas, the ethoxide ion obtained after the removal of a proton is not stabilised but destabilised due to + I effect of $-C_2H_5$ group. Therefore, phenol is a stronger acid than ethanol. + I effect of $CH_3 - CH_2$ group increase the electron density on $O-H$ bond in ethanol. As the electron density on the $O-H$ bond of ethanol is more than that of water. So, ethanol is a weaker acid than water. Thus, the increasing order of acidity is

ethanol < water < phenol

Matching The Columns

Q.57 Match the structures of the compounds given in Column I with the name of the compounds given in Column II.

	Column I		Column II
A.	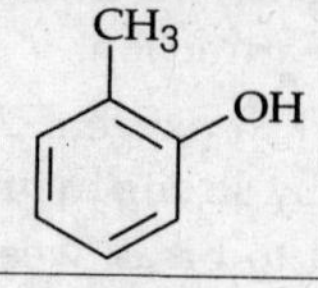 CH_3, OH	1.	Hydroquinone
B.	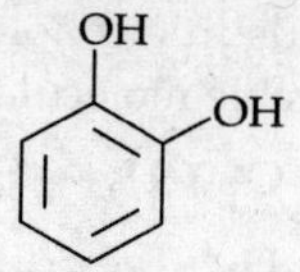 OH, OH	2.	Phenetole
C.	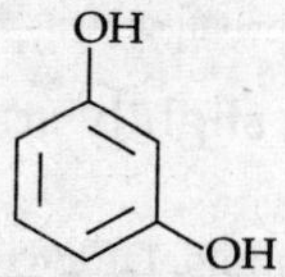 OH, OH	3.	Catechol
D.	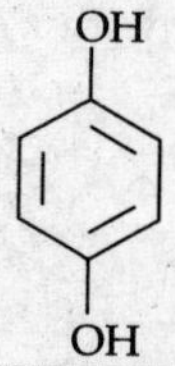 OH, OH	4.	*o*-cresol
E.	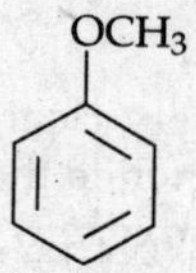 OCH_3	5.	Quinone
F.	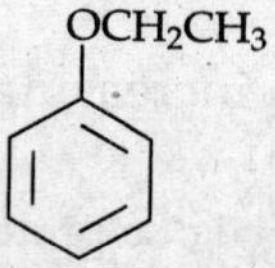 OCH_2CH_3	6.	Resorcinol
		7.	Anisole

Ans. **A.** → (4) **B.** → (3) **C.** → (6) **D.** → (1) **E.** → (7) **F.** → (2)

A. Cresols are organic compounds which are methyl phenols. There are three forms of cresol : *o*-cresol, *p* – cresol and *m* – cresol.

B. Catechol is also known as pyrocatechol. Its IUPAC name is 1, 2-dihydroxybenzene. It is used in the production of pesticides, perfumes and pharmaceuticals.

C. Its IUPAC name is 1, 3-dihydroxybenzene. Resorcinol is used to treat acne, seborrheic dermatitis and other skin disorder.

D. Hydroquinone is also known as quinol. Its IUPAC name is 1, 4-dihydroxybenzene. It is a white granular solid. It is a good reducing agent.

E. Anisole or methoxy benzene, is a colourless liquid with a smell reminiscent of anise seed.

F. Phenetole is an organic compound. It is also known as ethylphenyl ether. It is volatile in nature and its vapours are explosive in nature.

Q.58 Match the starting material given in Column I with the products formed by these (Column II) in the reaction with HI.

Column I	Column II
A. CH_3-O-CH_3	1. $C_6H_5OH + CH_3I$ (phenol)
B. $(CH_3)_2CH-O-CH_3$	2. $CH_3-C(CH_3)_2-I + CH_3OH$
C. $H_3C-C(CH_3)_2-O-CH_3$	3. $C_6H_5I + CH_3OH$ (iodobenzene)
D. $C_6H_5OCH_3$ (anisole)	4. $CH_3-OH + CH_3I$
	5. $(CH_3)_2CH-OH + CH_3I$
	6. $(CH_3)_2CH-I + CH_3OH$
	7. $CH_3-C(CH_3)_2-OH + CH_3I$

Ans. **A.** → (4) **B.** → (5) **C.** → (2) **D.** → (1)

A. CH_3-O-CH_3 is a symmetrical ether so the products obtained by the reaction with HI are CH_3I and CH_3OH.

B. In $(CH_3)_2CH-O-CH_3$ unsymmetrical ether, one alkyl group is primary while another is secondary. So, it follows S_N2 mechanism. Thus, the halide ion attacks the smaller alkyl group and the products are

$$(H_3C)_2CHOH + CH_3I$$

C. In this case, one of the alkyl group is tertiary and the other is primary. It follows S_N1 mechanism and halide ion attacks the tertiary alkyl group and the products are $(CH_3)_3C-I$ and CH_3OH.

D. Here, the unsymmetrical ether is alkyl aryl ether. In this ether, $O-CH_3$ bond is weaker than $O-C_6H_5$ bond which has partial double bond character due to resonance. So, the halide ion attacks on alkyl group and the products are C_6H_5-OH and CH_3I.

Q.59 Match the items of Column I with items of Column II.

	Column I		Column II
A.	Antifreeze used in car engine	1.	Neutral ferric chloride
B.	Solvent used in perfumes	2.	Glycerol
C.	Starting material for picric acid	3.	Methanol
D.	Wood spirit	4.	Phenol
E.	Reagent used for detection of phenolic group	5.	Ethylene glycol
F.	By product of soap industry used in cosmetics	6.	Ethanol

Ans. **A.** → (5) **B.** → (6) **C.** → (4) **D.** → (3) **E.** → (1) **F.** → (2)

A. IUPAC name of ethylene glycol is ethane –1, 2 - diol. It is primarily used as a raw material in the manufacturing of polyester fibers and fabric industry. A small percentage of it is used in antifreeze formulations.

B. Ethanol is a good solvent for fatty and waxy substances. Fats and waxes provide odour to the perfumes. Apart from being a good solvent, it is less irritating to the skin. So, it is used in perfumes.

C. Phenol is converted into picric acid (2, 4, 6-trinitrophenol) by the reaction of phenol with conc. HNO_3.

$$C_6H_5OH \xrightarrow[HNO_3]{Conc.} C_6H_2(NO_2)_3OH$$

(Picric acid)

D. Methanol, CH_3OH is also known as 'wood spirit' as it was produced by the destructive distillation of wood.

E. Neutral ferric chloride gives purple/red colour when treated with phenols. It is the reagent used for detection of phenolic group.

F. Soaps are prepared by the reactions of fatty acid with NaOH.

$$\begin{array}{l} CH_2-O-CO-C_{17}H_{35} \\ | \\ CH-O-CO-C_{17}H_{35} \\ | \\ CH_2-O-CO-C_{17}H_{35} \end{array} + 3NaOH \longrightarrow \underset{\text{Sodium stearate (soap)}}{3C_{17}H_{35}COONa} + \underset{\text{Glycerol}}{\begin{array}{l} CH_2OH \\ | \\ CHOH \\ | \\ CH_2OH \end{array}}$$

This glycerol (propan -1, 2, 3 - triol) is the by-product of soap industry and is used in cosmetics.

Q.60 Match the items of Column I with items of Column II.

	Column I		Column II
A.	Methanol	1.	Conversion of phenol to *o*- hydroxybenzoic acid
B.	Kolbe's reaction	2.	Ethyl alcohol
C.	Williamson's synthesis	3.	Conversion of phenol to salicylaldehyde
D.	Conversion of 2° alcohol to ketone	4.	Wood spirit
E.	Reimer-Tiemann reaction	5.	Heated copper at 573K
F.	Fermentation	6.	Reaction of alkyl halide with sodium alkoxide

Ans. A. → (4) B. → (1) C. → (6) D. → (5) E. → (3) F. → (2)

A. Methanol is also known as 'wood spirit' as it was produced by the destructive distillation of wood.

B. In Kolbe's reaction, 2 – hydroxybenzoic acid (salicylic acid) is prepared by the reaction of phenol with CO_2 gas and NaOH.

$$C_6H_5OH \xrightarrow{NaOH} C_6H_5ONa \xrightarrow[(ii)\ H^+]{(i)\ CO_2} o\text{-}HOC_6H_4COOH$$

2-Hydroxybenzoic acid
(Salicylic acid)

C. Williamson's synthesis is an important method for the preparation of ethers. In this method, an alkyl halide is allowed to react with sodium alkoxide.

$$R-X + R-ONa \longrightarrow ROR + NaX$$

D. When a 2° alcohol is allowed to pass over heated copper at 573 K, dehydrogenation takes place and a ketone is formed.

$$R-\underset{\underset{OH}{|}}{CH}-R' \xrightarrow[573\ K]{Cu} R-\underset{\underset{O}{||}}{C}-R'$$

E. On treating phenol with chloroform in the presence of NaOH, an aldehydic group is introduced at *ortho* position of benzene ring

$$C_6H_5OH \xrightarrow[aq.\ NaOH]{CHCl_3} \left[o\text{-}CHCl_2C_6H_4ONa\right] \xrightarrow{NaOH} o\text{-}CHOC_6H_4ONa \xrightarrow{H^+} o\text{-}HOC_6H_4CHO$$

Salicylaldehyde

F. Ethanol is prepared by the fermentation of sugars.

$$C_{12}H_{22}O_{11} + H_2O \xrightarrow{Invertase} C_6H_{12}O_6 + C_6H_{12}O_6$$

$$C_6H_{12}O_6 \xrightarrow{Zymase} 2C_2H_5OH + 2CO_2$$

Assertion and Reason

In the following questions a statement of Assertion followed by a statement of Reason is given. Choose the correct answer out of the following choices.

(a) Assertion and reason both are correct and reason is correct explanation of assertion.
(b) Assertion and reason both are wrong statements.
(c) Assertion is correct statement but reason is wrong statement.
(d) Assertion is wrong statement but reason is correct statement.
(e) Both assertion and reason are correct statements but reason is not correct explanation of assertion.

Q.61 Assertion Addition reaction of water to but-1-ene in acidic medium yields butan-1-ol.

Reason Addition of water in acidic medium proceeds through the formation of primary carbocation.

Ans. ***(b)*** Assertion and reason both are wrong statements.

Correct Assertion Addition reaction of water to but-1-ene in acidic medium yields butan-2-ol.

Correct Reason Addition of water in acidic medium proceeds through the formation of secondary carbocation.

Mechanism $H_2O + H^+ \longrightarrow H_3O^+$

$$CH_3-CH_2-CH=CH_2 + H-\overset{\overset{H}{|}}{\underset{\cdot\cdot}{O^+}}-H \longrightarrow H_3C-CH_2-\overset{+}{C}H-CH_3 + H_2O$$

(2° carbocation)

$$H_3C-CH_2-\overset{+}{C}H-CH_3 + H_2O \longrightarrow H_3C-CH_2-\underset{\underset{\underset{H}{|}}{:\overset{+}{O}-H}}{\underset{|}{CH}}-CH_3$$

$$H_3C-CH_2-\overset{\overset{CH_3}{|}}{CH}-\overset{\overset{H}{|}}{\underset{\cdot\cdot}{O^+}}-H + H_2O \rightarrow CH_3-CH_2-\overset{\overset{OH}{|}}{CH}-CH_3$$

Butan-2-ol

Q.62 Assertion *p*-nitrophenol is more acidic than phenol.

Reason Nitro group helps in the stabilisation of the phenoxide ion by dispersal of negative charge due to resonance.

Ans. ***(a)*** Assertion and reason both are correct and reason is correct explanation of assertion. *p*-Nitrophenol is more acidic than phenol because nitro group helps in the stabilisation of the phenoxide ion by dispersal of negative charge due to resonance.

Q.63 Assertion IUPAC name of the compund

$$CH_3-\underset{\underset{CH_3}{|}}{CH}-O-CH_2-CH_2-CH_3$$ is 2-ethoxy-2-methylethane

Reason In IUPAC nomenclature, ether is regarded as hydrocarbon derivative in which a hydrogen atom is replaced by —OR or —OAr group [where, R = alkyl group and Ar = aryl group].

Ans. ***(d)*** Assertion is wrong statement but reason is correct statement.

Correct Assertion The IUPAC name of the given compound is 1-(2-propoxy) propane.

Q.64 Assertion Bond angle in ethers is slightly less than the tetrahedral angle.

Reason There is a repulsion between the two bulky (– *R*) groups.

Ans. ***(d)*** Assertion is wrong statement but reason is correct statement.

Correct Assertion Bond angle in ether is slightly more than the tetrahedral angle due to a repulsion between the two bulky —*R* groups.

$$\underset{R \quad\quad R}{\ddot{O}} \quad 111.7^\circ$$

Q.65 Assertion Boiling points of alcohols and ethers are high.

Reason They can form intermolecular hydrogen-bonding.

Ans. ***(b)*** Assertion and reason both are wrong statements.

Correct Assertion Boiling points of alcohols are higher than that of ethers of comparable molecular mass.

Correct Reason Alcohols can form intermolecular hydrogen bonding while ethers cannot.

Q.66 Assertion Like bromination of benzene, bromination of phenol is also carried out in the presence of Lewis acid.

Reason Lewis acid polarises the bromine molecule.

Ans. ***(d)*** Assertion is wrong statement but reason is correct statement.

Correct Assertion Bromination of benzene but not of phenol is carried out in presence of a Lewis acid. In case of phenol, the polarisation of bromine molecule takes place even in the absence of Lewis acid, due to the presence of highly activating effect of —OH group.

Q.67 Assertion *o*-Nitrophenol is less soluble in water than the *m* and *p*-isomers.

Reason *m* and *p*-Nitrophenols exist as associated molecules.

Ans. ***(e)*** Both assertion and reason are correct statements but reason is not correct explanation of assertion.

Correct Explanation Due to the presence of intramolecular hydrogen bonding, *o*-nitrophenol does not form hydrogen bonds with H_2O but *m*- and *p*-nitrophenol form hydrogen bonds with water. Therefore, *o*-nitrophenol is less soluble in water than the *m*-and *p*-isomers.

Q.68 Assertion Ethanol is a weaker acid than phenol.

Reason Sodium ethoxide may be prepared by the reaction of ethanol with aqueous NaOH.

Ans. ***(c)*** Assertion is correct statement but reason is wrong statement.

Correct Reason Phenoxide ion is stabilised by resonance but ethoxide ion is not stabilised by resonance. Thus, ethanol is a weaker acid than phenol.

Resonance in phenoxide ion

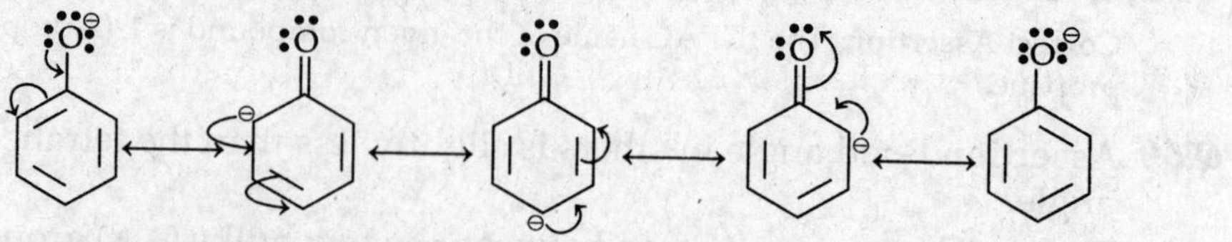

Q.69 Assertion Phenol forms 2, 4, 6-tribromophenol on treatment with Br_2 in carbon disulphide at 273K.

Reason Bromine polarises in carbon disulphide.

Ans. *(b)* Assertion and reason both are wrong statements.

Correct Assertion Phenol form 2, 4, 6-tribromophenol on treatment with bromine in water.

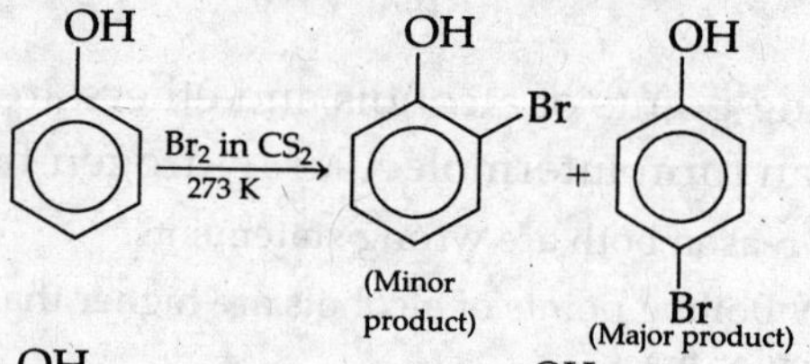

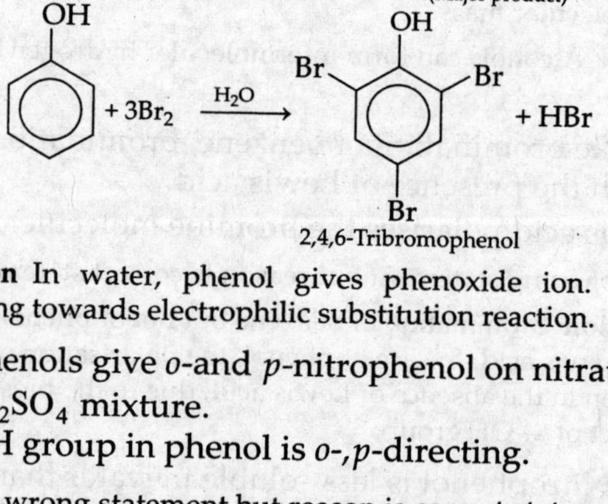

Br_2 in CS_2, 273 K: Phenol → o-Bromophenol (Minor product) + p-Bromophenol (Major product)

Phenol $+ 3Br_2 \xrightarrow{H_2O}$ 2,4,6-Tribromophenol $+ HBr$

Correct Reason In water, phenol gives phenoxide ion. This phenoxide ion activates the ring towards electrophilic substitution reaction.

Q.70 Assertion Phenols give *o*-and *p*-nitrophenol on nitration with conc. HNO_3 and H_2SO_4 mixture.

Reason —OH group in phenol is *o*-,*p*-directing.

Ans. *(d)* Assertion is wrong statement but reason is correct statement.

Correct Assertion Phenols give *o*- and *p*-nitrophenol on nitration with dil. HNO_3 at 298 K.

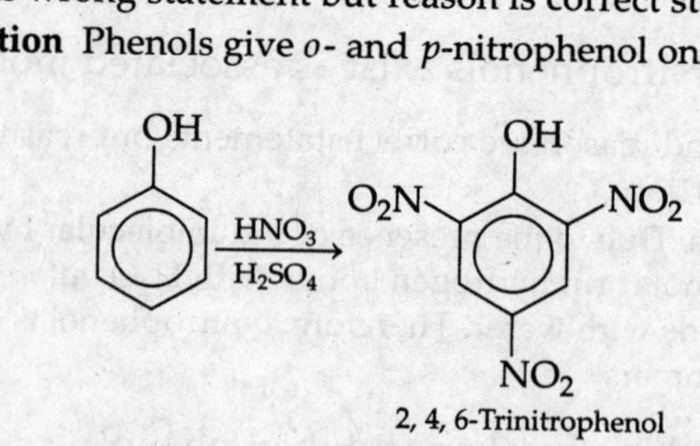

Phenol $\xrightarrow[H_2SO_4]{HNO_3}$ 2, 4, 6-Trinitrophenol

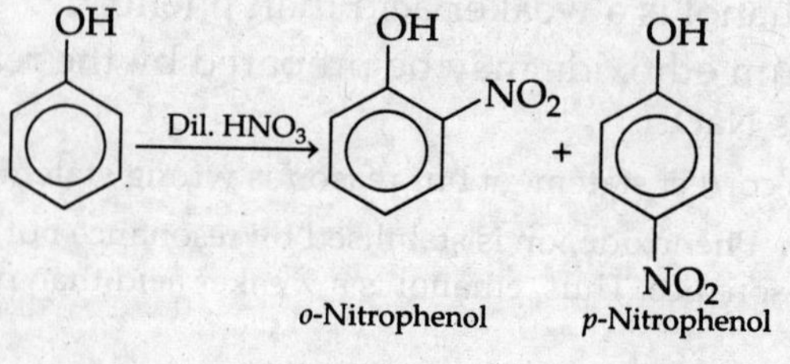

Phenol $\xrightarrow{\text{Dil. } HNO_3}$ *o*-Nitrophenol + *p*-Nitrophenol

Long Answer Type Questions

Q.71 Write the mechanism of the reaction of HI with methoxybenzene.

Ans. In case of alkyl aryl ethers, the products are always phenol and an alkyl halide because due to resonance C_6H_5 —O bond has partial double bond character. The mechanism is given below

Mechanism Protonation of anisole gives methylphenyl oxonium ion.

$$C_6H_5-\ddot{\underset{\cdot\cdot}{O}}CH_3 + H^+ \longrightarrow C_6H_5-\overset{+}{\underset{|\atop H}{O}}\!:-CH_3$$

In this ion, the bond between O — CH_3 is weaker than the bond between O—C_6H_5 which has partial double bond character. This partial double bond character is due to the resonance between the lone pair of electrons on the O-atom and the sp^2 hybridised carbon atom of the phenyl group. Therefore, attack by I^- ion exclusively breaks the weaker O — CH_3 bond forming methyl iodide and phenol.

$$C_6H_5-\overset{+}{\underset{|\atop H}{O}}-CH_3 + I^- \longrightarrow \underset{\text{Phenol}}{C_6H_5OH} + \underset{\text{Methyliodide}}{CH_3I}$$

Q.72 (a) Name the starting material used in the industrial preparation of phenol.

(b) Write complete reaction for the bromination of phenol in aqueous and non-aqueous medium.

(c) Explain why Lewis acid is not required in bromination of phenol?

Ans. (a) The starting material used in the industrial preparation of phenol is cumene.

$$\underset{\substack{\text{Cumene}\\\text{(Iso-propyl}\\\text{benzene)}}}{C_6H_5CH(CH_3)_2} \xrightarrow[368\text{-}408\,K]{O_2} \underset{\substack{\text{Cumene}\\\text{hydroperoxide}}}{C_6H_5C(CH_3)_2-O-O-H} \xrightarrow[H_2O]{H^+} \underset{\text{Phenol}}{C_6H_5OH} + \underset{\text{Propanone}}{CH_3COCH_3}$$

(b) Phenols when treated with bromine water gives polyhalogen derivatives in which all the hydrogen atoms present at *ortho* and *para* positions with respect to —OH group are replaced by bromine atoms.

$$C_6H_5OH + 3Br_2 \xrightarrow{H_2O} \underset{\substack{\text{2, 4, 6-tribromophenol}\\\text{(white ppt.)}}}{C_6H_2Br_3OH} + 3HBr$$

However, in non-aqueous medium such as CS_2, CCl_4 or $CHCl_3$, monobromophenols are obtained.

$$\text{Phenol} \xrightarrow[273\text{ K}]{Br_2 \text{ in } CS_2} \text{4-Bromophenol} + \text{2-Bromophenol}$$

In aqueous solution, phenol ionises to form phenoxide ion. This ion activates the benzene ring to a very large extent and hence the substitution of halogen takes place at all three positions.

On the other hand, in non-aqueous solution ionisation of phenol is greatly suppressed. Therefore, ring is activated slightly and hence monosubstitution occur.

(c) Lewis acid is an electron deficient molecule. In bromination of benzene, Lewis acid is used to polarise Br_2 to form Br^+ electrophile.

In case of phenol, oxygen atom of phenol itself polarises the bromine molecule to form Br^+ ion (electrophile). So, Lewis acid is not required in the bromination of phenol.

Q.73 How can phenol be converted to aspirin?

Ans. Phenol is converted into salicylic acid. This salicylic acid is treated with acetic anhydride. On acetylation of salicylic acid, aspirin (acetyl salicylic acid) is formed.

$$\text{Phenol} \xrightarrow[-H_2O]{NaOH} \text{Sodium phenoxide} \xrightarrow[4\text{-}7\text{ atm}]{CO_2/400\text{ K}} [\text{Sodium salicylate (OH, COONa)}] \xrightarrow{\text{Dil. HCl}} \text{Salicylic acid (OH, COOH)}$$

$$\text{Salicylic acid} \xrightarrow[\text{(acetylation)}]{(CH_3CO)_2O/H^+} \text{Aspirin } (OCOCH_3, COOH) + CH_3COOH$$

Q.74 Explain a process in which a biocatalyst is used in industrial preparation of a compound known to you.

Ans. Enzymes are biocatalyst. These biocatalysts (enzymes) are used in the industrial preparation of ethanol. Ethanol is prepared by the fermentation of molasses - a dark brown coloured syrup left after crystallisation of sugar which still contains about 40% of sugar.

The process of fermentation actually involves breaking down of large molecules into simple ones in the presence of enzymes. The source of these enzymes is yeast. The various reactions taking place during fermentation of carbohydrates are

$$\underset{\text{Sucrose}}{C_{12}H_{22}O_{11}} + H_2O \xrightarrow{\text{Invertase}} \underset{\text{Glucose}}{C_6H_{12}O_6} + \underset{\text{Fructose}}{C_6H_{12}O_6}$$

$$\underset{\text{Glucose}}{C_6H_{12}O_6} \xrightarrow{\text{Zymase}} \underset{\text{Ethyl alcohol}}{2C_2H_5OH} + 2CO_2$$

In wine making, grapes are the source of sugars and yeast. As grapes ripen, the quantity of sugar increases and yeast grows on the outer skin. When grapes are crushed, sugar and the enzyme come in contact and fermentation starts. Fermentation takes place in anaerobic conditions, *i.e.,* in absence of air. CO_2 gas is released during fermentation.

The action of zymase is inhibited once the percentage of alcohol formed exceeds 14 per cent. If air gets into fermentation mixture, the oxygen of air oxidises ethanol to ethanoic acid which in turn destroys the taste of alcoholic drinks which is widely used in industry.

Chapter 12

Aldehyde, Ketones and Carboxylic Acids

Multiple Choice Questions (MCQs)

Q.1 Addition of water to alkynes occurs in acidic medium and in the presence of Hg^{2+} ions as a catalyst. Which of the following products will be formed on addition of water to but-1-yne under these conditions?

(a) $CH_3-CH_2-CH_2-\overset{O}{\overset{\|}{C}}-H$

(b) $CH_3-CH_2-\overset{O}{\overset{\|}{C}}-CH_3$

(c) $CH_3-CH_2-\overset{O}{\overset{\|}{C}}-OH+CO_2$

(d) $CH_3-\overset{O}{\overset{\|}{C}}-OH+H-\overset{O}{\overset{\|}{C}}-H$

- **Concept Insight** The reaction illustrates the key concepts of Markovnikov's addition, acid catalyzed hydration, enol formation, tautomerisation and the use of catalyst in organic reactions, leading to the final product, 2-butanone.

Ans. ***(b)*** But-1-yne on reaction with water in presence of Hg^{2+} ions as a catalyst produces butan-2-one.

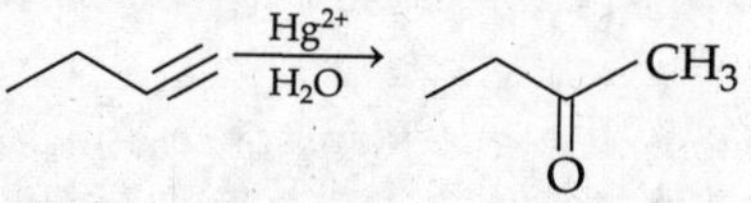

$$CH_3CH_2C\equiv CH \xrightarrow[H_2O]{Hg^{2+}} CH_3CH_2COCH_3$$

Mechanism

$$CH_3CH_2C\equiv CH \xrightarrow[H_2O]{Hg^{2+}} CH_3CH_2C(OH)=CH_2 \xrightarrow{\text{Tautomerism}} CH_3CH_2COCH_3$$

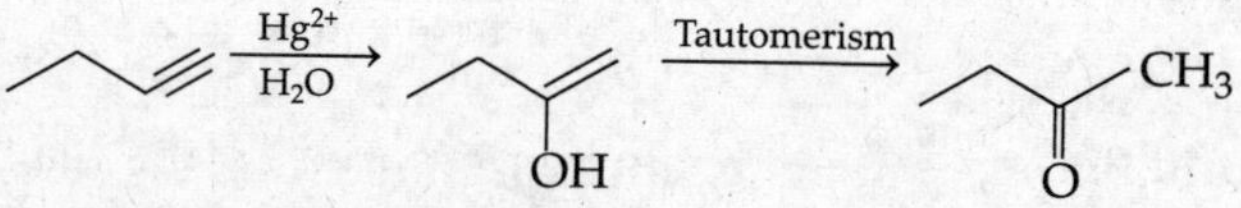

Q.2 Which of the following compounds is most reactive towards nucleophilic addition reactions?

(a) $CH_3-\overset{O}{\overset{\|}{C}}-H$

(b) $CH_3-\overset{O}{\overset{\|}{C}}-CH_3$

(c) 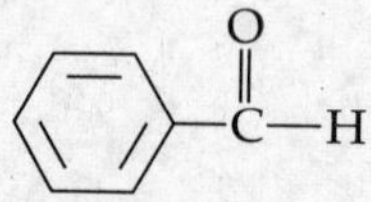 $C_6H_5-\overset{O}{\overset{\|}{C}}-H$

(d) 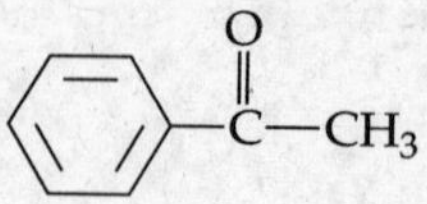 $C_6H_5-\overset{O}{\overset{\|}{C}}-CH_3$

Ans. *(a)* Reactivity of carbonyl compounds can be decided by two factors

(i) **Steric factor** Lesser the steric factor greater will be its reactivity.

(ii) **Electronic factor** Greater the number of alkyl group, lesser will be its electrophilicity and reactivity.

Hence, CH_3— CHO is most reactive towards nucleophilic addition reaction.

Q.3 The correct order of increasing acidic strength is ....

(a) phenol < ethanol < chloroacetic acid < acetic acid
(b) ethanol < phenol < chloroacetic acid < acetic acid
(c) ethanol < phenol < acetic acid < chloroacetic acid
(d) chloroacetic acid < acetic acid < phenol < ethanol

Ans. *(c)* Phenol is more stable than alcohol due to formation of more stable conjugate base after removal of H^+ from phenol.

$$CH_3-CH_2OH < C_6H_5OH < CH_3-\overset{O}{\overset{\|}{C}}-OH < Cl-CH_2-\overset{O}{\overset{\|}{C}}-OH$$

On the other hand, carboxylic acid is more acidic than phenol due to formation of more stable conjugate base after removal of H^+ as compared to phenol.

$$C_6H_5OH \xrightarrow{-H^+} C_6H_5O^-$$

$$CH_3-\overset{O}{\overset{\|}{C}}-O-H \xrightarrow{-H^+} \left[CH_3-\overset{O}{\overset{\|}{C}}-O^{\ominus} \longleftrightarrow CH_3-\overset{O^{\ominus}}{\overset{|}{C}}=O \right]$$

Resonance stabilised

Chloroacetic acid is more acidic than acetic acid due to the presence of electron withdrawing chlorine group attached to α-carbon of carboxylic acid.
Hence, correct choice is (c).

Mistake Alert! *Student might confuse the acidity order of ethanol and phenol, not recognize the electron withdrawing effect of chlorine in chloroacetic acid, or overlook the resonance stabilization in carboxylic acids i.e., acetic acid.*

Q.4 Compound $Ph-O-\overset{O}{\overset{\|}{C}}-Ph$ can be prepared by the reaction of ....

(a) phenol and benzoic acid in the presence of NaOH
(b) phenol and benzoyl chloride in the presence of pyridine
(c) phenol and benzoyl chloride in the presence of $ZnCl_2$
(d) phenol and benzaldehyde in the presence of palladium

Ans. *(b)* Compound Ph —COO— Ph can be prepared by the reaction of phenol and benzyl chloride in the presence of pyridine.

$$\underset{\text{Phenol}}{C_6H_5OH} + \underset{\text{Benzoyl chloride}}{C_6H_5\overset{O}{\overset{\|}{C}}Cl} \xrightarrow{\text{Pyridine}} C_6H_5-O-\overset{O}{\overset{\|}{C}}-C_6H_5$$

This is an example of **Schotten-Baumann reaction.**

Q.5 The reagent which does not react with both, acetone and benzaldehyde?

(a) Sodium hydrogensulphite (b) Phenyl hydrazine
(c) Fehling's solution (d) Grignard reagent

Ans. ***(c)*** Acetone and benzaldehyde both do not react with Fehling's solution. Fehling's solution reacts with aldehydes and do not react with ketones and aromatic aldehydes. Acetone is a ketone while benzaldehyde is an aromatic aldehyde having absence of α-hydrogen.

Q.6 Cannizzaro's reaction is **not** given by ....

(a) 1-methylcyclohexane-1-carbaldehyde (cyclohexane ring bearing CHO and CH_3) (b) C_6H_5—CHO

(c) HCHO (d) CH_3CHO

Ans. ***(d)*** Necessary condition for Cannizzaro reaction is absence of α-hydrogen atom. So, CH_3CHO will not give Cannizzaro reaction because it has α-hydrogen atom, while other three compounds have no α-hydrogen. Hence, they will give Cannizzaro reaction.

Q.7 Which products is formed when the compound C_6H_5—CHO is treated with concentrated aqueous KOH solution?

(a) $\overset{+}{K}\overset{-}{O}$—$C_6H_4$—CHO

(b) C_6H_5—C(=O)—$\overset{-}{O}\overset{+}{K}$ + C_6H_5—CH_2OH

(c) $\overset{+}{K}\overset{-}{O}$—$C_6H_4$—C(=O)—$\overset{-}{O}\overset{+}{K}$ + $\overset{+}{K}\overset{-}{O}$—$C_6H_4$—$\overset{-}{O}\overset{+}{K}$

(d) C_6H_5—C(=O)—$\overset{-}{O}\overset{+}{K}$ + C_6H_5—$\overset{-}{O}\overset{+}{K}$

Ans. ***(b)*** Benzaldehyde is an aromatic aldehyde having no α-hydrogen. So, on reaction with aqueous KOH solution it undergoes is Cannizzaro reaction to produce benzyl alcohol and potassium benzoate.

$$\underset{\text{Benzaldehyde}}{C_6H_5CHO} \xrightarrow{\text{KOH }(aq.)} \underset{\text{Benzyl alcohol}}{C_6H_5CH_2OH} + \underset{\text{Potassium benzoate}}{C_6H_5CO\overset{-}{O}\overset{+}{K}}$$

Mistake Alert ! *Student may mistakenly assume that benzaldehyde can undergo aldol condensation, not realising that it lacks a α-hydrogen.*

Q.8 $CH_3—C\equiv CH \xrightarrow[1\%\ HgSO_4]{40\%\ H_2SO_4} A \xrightarrow{\text{Isomerisation}} CH_3—\underset{\underset{O}{\parallel}}{C}—CH_3$

Structure of '*A*' and type of isomerism in the above reaction are respectively.

(a) Prop-1-en-2-ol, metamerism

(b) Prop-1-en-1-ol, tautomerism

(c) Prop-2-en-2-ol, geometrical isomerism

(d) Prop-1-en-2-ol, tautomerism

Ans. ***(d)*** Chemical reaction can be shown as

$$\underset{\text{Propyne}}{CH_3—C\equiv CH} \xrightarrow[1\%\ HgSO_4]{40\%\ H_2SO_4} \underset{\text{Prop-1-en-2-ol}}{CH_3—\overset{\overset{OH}{|}}{C}=\overset{\overset{H}{|}}{CH}} \xrightarrow{\text{keto- enol tautomerism}} \underset{\text{Acetone}}{CH_3—\overset{\overset{O}{\parallel}}{C}—CH_3}$$

[*A*] is prop-1-en-2-ol, which undergo tautomerism to form acetone.

Q.9 Compounds *A* and *C* in the following reaction are ....

$CH_3CHO \xrightarrow[(ii)\ H_2O]{(i)\ CH_3MgBr} (A) \xrightarrow{H_2SO_4,\ \Delta} (B) \xrightarrow{\text{Hydroboration oxidation}} (C)$

(a) identical

(b) positional isomers

(c) functional isomers

(d) optical isomers

Ans. ***(b)*** Chemical reaction can be shown as

$$\underset{\text{Ethanal}}{CH_3CHO} \xrightarrow[(ii)\ H_2O]{(i)\ CH_3MgBr} \underset{\underset{\text{Propan-2- ol}}{(A)}}{CH_3—\underset{\underset{CH_3}{|}}{CH}—OH} \xrightarrow[\text{Dehydration}]{H_2SO_4,\ \Delta} \underset{\underset{\text{Propene}}{(B)}}{CH_3—\underset{\underset{H}{|}}{C}=CH_2}$$

$$\xrightarrow[\text{(Hydroboration Oxidation)}]{(i)\ BH_3 \quad (ii)\ H_2O_2/OH^{\ominus}} \underset{\underset{\text{Propan–1–ol}}{(C)}}{CH_3—CH_2—CH_2OH}$$

Thus, $CH_3\underset{\underset{CH_3}{|}}{CH}—OH$ and $CH_3—CH_2—CH_2OH$ are positional isomers which differ in the position of — OH group.

Hence, option (b) is correct.

Q.10 Which is the most suitable reagent for the following conversion?

$$CH_3—CH=CH—CH_2—\overset{\overset{O}{\parallel}}{C}—CH_3 \longrightarrow$$

$$CH_3—CH=CH—CH_2—\overset{\overset{O}{\parallel}}{C}—OH$$

(a) Tollen's reagent

(b) Benzoyl peroxide

(c) I_2 and NaOH solution

(d) Sn and NaOH solution

Ans. *(c)* Iodoform test is used to test presence of — $COCH_3$ group, which is converted into — COOH group.

The reaction is shown as

$$CH_3-CH=CH-CH_2-\overset{\overset{O}{\|}}{C}-CH_3 \xrightarrow[\text{(Iodoform reaction)}]{I_2/NaOH\text{ solution}} \underset{\text{(Iodoform)}}{CHI_3}$$
Hex-4-en-2-one

$$+ CH_3-CH=CH-CH_2-\overset{\overset{O}{\|}}{C}-OH$$
Pent-3-en-1-oic acid

Other Options Tollen's reagent is used for the oxidation of aldehydes not ketones. Benzoyl peroxide is a radical initiator used in polymerization reactions. Sn and NaOH solution is not relevant for this transformation.

Mistake Alert! *Student may confuse reagents by not recognizing that I_2 and NaOH perform the idoform reaction, which oxidizes methyl ketones to carboxylic acids.*

Q.11 Which of the following compounds will give butanone on oxidation with alkaline $KMnO_4$ solution?

(a) Butan-1-ol (b) Butan-2-ol (c) Both (a) and (b) (d) None of these

Ans. *(b)* Butan-2-ol on oxidation with alkaline $KMnO_4$ solution produces butanone as follows

$$\underset{\text{Butan-2-ol}}{CH_3CH_2CH(OH)CH_3} \xrightarrow[KMnO_4]{[O]} \underset{\text{Butan-2-one}}{CH_3CH_2COCH_3}$$

Q.12 In Clemmensen reduction, carbonyl compound is treated with ....

(a) zinc amalgam + HCl (b) sodium amalgam + HCl

(c) zinc amalgam + nitric acid (d) sodium amalgam + HNO_3

Ans. *(a)* Clemmensen reduction is used to convert carbonyl group to CH_2 group as follows

$$>C=O \xrightarrow{Zn(Hg)+HCl} >CH_2 + H_2O$$

Zinc amalgam and HCl act as reagent in this reaction.

Mistake Alert! *Students may make a mistake of selecting sodium amalgam or the wrong acid like HNO_3, instead of recognizing that zinc amalgam and HCl are specifically required for this reaction.*

Multiple Choice Questions (More Than One Options)

Q.13 Which of the following compounds do not undergo aldol condensation?

(a) CH_3-CHO (b) C_6H_5-CHO

(c) $CH_3-\overset{\overset{O}{\|}}{C}-CH_3$ (d) $CH_3-\underset{CH_3}{\overset{CH_3}{\overset{|}{\underset{|}{C}}}}-CHO$

Ans. *(b, d)* Necessary condition for aldol condensation is the presence of atleast one α H-atom. Hence, C_6H_5CHO and $(CH_3)_3CCHO$ do not undergo aldol condensation as they lack α-hydrogen atom.

Q.14 Treatment of compound $Ph-O-\overset{O}{\overset{\|}{C}}-Ph$ with NaOH solution yields

(a) phenol
(b) sodium phenoxide
(c) sodium benzoate
(d) benzophenone

- **Concept Insight** This solution demonstrates the hydrolysis of an ether in basic conditions, where NaOH breaks down an ether, forming sodium phenoxide and sodium benzoate.

Ans. ***(b, c)*** Treatment of compound $Ph-O-\overset{O}{\overset{\|}{C}}-Ph$ with NaOH yields sodium phenoxide and sodium benzoate by means of nucleophillic substitution reaction, as shown below

$$Ph-O\underset{H+ONa}{+}\overset{O}{\overset{\|}{C}}-Ph \xrightarrow[\text{(Hydrolysis)}]{NaOH} [PhOH] + \underset{\text{Sodium benzoate}}{Ph-\overset{O}{\overset{\|}{C}}-ONa}$$

$$[PhOH] \xrightarrow{NaOH} \underset{\text{Sodium phenoxide}}{PhONa} + H_2O$$

Q.15 Which of the following conversions can be carried out by Clemmensen reduction?

(a) Benzaldehyde into benzyl alcohol
(b) Cyclohexanone into cyclohexane
(c) Benzoyl chloride into benzaldehyde
(d) Benzophenone into diphenyl methane

Ans. ***(b, d)*** Clemmensen reduction is used to convert cyclohexanone into cyclohexane and benzophenone into diphenyl methane.

The reagent used in Clemmensen reduction is zinc amalgam in hydrochloric acid, *i.e.*, Zn(Hg) in HCl.

Mechanism

$$\text{Cyclohexanone} \xrightarrow{Zn(Hg)\ \text{in}\ HCl} \text{Cyclohexane}$$

$$\text{Benzophenone} \xrightarrow{Zn(Hg)\ \text{in}\ HCl} \text{Diphenyl methane}$$

Q.16 Through which of the following reactions number of carbon atoms can be increased in the chain?

(a) Grignard reaction
(b) Cannizzaro's reaction
(c) Aldol condensation
(d) HVZ reaction

Ans. *(a, c)* Grignard reaction and aldol condensation are used to increase the number of carbon atom in the chain. The Grignard reaction adds carbon by forming a bond between a carbonyl group and a Grignard reagent (R–MgX), while aldol condensation joins two carbonyl compounds, increasing the chain length as shown below

Grignard reaction

$$CH_3COCH_3 \text{ (Acetone)} \xrightarrow[H_3O^+]{CH_3MgBr} (CH_3)_3C\text{–}OH \text{ (3°alcohol)}$$

Aldol condensation

$$CH_3COCH_3 \text{ (Acetone)} + CH_3COCH_3 \text{ (Acetone)} \xrightarrow{OH^{\ominus}} CH_3COCH_2C(OH)(CH_3)_2 \xrightarrow{\Delta, -H_2O} CH_3COCH{=}C(CH_3)_2$$

4-Hydroxy-4-methyl pentan-2 one (Aldol); 4-Methylpent-3-en-2 one or mesityl oxide

While other two reactions, Cannizzaro reaction and HVZ reaction do not lead to increase in number of carbon atom.

Q.17 Benzophenone can be obtained by ……… .

(a) benzoyl chloride + benzene + $AlCl_3$
(b) benzoyl chloride + diphenyl cadmium
(c) benzoyl chloride + phenyl magnesium chloride
(d) benzene + carbon monoxide + $ZnCl_2$

Ans. *(a, b)*

(a) Benzophenone can be obtained by **Friedel-Craft acylation** reaction. The reaction is shown as

$$C_6H_5COCl \text{ (Benzoyl chloride)} + C_6H_6 \xrightarrow{\text{Anhydrous } AlCl_3} C_6H_5COC_6H_5 \text{ (Benzophenone)} + HCl$$

(b) Benzophenone can also be obtained by the reaction between benzoyl chloride and diphenyl cadmium.

$$C_6H_5COCl \xrightarrow[\text{Dry ether}]{(C_6H_5)_2Cd} C_6H_5COC_6H_5 \text{ (Benzophenone)} + CdCl_2$$

Q.18 Which of the following is the correct representation for intermediate of nucleophilic addition reaction to the given carbonyl compound (*A*)?

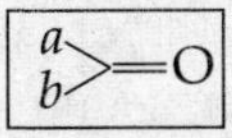

(*A*)

(a) 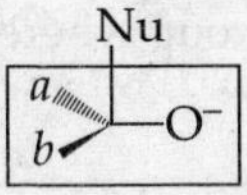 (b)

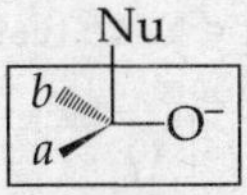

(c) 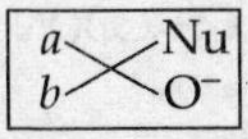 (d)

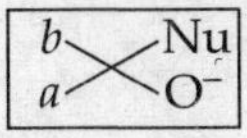

Ans. *(a, b)*

Since, carbonyl compound is a planar molecule hence two orientation of molecule regarding attack of nucleophile is possible as follows

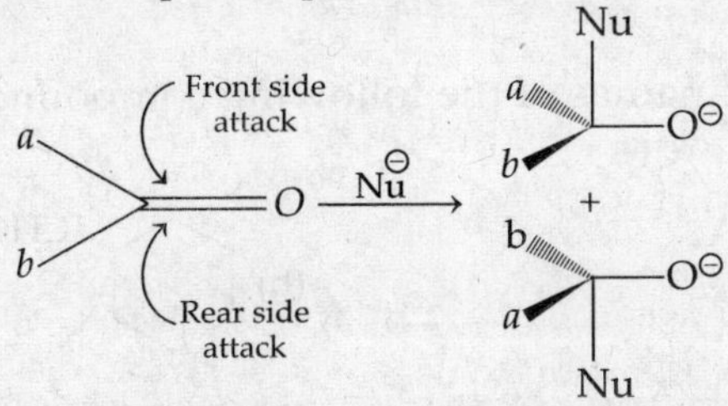

Front side attack

Rear side attack

Since, the product contains a chiral carbon, therefore, attack of nucleophile can occur either from front side attack or rear side attack, giving enantiomeric products. Hence, (a) and (b) are the correct choices.

Short Answer Type Questions

Q.19 Why is there a large difference in the boiling points of butanal and butan-1-ol?

Thinking Process This problem based upon the concept of H-bonding which is used in determination of boiling point.

Ans. Butan-1-ol has intermolecular H-bonding as shown below

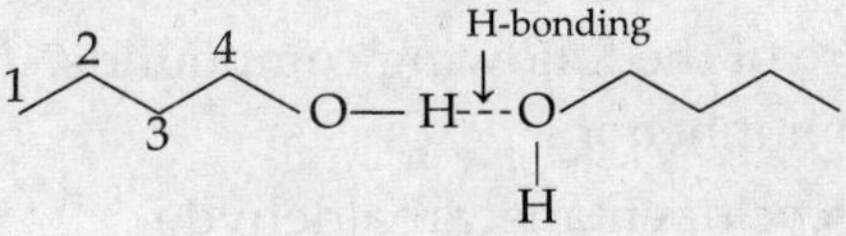

H-bonding

Intermolecular H-bonding in butan-1-ol

Butan-1-ol has a polar O—H bond, allowing for intermolecular hydrogen bonding, while butanal lacks this bond and only exhibits weaker dipole-dipole interactions. Therefore, butan-1-ol has higher boiling point than butanal.

Q.20 Write a test to differentiate between pentan-2-one and pentan-3-one.

Thinking Process This problem is based on the concept of iodoform test. The organic compound containing $-\overset{O}{\overset{||}{C}}-CH_3$ or $CH_3CH(OH)$ group undergoes iodoform test.

Ans. **Iodoform test** (yellow ppt. formed when heated with sodium hypohalite)
Pentan-2-one gives positive test as it contains — $COCH_3$ group whereas pentan-3-one does not.

$$\underset{\text{Pentan - 2 - one}}{CH_3CH_2CH_2-\overset{O}{\overset{||}{C}}-CH_3} \xrightarrow[\text{(Iodoform test)}]{I_2/NaOH} \underset{\substack{\text{Yellow}\\ \text{ppt}}}{CHI_3} + \underset{\substack{\text{Sodium}\\ \text{butanoate}}}{CH_3CH_2CH_2COONa}$$

$$\underset{\text{Pentan - 3 - one}}{CH_3CH_2-\overset{O}{\overset{||}{C}}-CH_2CH_3} \xrightarrow{I_2/NaOH} \text{No yellow ppt. of } CHI_3$$

Q.21 Give the IUPAC names of the following compounds.

(a) 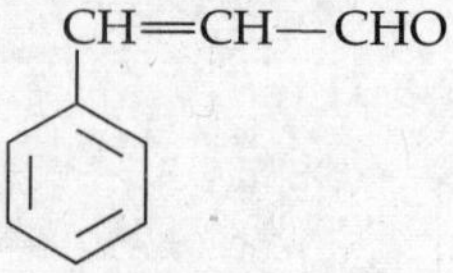 $C_6H_5-CH=CH-CHO$ (b) 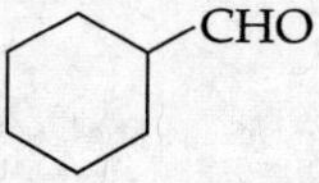 $C_6H_{11}-CHO$ (cyclohexane ring bearing CHO)

(c) $CH_3-CH_2-\underset{\underset{O}{||}}{C}-CH_2-CHO$ (d) $CH_2-CH=CH-CHO$

Ans. Following are the IUPAC names of the compounds

(a) 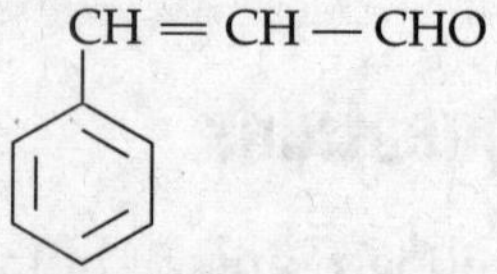 $C_6H_5-CH=CH-CHO$
3-Phenylprop-2-en-1-al

(b) 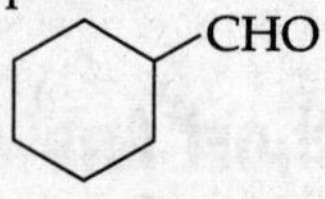 $C_6H_{11}-CHO$
Cyclohexanecarbaldehyde

(c) $CH_3-CH_2-\underset{\underset{O}{||}}{C}-CH_2-CHO$
3-oxo-pentan-1-al

(d) $CH_2-CH=CH-CHO$
But-2-en-1-al

Q.22 Give the structure of the following compounds.

(a) 4-Nitropropiophenone
(b) 2-Hydroxycyclopentanecarbaldehyde
(c) Phenyl acetaldehyde

Ans. (a) 4-Nitropropiophenone

$$O_2N\overset{4}{-}C_6H_4\overset{1}{-}\overset{O}{\overset{||}{C}}-CH_2CH_3$$

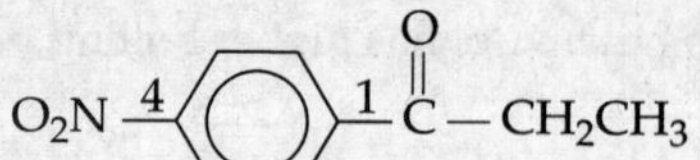

(b) 2-Hydroxycyclopentanecarbaldehyde

(c) Phenyl acetaldehyde

$C_6H_5-CH_2-CHO$

Q.23 Write IUPAC names of the following structures.

(a) CHO–CHO (b) (c)

Ans. The IUPAC names of the following structures are

(a) CHO–CHO

Ethan-1, 2-dial

(b)

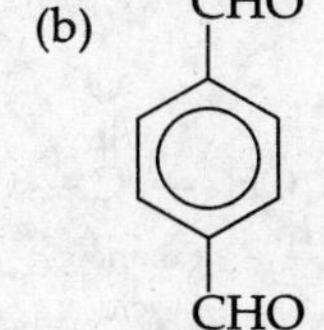

Benzene-1, 4-dicarbaldehyde

(c)

3-Bromobenzaldehyde

Q.24 Benzaldehyde can be obtained from benzal chloride. Write reactions for obtaining benzal chloride and then benzaldehyde from it.

Ans. Benzal chloride can be obtained by photochlorination of toluene *i.e.*, chlorination of toluene in presence of sunlight. Then, benzal chloride on hydrolysis produces benzaldehyde as shown below.

$C_6H_5CH_3$ (Toluene) $\xrightarrow[\text{(Side chain halogenation)}]{2Cl_2/hv,\ 383\ K}$ $C_6H_5CHCl_2$ (Benzal chloride) $\xrightarrow[\text{(Hydrolysis)}]{\text{(Dil. NaOH), 373K}}$ $[C_6H_5CH(OH)_2]$ $\xrightarrow{-H_2O}$ C_6H_5CHO (Benzaldehyde)

This method is commercially used for manufacture of benzaldehyde.

Q.25 Name the electrophile produced in the reaction of benzene with benzoyl chloride in the presence of anhydrous $AlCl_3$. Name the reaction also.

Ans. Benzene, on reaction with benzoyl chloride undergo formation of benzophenone through intermediate benzoylinium cation.

$C_6H_5-\overset{O}{\overset{\|}{C}}-Cl + AlCl_3\text{(anhydrous)} \longrightarrow C_6H_5-\overset{O}{\overset{\|}{C^+}}$ (Benzoylinium cation) $\xrightarrow{C_6H_6}$ $C_6H_5COC_6H_5$ (Benzophenone)

This is an example of Friedel-Craft acylation reaction.

Q.26 Oxidation of ketones involves carbon-carbon bond cleavage. Name the products formed on oxidation of 2, 5-dimethylhexan-3-one.

Thinking Process This problem is based on concept of cleavage of C—C bond. According to Popoff's rule, during cleavage of unsymmetrical ketone, keto group stays preferentially with the smaller group.

Ans. According to Popoff's rule, when an unsymmetrical ketone is oxidised, the C— C bond cleavage and keto group goes with $CH_3—\underset{|}{\overset{CH_3}{CH}}—$ group

$$\underset{(2,5\text{-Dimethylhexan-3-one})}{CH_3—\overset{CH_3}{\overset{|}{CH}}—\overset{O}{\overset{||}{C}}—CH_2—\overset{CH_3}{\overset{|}{CH}}—CH_3} \xrightarrow{[O]} \underset{(2\text{-Methylpropanoic acid})}{CH_3—\overset{CH_3}{\overset{|}{CH}}—COOH}$$

$$+ \underset{(3\text{-Methylpropanoic acid})}{CH_3—\overset{CH_3}{\overset{|}{CH}}—CH_2—COOH} + \underset{(\text{Propan-2-one})}{CH_3—\underset{O}{\underset{||}{C}}—CH_3}$$

$$\underset{\text{Propan-2-one}}{(CH_3)_2C{=}O} \xrightarrow{[O]} \underset{\text{Ethanoic acid}}{CH_3—\overset{O}{\overset{||}{C}}—OH} + \underset{\text{Methanoic acid}}{[HCOOH]} \xrightarrow{[O]} CO_2 + H_2O$$

Q.27 Arrange the following in decreasing order of their acidic strength and give reason for your answer.

CH_3CH_2OH, CH_3COOH, $ClCH_2COOH$, FCH_2COOH, $C_6H_5CH_2COOH$

Thinking Process This problem based on the concept of acidic strength, inductive effect and conjugation.

- Presence of $+I$ group decreases acidic strength.
- Presence of $-I$ group increases acidic strength.

Ans. $FCH_2COOH > ClCH_2COOH > C_6H_5CH_2COOH > CH_3COOH > CH_3CH_2OH$

Reasons

(i) FCH_2COOH— Fluorine has a strong electron withdrawing effect.

(ii) $ClCH_2COOH$—Chlorine is less electronegative than fluorine but still withdraw electrons.

(iii) CH_3COOH—No electronegative substituent.

(iv) CH_3CH_2COOH—Ethyl group donates electrons, weakening acidity.

(v) CH_3CH_2OH—Alcohol is much less acidic than carboxylic acids.

Q.28 What product will be formed on reaction of propanal with 2-methylpropanal in the presence of NaOH? What products will be formed? Write the name of the reaction also.

Thinking Process This problem based on the concept of cross aldol condensation.

Ans. It is an example of cross aldol condensation.

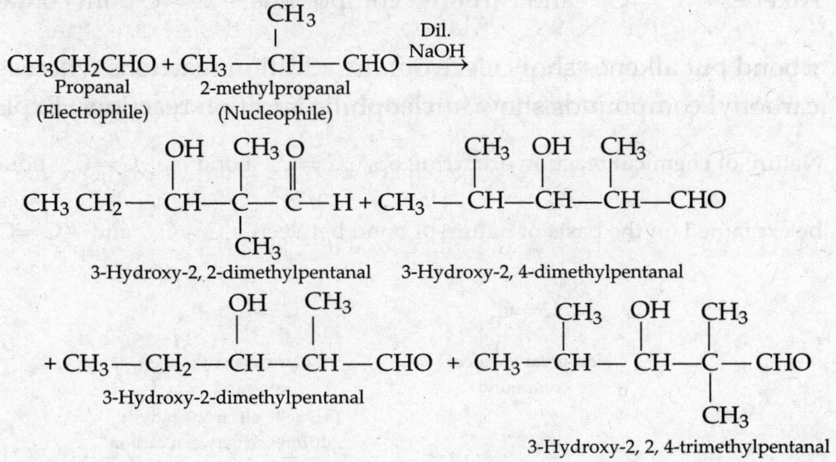

$$CH_3CH_2CHO + CH_3-\underset{}{\overset{CH_3}{\overset{|}{CH}}}-CHO \xrightarrow{\text{Dil. NaOH}}$$

Propanal (Electrophile)   2-methylpropanal (Nucleophile)

$$CH_3CH_2-\overset{OH}{\overset{|}{CH}}-\underset{CH_3}{\underset{|}{\overset{CH_3}{\overset{|}{C}}}}-\overset{O}{\overset{\|}{C}}-H + CH_3-\overset{CH_3}{\overset{|}{CH}}-\overset{OH}{\overset{|}{CH}}-\overset{CH_3}{\overset{|}{CH}}-CHO$$

3-Hydroxy-2, 2-dimethylpentanal   3-Hydroxy-2, 4-dimethylpentanal

$$+ CH_3-CH_2-\overset{OH}{\overset{|}{CH}}-\overset{CH_3}{\overset{|}{CH}}-CHO + CH_3-\overset{CH_3}{\overset{|}{CH}}-\overset{OH}{\overset{|}{CH}}-\underset{CH_3}{\underset{|}{\overset{CH_3}{\overset{|}{C}}}}-CHO$$

3-Hydroxy-2-dimethylpentanal   3-Hydroxy-2, 2, 4-trimethylpentanal

Q.29 Compound '*A*' was prepared by oxidation of compound '*B*' with alkaline $KMnO_4$. Compound '*A*' on reduction with lithium aluminium hydride gets converted back to compound '*B*'. When compound '*A*' is heated with compound *B* in the presence of H_2SO_4 it produces fruity smell of compound *C*. To which family the compounds '*A*', '*B*' and '*C*' belong to?

Thinking Process This problem includes conceptual mixing of preparation and properties of carboxylic acid and ester.

Ans. When compounds '*A*' and '*B*' are heated together in the presence of acid, it forms a fruity smell compound '*C*', which is an ester.

$$\underset{\text{Alcohol}}{[B]} \xrightarrow[\text{[O]}]{\text{AlkKMnO}_4} \underset{\text{Carboxylic acid}}{[A]}$$

$$\underset{\text{Acid}}{[A]} + \underset{\text{Alcohol}}{[B]} \overset{H_2SO_4}{\rightleftharpoons} \underset{\substack{\text{Ester} \\ \text{(fruity smell)}}}{[C]} + H_2O$$

Hence, (*A*) is a carboxylic acid, (*B*) is an alcohol and (*C*) is an ester.

Q.30 Arrange the following in decreasing order of their acidic strength. Give explanation for the arrangement.

$$C_6H_5COOH, FCH_2COOH, NO_2CH_2COOH$$

Thinking Process This problem includes the concept of electron withdrawing effect and acidic strength.

Ans. The decreasing order of their acidic strength is

$$NO_2CH_2COOH > FCH_2COOH > C_6H_5COOH$$

Acidic strength decreases as the number of electron withdrawing substituent(s) linked to α-carbon atom or carboxylic group of carboxylic acid decreases. Electron withdrawing ability of NO_2, F and C_6H_5 are as follows

$$-NO_2 > -F > C_6H_5-$$

Mistake alert! *Student may confuse the effects of electron withdrawing and electron donating groups on acidity.*

Q.31 Alkenes $>C=C<$ and carbonyl compounds $>C=O$ both contain a π bond but alkenes show electrophilic addition reactions whereas carbonyl compounds show nucleophilic addition reactions. Explain.

Ans. Nature of chemical reaction occurring on $>C=C<$ bond or $>C=C<$ bond can be explained on the basis of nature of bond between $>C=C<$ and $>C=C$.

$>C=C<$ — Non-polar covalent compound

$>C=C$ — Polar covalent compound (• Due to electronegativity difference between carbon and oxygen)

Thus, in $>C=O$ carbon acquires partially positive charge and O acquires partially negative charge and show nucleophilic addition reaction to the electrophilic carbonyl carbon. On the other hand, $>C=C<$ undergo electrophilic addition reaction due to nucleophilic nature of $>C=C<$ which contains π bond.

Q.32 Carboxylic acids contain carbonyl group but do not show the nucleophilic addition reaction like aldehydes or ketones. Why?

Ans. Carboxylic acids contain carbonyl group but do not show nucleophilic addition reaction like aldehydes and ketones. Due to resonance as shown below, the partial positive charge on carbonyl carbon atom is reduced.

$$-\overset{\overset{\Large O}{\|}}{C}-\ddot{O}-H \longleftrightarrow -\overset{\overset{\Large O^-}{|}}{C}=\overset{+}{O}-H$$

Q.33 Identify the compounds *A*, *B* and *C* in the following reaction.

$$CH_3-Br \xrightarrow{Mg/ether} [A] \xrightarrow[\text{(ii) Water}]{\text{(i) } CO_2} [B] \xrightarrow[\Delta]{CH_3OH/H^+} [C]$$

Ans. Complete chemical conversion can be done as

$$\underset{\text{Bromomethane}}{CH_3-Br} \xrightarrow{Mg/ether} \underset{\substack{[A]\\ \text{Methyl magnesium}\\ \text{bromide}}}{CH_3MgBr} \xrightarrow[\text{(ii) Water}]{\text{(i) } CO_2} \underset{\substack{[B]\\ \text{Ethanoic acid}}}{CH_3COOH} \xrightarrow{CH_3OH/H^+} \underset{\substack{[C]\\ \text{Methyl ethanoate}}}{CH_3COOCH_3}$$

Hence, $[A] = CH_3MgBr$, $[B] = CH_3COOH$, $[C] = CH_3-\overset{\overset{O}{\|}}{C}-O-CH_3$

Q.34 Why are carboxylic acids more acidic than alcohols or phenols although all of them have hydrogen atom attached to a oxygen atom (—O—H)?

Ans. Carboxylic acids are more acidic than alcohol or phenol, although all of them have O—H bond. This can be explained on the basis of stability of conjugate base obtained after removal of H^+ from acid or phenol.

$$R-\overset{O}{\overset{\|}{C}}-O-H \xrightarrow{-H^+} R-C(=O)-\ddot{O}:^{\ominus} \longleftrightarrow R-C(=O)-:\ddot{O}:^{\ominus}$$

(Carboxylic acid) [More stable carboxylate anion]

$$C_6H_5-O-H \xrightarrow{-H^+} C_6H_5-\ddot{O}:^{\ominus}$$

[Less stable phenoxide ion]

Hence, dissociation of O—H bond in case of carboxylic acid become easier than that of phenol. Hence, carboxylic acid are stronger acid than phenol.

Q.35 Complete the following reaction sequence.

$$CH_3-\overset{O}{\overset{\|}{C}}-CH_3 \xrightarrow[\text{(ii) } H_2O]{\text{(i) } CH_3MgBr} [A] \xrightarrow[\text{Ether}]{\text{Na metal}} [B] \xrightarrow{CH_3-Br} [C]$$

Ans. The complete chemical transformation can be shown as

$$\underset{\text{Propanone}}{CH_3-\overset{O}{\overset{\|}{C}}-CH_3} \xrightarrow[\text{(ii) } H_2O]{\text{(i) } CH_3MgBr} \underset{\substack{[A] \\ \text{2-Methylpropane-2-ol}}}{\overset{1}{C}H_3-\overset{OH}{\overset{|}{\underset{\underset{^3CH_3}{|}}{\overset{2}{C}}}}-CH_3} \xrightarrow[\text{Ether}]{\text{Na metal}} \underset{\substack{[B] \\ \text{Sodium tert-butoxide}}}{CH_3-\overset{\bar{O}\overset{+}{Na}}{\overset{|}{\underset{\underset{CH_3}{|}}{C}}}-CH_3}$$

$$\xrightarrow[\text{(Williamson's synthesis)}]{CH_3-Br} \underset{\substack{\text{2-Methyl-2-methoxypropane} \\ [C]}}{\overset{1}{C}H_3-\overset{OCH_3}{\overset{|}{\underset{\underset{CH_3}{|}}{\overset{2}{C}}}}-\overset{3}{C}H_3}$$

Hence, $[A] = CH_3-\overset{OH}{\overset{|}{\underset{\underset{CH_3}{|}}{C}}}-CH_3$, $[B] = CH_3-\overset{\bar{O}\overset{+}{Na}}{\overset{|}{\underset{\underset{CH_3}{|}}{C}}}-CH_3$, $[C] = CH_3-\overset{O-CH_3}{\overset{|}{\underset{\underset{CH_3}{|}}{C}}}-CH_3$

Q.36 Ethyl benzene is generally prepared by acetylation of benzene followed by reduction and not by direct alkylation. Think of a possible reason.

Ans. Preparation of ethyl benzene from acylation of benzene and reduction can be shown as

$$\underset{\text{Benzene}}{C_6H_6} + \underset{\text{Acetyl chloride}}{CH_3COCl} \xrightarrow[\text{(Friedel-Craft's acylation)}]{\text{Anhydrous } AlCl_3} \underset{\text{Acetophenone}}{C_6H_5COCH_3} \xrightarrow[\text{[H]}]{\text{Zn–Hg, HCl}} \underset{\text{Ethyl benzene}}{C_6H_5CH_2CH_3}$$

The direct alkylation cannot be performed because there is polysubstitution product is formed. Due to disadvantage of polysubstitution, Friedel-Craft's alkylation reaction is not used for preparation of alkylbenzenes. Hence, of Friedel-Craft's acylation is used for preparation of ethyl benzene.

Q.37 Can Gatterman-Koch reaction be considered similar to Friedel-Craft's acylation? Discuss.

Ans. In Gatterman-Koch reaction, benzene or its derivative is treated with CO and HCl in presence of anhydrous aluminium chloride to produce benzaldehyde.

$$C_6H_6 \xrightarrow[\text{Anhyd. } AlCl_3]{CO + HCl} C_6H_5CHO$$

While in Friedel-Craft acylation, acyl group is transferred to carbon of benzene and acyl benzene is obtained as a result.

This can be done by reaction of benzene with acyl chloride in the presence of anhydrous $AlCl_3$.

$$C_6H_6 + RCOCl \xrightarrow{\text{Anhyd. } AlCl_3} C_6H_5COR$$

Formyl chloride is unstable in nature. So, it can be transferred by only Gattermann-Koch reaction not by Friedel-Craft reaction.

Matching The Columns

Q.38 Match the common names given in Column I with the IUPAC names given in Column II.

	Column I (Common names)		Column II (IUPAC names)
A.	Cinnamaldehyde	1.	Pentanal
B.	Acetophenone	2.	Prop-2-enal
C.	Valeraldehyde	3.	4-Methylpent-3-en-2-one
D.	Acrolein	4.	3-Phenylprop-2- enal
E.	Mesityl oxide	5.	1-Phenylethanone

Ans. **A.** → (4) **B.** → (5) **C.** → (1) **D.** → (2) **E.** → (3)

	Common names	Structure	IUPAC names
A.	Cinnamaldehyde	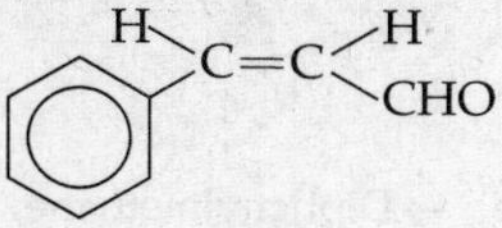 C_6H_5–CH=CH–CHO	3-Phenylprop-2 -enal
B.	Acetophenone	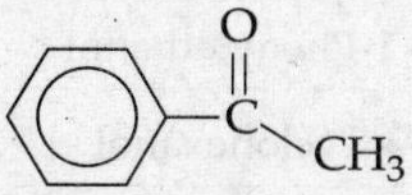 C_6H_5–C(=O)–CH_3	1-Phenylethanone
C.	Valeraldehyde	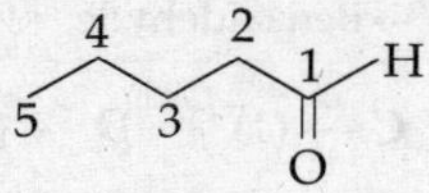 5 4 3 2 1, H, O	Pentanal
D.	Acrolein	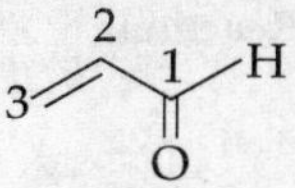 3 2 1, H, O	Prop-2-enal
E.	Mesityl oxide	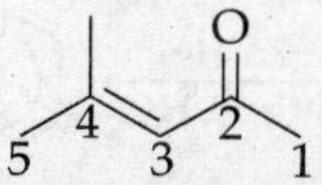 5 4 3 2 1, O	4-Methylpent-3-en-2-one

Q.39 Match the acids given in Column I with their correct IUPAC names given in Column II.

	Column I (Acids)	Column II (IUPAC names)
A.	Phthalic acid	1. Hexane- 1, 6-dioic acid
B.	Oxalic acid	2. Benzene-1, 2-dicarboxylic acid
C.	Succinic acid	3. Pentane-1, 5-dioic acid
D.	Adipic acid	4. Butane-1, 4-dioic acid
E.	Glutaric acid	5. Ethane-1, 2-dioic acid

Ans. **A.** → (2) **B.** → (5) **C.** → (4) **D.** → (1) **E.** → (3)

	Acids	IUPAC names	Structure
A.	Phthalic acid	Benzene-1, 2-dicarboxylic acid	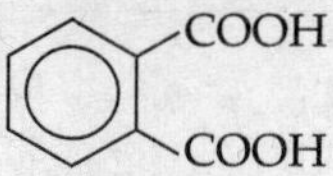 $C_6H_4(COOH)_2$ (COOH, COOH)
B.	Oxalic acid	Ethane-1, 2-dioic acid	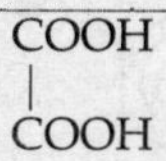 COOH–COOH
C.	Succinic acid	Butane-1, 4-dioic acid	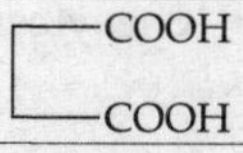 COOH, COOH
D.	Adipic acid	Hexane- 1, 6-dioic acid	 COOH, COOH
E.	Glutaric acid	Pentane-1, 5-dioic acid	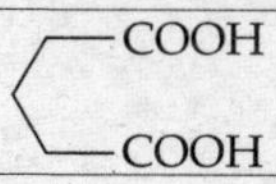 COOH, COOH

Q.40 Match the reactions given in Column I with the suitable reagents given in Column II.

	Column I (Reactions)		Column II (Reagents)
A.	Benzophenone → Diphenylmethane	1.	$LiAlH_4$
B.	Benzaldehyde → 1-Phenylethanol	2.	DIBAL-H
C.	Cyclohexanone → Cyclohexanol	3.	Zn(Hg)/Conc. HCl
D.	Phenyl benzoate → Benzaldehyde	4.	CH_3MgBr

Ans. **A.** → (3) **B.** → (4) **C.** → (1) **D.** → (2)

	Reactions	Reagents
A.	Benzophenone $\xrightarrow[\text{Conc. HCl}]{\text{Zn(Hg)}}$ Diphenylmethane	Zn(Hg)/Conc. HCl
B.	Benzaldehyde (C_6H_5CHO) $\xrightarrow[H_3O^+]{CH_3MgBr}$ 1-Phenylethanol ($C_6H_5CH(OH)CH_3$)	CH_3MgBr
C.	Cyclohexanone $\xrightarrow{LiAlH_4}$ Cyclohexanol	$LiAlH_4$
D.	Phenylbenzoate (C_6H_5–O–CO–C_6H_5) $\xrightarrow[H_2O]{\text{DIBAL-H}}$ Benzaldehyde (C_6H_5CHO)	DIBAL-H

Q.41 Match the example given in Column I with the name of the reaction in Column II.

	Column I (Example)	Column II (Reaction)
A.	$CH_3-\overset{O}{\overset{\|\|}{C}}-Cl + H_2 \xrightarrow{Pd-C/BaSO_4} CH_3-\overset{O}{\overset{\|\|}{C}}-H$	1. Friedel-Crafts acylation
B.	$C_6H_5CHO \xrightarrow{NaOH} C_6H_5CH_2OH + C_6H_5COO^-Na^+$	2. HVZ reaction
C.	$C_6H_6 + CH_3-\overset{O}{\overset{\|\|}{C}}-Cl \xrightarrow{AlCl_3} C_6H_5-\overset{O}{\overset{\|\|}{C}}-CH_3$	3. Aldol condensation
D.	$R-CH_2-COOH \xrightarrow{Br_2/Red\ P} R-\underset{Br}{\underset{\|}{CH}}-COOH$	4. Cannizzaro's reaction
E.	$CH_3-CN \xrightarrow[(ii)\ H_2O/H^+]{(i)\ SnCl_2/HCl} CH_3CHO$	5. Rosenmund's reduction
F.	$2CH_3CHO \xrightarrow{NaOH} CH_3-CH=CHCHO$	6. Stephen's reaction

Ans. A.→ (5) B.→ (4) C.→ (1) D.→ (2) E.→ (6) F.→ (3)

	Example	Name of the reaction
A.	$CH_3-\overset{O}{\overset{\|\|}{C}}-Cl + H_2 \xrightarrow{Pd-C/BaSO_4} CH_3-\overset{O}{\overset{\|\|}{C}}-H$	Rosenmund's reduction
B.	$C_6H_5CHO \xrightarrow{NaOH} C_6H_5CH_2OH + C_6H_5CO\bar{O}\overset{+}{Na}$	Cannizzaro's reaction
C.	$C_6H_6 + CH_3-\overset{O}{\overset{\|\|}{C}}-Cl \xrightarrow{AlCl_3} C_6H_5-\overset{O}{\overset{\|\|}{C}}-CH_3$	Friedel-Crafts acylation

	Example	Name of the reaction
D.	$R—CH_2—COOH \xrightarrow{Br_2/Red\ P} R—\underset{\underset{Br}{\vert}}{CH}—COOH$	HVZ reaction
E.	$CH_3—CN \xrightarrow[(ii)\ H_2O/H^+]{(i)\ SnCl_2/HCl} CH_3CHO$	Stephen's reaction
F.	$2CH_3CHO \xrightarrow{NaOH} CH_3—CH=CHCHO$	Aldol condensation

Assertion and Reason

In the following questions a statement of Assertion followed by a statement of Reason is given. Choose the correct answer out of the following choices.

(a) Assertion and reason both are correct and reason is correct explanation of assertion.
(b) Assertion and reason both are wrong statements.
(c) Assertion is correct statement but reason is wrong statement.
(d) Assertion is wrong statement but reason is correct statement.
(e) Assertion and reason both are correct statements but reason is not correct explanation of assertion.

Q.42 Assertion Formaldehyde is a planar molecule.
Reason It contains sp^2 hybridised carbon atom.

Ans. ***(a)*** Assertion and reason are correct and reason is the correct explanation of assertion.

Formaldehyde is a planar molecule due to sp^2 hybridised carbon atom.

$$\underset{H}{\overset{H}{>}}C=O$$

↑ sp^2 hybridised carbon

Q.43 Assertion Compounds containing —CHO group are easily oxidised to corresponding carboxylic acids.
Reason Carboxylic acids can be reduced to alcohols by treatment with $LiAlH_4$.

Ans. ***(e)*** Assertion and reason both are correct but reason is not the correct explanation of assertion.

Compounds containing —CHO group are easily oxidised to corresponding carboxylic acids. Due to electron withdrawing nature of C = O group, C — H bond in aldehydes is weak and easily oxidised to the corresponding carboxylic acids even with mild oxidising agent like Fehling's solution and Tollen's reagents.

Carboxylic acids can be reduced easily to alcohols by treatment with $LiAlH_4$.

Q.44 **Assertion** The α-hydrogen atom in carbonyl compounds is less acidic.
Reason The anion formed after the loss of α-hydrogen atom is resonance stabilised.

Ans. *(d)* Assertion is wrong statement but reason is correct statement.

Correct assertion is the α-hydrogen atom in carbonyl compounds is acidic in nature due to presence of electron withdrawing carbonyl group. The anion formed after loss of α-hydrogen atom is resonance stabilised.

Q.45 **Assertion** Aromatic aldehydes and formaldehyde undergo Cannizzaro reaction.
Reason Aromatic aldehydes are almost as reactive as formaldehyde.

Ans. *(c)* Assertion is the correct statement but reason is the wrong statement.

Aromatic aldehyde and formaldehyde undergo Cannizzaro reaction due to absence of α-H atom, which leads to the formation of carboxylic acid and alcohol of corresponding aldehyde. Formaldehyde is more reactive than aromatic aldehydes.

Q.46 **Assertion** Aldehydes and ketones, both react with Tollen's reagent to form silver mirror.
Reason Both, aldehydes and ketones contain a carbonyl group.

Ans. *(d)* Assertion is wrong statement but reason is the correct statement.

Ketones do not react with Tollen's reagent because they are not easily oxidised like aldehydes.

Reason is the correct Statement as aldehyde and ketones are both organic compounds that contains a carbonyl group.

Long Answer Type Questions

Q.47 An alkene '*A*' (molecular formula C_5H_{10}) on ozonolysis gives a mixture of two compounds '*B*' and '*C*'. Compound '*B*' gives positive Fehling's test and also forms iodoform on treatment with I_2 and NaOH. Compound '*C*' does not give Fehling's test but forms iodoform. Identify the compounds *A*, *B* and *C*. Write the reaction for ozonolysis and formation of iodoform from *B* and *C*.

Thinking Process This problem is based on conceptual mixing of preparation and properties of carbonyl compound including ozonolysis and iodoform test.

Only aldehydes (not ketones) undergo Fehlings test.

Compound containing $-\overset{\overset{\displaystyle O}{\|}}{C}-CH_3$ group undergo iodoform test.

Draw all possible structures of *A* using degree of unsaturation calculations and then choose the correct structure using information provided above in the question.

Ans. Molecular formula $= C_5H_{10}$

$$\text{Degree of unsaturation} = (C_n + 1) - \frac{H_n}{2}$$

where, C_n = number of carbon atoms

H_n = number of hydrogen atoms

Degree of unsaturation $= (5+1) - \frac{10}{2} = 1$

Compound A will be either alkene or cyclic hydrocarbon. Since, A is undergoing ozonolysis hence A must be an alkene.

Possible structures of alkene are

I. $CH_3-CH_2-CH_2-CH=CH_2$

II. $CH_3-CH_2-CH=CH-CH_3$

III. $CH_3-\underset{\underset{CH_3}{|}}{CH}-CH=CH_2$

IV. $CH_3-\underset{\underset{CH_3}{|}}{C}=CH-CH_2$

Ozonolysis of structure I produces aldehyde only.

$$CH_3-CH_2-CH_2-CH=CH_2 \xrightarrow[\text{(ii) Zn/H}_2\text{O}]{\text{(i) O}_3} CH_3-CH_2-CH_2-\underset{\underset{H}{|}}{C}=O + O=C\begin{matrix}H\\H\end{matrix}$$

Ozonolysis of structure II produces aldehyde only.

$$CH_3-CH_2-CH=CH-CH_3 \xrightarrow[\text{(ii) Zn/H}_2\text{O}]{\text{(i) O}_3} CH_3-CH_2-CHO + CH_3CHO$$

Ozonolysis of structure III produces aldehyde only.

$$CH_3-\underset{\underset{CH_3}{|}}{CH}-CH=CH_2 \xrightarrow[\text{(ii) Zn/H}_2\text{O}]{\text{(i) O}_3} CH_3-\underset{\underset{CH_3}{|}}{CH}-CHO + HCHO$$

Ozonolysis of structure IV produces both aldehyde and ketone

$$CH_3-\underset{\underset{CH_3}{|}}{CH}=CH-CH_3 \xrightarrow[\text{(ii) Zn/H}_2\text{O}]{\text{(i) O}_3} CH_3-\underset{\underset{CH_3}{|}}{C}=O + CH_3CHO$$

After ozonolysis, each of structures I, II and III produces only aldehydes as both components. But as given in the question one compound does not give Fehling's test but must give iodoform test. Hence, compound must be a ketone with $CH_3-\overset{\overset{O}{||}}{C}-$ group. Hence, correct structure is IV.

$$\underset{\substack{\text{2-Methylbut-2-ene}\\[A]}}{CH_3-CH=\underset{\underset{CH_3}{|}}{C}-CH_3} \xrightarrow[\text{(ii) Zn/H}_2\text{O}]{\text{(i) O}_3} \underset{\substack{\text{Acetaldehyde}\\[B]}}{H_3C-CHO} + \underset{\substack{\text{Acetone}\\[C]}}{O=\underset{\underset{CH_3}{|}}{C}-CH_3}$$

Formation of iodoform from 'B' and 'C' may be explained as follows

$$\underset{\substack{\text{Acetaldehyde}\\[B]}}{CH_3CHO} + 3I_2 + 4NaOH \xrightarrow{\Delta} \underset{\text{Iodoform}}{CHI_3} + \underset{\substack{\text{Sodium}\\\text{formate}}}{HCOONa} + 3NaI + 3H_2O$$

$$\underset{\substack{\text{Acetone}\\ [C]}}{CH_3COCH_3} + 3I_2 + 4NaOH \xrightarrow{\Delta} \underset{\text{Iodoform}}{CHI_3} + \underset{\substack{\text{Sodium}\\ \text{acetate}}}{CH_3COONa} + 3NaI + 3H_2O$$

Hence, compound *A* is 2-methylbut-2-ene, *B* is acetaldehyde and *C* is acetone.

Q.48 An aromatic compound '*A*' (molecular formula C_8H_8O) gives positive 2, 4-DNP test. It gives a yellow precipitate of compound '*B*' on treatment with iodine and sodium hydroxide solution. Compound '*A*' does not give Tollen's or Fehling's test. On drastic oxidation with potassium permanganate it forms a carboxylic acid '*C*' (molecular formula $C_7H_6O_2$), which is also formed alongwith the yellow compound in the above reaction. Identify *A*, *B* and *C* and write all the reactions involved.

Thinking Process This problem is based on conceptual mixing of 2, 4-DNP test, iodoform test and oxidation reactions. Follow the following stepwise approach to solve this question.

(i) Determine all possible structures of molecule using degree of unsaturation.

(ii) Use the concept of chemical test given by aldehydes and ketones to identify the correct structure.

(iii) After choosing any predicted structure complete the sequence of reactions.

Ans. Molecular formula = C_8H_8O

$$\text{Degree of unsaturation} = (C_n + 1) - \frac{H_n}{2}$$

$$= (8 + 1) - \frac{8}{2}$$

$$= 9 - 4 = 5$$

Degree of unsaturation > 5, *i.e.*, it may contain benzene ring having degree of unsaturation equal to 4 and one degree of unsaturation must be carbonyl group.

Thus, possible structures are

(I) $C_6H_5COCH_3$ (II) $C_6H_5CH_2-\overset{O}{\overset{||}{C}}-H$ (III) p-$CH_3C_6H_4CHO$

(IV) o-$CH_3C_6H_4CHO$ (V) m-$CH_3C_6H_4CHO$

According to question, compound '*A*' does not respond to Tollen's or Fehling's test, So, it is a ketone not aldehyde. Therefore, structure I is correct. Complete reaction sequence is as follows

Reaction scheme: Acetophenone [A] [C_8H_8O] (CH_3–C(=O)–C_6H_5)

- with 2, 4-DNP → C_6H_5–C(CH_3)=N–NH–$C_6H_3(NO_2)_2$, Acetophenone (2,4-dinitrophenyl) hydrazone
- with (i) I_2/NaOH (ii) H^+ → CHI_3 [B] (Yellow ppt.) Iodoform + C_6H_5COONa Sodium benzoate
- with $KMnO_4$ [O] → C_6H_5COOH [C] [$C_7H_6O_2$] Benzoic acid

Q.49 Write down functional isomers of a carbonyl compound with molecular formula C_3H_6O. Which isomer will react faster with HCN and why? Explain the mechanism of the reaction also. Will the reaction lead to the completion with the conversion of whole reactant into product at reaction conditions? If a strong acid is added to the reaction mixture what will be the effect on concentration of the product and why?

Ans. Functional isomers of C_3H_6O containing carbonyl group are

$$\underset{\text{Propanal}}{CH_3CH_2CHO} \text{ and } \underset{\text{Propanone}}{CH_3COCH_3}$$

(a) Propanal, CH_3CH_2CHO will react faster with HCN because there is less steric hindrance and electronic factors, which increases its electrophilicity.

(b) The reaction mechanism is as follow

$$HCN + OH^- \rightleftharpoons :\bar{C}N + H_2O$$

$$\underset{H}{\overset{H}{>}}\overset{\delta+}{C}=\overset{\delta-}{O} + :\bar{C}N \rightleftharpoons \left[>C\begin{matrix}O^{\ominus}\\CN\end{matrix}\right] \underset{}{\overset{H^+}{\rightleftharpoons}} >C\begin{matrix}OH\\CN\end{matrix}$$

Tetrahedral Intermediate — Cyanohydrin

The reaction does not lead to completion because it is a reversible reaction. Hence, equilibrium is established.

(c) If a strong acid is added to the reaction mixture, the reaction is inhibited because production of $\bar{C}N$ ions from HCN is prevented.

Q.50 When liquid '*A*' is treated with a freshly prepared ammoniacal silver nitrate solution it gives bright silver mirror. The liquid forms a white crystalline solid on treatment with sodium hydrogensulphite. Liquid '*B*' also forms a white crystalline solid with sodium hydrogen sulphite but it does not give test with ammoniacal silver nitrate. Which of the two liquids is aldehyde? Write the chemical equations of these reactions also.

Ans. Since the liquid *A* reduces ammoniacal silver nitrate (Tollen's reagent), hence, '*A*' is aldehyde. Liquid *B* does not give test with Tollen's reagent, it means liquid '*B*' is a ketone.

1. $$\underset{\text{Aldehydes or ketones}}{>C{=}O} + \underset{\text{Sodium hydrogen-sulphite}}{NaHSO_3} \rightleftharpoons >C<^{OSO_2H}_{OH} \xrightleftharpoons{\text{Proton transfer}} \underset{\substack{\text{Bisulphite addition compound}\\\text{(white crystalline solid)}}}{>C<^{OSO_2Na}_{OH}}$$

2. $$\underset{\text{Aldehyde}}{RCHO} + 2[Ag(NH_3)_2]\,NO_3 + 2NH_4OH \longrightarrow RCOOH + \underset{\text{Silver mirror}}{2Ag\downarrow} + H_2O + 4NH_3 + 2NH_4NO_3$$

Mistake Alert! *Aldehydes and ketones both gives white crystallie solid with sodium hydrogen sulphite but only aldehydes gives Tollen's test and Fehling's test.*

Chapter 13

Amines

Multiple Choice Questions (MCQs)

Q.1 Which of the following is a 3° amine?

(a) 1-methylcyclohexylamine
(b) Triethylamine
(c) *tert*-butylamine
(d) N-methylaniline

Ans. ***(b)*** The structures of given amines are as follows

(a) 1-Methylcyclohexylamine (2° amine) — cyclohexane ring bearing NH–CH_3

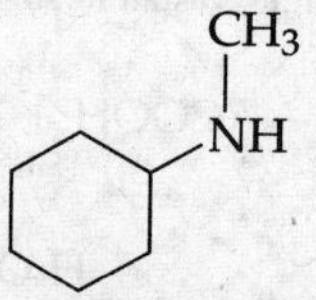

(b) CH_3CH_2–$\ddot{N}$(CH_2CH_3)–CH_2CH_3 Triethylamine (3° amine)

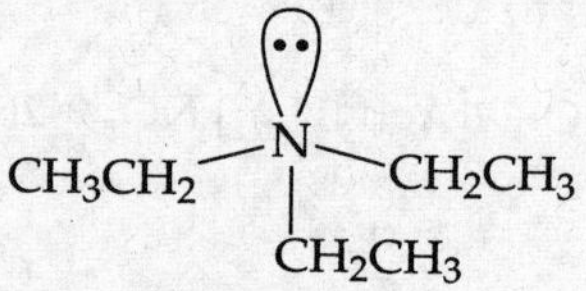

(c) CH_3–C(CH_3)(CH_3)–NH_2 tert-butylamine (1° amine)

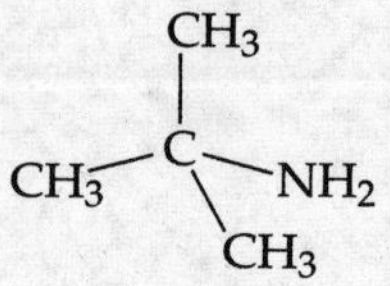

(d) H_3C–N(H)–C_6H_5 N-methylaniline (2° amine)

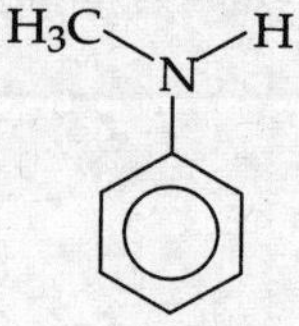

Hence, triethylamine is a tertiary amine. The correct choice is (b).

Q.2 The correct IUPAC name for $CH_2=CHCH_2NHCH_3$ is

(a) Allylmethylamine
(b) 2-amino-4-pentene
(c) 4-aminopent-1ene
(d) N-methylprop-2-en-1-amine

Ans. ***(d)*** IUPAC name of $\overset{3}{C}H_2=\overset{2}{C}H\overset{1}{C}H_2\,NHCH_3$ is N-methylprop-2-en-1-amine

Hence, option (d) is correct.

Q.3 Amongst the following, the strongest base in aqueous medium is ....

(a) CH_3NH_2
(b) $NCCH_2NH_2$
(c) $(CH_3)_2NH$
(d) $C_6H_5NHCH_3$

Thinking Process This problem is based on the concept of basic strength of various types of amine depending upon inductive effect, resonance and solvation.

Ans. *(c)*

	Compound	Factors responsible for basic character are
(a)	$CH_3—NH_2$	Inductive effect (+ *I*)
(b)	$NC—CH_2—NH_2$	Inductive effect (− *I*)
(c)	$(CH_3)_2NH$	Inductive effect (+ *I*) and Solvation
(d)	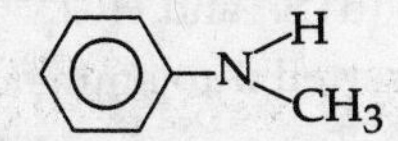 $C_6H_5—N(H)CH_3$	− *I* effect and resonance

Since, + *I* effect and solvation increases basic character, while −*I* effect and resonance decreases basic character. Hence, correct choice is option (c).

Mistake Alert ! *Students may be confused about the effects of + I (Inductive effect), solvation and resonance on basicity, especially in complex amines.*

Q.4 Which of the following is the weakest Bronsted base?

(a) 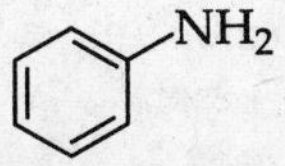 $C_6H_5NH_2$ (b) piperidine (N—H) (c) cyclohexylamine (NH_2) (d) CH_3NH_2

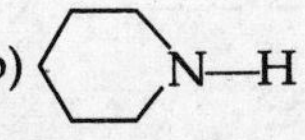

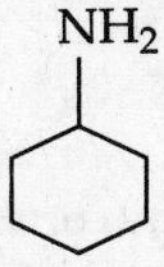

Thinking Process This problem is based on the concept of basicity and resonance effects in aromatic amines.

Ans. *(a)* Aniline is weakest Bronsted base among the given four compounds due to resonance present in case of aniline.

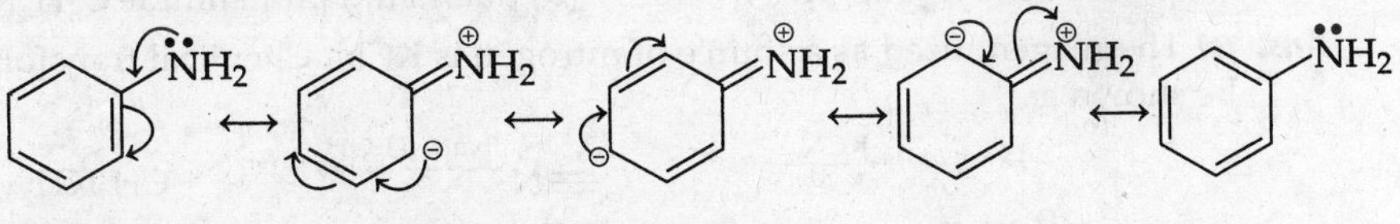

$\ddot{N}H_2 \longleftrightarrow \overset{\oplus}{N}H_2 \longleftrightarrow \overset{\oplus}{N}H_2 \longleftrightarrow \overset{\oplus}{N}H_2 \longleftrightarrow \ddot{N}H_2$

(Resonating structure of aniline)

Hence, lone pair of nitrogen are less available for donation to the acid.

Q.5 Benzylamine may be alkylated as shown in the following equation

$$C_6H_5CH_2NH_2 + R—X \longrightarrow C_6H_5CH_2NHR$$

Which of the following alkylhalides is best suited for this reaction through S_N1 mechanism?

(a) CH_3Br (b) C_6H_5Br (c) $C_6H_5CH_2Br$ (d) C_2H_5Br

Ans. *(c)* S_N1 reaction proceeds through formation of carbocation. Hence, more stable the carbocation, more reactivity towards S_N1 mechanism.

	Alkyl halides		Intermediate
(a)	CH_3Br	$\longrightarrow$	$CH_3^{\oplus}$
(b)	C_6H_5Br	$\longrightarrow$	$C_6H_5^{\oplus}$
(c)	$C_6H_5CH_2Br$	$\longrightarrow$	$C_6H_5—CH_2^{\oplus}$ (more stable)
(d)	C_2H_5Br	$\longrightarrow$	$C_2H_5^{\oplus}$

Hence, the reaction will proceed through S_N1 mechanism, when, $C_6H_5CH_2Br$ is the substrate. because on ionisation it gives a resonance stabilised carbocation $(C_6H_5\overset{+}{C}H_2)$.

Q.6 Which of the following reagents would **not** be a good choice for reducing an aryl nitro compound to an amine?

(a) H_2(excess) / Pt
(b) $LiAlH_4$ in ether
(c) Fe and HCl
(d) Sn and HCl

Ans. ***(b)*** Aryl nitro compound **can not** be converted into amine using $LiAlH_4$ in ether.

$$C_6H_5NO_2 \xrightarrow{H_2(\text{excess})/Pt} C_6H_5NH_2$$
$$C_6H_5NO_2 \xrightarrow{Fe/HCl} C_6H_5NH_2$$
$$C_6H_5NO_2 \xrightarrow{Sn/HCl} C_6H_5NH_2$$
$$C_6H_5NO_2 \xrightarrow{LiAlH_4/\text{ether}} \text{No reaction}$$

Hence, option (b) is the correct choice.

Q.7 In order to prepare a 1° amine from an alkyl halide with simultaneous addition of one CH_2 group in the carbon chain, the reagent used as source of nitrogen is ....

(a) sodium amide, $NaNH_2$
(b) sodium azide, NaN_3
(c) potassium cyanide, KCN
(d) potassium phthalimide $C_6H_4(CO)_2N^-K^+$

Ans. ***(c)*** The reagent used as a source of nitrogen is KCN. Chemical transformation can be shown as

$$\underset{\text{1°-carbon containing haloalkane}}{CH_3CH_2-X} \xrightarrow[-KX]{KCN} CH_3CH_2-C\equiv N \xrightarrow{Na/C_2H_5OH} \underset{\text{1°-carbon containing amine}}{CH_3CH_2CH_2NH_2}$$

Q.8 The source of nitrogen in Gabriel synthesis of amines is ....

(a) sodium azide, NaN_3
(b) sodium nitrite, $NaNO_2$
(c) potassium cyanide, KCN
(d) potassium phthalimide $C_6H_4(CO)_2N^-K^+$

Ans. ***(d)*** Source of nitrogen in Gabriel phthalimide synthesis is potassium phthalimide.

$$\underset{\text{Phthalimide}}{C_6H_4(CO)_2NH} + KOH\,(\text{alc.}) \xrightarrow{-H_2O} C_6H_4(CO)_2\overset{-}{N}\overset{+}{K} \xrightarrow[-KI]{RI,\ \Delta}$$

$$C_6H_4(CO)_2N-R \xrightarrow[HO^-/H_2O,\ \Delta]{H^+/H_2O,\ \Delta \text{ or}} \underset{\text{Phthalic acid}}{C_6H_4(COOH)_2} + \underset{\text{1° amine}}{RNH_2}$$

Q.9 Amongst the given set of reactants, the most appropriate for preparing 2° amine is ....

(a) $2^{\circ} R-Br+NH_3$

(b) $2^{\circ} R-Br+NaCN$ followed by H_2 / Pt

(c) $1^{\circ} R-NH_2+RCHO$ followed by H_2 / Pt

(d) $1^{\circ} R-Br$(2 mol) +potassium phthalimide followed by H_3O^+/ heat

Ans. ***(c)*** Chemical transformation can be shown as

$$R-NH_2+RCHO \xrightarrow[\text{Reductive amination}]{} [R-N=\underset{\underset{H}{|}}{C}-R] \xrightarrow[\text{Reducton)}]{\text{H}_2\text{/Pt}} \underset{\text{2° amine}}{R-\underset{\underset{H}{|}}{N}-\overset{\overset{H}{|}}{\underset{\underset{H}{|}}{C}}-R}$$

While other given set of reactants give primary amines only.

Q.10 The best reagent for converting 2-phenylpropanamide into 2-phenylpropanamine is ....

(a) excess H_2

(b) Br_2 in aqueous NaOH

(c) iodine in the presence of red phosphorus

(d) $LiAlH_4$ in ether

Ans. ***(d)*** The best reagent tor converting 2-phenylpropanamide into 2-phenylpropanamine is $LiAlH_4$ in ether. Reaction is as given below :

$$\text{2-Phenylpropanamide} \xrightarrow{\text{LiAlH}_4\text{ in ether}} \text{2-Phenylpropanamine}$$

Q.11 The best reagent for converting, 2-phenylpropanamide into 1-phenylethanamine is ....

(a) excess H_2 /Pt

(b) NaOH / Br_2

(c) $NaBH_4$ /methanol

(d) $LiAlH_4$ /ether

Thinking Process This problem is based on the concept of amide reduction reactions.

Ans. ***(b)*** The best reagent for converting 2-phenylpropanamide into 1-phenylethanamine is by NaOH / Br_2 and chemical transformation can be done as

$$\text{2-Phenylpropapanide} \xrightarrow{\text{NaOH/Br}_2} \underset{\text{1-Phenylethanamine}}{C_6H_5-\overset{\overset{CH_3}{|}}{CH}-NH_2}$$

This occurs due to intramolecular migration of alkyl group. It is an example of Hofmann bromamide reaction.

Q.12 Hofmann bromamide degradation reaction is shown by ....
(a) $ArNH_2$
(b) $ArCONH_2$
(c) $ArNO_2$
(d) $ArCH_2NH_2$

Ans. *(b)* Hofmann bromamide degradation is shown by $Ar-\overset{O}{\overset{\|}{C}}-NH_2$ in which amide is converted into amine *via* undergoing intramolecular migration of phenyl group.

$$\underset{\text{Benzamide}}{C_6H_5CONH_2} \xrightarrow{Br_2/NaOH} \underset{\text{Aniline}}{C_6H_5NH_2} + K_2CO_3 + KBr + 2H_2O$$

Q.13 The correct increasing order of basic strength for the following compounds is ....

(I) Aniline ($C_6H_5NH_2$); (II) p-nitroaniline (NH_2 with NO_2 para); (III) p-toluidine (NH_2 with CH_3 para)

(a) II < III < I
(b) III < I < II
(c) III < II < I
(d) II < I < III

Ans. *(d)* The correct increasing order of basic strength is as follows

p-nitroaniline (II) < aniline (I) < p-toluidine (III)

Greater the electron density towards ring, greater will be its basic strength. Electron withdrawing group ($-NO_2$) decreases basic strength, while electron donating group ($-CH_3$) increases basic strength of amine.

Q.14 Methylamine reacts with HNO_2 to form ....
(a) $CH_3-O-N=O$
(b) CH_3-O-CH_3
(c) CH_3OH
(d) CH_3CHO

Ans. *(c)* Methylamine reacts with HNO_2 (nitrous acid) to form methanol.

$$CH_3NH_2 + HNO_2 \xrightarrow{0°+05°C} CH_3OH + N_2\uparrow + H_2O$$

Q.15 The gas evolved when methylamine reacts with nitrous acid is ....
(a) NH_3
(b) N_2
(c) H_2
(d) C_2H_6

Ans. ***(b)*** Chemical reaction that takes place during reaction of methylamine with nitrous acid is as follows

$$\underset{\text{Methylamine}}{CH_3—NH_2} \xrightarrow{HNO_2} CH_3—\overset{+}{N}\equiv NCl^- \xrightarrow{\Delta,\ H_2O} \underset{\text{Methanol}}{CH_3OH} + N_2 \uparrow$$

Q.16 In the nitration of benzene using a mixture of conc. H_2SO_4 and conc. HNO_3, the species which initiates the reaction is ....

(a) NO_2 (b) NO^+ (c) NO_2^+ (d) NO_2^-

● **Concept Insight** This reaction involves electrophilic aromatic substitution, where a nitrogen ion, generated by the reaction between conc. H_2SO_4 and HNO_3, acts as electrophile.

Ans. ***(c)*** Nitration of benzene using a mixture of conc. H_2SO_4 and conc. HNO_3 proceeds as :

$$HO—N(=O)—O—H + H_2SO_4 \longrightarrow H_3\overset{\oplus}{O} + \overset{\oplus}{N}O_2 + 2H_2O + SO_2$$

$$C_6H_6 \xrightarrow{\overset{\oplus}{N}O_2} C_6H_5NO_2$$

This reaction is known as electrophilic substitution reaction.

Q.17 Reduction of aromatic nitro compounds using Fe and HCl gives ....

(a) aromatic oxime (b) aromatic hydrocarbon

(c) aromatic primary amine (d) aromatic amide

Ans. ***(c)*** Aromatic nitro compound on reaction with Fe and HCl gives aromatic primary amine as shown below :

$$\underset{\text{Aromatic nitro compound}}{C_6H_5NO_2} + 3H_2 \xrightarrow{Fe/HCl} \underset{\text{Aromatic primary amine}}{C_6H_5NH_2} + 2H_2O$$

Q.18 The most reactive amine towards dilute hydrochloric acid is ....

(a) CH_3-NH_2

(b) $(CH_3)_2NH$

(c) $(CH_3)_2N—CH_3$

(d) $C_6H_5NH_2$

💡 **Thinking Process** This problem is based on the concept of basicity of amines and their reactivity with acids.

Ans. ***(b)*** Greater will be the strength of base, greater will be its reactivity towards dilute HCl. Hence, $(CH_3)_2NH$ has highest basic strength as it has highest reactivity.

$$(H_3C)_2N{-}H \xrightarrow{HCl} (H_3C)_2\overset{\oplus}{N}H_2 + \overset{\ominus}{Cl}$$

Q.19 Acid anhydrides on reaction with primary amines give ....

(a) amide (b) imide

(c) secondary amine (d) imine

Ans. ***(a)*** Acid anhydride on reaction with primary amine produces amide as

$$R{-}CO{-}O{-}CO{-}R \xrightarrow{R\ddot{N}H_2} R{-}CO{-}O{-}C(O^{\ominus})(\overset{\oplus}{N}H_2R){-}R \longrightarrow R{-}\overset{\oplus}{N}H_2{-}CO{-}R + R{-}CO\overset{\ominus}{O} \longrightarrow \underset{\text{Amide}}{R{-}NH{-}CO{-}R} + RCOOH$$

Q.20 The reaction $Ar\overset{+}{N_2}Cl^- \xrightarrow{Cu/HCl} ArCl + N_2 + CuCl$ is named as ....

(a) Sandmeyer reaction (b) Gattermann reaction

(c) Claisen reaction (d) Carbylamine reaction

Thinking Process This problem is based on the concept of substitution reactions of aryl diazonium salts. To identify the correct reaction, recognise that the Gattermann reaction uses Cu and HCl (or HBr) to replace the diazonium group with a halogen, while Sandmeyer reaction requires CuCl or CuBr salts for the same transformation.

Ans. ***(b)***

$$\underset{\text{Benzene diazonium chloride}}{C_6H_5\overset{+}{N_2}Cl^-} \xrightarrow{Cu/HCl} \underset{\text{Chlorobenzene}}{C_6H_5Cl} + N_2 + CuCl$$

This reaction is called Gattermann reaction. In this reaction, Cl, Br and CN can be introduced into the benzene ring by simply treating diazonium salts with HCl, HBr, KCN, respectively in presence of copper powder instead of using Cu (I) salts.

Q.21 Best method for preparing primary amines from alkyl halides without changing the number of carbon atoms in the chain is

(a) Hoffmann bromamide reaction (b) Gabriel phthalimide synthesis

(c) Sandmeyer reaction (d) reaction with NH_3

Concept Insight This solution includes the concept of selective preparation of primary amines using Gabriel Phthalimide synthesis.

Ans. ***(b)*** Best method of preparing primary amines from alkyl halides without changing the number of carbon atoms in the chain is Gabriel phthalimide synthesis.

NH $\xrightarrow{\text{KOH (alc.)}}$ $\overset{\ominus}{N}\overset{+}{K}$ $\xrightarrow{R-X}$ N—R $\xrightarrow{NaOH/H_2O}$ $R-NH_2$ + (phthalate, $ONa^{\oplus}$, $\overset{\ominus}{O}Na^{\oplus}$)

Primary amine

Q.22 Which of the following compound will not undergo azo coupling reaction with benzene diazonium chloride?

(a) Aniline (b) Phenol (c) Anisole (d) Nitrobenzene

Ans. ***(d)*** Nitrobenzene will not undergo azo coupling reaction with benzene diazonium chloride while other three undergo diazo coupling reaction very easily. Diazonium cation is a weak E^+ and hence reacts with electron rich compounds cotaining electron donating group, *i.e.*, —OH, —NH_2 and —OCH_3 groups and not with compounds containing electron withdrawing group, *i.e.*, NO_2, etc.

Q.23 Which of the following compounds is the weakest Bronsted base?

(a) 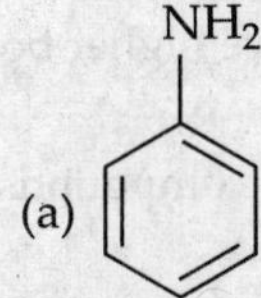

(b) NH_2 (c) OH (d) 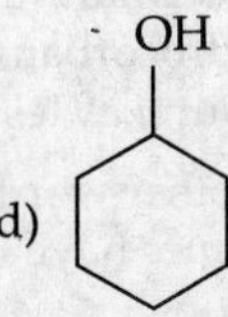

Ans. ***(c)*** Phenol is weakest Bronsted base as phenol after gaining H^+ produces least stable conjugate acid among the compounds.

Oxygen has more electronegativity than N. So, O—H bond is more polar and it has highest value of acidic character. Since, phenol is more acidic than alcohol. Therefore, phenol has the least tendency to accept a proton and hence it is weak Bronsted base. Hence, phenol is least basic among the given four choices.

Q.24 Among the following amines, the strongest Bronsted base is ....

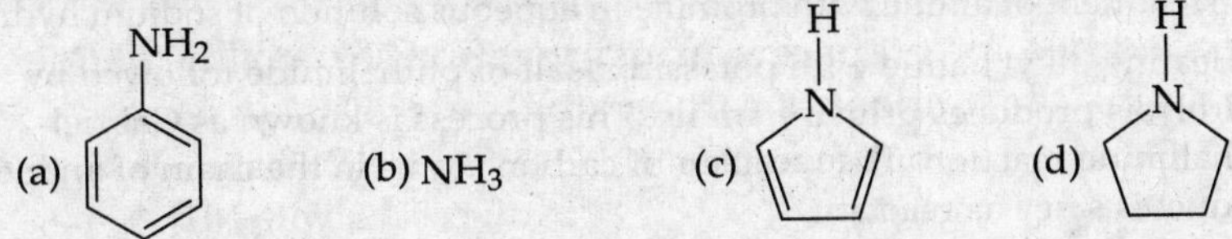

Ans. ***(d)*** Aniline is a weaker base than NH_3 due to delocalisation of lone pair of electrons of the N-atom over the benzene ring. Pyrrole is not more basic because the lone pair of electrons on the N-atom is donated towards aromatic sextet formation.

Therefore, pyrrolidine is strongest base as lone pair of nitrogen is not involved in resonance and also due to presence of two alkyl ring residue, basic strength becomes high among given four compounds.

Q.25 The correct decreasing order of basic strength of the following species is .... H_2O, NH_3, OH^-, NH_2^-

(a) $NH_2^- > OH^- > NH_3 > H_2O$
(b) $OH^- > NH_2^- > H_2O > NH_3$
(c) $NH_3 > H_2O > NH_2^- > OH^-$
(d) $H_2O > NH_3 > OH^- > NH_2^-$

Ans. *(a)*

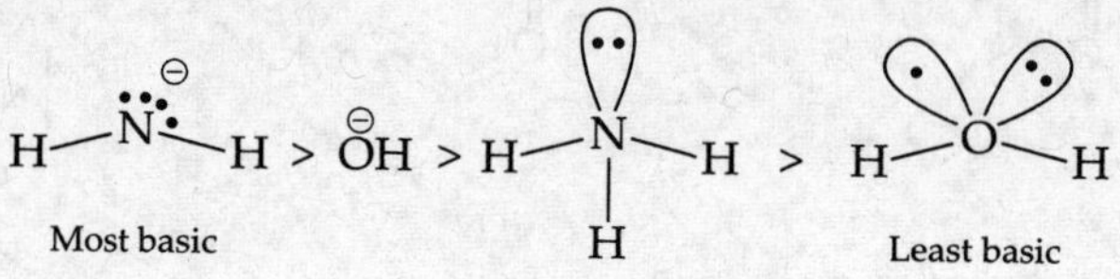

$$H-\ddot{N}^{\ominus}-H > \overset{\ominus}{O}H > H-\underset{\underset{H}{|}}{\ddot{N}}-H > H-\ddot{O}-H$$

Most basic ... Least basic

Basic strength of the above species can be explained on the basis of electronegativity of central atom and its proton accepting tendency. Here, amide ion is most basic among given compounds due to presence of negative charge and two pair of electrons on nitrogen atom.

Q.26 Which of the following should be most volatile?

I. $CH_3CH_2CH_2NH_2$
II. $(CH_3)_3N$
III. $CH_3CH_2 \searrow NH$ / $CH_3 \nearrow$
IV. $CH_3CH_2CH_3$

(a) II (b) IV (c) I (d) III

Ans. *(b)* 1° and 2° amines have higher boiling points due to intermolecular H-bonding and they are less votatile than 3° amines and hydrocarbons of comparable molecular mass. Due to polar C-N bonds, 3° amines are more polar than hydrocorbans which are almost non-polar. Hence, 3° amines have higher boiling point (*i.e.*, less volatile) than hydrocarbons.

In other words, hydrocarbons are more volatile among the given compounds as amines have higher boiling points than hydrocarbons.

Q.27 Which of the following methods of preparation of amines will give same number of carbon atoms in the chain of amines as in the reactant?

(a) Reaction of nitrite with $LiAlH_4$.
(b) Reaction of amide with $LiAlH_4$ followed by treatment with water.
(c) Heating alkylhalide with potassium salt of phthalimide followed by hydrolysis.
(d) Treatment of amide with bromine in aqueous solution of sodium hydroxide.

Ans. *(c)* Heating alkyl halide with potassium salt of phthalimide followed by hydrolysis produces primary amine. This process is known as Gabriel phthalimide reaction. The number of carbon atoms in the chain of amines of product is same as reactant.

$$\text{Phthalimide (C}_6\text{H}_4(\text{CO})_2\text{NH)} \xrightarrow{\text{KOH(alc.)}} \text{C}_6\text{H}_4(\text{CO})_2\overset{\ominus}{\text{N}}\overset{\oplus}{\text{K}} \xrightarrow[\Delta]{R\text{—}X} \text{C}_6\text{H}_4(\text{CO})_2\text{N—}R \longrightarrow \text{C}_6\text{H}_4(\text{CO}\overset{\ominus}{\text{O}}\overset{\oplus}{\text{K}})_2 + R\text{—NH}_2$$

Multiple Choice Questions (More Than One Options)

Q.28 Which of the following cannot be prepared by Sandmeyer's reaction?

(a) Chlorobenzene (b) Bromobenzene

(c) Iodobenzene (d) Fluorobenzene

Ans. ***(c, d)*** Sandmeyer's reaction is used for preparation of chlorobenzene and bromobenzene.

$$C_6H_5N_2^+Cl^- \xrightarrow{Cu_2Cl_2} C_6H_5Cl$$

$$C_6H_5N_2^+Cl^- \xrightarrow{Cu_2Br_2} C_6H_5Br$$

Iodobenzene and fluorobenzene can be prepared by direct reaction of diazonium salt with KI and HBF_4/Δ.

$$C_6H_5\overset{+}{N}_2\overline{Cl} \xrightarrow{KI} C_6H_5I$$

$$C_6H_5\overset{+}{N}_2\overline{Cl} \xrightarrow[\Delta]{HBF_4} C_6H_5F$$

Q.29 Reduction of nitrobenzene by which of the following reagent gives aniline?

(a) Sn/HCl (b) Fe/HCl (c) H_2-Pd (d) Sn/NH_4OH

Ans. ***(a, b, c)*** Reduction of nitrobenzene by Sn/HCl, Fe/HCl and H_2- Pd gives aniline as follows

$$\underset{\text{Nitrobenzene}}{C_6H_5—NO_2} \xrightarrow{\text{Sn/HCl, Fe/HCl or } H_2—Pd} \underset{\text{Aniline}}{C_6H_5—NH_2}$$

Q.30 Which of the following species are involved in the carbylamine test?

(a) $R-NC$ (b) $CHCl_3$ (c) $COCl_2$ (d) $NaNO_2 + HCl$

Ans. *(a, b)* **Carbylamine reaction** Amine on reaction with a mixture of $CHCl_3$ and KOH produces alkyl isocyanate.

$$R—NH_2 + CHCl_3 + 3\,KOH \longrightarrow RNC + 3KCl + 3H_2O$$

Only R–NC and $CHCl_3$ are involved in carbylamine reaction. Hence, (a) and (b) are correct.

Mistake Alert! *Students may be confused about the reagents and products involved in the carbylamie test. This test is used to detect primary amines by reacting it with* $CHCl_3$ *and* NaOH, *leading to the formation of an isocyanide* ($R-NC$).

Q.31 The reagents that can be used to convert benzenediazonium chloride to benzene are ....

(a) $SnCl_2 / HCl$ (b) CH_3CH_2OH (c) H_3PO_2 (d) $LiAlH_4$

Ans. *(b, c)* Benzene diazonium chloride can be converted into benzene using protic acid like hypophosphorus acid (phosphoric acid) or ethanol as follows :

$$C_6H_5\overset{+}{N_2}Cl^- \xrightarrow[H_3PO_2]{CH_3CH_2OH} C_6H_6$$

Q.32 The product of the following reaction is ....

$$C_6H_5NHCOCH_3 + Br_2/CH_3COOH \longrightarrow$$

(a) p-Br-C_6H_4-$NHCOCH_3$ (NHCOCH₃ at top, Br at para position)

(b) o-Br-C_6H_4-$NHCOCH_3$ (NHCOCH₃, Br at ortho position)

(c) m-Br-C_6H_4-$NHCOCH_3$ (NHCOCH₃, Br at meta position)

(d) 2,4,6-tribromo-C_6H_2-$NHCOCH_3$ (NHCOCH₃ with Br, Br, Br)

Ans. *(a, b)* N-acetylaniline on reaction with Br_2 in presence of acetic acid produces *p*-bromo N-acetyl aniline (major) and *o*-bromo-N-acetyl aniline (minor) as follows

$$C_6H_5NHCOCH_3 \xrightarrow{Br_2/CH_3COOH} p\text{-}BrC_6H_4NHCOCH_3 + o\text{-}BrC_6H_4NHCOCH_3$$

The N-acetyl group is a *ortho, para* directing group.

Hence, (a) and (b) are correct.

Q.33 Arenium ion involved in the bromination of aniline is ....

(a) 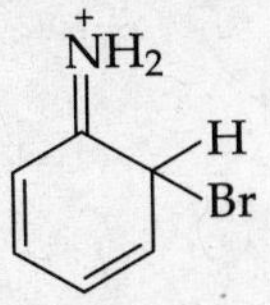 $\overset{+}{N}H_2$, H, Br (b) 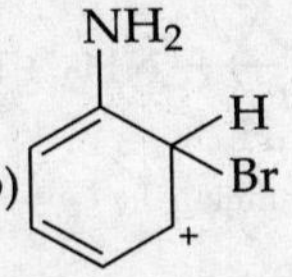 NH_2, H, Br, + (c) 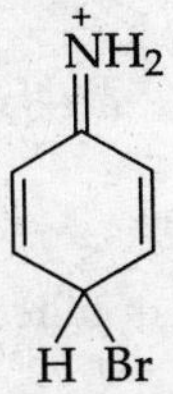 $\overset{+}{N}H_2$, H Br (d) 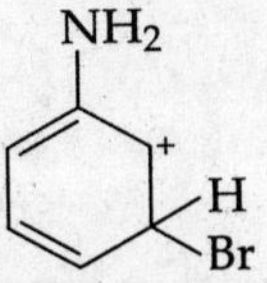 NH_2, +, H, Br

Ans. ***(a, b, c)*** Arenium ion involved in the bromination of aniline are as follows :

(i) 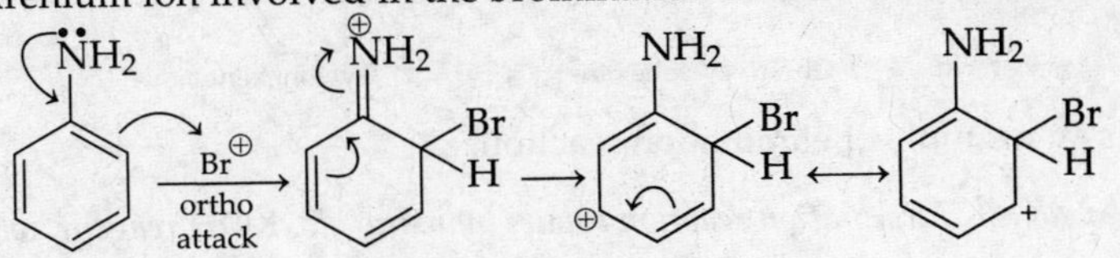 $\ddot{N}H_2$ $\xrightarrow[\text{ortho attack}]{Br^{\oplus}}$ $\overset{\oplus}{N}H_2$, Br, H $\longrightarrow$ NH_2, Br, H, $\oplus$ $\longleftrightarrow$ NH_2, Br, H, +

(ii) 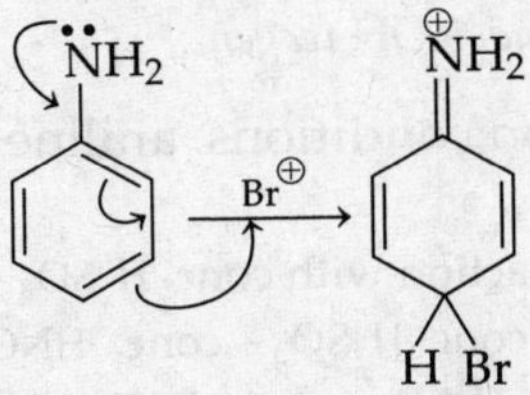 $\ddot{N}H_2$ $\xrightarrow{Br^{\oplus}}$ $\overset{\oplus}{N}H_2$, H Br

Q.34 Which of the following amines can be prepared by Gabriel synthesis?

(a) Isobutyl amine (b) 2-Phenylethylamine

(c) N-methylbenzylamine (d) Aniline

Ans. ***(a, b)*** Isobutylamine and 2-phenylethyl amine are primary amines, which can be prepared easily by Gabriel phthalimide reaction.

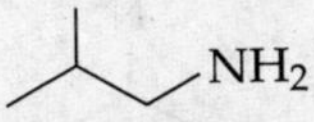

NH_2 isobutyl amine NH_2 2 Phenylethylamine

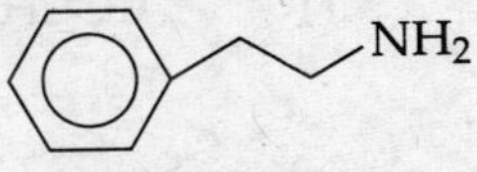

2° amines N-methyl benzylamine and 1° amine however cannot be prepared.

Q.35 Which of the following reactions are correct?

(a) 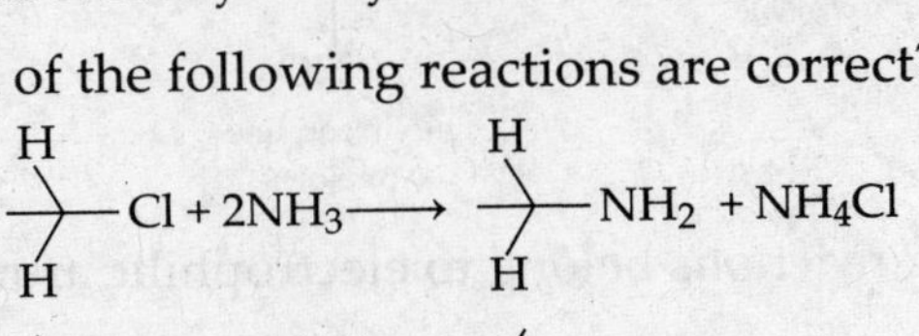 $H_2C(H)(H)-Cl + 2NH_3 \longrightarrow H_2C(H)(H)-NH_2 + NH_4Cl$

(b) 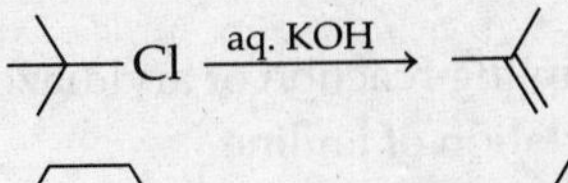 —Cl $\xrightarrow{\text{aq. KOH}}$

(c) 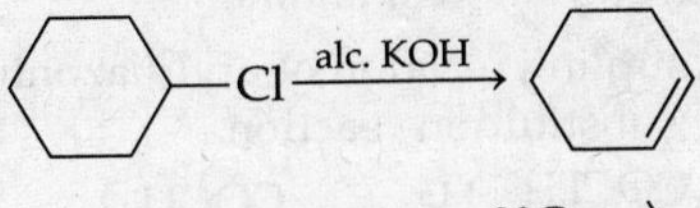 —Cl $\xrightarrow{\text{alc. KOH}}$

(d) 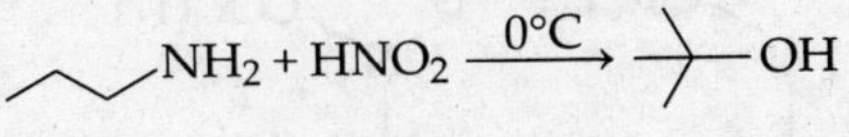 $NH_2 + HNO_2 \xrightarrow{0°C}$ —OH

Ans. *(a, c)*

(a)

$$\text{H}_2\text{C(H)(H)}{-}\text{Cl} + 2\text{NH}_3 \longrightarrow \text{H}_2\text{C(H)(H)}{-}\text{NH}_2 + \text{NH}_4\text{Cl}$$

1° alkylhalides → amine

This is an example of nucleophilic substitution reaction.

(c) Chloro cyclohexane $\xrightarrow{\text{alc. KOH}}$ Cyclohexene

This is an example of elimination reaction.

Mistake Alert! *Elimination reaction occurs by using alc.* KOH *reagent, whereas substitution reaction (of* $\bar{O}$H*) occurs by using aq.* KOH *reagent.*

Q.36 Under which of the following reaction conditions, aniline gives *p*-nitro derivative as the major product?

(a) Acetyl chloride/pyridine followed by reaction with conc. H_2SO_4 + conc. HNO_3.

(b) Acetic anhydride/pyridine followed by conc. H_2SO_4 + conc. HNO_3.

(c) Dil. HCl followed by reaction with conc. H_2SO_4 + conc. HNO_3.

(d) Reaction with conc. HNO_3 + conc. H_2SO_4.

Ans. *(a, b)* Aniline on reaction with acetyl chloride or acetic anhydride in the presence of pyridine produces N-acetyl aniline which is a *ortho, para* directing group, which on further reaction with nitrating mixture (conc. HNO_3 + conc. H_2SO_4) produces *p*-nitroaniline preferentially as shown below.

Aniline ($C_6H_5NH_2$) $\xrightarrow[\text{pyridine}]{CH_3COCl \text{ or } (CH_3CO)_2O}$ Acetanilide ($C_6H_5NHCOCH_3$) $\xrightarrow{\text{Conc. } HNO_3 + \text{Conc. } H_2SO_4}$ *p*-Nitroaniline (p-$O_2NC_6H_4NHCOCH_3$) (major) + o-isomer (minor)

Q.37 Which of the following reactions belong to electrophilic aromatic substitution?

(a) Bromination of acetanilide

(b) Coupling reaction of aryldiazonium salts

(c) Diazotisation of aniline

(d) Acylation of aniline

Ans. *(a, b)* Bromination of acetanilide and coupling reaction of aryldiazonium salts are associated with electrophilic aromatic substitution reaction.

$C_6H_5NHCOCH_3 \xrightarrow{Br^{\oplus}}$ p-$BrC_6H_4NHCOCH_3$ + o-$BrC_6H_4NHCOCH_3$

Coupling reaction of aryldiazonium salts

$$C_6H_5-\overset{\oplus}{N}\equiv N\overset{\ominus}{Cl} + C_6H_5-OH \longrightarrow C_6H_5-N=N-C_6H_4-OH + HCl$$

Benzenediazonium chroride

p-Hydroxyazobenzene (Orange)

Short Answer Type Questions

Q.38 What is the role of HNO_3 in the nitrating mixture used for nitration of benzene?

Ans. HNO_3 acts as a base in the nitrating mixture and provides the electrophile, NO_2^+ on reaction with H_2SO_4 as follows

$$\underset{\text{acts as a base}}{HNO_3} + \underset{\text{Acid}}{H_2SO_4} \longrightarrow \underset{\text{conjugate acid}}{H_2NO_3^+} + HSO_4^- \longrightarrow \underset{\text{Electrophile}}{NO_2^+} + HSO_4^- + H_2O$$

$$C_6H_6 \xrightarrow{NO_2^{\oplus}} C_6H_5NO_2$$

Q.39 Why is NH_2 group of aniline acetylated before carrying out nitration?

Ans. The NH_2 group is a strong electron-donating group, activating the aromatic ring towards electrophilic substitution. This increased reactivity often leads to multiple substitution at the ortho and para position, making it difficult to stop the reaction at the monosubstitution stage.

In order to check the activation of benzene ring by amino group, first it is acetylated with acetic anhydride or acetyl chloride in presence of pyridine to form acetanilide, which can be further nitrated easily by nitrating mixture.

$$C_6H_5NH_2 \xrightarrow[\text{Pyridine}]{(CH_3CO)_2O} C_6H_5NHCOCH_3 \xrightarrow[\text{Conc. } H_2SO_4 \text{ 228 k}]{\text{Conc. } HNO_3} p\text{-}O_2NC_6H_4NHCOCH_3 + o\text{-}O_2NC_6H_4NHCOCH_3$$

p-Nitroacetanilide (major product)

o-Nitroacetanilide (minor product)

Q.40 What is the product when $C_6H_5CH_2NH_2$ reacts with HNO_2?

Ans. $C_6H_5CH_2NH_2$ on reaction with HNO_2 produces $C_6H_5CH_2N_2^+Cl^-$ as follows

$$C_6H_5CH_2-NH_2 \xrightarrow{HNO_2} \underset{\text{Diazonium salt}}{C_6H_5CH_2-\overset{\oplus}{N}\equiv N\overset{\ominus}{Cl}} \xrightarrow{H_2O,\ \Delta} \underset{\text{Benzyl alochol}}{C_6H_5CH_2-OH} + N_2 + H_2O$$

Q.41 What is the best reagent to convert nitrile to primary amine?

Ans. Best reagent to convert nitrile to aniline is sodium/alcohol or $LiAlH_4$.

$$\underset{\text{Methylnitrile}}{CH_3—C\equiv N} \xrightarrow[\text{Na/alcohol}]{LiAlH_4} \underset{\text{Ethylamine}}{CH_3—CH_2—NH_2}$$

Q.42 Give the structure of '*A*' in the following reaction.

(4-methyl-2-nitroaniline: ring with CH_3, NO_2, NH_2) $\xrightarrow[\text{(ii) } H_3PO_2,\ H_2O]{\text{(i) } NaNO_2 + HCl,\ 273\text{-}278\ K}$ *A*

Thinking Process This problem is based on the concept of preparation of diazonium salt and its chemical properties.

Ans. Complete conversion can be shown as

2-Nitro-4 methyl aniline (CH_3, NO_2, NH_2) $\xrightarrow[\text{Diozotisation}]{NaNO_2 + HCl,\ 273\text{-}278\ K}$ (CH_3, NO_2, $\overset{+}{N_2}\overset{-}{Cl}$) $\xrightarrow{H_3PO_2,\ H_2O}$ 3-Methyl nitrobenzene (*A*) (CH_3, NO_2) $+ H_3PO_3 + HCl + N_2$

Q.43 What is Hinsberg reagent?

Ans. Benzene sulphonyl chloride ($C_6H_5SO_2Cl$) is known as Hinsberg reagent. It is used to distinguish between primary, secondary and tertiary amine.

Q.44 Why is benzene diazonium chloride not stored and is used immediately after its preparation?

Ans. Benzene diazonium chloride is very unstable. Due to its instability, it is used immediately after its preparation.

Q.45 Why does acylation of $—NH_2$ group of aniline reduce its activating effect?

Ans. Acylation of $—NH_2$ group of aniline reduces its activity due to resonance of lone pair of nitrogen towards the carbonyl group, hence $o - p^{-}$ – directive influence of amino group get less effective.

$$C_6H_5NH_2 \xrightarrow[\text{Pyridine}]{RCOCl} C_6H_5NHCOR$$

The resonating structures of acylated product of aniline are

$$\left[C_6H_5-\ddot{N}H-C(=O)-R \longleftrightarrow C_6H_5-\overset{\oplus}{N}H=C(-O^{\ominus})-R \right]$$

Q.46 Explain why $MeNH_2$ is stronger base than MeOH?

Ans. Basicity of $MeNH_2$ and MeOH can be explained on the basis of electronegativity of N and O atom. $MeNH_2$ is a stronger base than MeOH. Because of low electronegativity value of N, it is easy for nitrogen to loose its lone pair readily as compared to MeOH.

Q.47 What is the role of pyridine in the acylation reaction of amines?

Ans. Pyridine being a base, is used to remove the side product *i.e.*, HCl from reaction mixture.

$$C_6H_5NH_2 \xrightarrow[\text{pyridine}]{CH_3COCl} C_6H_5NHCOCH_3 + HCl,$$

$$C_5H_5N + HCl \longrightarrow C_5H_5\overset{\oplus}{N}H\,Cl^-$$

Q.48 Under what reaction condition (acidic, basic) the coupling reaction of aryl diazonium chloride with aniline is carried out?

Ans. In strongly basic conditions, benzenediazonium chloride is converted into diazohydroxide and diazoate, both of which are not electrophilic and do not couple with aniline.

$$C_6H_5\overset{+}{N}\equiv N\overset{-}{Cl} + OH \longrightarrow \underset{\text{Diazohydroxide}}{C_6H_5-N=N-OH} \overset{NaOH}{\rightleftharpoons} \underset{\text{Sodium diazoate}}{C_6H_5-N=N-\overset{-}{O}Na^+}$$

Similarly, in highly acidic conditions, aniline gets converted into anilinium ion. As a result, aniline is no longer nucleophilic and hence will not couple with diazonium chloride. Hence, the reaction is carried out under mild acidic conditions, *i.e.*, pH′= 4 − 5

$$\underset{\text{Aniline}}{C_6H_5NH_2} + H^+ \rightarrow \underset{\substack{\text{Anilinium ion}\\\text{(coupling do not occur)}}}{C_6H_5-\overset{+}{N}H_3}$$

Q.49 Predict the product of reaction of aniline with bromine in non-polar solvent such as CS_2.

Ans. Aniline on reaction with Br_2 in non-polar solvent CS_2 produces 2, 4, 6 tribromo aniline.

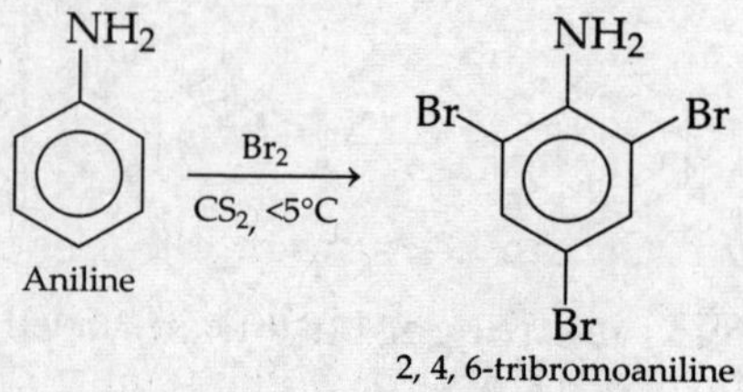

NH_2 — Br_2 / CS_2, <5°C → NH_2, Br, Br, Br

Aniline

2, 4, 6-tribromoaniline

Aniline has high reactivity towards bromine as it gives the *tri* substituted product.

Q.50 Arrange the following compounds in increasing order of dipole moment.

$$CH_3CH_2CH_3, CH_3CH_2NH_2, CH_3CH_2OH$$

Ans. Dipole moment of amine, alcohol and hydrocarbon can be explained on the basis of bond polarity of C—H, N—H and O—H bond. As the bond polarity increases, dipole moment increases. The correct order of increasing dipole moment is :

$$CH_3CH_2CH_3 < CH_3CH_2NH_2 < CH_3CH_2OH$$

Q.51 What is the structure and IUPAC name of the compound, allyl amine?

Ans. Structural formula of allyl amine is as follows

$$\overset{3}{C}H_2 = \overset{2}{C}H - \overset{1}{C}H_2 - NH_2$$

Prop-2-ene-1-amine (IUPAC name)

Q.52 Write down the IUPAC name of

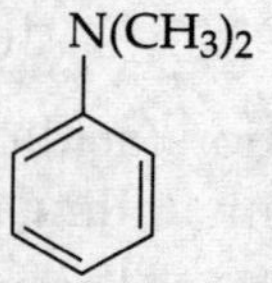

$N(CH_3)_2$

Ans.

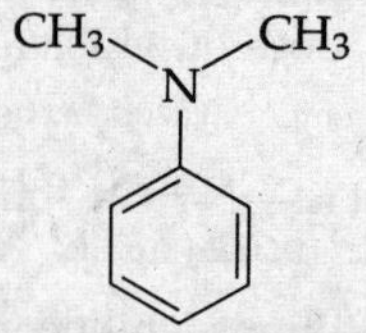

CH_3, CH_3, N

N, N-dimethylbenzenamine

Q.53 A compound Z with molecular formula C_3H_9N reacts with $C_6H_5SO_2Cl$ to give a solid, insoluble in alkali. Identify Z.

Thinking Process This process is based on concept of Hinsberg's is test. Only amine containing replaceable H gives Hinsberg's is test.

Ans. $Z(C_3H_9N)$ is an aliphatic amine. On reaction with $C_6H_5SO_2Cl$ (Hinsberg's reagent), it gives a product insoluble in alkali. It means that the product does not have a replaceable H-atom attached to the N- atom. So, compound Z is a secondary amine (ethylmethylamine).

$$\underset{\substack{\text{Ethymethylamine}\\ [Z = C_3H_9N]}}{CH_3-\underset{\underset{C_2H_5}{|}}{NH}} + C_6H_5SO_2Cl \longrightarrow \underset{\substack{\text{N-ethyl-N-methyl}\\ \text{benzene sulphonamide}\\ \text{(Insoluble in alkali)}}}{CH_3-\underset{\underset{C_2H_5}{|}}{N}-SO_2C_6H_5}$$

Q.54 A primary amine, RNH_2 can be reacted with $CH_3—X$ to get secondary amine, $R—NHCH_3$ but the only disadvantage is that 3° amine and quaternary ammonium salts are also obtained as side products. Can you suggest a method where RNH_2 forms only 2° amine?

Ans.

$$\underset{\text{Primary amine}}{RNH_2} \xrightarrow[\text{Carbylamine reaction}]{KOH/CHCl_3} \underset{\text{Alkyl Iso cyanide}}{RNC} \xrightarrow{H_2\,/\,Pd} \underset{\text{Secondary amine}}{RNHCH_3}$$

Primary amines show carbylamine reaction in which two H-atoms attached to N-atoms of NH_2 are replaced by one C-atom. On catalytic reduction, isocyanide (formed) produces secondary amine and not tertiary or quaternary salts.

Q.55 Complete the following reaction.

$$C_6H_5OH \xrightarrow[\bar{O}H]{Ar\overset{+}{N}_2Cl^-}$$

Ans. The reaction exhibits azo-coupling reaction of phenols. Benzene diazonium chloride reacts with phenol in such a manner that the *para* position of phenol is coupled with diazonium salt to form *p*-hydroxyazobenzene.

$$\underset{\substack{\text{Benzene diazonium chloride}\\ (Ar\overset{+}{N}_2\overset{-}{Cl})}}{C_6H_5-\overset{+}{N}\equiv NCl^-} + \underset{\text{Phenol}}{H-C_6H_4-OH} \xrightarrow{OH^-} \underset{\substack{\text{p-hydroxyazobenzene}\\ \text{(Orange dye)}}}{C_6H_5-N=N-C_6H_4-OH} + H_2O + Cl^-$$

Q.56 Why is aniline soluble in aqueous HCl?

Ans. Aniline is soluble in aqueous HCl due to formation of ionic anilinium chloride.

$$\underset{\substack{\text{Aniline}\\ \text{(colourless liquid,}\\ \text{insoluble in water)}}}{C_6H_5NH_2} \xrightarrow{HCl\,(aq)} \underset{\substack{\text{Anilinium chloride}\\ \text{(soluble in water)}}}{C_6H_5\overset{\oplus}{N}H_3Cl^{\ominus}}$$

Q.57 Suggest a route by which the following conversion can be accomplished.

Cyclohexyl–$CONH_2$ ⟶ Cyclohexyl–$NH—CH_3$

Ans. Complete conversion can be performed as

Cyclohexyl–$CONH_2$ (Cyclohexyl amide) $\xrightarrow[\text{Hoffmann bromamide reaction}]{Br_2/KOH}$ Cyclohexyl–NH_2 (Cyclohexyl amine) $\xrightarrow[\text{Carbylamine reactioin}]{CHCl_3/KOH}$ Cyclohexyl–$\overset{+}{N}\equiv\overset{-}{C}$ (Cyclohexyl isocyanide) $\xrightarrow{H_2/Pd}$ Cyclohexyl–$NH—CH_3$ (Cyclohexyl methyl amine)

Q.58 Identify *A* and *B* in the following reaction.

2-(2-chloroethyl)cyclohexan-1-one (ring C=O, side chain CH_2CH_2Cl) $\xrightarrow{KCN}$ A $\xrightarrow{H_2/Pd}$ B

Ans. Complete conversion can be performed as :

2-(2-chloroethyl)cyclohexanone (–CH_2CH_2Cl) $\xrightarrow[\text{(Nucleophilic substitution)}]{KCN}$ 2-oxocyclohexyl–CH_2CH_2CN (*A*) $\xrightarrow[\text{(Catalytic hydrogenation)}]{H_2/Pd}$ 2-oxocyclohexyl–CH_2CH_2–$CH_2—NH_2$ (*B*)

Hence, *A* = 2-oxocyclohexyl–CH_2CH_2CN
3-(2-oxocyclohexyl) propanenitrile

B = 2-oxocyclohexyl–$CH_2CH_2CH_2NH_2$
2-(3-aminopropyl) -cyclohex-1-one

Q.59 How will you carry out the following conversions?

(i) Toluene $\longrightarrow$ *p*-toluidine

(ii) *p*-toluidine diazonium chloride $\longrightarrow$ *p*-toluic acid

Ans. (i) Conversion of toluene to *p*-toluidine can be done as :

$$\text{Toluene } (C_6H_5CH_3) \xrightarrow{HNO_3/H_2SO_4} \text{4-Methylnitrobenzene } (CH_3C_6H_4NO_2) \xrightarrow[\text{[H]}]{Fe/HCl} p\text{-toluidine } (CH_3C_6H_4NH_2)$$

(ii) Conversion of *p*-toluidine diazonium chloride to *p*-toluic acid can be done as :

$$p\text{-toluidine diazonium chloride } (CH_3C_6H_4\overset{+}{N}\equiv N\overset{-}{Cl}) \xrightarrow{CuCN} CH_3C_6H_4CN \xrightarrow{H_2O/H^+} p\text{-tolulic acid } (CH_3C_6H_4COOH)$$

Q.60 Write following conversions

(i) Nitrobenzene $\longrightarrow$ Acetanilide

(ii) Acetanilide $\longrightarrow$ *p*-nitroaniline

Ans. **(i)** Nitrobenzene can be converted into acetanilide as follows

$$\text{Nitrobenzene } (C_6H_5NO_2) \xrightarrow[\text{(Reduction)}]{Sn/HCl} C_6H_5NH_2 \xrightarrow[\text{(Acetylation)}]{CH_3COCl,\ \text{pyridine}} \text{Acetanilide } (C_6H_5NHCOCH_3)$$

(ii) Acetanilide can be converted into *p* - nitroaniline as follows

$$\text{Acetanilide } (C_6H_5NHCOCH_3) \xrightarrow[\text{288 K (Nitration)}]{\text{conc } HNO_3 + \text{conc } H_2SO_4} p\text{-Nitroacetanilide } (NO_2C_6H_4NHCOCH_3) \xrightarrow{\overline{O}H \text{ or } H_3O^+} p\text{-Nitroaniline (major product) } (NO_2C_6H_4NH_2)$$

Q.61 A solution contains 1 g mol. each of *p*-toluene diazonium chloride and *p*-nitrophenyl diazonium chloride. To this 1 g mol. of alkaline solution of phenol is added. Predict the major product. Explain your answer.

Thinking Process This problem is based upon conceptual mixing of electrophilicity of ring system and diazo-coupling reaction.

Ans. The above stated reaction is an example of electrophilic aromatic substitution. In alkaline medium, phenol generates phenoxide ion which is more electron rich than phenol and more reactive for electrophilic attack.

The electrophile in this reaction is aryldiazonium cation. As we know, stronger the electrophile faster is the reaction. *p*-nitrophenyldiazonium cation is a stronger electrophile than *p*-toluene diazonium cation.

So, nitrophenyl diazonium chloride couples preferentially with phenol.

$O_2N-C_6H_4-\overset{+}{N_2}\overset{-}{Cl}$ + $CH_3-C_6H_4-\overset{+}{N_2}\overset{-}{Cl}$ $\xrightarrow[\text{(NaOH)}]{C_6H_5OH}$ $O_2N-C_6H_4-N=N-C_6H_4-OH$

(Major product)

Q.62 How will you bring out the following conversion?

p-Nitroaniline ⟶ 3, 4, 5-Tribromonitrobenzene

Thinking Process This problem includes conceptual mixing of bromination, nitration and Sandmeyer's reaction. Bromination of *p*-nitroaniline followed by diazotisation and Sandmeyer's reaction.

Ans. Complete conversion of above reaction can be shown as :

p-nitroaniline $\xrightarrow{Br_2/CH_3COOH}$ 2,6-dibromo-4-nitroaniline $\xrightarrow[273\text{-}278\ K]{NaNO_2/HCl}$ 2,6-dibromo-4-nitrobenzenediazonium chloride ($\overset{+}{N_2}Cl^-$) $\xrightarrow{Cu_2Br_2/HBr}$ 3, 4, 5-tribromonitrobenzene

Q.63 How will you carry out the following conversion?

NO_2

→

NH_2

Ans. Conversion of benzene to *p*-nitroaniline can be done as :

Benzene $\xrightarrow[\text{conc. } H_2SO_4]{\text{conc. } HNO_3 +}$ $C_6H_5NO_2$ $\xrightarrow{\text{Sn/HCl}}$ $C_6H_5NH_2$ $\xrightarrow[\text{Pyridine}]{(CH_3CO_2)_2O}$ $C_6H_5NHCOCH_3$ $\xrightarrow[\text{conc. } H_2SO_4]{\text{conc. } HNO_3 +}$ $p\text{-}NO_2C_6H_4NHCOCH_3$ $\xrightarrow{H_2O/H^+}$ $p\text{-}NO_2C_6H_4NH_2$

p-nitroaniline

Q.64 How will you carry out the following conversion?

NH_2 → NO_2, Br

Ans. Conversion of aniline to *m*-bromonitrobenzene can be completed as :

Aniline (NH_2) $\xrightarrow[273\text{-}278 \text{ K}]{HNO_2}$ $N_2^+Cl^-$ (Benzene diazonium chloride) $\xrightarrow{HBF_4}$ $N_2^+BF_4^-$ (Benzene diazonium tetrafuoroborate) $\xrightarrow[\text{Cu, }\Delta]{NaNO_2}$ NO_2 (Nitrobenzene) $\xrightarrow{Br_2/CH_3COOH}$ NO_2, Br

m-Bromonitrobenzene

Q.65 How will you carry out the following conversions?

(i) NH_2 → NO_2, Br, Br

(ii) NH_2 → NO_2, Br, Br, I

Ans. (i) Conversion of aniline to 3, 5-dibromonitrobenzene can be completed as

Aniline (NH_2) $\xrightarrow[\text{pyridine}]{(CH_3CO_2)_2O}$ Acetanilide ($NHCOCH_3$) $\xrightarrow[\text{conc. } H_2SO_4]{\text{conc. } HNO_3}$ *p*-Nitroacetanilide ($NHCOCH_3$, NO_2) $\xrightarrow{H_2O/H^+}$ *p*-Nitroaniline (NH_2, NO_2)

p-Nitroaniline $\xrightarrow{Br_2/CH_3COOH}$ 2,6-dibromo-4-nitroaniline (NH_2, Br, Br, NO_2) $\xrightarrow[273\text{-}278\text{ K}]{HNO_2}$ ($\overset{+}{N_2}Cl^-$, Br, Br, NO_2) $\xrightarrow{H_3PO_2}$ 3,5-Dibromonitrobenzene (Br, Br, NO_2)

(ii) Conversion (*A*) given below is same as in part (i) given above after that reaction (*B*) can be carried out.

(A) (NH_2) $\longrightarrow$ ($\overset{+}{N_2}Cl^-$, Br, Br, NO_2) $\xrightarrow{KI}$ (I, Br, Br, NO_2)

Matching The Columns

Q.66 Match the reactions given in Column I with the statements given in Column II.

	Column I		Column II
A.	Ammonolysis	1.	Amine with lesser number of carbon atoms
B.	Gabriel phthalimide synthesis	2.	Detection test for primary amines.
C.	Hoffmann bromamide reaction	3.	Reaction of phthalimide with KOH and $R-X$
D.	Carbylamine reaction	4.	Reaction of alkylhalides with NH_3

Ans. A. → (4) B. → (3) C. → (1) D. → (2)

	Reaction	Statements
A.	Ammonolysis	Reaction of alkylhalide with NH_3 $R-X \xrightarrow{NH_3} RNH_2 + HCl$.
B.	Gabriel phthalimide synthesis	Reaction of phthalimide with KOH and $R-X$. Phthalimide $\xrightarrow[R-X]{KOH}$ $C_6H_4(CO\ddot{O}K^+)_2 + RNH_2$
C.	Hoffmann bromamide reaction	Amine with lesser number of carbon atoms. $RCONH_2 \xrightarrow{NaOX} RNH_2$
D.	Carbylamine reaction	Detection test of primary amines.

Q.67 Match the compounds given in Column I with the items given in Column II.

	Column I		Column II
A.	Benzene sulphonyl chloride	1.	Zwitter ion
B.	Sulphanilic acid	2.	Hinsberg reagent
C.	Alkyl diazonium salts	3.	Dyes
D.	Aryl diazonium salts	4.	Conversion to alcohols

Ans. A. → (2) B. → (1) C. → (4) D. → (3)

	Compounds	Items
A.	Benzene sulphonyl chloride	Hinsberg reagent $C_6H_5-SO_2Cl$
B.	Sulphanilic acid	Zwitter ion (dipolar ion) $\overset{\oplus}{N}H_3-C_6H_4-SO_3^{\ominus}$
C.	Alkyl diazonium salts	Conversion to alcohols $R-N_2^+X^- \xrightarrow{H_2O} ROH$
D.	Aryl diazonium salts	Dyes

Assertion and Reason

In the following questions a statement of Assertion followed by a statement of Reason is given. Choose the correct answer out of the following choices.

(a) Both assertion and reason are wrong.

(b) Both assertion and reason are correct statements but reason is not correct explanation of assertion.

(c) Assertion is correct statement but reason is wrong statement.

(d) Both assertion and reason are correct statements and reason is correct explanation of assertion.

(e) Assertion is wrong statement but reason is correct statement.

Q.68 **Assertion** Acylation of amines gives a monosubstituted product whereas alkylation of amines gives polysubstituted product.

Reason Acyl group sterically hinders the approach of further acyl groups.

Ans. *(c)* Assertion is correct statement but reason is wrong statement.

Acylation of amine gives a monosubstituted product whereas alkylation of amine gives polysubstituted product because acylation in amine takes place at N-atom and alkylation takes place at *o* and *p* positions.

Q.69 **Assertion** Hoffmann's bromamide reaction is given by primary amines.

Reason Primary amines are more basic than secondary amines.

Ans. *(a)* Both assertion and reason are wrong.

Correct Assertion Hoffmann's bromamide reaction is given by amides.

Correct Reason Amide on reaction with NaOX produces amine having one carbon less than amide.

Note Secondary amines are more basic than primary amines.

Q.70 **Assertion** N-ethylbenzene sulphonamide is soluble in alkali.

Reason Hydrogen attached to nitrogen in sulphonamide is strongly acidic.

Ans. *(d)* Both assertion and reason are correct and reason is the correct explanation of assertion.

N-ethylbenzene sulphonamide is soluble in alkali because hydrogen attached to nitrogen in sulphonamide is strongly acidic and forms a salt during reaction between these two.

Q.71 **Assertion** N, N-diethylbenzene sulphonamide is insoluble in alkali.

Reason Sulphonyl group attached to nitrogen atom is strong electron withdrawing group.

Ans. *(b)* Both assertion and reason are correct but reason is not the correct explanation of assertion.

N, N-diethylbenzene sulphonamide is insoluble in alkali due to absence of acidic H attached to nitrogen.

Q.72 **Assertion** Only a small amount of HCl is required in the reduction of nitro compounds with iron scrap and HCl in the presence of steam.
Reason (R) $FeCl_2$ formed gets hydrolysed to release HCl during the reaction.

Ans. *(d)* Assertion and reason both are correct and reason is the correct explanation of assertion.

Only small amount of HCl is required in the reduction of nitro compounds with iron scrap and HCl in the presence of steam because $FeCl_2$ formed gets hydrolysed to release HCl during the reaction.

Q.73 **Assertion** Aromatic 1° amines can be prepared by Gabriel phthalimide synthesis.
Reason Aryl halides undergo nucleophilic substitution with anion formed by phthalimide.

Ans. *(a)* Both assertion and reason are wrong. Aryl 1° amine cannot be prepared by Gabriel phthalimide reaction because aryl halide do not undergo nucleophilic substitution with anion formed by phthalimide.

Q.74 **Assertion** Acetanilide is less basic than aniline.
Reason Acetylation of aniline results in decrease of electron density on nitrogen.

Ans. *(d)* Assertion and reason both are correct and reason is the correct explanation of assertion.

Acetanilide is less basic than aniline because acetylation of aniline results in decrease of electron density on nitrogen.

Long Answer Type Questions

Q.75 A hydrocarbon 'A' (C_4H_8) on reaction with HCl gives a compound 'B,' (C_4H_9Cl), which on reaction with 1 mol of NH_3 gives compound 'C,' ($C_4H_{11}N$). On reacting with $NaNO_2$ and HCl followed by treatment with water, compound 'C' yields an optically active alcohol, 'D'. Ozonolysis of 'A' gives 2 mols of acetaldehyde. Identify compounds 'A' to 'D'. Explain the reactions involved.

Thinking Process This problem includes conceptual mixing of ozonolysis, optical activity, ammonolysis and diazotisation. Follow the steps to solve the problem. Analyse the overall reaction once then sequentially predict a molecule for each A,B,C and D on the basis of information provided in the question.
Fit every molecule in a flow chart made by using information provided in the question and reach to the correct compounds.

Ans. (i) Addition of HCl to compound 'A' shows that compound 'A' is alkene. Compound 'B' is C_4H_9Cl.

(ii) Compound 'B' reacts with NH_3 it forms amine 'C'.

$$\underset{[A]}{C_4H_8} \xrightarrow{HCl} \underset{[B]}{C_4H_9Cl} \xrightarrow{NH_3} \underset{[C]}{C_4H_{11}N \text{ or } C_4H_9NH_2}$$

(iii) 'C' gives diazonium salt with $NaNO_2$ / HCl, which yields an optically active alcohol. So, 'C' is aliphatic amine.

(iv) 'A' on ozonolysis produces 2 moles of CH_3CHO. So, 'A' is $CH_3-CH=CH-CH_3$ (But-2-ene).

Reactions

(i) $\overset{4}{C}H_3-\overset{3}{C}H=\overset{2}{C}H-\overset{1}{C}H_3 \xrightarrow{HCl} \overset{4}{C}H_3-\overset{3}{C}H_2-\overset{2}{C}H(Cl)-\overset{1}{C}H_3$

But-2-ene [A] [C_4H_8] → 2-chorobutane [B] [C_4H_9Cl]

(ii) $CH_3-CH_2-CH(Cl)-CH_3 \xrightarrow{NH_3} CH_3-CH_2-CH(NH_2)-CH_3$

2-chlorobutane [A] → 2-Aminobutane [C] [$C_4H_{11}N$]

(iii) $CH_3-CH_2-CH(NH_2)-CH_3 \xrightarrow[H_2O]{NaNO_2\ /\ HCl} \overset{1}{C}H_3-\overset{2}{C}(H)(OH)-\overset{3}{C}H_2-\overset{4}{C}H_3$

2-Aminobutane [C] [$C_4H_{11}N$] → Butan-2-ol [D] (Optically active)

(iv) $CH_3-CH=CH-CH_3 + O_3 \longrightarrow CH_3-CH\overset{O}{\frown}CH-CH_3$ (with O—O bridge)

But-2-ene [A] → Ozonide

$\xrightarrow{Zn+H_2O} CH_3CHO + CH_3CHO$

2 moles of acetaldehyde

Q.76 A colourless substance 'A' (C_6H_7N) is sparingly soluble in water and gives a water soluble compound 'B' on treating with mineral acid. On reacting with $CHCl_3$ and alcoholic potash 'A' produces an obnoxious smell due to the formation of compound 'C'. Reaction of 'A' with benzenesulphonyl chloride gives compound 'D' which is soluble in alkali. With $NaNO_2$ and HCl, 'A' forms compound 'E' which reacts with phenol in alkaline medium to give an orange dye 'F'. Identify compounds 'A' to 'F'.

Thinking Process This problem is based on chemical properties of aniline and property and solubility of their derivatives.

Ans.

(i) Aniline $[C_6H_7N]$ [*A*] + HCl → Anilinium chloride ($C_6H_5NH_3^+Cl^-$) [*B*]

(ii) Aniline [*A*] + $CHCl_3$ + KOH $\xrightarrow[\text{reaction}]{\text{Carbylamine}}$ Benzene isonitrile (C_6H_5NC) [C] + 3KCl + $3H_2O$

(iii) Aniline [*A*] + Benzene sulphonyl chloride ($C_6H_5SO_2Cl$) $\xrightarrow{-HCl}$ N-phenylbenzene sulphonamide ($C_6H_5NH—SO_2—C_6H_5$) (Soluble in alkali)

(iv) Aniline [*A*] $\xrightarrow[\text{273-278 K}]{NaNO_2/HCl}$ Benzene diazonium chloride ($C_6H_5N_2^+Cl^-$) [*E*] $\xrightarrow[OH^-]{C_6H_5OH}$ *p*-Hydroxyazobenzene ($C_6H_5—N{=}N—C_6H_4—OH$) (Orange dye) [*F*]

Q.77 Predict the reagent or the product in the following reaction sequence.

p-Nitrotoluene (CH_3, NO_2) $\xrightarrow{1}$ p-Toluidine (CH_3, NH_2) $\xrightarrow[\text{Pyridine}]{(CH_3CO_2)_2O}$ (CH_3, $NHCOCH_3$) $\xrightarrow[H_2SO_4]{HNO_3}$ 2 $\xrightarrow{3}$ (CH_3, NO_2, NH_2) $\xrightarrow{NaNO_2/HCl}$ 4 $\xrightarrow{5}$ m-Nitrotoluene (CH_3, NO_2)

Ans. Correct sequence can be represented as follows, including all reagents.

$$\underset{\text{(p-nitrotoluene)}}{CH_3C_6H_4NO_2} \xrightarrow[(1)]{Sn/HCl} CH_3C_6H_4NH_2 \xrightarrow[\text{pyridine}]{(CH_3CO)_2O} CH_3C_6H_4NHCOCH_3 \xrightarrow[H_2SO_4]{HNO_3} \underset{(2)}{CH_3C_6H_3(NO_2)NHCOCH_3}$$

$$\xrightarrow[(3)]{H_2O/H^+} CH_3C_6H_3(NO_2)NH_2 \xrightarrow[\text{Diazotisation}]{NaNO_2/HCl} \underset{(4)}{CH_3C_6H_3(NO_2)N_2^+Cl^-} \xrightarrow[(5)]{H_3PO_2/H_2O} CH_3C_6H_4NO_2 \text{ (m-nitrotoluene)}$$

Hence,

(i) 1 = Sn/HCl

(ii) 2 = $CH_3C_6H_3(NO_2)NHCOCH_3$ (4-methyl-2-nitroacetanilide: CH_3 at top, NO_2 meta to CH_3, $NHCOCH_3$ para to CH_3)

(iii) 3 = H_2/H^+

(iv) 4 = $CH_3C_6H_4N_2^+Cl^-$ (CH_3 and $\overset{+}{N_2}\bar{Cl}$ para)

(v) 5 = H_3PO_2/H_2O

Chapter

14 Biomolecules

Multiple Choice Questions (MCQs)

Q.1 Glycogen is a branched chain polymer of α-*D* glucose units in which chain is formed by $C_1 - C_4$ glycosidic linkage whereas branching occurs by the formation of $C_1 - C_6$ glycosidic linkage. Structure of glycogen is similar to ....

(a) amylose (b) amylopectin (c) cellulose (d) glucose

Ans. ***(b)*** Structure of glycogen is similar to a amylopectin. Glycogen is a branched chain polymer of α-D glucose units in which chain is formed by $C_1 - C_4$ glycosidic linkage whereas branching occurs by the formation of $C_1 - C_6$ glycosidic linkage. Structure of glycogen can be shown as

Structure of amylopectin

Glycogen is also known as animal starch and it is present in liver, muscles and brain.

Q.2 Which of the following polymer is stored in the liver of animals?

(a) Amylose (b) Cellulose
(c) Amylopectin (d) Glycogen

Ans. ***(d)*** Glycogen is a polymer of α-*D* glucose stored in the liver, brain and muscles of animals. It is also known as animal starch.

Q.3 Sucrose (cane sugar) is a disaccharide. One molecule of sucrose on hydrolysis gives ....

(a) 2 molecules of glucose
(b) 2 molecules of glucose + 1 molecule of fructose
(c) 1 molecule of glucose +1 molecule of fructose
(d) 2 molecules of fructose

Ans. *(c)* Sucrose (cane sugar) is a disaccharide. One molecule of sucrose on hydrolysis gives one molecule of glucose and one molecule of fructose.

$$\underset{\text{Cane sugar}}{C_{12}H_{22}O_{11}} \xrightarrow[H^+]{H_2O} \underset{\text{D (+) glucose}}{C_6H_{12}O_6} + \underset{\text{D (–) fructose}}{C_6H_{12}O_6}$$

Note Sucrose is a dextro-rotatory sugar, which on hydrolysis produces a laevorotatory mixture so, it is known as invert sugar. Sucrose is a non-reducing sugar while maltose and lactose are reducing sugars.

Q.4 Which of the following pairs represents anomers?

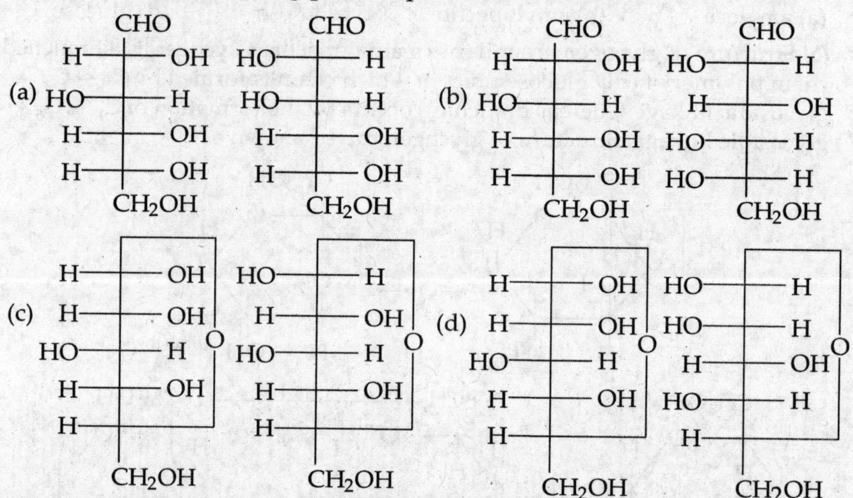

Thinking Process This problem is based on the concept of anomers. Saccharides which differ in configuration at C_1 are known as anomers.

Ans. *(c)* Anomers have different configuration at C_1. If —OH is present at right side of anomeric carbon, then it is known as α- form and if –OH is present at left side of anomeric carbon, then it is known as β- form.

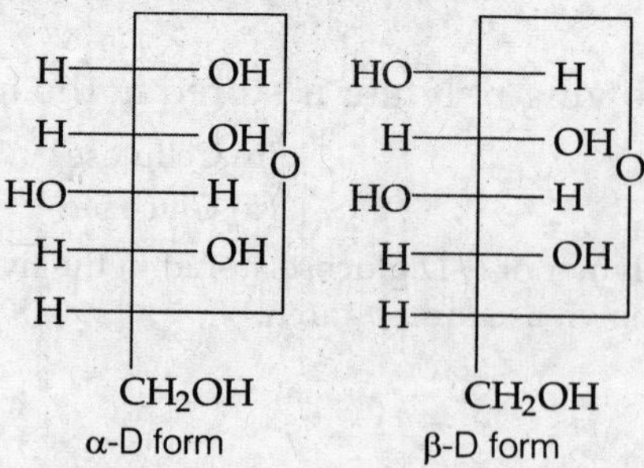

α-D form β-D form

Q.5 Proteins are found to have two different types of secondary structures *viz.* α-helix and β-pleated sheet structure. α-helix structure of protein is stabilised by :

(a) peptide bonds (b) van der Waals forces

(c) hydrogen bonds (d) dipole-dipole interactions

Ans. *(c)* In α- helix structure, a polypeptide chain forms all possible hydrogen bonds by twisting into a right handed screw with $-NH$ group of each amino acid residue hydrogen bonded to the $>C=O$ of an adjacent turn of the helix.

Q.6 In disaccharides, if the reducing groups of monosaccharides, *i.e.*, aldehydic or ketonic groups are bonded, these are non-reducing sugars. Which of the following disaccharide is a non-reducing sugar?

(a)

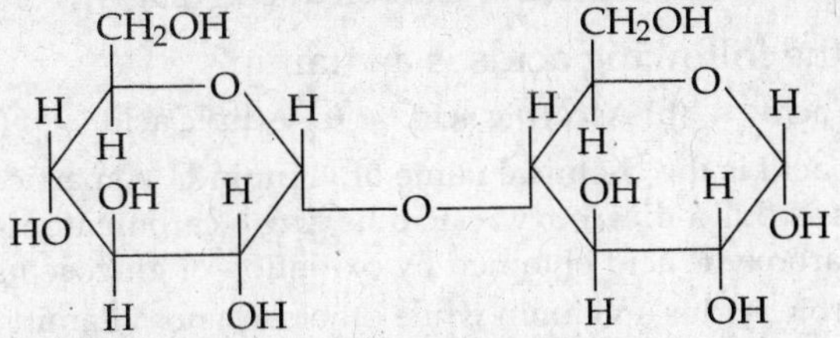

(b)

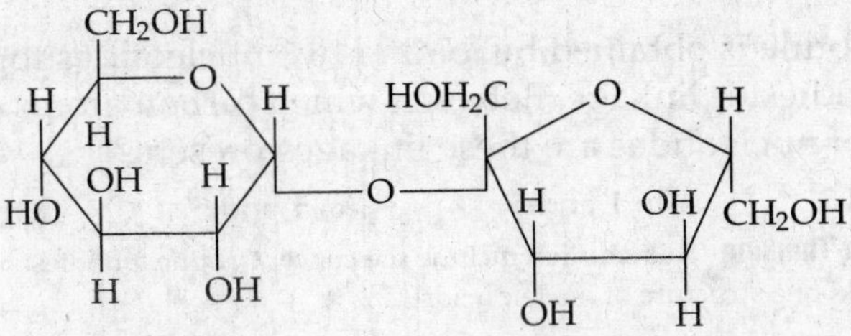

(c)

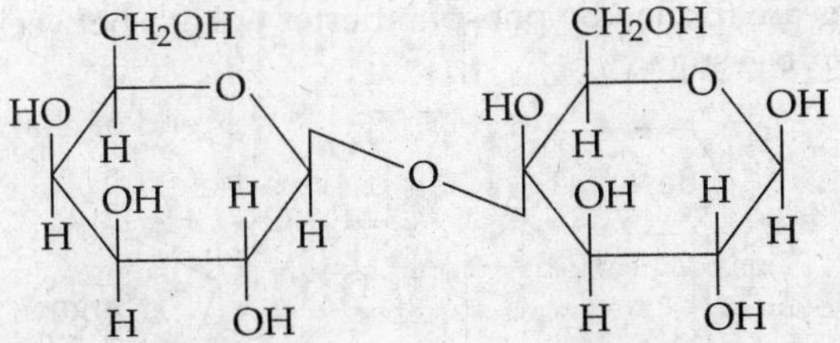

(d)

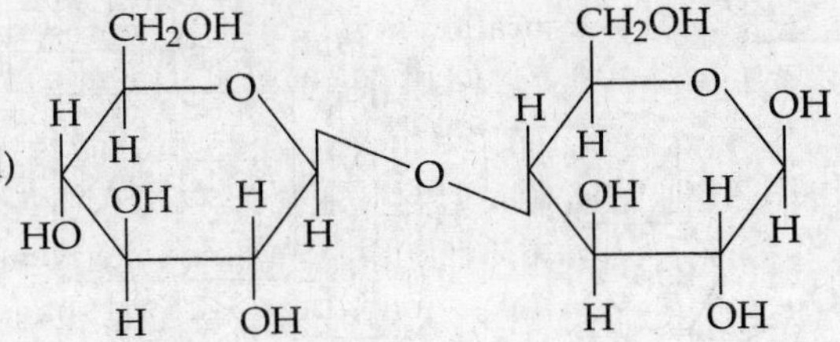

Ans. ***(b)***

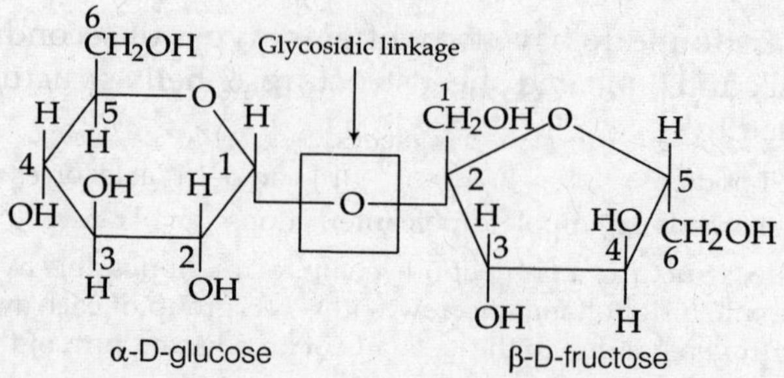

This structure represents sucrose in which α -D glucose and β-D- fructose is attached to each other by C_1—C_2 glycosidic linkage.

Since, reducing groups of glucose and fructose are involved in glycosidic bond formation, thus it is considered as a non-reducing sugar.

Q.7 Which of the following acids is a vitamin?

(a) Aspartic acid (b) Ascorbic acid (c) Adipic acid (d) Saccharic acid

Ans. ***(b)*** Ascorbic acid is the chemical name of vitamin C. Aspartic acid is an amino acid. Adipic acid is a dicarboxylic acid having 6 carbon atoms in chain. Saccharic acid is a dicarboxylic acid obtained by oxidation of glucose using HNO_3. Hence, ascorbic acid is a vitamin while others are not vitamins.

Q.8 Dinucleotide is obtained by joining two nucleotides together by phosphodiester linkage. Between which carbon atoms of pentose sugars of nucleotides are these linkages present?

(a) 5′ and 3′ (b) 1′ and 5′ (c) 5′ and 5′ (d) 3′ and 3′

- **Concept Thinking** This solution include the concept of phosphodiester linkage, which is the backbone structure of nucleic acids.

Ans. ***(a)*** Dinucleotides are formed by phosphodiester linkage between 5′ and 3′ carbon atoms of the pentose sugar.

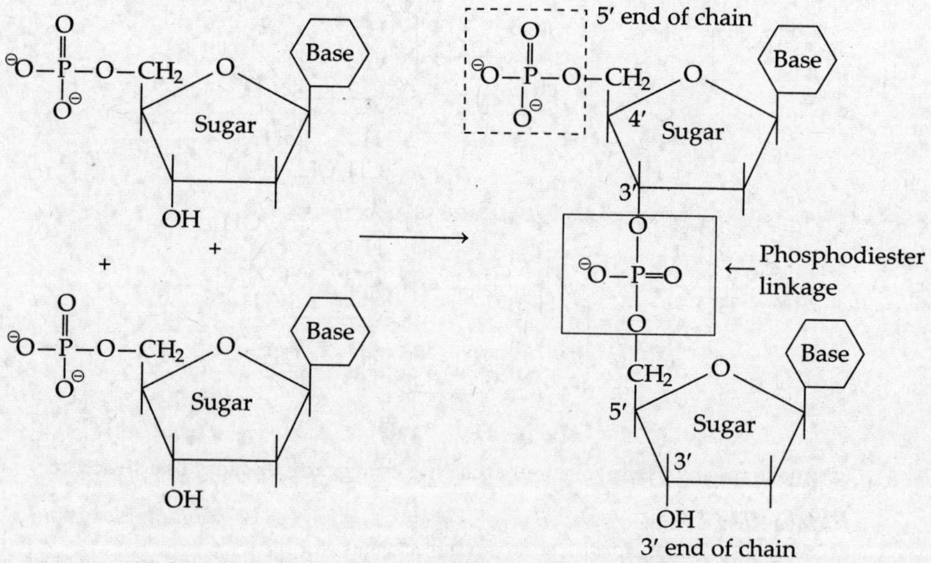

Q.9 Nucleic acids are the polymers of

(a) nucleosides (b) nucleotides (c) bases (d) sugars

Ans. ***(b)*** Nucleic acids are polymer of nucleotides in which nucleic acids are linked together by phosphodiester linkage.

Base Base Base

—Sugar—phoshate—(sugar—phosphate)$_n$—sugar—

e.g., DNA, RNA, etc.

Q.10 Which of the following statements is **not** true about glucose?

(a) It is an aldohexose.

(b) On heating with HI it forms *n*-hexane.

(c) It is present in furanose form.

(d) It does not give 2, 4- DNP test.

Ans. ***(c)*** Glucose is a aldohexose having structural formula :

CHO
H—C—OH
HO—C—H
H—C—OH
H—C—OH
CH_2OH

Glucose on heating with HI produces *n*-hexane.

$$C_6H_{12}O_6 \xrightarrow[\Delta]{HI} C_6H_{14}$$

Glucose does not give 2,4-DNP test due to its existence as cyclic structure shown below :

H—C—OH
H—C—OH
HO—C—H O
H—C—OH
H—C
CH_2OH

It is present in pyranose form, as shown below :

CH_2OH
O
HO H
H
HO H
H OH
H OH

Pyranose means pyran (6-membered ring containing oxygen) like structure.

Mistake Alert ! *Students may be confused about option (c), as glucose predominantly exists in the pyranose form, not the furanose form.*

Q.11 Each polypeptide in a protein has amino acids linked with each other in a specific sequence. This sequence of amino acids is said to be ....

(a) primary structure of proteins
(b) secondary structure of proteins
(c) tertiary structure of proteins
(d) quateranary structure of proteins

Ans. ***(a)*** In primary structure of proteins, each polypeptide in a protein has amino acids linked with each other in a specific sequence.

Q.12 DNA and RNA contain four bases each. Which of the following bases is **not** present in RNA?

(a) Adenine (b) Uracil (c) Thymine (d) Cytosine

Thinking Process This problem is based on the concept of base composition differences between DNA and RNA, where RNA contains uracil instead of thymine.

Ans. ***(c)*** DNA contains four bases adenine, guanine, thymine and cytosine. While RNA contains four bases adenine, uracil, guanine and cytosine. Thus, RNA does not contain thymine.

Hence, statement (c) is the correct choice.

Q.13 Which of the following B group vitamins can be stored in our body?

(a) Vitamin B_1 (b) Vitamin B_2 (c) Vitamin B_6 (d) Vitamin B_{12}

Ans. ***(d)*** Vitamin B_{12} belongs to B group vitamins, which can be stored in our body because it is not water soluble.

Q.14 Which of the following bases is **not** present in DNA?

(a) Adenine (b) Thymine (c) Cytosine (d) Uracil

Ans. ***(d)*** DNA contains following four bases :

(i) adenine (A) (ii) thymine (T) (iii) guanine (G) (iv) cytosine (C)

It does not contain uracil.

Mistake Alert ! *Students may be confused about compositional differences between DNA and RNA, uracil is not present in DNA, instead thymine is present.*

Q.15 Three cyclic structures of monosaccharides are given below, which of these are anomers.

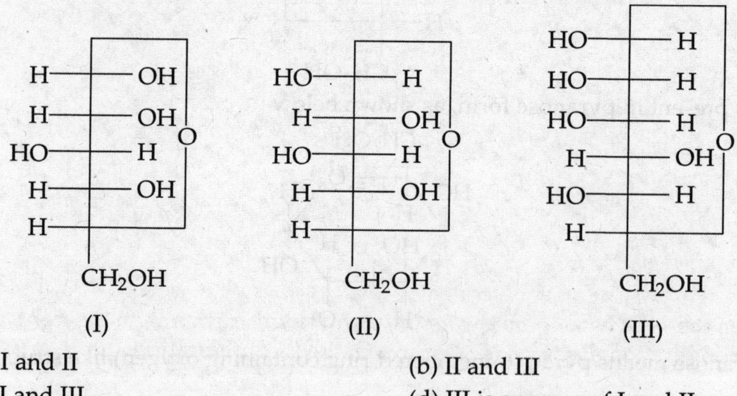

(a) I and II
(b) II and III
(c) I and III
(d) III is anomer of I and II

Ans. *(a)* **Anomers** Cyclic structures of monosaccharides which differ in structure at carbon-1 are known as anomers.

Here, I and II are anomers because they differ from each other at carbon- 1 only.

Q.16 Which of the following reactions of glucose can be explained only by its cyclic structure?

(a) Glucose forms pentaacetate.

(b) Glucose reacts with hydroxylamine to form an oxime.

(c) Pentaacetate of glucose does not react with hydroxylamine.

(d) Glucose is oxidised by nitric acid to gluconic acid.

- **Concept Insight** This solution includes the concept of cyclic structure formation in glucose. The lack of reaction with hydroxylamine indicates that glucose predominantly exists in a cyclic form without a free —CHO group.

Ans. *(c)* "Pentaacetate of glucose does not react with hydroxylamine" showing absence of free CHO group. This cannot be explained by open structure of glucose. While all other properties are easily explained by open structure of glucose.

Hence, option (c) is the correct choice.

Q.17 Optical rotations of some compounds along with their structures are given below which of them have D configuration.

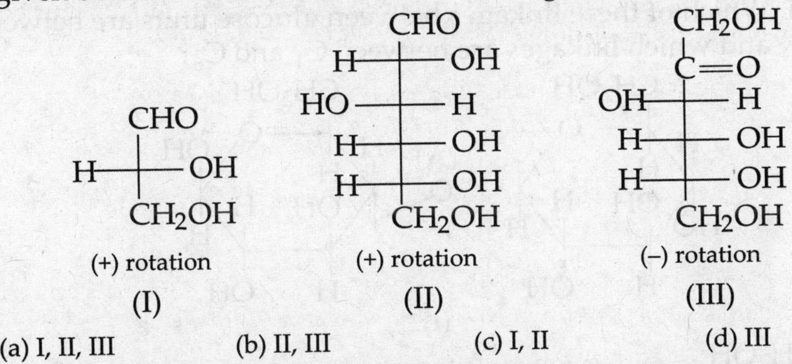

(a) I, II, III (b) II, III (c) I, II (d) III

Ans. *(a)* *D* and *L* configuration are relative configuration decided by relative structure of given saccharide with *D* or *L* glyceraldehyde.

(I)	(II)	(III)
CHO	CHO	CH_2OH
H—C—OH	H—C—OH	C=O
CH_2OH	HO—C—H	HO—C—H
	H—C—OH	H—C—OH
	H—C—OH	H—C—OH
	CH_2OH	CH_2OH
(+)	(+)	(–)

When the —OH group on the lowest asymmetric carbon is on the right, it is in the D-configuration; if it's on the left, it is in the L-configuration.

Q.18 Structure of disaccharide formed by glucose and fructose is given below. Identify anomeric carbon atoms in monosaccharide units.

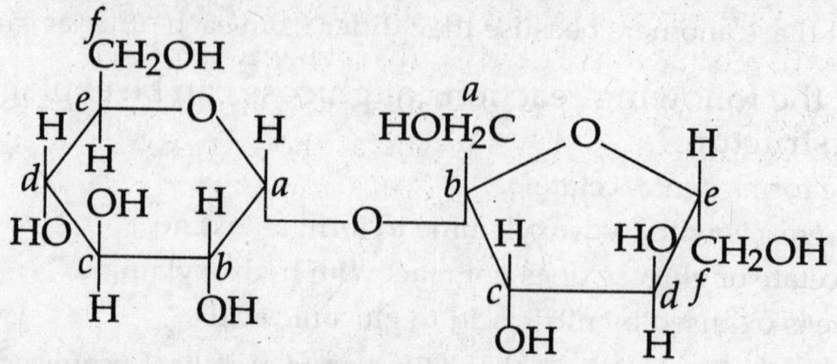

(a) '*a*' carbon of glucose and '*a*' carbon of fructose.
(b) '*a*' carbon of glucose and '*e*' carbon of fructose.
(c) '*a*' carbon of glucose and '*b*' carbon of fructose.
(d) '*f*' carbon of glucose and '*f*' carbon of fructose.

Ans. ***(c)*** Carbon adjacent to oxygen atom in the cyclic structure of glucose or fructose is known as anomeric carbon. As shown in the structure above '*a*' and '*b*' are present at adjacent to oxygen atom. Both carbons differ in configurations of the hydroxyl group.

Hence, '*a*' carbon of glucose and '*b*' carbon of fructose are anomeric carbon atoms.

Q.19 Three structures are given below in which two glucose units are linked. Which of these linkages between glucose units are between C_1 and C_4 and which linkages are between C_1 and C_6?

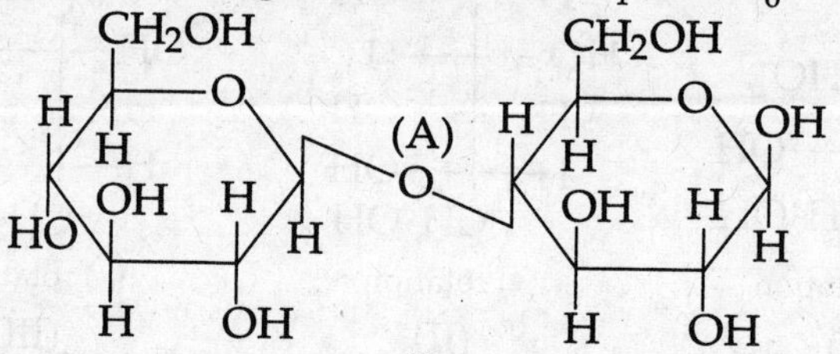

(i)

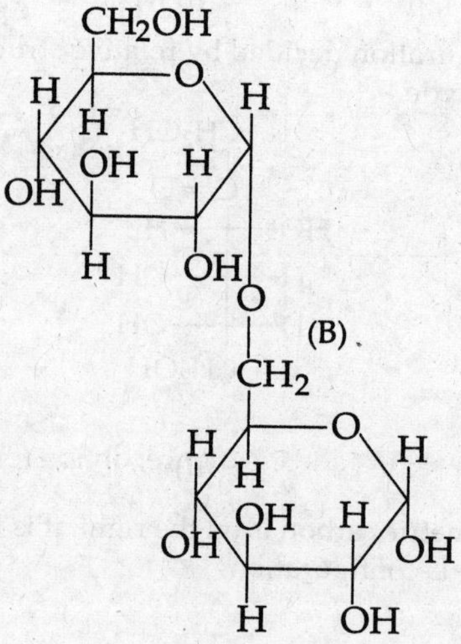

(ii)

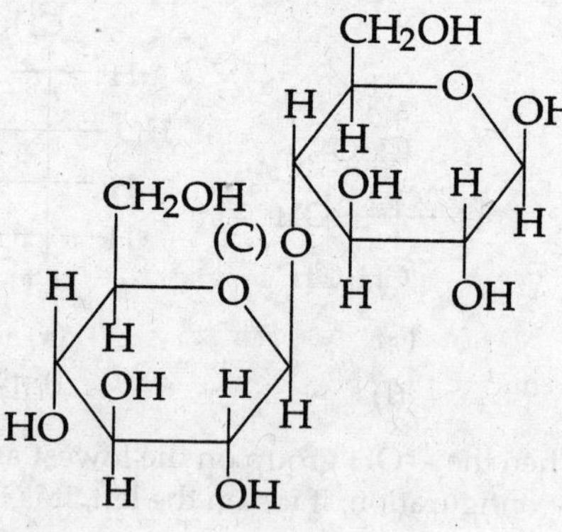

(iii)

(a) (A) is between C_1 and C_4, (B) and (C) are between C_1 and C_6
(b) (A) and (B) are between C_1 and C_4, (C) is between C_1 and C_6
(c) (A) and (C) are between C_1 and C_4, (B) is between C_1 and C_6
(d) (A) and (C) are between C_1 and C_6, (B) is between C_1 and C_4

Ans. ***(c)*** Numbering of glucose starts from adjacent carbon of O-atom to the other carbon atom ending at last CH_2OH group as shown below

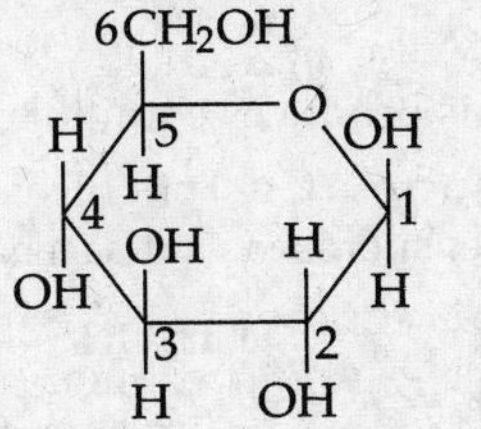

6CH_2OH ... H 5 O OH H 4 1 OH H OH H 3 2 H OH

In this way, numbering for the disaccharides can be done as

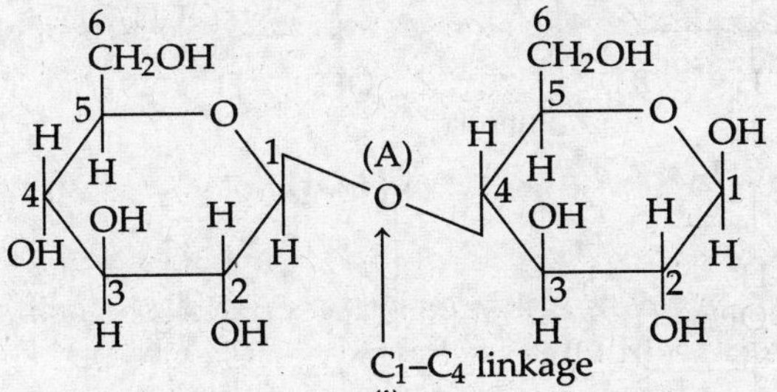

6 CH_2OH 5 O H H 1 (A) O 4 OH H OH H 3 2 H OH — 6 CH_2OH 5 O H OH H 4 1 OH H H 3 2 H OH

C_1–C_4 linkage
(i)

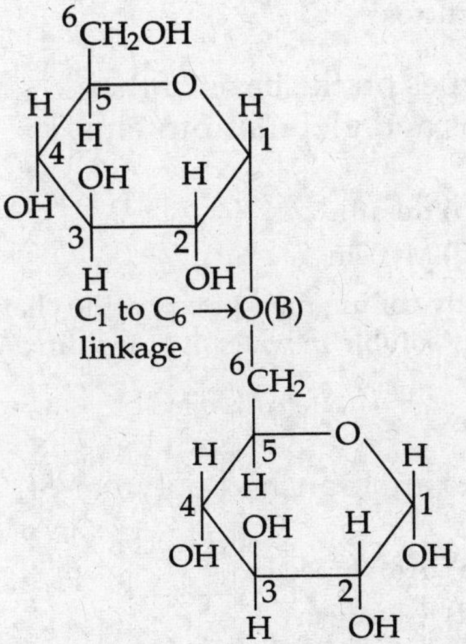

$^6CH_2OH$ H 5 O H H 4 1 OH H OH 3 2 H OH

C_1 to C_6 ⟶ O(B) linkage

$^6CH_2$ H 5 O H H 4 1 OH H OH OH 3 2 H OH

(ii)

$^6CH_2OH$ H 5 O OH H 4 1 OH H H 3 2 H OH

$^6CH_2OH$(C) O ← C_1–C_4 linkage

H 5 O H 4 1 OH H HO H 3 2 H OH

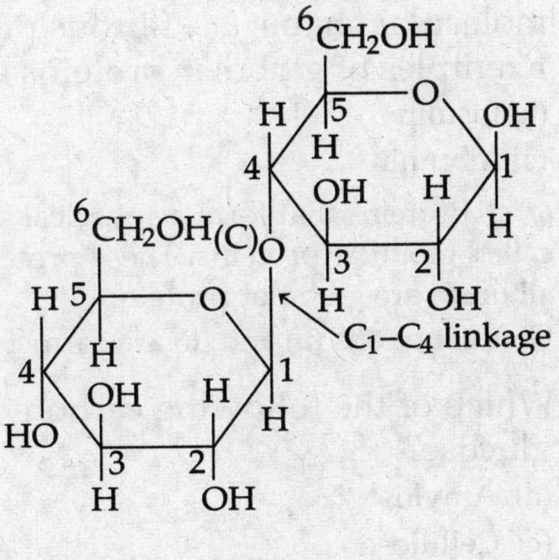

(iii)

(A) and (C) are between C_1 and C_4, (B) is between C_1 and C_6. Hence, option (c) is the correct choice.

Multiple Choice Questions (More Than One Options)

Q.20 Carbohydrates are classified on the basis of their behaviour on hydrolysis and also as reducing or non-reducing sugar. Sucrose is a ....

(a) monosaccharide (b) disaccharide

(c) reducing sugar (d) non-reducing sugar

Ans. ***(b, d)*** Sucrose on hydrolysis produces equimolar mixture of $\alpha - D(+)$ glucose and β-D(–). fructose. Since in sucrose C – 1 of glucose and C – 2 of fructose are linked with each other. Therefore, sucrose is a disaccharide and non-reducing sugar.

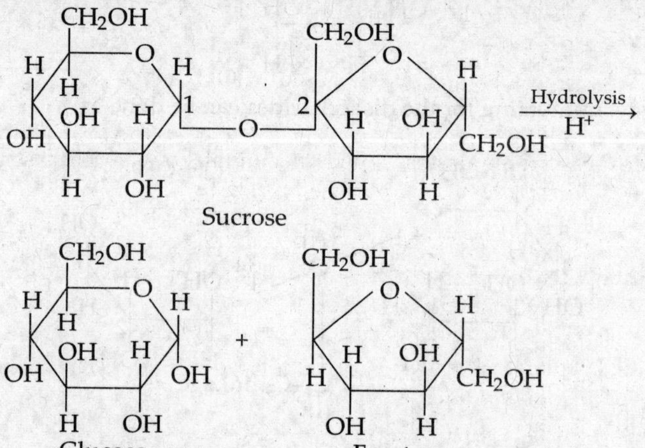

CH_2OH CH_2OH
H O H O H
H 1 2
OH H O H OH Hydrolysis $\xrightarrow{H^+}$
OH CH_2OH
H OH OH H

Sucrose

CH_2OH CH_2OH
H O H O H
H +
OH H H OH
OH OH H CH_2OH
H OH OH H

Glucose Fructose

Q.21 Proteins can be classified into two types on the basis of their molecular shape, *i.e.*, fibrous proteins and globular proteins. Examples of globular proteins are

(a) Insulin (b) Keratin

(c) Albumin (d) Myosin

Ans. ***(a, c)*** Proteins that form a spherical shape by coiling their polypeptide chains are called globular proteins. These proteins are soluble in water, *e.g.*, insulin and albumin are globular protein.

Hence, options (a) and (c) are correct choices.

Q.22 Which of the following carbohydrates are branched polymer of glucose?

(a) Amylose (b) Amylopectin

(c) Cellulose (d) Glycogen

Thinking Process This problem is based on the concept of polymers of glucose and their branching patterns. Amylopectin and glycogen are branched polymers, while amylose and cellulose are unbranched.

Ans. ***(b, d)*** Amylopectin and glycogen have almost similar structure, where glucose units are linked linearly to each other by $C_1 - C_4$ glycosidic linkage and branched at $C_1 - C_6$ glycosidic linkage.

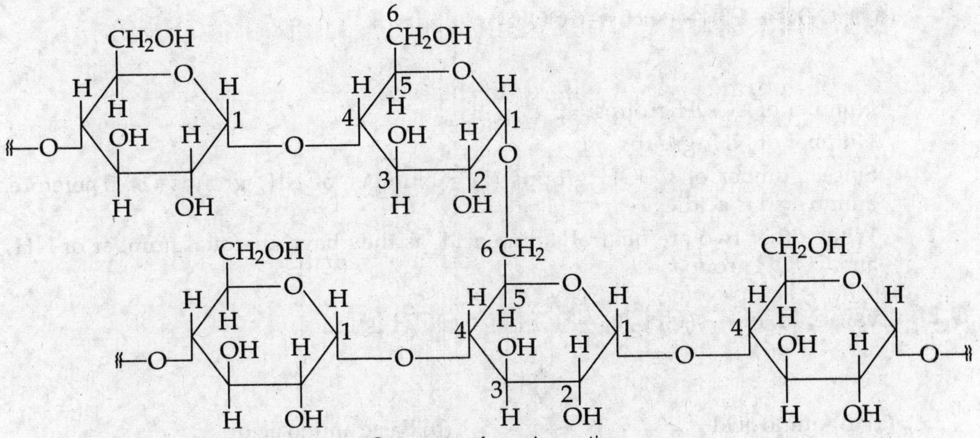

Structure of amylopectin

Glycogen are carbohydrates stored in animal body, with a structure similar to amylopectin but more highly branched.

Q.23 Amino acids are classified as acidic, basic or neutral depending upon the relative number of amino and carboxyl groups in their molecule. Which of the following are acidic?

(a) $(CH_3)_2CH—CH(NH_2)—COOH$

(b) $HOOC—CH_2—CH_2—CH(NH_2)—COOH$

(c) $H_2N—CH_2—CH_2—CH_2—COOH$

(d) $HOOC—CH_2—CH(NH_2)—COOH$

Thinking Process This problem is based on concept of nature of amino acid, *i.e.*, either it is acidic, basic or neutral.

Depending upon the number of acidic COOH group and basic $—NH_2$ group, amino acid can be classified as

(i) If number of COOH groups = number of NH_2 groups, amino acid is neutral.

(ii) If number of COOH groups > number of NH_2 groups, amino acid is acidic.

(iii) If number of COOH group < number of NH_2 group, amino acid is basic.

Ans. ***(b, d)***

(b) $HOOC—CH_2—CH_2—CH(NH_2)—COOH$

Number of COOH groups = 2

Number of NH_2 group = 1

Since, number of COOH groups (2) > number of NH_2 group (1). Therefore, this amino acid is acidic.

(d) $HOOC—CH_2—\underset{\displaystyle NH_2}{\underset{|}{CH}}—COOH$

Number of COOH groups = 2
Number of NH_2 groups = 1
Since, number of COOH groups (2) > Number of NH_2 groups (1). Therefore, amino acid is acidic.

While other two are neutral amino acid, as they have an equal number of NH_2 and COOH groups.

Q.24 Lysine, $H_2N—(CH_2)_4—\underset{\displaystyle NH_2}{\underset{|}{CH}}—COOH$ is ....

(a) α-Amino acid
(b) Basic amino acid
(c) Amino acid synthesised in body
(d) β-Amino acid

● **Concept Insight** This solution includes the concept of amino acid classification based on functional groups.

Ans. ***(a, b)*** Lysine whose structural formula is written below as :

$$H_2N—(CH_2)_4—\underset{\displaystyle NH_2}{\underset{|}{CH}}—COOH$$

(a) It is an α-amino acid.

(b) It is a basic amino acid because number of NH_2 groups (2) is greater than number of COOH group (1).

Mistake Alert ! *Students may make a mistake in considering lysine as an amino acid which can be synthesised in the body. Lysine is not synthesised in the body and is considered an essential amino acid. It must be obtained through diet rather than being produced by the body.*

Q.25 Which of the following monosaccharides are present as five membered cyclic structure (furanose structure)?

(a) Ribose (b) Glucose (c) Fructose (d) Galactose

Ans. ***(a, c)*** Ribose and fructose has five membered cyclic furanose structure because it includes 5 carbon atoms containing polyhydroxy carbonyl compound.
Hence, option (a) and (c) are correct choice.

Q.26 In fibrous proteins, polypeptide chains are held together by ....

(a) van der Waal's forces
(b) disulphide linkage
(c) electrostatic forces of attraction
(d) hydrogen bonds

Thinking Process This problem is based on the concept of structural characteristics of fibrous proteins.

Ans. ***(b, d)*** In fibrous proteins, polypeptide chains run parallel to each other and are held together by hydrogen bonds and disulphide bonds, creating a fibre-like structure. These proteins are generally insoluble in water, *e.g.*, keratin and myosin.

Q.27 Which of the following are purine bases?

(a) Guanine
(b) Adenine
(c) Thymine
(d) Uracil

Ans. ***(a, b)*** Purines consist of six membered and five membered nitrogen containing ring fused together.

Guanine and adenine are purine bases whose structures are :

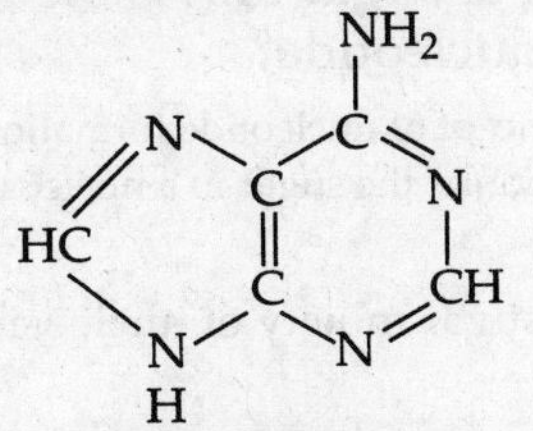

Adenine (A) 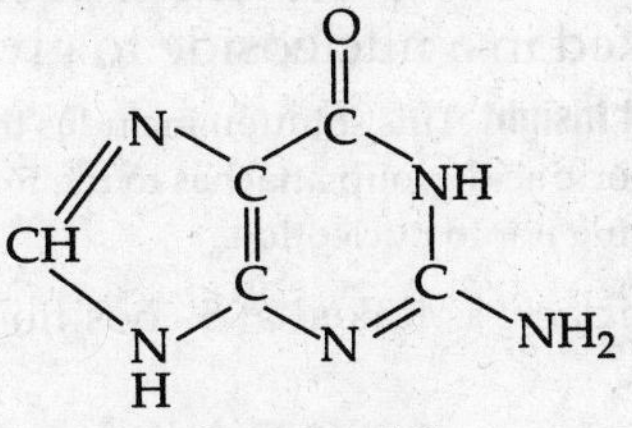 Guanine (G)

While thymine and uracil are pyrimidine bases.

Hence, (a) and (b) are correct choices.

Q.28 Which of the following terms are correct about enzyme?

(a) Proteins (b) Dinucleotides (c) Nucleic acids (d) Biocatalysts

Ans. ***(a, d)*** Enzymes are proteins which acts as biocatalysts having specific role/action in specific biochemical reactions.

e.g., Maltase decomposes maltose to glucose.

$$\underset{\text{Maltose}}{C_{12}H_{22}O_{11}} \xrightarrow{\text{Maltase}} \underset{\text{Glucose}}{2C_6H_{12}O_6}$$

Short Answer Type Questions

Q.29 Name the sugar present in milk. How many monosaccharide units are present in it? What are such oligosaccharides called?

Ans. Sugar present in milk is known as lactose sugar. Two units of monosaccharides, β-D-galactose and β -D-glucose are linked together in lactose.

Hence, such oligosaccharides are known as disaccharides.

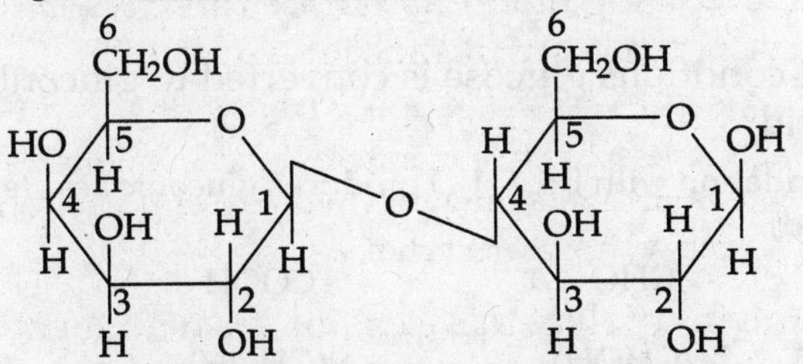

β-D-galactose β-D-glucose

Q.30 How do you explain the presence of all the six carbon atoms in glucose in a straight chain?

Ans. Glucose on heating with HI produces *n*-hexane.

$$\underset{\text{Glucose}}{CHO-(CHOH)_4-CH_2OH} \xrightarrow[\Delta]{HI} \underset{n\text{-Hexane}}{CH_3-CH_2-CH_2-CH_2-CH_2-CH_3}$$

This shows that all the six carbon atoms of glucose are linked in a straight chain.

Q.31 In nucleoside, a base is attached at 1′ position of sugar moiety. Nucleotide is formed by linking of phosphoric acid unit to the sugar unit of nucleoside. At which position of sugar unit is the phosphoric acid linked in a nucleoside to give a nucleotide?

- **Concept Insight** This solution includes the concept of nucleotide formation, where a phosphoric acid group attaches to the 5′-position of the sugar in a nucleoside, converting it into nucleotide.

Ans. Phosphoric acid is linked at 5′- position of sugar moiety of nucleoside to give a nucleotide.

O
‖
⊖O–P–O–CH₂ (5′) — O — Base
|
⊖O
Phosphoric acid
4′, 1′, H H H H, 3′, 2′
OH OH

Q.32 Name the linkage connecting monosaccharide units in polysaccharides.

Ans. Glycosidic linkage connects monosaccharide units in polysaccharides.

CH_2OH ... CH_2OH (6)
OH, 5, O ... H, 5, O, OH
4, H, 1, O, 4, H, 1
OH, H ... OH, H
H, H ... H
3, 2 ... 3, 2
H, OH ... H, OH
β-D-Galactose ... β-D-Glucose

Glycosidic linkage in lactose

Q.33 Under what condtions glucose is converted to gluconic acid and saccharic acid?

Ans. Glucose on oxidation with Br_2 / H_2O produces gluconic acid (six carbon carboxylic acid).

$$\underset{\text{Glucose}}{\begin{matrix} CHO \\ | \\ (CHOH)_4 \\ | \\ CH_2OH \end{matrix}} \xrightarrow{Br_2\ /\ H_2O} \underset{\text{Gluconic acid}}{\begin{matrix} COOH \\ | \\ (CHOH)_4 \\ | \\ CH_2OH \end{matrix}}$$

Glucose on oxidation with nitric acid produces saccharic acid (dicarboxylic acid).

$$\underset{\text{Glucose}}{\begin{matrix} CHO \\ | \\ (CHOH)_4 \\ | \\ CH_2OH \end{matrix}} \xrightarrow{HNO_3} \underset{\text{Saccharic acid}}{\begin{matrix} COOH \\ | \\ (CHOH)_4 \\ | \\ COOH \end{matrix}}$$

Q.34 Monosaccharides contain carbonyl group hence are classified, as aldose or ketose. The number of carbon atoms present in the monosaccharide molecule are also considered for classification. In which class of monosaccharide will you place fructose?

Ans. Monosaccharides contain carbonyl group. Hence, they are are classified as aldose or ketose.

When an aldehyde group is present, the monosaccharides are known as aldose.

When a ketone group is present, the monosaccharides are known as ketose. Fructose has molecular formula $C_6H_{12}O_6$ containing 6 carbon and keto group and is classified as ketohexose.

$$\begin{array}{ccc} & CH_2OH & \\ & | & \\ & C{=}O & \\ HO & - & H \\ H & - & OH \\ H & - & OH \\ & CH_2OH & \end{array}$$

D (–) fructose

Q.35 The letters '*D*' or '*L*' before the name of a stereoisomer of a compound indicate the correlation of configuration of that particular stereoisomer. This refers to their relation with one of the isomers of glyceraldehyde. Predict whether the following compound has '*D*' or '*L*' configuration.

$$\begin{array}{ccc} & CHO & \\ HO & - & H \\ H & - & OH \\ HO & - & H \\ HO & - & H \\ & CH_2OH & \end{array}$$

Thinking Process This problem is based on relative configuration, *i.e.*, *D* and *L* configuration. This can be done by comparing relative structure of monosaccharides with structure of glyceraldehyde.

If OH is present at right side of second last carbon of monosaccharide, then it is considered as *D* configuration.

If OH is present at left side of second last carbon of monosaccharide, then it is considered as *L* configuration.

Ans. Here, OH group is present on second last carbon at left side, hence this has L configuration.

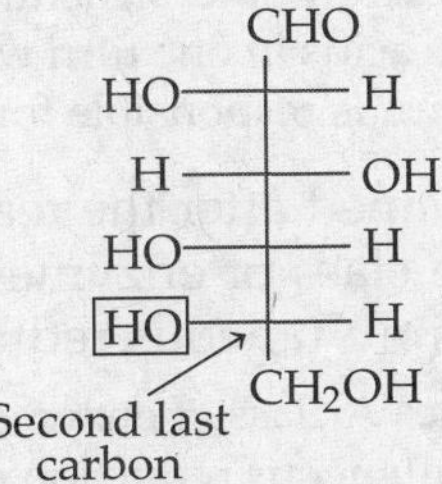

Q.36 Aldopentoses named as ribose and 2-deoxyribose are found in nucleic acids. What is their relative configuration?

Ans.

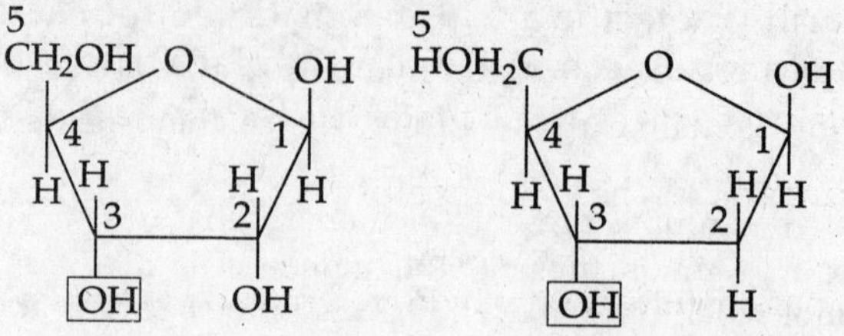

$$\text{β-D-ribose: furanose ring } C_1\text{–}C_4\text{ with O; } C_5H_2OH \text{ on } C_4;\ C_1: OH \text{ (up)}, H;\ C_2: H, OH \text{ (down)};\ C_3: H, \boxed{OH} \text{ (down)};\ C_4: H$$

$$\text{β-D-2-deoxyribose: } HOH_2C_5 \text{ on } C_4;\ C_1: OH \text{ (up)}, H;\ C_2: H, H;\ C_3: H, \boxed{OH} \text{ (down)};\ C_4: H$$

β-D-ribose β-D-2-deoxyribose

In case of cyclic structure of saccharide, if —OH group present at second last carbon is present at bottom side, then it is considered as *D* configuration (as shown above).

Q.37 Which sugar is called invert sugar? Why is it called so?

Ans. Sucrose is dextrorotatory, but sucrose upon hydrolysis, produces dextrorotatory glucose and laevorotatory fructose, resulting in an overall laevorotatory mixture. A sugar that changes its optical rotation from *dextro* to *laevo* upon hydrolysis is called an invert sugar.

Q.38 Amino acids can be classified as α-, β-, γ-, δ- and so on depending upon the relative position of amino group with respect to carboxyl group. Which type of amino acids form polypeptide chain in proteins?

Ans. α-Amino acid forms polypeptide chain by elimination of water molecules.

$$\alpha\text{-amino acid} \rightarrow R - \overset{\alpha}{C}H(NH_2) - COOH$$

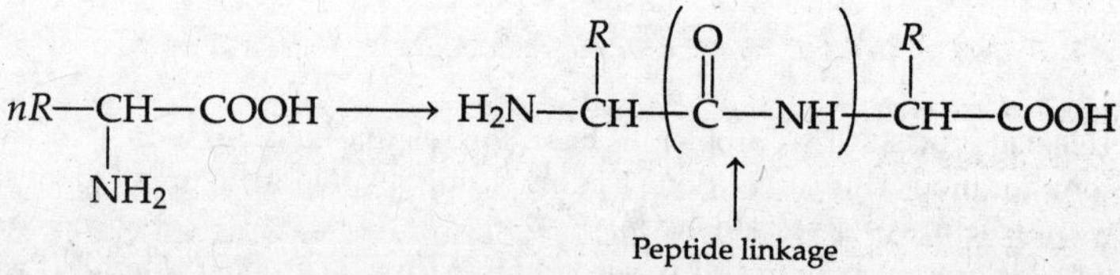

$$nR\text{—}CH(NH_2)\text{—}COOH \longrightarrow H_2N\text{—}CH(R)\text{—}\left(\overset{O}{\overset{\|}{C}}\text{—}NH\right)\text{—}CH(R)\text{—}COOH$$

Peptide linkage

Q.39 α-Helix is a secondary structure of proteins formed by twisting of polypeptide chain into right handed screw like structure. Which type of interactions are responsible for making the α-helix structure stable?

Ans. α-Helix is a secondary structure of proteins formed by twisting of polypeptide chain to right handed screw like structure. Hydrogen bonds formed between —NH— group of amino acids in one turn with the $>C=O$ groups of amino acids belonging to adjacent turn is responsible for making the α-helix structure stable.

Q.40 Some enzymes are named after the reaction, where they are used. What name is given to the class of enzymes which catalyse the oxidation of one substrate with simultaneous reduction of another substrate?

Ans. **Oxidoreductase enzymes** A class of enzymes which catalyses the oxidation of one substrate with simultaneous reduction of another substrate is known as oxidoreductase enzymes.

Q.41 During curdling of milk, what happens to sugar present in it?

Ans. Curdling of milk is caused due to formation of lactic acid by the bacteria present in milk. It is an example of denaturation of protein, *i.e.*, when a protein is subjected to some physical or chemical changes, hydrogen bond get disturbed and globules unfold and helix get uncoiled, and protein loses its biological activity.

Q.42 How do you explain the presence of five —OH groups in glucose molecule?

Ans. Glucose on reaction with acetic anhydride produces glucose pentaacetate.

$$\begin{array}{c} CHO \\ | \\ (CHOH)_4 \\ | \\ CH_2OH \end{array} \xrightarrow{\text{Acetic anhydride}} \begin{array}{c} CHO \\ | \\ (CHOAc)_4 \\ | \\ CHOAc \end{array}$$

Glucose pentacetate

This reaction explains the presence of five — OH groups.

Q.43 Why does compound (*A*) given below not form an oxime?

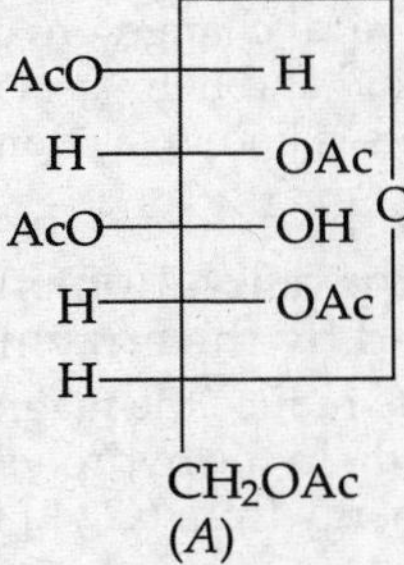

(*A*)

Ans. Compound (*A*) does not form an oxime on reaction with NH_2OH due to absence of CHO group or >C=O group.

Q.44 Why must vitamin C be supplied regularly in diet?

Ans. Vitamin C is water soluble, hence it is regularly excreted in urine and cannot be stored in our body. So, it must be supplied regularly in diet.

Q.45 Sucrose is dextrorotatory but the mixture obtained after hydrolysis is laevorotatory. Explain.

Ans. Sucrose is dextrorotatory. On hydrolysis, it produces a mixture of glucose and fructose having specific rotation +52.5° and –92.4°. Thus, the net resultant mixture become laevorotatory.

Hence, the mixture is laevorotatory and product is known as invert sugar.

Q.46 Amino acids behave like salts rather than simple amines or carboxylic acids. Explain.

Ans. Amino acids have acidic COOH group as well as NH_2 group. Hence, COOH give its H to NH_2, hence they exist as Zwitter ion.

$$\begin{array}{c} R\text{—CH—}COO^- \\ | \\ \overset{\oplus}{N}H_3 \end{array}$$

Zwitter ion

Q.47 Structures of glycine and alanine are given below. Show the peptide linkage in glycylalanine.

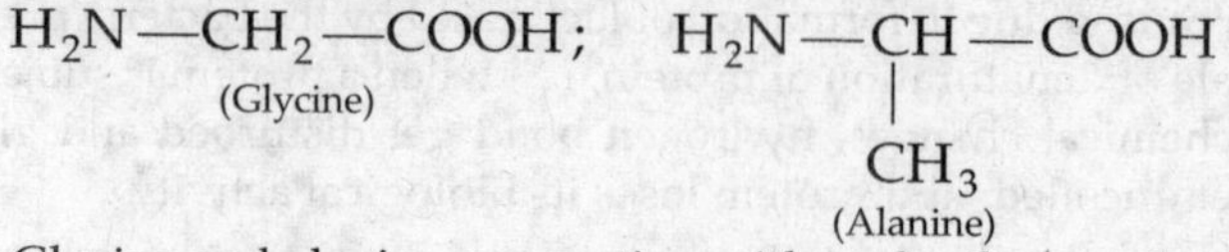

$$H_2N—CH_2—COOH \text{ (Glycine)}; \quad H_2N—\underset{\underset{CH_3}{|}}{CH}—COOH \text{ (Alanine)}$$

Ans. Glycine and alanine on reaction with each other produces glycylalanine as

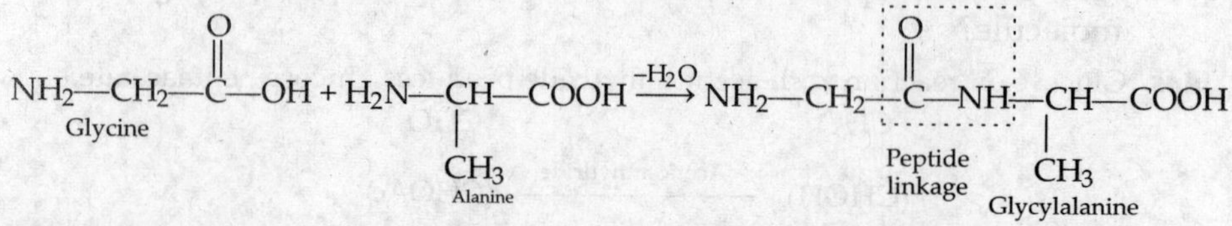

$$\underset{\text{Glycine}}{NH_2—CH_2—\overset{\overset{O}{||}}{C}—OH} + \underset{\text{Alanine}}{H_2N—\underset{\underset{CH_3}{|}}{CH}—COOH} \xrightarrow{-H_2O} \underset{\text{Glycylalanine}}{NH_2—CH_2—\underset{\text{Peptide linkage}}{\boxed{\overset{\overset{O}{||}}{C}—NH}}—\underset{\underset{CH_3}{|}}{CH}—COOH}$$

Q.48 Protein found in a biological system with a unique three-dimensional structure and biological activity is called a native protein. When a protein in its native form, is subjected to a physical change like change in temperature or a chemical change like, change in pH, denaturation of protein takes place. Explain the cause.

Ans. Due to physical and chemical changes, hydrogen bonds in proteins are disturbed. Due to this globules unfold and helix gets uncoiled and therefore, protein loses its biological activity. This is known as **denaturation** of **proteins**.

Q.49 Activation energy for the acid catalysed hydrolysis of sucrose is 6.22 kJ mol^{-1}, while the activation energy is only 2.15 kJ mol^{-1}, when hydrolysis is catalysed by the enzyme sucrase. Explain.

Ans. Enzymes, the biocatalysts reduce the magnitude of activation energy by providing alternative path. In the hydrolysis of sucrose, the enzyme sucrase reduces the activation energy from 6.22 kJ mol^{-1} to 2.15 kJ mol^{-1}.

Q.50 How do you explain the presence of an aldehydic group in a glucose molecule?

Ans. Glucose on reaction with bromine water produces gluconic acid. This indicates the presence of CHO group.

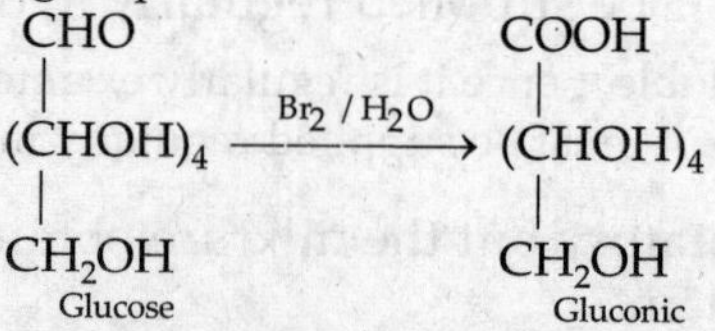

$$\underset{\text{Glucose}}{\begin{array}{c} CHO \\ | \\ (CHOH)_4 \\ | \\ CH_2OH \end{array}} \xrightarrow{Br_2/H_2O} \underset{\text{Gluconic}}{\begin{array}{c} COOH \\ | \\ (CHOH)_4 \\ | \\ CH_2OH \end{array}}$$

Q.51 Which moieties of nucleosides are involved in the formation of phosphodiester linkages present in dinucleotides? What does the word diester in the name of linkage indicate? Which acid is involved in the formation of this linkage?

Ans. (i) 5′ and 3′ carbon atoms of pentose sugar are involved in the formation of phosphodiester linkages present in dinucleotides.

(ii) Most probably the resemblance with 2 ester $(-COO)^{2-}$ groups joined together indicates the word diester in the name of linkage.

$$\begin{array}{c} | \\ O \\ | \\ O^-—P{=}O \\ | \\ O \\ | \end{array}$$

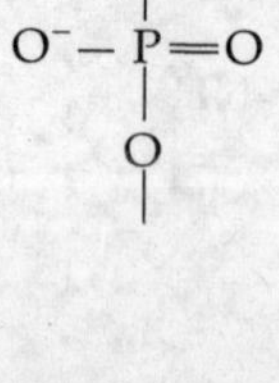

(iii) Phosphoric acid (H_3PO_4) is involved in the formation of this linkage.

Nucleosides are joined together by phosphodiester linkage between 5' and 3' carbon atoms of pentose sugar and a dinucleotide with phosphoric acid (H_3PO_4) is formed.

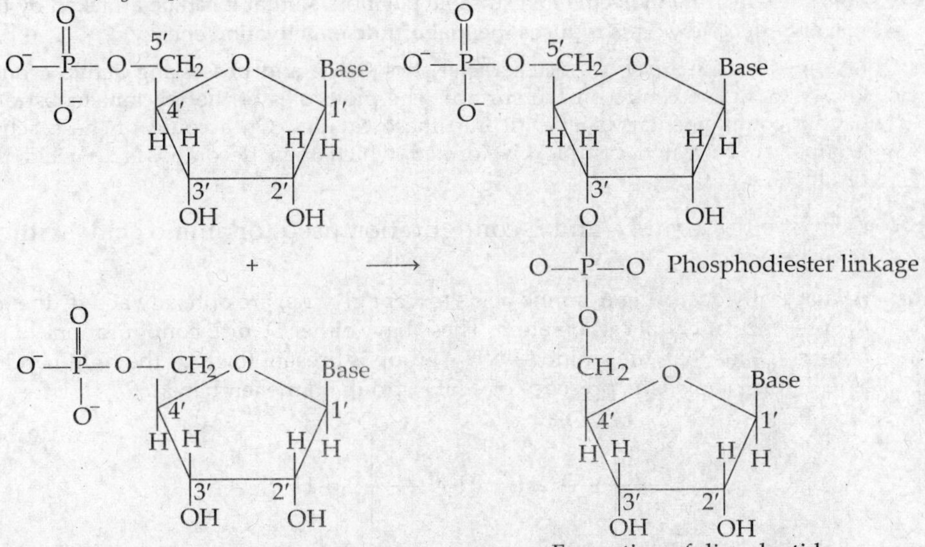

Formation of dinucleotide

Q.52 What are glycosidic linkages? In which type of biomolecules are they present?

Ans. Linkage between two monosaccharides due to oxide linkage formed by the loss of a water molecule, is known as glycosidic linkage as shown below :

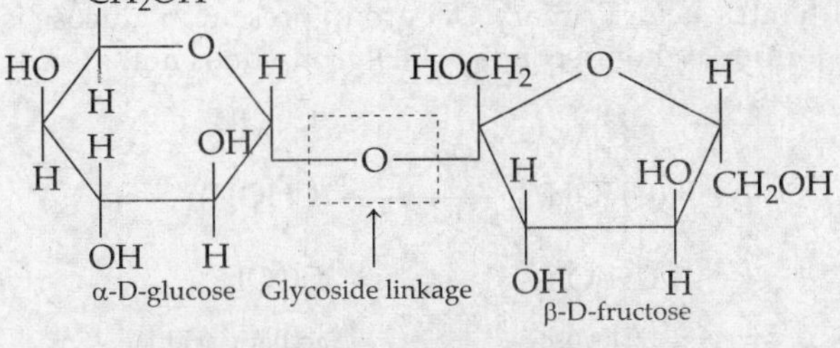

α-D-glucose Glycoside linkage β-D-fructose

Q.53 Which monosaccharide units are present in starch, cellulose and glucose and which linkages link these units?

Ans. Monosaccharides units present in starch, cellulose and glucose can be determined by knowing the product of their hydrolysis.

(i) Starch is a polysaccharide of α-glucose in which two types of linkage are observed, *i.e.*, $C_1 — C_6$ and $C_1 — C_4$ glycosidic linkage.

(ii) Cellulose is a straight chain polysaccharide of β-D glucose in which glucose are linked together by $C_1 — C_4$ glycosidic linkage.

(iii) Glucose is a monosaccharide.

Q.54 How do enzymes help a substrate to be attacked by the reagent effectively?

Ans. At the surface of enzyme, active sites are present. These active sites of enzymes hold the substrate molecule in a suitable position, so that it can be attacked by the reagent effectively. This reduces the magnitude of activation energy.

Enzymes contains cavities of characteristics shape and possessing active groups known as active centre on the surface. The molecules of the reactant (substrate) having complementary shape, fit into these cavities. On account of these active groups, an activated complex is formed which then decomposes to yield the products.

Q.55 Describe the term *D*- and *L*-configuration used for amino acids with examples.

Ans. All naturally occurring α-amino acids (except glycine) are optically active due to the presence of chiral carbon atom. These have either *D*- or *L*-configuration. *D*-form means that, the amino ($-NH_2$) group is present towards the right hand side. *L*-form shows the presence of $-NH_2$ group on the left hand side.

```
        COOH                  COOH
         |                     |
H ———————+——————NH2   H2N——————+——————H
         |                     |
        CH3                   CH3
     D-alanine             L-alanine
```

Q.56 How will you distinguish 1° and 2° hydroxyl groups present in glucose? Explain with reactions.

Ans. 1° and 2° hydroxyl groups present in glucose can be identified by the reaction of glucose with nitric acid. Primary OH group present in glucose is easily oxidised to $-COOH$ group, while secondary OH group does not.

```
  CHO                       COOH
   |           HNO3          |
(CHOH)4  ——————————————→  (CHOH)4
   |                         |
 CH2OH                     COOH
Glucose               Saccharic acid
```

Hence, one hydroxyl is primary hydroxyl group.

Q.57 Coagulation of egg white on boiling is an example of denaturation of protein. Explain it in terms of structural changes.

Ans. **Denaturation of proteins** Protein present in egg white has an unique three dimensional structure. When it is subjected to physical change like change in temperature, *i.e.*, on boiling, coagulation of egg white occurs due to denaturation of protein.

During denaturation, hydrogen bonds are disturbed and due to this globules unfold and helix gets uncoiled and protein loses its biological activity.

Matching The Columns

Q.58 Match the vitamins given in Column I with the deficiency disease they cause given in Column II.

Column I (Vitamins)		Column II (Diseases)	
A.	Vitamin A	1.	Pernicious anaemia
B.	Vitamin B_1	2.	Increased blood clotting time
C.	Vitamin B_{12}	3.	Xerophthalmia
D.	Vitamin C	4.	Rickets
E.	Vitamin D	5.	Muscular weakness
F.	Vitamin E	6.	Night blindness
G.	Vitamin K	7.	Beri-beri
		8.	Bleeding gums
		9.	Osteomalacia

Ans. **A.** → (3, 6) **B.** → (7) **C.** → (1) **D.** → (8) **E.** → (4, 9) **F.** → (5) **G.** → (2)

Column I (Vitamins)		Column II (Diseases)
A.	Vitamin A	Xerophthalmia Night blindness
B.	Vitamin B_1	Beri beri
C.	Vitamin B_{12}	Pernicious anaemia
D.	Vitamin C	Bleeding gums
E.	Vitamin D	Rickets Osteomalacia
F.	Vitamin E	Muscular weakness
G.	Vitamin K	Incresed blood clotting time

Q.59 Match the following enzymes given in Column I with the reactions they catalyse given in Column II.

Column I (Enzymes)		Column II (Reactions)	
A.	Invertase	1.	Decomposition of urea into NH_3 and CO_2.
B.	Maltase	2.	Conversion of glucose into ethyl alcohol.
C.	Pepsin	3.	Hydrolysis of maltose into glucose.
D.	Urease	4.	Hydrolysis of cane sugar.
E.	Zymase	5.	Hydrolysis of proteins into peptides.

Ans. A. → (4) B. → (3) C. → (5) D. → (1) E. → (2)

	Column I (Enzymes)	Column II (Reaction)
A.	Invertase	Hydrolysis of cane sugar.
B.	Maltase	Hydrolysis of maltose into glucose.
C.	Pepsin	Hydrolysis of protein into peptides.
D.	Urease	Decomposition of urea into NH_3 and CO_2
E.	Zymase	Conversion of glucose into ethyl alcohol.

Assertion and Reason

In the following questions a statement of Assertion followed by a statement of Reason is given. Choose the correct answer out of the following choices.

(a) Assertion and reason both are correct statements and reason explains the assertion.
(b) Both assertion and reason are wrong statements.
(c) Assertion is correct statement and reason is wrong statement.
(d) Assertion is wrong statement and reason is correct statement.
(e) Assertion and reason both are correct statements but reason does not explain assertion.

Q.60 **Assertion** D (+) – Glucose is dextrorotatory in nature.

Reason 'D' represents its dextrorotatory nature.

Ans. *(c)* Assertion is correct but reason is wrong statement, *D* (+) glucose is dextrorotatory because it rotates the plane polarised light to right.

Here, D represents relative configuration of glucose with respect to glyceraldehyde.

Q.61 **Assertion** Vitamin D can be stored in our body.

Reason Vitamin D is fat soluble vitamin.

Ans. *(a)* Assertion and reason both are correct statements and reason explains assertion. Vitamin D can be stored in our body because vitamin D is fat soluble vitamin.

Q.62 **Assertion** β-glycosidic linkage is present in maltose.

CH₂OH CH₂OH
O O
H H H H
H H
OH H O OH H
HO OH
H
H OH H OH

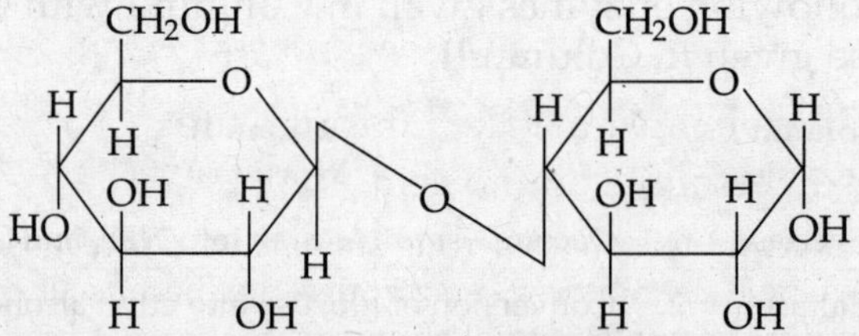

Reason Maltose is composed of two glucose units in which C_1 of one glucose unit is linked to C_2 of another glucose unit.

Ans. *(d)* Assertion is wrong statement and reason is correct statement. α-glycosidic linkage is present in maltose.

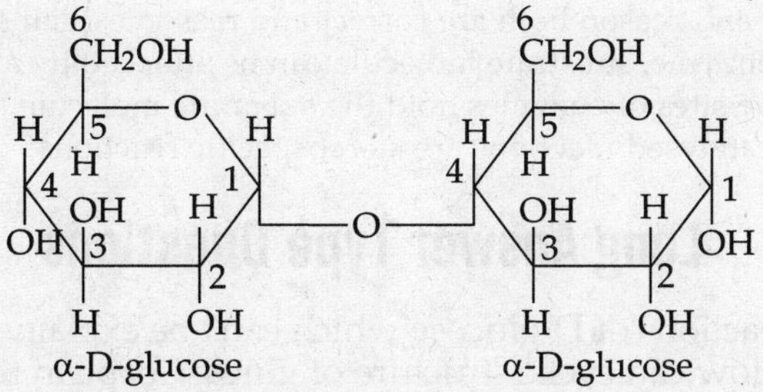

Maltose is composed of two glucose unit in which C-1 of one glucose unit is linked to C-4 of another glucose unit.

Q.63 Assertion All naturally occurring α-amino acids except glycine are optically active.

Reason Most naturally occurring amino acids have L-configuration.

Ans. *(e)* Assertion and reason both are correct and reason does not explain assertion. All naturally occurring α-amino acids except glycine are optically active. Glycine is optically inactive because glycine does not have all four different substituent as shown below.

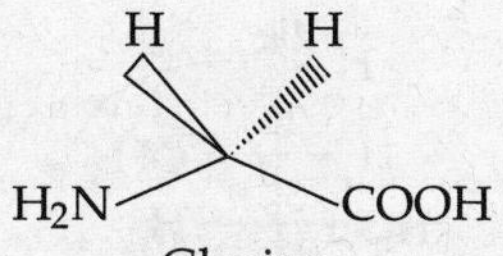

Glycine

Q.64 Assertion Deoxyribose, $C_5H_{10}O_4$ is not a carbohydrate.

Reason Carbohydrates are hydrates of carbon so compounds which follow $C_x(H_2O)_y$ formula are carbohydrates.

Ans. *(b)* Both assertion and reason are wrong statements. Deoxyribose, $C_5H_{10}O_4$ is a carbohydrate because it follow $C_5(H_2O)_2$ formula and exist as polyhydroxy carbonyl compound, whose cyclic structure is as shown below

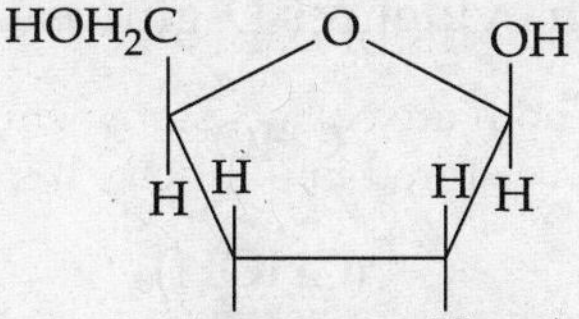

β-D-2-deoxyribose

Q.65 Assertion Glycine must be taken through diet.

Reason It is an essential amino acid.

Ans. *(b)* Both assertion and reason are wrong statements. Correct asserstion and reason are Glycine must not be taken through diet because it can be synthesised in our body and it is a non-essential amino acid.

Q.66 Assertion In presence of enzyme, substrate molecule can be attacked by the reagent effectively.

Reason Active sites of enzymes hold the substrate molecule in a suitable position.

Ans. ***(a)*** Assertion and reason both are correct and reason explains assertion. In presence of enzyme, substrate molecule can be attacked by a reagent effectively because active sites of enzymes hold the substrate molecule in a suitable position. So, enzyme catalysed reactions are stereospecific reactions.

Long Answer Type Questions

Q.67 Write the reactions of D-glucose which can't be explained by its open chain structure. How can cyclic structure of glucose explain these reactions?

Ans. Chemical reactions of D-glucose which can't be explained by its open chain structure are

(i) Glucose does not give Schiff's test and does not produce hydrogensulphite addition product with $NaHSO_3$, despite having aldehyde group.

(ii) The pentaacetate of glucose does not react with hydroxylamine.

In actual, glucose exist in two different crystalline form α form and β form. It was proposed that one of the OH groups may add to the —CHO group and form cyclic hemiacetal structure. Glucose forms a 6 membered pyranose structure.

Cyclic structure exist in equilibrium with open structure and can be represented as :

α - D (+) glucose		open chain		β - D (+) glucose
H—C1—OH (ring O)		H—C1(=O)		HO—C1—H (ring O)
H—C2—OH		H—C2—OH		H—C2—OH
HO—C3—H	⇌	HO—C3—H	⇌	HO—C3—H
H—C4—OH		H—C4—OH		H—C4—OH
H—C5— (ring O)		H—C5—OH		H—C5— (ring O)
$_6CH_2OH$		$_6CH_2OH$		$_6CH_2OH$

α - D (+) glucose β - D (+) glucose

Due to formation of cyclic structure of glucose CHO group of glucose remain no longer free due to which they do not show above given reactions.

Q.68 On the basis of which evidences D-glucose was assigned the following structure?

$$\begin{array}{c} CHO \\ | \\ (CHOH)_4 \\ | \\ CH_2OH \end{array}$$

Ans. Evidences on the basis of which glucose was assigned the following structure are as follows

(i) Glucose on reaction with HI produces *n*-hexane which indicates presence of six carbon atoms linked in a straight chain.

$$C_6H_{12}O_6 \xrightarrow{HI} n \text{ hexane}$$

(ii) Glucose on reaction with acetic anhydride produces glucose pentaacetate which indicates presence of five OH groups.

$$C_6H_{12}O_6 \xrightarrow{Ac_2O} \text{Glucose pentaacetate}$$

(iii) Glucose on oxidation with bromine water produces gluconic acid indicates presence of —CHO group.

$$\text{Glucose} \xrightarrow{Br_2/H_2O} \text{Gluconic acid}$$

(iv) Glucose on reaction with HNO_3 produces saccharic acid which indicates presence of one primary OH group.

Q.69 Carbohydrates are essential for life in both plants and animals. Name the carbohydrates that are used as storage molecules in plants and animals, also name the carbohydrate which is present in wood or in the fibre of cotton cloth.

Ans. Carbohydrates that are used as storage molecules in plants and animals are as follows

(i) Plant contains mainly starch, cellulose, sucrose, etc.

(ii) Animals contain glycogen in their body. So, glycogen is also known as animal starch. Glycogen is present in liver, muscles and brain. When body needs glucose, enzyme breaks glycogen down to glucose.

(iii) Cellulose is present in wood and fibre of clothes.

Q.70 Explain the terms primary and secondary structure of proteins. What is the difference between α-helix and β-pleated sheet structure of proteins?

Ans. **Primary structure of proteins** Proteins consist of one or more polypeptide chains. Each polypeptide is a protein, which contains **amino acids** joined with each other in a **specific sequence.**

Secondary structure of proteins It refers to the **shape** in which **a long polypeptide chain** can exist.

α-helix structure	β-pleated sheet structure
A structure of twisting of all a polypeptide chain formed by possible H-bonds into a right handed screw (helix) with the —NH group of each amino acid, and residue hydrogen bonded to the — CO — of an adjacent turn of the helix. Hence, called α-helix.	All peptide chains are stretched out to nearly maximum extension and then laid side by side which are held together by intermolecular hydrogen bonds. This structure resembles the pleated folds of the drapery. Hence, called β-pleated sheet structure.

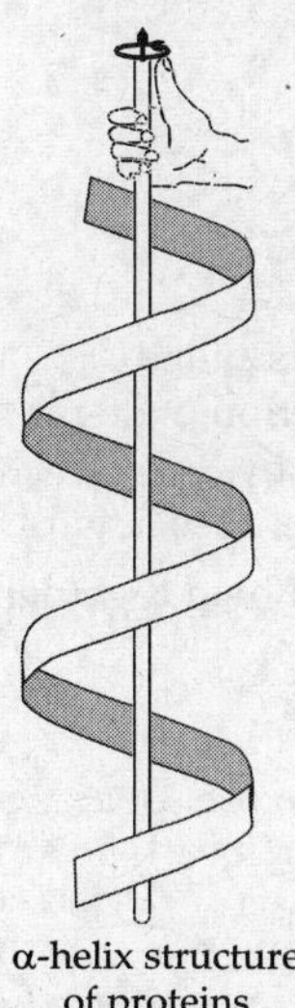

α-helix structure of proteins

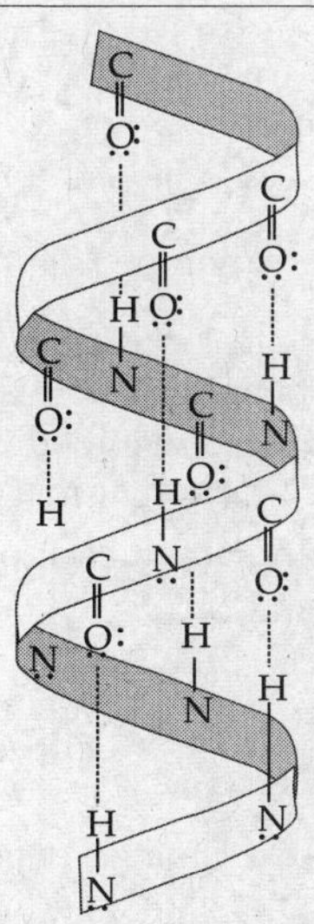

β-pleated sheet structure of proteins

Q.71 Write the structures of fragments produced on complete hydrolysis of DNA. How are they linked in DNA molecule? Draw a diagram to show pairing of nucleotide bases in double helix of DNA.

Ans. On complete hydrolysis of DNA, following fragments are formed, a pentose sugar (β-D-2-deoxyribose), phosphoric acid (H_3PO_4) and bases (nitrogen containing heterocyclic compounds).

Structures

(i) **Sugar**

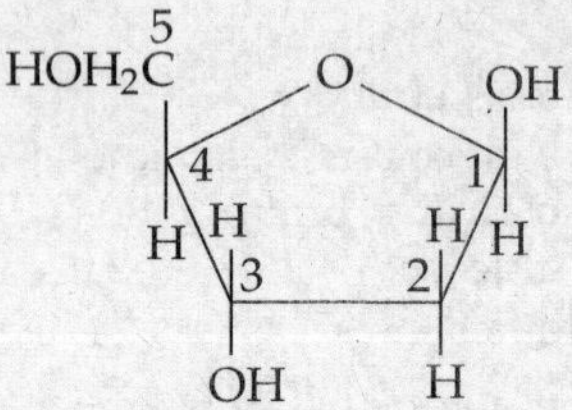

HOH_2C (5), O, OH, 4, 1, H, H, H, H, 3, 2, OH, H

β-D-2-deoxyribose

(ii) **Phosphoric acid**

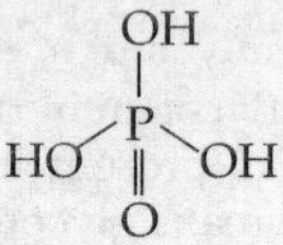

OH, HO–P–OH, ‖ O

(iii) **Nitrogen bases** DNA contains four bases Adenine, Guanine (G), Cytosine (C) and Thymine (T).

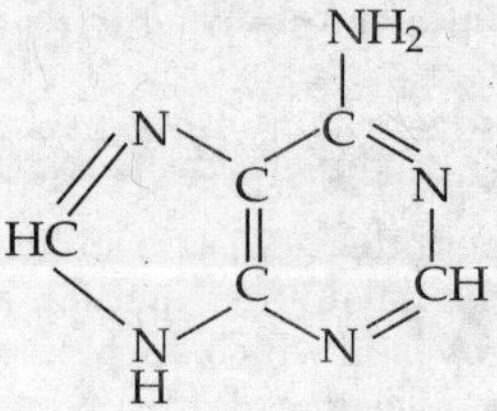

Adenine [A]

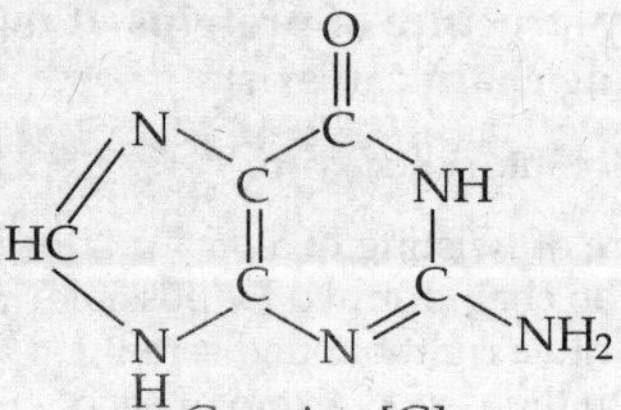

Guanine [G]

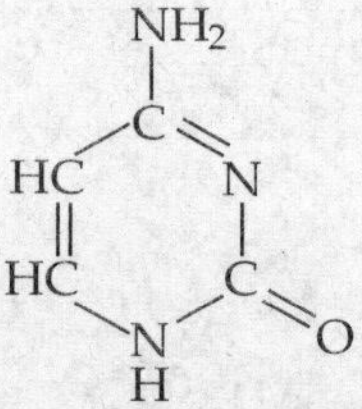

Cytosine [C]

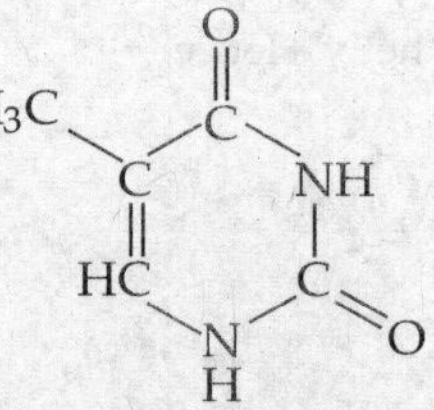

Thymine [T]

A unit formed by the attachment of a base to 1′-position of sugar is called **nucleoside**. When nucleoside links to phosphoric acid at 5′-position of sugar moiety, a **nucleotide** is formed. Nucleotides are joined together by phosphodiester linkage between 5′ and 3′ carbon atoms of the pentose sugar.

In DNA, two nucleic acid chains are wound about each other and held together by hydrogen bonds between pairs of bases.

The two strands are complementary to each other because hydrogen bonds are formed between specific pair of bases, adenine form hydrogen bonds with thymine whereas cytosine form hydrogen bonds with guanine.

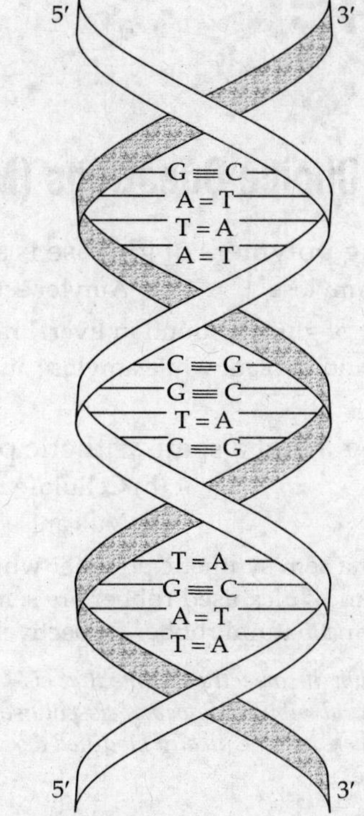

Double stranded helix structure of DNA

Chapter

15 Polymer*

Multiple Choice Questions (MCQs)

Q.1 Which of the following polymers of glucose is stored by animals?

(a) Cellulose (b) Amylose (c) Amylopectin (d) Glycogen

Ans. ***(d)*** Glycogen is a polymer of glucose found in liver, brain and muscles of animals. Cellulose is a polymer found in plant while amylose and amylopectin are structural units of starch.

Q.2 Which of the following is **not** a semisynthetic polymer?

(a) *cis*-polyisoprene (b) Cellulose nitrate

(c) Cellulose acetate (d) Vulcanised rubber

Ans. ***(a)*** *cis*-polyisoprene is not a semisynthetic polymer while other three cellulose nitrate, cellulose acetate and vulcanised rubber are semisynthetic polymers made from cellulose, cellulose and natural rubber respectively.

Mistake Alert! *Students may incorrectly assume that cis-polyisoprene is semisynthetic because it is realated to natural rubber. However, cis-polyisoprene is a natural polymer, not semisynthetic, while others are chemically modified derivatives of natural polymers, making them semi-synthetic.*

Q.3 The commercial name of polyacrylonitrile is ....

(a) dacron (b) orlon (acrilan) (c) PVC (d) bakelite

Ans. ***(b)*** The commercial name of polyacrylonitrile is orlon (acrilan).

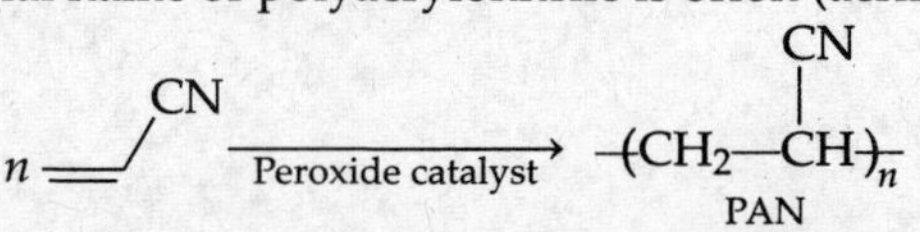

$$n\ CH_2{=}CH{-}CN \xrightarrow{\text{Peroxide catalyst}} \left(CH_2 - \underset{|}{\overset{CN}{C}}H \right)_n$$

PAN
or orlon
or acrilan

Q.4 Which of the following polymer is biodegradable?

(a) $\left(CH_2 - \underset{Cl}{\underset{|}{C}} = CH - CH_2 \right)_n$

(b) $\left(CH_2 - CH = CH - CH_2 - CH_2 - \overset{CN}{\overset{|}{C}}H \right)_n$

(c) $\left(O - \underset{CH_3}{\underset{|}{C}}H - CH_2 - \underset{O}{\underset{||}{C}} - O - \underset{CH_2CH_3}{\underset{|}{C}}H - CH_2 - \underset{O}{\underset{||}{C}} \right)_n$

(d) $\left(\overset{H}{\overset{|}{N}} - (CH_2)_6 - \overset{H}{\overset{|}{N}} - \overset{O}{\overset{||}{C}} - (CH_2)_4 - \overset{O}{\overset{||}{C}} \right)_n$

Note (*) This chapter has been deleted from latest NCERT.

Ans. ***(c)*** $\left(\!-O-\underset{\displaystyle CH_3}{\underset{|}{CH}}-CH_2-\underset{\displaystyle O}{\underset{\|}{C}}-O-\underset{\displaystyle CH_2CH_3}{\underset{|}{CH}}-CH_2-\underset{\displaystyle O}{\underset{\|}{C}}-\!\right)_n$

Poly β –hydroxybutyrate - co-β –hydroxy valerate is an example of biodegradable polymer.

Q.5 In which of the following polymers ethylene glycol is one of the monomer units?

(a) $\left(\!-OCH_2-CH_2OOC-C_6H_4-CO-\!\right)_n$ (benzene ring, ortho-substituted)

(b) $\left(\!-CH_2-CH_2-\!\right)_n$

(c) $\left(\!-CH_2-CH{=}CH-CH_2-\underset{}{\overset{C_6H_5}{\overset{|}{CH}}}-CH_2-\!\right)_n$

(d) $\left(\!-O-\underset{\displaystyle CH_3}{\underset{|}{CH}}-CH_2-\underset{\displaystyle O}{\underset{\|}{C}}-O-\underset{\displaystyle CH_2CH_3}{\underset{|}{CH}}-CH_2-\underset{\displaystyle O}{\underset{\|}{C}}-\!\right)_n$

Ans. ***(a)*** Given polymer can be obtained by the condensation polymerisation of ethylene glycol and phthalic acid with the elimination of water molecule.

$$\underset{\text{Glycol}}{n\,HOCH_2-CH_2OH} + \underset{\text{Phthalic acid}}{n\,HOOC-C_6H_4-COOH} \xrightarrow[-\,nH_2O]{\substack{420\text{-}460\text{ K}\\ Zn(OCOCH_3)_2+Sb_2O_3}} \underset{\text{Terylene or dacron}}{\left(\!-O-CH_2-CH_2OOC-C_6H_4-\overset{\displaystyle O}{\overset{\|}{C}}-\!\right)_n}$$

Q.6 Which of the following statements is **not** true about low density polyethene?

(a) Tough

(b) Hard

(c) Poor conductor of electricity

(d) Highly branched structure

Ans. ***(b)*** Low density polyethylene is tough, flexible, has a highly branched structure and is a poor conductor of electricity. However, it is not hard, it is soft and pliable. Hence, option (b) is correct choice.

Q.7 $\left(\!-CH_2-\underset{\displaystyle CH_3}{\overset{\displaystyle CH_3}{\overset{|}{\underset{|}{C}}}}-CH_2-\underset{\displaystyle CH_3}{\overset{\displaystyle CH_3}{\overset{|}{\underset{|}{C}}}}-\!\right)_n$ is a polymer having monomer units ....

(a) $CH_2{=}C(CH_3)_2$ (b) $CH_2{=}CH-CH_3$ (c) $CH_3-CH{=}CH-CH_3$ (with H, H) (d) $(CH_3)_2C{=}C(CH_3)_2$

Ans. *(a)* $-\!\!\left(CH_2-\underset{CH_3}{\overset{CH_3}{\overset{|}{\underset{|}{C}}}}-CH_2-\underset{CH_3}{\overset{CH_3}{\overset{|}{\underset{|}{C}}}}\right)\!\!-_n$ can be obtained by addition polymerisation of $=\!\!\!<$ as shown below.

$$n=\!\!< \text{ or } {}_nCH_2=C\begin{matrix}CH_3\\CH_3\end{matrix} \xrightarrow{\text{Polymerisation}} -\!\!\left(CH_2-\underset{CH_3}{\overset{CH_3}{\overset{|}{\underset{|}{C}}}}-CH_2-\underset{CH_3}{\overset{CH_3}{\overset{|}{\underset{|}{C}}}}\right)\!\!-_n$$

(Monomer) 2-Methylpropene — Polymer

Q.8 Which of the following polymer can be formed by using the following monomer unit?

(Ring structure: N–H bonded to H_2C and C=O; ring H_2C, H_2C, H_2C—CH_2, CH_2)

(a) Nylon-6, 6 (b) Nylon-2-nylon-6
(c) Melamine polymer (d) Nylon-6

Ans. *(d)* Given, monomer is the structure of caprolactum which on polymerisation produces Nylon-6.

$$\text{Caprolactum} \xrightarrow[-(n-1)H_2O]{\Delta,\ \text{Polymerisation}} \left[NH-(CH_2)_5-\overset{O}{\overset{\|}{C}}\right]_n$$

Caprolactum — Nylon-6

Multiple Choice Questions (More Than One Options)

Q.9 Which of the following polymers, need atleast one diene monomer for their preparation?

(a) Dacron (b) Buna-S
(c) Neoprene (d) Novolac

Ans. *(b,c)* Buna-S and neoprene are two such polymers which needs atleast one diene monomer for their preparation.

(b) Buna-S is prepared by copolymerisation of 1, 3-butadiene and styrene.

$$nCH_2=CH-CH=CH_2 + C_6H_5CH=CH_2 \xrightarrow{Na/\Delta} \left[CH_2-CH=CH-CH_2-\underset{C_6H_5}{\underset{|}{CH}}-CH\right]_n$$

1, 3-butadiene; Styrene; Styrene butadiene Rubber (buna-S)

(c) Neoprene is prepared by polymerisation of chloroprene.

$$n\underset{\text{Chloroprene}}{CH_2{=}\overset{\overset{\Large Cl}{|}}{C}{-}CH{=}CH_2} \xrightarrow[O_2/\text{peroxides}]{\text{Polymerisation}} \underset{\text{Neoprene}}{\left(CH_2{-}\overset{\overset{\Large Cl}{|}}{C}{=}CH{-}CH_2\right)_n}$$

Q.10 Which of the following are characteristics of thermosetting polymers?

(a) Heavily branched cross linked polymers.

(b) Linear slightly branched long chain molecules .

(c) Become infusible on moulding so cannot be reused.

(d) Soften on heating and harden on cooling, can be reused.

Ans. ***(a, c)*** Thermosetting polymer

(i) These are cross linked or heavily branched molecule.

(ii) These on heating undergo extensive cross linking in moulds and become infusible.

(iii) These cannot be reused.

(iv) Examples are bakelite, urea-form aldehyde resin.

Q.11 Which of the following polymers are thermoplastic?

(a) Teflon (b) Natural rubber (c) Neoprene (d) Polystyrene

Ans. ***(a, d)*** Teflon and polystyrene both are thermoplastic as they can be moulded by heating and melting.

Q.12 Which of the following polymers are used as fibre?

(a) Polytetrafluoroethane (b) Polychloroprene

(c) Nylon (d) Terylene

Ans. ***(c, d)*** Nylon and terylene are used as fibre due to strong intermolecular forces like H-bonding which leads to close packing in chain and thus impart crystalline nature.

Q.13 Which of the following are addition polymers?

(a) Nylon (b) Melamine formaldehyde resin

(c) Orlon (d) Polystyrene

Ans. ***(c, d)*** Addition polymers are formed by the repeated addition of a large number of same or different monomers possessing double and triple bonds. .

e.g.,

(i) Orlon is obtained by addition polymerisation of acrylonitrile in presence of a peroxide catalyst.

$$n\, CH_2{=}CH{-}CN \xrightarrow[\text{Peroxides}]{\text{Polymerisation}} \underset{\substack{\text{Orlon}\\ \text{(polyacrylonitrile)}}}{\left(CH_2{-}\overset{\overset{\Large CN}{|}}{CH}\right)_n}$$

(ii) Polystyrene is obtained by addition polymeriration of styrene.

$$n\, \underset{\text{Styrene}}{C_6H_5{-}CH{=}CH_2} \xrightarrow{\text{Polymerisation}} \underset{\text{Polystyrene}}{\left[\underset{C_6H_5}{CH}{-}CH_2\right]_n}$$

Q.14 Which of the following polymers are condensation polymers?

(a) Bakelite
(b) Teflon
(c) Butyl rubber
(d) Melamine formaldehyde resin

Thinking Process Identify polymers formed by the elimination of small molecules (condensation). Bakaelite and melamine formaldehyde resin are condensation polymers, while Teflon and butyl rubber are addition polymers.

Ans. ***(a, d)*** Condensation polymers are formed by repeated condensation reaction between two bifunctional or trifunctional monomer units usually with the elimination of small molecules like water, alcohol, ammonia, CO_2, HCl.

e.g.,

(i) Bakelite is obtained by polymeristation of phenol and formaldehyde.

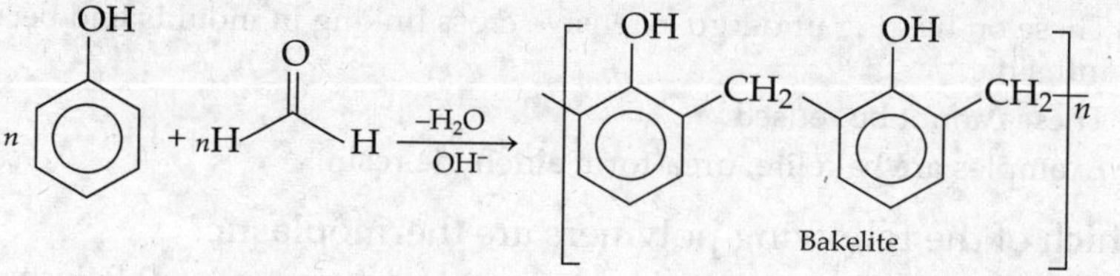

$$n\,C_6H_5OH + nH-\overset{O}{\overset{\|}{C}}-H \xrightarrow[OH^-]{-H_2O} \left[-C_6H_3(OH)-CH_2-C_6H_3(OH)-CH_2- \right]_n$$

Bakelite

(ii) Melamine formaldehyde resin

$$\text{Melamine} + \underset{\text{Formaldehyde}}{HCHO} \longrightarrow \text{Melamine-formaldehyde resin intermediate } (H_2N-C_3N_3(NH_2)-NH_2CH_2OH) \xrightarrow{\text{Polymerisation}} \left[-HN-C_3N_3(NH)-NHCH_2- \right]_n$$

Melamine

Melamine-formaldehyde resin intermediate

Polymerisation

Melamine-formaldehyde polymer

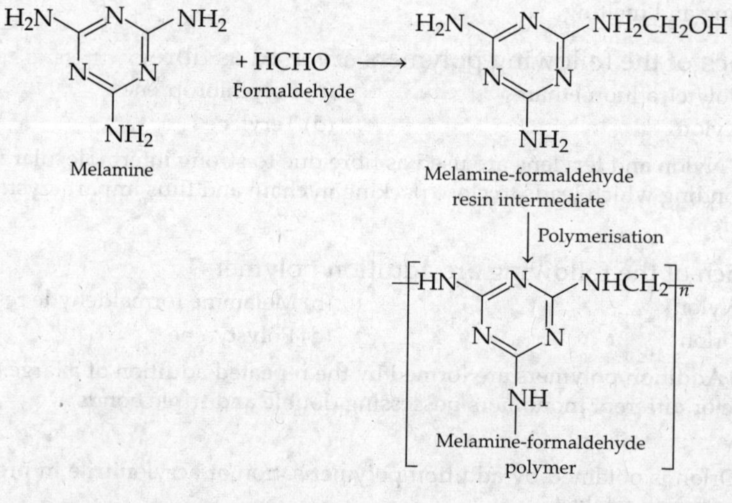

Q.15 Which of the following monomers form biodegradable polymers?

(a) 3-hydroxybutanoic acid + 3-hydroxypentanoic acid
(b) Glycine + amino caproic acid
(c) Ethylene glycol + phthalic acid
(d) Caprolactum

Ans. ***(a, b)*** **Biodegradable Polymer** The polymers which are easily decomposed and not harmful for the environment are known as biodegradable polymers.

e.g.,

(i) PHBV is obtained by condensation polymerisation of 3-hydroxybutanoic acid and 3 hydroxypentanoic acid.

$$n\,CH_3-\underset{\displaystyle |}{\overset{\displaystyle OH}{CH}}-CH_2-COOH + n\,CH_3-CH_2-\overset{\displaystyle OH}{\overset{|}{CH}}-CH_2-COOH \xrightarrow{\text{Polymerisation}}$$

$$\left[O-\underset{\displaystyle CH_2}{\underset{|}{CH}}-CH_2-\underset{\displaystyle O}{\underset{\|}{C}}-O-CH-CH_2-\underset{\displaystyle O}{\underset{\|}{C}}\right]_n + (2n-1)\,H_2O$$

(ii) Glycine and aminocaproic acid produces nylon-2 nylon-6 polymer.

$$n\,\underset{\text{Glycine}}{NH_2-CH_2-COOH} + n\,\underset{\text{Aminocaproic acid}}{NH_2(CH_2)_5\,COOH} \longrightarrow$$

$$\underset{\text{Nylon-2-nylon-6}}{\left[NH-CH_2-\underset{\displaystyle O}{\underset{\|}{C}}-NH-(CH_2)_5-\underset{\displaystyle O}{\underset{\|}{C}}\right]_n} + (2n-1)\,H_2O$$

Q.16 Which of the following are example of synthetic rubber?

(a) Polychloroprene
(b) Polyacrylonitrile
(c) Buna-N
(d) *cis*-polyisoprene

Ans. ***(a, c)*** **Synthetic Polymer** Polymer which are not found in nature and can be synthesised in laboratory and industry are known as synthetic polymer.

e.g.,

(i) Polychloroprene also known as neoprene is a polymer of chloroprene [monomer]. It is known as synthetic rubber.

$$\underset{\text{Chloroprene}}{{}_nCH_2=\underset{\displaystyle Cl}{\underset{|}{C}}-CH=CH_2} \xrightarrow[\text{peroxide}]{O_2\text{ or}} \underset{\text{Polychloroprene}}{\left[CH_2-\underset{\displaystyle Cl}{\underset{|}{C}}=CH-CH_2\right]}$$

(ii) Buna-N can be obtained by copolymerisation of 1,3-Butadiene and acyrlonitrile as shown below

$$\underset{\text{1, 3 Butadiene}}{{}_nCH_2=CH-CH=CH_2} + \underset{\text{Acrylonitrile}}{CH_2=CH-CN}$$

$$\xrightarrow{\text{Peroxide}/\Delta} \underset{\text{Buna-N}}{\left[CH_2-CH=CH-CH_2-CH_2-\underset{\displaystyle CN}{\underset{|}{CH}}\right]_n}$$

Q.17 Which of the following polymers can have strong intermolecular forces?

(a) Nylon (b) Polystyrene
(c) Rubber (d) Polyesters

Ans. ***(a, d)*** Nylon and polyesters have strong intermolecular forces of attractions due to presence of either H-bonding or dipole-dipole interactions.

Q.18 Which of the following polymers have vinylic monomer units?

(a) Acrilan (b) Polystyrene
(c) Nylon (d) Teflon

Ans. ***(a, b, d)*** Acrilan, polystyrene and teflon has vinylic monomer units as shown below.

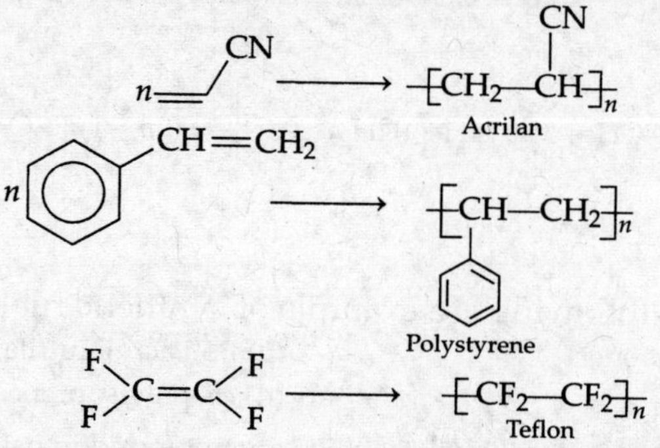

$$n\,CH_2{=}CH{-}CN \longrightarrow {+}CH_2{-}\underset{}{\overset{CN}{\overset{|}{C}H}}{+}_n$$
Acrilan

$$n\,C_6H_5{-}CH{=}CH_2 \longrightarrow {+}\underset{C_6H_5}{\underset{|}{C}H}{-}CH_2{+}_n$$
Polystyrene

$$n\,F_2C{=}CF_2 \longrightarrow {+}CF_2{-}CF_2{+}_n$$
Teflon

Q.19 Vulcanisation makes rubber ....

(a) more elastic (b) soluble in inorganic solvent
(c) crystalline (d) more stiff

Thinking Process This problem includes the concept of vulcanistion of rubber and characteristic of vulcanized rubber. Vulcanisation of rubber produces more elastic and more stiff rubber due to presence of sulphide linkage.

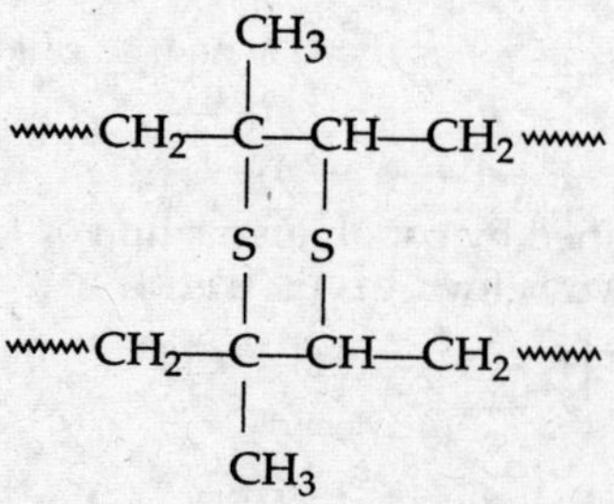

$$\begin{array}{c} CH_3 \\ | \\ \sim\sim CH_2{-}C{-}CH{-}CH_2\sim\sim \\ \quad\;\; | \quad\;\; | \\ \quad\;\; S \quad\;\; S \\ \quad\;\; | \quad\;\; | \\ \sim\sim CH_2{-}C{-}CH{-}CH_2\sim\sim \\ | \\ CH_3 \end{array}$$

Ans. ***(a, d)*** In vulcanised rubber, the polymer chains are held together by sulphur cross-linkages (—S—S—). These cross links make rubber more hard, elastic and stronger.

Short Answer Type Questions

Q.20 A natural linear polymer of 2-methyl-1, 3-butadiene becomes hard on treatment with sulphur between 373 to 415 K and —S—S—bonds are formed between chains. Write the structure of the product of this treatment?

Thinking Process This problem is based on vulcanised rubber and its structure.

Ans. The product is called vulcanised rubber. Its structure is

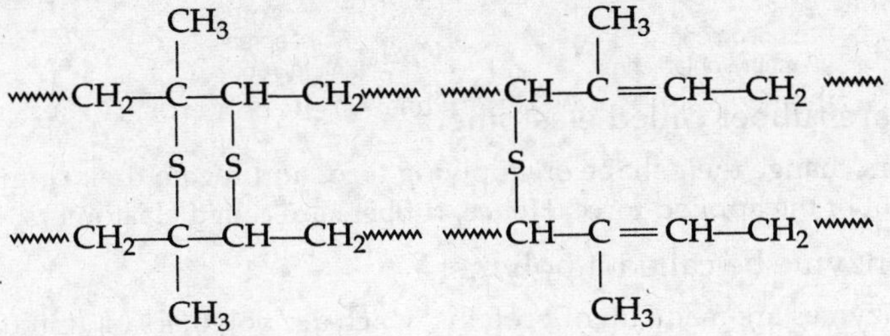

```
           CH3                              CH3
           |                                |
~~~~CH2—C—CH—CH2~~~~    ~~~~CH—C=CH—CH2 ~~~~
           |   |                  |
           S   S                  S
           |   |                  |
~~~~CH2—C—CH—CH2~~~~    ~~~~CH—C=CH—CH2 ~~~~
           |                                |
           CH3                              CH3
```

Q.21 Identify the type of polymer

$$—A—A—A—A—A—A—$$

Ans. Homopolymer as it contains only one type of monomer units, *i.e.*, only *A* monomer units.

Q.22 Identify the type of polymer

$$—A—B—B—A—A—A—B—A—$$

Ans. Copolymer, as it contains more than one type of monomer units. Here, *A* and *B* are two types of monomer units.

Q.23 Out of chain growth polymerisation and step growth polymerisation, in which type will you place the following.

$$(\!-A-\!)_m + (\!-A-\!)_n \longrightarrow (\!-A)_n\text{—}(A)_n \text{ or } (\!-A\text{—}A-\!)_{m+n}$$

Ans. Chain growth polymerisation, as there is no loss of small molecules like water; methanol, etc.

$$(\!-A-\!)_m + (\!-A-\!)_n \longrightarrow (\!-A)_m\text{—}(A)_n \text{ or } (\!-A\text{—}A-\!)_{m+n}$$

Q.24 Identify the type of polymer given in the following figure.

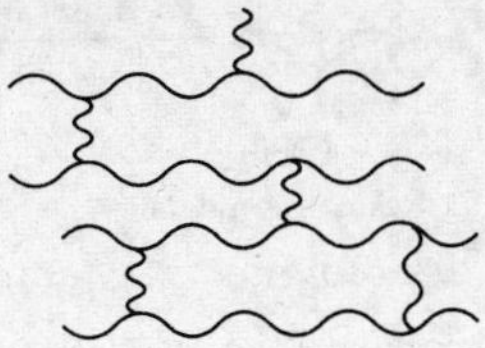

Ans. Cross-linked or network polymer.

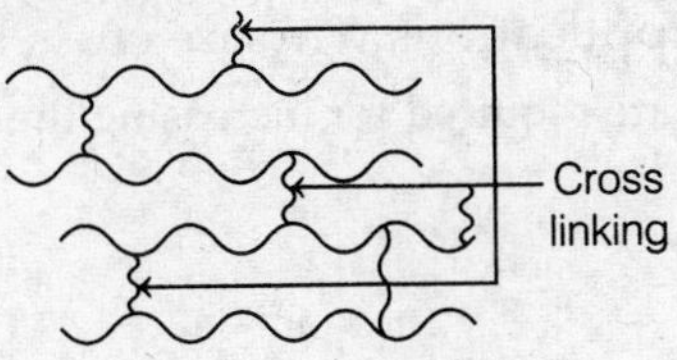

Cross
linking

Q.25 Identify the polymer given below.

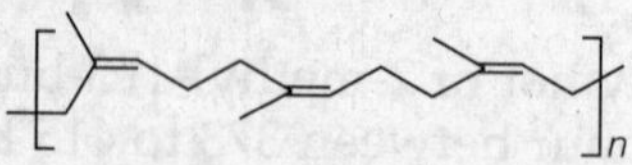

Ans. The given polymer is formed by 1, 4-addition of 2- methylbuta- 1,3- diene (isoprene) and stereochemistry is '*cis*' throughout. Therefore, the given polymer is '*cis*'- polyisoprene, *i.e.*, natural rubber.

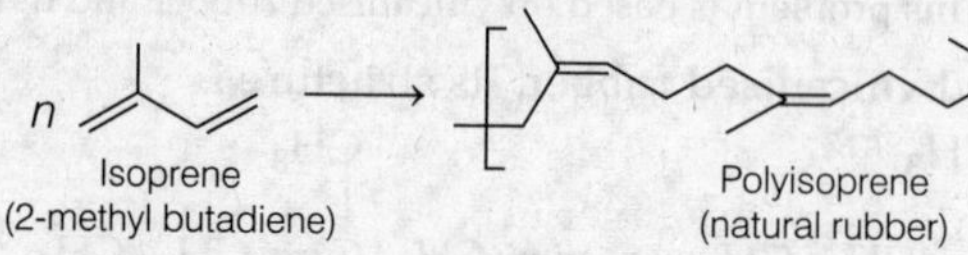

n Isoprene (2-methyl butadiene) → Polyisoprene (natural rubber)

Q.26 Why are rubber called elastomers?

Ans. Rubbers change their shape on applying force and regain their original shape on removal of the applied force. Hence, rubbers are called elastomers.

Q.27 Can enzyme be called a polymer?

Ans. Yes, enzymes are made up of proteins which are polymers of amino acids.

Q.28 Can nucleic acids, proteins and starch be considered as step growth polymers?

Ans. *Yes,* nucleic acids, proteins and starch can be considered as step growth polymers as during their polymerisation reaction, they lead to removal of water molecule or any neutral molecule also. Thus, these are the examples of condensation polymers or step growth polymers.

Q.29 How is the following resin intermediate prepared and which polymers is formed by this monomer unit?

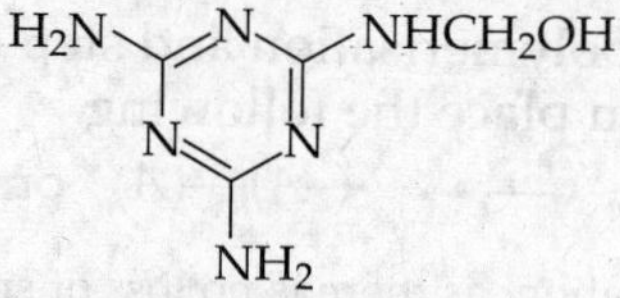

H_2N, $NHCH_2OH$, NH_2 (Resin intermediate)

Ans. Reaction between melamine and formaldehyde can be shown as

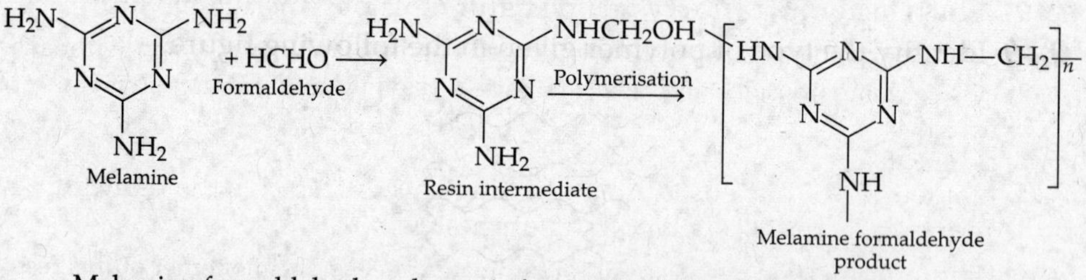

Melamine + HCHO (Formaldehyde) → Resin intermediate $\xrightarrow{\text{Polymerisation}}$ $[HN-C_3N_3(NH-)-NH-CH_2]_n$ Melamine formaldehyde product

Melamine-formaldehyde polymer is formed by this monomer unit.

Q.30 To have practical applications why are cross links required in rubber?

Ans. Cross links in rubber are required for increasing the elasticity of rubber.

Q.31 Why does *cis*-polyisoprene possess elastic property?

Ans. *cis*-polyisoprene is also known as natural rubber. Its elastic property is due to the existence of weak van der Waals interactions between their various polymer chains.

Q.32 What is the structural difference between HDP and LDP? How does the structure account for different behaviour and nature, hence use of a polymer?

Ans. HDP (high density polymer) consists of linear molecule and has a high density due to close packing. It is a translucent polymer. While LDP (low density polymer) has highly branched structure and hence, does not pack well resulting in low density. It is a transparent material.

Q.33 What is the role of benzoyl peroxide in addition polymerisation of alkenes? Explain its mode of action with the help of an example.

Ans. Role of benzoyl peroxide is to initiate the free radical polymerisation reaction which can be easily understood by taking an example of polymerisation of ethene to polyethene.

(i) Chain initiation

$$Ph-\overset{O}{\overset{\|}{C}}-O-O-\overset{O}{\overset{\|}{C}}-Ph \longrightarrow 2\left[C_6H_5-\overset{O}{\overset{\|}{C}}-\dot{O}\right] \longrightarrow 2\dot{C}_6H_5 + 2CO_2$$

Phenyl free radical

(ii) Chain propagation

$$\dot{C}_6H_5 + \underset{\text{Ethene}}{CH_2=CH_2} \longrightarrow C_6H_5-CH_2-\dot{C}H_2$$

$$\xrightarrow{CH_2=CH_2} C_6H_5 \left(CH_2-CH_2 \right)_n CH_2-\dot{C}H_2$$

(iii) Chain terminator step

$$2C_6H_5 \left(CH_2CH_2 \right)_n \dot{C}H_2 \longrightarrow$$

$$\underset{\text{Polythene}}{C_6H_5 \left(CH_2-CH_2 \right)_n CH_2CH_2CH_2CH_2 \left(CH_2-CH_2 \right)_n C_6H_5}$$

Q.34 Which factor imparts crystalline nature to a polymer like nylon?

Ans. Strong intermolecular forces like hydrogen bonding and linear structure leads to close packing of chains and hence, imparts crystalline character to polymer, *e.g.*, nylon.

Q.35 Name the polymer used in laminating sheets and give the name of monomeric units involved in its formation.

Ans. Urea formaldehyde resin is used for laminated sheets. The monomer of this resin is urea (NH_2CONH_2) and formaldehyde (HCHO).

$$n\underset{\text{Urea}}{NH_2-CO-NH_2} + n\underset{\text{Formaldehyde}}{HCHO} \xrightarrow[\text{Condensation polymerisation}]{-H_2O} \left[NH-CO-NH-CH_2 \right]_n$$

Q.36 Which type of biomolecules have some structural similarity with synthetic polyamides? What is similarity?

Ans. Polyamides have structural repetition of amide linkages which is similar to peptide bond as present in polypeptide chains of proteins.

$$n\underset{\underset{NH_2}{|}}{CH_2}-COOH \longrightarrow -\!\!\left[NH-CH_2-\boxed{\overset{O}{\overset{\|}{C}}-NH}-CH_2-\overset{O}{\overset{\|}{C}}\right]\!\!-_n$$

Peptide bond

Q.37 Why should the monomer used in addition polymerisation through free radical pathway be very pure?

Ans. During free radical polymerisation, monomers should be very pure because even very trace amounts of impurities may act as inhibitors which leads to the formation of polymers with shorter length.

Matching The Columns

Q.38 Match the polymer of Column I with correct monomer of Column II.

	Column I		Column II
A.	High density polyethene	1.	Isoprene
B.	Neoprene	2.	Tetrafluoro ethene
C.	Natural rubber	3.	Chloroprene
D.	Teflon	4.	Acrylonitrile
E.	Acrilan	5.	Ethene

Ans. **A.** → (5) **B.** → (3) **C.** → (1) **D.** → (2) **E.** → (4)

Column I represents various kind of polymer and Column II represents their monomer units. Correct matching can be done as :

	Column I	Column II
A.	High density polymer	Ethene
B.	Neoprene	Chloroprene
C.	Natural rubber	Isoprene
D.	Teflon	Tetrafluoroethene
E.	Acrilan	Acrylonitrile

Q.39 Match the polymers given in Column I with their chemical names given in Column II.

	Column I		Column II
A.	Nylon-6	1.	Polyvinyl chloride
B.	PVC	2.	Polyacrylonitrile
C.	Acrilan	3.	Polycaprolactum
D.	Natural rubber	4.	Low density polythene
E.	LDP	5.	*cis*-polyisoprene

Ans. **A.** → (3) **B.** → (1) **C.** → (2) **D.** → (5) **E.** → (4)

Column I represents various polymers and Column II represents their chemical names.

	Column I	Column II
A.	Nylon-6	Polycaprolactum
B.	PVC	Polyvinyl chloride
C.	Acrilan	Polyacrylonitrile
D.	Natural rubber	*cis*-polyisoprene
E.	LDP	Low density polythene

Q.40 Match the polymers given in Column I with their commercial names given in Column II.

	Column I		Column II
A.	Polyester of glycol and phthalic acid	1.	Novolac
B.	Copolymer of 1, 3-butadiene and styrene	2.	Glyptal
C.	Phenol and formaldehyde resin	3.	Buna-S
D.	Polyester of glycol and terephthalic acid	4.	Buna-N
E.	Copolymer of 1,3- butadiene and acrylonitrile	5.	Dacron

Ans. **A.** → (2) **B.** → (3) **C.** → (1) **D.** → (5) **E.** → (4)

Column I represents monomers of polymer and Column II represents their commercial name.

	Column I	Column II
A.	Polyester of glycol and phthalic acid	Glyptal
B.	Copolymer of 1, 3-butadiene and styrene	Buna-S
C.	Phenol and formaldehyde resin	Novolac
D.	Polyester of glycol and terephthalic acid	Dacron
E.	Copolymer of 1, 3-butadiene and acrylonitrile	Buna-N

Q.41 Match the polymers given in Column I with their main applications given in Column II.

	Column I		Column II
A.	Bakelite	1.	Unbreakable crockery
B.	Low density polythene	2.	Non-stick cookwares
C.	Melamine-formaldehyde resin	3.	Packaging material for shock absorbance
D.	Nylon-6	4.	Electrical switches
E.	Polytetrafluoroethane	5.	Squeeze bottles
F.	Polystyrene	6.	Tyre, cords

Ans. **A.** → (4) **B.** → (5) **C.** → (1) **D.** → (6) **E.** → (2) **F.** → (3)

	Column I	Column II
A.	Bakelite	Electrical switches
B.	Low density polythene	Squeeze bottles
C.	Melamine-formaldehyde resin	Unbreakable crockery
D.	Nylon-6	Tyre, cords
E.	Polytetrafluoroethane	Non-stick cookwares
F.	Polystyrene	Packaging material for shock absorbance

Q.42 Match the polymers given in Column I with the preferred mode of polymerisation followed by their monomers in Column II.

	Column I		Column II
A.	Nylon-6,6	1.	Free radical polymerisation
B.	PVC	2.	Ziegler-Natta polymerisation or coordination polymerisation
C.	HDP	3.	Anionic polymerisation
		4.	Condensation polymerisation

Ans. **A.** → (4) **B.** → (1) **C.** → (2)

Column I represents name of various polymer and Column II represents mechanism of polymerisation. Correct matching can be done as.

	Column I (Polymer)	Column II (Mechanism of polymerisation)
A.	Nylon- 6, 6	Condensation polymerisation
B.	PVC	Free radical polymerisation
C.	HDP	Ziegler-Natta polymerisation or coordination polymerisation

Q.43 Match the polymers given in Column I with the type of linkage present in them given in Column II.

	Column I		Column II
A.	Terylene	1.	Glycosidic linkage
B.	Nylon	2.	Ester linkage
C.	Cellulose	3.	Phosphodiester linkage
D.	Protein	4.	Amide linkage
E.	RNA		

Ans. A. → (2) B. → (4) C. → (1) D. → (4) E. → (3)

Column I represents name of polymer and Column II represents types of linkage. Hence, correct matching can be done as.

	Column I	Column II
A.	Terylene	Ester linkage
B.	Nylon	Amide linkage
C.	Cellulose	Glycosidic linkage
D.	Protein	Amide linkage
E.	RNA	Phosphodiester linkage

Q.44 Match materials given in Column I with the polymers given in Column II.

	Column I		Column II
A.	Natural rubber latex	1.	Nylon
B.	Wood laminates	2.	Neoprene
C.	Ropes and fibres	3.	Dacron
D.	Polyester fabric	4.	Melamine formaldehyde resins
E.	Synthetic rubber	5.	Urea-formaldehyde resins
F.	Unbreakable crockery	6.	*cis*-polyisoprene

Ans. A. → (6) B. → (5) C. → (1) D. → (3) E. → (2) F. → (4)

Column I represents various uses or precursors of polymers and Column II represents name of related polymer. The correct matching can be done as :

	Column I	Column II
A.	Natural rubber latex	*cis*-polyisoprene
B.	Wood laminates	Urea-formaldehyde resins
C.	Ropes and fibres	Nylon
D.	Polyester fabric	Dacron
E.	Synthetic rubber	Neoprene
F.	Unbreakable crockery	Melamine formaldehyde resins

Q.45 Match the polymers given in Column I with their repeating units given in Column II.

	Column I		Column II
A.	Acrilan	1.	$-[CH_2-CH(C_6H_5)]_n-$
B.	Polystyrene	2.	$-[CH_2-C(Cl)=CH-CH_2]_n-$
C.	Neoprene	3.	$-[CH_2-CH=CH-CH_2-CH_2-CH(CN)]_n-$
D.	Novolac	4.	$-[CH_2-CH(CN)]_n-$
E.	Buna–N	5.	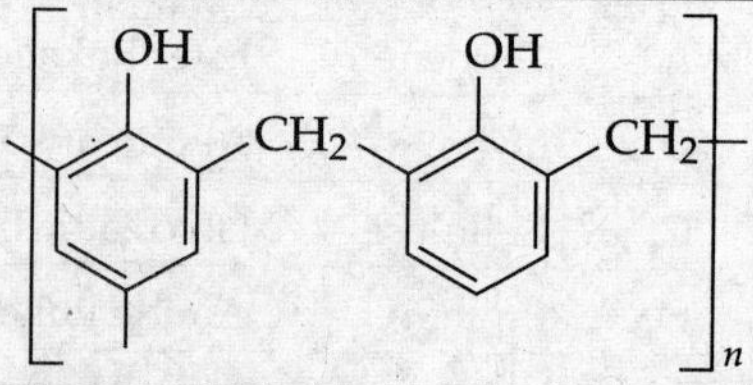 $\left[\text{(phenol ring with OH)}-CH_2-\text{(phenol ring with OH)}-CH_2\right]_n$
		6.	$-[CH_2-CH(Cl)]_n-$

Ans. **A.** → (4) **B.** → (1) **C.** → (2) **D.** → (5) **E.** → (3)

Column I represents name of polymer and Column II represents their molecular formula. The correct matching can be done as.

	Column I	Column II
A.	Acrilan	$-[CH_2-CH(CN)]_n-$
B.	Polystyrene	$-[CH_2-CH(C_6H_5)]_n-$
C.	Neoprene	$-[CH_2-C(Cl)=CH-CH_2]_n-$
D.	Novolac	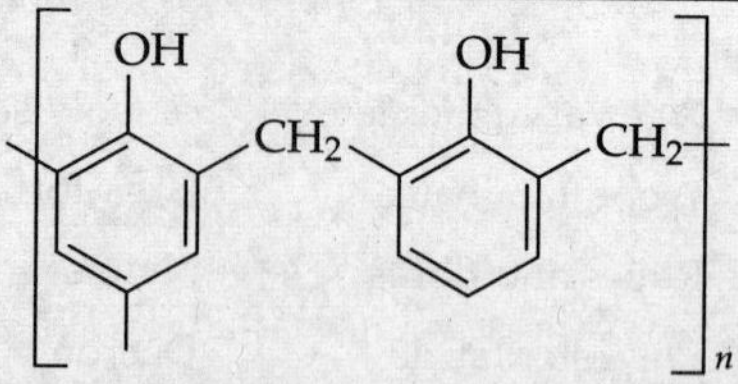 $\left[\text{(phenol ring with OH)}-CH_2-\text{(phenol ring with OH)}-CH_2\right]_n$
E.	Buna–N	$-[CH_2-CH=CH-CH_2-CH_2-CH(CN)]_n-$

Assertion and Reason

In the following questions a statement of assertion followed by a statement of reason is given. Choose the correct answer out of the following choices.

(a) Assertion and reason both are correct statement But reason does not explain assertion.

(b) Assertion and reason both are correct statements and reason explain the assertion.

(c) Both assertion and reason are wrong statements.

(d) Assertion is correct statement and reason is wrong statement.

(e) Assertion is wrong statement and reason is correct statement.

Q.46 **Assertion** Rayon is a semisynthetic polymer and is taken as a better choice than cotton fabric.

Reason Mechanical and aesthetic properties of cellulose can be improved by Acetylation.

Ans. *(b)* Assertion and reason both are correct and reason explains the assertion.

Rayon is a semisynthetic polymer and is taken as a better choice than cotton fabric because mechanical and aesthetic properties of cellulose can be improved by acetylation.

Q.47 **Assertion** Most of the synthetic polymers are not biodegradable.

Reason Polymerisation process induces toxic character in organic molecules.

Ans. *(d)* Assertion is correct statement but reason is not correct statement. Most of synthetic polymers are not biodegradable because they are not easily broken by soil organisms and are hazardous to the environment.

Q.48 **Assertion** Olefinic monomers undergo addition polymerisation.

Reason Polymerisation of vinyl chloride is initiated by peroxides/persulphates.

Ans. *(a)* Assertion and reason both are correct but reason does not explain assertion.

Olefin monomers undergo addition polymerisation because it adds on to other monomers of olefin through free radical mechanism due to the presence of peroxide initiator and double bond, and the produces high molecular mass polymers.

Q.49 **Assertion** Polyamides are best used as fibres because of high tensile strength.

Reason Strong intermolecular forces (like hydrogen bonding within polyamides) lead to close packing of chains and increase the crystalline character, hence, provide high tensile strength to polymers.

Ans. *(b)* Assertion and reason both are correct and reason explains assertion.
Polyamides are best used as fibres because of high tensile strength. This is due to strong intermolecular forces (like hydrogen bonding within polyamides) which leads to close packing of chains and increase in the crystalline character, hence, it provide high tensile strength to polymers.

Q.50 **Assertion** For making rubber synthetically, isoprene molecules are polymerised.

Reason Neoprene (a polymer of chloroprene) is a synthetic rubber.

Ans. *(e)* Assertion is wrong and reason is correct statement. Correct assertion is, synthetic rubbers are prepared by polymerisation of 1, 3- butadiene.

Neoprene is a synthetic rubber, which is formed by the free radical polymerisation of chloroprene.

Cl Cl

n n

Chloroprene Neoprene

Q.51 **Assertion** Network polymers are thermosetting.

Reason Network polymers have high molecular mass.

Ans. *(a)* Assertion and reason both are correct and reason does not explain assertion. Network polymers are thermosetting because they cannot be reused after heating once. Because after heating, it undergoes extensive cross linking in moulds and again become infusible.

Q.52 **Assertion** Polytetrafluoroethene is used in making non-stick cookwares.

Reason Fluorine has highest electronegativity.

Ans. *(a)* Assertion and reason both are correct but reason does not explain assertion.

Polytetrafluoroethene (teflon) is used in making non-stick cookwares because it is chemically inert, thermally stable and resistant to attack by corrosive reagents.

Long Answer Type Questions

Q.53 Synthetic polymers do not degrade in the environment for a long time. How can biodegradable synthetic polymers be made. Differentiate between biopolymers and biodegradable polymers and give examples of each type.

Ans. Synthetic polymers are quite resistant to environmental degradation process and are responsible for accumulation of polymer solid waste material. New biodegradable synthetic polymers have been designed and developed. These polymers contain similar functional groups as present in biopolymers.

e.g., aliphatic polyesters

Biopolymer are polymers of amino acid or carbohydrates which are linked to each other by peptide or glycosidic linkages as shown below.

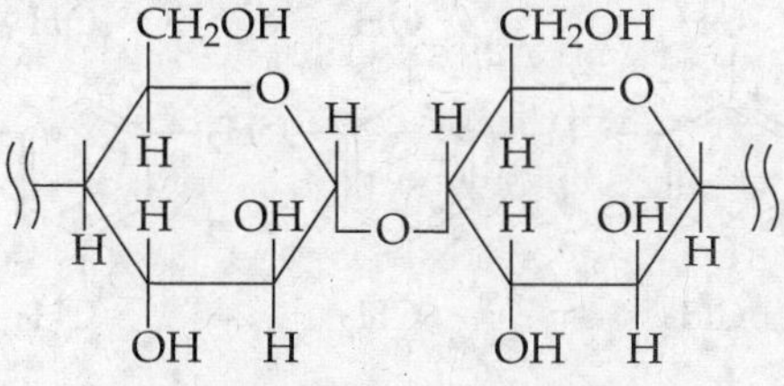

Starch (polymer of glucose)

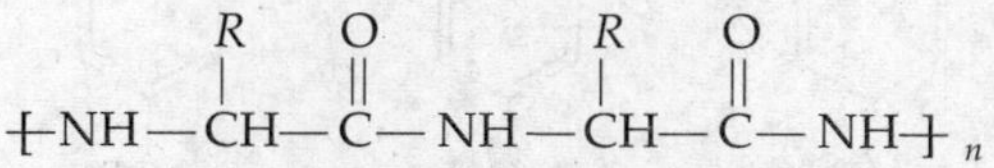

$$-\!\!\left[NH-\underset{}{\overset{R}{\overset{|}{C}}}H-\overset{O}{\overset{||}{C}}-NH-\overset{R}{\overset{|}{C}}H-\overset{O}{\overset{||}{C}}-NH\right]\!\!-_n$$

Polymer of amino acid

Biopolymer can or cannot be biodegradable. *e.g.*, protein, starch etc., are biodegradable but keratin is non-biodegradable. Biodegradable polymers are polymers which can be degradable. *e.g.*, PHBV, Nylon-2, Nylon-6.

Q.54 Differentiate between rubbers and plastics on the basis of intermolecular forces.

Ans. Rubber is a natural polymer which possess elastic properties. Natural rubber is a linear polymer of isoprene (2-methyl-1,3-butadiene).

In natural rubber, *cis*-polyisoprene molecules consist of various chains held together by weak van der Waals interaction and has coiling structure. So, it can be stretched like a spring. Plastics are generally polymer of ethene known as polythene. Polythene is thermoplastic polymer which may be linear (HDP) or branched (LDP). These type of polymers, possesses intermediate intermolecular forces of attraction. It has linear, structure that can be moulded but cannot be regained to its original shape after stretching.

Q.55 Phenol and formaldehyde undergo condensation to give a polymer which on heating with formaldehyde gives a thermosetting polymer (*B*). Name the polymers. Write the reactions involved in the formation of (A). What is the structural difference between two polymers?

Ans. Phenol and formaldehyde undergo condensation to give a polymer novolac which on heating with formaldehyde gives bakelite (*B*) which is a thermosetting polymer. Sequence of the reaction can be written as.

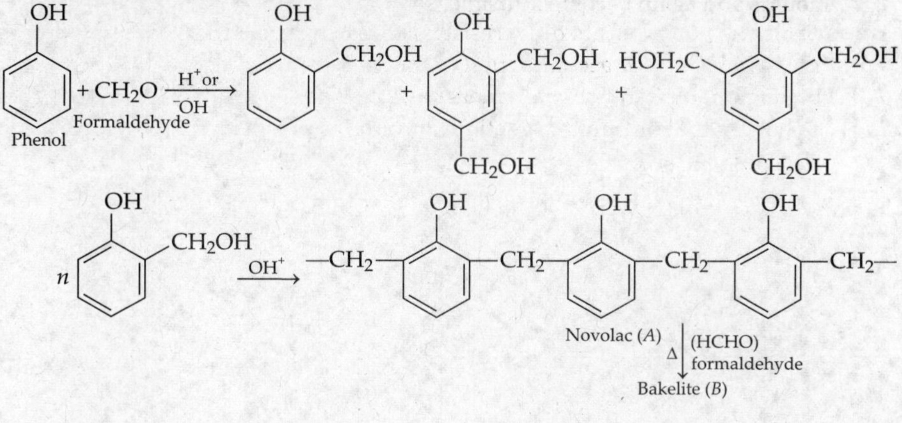

Phenol + CH_2O (Formaldehyde) $\xrightarrow[^-OH]{H^+ \text{ or}}$ o-hydroxymethylphenol (OH, CH_2OH) + 2,4-bis(hydroxymethyl)phenol (OH, CH_2OH, CH_2OH) + 2,4,6-tris(hydroxymethyl)phenol (HOH_2C, OH, CH_2OH, CH_2OH)

n o-hydroxymethylphenol (OH, CH_2OH) $\xrightarrow{OH^+}$ $-CH_2-$[phenol]$-CH_2-$[phenol]$-CH_2-$[phenol]$-CH_2-$

Novolac (*A*) $\xrightarrow[\Delta]{\text{(HCHO) formaldehyde}}$ Bakelite (*B*)

Structural difference in between these two is that novolac is a linear polymer while bakelite is a cross linked polymer.

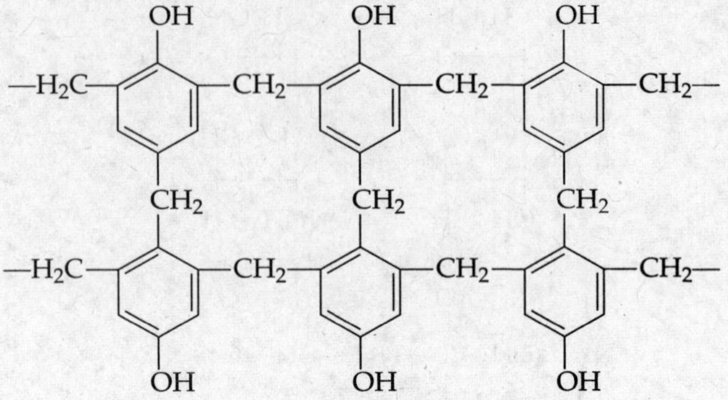

Bakelite (*B*) (cross linked polymer)

Q.56 Low density polythene and high density polythene, both are polymers of ethene but there is marked difference in their properties. Explain.

Ans. Low density and high density polythenes are obtained under different conditions. These differ in their structural features. Low density polythenes are highly branched structures while high density polythene consists of closely packed linear molecules. Close packing increases the density.

Low density polymer is obtained through free radical addition at high pressure and temperature. High density polymer is obtained by addition polymerisation of ethene in presence of hydrocarbon solvent at low pressure and temperature.

Q.57 Which of the following polymers soften on heating and harden on cooling? What are the polymers with this property collectively called? What are the structural similarities between such polymers? Bakelite, urea-formaldehyde resin, polythene, polyvinyls, polystyrene.

Ans. Polythene, polyvinyls and polystyrene soften on heating and harden on cooling. Such polymers are called thermoplastic polymers. These polymers are linear array of slightly branched long chain molecules.

These possess intermolecular forces whose strength lies between strength of intermolecular forces of elastomers and fibres. Bakelite, urea formaldehyde resin are thermosetting polymers which on heating undergo extensive cross linking in moulds and again become infusible.

Chapter

16 Chemistry in Everyday Life*

Multiple Choice Questions (MCQs)

Q.1 Which of the following statements is **not** correct?

(a) Some antiseptics can be added to soaps.
(b) Dilute solutions of some disinfectants can be used as antiseptic.
(c) Disinfectants are antimicrobial drugs.
(d) Antiseptic medicines can be ingested.

Ans. *(d)* An antiseptic is an antimicrobial drug. It tends to destroy/prevent development or inhibit the pathogenic action of microbes. Antiseptics are applied to the living tissues such as wounds, cuts, ulcers and diseased skin surfaces. Example of antiseptic is soframicine.

Bithionol (the compound is also called bithional) is added to soaps to impart antiseptic properties.

Dilute solutions of some disinfectants can be used as antiseptic *e.g.,* 0.2 per cent solution of phenol is an antiseptic while its one per cent solution is disinfectant. But, antiseptic medicines can not be ingested like antibiotics.

Q.2 Which is the correct statement about birth control pills?

(a) Contain estrogen only.
(b) Contain progesterone only.
(c) Contain a mixture of estrogen and progesterone derivatives.
(d) Progesterone enhances ovulation.

Ans. *(c)* Chemical substances which are used to prevent pregnancy in women are called birth control pills. Birth control pills essentially contain a mixture of synthetic estrogen and progesterone derivatives, both of these are sex hormones. It is known that progesterone suppresses ovulation and estrogen controls the menstrual cycle.

Some of the commonly used pills contain a mixture of norethindrone (a progesterone derivative) and novestrol (an oestrogen).

Q.3 Which statement about aspirin is **not** true?

(a) Aspirin belongs to narcotic analgesics.
(b) It is effective in relieving pain.
(c) It has antiblood clotting action.
(d) It is a neurologically active drug.

Thinking Process This problem is based on the concept of classification of drugs based on their action. It can be solved by identifying aspirin's properties and distinguishing narcotic from non-narcotic analgesics.

Note (*) This chapter has been deleted from latest NCERT.

Ans. *(a)* Aspirin can be prepared as follows :

$$\text{Salicylic acid (C}_6\text{H}_4\text{(COOH)(OH))} + (CH_3CO)_2O \xrightarrow{H^+} \text{2-Acetoxybenzoic acid (C}_6\text{H}_4\text{(COOH)(OCOCH}_3\text{))} + CH_3COOH$$

Salicylic acid — 2-Acetoxybenzoic acid (Aspirin)

Aspirin inhibits the synthesis of compounds known as prostaglandins which stimulate inflammation in the tissues and cause pain. So, it is effective in relieving pain.

Beside this, aspirin has many other effects such as reducing fever (antipyretic) and preventing blood platelet coagulation. Because of this anti-blood clotting action, it is widely used to prevent heart attacks. It does not make a person addictive as it is non-narcotic drug.

Q.4 The most useful classification of drugs for medicinal chemists is ....

(a) on the basis of chemical structure
(b) on the basis of drug action
(c) on the basis of molecular targets
(d) on the basis of pharmacological effect

Ans. *(c)* Drugs can be classified in the following ways

(a) **On the basis of chemical structure** Drugs have been classified on the basis of their chemical structures because drugs having common structural features often have similar pharmacological activity, *e.g.*, all sulphonamides having the common structural feature as given below are mostly antibacterial.

(b) **On the basis of drug action** This classification is based on the action of a drug on a particular biochemical process.

(c) **On the basis of molecular target** Drugs usually interact with the biomolecules or biological macromolecules such as proteins, nucleic acids and lipids. These are called drug targets.

Drugs possessing some common structural features may have the same mechanism of action on a specific drug target. This classification is most useful for the medicinal chemists.

(d) **On the basis of pharmacological effect** This classification is based upon the pharmacological effects of the drugs. It is more useful for the doctors because it provides them the whole range of drugs available for the treatment of a particular disease. *e.g.,* analgesics reduce or kill pain while antiseptic either kill or arrest the growth of microorganisms.

Q.5 Which of the following statements is correct?

(a) Some tranquilizers function by inhibiting the enzymes, which catalyse the degradation of noradrenaline.
(b) Tranquilizers are narcotic drugs.
(c) Tranquilizers are chemical compounds that do not affect the message transfer from nerve to receptor.
(d) Tranquilizers are chemical compounds that can relieve pain and fever.

Ans. *(a)* Tranquilizers are used for the treatment of stress, fatigue, mild and severe mental diseases. They relieve anxiety, stress, irritability or excitement by inducing a sense of well-being. Noradrenaline is one of the several neurotransmitters which play an important role in mood changes. These drugs inhibits the enzymes which catalyse the degradation of noradrenaline.

Note If the level of noradrenaline in the body is low for some reasons, then the message transfer process becomes slow and the person suffer from depression. In such cases, antidepressant drugs are used. These drugs inhibit the enzymes which catalyse the degradation of noradrenaline.

Q.6 Salvarsan is arsenic containing drug which was first used for the treatment of ....

(a) syphilis (b) typhoid (c) meningitis (d) dysentry

Ans. *(a)* Syphilis is an acute and chronic infections disease caused by the bacterium *Treponema pallidum*. It is a sexually transmitted infection. The primary route of transmission is through sexual contact but it may also be transmitted from mother to foetus during pregnancy or at birth.

Paul Ehrlich investigated arsenic based structures in order to produce less toxic substances for the treatment of syphilis as he got Nobel prize for medicine in 1908 for this discovery. Salvarsan was the first effective medicine discovered for syphilis. Although salvarsan is toxic to human beings, its effect on bacteria is much greater than on human being. Structure of salvarsan is

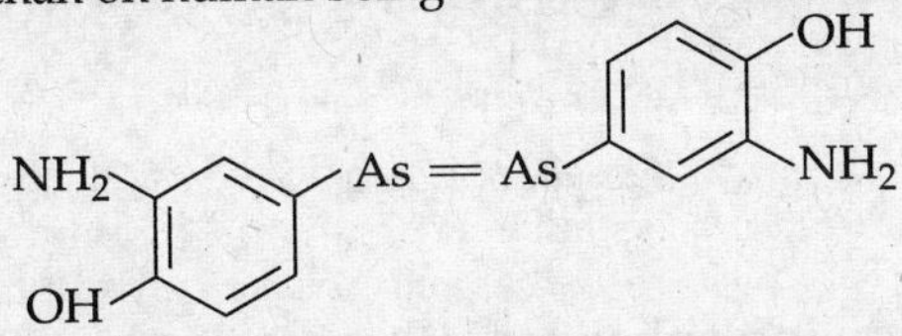

Q.7 A narrow spectrum antibiotic is active against ....

(a) gram positive or gram negative bacteria
(b) gram negative bacteria only
(c) single organism or one disease
(d) both gram positive and gram negative bacteria

Ans. *(a)* Broad spectrum antibiotics are effective against a wide range of harmful bacteria, including both gram-positive and gram-negative bacteria. However, narrow-spectrum antibiotics target either gram-positive or gram-negative bacteria specifically.

Q.8 The compound that causes general antidepressant action on the central nervous system belongs to the class of......

(a) analgesics (b) tranquilizers
(c) narcotic analgesics (d) antihistamines

Ans. *(b)* Analgesics reduces or abolish pain without causing impairment of consciousness, mental confusion, incordination, paralysis or some other disturbances of nervous system. Analgesics are non-narcotic or narcotic. Narcotic analgesics when administered in small doses relieve pain and produce sleep.

Tranquilisers are a class of chemical compounds used for the treatment of stress, and mild or even severe mental diseases. The class of tranquilizers are used as antidepressant drugs which act on the central nervous system.

Q.9 Compound which is added to soap to impart antiseptic properties is ....

(a) sodium laurylsulphate (b) sodium dodecylbenzenesulphonate
(c) rosin (d) bithional

- **Concept Insight** This solution includes the concept of soap and detergent composition and their functional additives. It explains how different substances like rosin enhance lathering and bithional provides antiseptic properties.

Ans. ***(d)*** Basically, all soaps are made by boiling fats or oils with suitable hydroxide. Variations are made by adding different raw materials. Sodium laurylsulphate and sodium dodecylbenzenesulphonate are anionic detergents.

A gum rosin is added to soap to make it lather well. Bithional is added to soaps to impart antiseptic properties to soap.

Q.10 Equanil is ....

(a) artificial sweetener (b) tranquilizer
(c) antihistamine (d) antifertility drug

Ans. ***(b)*** Equanil is a tranquilizer.

$$H_2N-\overset{\overset{\large O}{\|}}{C}-O-CH_2-\overset{\overset{\large CH_3}{|}}{\underset{\underset{\large CH_3}{|}}{C}}-CH_2-O-\overset{\overset{\large O}{\|}}{C}-NH_2$$

Structure of equanil

(*Also, refer to Q.* 5)

Q.11 Which of the following enhances lathering property of soap?

(a) Sodium carbonate (b) Sodium rosinate
(c) Sodium stearate (d) Trisodium phosphate

Ans. ***(b)*** Shaving soaps contain glycerol to prevent rapid drying. While preparing the soaps, a gum called rosin is added to them. It forms sodium rosinate which lathers well. Laundary soaps contain fillers like sodium rosinate, sodium silicate, borax and sodium carbonate.

Trisodium polyphosphate is an important filler added to detergent powders and liquid detergents.

Q.12 Glycerol is added to soap. It functions ....

(a) as a filler (b) to increases lathering
(c) to prevent rapid drying (d) to make soap granules

Ans. ***(c)*** Glycerol is added to shaving soap to prevent rapid drying while to enhance the lathering property of soap, a gum called rosin is added to them. It forms sodium rosinate which lathers well. Soap granules are dried miniature soap bubbles.

Builders/fillers make the soap act more rapidly. Builder or filler (*e.g.* sodium tripolyphosphate) is added to detergent powder. Its main function is to act as water softener by removing Mg^{2+} and Ca^{2+} ions from hard water by forming stable soluble complexes.

Q.13 Which of the following is an example of liquid dishwashing detergent?

(a) $CH_3(CH_2)_{10}CH_2OSO_3^-Na^+$

(b) $C_9H_{19}-C_6H_4-O+CH_2-CH_2-O+_5CH_2CH_2OH$

(c) $CH_3-C_6H_4-SO_3^- Na^+$

(d) $\left[CH_3(CH_2)_{15}-\underset{CH_3}{\overset{CH_3}{|}}{N}-CH_3 \right]^+ Br^-$

Ans. ***(b)*** Liquid dishwashing detergents are non-ionic type. Non-ionic detergents do not contain any ion in their constitution. Mechanism of cleansing action of this type of detergents is the same as that of soaps. These remove grease and oil by micelle formation.

$$C_9H_{19}-C_6H_4-O(CH_2CH_2O)_n-CH_2CH_2OH$$

Liquid dishwashing detergent

Other two classes of detergents are anionic detergents and cationic detergents. Anionic detergents are sodium salts of sulphonated long chain alcohols or hydrocarbons.

$$\underset{\text{Lauryl alcohol}}{H_3C-(CH_2)_{10}CH_2OH} \xrightarrow{H_2SO_4} \underset{\text{Lauryl hydrogensulphate}}{CH_3(CH_2)_{10}CH_2OSO_3H}$$

$$\xrightarrow{NaOH} \underset{\text{Anionic detergent (sodium lauryl sulphate)}}{CH_3(CH_2)_{10}CH_2OSO_3^-Na^+}$$

They are mostly used for household work.

Cationic detergents are quaternary ammonium salts of amines with acetates, chlorides or bromides as anions. Cetyltrimethylammonium bromide is a popular cationic detergent and is used in hair conditioners.

$$\left[CH_3(CH_2)_{15}-\underset{CH_3}{\overset{CH_3}{|}}{N}-CH_3 \right]^+ Br^-$$

Cetyltrimethylammonium bromide

Q.14 Polyethyleneglycols are used in the preparation of which type of detergents?

(a) Cationic detergents (b) Anionic detergents

(c) Non-ionic detergents (d) Soaps

Ans. ***(c)*** Polyethyleneglycols are used in the preparation of non-ionic detergents. Non-ionic detergents do not contain any ion in their constitution.

Reaction is as follows

$$\underset{\text{Stearic acid}}{CH_3(CH_2)_{16}COOH} + \underset{\text{Polyethylene glycol}}{HO(CH_2CH_2O)_nCH_2CH_2OH} \xrightarrow{-H_2O}$$

$$\underset{\text{Non-ionic detergent}}{CH_3(CH_2)_{16}COO(CH_2CH_2O)_nCH_2CH_2OH}$$

Q.15 Which of the following is **not** a target molecule for drug function in body?

(a) Carbohydrates (b) Lipids (c) Vitamins (d) Proteins

Ans. ***(c)*** Drugs usually interact with biomolecules such as carbohydrates, lipids, proteins and nucleic acids. These are called drug targets. Vitamins are not a target molecule for drug function in body.

Q.16 Which of the following statements is **not** true about enzyme inhibitors?

(a) Inhibit the catalytic activity of the enzyme.

(b) Prevent the binding of substrate.

(c) Generally a strong covalent bond is formed between an inhibitor and an enzyme.

(d) Inhibitors can be competitive or non-competitive.

Ans. ***(c)*** Drugs can block the binding site of the enzyme and prevent the binding of substrate, or can inhibit the catalytic activity of the enzyme. Such drugs are called enzyme inhibitors.

Generally, a weak bond such as hydrogen bonding, van der Waals interactions, etc., is formed between the enzyme and inhibitor.

Hence, option (c) is correct choice.

Q.17 Which of the following chemicals can be added for sweetening of food items at cooking temperature and does not provide calories?

(a) Sucrose (b) Glucose (c) Aspartame (d) Sucralose

Ans. ***(d)*** Sucrose and glucose are natural sweetening agent while aspartame and sucralose are artificial sweetening agent.

Aspartame is roughly 100 times as sweet as cane sugar. It is methyl ester of dipeptide formed from aspartic acid and phenylalanine. Use of aspartame is limited to cold foods and soft drinks because it is unstable at cooking temperature.

Sucralose is trichloro derivative of sucrose. Its appearance and taste are like sugar. It is stable at cooking temperature. It does not provide calories.

Q.18 Which of the following will **not** enhance nutritional value of food?

(a) Minerals (b) Artificial sweeteners

(c) Vitamins (d) Amino acids

Ans. ***(b)*** Vitamins and minerals are essential nutrients because they perform hundred of roles in the body. They help in building strong bones, heal wounds and boost immune system. They also convert food into energy, and repair cellular damage.

Artificial sweeteners are non-caloric substitutes for sugar. They are often intensly more sweet than sugar but do not enhance nutritional value of food.

Amino acids are the monomers of proteins. Proteins are required for the growth and maintenance of the body. Therefore, amino acids will also enhance the nutritional value of food.

Multiple Choice Questions (More Than One Options)

Q.19 Which of the following statements are **incorrect** about receptor proteins?

(a) Majority of receptor proteins are embedded in the cell membranes.

(b) The active site of receptor proteins opens on the inside region of the cell.

(c) Chemical messengers are received at the binding sites of receptor proteins.

(d) Shape of receptor doesn't change during attachment of messenger.

Ans. *(b, d)* Receptors are proteins that are crucial to body's communication process. Majority of these are embedded in cell membranes in such a way that their small part possessing active site projects out of the surface of the membrane and opens on the outside region of the cell membrane.

In the body, message between two neurons and that between neuron to muscles is communicated through certain chemicals. These chemicals, known as chemical messengers are received at the binding site of receptors proteins.

To accommodate a messenger, shape of the receptor site changes. This brings about the transfer of message into the cell. Thus, chemical messenger gives message to the cell without entering the cell.

Q.20 Which of the following are **not** used as food preservatives?

(a) Table salt

(b) Sodium hydrogencarbonate

(c) Cane sugar

(d) Benzoic acid

Ans. *(b, c)* Food preservatives prevent spoilage of food due to microbial growth. The most commonly used preservatives include table salt, sugar, vegetable oils and sodium benzoate. Sodium hydrogen carbonate and cane sugar are not used as food preservatives.

Q.21 Compounds with antiseptic properties are ....

(a) $CHCl_3$

(b) CHI_3

(c) boric acid

(d) 0.3 ppm aqueous solution of Cl_2

Ans. *(b, c)* Antiseptics are the chemical substances which either kill or prevent the growth of microorganisms.

(a) $CHCl_3$ (chloroform) was used as an anaesthesia in surgery but now it is used in the production of the freon refrigerant R-22.

(b) Iodoform (CHI_3) produces iodine on coming in contact with skin, so it is used as an antiseptic for wounds.

(c) Boric acid (H_3BO_3) in dilute aqueous solution is a weak antiseptic for eyes.

(d) Chlorine in the concentration of 0.2 to 0.4 ppm in aqueous solution and sulphur dioxide in very low concentrations, are disinfectants.

Q.22 Which of the following statements are correct about barbiturates?

(a) Hypnotics or sleep producing agents.

(b) These are tranquilizers.

(c) Non-narcotic analgesics.

(d) Pain reducing without disturbing the nervous system.

Ans. *(a, b)* Barbituric acid and its derivatives such as veronal, luminal, seconal, amytal and nembutal constitute an important class of tranquilizers called barbiturates. They are used as hypnotics, *i.e.*, sleep producing agents.

Q.23 Which of the following are sulpha drugs?

(a) Sulphapyridine (b) Prontosil

(c) Salvarsan (d) Nardil

Ans. ***(a, b)*** Sulpha drugs kill bacteria and fungi by interfering with their metabolism.

(a) Sulphapyridine is a sulphonamide antibacterial drug. It is no longer prescribed for the treatment of infections in humans. It is a good antibacterial drug, but its water solubility is very pH dependent. Thus, there is a risk of crystallisation within the bladder or urethra, which could lead to pain or blockage.

(b) Prontosil is also called sulphamidochrysoidine. It is used in the treatment of general bacterial infection in humans.

(c) Salvarsan is arsenic based antibacterial drug. It is used in the treatment of syphilis.

(d) Nardil is an antidepressant drug.

Q.24 Which of the following are antidepressants?

(a) Iproniazid (b) Phenelzine

(c) Equanil (d) Salvarsan

Ans. ***(a, b, c)***

Antidepressants are the substances which correct chemical imbalances of neurotransmitters in the brain and probably cause changes in mood and behaviour.

Iproniazid is a hydrazine drug used as an antidepressant. Phenelzine is also known as Nardil. It is used in the treatment of major depressive disorder. Equanil is used in controlling depression and hypertension.

Salvarsan is an antibacterial drug. It is used in the treatment of Syphilis.

Q.25 Which of the following statements are **incorrect** about penicillin?

(a) An antibacterial fungus.

(b) Ampicillin is its synthetic modification.

(c) It has bacteriostatic effect.

(d) It is a broad spectrum antibiotic.

Ans. ***(c, d)*** Penicillin is a group of antibiotics derived from *Penicillium* fungi. Ampicillin and Amoxycillin are synthetic modifications of penicillin. Pencillin destroys bacteria by destroying the cell wall of the microorganism or kill the bacteria so, it has bacteriocidal effect.

Penicillin as a class of antibiotics are generally narrow spectrum but when used in the combination with other antibiotics, it can make up a part of broad spectrum antibiotics.

Q.26 Which of the following compounds are administered as antacids?

(a) Sodium carbonate (b) Sodium hydrogencarbonate

(c) Aluminium carbonate (d) Magnesium hydroxide

Ans. ***(b, d)*** Antacid is a substance which neutralizes excess of acid in stomach. The chemical formula of sodium hydrogen carbonate is $NaHCO_3$. It is often used as an antacid because it neutralises excess of HCl secreted from the walls of stomach.

$$NaHCO_3(s) + HCl(aq.) \longrightarrow NaCl(aq.) + H_2O(l) + CO_2$$

However, excessive hydrogen carbonate can make the stomach alkaline and trigger the production of even more acid.

Milk of magnesia, which is an aqueous solution of magnesium hydroxide is also used as an antacid.

Q.27 Amongst the following antihistamines, which are antacids?

(a) Ranitidine (b) Brompheniramine (c) Terfenadine (d) Cimetidine

Thinking Process This question is based on the inter-relation between the antihistamines and antacids. Antihistaminies drugs are used in the treatment of hyperacidity as histamine, stimulates the secreation of pepsin and hydrochloric acid in the stomach.

Ans. ***(a, d)*** Ranitidine and cimetidine are anti-histamines, which are used as antacids. These drugs release lesser amount of acid.

Brompheniramine is an antihistamine. It is used to treat runny nose, sneezing, itching and watery eyes caused by allergy.

Terfenadine, an antihistamine, was used for allergy.

Q.28 Veronal and luminal are derivatives of barbituric acid which are ....

(a) tranquilizers (b) non-narcotic analgesic
(c) anti allergic drugs (d) neurologically active drugs

Ans. ***(a, d)*** Derivatives of barbituric acid *viz.*, veronal and luminal are called barbiturates. These barbiturates constitute an important class of tranquilizers. Tranquilizers are a class of chemical compounds used for the treatment of stress and mild or severe mental diseases. Tranquilizers are neurologically active drugs. These drugs affect the message transfer mechanism from nerve to receptor.

Q.29 Which of the following are anionic detergents?

(a) Sodium salts of sulphonated long chain alcohol.
(b) Ester of stearic acid and polyethylene glycol.
(c) Quarternary ammonium salt of amine with acetate ion.
(d) Sodium salts of sulphonated long chain hydrocarbons.

Ans. ***(a, d)*** Detergents are cleansing agents which have all the properties of soap, but which actually do not contain any soap.

Anionic detergents These are sodium salts of sulphonated long chain alcohols or hydrocarbons.

$$\underset{\text{Lauryl alcohol}}{H_3C-(CH_2)_{10}-CH_2OH} \xrightarrow{H_2SO_4} \underset{\text{Lauryl hydrogen sulphate}}{CH_3(CH_2)_{10}-CH_2OSO_3H} \xrightarrow{NaOH(aq)} \underset{\text{Sodium lauryl sulphate}}{CH_3(CH_2)_{10}CH_2O\overset{-}{S}O_3Na^+}$$

$$\underset{\text{Dodecylbenzene}}{CH_3(CH_2)_{11}-C_6H_5} \xrightarrow{H_2SO_4} \underset{\text{Dodecylbenzene sulphonic acid}}{CH_3(CH_2)_{11}-C_6H_4-SO_3H} \xrightarrow{NaOH\,(aq.)} \underset{\text{Sodium dodecylbenzenesulphonate}}{CH_3(CH_2)_{11}-C_6H_4-\overset{-}{S}O_3\overset{+}{Na}}$$

Q.30 Which of the following statements are correct?

(a) Cationic detergents have germicidal properties.

(b) Bacteria can degrade the detergents containing highly branched chains.

(c) Some synthetic detergents can give foam even in ice cold water.

(d) Synthetic detergents are not soaps.

Ans. *(a, c, d)*

(a) Cationic detergents are quarternary ammonium salts of amines with acetates, chlorides or bromides as anions. These detergents have germicidal properties. Hence, option (a) is correct.

(b) Bacteria cannot degrade the detergents containing highly branched chains, therefore, in most of the detergents used these days, the branching is kept to a minimum so that the detergents become easily biodegradable. Hence, option (b) is incorrect.

(c) Some synthetic detergents can give foam even in ice cold water. Hence, option (c) is correct.

(d) Synthetic detergents are cleansing agents which have all the properties of soaps, but which actually do not contain any soap. Hence, option (d) is correct.

Short Answer Type Questions

Q.31 What is the average molecular mass of drugs?

Ans. Drugs are the chemicals of low molecular masses, *i.e.*, (~ 100 – 500 u). They interact with macromolecular targets and produce a biological response. When the biological response is therapeutic and useful, these chemicals are called medicines.

Q.32 Write the uses of medicines.

Ans. Chemical substances whose biological response is therapeutic and useful are called medicines. Medicines are used in diagnosis, prevention and treatment of diseases.

Note If drugs taken in doses higher than those recommended, most of the drugs used as medicines are potential poisons. Use of chemicals for therapeutic effect is called chemotherapy.

Q.33 What are antiseptics?

Ans. Antiseptics are the antimicrobes. Antiseptics are the chemical which either kill or prevent the growth of microorganism and are safe to be applied to the living tissues *e.g.*, soframicine. They can not be taken orally like antibiotics.

Q.34 Which type of drugs come under antimicrobial drugs?

Ans. Disease in human beings and animals may be caused by a variety of microorganisms such as bacteria, virus, fungi and other pathogens.

An antimicrobial drug tends to destroy/prevent development or inhibit the pathogenic action of microbes such as bacteria (antibacterial drugs), fungi (antifungal agents), virus (antiviral agents), or other parasites (antiparasitic drugs) selectively. Antiseptic, disinfectants, antibiotics and sulpha drugs are antimicrobial drugs.

Q.35 Where are receptors located?

Ans. Receptors are proteins that are crucial to body's communication process. Receptors are embedded on the outer surface of the cell membrane in such a way that their small part possessing active site projects out of the surface of the membrane and opens on the outside region of the cell membrane.

Q.36 What is the harmful effect of hyperacidity?

Ans. Hyperacidity produces sudden stomach pain. It may lead to vomiting, loss of appetite, flatulence and heart burn. It is also responsible for chronic indigestion and in severe cases cause gastric ulcers.

Q.37 Which site of an enzyme is called allosteric site?

Ans. Sites different from active site of enzyme where a molecule can bind and change the shape of the active site is called allosteric site.

Q.38 What type of forces are involved in binding of substrate to the active site of enzyme?

Ans. During the catalytic action of an enzyme, enzyme hold the substrate for a chemical reaction. Active sites of enzymes hold the substrate molecule in a suitable position, so that it can be attacked by the reagent effectively.
Substrate bind to the active site of the enzyme through a variety of interactions. These forces are van der Waals interactions, ionic bonding, hydrogen bonding or dipole-dipole interaction.

Q.39 What is the commonality between the antibiotic arsphenamine and azo dye?

Ans. Arsphenamine is also known as salvarsan. It is a synthetic organic arsenic compound that was previously used for treating syphilis. Arsphenamine possess $-As=As-$ linkage.

Azo dyes are used to promote epithelial growth in the treatment of ulcers, burns and other wounds. Many azodyes have anticoagulation action. Azo dyes possess $-N=N-$ linkage like arsphenamine which possess $-As=As-$ linkage.

H_2N, HO, As, As, HO, H_2N

Salvarsan

N, N, OH

Azo dye

Q.40 Which class of drugs is used in sleeping pills?

Ans. Tranquilizers are essential components of sleeping pills. It is the class of chemical compounds used for the treatment of stress and mild or even severe mental diseases. These relieve anxiety stress, irritability or excitement by inducing a sense of well-being.

Q.41 Aspirin is pain relieving antipyretic drug but can be used to prevent heart attack. Explain.

Ans. Aspirin is 2- acetoxybenzoic acid. It is very effective in reducing or abolishing pain without causing impairment of consciousness, mental confusion, in incoordination or paralysis or some other disturbance or disorder of the nervous system. It reduces fever (antipyretics) and prevents platelet coagulation. Due to this, it has anti blood clotting action and, therefore, it is widely used to prevent heart attack.

Q.42 Both antacids and antiallergic drugs are antihistamines but they cannot replace each other. Explain why?

Ans. Histamine is a chemical substance that stimulates the secretion of pepsin and hydrochloric acid in stomach. Antacids are designed to prevent the interaction of histamine with the receptors present in the stomach wall. As a result, less HCl is released in stomach.

Histamine contracts the smooth muscles in the bronchi and gut and relaxes other muscles in walls of fine blood vessels. As a result, histamine causes allergy. Antihistamines interfere with the natural action of histamine by competing with histamine for binding sites of receptor where histamine exerts its effect.

Since, antiallergic and antacids drugs work on different receptors, therefore, antihistamines remove allergy while antacids remove acidity.

Q.43 What is a soft soap?

Ans. Chemical substances which concentrates at the surface of the solution or interfaces, from surface films, reduces surface tension of the solution and help in removing dirt and dust by emulsifying grease are called surfactants *i.e.*, soap and detergents.

Soaps are sodium or potassium salts of long chain fatty acids such as palmitic acid ($C_{15}H_{31}COOH$), stearic acid ($C_{17}H_{35}COOH$) and linolic acid ($C_{17}H_{31}COOH$)

Potassium salts of fatty acids such as palmitic acid, stearic acid and oleic acid are called soft soap.

$$\underset{\text{Glyceryl ester of stearic acid (fat)}}{\begin{matrix} CH_2-O-\overset{O}{\overset{\|}{C}}-C_{17}H_{35} \\ | \\ CH-O-\underset{O}{\underset{\|}{C}}-C_{17}H_{35} \\ | \\ CH_2-O-\underset{O}{\underset{\|}{C}}-C_{17}H_{35} \end{matrix}} + \underset{\text{Potassium hydroxide}}{KOH} \longrightarrow \underset{\text{Potassium stearate}}{3C_{17}H_{35}COOK} + \underset{\text{Glycerol}}{\begin{matrix} CH_2OH \\ | \\ CHOH \\ | \\ CH_2OH \end{matrix}}$$

Generally, potassium soaps are soft to the skin so, they are named as soft soap.

Q.44 If soap has high alkali content it irritates skin. How can the amount of excess alkali be determined? What can be the source of excess alkali?

Ans. A solution of soap is titrated with standard hydrochloric acid. It is an acid-base titration. In this titration, phenolphthalein is used as an indicator. During the preparation of soap, fat (*i.e.*, glyceryl ester of fatty acid) is heated with aqueous sodium hydroxide.

$$\underset{\text{Glyceryl ester of stearic acid (fat)}}{\begin{matrix} CH_2-O-\overset{O}{\overset{\|}{C}}-C_{17}H_{35} \\ | \\ CH-O-\underset{O}{\underset{\|}{C}}-C_{35}H_{35} \\ | \\ CH_2-O-\underset{O}{\underset{\|}{C}}-C_{35}H_{35} \end{matrix}} + \underset{\text{Potassium hydroxide}}{KOH} \longrightarrow \underset{\text{Potassium stearate}}{3C_{17}H_{35}COOK} + \underset{\text{Glycerol}}{\begin{matrix} CH_2OH \\ | \\ CHOH \\ | \\ CH_2OH \end{matrix}}$$

Thus, the source of this excess alkali (which irritates skin) is the alkali left unused when the soap is prepared by hydrolysis of fat.

Q.45 Explain why some times foaming is seen in river water near the place where sewage water is poured after treatment?

Ans. Detergents have long hydrocarbon chains. If their hydrocarbon chain is highly branched, then bacteria cannot degrade this easily. Such detergents are non-biodegradable. Slow degradation of detergents leads to their accumulation. These non-biodegradable detergents persist in water even after sewage treatment and cause foaming in rivers ponds and their water get polluted. In order to overcome this issue branching of the hydrocarbon chain is controlled and kept to minimum.

Q.46 Which category of the synthetic detergents is used in toothpaste?

Ans. Anionic detergents such as sodium laurylsulphate, sodium dodecylbenzenesulphonate, etc., are used in toothpaste. They are responsible to clean the teeth and to provide a foam that helps to carry away the debris. Further, sodium laurylsulphates have significant antibacterial properties, and can penetrate as well as dissolve the plaque.

$$\underset{\text{Lauryl alcohol}}{H_3C(CH_2)_{10}—CH_2OH} \xrightarrow{H_2SO_4} \underset{\text{Lauryl hydrogensulphate}}{CH_3—(CH_2)_{10}—CH_2—O—SO_3H}$$

$$\xrightarrow{\text{NaOH (aq)}} \underset{\text{Sodium laurylsulphate}}{CH_3(CH_2)_{10}\,CH_2OSO_3^-\,Na^+}$$

$$\underset{\text{Dodecylbenzene}}{H_3C—(CH_2)_{11}—C_6H_5} \xrightarrow{H_2SO_4} \underset{\text{Dodecylbenzenesulphonic acid}}{H_3C—(CH_2)_{11}—C_6H_4—SO_3H}$$

$$\xrightarrow{\text{NaOH } (aq.)} \underset{\text{Sodium dodecylbenzenesulphonate}}{H_3C—(CH_2)_{11}—C_6H_4—SO_3^-\,Na^+}$$

Q.47 Hair shampoos belong to which class of synthetic detergent?

Ans. Hair shampoos are made up of cationic detergents. These are quarternary ammonium salts of amines with acetates, chlorides or bromides as anions, *e.g.*, cetyltrimethyl ammonium bromide.

$$\left[H_3C—(CH_2)_{15}—\overset{\overset{\large CH_3}{|}}{\underset{\underset{\large CH_3}{|}}{N}}—CH_3 \right]^+ Br^-$$

Cetyltrimethyl ammonium bromide

Q.48 Dishwashing soaps are synthetic detergents. What is their chemical nature?

Ans. Dishwashing soaps are non-ionic detergents. It can be prepared by the reaction of stearic acid with polyethylene glycol.

$$\underset{\text{Stearic acid}}{CH_3—(CH)_{16}COOH} + \underset{\text{Polyethylene glycol}}{HO—(CH_2CH_2O)_n—CH_2CH_2OH} \xrightarrow{-H_2O}$$

$$CH_3—(CH_2)_{16}COO(CH_2CH_2O)_nCH_2CH_2OH$$

Since, non-ionic detergents do not contain any ion in their constitution, it is neutral in nature.

Q.49 Draw the diagram showing micelle formation by the following detergent. $CH_3(CH_2)_{10}CH_2OSO_3^-Na^+$

Ans. An aggregate thus formed is known as micelle.

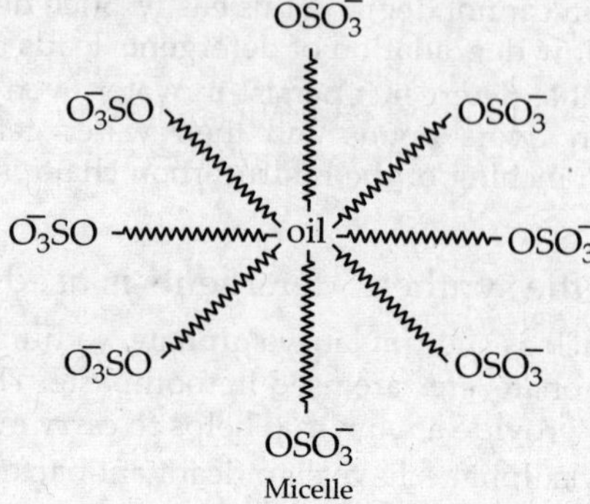

Micelle

Q.50 How does the branching of hydrocarbon chain of synthetic detergents affect their biodegradability?

Ans. Detergents having highly branched hydrocarbon chains cause pollution in rivers. The reason being that side chains stop bacteria from attacking and breaking the chains.

Thus, lesser the branching, more is the biodegradability, *i.e.*, detergents with long straight hydrocarbon chains are more easily degraded than those having branched hydrorcarbon chains.

$SO_3^-Na^+$

side chain (branching)

Since, unbranched (*i.e.*, straight) chains are more prone to attack by bacteria, therefore, in most of the detergents used these days, the branching is kept to be minimum, so that the detergents become easily biodegradable.

Q.51 Why is it safer to use soap from the environmental point of view?

Ans. Soaps are biodegradable while detergents containing branched hydrocarbon chains are quite stable, *i.e.*, they are not degraded by the action of microorganism and therefore, it causes water pollution in rivers and other water ways.

Q.52 What are analgesics?

Ans. Analgesics reduce or abolish pain without causing impairment of consciousness, mental confusion, incoordination or paralysis or some other disturbances of nervous system.

These are classified in two groups

(i) **Non-narcotic analgesics** These are non-addictive analgesics, *e.g.*, aspirin.

(ii) **Narcotic analgesics** Morphine is an example of narcotic analgesics. They relieve pain and produce sleep.

Q.53 What is the scientific explanation for the feeling of depression ?

Ans. Noradrenaline is a neuro-transmitter which plays a crucial role in mood changes. If any person has low level of noradrenaline, then the message transfer process becomes slow and the person suffers from of depression.

Q.54 What is the basic difference between antiseptics and disinfectants ?

Ans. Antiseptics and disinfectants both are antimicrobials. Antiseptics prevent or destroy development or inhibit the pathogenic action of microbes. They are safe to be applied on living tissues.

On the other hand, disinfectants also kill microorganisms but are not safe to be applied on living tissues. They are generally applied on non-living objects such as drains, toilets, floors and living rooms infected with bacteria and disease carrying germs.

Q.55 Between sodiumhydrogencarbonate and magnesium hydroxide which is a better antacid and why ?

Ans. Magnesium hydroxide [$Mg(OH)_2$] is a better antacid because being insoluble, it does not allow the pH to increase above neutrality. On the other hand, sodium hydrogen carbonate being soluble, so, its excess amount can make the stomach alkaline and trigger the production of even more acid.

Q.56 Which analgesics are called opiates?

Ans. Analgesics reduce or abolish pain without causing impairment of consciousness, mental confusion, incoordination or paralysis or some other disturbances of nervous system. These are classifieds in two categories

(i) **Non-narcotic (non-addicitive) analgesics** - Aspirin and paracetamol belong to the class of non-narcotic analgesics.

(ii) **Narcotic analgesics**–Morphine and many of its homologues, when administered in medicinal doses, relieve pain and produce sleep. In poisonous doses, these produce stupor, coma, convulsions and ultimately death. Morphine narcotics are sometimes referred to as opiates, since they are obtained from the opium poppy.

Q.57 What is the medicinal use of narcotic drugs?

Ans. Narcotic analgesics (morphine and many of its homologous) when administered in medicinal doses, relieve pain and produce sleep. Since, these drugs relieve pain and produce sleep, therefore are chiefly used for the relief of postoperative pain, cardian pain and pains of terminal cancer, and in child birth.

Q.58 What are antagonistic drugs?

Ans. Drugs that bind to the receptor site and inhibit its natural function are called antagonistic drugs *e.g.*, cimetidine is an antagonist drug because it binds to the receptor site in stomach otherwise histamine will bind to the receptor site and induce the secretion of HCl in stomach.

Thus, this antacid blocks the receptor site and hence, the secretion of HCl is reduced thereby reducing/removing hyperacidity.

Q.59 What is the mode of action of antimicrobial drugs?

Ans. An antimicrobial drug tend to destroy/prevent development or inhibit the pathogenic action of microbes such as bacteria, fungi, virus or other parasites selectively. Thus, antimicrobial are drugs which cure diseases caused by microorganisms.

Q.60 What is the side product of soap industry ? Give reactions showing soap formation.

Ans. Soaps are sodium or potassium salts of long chain fatty acids such as stearic acid, oleic acid and palmitic acid. Soaps containing sodium salts are formed by heating fat (*i.e.*, glyceryl ester of fatty acid) with aqueous sodium hydroxide.

$$\begin{array}{l} H_2C-O-\overset{\displaystyle O}{\overset{\|}{C}}-C_{17}H_{35} \\ | \\ HC-O-\overset{\displaystyle O}{\overset{\|}{C}}-C_{17}H_{35} \\ | \\ H_2C-O-\underset{\displaystyle O}{\underset{\|}{C}}-C_{17}H_{35} \end{array} + \underset{\text{Sodium hydroxide}}{3NaOH} \longrightarrow \underset{\text{Sodium stearate}}{3C_{17}H_{35}COONa} + \begin{array}{l} CH_2OH \\ | \\ CHOH \\ | \\ CH_2OH \end{array}$$

Glyceryl ester of stearic acid (Fat) — Glycerol (or glycerine)

This reaction is known as saponification. In this reaction, esters of fatty acids are hydrolysed and the soap obtained remains in colloidal form. It is precipitated from the solution by adding NaCl. The solution left after removing the soap contains glycerol as side product.

Q.61 What is the difference between bathing soap and washing soaps?

Ans. Bathing soaps are potassium salts of long chain fatty acids. They are usually soft and are also free from unused alkali. On the other hand, washing soaps are sodium salts of long chain fatty acids.They are usually hard and also contain some residual alkali.

Q.62 How are transparent soaps manufactured?

Ans. Transparent soaps are made by dissolving the soap in ethanol and then evaporating the excess solvent.

Q.63 What is the advantage of using antihistamines over antacids in the treatment of acidity?

Ans. Usual antacid like sodium hydrogencarbonate control only the symptom and not the cause. They neutralize the excess of acid produced in the stomach, but do not control the cause of production of excess of HCl in stomach.

Histamine, a chemical, is responsible for the secretion of pepsin and HCl in the stomach. Antihistamine are the drugs which supress the action of histamine, which in turn supress the secretion of pepsin and HCl in the stomach. Antihistamine prevent the binding of histamine with the receptors present in the stomach wall.

As a result, less HCl is produced and hyperacidity is cured. Thus, a better treatment for curing acidity is to use antihistamines over antacids.

Q.64 What are the functions performed by histamine in the body?

Ans. Histamine is a potent vasodilator. It performs various functions in the body

(i) It contracts smooth muscles in gut and bronchi.

(ii) It relaxes some other muscles, *e.g.*, in the walls of fine blood vessels.

(iii) It is responsible for congestion in the nose associated with common cold and allergies.

(iv) It stimulates the release of pepsin and HCl in stomach.

Q. 65 **With the help of an example explain how do tranquilizers control the feeling of depression?**

Ans. Noradrenaline is a neurotransmitter which plays a crucial role in mood changes. If somehow any person has low level of noradrenaline in the body, then the signal sending activity becomes slow and the person suffers from depression.

For treating depression and to boost the mood, tranquilizers are used. These drugs inhibit the enzyme which catalyse the degradation of noradrenaline.

Tranquilizers affect the central nervous system and induce the sleep for the patients as well as climinate the symptoms of emotional distress.

From this result, neurotransmitter noradrenaline is slowly metabolised and can activate the receptor for longer periods of time, thus counteracting the effect of depression.

Q.66 **Why are certain drugs called enzyme inhibitors?**

Ans. Some drugs can block the binding site of the enzyme and prevent the binding of the substrate, or can inhibit the catalytic activity of the enzyme. Such drugs are called enzyme inhibitors.

(Also, refer to Q. 16.)

Q.67 **What are fillers and what role these fillers play in soap?**

Ans. Substances which are added to soaps to change their properties in order to make them more useful for a particular application, are called fillers. Some important examples are given below.

(i) Sodium rosinate, sodium silicate, borax and sodium carbonate are added to laundary soaps to increase their lather forming ability.

(ii) Glycerol is added to shaving soaps to prevent them from rapid drying.

(iii) In medicated soaps, substances of medicinal values are added.

Q.68 **Sugar is the main source of energy as it produces energy on metabolic decomposition. But these days low calorie drinks are more popular, why?**

Ans. Natural sweetners, *e.g.*, sucrose add to calorie intake. Due to occurrence of more cases of diabetes and obesity among young and old people, these days people usually take low calorie drinks. These are made up of artificial sweetening agents which are given below.

Saccharin It is 550 times as sweet as cane sugar. It is excreted from the body through urine.

Aspartame It is 100 times as sweet as cane sugar. Its use is limited to cold foods and soft drinks because it is unstable at cooking temperature.

Alitame It is more stable than aspartame but the control of sweetness of food is difficult while using it.

Sucralose It is stable at cooking temperature. It does not provide calories.

These artificial sweetening agents do not metabolize and hence do not produce any energy.

Q.69 **Pickles have a long shelf life and do not get spoiled for months, why?**

Ans. Plenty of salt and cover of oil act as preservatives. These food preservatives prevent spoilage of food due to microbial growth. Salt and oil do not allow moisture and air to enter the material and hence bacteria cannot thrive on them. Therefore, pickles do not get spoiled for months.

Q.70 What is the difference between saccharin and saccharic acid?

Ans. Saccharin is an artificial sweetening agent. It is about 550 times as sweet as cane sugar. It is excreted from the body in urine unchanged. It appears to be entirely inert and harmless when taken. Its use is of great value to diabetic people who needs to control intake of calories.

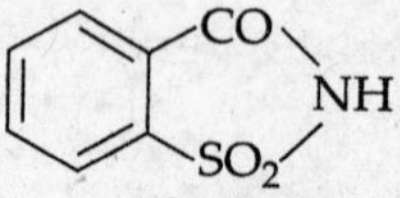

Saccharin

On the other hand, saccharic acid, is a dibasic acid obtained by the bacterial oxidation of glucose in the mouth or by conc. HNO_3 in the laboratory.

$$\underset{\text{Glucose}}{\begin{array}{c} CHO \\ | \\ (CHOH)_4 \\ | \\ CH_2OH \end{array}} \xrightarrow[\text{or conc. } HNO_3]{\text{Bacterial oxidation}} \underset{\text{Saccharic acid}}{\begin{array}{c} COOH \\ | \\ (CHOH)_4 \\ | \\ COOH \end{array}}$$

Q.71 Name an artificial sweetener which is derivative of sucrose.

Ans. **Sucralose** is trichloro derivative of the sucrose. Its appearance and taste are like sugar. It is stable at cooking temperature. Sucralose contributes zero calories to the diet, compared with sucrose, which contributes 16 calories per teaspoon. Structure of sucralose is

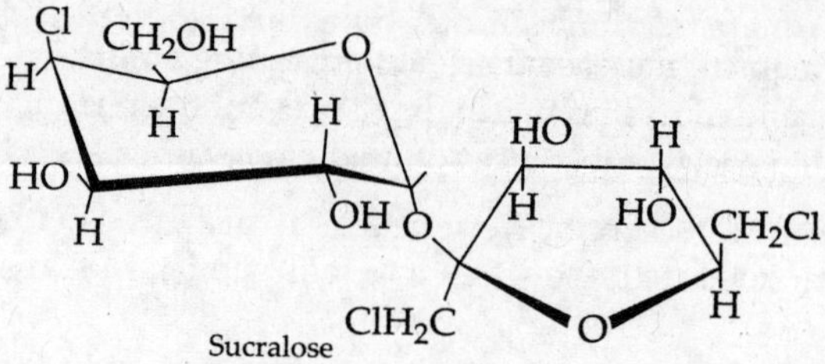

Sucralose

Q.72 Name two α-amino acids which form a dipeptide which is 100 times more sweet than cane sugar ?

Ans. Aspartic acid and phenylalanine are the two α-amino acids and they form a dipeptide which is 100 times more sweet than cane sugar. It is methyl ester of dipeptide formed from aspartic acid and phenylalanine. Its use is limited to cold foods and soft drinks because it is unstable at cooking temperature.

Structure of aspartame is

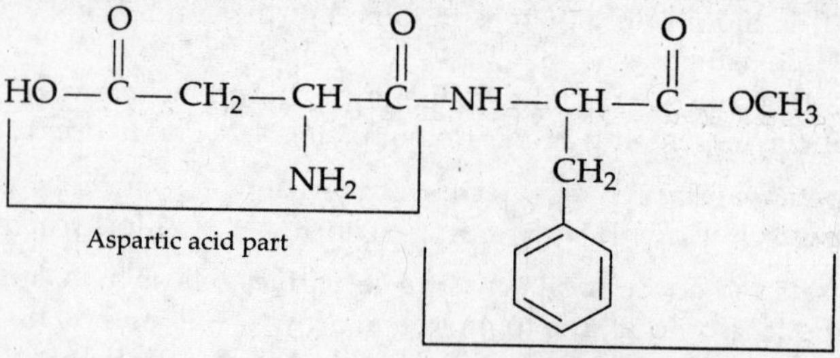

$$HO-\overset{O}{\overset{\|}{C}}-CH_2-\underset{NH_2}{\underset{|}{CH}}-\overset{O}{\overset{\|}{C}}-NH-\underset{CH_2C_6H_5}{\underset{|}{CH}}-\overset{O}{\overset{\|}{C}}-OCH_3$$

Aspartic acid part

Phenylalanine (methyl ester part)

Q.73 Aspartame is unstable at cooking temperature, where would you suggest aspartame to be used for sweetening?

Ans. Aspartame is used in cold foods and soft drinks. It is an artifical sweetening agent.

(*Also, refer to Q.* 72)

Q.74 Sodium salts of some acids are very useful as food preservatives. Suggest a few such acids.

Ans. A preservative is naturally occuring or synthetically produced substance that is added to foods to prevent decomposition by microbial growth or by undesirable chemical changes. Sodium salts of some acids are very useful as food preservatives. Some examples of such acids are as follows :

(i) Benzoic acid in the form of its sodium salt, constitutes one of the most common food preservative. Sodium benzoate is a common preservative in acid or acidified foods such as fruit, juices, pickles, etc. Yeasts are inhibited by benzoate to a greater extent than are moulds and bacteria.

(ii) Sorbic acid and its salts (sodium, potassium and calcium) also have preservative activities but the applications of sodium sorbate $C_6H_7NaO_2$ are limited compared to that for potassium salt.

(iii) Sodium erythorbate $C_6H_7NaO_6$ is a food additive used predominate in meats, poultry and soft drinks.

(iv) Sodium propanoate, $Na(C_2H_5COO)$ is used in bakery products as mold inhibitor.

Q.75 Explain the role of allosteric site in enzyme inhibition?

Ans. Some drugs do not bind to the active site of enzymes to inhibit their activities. These bind to a different site of enzyme. This binding of inhibitor (drug) changes the shape of the active site in such a way that substrate cannot recognise it.

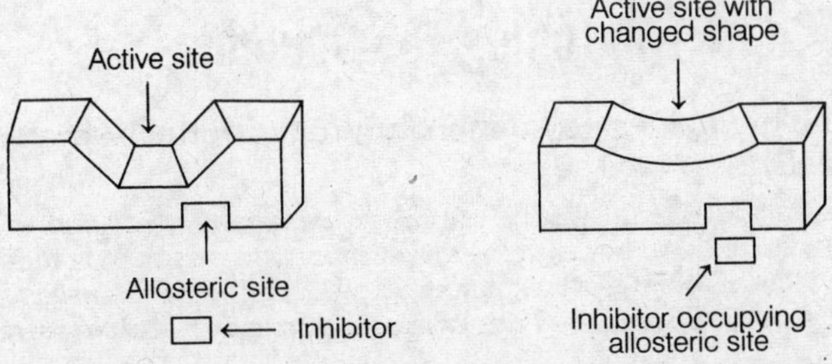

Non-competitive inhibitor changes the active site of enzyme after binding at allosteric site

The site different from active site of an enzyme where a drug molecule can bind is called the allosteric site.

Non-competitive inhibitor changes the active site of enzyme after binding at allosteric site.

Q.76 How are receptor proteins located in the cell membrane?

Ans. Receptor proteins are embedded in the cell membrane in such a way that their small part possessing active site projects out of the surface of the membrane and opens on the outside region of the cell membrane.

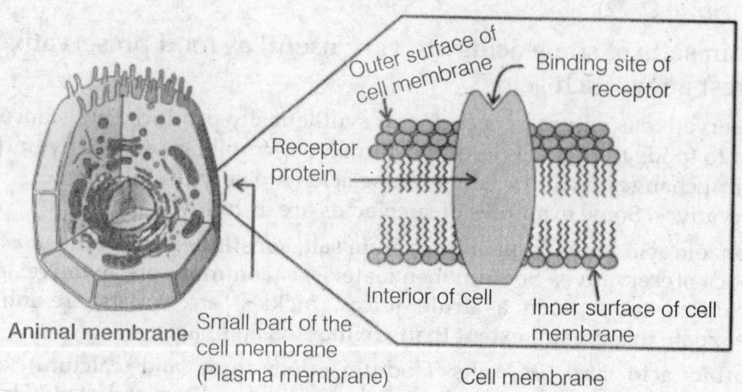

Receptor protein embedded in the cell membrane, the active site of the receptor opens on the outside region of the cell

Q.77 What happens when the bond formed between an enzyme and an inhibitor is a strong covalent bond?

Ans. Generally, a weak bond such as H-bonding, van der Waals interactions, etc., is formed between the enzyme and inhibitor. If a strong covalent bond is formed between the enzyme and the inhibitor which cannot be broken easily, then the enzyme is blocked permanently. The body then degrades the enzyme-inhibitor complex and synthesises the new enzyme.

Matching The Columns

Q.78 Match the medicines given in Column I with their use given in Column II.

Column I		Column II	
A.	Ranitidine	1.	Tranquilizer
B.	Furacine	2.	Antibiotic
C.	Phenelzine	3.	Antihistamine
D.	Chloramphenicol	4.	Antiseptic
		5.	Antifertility drug

Ans. A. → (3) B. → (4) C. → (1) D. → (2)

A. **Ranitidine** It prevents the interaction of histamine with the receptors present in the stomach wall. Thus, it controls the secretion of HCl and pepsin in stomach.

B. **Furacine** Furacine is an antiseptic. It can be applied to the living tissues to kill or to prevent the growth of microorganisms.

C. **Phenelzine** It is also known as Nardil. Its structure is

(Structure: benzene ring–CH_2CH_2–NH.NH_2)

It is used to treat depression.

D. **Chloramphenicol** It is a broad spectrum antibiotic. It can be given orally in case of typhoid, acute fever, dysentary, certain urinary infections, meningitis and pneumonia.

Q.79 Match the soaps given in Column I with items given in column II.

	Column I		Column II
A.	Soap chips	1.	dried miniature soap bubbles
B.	Soap granules	2.	small broken pieces of soap formed from melted soaps
C.	Soap powder	3.	soap powder + abrasives + builders (Na_2CO_3, Na_3PO_4)
D.	Scouring soap	4.	soap powder + builders like Na_2CO_3 and Na_3PO_4

Ans. A. → (2) **B.** → (1) **C.** → (4) **D.** → (3)

A. Soap chips are made by running a thin sheet of melted soap into a cool cylinder and scraping off the soaps in small broken pieces.

B. Soap granules are dried miniature soap bubbles.

C. Soap powders contain soap powder and builders like sodium carbonate and trisodium phosphate. Builders make the soap act more rapidly.

D. Scouring soaps contain soap powder, a scouring agent (abrasive) such as powdered pumice or finely divided sand and builders.

Q.80 Match structures given in Column I with the type of detergents given in Column II.

	Column I		Column II
A.	$CH_3(CH_2)_{16}COO(CH_2CH_2O)_nCH_2CH_2OH$	1.	Cationic detergent
B.	$C_{17}H_{35}COO^-Na^+$	2.	Anionic detergent
C.	$CH_3—(CH_2)_{10}CH_2SO_3^-Na^+$	3.	Nonionic detergent
D.	$\left[CH_3(CH_2)_{15}—\overset{CH_3}{\underset{CH_3}{N}}—CH_3\right]^+ Br^-$	4.	Soap

Ans. A. → (3) B. → (4) C. → (2) D. → (1)

Non-ionic detergent – $CH_3(CH_2)_{16}COO(CH_2CH_2O)_nCH_2CH_2OH$
Soap – $C_{17}H_{35}COO^-Na^+$
Anionic detergent – $CH_3—(CH_2)_{10}CH_2SO_3^-Na^+$

Cationic detergent $\left[CH_3(CH_2)_{15}—\underset{CH_3}{\overset{CH_3}{N}}—CH_3\right]^+ Br^-$

Q. 81 Match the detergents given in Column I with their uses in Column II.

	Column I		Column II
A.	$\left[CH_3(CH_2)_{15}—\underset{CH_3}{\overset{CH_3}{N}}—CH_3\right]^+ Br^-$	1.	Dishwashing powder
B.	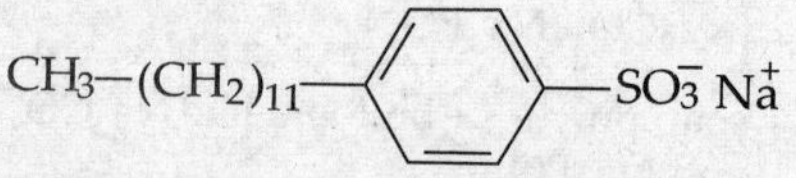 $CH_3—(CH_2)_{11}—C_6H_4—SO_3^- \overset{+}{Na}$	2.	Laundry soap
C.	$C_{17}H_{35}CO\overset{-}{O}\overset{+}{Na} + Na_2CO_3 + \text{Rosin}$	3.	Hair conditioners
D.	$CH_3(CH_2)_{16}COO(CH_2CH_2O)_n CH_2CH_2OH$	4.	Toothpaste

Ans. A. → (3) B. → (4) C. → (2) D. → (1)

A. Hair shampoos /conditioners are made up of cationic detergents. These are quarternary ammonium salts of amines with chlorides, bromides or acetates, *e.g.*, cetyltrimethyl ammonium bromide.

B. Anionic detergents are used in toothpaste, *e.g.*, sodium dodecyl benzene sulphonate. It can be prepared as follows.

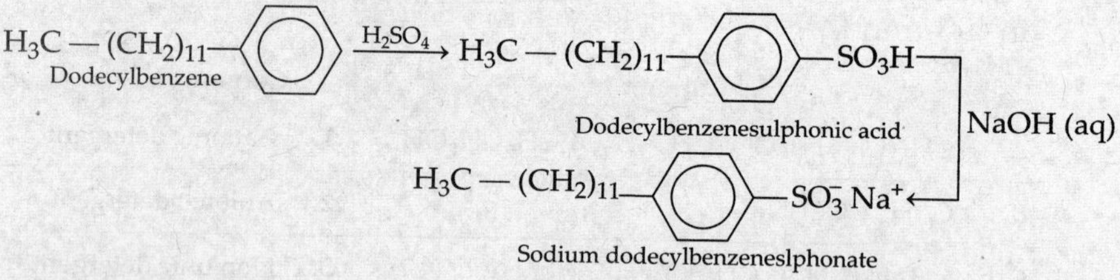

$$\underset{\text{Dodecylbenzene}}{H_3C—(CH_2)_{11}—C_6H_5} \xrightarrow{H_2SO_4} \underset{\text{Dodecylbenzenesulphonic acid}}{H_3C—(CH_2)_{11}—C_6H_4—SO_3H} \xrightarrow{NaOH (aq)} \underset{\text{Sodium dodecylbenzeneslphonate}}{H_3C—(CH_2)_{11}—C_6H_4—SO_3^- Na^+}$$

C. Laundary soaps contain fillers like sodium rosinate, sodium silicate, borax and sodium carbonate. Sodium rosinate makes the soap to lather well.

D. Dishwashing powder are non–ionic detergents

$$\underset{\text{Stearic acid}}{CH_3—(CH_2)_{16}—COOH} + \underset{\text{Polyethylene glycol}}{HO—(CH_2CH_2O)_n—CH_2—CH_2OH} \xrightarrow{-H_2O}$$

$$H_3C-(CH_2)_{16}COO(CH_2CH_2O)_nCH_2CH_2OH$$

Q.82 Match the class of compounds given in Column I with their functions given in Column II.

Column I		Column II	
A.	Antagonists	1.	Communicate message between two neurons and that between neurons to muscles.
B.	Agonists	2.	Bind to the receptor site and inhibit its natural function.
C.	Chemical messenger	3.	Crucial to body's communication process.
D.	Inhibitors	4.	Mimic the natural messenger.
E.	Receptors	5.	Inhibit activities of enzymes.

Ans. **A.** → (2) **B.** → (4) **C.** → (1) **D.** → (5) **E.** → (3)

A. **Antagonist** drugs are used when blocking of message is required. *e.g.*, dopamine antagonist is a drug which blocks the dopamine receptors by receptor antagonism.

B. **Agonist** drugs are useful when there is lack of chemical messenger. *e.g.*, heroin. They mimic the natural messenger by switching on the receptor.

C. These **chemical messengers** are received at the binding sites of receptor. These communicate message between two neurons and that between neurons to muscles.

D. **Inhibitors** block the binding site of the enzyme and prevent the binding of the substrate, or inhibit the catalytic activity of the enzyme.

E. **Receptors** are proteins that are crucial to body's communication. They are embedded in the cell membrane in such a way that their small part possessing active site projects out of the surface of the membrane and opens on the outside region of the cell membrane.

Q.83 Match the classes of drugs given in Column I with their action given in Column II.

Column I		Column II	
A.	Analgesics	1.	Inhibit the growth of microorganisms can be given orally
B.	Antiseptics	2.	Treatment of stress
C.	Antihistamines	3.	Applied to inanimate objects
D.	Antacids	4.	Prevents the interaction of histamine with its receptor
E.	Tranquilizers	5.	Pain killing effect
F.	Antibiotics	6.	Applied to diseased skin surfaces
G.	Disinfectants	7.	Treatment of acidity

Ans. A. → (5) B. → (6) C. → (4) D. → (7) E. → (2) F. → (1) G. → (3)

A. **Analgesics** reduce or abolish pain without causing impairment of consciousness, mental confusion, in coordination or paralysis or some other disturbances of nervous system, *e.g.*, aspirin.

B. **Antiseptics** are the chemicals which either kill or prevent the growth of mircoorganisms. They are applied to living tissues such as wounds, cuts, etc. *e.g.*, tincture of iodine.

C. **Antihistamines** are anti-allergic drugs. These drugs interfere with the natural action of histamine by competing with histamine for binding sites of receptor where histamine exerts its effect. *e.g.*, seldane.

D. **Antacids** are used to neutralise excess of acid released in stomach. *e.g.*, milk of magnesia $Mg(OH)_2$.

E. **Tranquilizers** are used for the treatment of stress, and mild or even severe mental diseases *e.g.*, equanil.

F **Antibiotics** are antimicrobial drugs. Antibiotics are used as drugs to treat infections because of their low toxicity for humans and animals *e.g.*, chloramphenicol.

G. **Disinfectants** are the chemicals which either kill or prevent the growth of microorganisms but they can be applied on non-living objects *e.g.*, 1 per cent solution of phenol.

Assertion and Reason

In the following questions a statement of assertion followed by a statement of reason is given. Choose the correct answer out of the following choices.

(a) Assertion and reason both are correct statements but reason does not explain assertion.

(b) Assertion and reason both are correct and reason explains the assertion.

(c) Both assertion and reason are wrong statements.

(d) Assertion is correct statement reason is wrong statement.

(e) Assertion is wrong statement reason is correct statement.

Q.84 Assertion Penicillin (G) is an antihistamine.
Reason Penicillin (G) is effective against gram positive as well as gram negative bacteria.

Ans. *(c)* Both assertion and reason are wrong statements. **Correct assertion** Penicillin (G) is an antibiotic.

Correct reason Penicillin is effective against some gram positive bacteria.

Q.85 Assertion Sulpha drug contain sulphonamide group.
Reason Salvarsan is a sulpha drug.

Ans. *(d)* Asssertion is correct statement reason is wrong statement. **Correct reason** Salvarsan is an antibacterial but does not contain sulphonamide group.

Q.86 Assertion Receptors are crucial to body's communication process.
Reason Receptors are proteins.

Ans. *(a)* Assertion and reason both are correct statements but reason does not explain assertion. **Correct Explanation** Neurotransmitters are small molecules which bind to the receptor for a very short time to transfer message to it and depart quickly unchanged after transferring the message. The receptor then forwards the message inside the cell.

Q.87 **Assertion** Enzymes have active sites that hold substrate molecule for a chemical reaction.

Reason Drugs compete with natural substrate by attaching covalently to the active site of enzyme.

Ans. *(d)* Assertion is correct statement reason is wrong statement **Correct reason** Drug compete with natural substrate by attaching by weak bonds such as hydrogen bond, van der Waals interaction and ionic bonding, etc., to the active site of the enzyme.

Q.88 **Assertion** Chemical messengers are chemicals that enable communication of message between two neurons or between neurons and muscles.

Reason Chemicals enter the cell through receptor.

Ans. *(d)* Assertion is correct statement reason is wrong statement.

Correct reason Chemicals bind to the receptor sites present on the surface of the membrane or the cell. They give message to the cell without entering the cell.

Q.89 **Assertion** Transparent soaps are made by dissolving soaps in ethanol.
Reason Ethanol makes things invisible.

Ans. *(d)* Assertion is correct statement reason is wrong statement. **Correct reason** Ethanol removes air and moisture which scatter light.

Q.90 **Assertion** Sodium chloride is added to precipitate soap after saponification.
Reason Hydrolysis of esters of long chain fatty acids by alkali produces soap in colloidal form.

Ans. *(b)* Assertion and reason both are correct and reason explains the assertion. Sodium chloride is added to precipitate soap after saponification because hydrolysis of esters of long chain fatty acids by alkali produces soap in colloidal form.

Q.91 **Assertion** Competitive inhibitors compete with natural substrate for their attachment on the active sites of enzymes.

Reason In competitive inhibition, inhibitor binds to the allosteric site of the enzyme.

Ans. *(d)* Assertion is correct statement reason is wrong statement. **Correct reason** In competitive inhibition, inhibitor binds to the active site of the enzyme.

Q.92 **Assertion** Non-competitive inhibitor inhibits the catalytic activity of enzyme by binding with its active site.

Reason Non-competitive inhibitor changes the shape of the active site in such a way that substrate can't recognise it.

Ans. *(e)* Assertion is wrong statement reason is correct statement. **Correct** assertion Non-competitive inhibitor inhibits the catalytic activity by binding the enzyme at allosteric site.

Q.93 **Assertion** Chemical messenger gives message to the cell without entering the cell.

Reason Chemical messenger is received at the binding site of receptor proteins.

Ans. *(b)* Assertion and reason both are correct and reason explains the assertion. Chemical messenger gives message to the cell without entering the cell because it is received at the binding site of receptor proteins.

Q.94 **Assertion** Receptor proteins show selectivity for one chemical messenger over the other.
Reason Chemical messenger binds to the receptor site and inhibits its natural function.

Ans. *(d)* Assertion is correct statement reason is wrong statement. **Correct reason** Chemical messenger binds the receptor site and gives the message to the cell without entering the cell.

Q.95 **Assertion** All chemicals added to food items are called food preservatives.
Reason All these chemicals increase the nutritive value of the food.

Ans. *(c)* Both assertion and reason are wrong statements. **Correct assertion** Chemicals which are used to protect food against bacteria, yeasts and moulds are called food preservatives.

Correct reason Preservatives do not increase the nutritive values of food.

Q.96 **Assertion** Preservative are added to food items.
Reason Preservatives inhibit the growth of mircroorganisms.

Ans. *(b)* Assertion and reason both are correct and reason explains the assertion. Preservatives are added to food items because it inhibits the growth of microorganisms.

Q.97 **Assertion** Artificial sweeteners are added to the food to control the intake of calories.
Reason Most of the artificial sweeteners are inert and do not metabolise in the body.

Ans. *(b)* Assertion and reason both are correct and reason explains the assertion. Aritificial sweeteners are added to the food to control the intake of calories because most of the artificial sweeteners are inert and do not metabolise in the body.

Long Answer Type Questions

Q.98 In what respect do prontosil and salvarsan resemble. Is there any resemblance between azo dye and prontosil? Explain.

Ans. Prontosil, also called sulfamido chrysoidine, trade name of the first synthetic drug used in the treatment of general bacterial infections in humans.

Prontosil resulted from research, directed by German chemist and pathologist Gerhard Domagk, on the antibacterial action of azo dyes. A red azo dye of low toxicity, prontosil was shown by Domagk to prevent mortality in mice infected with Streptococcus bacteria.

The dye was also effective in controlling staphylococcus infections in rabbits. Within a relatively short period, it was demonstrated that prontosil was effective not only in combating experimental infections in animals but also against Streptococcal disease in humans, including meningitis and puerperal sepsis. Structural formula of prontosil is

Prontosil

From the structure of prontosil, it is very clear that it has —N=N— linkage. It was discovered that the part of the structure of prontosil molecule shown in box, *i.e.*, p-aminobenzenesulphonamide has antibacterial activity.

Salvarsan is also known as arsphenamine. It was introduced at the begining of 1910s as the first effective treatment for syphilis. It is an organoarsenic molecule and has –As = As– double bond.

Salvarsan

Salvarsan and prontosil show similarity in their structure. Both of these drugs are antimicrobials. Salvarsan contains —As =As — linkage whereas prontosil has —N = N— linkage.

Prontosil (a red azo dye) and azo dye both have — N=N— linkage.

Azodye

Q.99 How do enzymes catalyse a chemical reaction in the living system? Explain drug target interaction taking the example of enzyme as target.

Ans. In the catalytic activity, enzymes perform the following two major functions :

(i) The first function of an enzyme is to hold the substrate molecule for a chemical reaction. The active sites of the enzymes hold the substrate molecule in a suitable position, so that it can be attacked by the reagent effectively.

The substrate molecules bind to the amino acid residues of the protein present the active site of the enzyme through a variety of interactions such as hydrogen bonding, dipole-dipole interactions, van der Waals interactions and ionic bonding.

These binding forces should be strong enough to hold the substrate long enough so that the enzyme can catalyse the reaction, but weak enough to allow the products to depart after their formation.

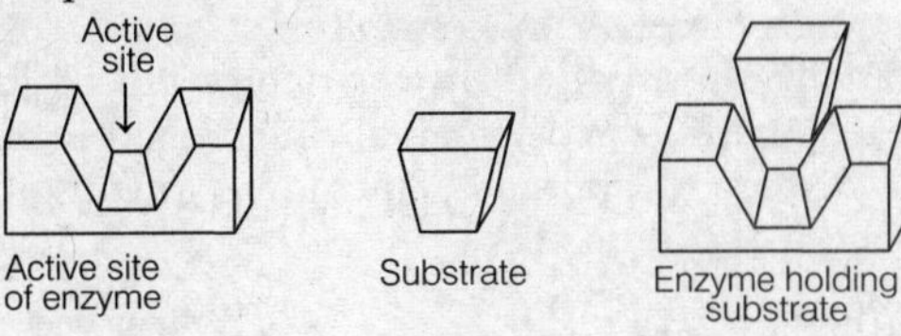

(ii) The second function of the enzyme is to provide functional groups which will attack the substrate to carry out the chemical reaction. This function is carried out by some other amino acid residues of protein present on the active site of the enzyme.

These provide free amino groups to attack the substrate and bring about the chemical reaction. If the amino acid serine is present nearby the substrate held on the active site, then its — OH group is free to act as a nucleophile in the enzyme catalysed reaction.

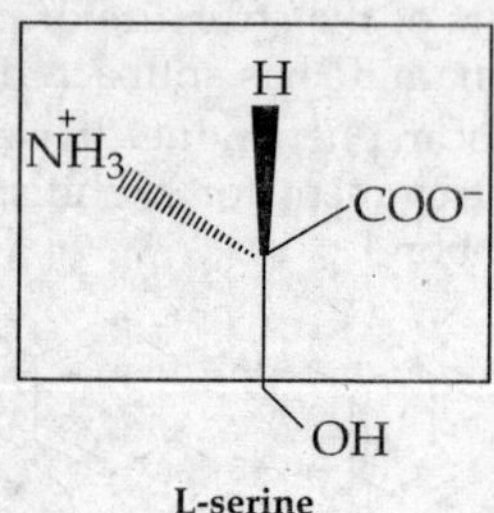

L-serine

The part of the amino acid which lies outside the box act as a nucleophile in enzyme catalysed reactions, but the part of the amino acid which is enclosed in the box is involved in the formation of peptide bond in protein molecule.

Q.100 Sythetic detergents have advantage over usual soaps as far as cleansing power is concerned. But use of synthetic detergents over a long time creates environmental pollution. How can the pollution caused by synthetic detergents be minimised? Classify the detergents according to their chemical nature.

Ans. Synthetic detergents are cleansing agents which have all the properties of soaps, but they actually do not contain any soap. These can be used in soft as well as in hard water.

They are mainly classified into three categories

(1) **Anionic Detergents** Anionic detergents are sodium salts of sulphonated long chain alcohols or hydrocarbons. Alkyl hydrogen sulphates formed by treating long chain alcohols with conc. H_2SO_4 are neutralised with alkali to form anionic detergents. Similarly alkyl benzene sulphonates are obtained by neutralising alkyl benzene sulphonic acids with alkali.

$$\underset{\text{Lauryl alcohol}}{CH_3(CH_2)_{10}CH_2OH} \xrightarrow{H_2SO_4} \underset{\text{Laurylhydrogen sulphate}}{CH_3(CH_2)_{10}CH_2OSO_3H} \xrightarrow{NaOH\,(aq)} \underset{\substack{\text{Sodium Laurylsulphate}\\ \text{(Anionic detergent)}}}{CH_3(CH_2)_{10}CH_2O\overset{-}{S}O_3\,Na^+}$$

$$\underset{\text{Dodecyl benzene}}{CH_3-(CH_2)_{11}-C_6H_5} \xrightarrow{H_2SO_4} \underset{\substack{\text{Dodecyl benzene}\\ \text{sulphonic acid}}}{H_3C-(CH_2)_{11}-C_6H_4-SO_3H} \xrightarrow{NaOH\,(aq.)} \underset{\substack{\text{Sodium dodecyl}\\ \text{benzene sulphonate}}}{H_3C-(CH_2)_{11}-C_6H_4-SO_3^-\,Na^+}$$

In these detergents, the anionic part of the molecule is involved in the cleansing action. They are mostly used for household work. They are also used in toothpaste.

(2) **Cationic Detergents** They are quarternary ammonium salts of amines with acetates, chlorides or bromides as anions. Cationic part possess a long hydrocarbon chain and a positive charge on nitrogen atom.

Cetyltrimethylammonium bromide is a popular cationic detergent and is used in hair conditioners.

$$\left[\begin{array}{c} CH_3 \\ | \\ CH_3(CH_2)_{15}-N-CH_3 \\ | \\ CH_3 \end{array}\right]^+ Br^-$$

Cationic detergents have germicidal properties and are expensive, therefore, these are of limited use.

(3) **Non-ionic Detergents** Non-ionic detergents do not contain any ion in their constitution. One such detergent is formed when stearic acid reacts with polyethylene glycol.

$$\underset{\text{Stearic acid}}{H_3C-(CH_2)_{16}COOH} + \underset{\text{Polyethyleneglycol}}{HO(CH_2CH_2O)_nCH_2CH_2OH} \xrightarrow{-H_2O}$$

$$\underset{\text{Polyethyleneglycol stearate}}{CH_3(CH_2)_{16}COO(CH_2CH_2O)_nCH_2CH_2OH}$$

Liquid dishwashing detergents are non-ionic type.

Advantages of Synthetic Detergents over Soaps

(i) Synthetic detergents can be used in hard water without any wastage while some of the soaps gets wasted.

(ii) Synthetic detergents can be used in acidic medium while soaps get precipitated.

(iii) Synthetic detergents are more soluble in water and hence produce lather more easily than soaps. Some synthetic detergents produce lather even in ice cold water.

(iv) Synthetic detergents decrease the surface tension of water to greater extent and hence have a stronger cleansing action than soap.

Synthetic detergents have advantages over usual soaps but use of synthetic detergents over a long time creates environmental pollution because some detergents have hisghly branched hydrocarbon chains.

These branches or side chains stop bacteria from attacking and breaking the chains. This result in slow degradation of detergent molecule leading to their accumulation. Effluents containing these detergents reach the rivers, ponds, etc. These persist in water even after sewage treatment and thus water gets polluted.

Since, unbranched (*i.e.*, straight) chains are more prone to attack by bacteria, therefore, in most of the detergents used these days, the branching is kept to a minimum, so that the detergents become easily biodegradable and hence, pollution is prevented.

Q. 101 What are enzyme inhibitors? Classify them on the basis of their mode of attachments on the active site of enzymes. With the help of diagrams explain how do inhibitors inhibit the enzymatic activity.

Ans. Enzymes are responsible to hold the substrate molecule for a chemical reaction and they provide functional groups which will attack the substrate to carry out the chemical reaction. Drugs which inhibit any of the two activities of enzymes are called enzyme inhibitors.

Enzyme inhibitors can block the binding site thereby preventing the binding of the substrate to the active site and hence inhibiting the catalytic activity of the enzyme. Drugs inhibit the attachment of natural substrate on the active site of enzymes in two different ways as explained below.

(i) Drugs which compete with natural substrate for their attachment on the active sites of enzymes are called competitive inhibitors.

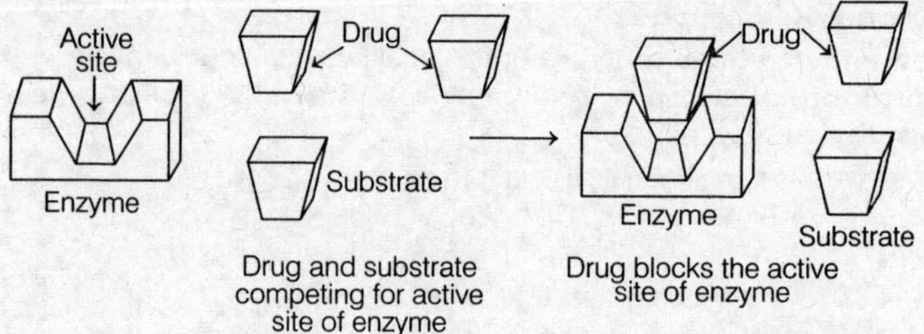

(ii) Some drugs, however, do not bind to the active site but bind to a different site of the enzyme which is called allosteric site. This binding of the drug at allosteric site changes the shape of the active site of the enzyme in such a way that the natural substrate cannot recognise it. Such enzymes are called non-competitive inhibitors.

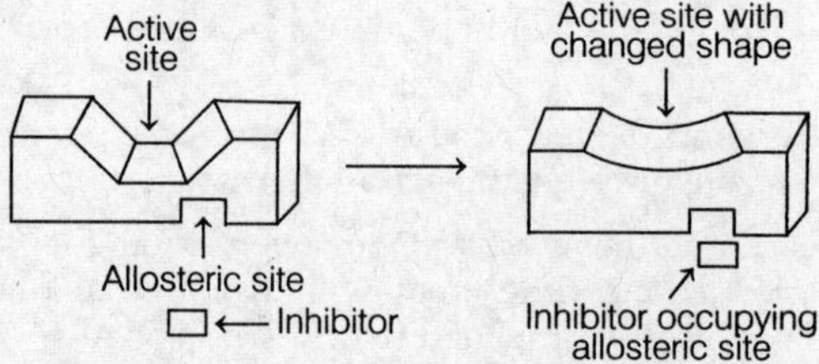